HOW TO BUY AND SELL
just about
every- thing

Also in this series

How To Do (Just About) Everything
by Courtney Rosen

HOW TO BUY AND SELL just about every-thing

Jeff Wuorio

Collins

Harper Collins Publishers
Westerhill Road, Glasgow G64 2QT
www.collins.co.uk

UK Edition
Produced by Grant Laing Partnership
Contributing Editors: Alison Bolus, Terry Burrows,
Reg Grant, James Harrison, Jane Laing, Helen Ridge,
Jane Simmonds
Designer: Christine Lacey
Indexer: Kay Ollerenshaw

●com|press

Designed and produced by .com press
.com press is a division of Weldon Owen Inc.,
814 Montgomery Street, San Francisco, CA 94133

CEO: John Owen
President: Terry Newell
COO: Larry Partington
VP, International Sales: Stuart Laurence
VP, Publisher: Roger Shaw
Creative Director: Gaye Allen
Production Manager: Chris Hemesath
Series Editor: Brynn Breuner
Managing Editor: Jennifer Block Martin
Consulting Editor: Bill Marken
Production & Layout: Joan Olson, Phoebe Bixler
Illustrator: William Laird
Copy Editors: Jacqueline Aaron, Rick Clogher,
Gail Nelson-Bonebrake
Contributing Editors: Donald Breuner,
Elizabeth Dougherty, Kevin Ireland, Jane Mason,
Sarah Stephens, Julie Thompson, Robert von Goeben,
Laurie Wertz
Editorial Assistance: Sinclair Crockett, Dave Martin,
Lindsay Powers, Juli Vendzules, Heidi Wilson
Proofreaders: Jacqueline Aaron, Andrew Alden,
Cynthia Rubin
Indexer: Ken DellaPenta

Printed and bound in Dubai by Oriental Press

10 9 8 7 6 5 4 3 2 1

A catalogue record for this book is available from the
British Library.

ISBN 0-00-719370-X

CONTENTS
FOREWORD

A NOTE TO READERS

SMART STRATEGIES

DAILY LIFE

SPECIAL OCCASIONS

SPLURGES & RARE EVENTS

PERSONAL FINANCE

CAREERS

PROPERTY

HOME & GARDEN

FOOD & DRINK

FAMILY AFFAIRS

HEALTH & BEAUTY

COLLECTIBLES

COMPUTERS & HOME ELECTRONICS

TRAVEL

SPORTS & OUTDOOR RECREATION

CLOTHING & ACCESSORIES

CARS & OTHER VEHICLES

INDEX

CONTRIBUTOR CREDITS

A NOTE TO READERS

When attempting to follow any of the advice in this book, please note the following:

Risky activities: Certain activities described in this book are inherently dangerous or risky. Before attempting any new activity, know your own limitations and consider all applicable risks (whether listed or not).

Professional advice: While we strive to provide complete and accurate information, this is not intended as a substitute for professional advice. You should always consult a professional whenever appropriate or if you have any questions or concerns regarding medical, legal or financial advice.

Physical or health-related activities: Be sure to consult a doctor before attempting any health- or diet-related activity or any activity involving physical exertion, particularly if you have any condition that could impair or limit your ability to engage in such an activity.

Adult supervision: The activities described in this book are intended for adults only, and they should not be performed by children without responsible adult supervision.

Violations of law: The information provided in this book should not be used to violate any applicable law or regulation.

Sources and prices: Prices and sources for products and services listed in this edition were accurate at press time. Since the nature of any market is changeable, however, we cannot guarantee that any source listed in these pages will continue to carry items mentioned or even remain in business. Similarly, all prices mentioned in this book are approximate only and are subject to change.

All of the information in this book is obtained from sources that the author and publisher believe to be accurate and reliable. However, we make no warranty, expressed or implied, that the information is sufficient or appropriate for every individual, situation or purpose. Further, the information may become outdated over time. You assume the risk and full responsibility for all of your actions, and neither the author nor the publisher will be liable for any loss or damage of any sort, whether consequential, incidental, special or otherwise, that may result from the information presented. The descriptions of third-party products, websites and services are for informational purposes only and are not intended as an endorsement of any particular product or service.

Foreword

When we set out to write the weighty buying and selling guide you hold
in your hands, we hardly knew what we were in for. Certainly, we've all
bought a toothbrush before, or many pairs of sports shoes, and certainly
we've chosen a ripe juicy peach, but have we ever really thought about what
goes into making smart choices? To make astute decisions, you need not
only the collective knowledge of past purchasing experiences, but also
expert advice, rules of thumb, shrewd insider tips, and brand comparisons.
We laboured to bring this level of guidance to each one of the 556 topics
covered in *How to Buy and Sell (Just About) Everything*.

The book is simple to use. For a snapshot of each topic, check out its
"What to Look For" list and note the number of calculators, which indicate the
difficulty level of the buying or selling decision. To continue, read the concise
steps, useful tips and warnings, and charts. You'll get the information you
need to make better informed, more confident buying and selling decisions.

Your first tip: Start with the "Smart Strategies" chapter, then sail on to the
other sections. You'll become a smarter consumer and pick up tricks of
the trade that you'll be able to apply to a wealth of other buying and selling
ventures. You'll also get an insider's edge to stretching every pound further.

We included such topics as "Buy Bargain Clothing" (11) and "Save on Your Mortgage" (174)
to help you fatten your wallet. You'll find advice on ways to get rid of things you're finished
with (and make some money in the process), like selling your wedding dress (76), parting
company with a football-card collection (394), or losing that old banger in the driveway
(539). For those exalted few for whom money is no object, you'll be able to brush up on
how to "Employ a Butler" (102), "Buy a Journey into Space" (115), or "Buy a Racehorse"
(112). And who could pass up the "Buy Happiness" (15) or "Sell Your Story to the Tabloids"
(124) entries? Just for good measure, we have "Buy a Better Mousetrap" (16) in here, too.
And though you may not know when you'll be in the market for a private island, if that day
comes, rest assured you'll find out how to buy one in this book.

Thanks to all our authors for spending hours researching mountains of information and
distilling it into concise, readable topics (and for going the extra mile to find out exactly how
you donate your body to science and which adhesive works with what material). A special
thank you to Derek Wilson, Marcia Layton Turner and Robert von Goeben for their expert
contributions to many chapters. (You'll find the names of all the talented and skilled authors
on the Contributors page in the back of the book.) A deep bow to managing editor Jennifer
Block Martin for her expertise, vigilance and talent, and for going above and beyond time
and time again.

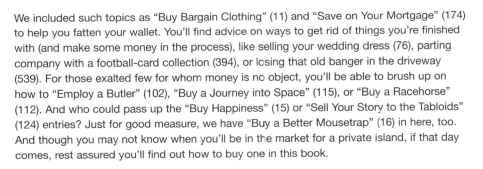

Jeff Wuorio

...TION SITES • BUY BARGAIN CLOTHING • BUY WHOLESALE • GET OUT OF DEBT • BUY NOTHING • BUY HAPPINESS • BUY A BETTER MOUS

...UY YOUR WAY INTO SOMEONE'S FAVOUR • BUY LOVE • FIND THE RIGHT RELAXATION TECHNIQUE FOR YOU • BUY HEALTHY FAST FOOD • B

...ING SERVICE • SELL YOURSELF ON AN ONLINE DATING SERVICE • SELL YOURSELF TO YOUR GIRLFRIEND/BOYFRIEND'S FAMILY • BUY FLO

...HOOSE FILM FOR YOUR CAMERA • BUY RECHARGEABLE BATTERIES • GIVE TO A GOOD CAUSE • TAKE PART IN A CAR BOOT SALE • EMPLO

...DENT DISCOUNTS • BUY FLOWERS WHOLESALE • GET A PICTURE FRAMED • EMPLOY A REMOVAL COMPANY • EMPLOY A LIFESTYLE MAN

...Y FOR A HALLOWE'EN PARTY • BUY A GREAT BIRTHDAY PRESENT FOR UNDER £10 • SELECT GOOD CHAMPAGNE • BUY A DIAMOND • BUY J

...A GIFT LIST • BUY WEDDING GIFTS • SELECT BRIDESMAIDS' DRESSES • HIRE AN EVENTS ORGANISER • HIRE A BARTENDER FOR A PARTY

...NOUNCEMENTS • SELL YOUR WEDDING DRESS • BUY AN ANNIVERSARY GIFT • ARRANGE ENTERTAINMENT FOR A PARTY • COMMISSION A

...SON WHO HAS EVERYTHING • BUY A GIFT FOR PASSING EXAMS • SELECT A CHRISTMAS TURKEY • BUY A HOUSEWARMING GIFT • PURCH

...AND • WRITE A MESSAGE IN THE SKY • HIRE A BIG-NAME BAND • GET INTO A PRIVATE GAMBLING ROOM IN LAS VEGAS • BUY SOMEONE A

TIMES • EMPLOY A BUTLER • BUY A FOOTBALL CLUB • BUY A PERSONAL JET • SELECT A CLASSIC CAR • ACQUIRE A BODY GUARD • BO

...YHOUND TO RACE • BUY A RACEHORSE • BUY A VILLA IN TUSCANY • EMPLOY A PERSONAL CHEF • BUY A JOURNEY INTO SPACE • EMPL

...TUNE • HIRE AN EXPERT WITNESS • MAKE MONEY FROM ACCIDENT COMPENSATION • DONATE YOUR BODY TO SCIENCE • MAKE MONEY

...ANCIAL ADVISER • PLAN FOR RETIREMENT • COPE WITH HIGHER EDUCATION COSTS • BUY AND SELL SHARES • CHOOSE A STOCKBROKER

...S INSURANCE • BUY LIFE INSURANCE • GET PRIVATE HEALTH INSURANCE • BUY PERSONAL FINANCE SOFTWARE • CHOOSE AN ACCOUNTA

...E OUT A PATENT • MARKET YOUR INVENTION • FINANCE YOUR BUSINESS IDEA • BUY A SMALL BUSINESS • BUY A FRANCHISE • LEASE RET

...BSITE • HIRE A GRAPHIC DESIGNER • ACQUIRE CONTENT FOR YOUR WEBSITE • BUY ADVERTISING ON THE WEB • SELL YOUR ART • HIRE A

...LISH YOUR BOOK • START A BED-AND-BREAKFAST • SELL A FAILING BUSINESS • BUY A HOT DOG STAND • SHOP FOR A MORTGAGE • GET

...SE AT AUCTION • SHOP FOR A HOUSE ONLINE • BUY A PROPERTY FOR RENOVATION AND RESALE • EVALUATE BEFORE BUYING INTO A NE

...A PLOT OF LAND • HAVE YOUR HOUSE DESIGNED • HIRE AN ARCHITECT • HIRE A BUILDER • GET PLANNING PERMISSION • BUY A HOLIDA

...OAD • BUY TO LET • RENT YOUR HOME FOR A LOCATION SHOOT • FURNISH YOUR HOME • FURNISH YOUR STUDIO FLAT • BUY USED FUR

...Y HOUSEHOLD APPLIANCES • BUY FLOOR-CARE APPLIANCES • BUY EXTENDED WARRANTIES ON APPLIANCES • FIND PERIOD FIXTURES •

...E • SELECT PAINT, STAIN AND VARNISH • CHOOSE DECORATIVE TILES • CHOOSE A DEHUMIDIFIER • BUY A WHIRLPOOL BATH • BUY A SHO

...LPAPER • BUY A WOOD-BURNING STOVE • SELECT FLOORING • SELECT CARPETING • CHOOSE KITCHEN CABINETS • CHOOSE A KITCHEN

...KE ALARMS • BUY CARBON MONOXIDE DETECTORS • BUY FIRE EXTINGUISHERS • CHOOSE AN ENTRY DOOR • BUY A GARAGE-DOOR OPE

...DOOR FURNITURE • BUY THE PERFECT ROSE • BUY FLOWERING BULBS • BUY FLOWERS FOR YOUR GARDEN • SELECT PEST CONTROLS •

...OMATIC WATERING SYSTEM • START A NEW LAWN • BUY A LAWN MOWER • BUY KOI FOR YOUR FISH POND • BUY A STORAGE SHED • HIR

...DUCE • CHOOSE A PERFECT PEACH • BUY AND SELL AT FARMERS' MARKETS • SELECT KITCHEN KNIVES • DECIPHER FOOD LABELS • SEL

...FECT BURGER • PURCHASE A CHRISTMAS HAM • BUY ORGANIC BEEF • BUY HAGGIS • PURCHASE LOCAL HONEY • CHOOSE A CHICKEN •

...TRUFFLES • BUY ARTISAN BREADS • BUY ARTISAN CHEESES • PURCHASE KOSHER FOOD • BUY SENSIBLY IN SUPERMARKETS • CHOOSE

...ER A GREAT CUP OF COFFEE • BUY A COFFEEMAKER OR ESPRESSO MACHINE • PURCHASE PARTY BEER • CHOOSE THE RIGHT WINE • CH

...RM • CHOOSE AN OVULATION PREDICTOR KIT • PICK A PREGNANCY TEST KIT • CHOOSE BIRTH CONTROL • CHOOSE WHERE TO GIVE BIRT

...BABY CLOTHES • CHOOSE NAPPIES • BUY OR RENT A BREAST PUMP • CHOOSE A CAR SEAT • BUY CHILD-PROOFING SUPPLIES • FIND RE

...A GARDEN PLAY STRUCTURE • FIND A FAMILY-FRIENDLY HOTEL • ORGANISE A FUND-RAISING EVENT • BUY BRACES FOR YOUR KID • BU

...MODEL • SELL USED BABY GEAR, TOYS, CLOTHES AND BOOKS • FIND A COUPLES COUNSELLOR • HIRE A FAMILY SOLICITOR • BUY OR R

...CHASE A TOOTHBRUSH • BUY MOISTURISERS AND ANTIWRINKLE CREAMS • SELECT PAIN RELIEF AND COLD MEDICINES • CHOOSE A COM

...DUCTS • BUY WAYS TO COUNTER HAIR LOSS • BUY A WIG OR HAIRPIECE • BUY A NEW BODY • GET A TATTOO OR BODY PIERCING • OBTA

...H • SELECT SPECTACLES AND SUNGLASSES • HIRE A PERSONAL TRAINER • SIGN UP FOR A YOGA CLASS • TREAT YOURSELF TO A DAY AT

...N ANTIQUE MARKET • BUY AT AUCTION • KNOW WHAT YOUR COLLECTIBLES ARE WORTH • BARTER WITH DEALERS • GET AN ANTIQUE APP

...S • BUY AN ANTIQUE QUILT • BUY FILM POSTERS • LIQUIDATE YOUR BEANIE BABY COLLECTION • SCORE AUTOGRAPHS • TRADE YU-GI-O

...SELL SPORTS MEMORABILIA • SELL YOUR FOOTBALL-CARD COLLECTION • CHOOSE A DESKTOP COMPUTER • SHOP FOR A USED COMPU

...PUTER PERIPHERALS • CHOOSE AN INTERNET SERVICE PROVIDER • GET AN INTERNET DOMAIN NAME • NETWORK YOUR COMPUTERS • U

...PLAYER • BUY A VIDEO RECORDER • CHOOSE A PERSONAL DIGITAL ASSISTANT • CHOOSE A MOBILE PHONE SERVICE • GET A BETTER DE

...AL CAMERA • BUY A HOME AUTOMATION SYSTEM • BUY A STATE-OF-THE-ART SOUND SYSTEM • BUY AN AUDIO/VIDEO DISTRIBUTION SYS

...YSTEM • BUY VIRTUAL-REALITY FURNITURE • BUY TWO-WAY RADIOS • BUY A MOBILE ENTERTAINMENT SYSTEM • GET A PASSPORT, QUIC

...LUGGAGE • FLY FOR NEXT TO NOTHING • TAKE A TRIP ON THE TRANS-SIBERIAN EXPRESS • BUY DUTY-FREE • SHIP FOREIGN PURCHASE

...AN CYCLING HOLIDAY • CHOOSE A CHEAP CRUISE • BOOK A HOTEL PACKAGE FOR THE GREEK ISLANDS • RAFT THE GRAND CANYON • BO

...SHAW IN RANGOON • TAKE SALSA LESSONS IN CUBA • BUY A CAMERA IN HONG KONG • BUY YOUR WAY ONTO A MOUNT EVEREST EXPED

...TEAM • BUY ANKLE AND KNEE BRACES • CHOOSE RUGBY PROTECTION KIT • BUY GOLF CLUBS • SELL FOUND GOLF BALLS • BUY PORTS

...LOY A SCUBA INSTRUCTOR • BUY A SKATEBOARD AND PROTECTIVE GEAR • BUY SKATES • GO BUNJEE JUMPING • GO SKYDIVING • BUY V

...'S AND BINDINGS • BUY SKI BOOTS • BUY A BICYCLE • BUY AN ELECTRIC BICYCLE • BUY CYCLE CLOTHING • BUY A PROPERLY FITTING H

... BUY A SURFBOARD • BUY FLY-FISHING GEAR • BUY ROCK-CLIMBING EQUIPMENT • BUY A CASHMERE JUMPER • PURCHASE VINTAGE C

...KTAIL DRESS • BUY DESIGNER CLOTHES AT A DISCOUNT • CHOOSE A BASIC WARDROBE FOR A MAN • BUY A MAN'S DRESS SHIRT • PICK

...HER JACKET • BUY MATERNITY CLOTHES • GET A GREAT-FITTING BRA • CHOOSE A HIGH-PERFORMANCE SWIM SUIT • BUY PERFORMANC

...ORY SHOPS • BUY A NEW CAR • BUY THE BASICS FOR YOUR CAR • BUY A USED CAR • BUY OR SELL A CAR ONLINE • BUY A HYBRID CAR

BUY TIME • BUY A BOUQUET OF ROSES • BUY SOMEONE A DRINK • GET SOMEONE TO BUY YOU A DRINK • BUY YOUR WAY INTO THE B
NSCREEN • BUT FURTHER EDUCATION • ORDER EXOTIC FOOD • ORDER AT A SUSHI BAR • BUY DINNER AT A FRENCH RESTAURANT • EMPL
TO SAY SORRY TO YOUR PARTNER • BUY MUSIC ONLINE • EMPLOY MUSICIANS • ORDER A GOOD BOTTLE OF WINE • BUY AN ERGONOMIC
EANER • EMPLOY AN AU PAIR • BUY A GUITAR • BUY DUCT TAPE • GET A GOOD DEAL ON A MAGAZINE SUBSCRIPTION • GET SENIOR CITIZ
FIND A VET • BUY PET FOOD • BUY A PEDIGREE DOG OR CAT • BREED YOUR PET AND SELL THE LITTER • BUY OR RENT FOR A FANCY DR
LERY MADE OF PRECIOUS METALS • BUY COLOURED GEMSTONES • CHOOSE THE PERFECT WEDDING DRESS • BUY OR RENT MEN'S FORM
A PHOTOGRAPHER • HIRE A CATERER • FIND THE IDEAL CIVIL WEDDING VENUE • THE COST OF MARRYING • ORDER PERSONALISED INVIT
ORKS SHOW • BUY A MOTHER'S DAY GIFT • BUY A FATHER'S DAY GIFT • SELECT AN APPROPRIATE COMING-OF-AGE GIFT • GET A GIFT FOR
HRISTMAS CARDS • BUY CHRISTMAS STOCKING FILLERS • BUY CHRISTENING GIFTS • PURCHASE A PERFECT CHRISTMAS TREE • BUY A P
PAY A RANSOM • GET HOT TICKETS • HIRE A LIMOUSINE • BUY A CRYONIC CHAMBER • RENT YOUR OWN HOARDING • TAKE OUT A FULL-
UXURY CRUISE AROUND THE WORLD • BUY A TICKET TO TRAVEL FOR A YEAR • BOOK A TRIP ON THE ORIENT-EXPRESS • OWN A VINEYARD
HOSTWRITER TO WRITE YOUR MEMOIRS • COMMISSION ORIGINAL ARTWORK • IMMORTALISE YOUR SPOUSE IN A SCULPTURE • GIVE AWA
EDICAL GUINEA PIG • SELL YOUR STORY TO THE TABLOIDS • SELL YOUR SOUL TO THE DEVIL • NEGOTIATE A BETTER CREDIT CARD DEAL
-TRADE (OR NOT) • BUY ANNUITIES • BUY AND SELL MUTUAL FUNDS • BUY BONDS • SELL SHORT • INVEST IN PRECIOUS METALS • BUY S
FIND CASUAL WORK • SELL YOUR PRODUCT O   HEADHUNTER • SELL YOURSELF IN A JOB INT
PACE • LEASE INDUSTRIAL SPACE • LEASE OFFI   MENT • HIRE SOMEONE TO DESIGN AND BUILD
COACH • SELL ON THE CRAFT CIRCUIT • HIRE A   RY • SELL A SCREENPLAY • SELL YOUR NOVEL
TER MORTGAGE DEAL • SAVE ON YOUR MORTC   D • OBTAIN HOUSE INSURANCE • BUY A HOUSE
EA • EXCHANGE CONTRACTS ON A PROPERTY   AN ESTATE AGENT • RELEASE CAPITAL FROM YO
ME • RENT A HOLIDAY HOME • BUY A FLAT • REI   COUNTRY • BUY A LOFT APARTMENT • BUY PR
E • BUY DOOR AND WINDOW LOCKS • CHOOSE   GHT FIXTURES • BUY A PROGRAMMABLE LIGH
BED AND MATTRESS • HIRE AN INTERIOR DES   NCORPORATE A GREATER SENSE OF SPACE INT
BUY A TOILET • CHOOSE A TAP • BUY GLUES   MENTS • GET SELF-CLEANING WINDOWS • CHO
KTOP • BUY GREEN HOUSEHOLD CLEANERS • S   SECURITY SYSTEM • BUY A HOME ALARM SYS
BUY TIMBER FOR A DIY PROJECT • HOW TO S   R, PAINTER OR ELECTRICIAN • HIRE A GARDEN
SOIL IMPROVERS • BUY MULCH • BUY A COMP   BLE GARDEN • HIRE A GARDEN DESIGNER • BU
EE SURGEON • BUY BASIC GARDEN TOOLS • B   • BUY AN OUTDOOR LIGHTING SYSTEM • BUY
ERBS AND SPICES • STOCK YOUR KITCHEN WIT   RESH PRODUCE • SELECT MEAT • STOCK UP F
CT FRESH FISH • SELECT RICE • PURCHASE PR   LTON • GET FRESH FISH DELIVERED TO YOUR D
KING OILS • SELECT OLIVE OIL • SELECT OLIVES   VINEGAR • CHOOSE PASTA • BUY TEA • BUY CO
A REAL ALE • ORDER A COCKTAIL • CHOOSE A   STOCK A WINE CELLAR • STOCK YOUR BAR •
RE A MIDWIFE OR DOULA • PLAN A HOME BIRT   R A NEW BABY • BUY A NEW COT • CHOOSE A
E CHILDCARE • FIND A GREAT NANNY • FIND T   TER-SCHOOL CARE • SIGN YOUR CHILD UP FO
S • BUY BOOKS, VIDEOS AND MUSIC FOR YOU   HIRE A TUTOR • ADOPT A CHILD • GET YOUR
HELTERED HOUSING • CHOOSE A CARE HOME   LOT • PAY FOR FUNERAL EXPENSES • GET VIA
ENTARY MTHERAPY • SEE A MENTAL-HEALTH P   BUY HOME-USE MEDICAL SUPPLIES • SELECT
EAST IMPLANTS • GET WRINKLE-FILLER INJECT   ACTITIONERS • CHOOSE A MANICURIST • GET V
ISPA • BOOK A MASSAGE • GET ON ANTIQUES   SHOP AT AN ANTIQUE FAIR OR FLEA MARKET •

Smart Strategies

ED • BUY SILVERWARE • EVALUATE CARNIVAL GLASS • BUY AND SELL STAMPS • BUY ANTIQUE FURNITURE • GET CLUED UP ON CLARICE
RDS • SEIZE STAR WARS ACTION FIGURES • SELL YOUR VINYL RECORD COLLECTION • SELL TO A PAWNSHOP • BUY AND SELL COMIC BO
OR PERIPHERALS • CHOOSE A LAPTOP OR NOTEBOOK COMPUTER • SELL OR DONATE A COMPUTER • BUY PRINTER PAPER • BUY A PRINT
DE THE MEMORY IN YOUR COMPUTER • BUY COMPUTER SOFTWARE • CHOOSE A CD PLAYER • BUY BLANK CDS • BUY AN MP PLAYER •
OM YOUR PHONE COMPANY • BUY VIDEO AND COMPUTER GAMES • CHOOSE A FILM CAMERA • CHOOSE A DIGITAL CAMCORDER • DECID
BUY A SERIOUS TV • CHOOSE BETWEEN DIGITAL TV PROVIDERS • GET A DIGITAL VIDEO RECORDER • GET A UNIVERSAL REMOTE • BUY
URCHASE CHEAP AIRLINE TICKETS • FIND GREAT HOTEL DEALS • HIRE THE BEST CAR FOR THE LEAST MONEY • GET TRAVEL INSURANCE
THE UNITED KONGDOM • TIP IN A FOREIGN COUNTRY • TIP PROPERLY IN THE UK • BRIBE A FOREIGN OFFICIAL • GET AN INTERRAIL PASS
CHEAP BUT FANTASTIC SAFARI • RENT A CAMEL IN CAIRO • GET SINGLE-MALT WHISKY IN SCOTLAND • BUY A SAPPHIRE IN BANGKOK •
N • HIRE A TREKKING COMPANY IN NEPAL • RENT OR BUY A SATELLITE PHONE • BUY YOUR CHILD'S FIRST CRICKET BAT • ORDER A STRIP
DES • BUY A RACKET • BUY A HEALTH CLUB MEMBERSHIP • BUY AN AEROBIC FITNESS MACHINE • BUY SWIMMING EQUIPMENT • BUY A J
TLIFTING EQUIPMENT • CHOOSE A CAR RACK • BUY SKIS • BUY CLOTHES FOR COLD-WEATHER ACTIVITIES • SELL USED SKIS • BUY A SN
ET • BUY THE OPTIMAL SLEEPING BAG • BUY A TENT • BUY A BACKPACK • BUY A CAMPING STOVE • BUY A KAYAK • BUY A LIFEJACKET •
ING • SELL USED CLOTHING • ORDER CUSTOM-MADE COWBOY BOOTS • BUY CLOTHES ONLINE • FIND NON-STANDARD SIZES • BUY THE
A TIE • BUY A WOMAN'S SUIT • BUY A MAN'S SUIT • HIRE A TAILOR • BUY CUSTOM-TAILORED CLOTHES IN ASIA • BUY A BRIEFCASE • SHO
RKOUT CLOTHES • BUY A HEART-RATE MONITOR • SELECT A WATCH • BUY KIDS' CLOTHES • CHOOSE CHILDREN'S SHOES • PURCHASE O
LL A CAR • BUY A MOTORCYCLE • BUYING AND CHANGING MOTOR OIL • WASH A CAR • WAX A CAR • BUY CAR INSURANCE • SPRING FOR

1 Be a Smart Consumer

You work hard for your money. Retailers work equally hard to separate you from it. Being a smart consumer means looking beyond the sales pitch and assessing the true value of a product.

Steps

1 Use the full potential of the internet to research prices, options and product reviews before you buy.

2 Read the consumer reports in *Which?* magazine. Subscribe to the magazine or, better still, to the website (which.net). If you don't want to pay for *Which?*, go to your local reference library to consult current and back copies.

3 Get feedback and recommendations from friends or family who have made similar purchases. Their first-hand experience and tips will be invaluable.

4 Know what features you need and what you can afford to spend before you enter a shop.

5 Ask plenty of questions. Be wary of salespeople who are overly aggressive or evasive in answering them. If you're not getting the service and information you need, find the manager.

6 Research and read labels to determine if products are made with potentially toxic materials or pose any danger to people, pets or the environment by their use. Investigate non-toxic alternatives.

7 Always find out what the return and exchange policy is before you buy (see 4 "Take Goods Back"). If you're buying online, call the free customer-service phone number with return questions.

8 Read the fine print on a warranty or contract and ask for a clarification if it's unclear. Important information is often obfuscated by legal mumbo-jumbo.

9 Get a signed and dated contract that spells out particulars whenever you hire someone to do a job for you. Before you hire a car mechanic, a builder or any professional person, get an estimate and a description of the scope of the work in writing.

10 Use a credit card, especially if you're making an online, phone or mail-order purchase. Credit card companies won't hold you liable for fraudulent charges and will reclaim the money from the seller if you receive falsely advertised, defective or damaged goods.

11 Be cautious when confronted with doorstep salespeople or offers on the phone. Resist efforts to make you commit yourself on the spot. Remember you have the legal right to cancel on reflection.

12 Keep all receipts, warranties, owner's manuals, contracts and written estimates in a well-organised filing system. A complaint is much harder to prove without documentation. Save packaging for the first week in case you discover defects or unsatisfactory performance; returns may need to be in their original packaging.

What to Look For

- Price comparisons
- Product reviews
- Return and exchange policy
- Customer service number
- Contract and warranty

Tips

Use a credit card that rewards you with air travel miles and other incentives to reap even more benefits from your purchases.

Don't be duped by "sale" signs. Ask yourself, "Am I really getting a good deal for my money?"

Avoid buying things you don't really want or need just because they are offered at a knockdown price. Junk is junk however little it costs.

Check the packaging and condition of a product. If a box has been retaped, ask if the item was a return, a display model, or a reconditioned item. If so, ask for a discount and make sure the warranty is still in full effect.

Warning

Never pay money up front for goods or services offered over the phone, and don't give your credit card number to anyone or any company you don't know.

2 Get Something for Nothing

There's truth behind the saying "There's no such thing as a free lunch". Some freebies require that you register your address, which may bury you in junk mail. Others require your time or energy. However, for the intrepid bargain hunter, true deals make exciting prey.

FREEBIE STRATEGY

Search the web for "free stuff". You'll find websites that index online freebies from manufacturers and retailers.

Imitate professional dealers by arriving at jumble sales or car-boot sales early to pick up really desirable items for next to nothing.

Visit street markets late in the day, especially on a Saturday. Traders keen to get rid of unsold fruit, vegetables and other perishables will be knocking down prices or throwing in extra produce for free.

Participate in market research groups to get free meals, products or services and, possibly, even a payment for your services. Search online to find opportunities in your area.

Take advantage of two-for-one offers in supermarkets whenever you can. If there's enough room in your freezer and the item is one you're keen on, get four for the price of two.

Look out for new shops, restaurants or cafés opening. They may be offering freebies to attract customers during their first few weeks in business.

Call customer service if you have a legitimate complaint on an item. You may get a replacement product, plus freebies to keep you happy.

When making a large purchase, such as a computer, sofa or big-screen TV, ask the salesperson, "What else will I get if I buy this here?" You may discover rebates, offers and give-aways.

Volunteer for concerts, athletic events and other fund-raisers for charities. You'll find plenty of free food, T-shirts and products donated by corporate sponsors.

Respond to competitions in newspapers and magazines offering free goods or holidays as prizes. Often surprisingly few people try these, so your chances of winning may be better than you think.

Listen to radio stations that give away tickets and other prizes to listeners. Use speed-dial and multiple lines to better your chances when you call in.

WARNING   Naturally, many freebies have a catch. If they come from manufacturers or retailers, they are not being provided simply out of goodness of heart. Pay careful attention to any conditions that apply or commitments you might unwittingly be making.

3 Buy Products and Services Online

No longer just for techno-nerds, online shopping has been embraced wholeheartedly by the mainstream community. In fact, more than 60 per cent of people worldwide are reckoned to have bought at least some product or service online.

Steps

1 Buy from retailers with a reputation for quality products and excellent customer service. Bookmark them for easy access. Pay attention to the experiences of friends and colleagues, and avoid shady or unscrupulous traders.

2 Shop at websites that are quick to load and easy to navigate through so you can find what you want quickly. Look for secure and simple ordering procedures.

3 Use price comparison tools – for example, DealTime.co.uk, shopping.net, or uk.shopping.yahoo.com – to compare brands, prices and product features across several sites. Consider buying an online subscription to *Which?* Online (which.net) to obtain critical information on large and small purchases.

4 Read customer and media reviews to find out more about a product or service. Amazon.co.uk lists editorial and customer reviews. The ZDNet UK website (zdnet.co.uk) is one of several good sources for technology reviews.

5 Read the "About Us" section if you're buying from an unfamiliar website to find out how long the company has been in business and whether it has third-party recommendations. Check for a free customer-service phone number.

6 Look for enhanced shopping guides and options. For example, the Marks & Spencer website (marksandspencer.com) allows you to shop for clothing by product, size and colour, and even offers tips on self-measurement for different clothing items to help you choose the correct size (see 500 "Buy Clothes Online"). Other merchants allow you to listen to partial tracks from CDs or read book excerpts before you buy.

7 If you're shopping for a service, such as a plumber, look for clearly posted cancellation policies and free, instant quotes. Sites such as Scoot (scoot.co.uk) provide lists of service providers of different kinds in your area.

8 If you're buying a product, review the delivery and handling costs, the return policy and whether the company pays postage on returned items (see 4 "Take Goods Back").

9 Charge your purchases on a credit or debit card (see 1 "Be a Smart Consumer").

What to Look For

- Reputable retailer
- Easy browsing or searching
- Customer ratings
- Price and feature comparisons
- Buying guides
- Delivery costs and return policy
- Secure transactions
- Receipt or confirmation

Tip

Make sure any online retailer posts its privacy policy prominently and allows you to opt out of having your information used for marketing purposes or shared with other parties.

Warnings

Make sure that any purchase transactions you conduct are secure. A URL that begins with *https://* (instead of *http://*) signals that you are sending and receiving encrypted information, for security purposes.

Keep your passwords private. Never share your bank account number when making a purchase, and never send your credit card number via e-mail.

10 Save a copy of the receipt and confirmation number on your
    hard drive, or print it out and keep a record of the transaction.

11 Take the opportunity offered by many sites to store your address
    and credit card information in order to avoid retyping them
    every time you make a purchase. American Express ID Keeper
    (american express.com/idkeeper) is a Windows-based application
    that lets users securely store personal data, credit card infor-
    mation, and website log-ins and passwords. Additionally, this
    data is stored directly on the embedded chip on the American
    Express Blue card.

4 Take Goods Back

With a surge in retail fraud, many shops are tightening up their policy
on returned goods. Shops are not legally bound to take goods back
unless a product was defective or falsely advertised. The lesson?
Know the shop's policy before you buy, be courteous, don't expect
something you're not entitled to, and hold on to those receipts.

Steps

1 Present the item in its original packaging, with the receipt and
   the credit card number, if any, used in the purchase. Most shops
   require that you return goods within 30 days, although some
   allow 90 days.

2 Go to the customer service counter or to a cashier. Early mornings are a good time to take goods back. Tell the person behind
   the counter that you'd like to return something. Provide a short
   explanation if necessary.

3 Expect to receive a credit card refund or cash or, if not, to be
   given a credit towards the purchase of another item from the
   same shop.

4 Suggest an exchange for a product of equal value if the
   salesperson refuses take the product back. Be patient with the
   employees. Being aggressive is unlikely to help. Most salespeople know that a happy customer is good for them and will
   find a way to make you happy, if they possibly can.

5 Asking to speak to a manager or supervisor may be necessary
   but may anger the salesperson. As a first attempt, try something
   like "I understand your hands are tied. Is there someone else that
   I can talk to?"

6 Be prepared to give up on an attempt if you meet unreasonable
   resistance. Try to come back when more knowledgeable staff are
   on hand. Do not make insults or threats as this will prejudice
   future negotiations against you.

What to Look For

- Shop policy on returns
- Original packaging and
  receipt
- Refund or credit towards
  purchase of other goods
- Item-for-item exchange

Tip

If a product is defective or
was falsely advertised and
the store refuses to take it
back, seek help from your
local Citizens Advice Bureau
(see 5 "Deal With an
Unsatisfactory Purchase").

5 Deal With an Unsatisfactory Purchase

As a consumer, you have the right to assume that a product will work as advertised. This is the product's implied warranty. It doesn't matter whether you bought something through mail order, over the phone, online or at a high street store. But if something does go wrong, there are a number of ways you can get satisfaction.

Steps

1 See 4 "Take Goods Back".

2 Arm yourself with information before you buy. Make sure you know where to direct a complaint in case there's a problem. If you're getting an item delivered, be sure you know the retailer's policy on goods that are lost or damaged in transit. Review the warranty on an item (see 209 "Buy Extended Warranties on Appliances").

3 Visit the shop with the item and receipt. For an online purchase, e-mail customer services and include your order number. In a friendly but firm tone, explain the problem and your desired solution. If this fails to remedy the situation, call customer services. Most websites list customer-service phone numbers (in their "About Us" or "Contact Us" section).

4 If a shop salesperson doesn't give you adequate help, or isn't able to remedy the situation, ask to speak to a supervisor. If the supervisor won't help, ask for the name of the shop's manager or owner. Continue up the chain to the regional manager or the manager at the national headquarters.

5 Be persistent but polite on the phone, and get the name, title and direct number of each person you speak to. To avoid aggravating disconnections during transfers, and getting stuck in the voice mail quagmire, always ask for the number you are being transferred to. Address the salesperson by name in a friendly manner and make it clear that you are confident that, although he or she is not personally responsible for the problem, he or she will want to rectify the problem and reward your loyalty to the company.

6 Be prepared to insist on having the problem resolved. If the company admits fault, ask how they intend "to make it right". For example, if a bank messes up your account, ask for free banking for a year. If a mail-order company fails to deliver goods on time, ask for 50 per cent off the price of the product. If you're stumped for a specific request to make, ask the sales representative, "What can you do to make this right and restore my faith in your company again?"

What to Look For

- Product return policy
- Customer-service contact information
- Citizens Advice Bureau
- Small claims court
- Public attention

Tips

If you have a complaint about goods purchased elsewhere in the European Union, look for advice online at euroconsumer.org.uk.

Document everything. Write down names, titles and phone numbers of people you speak to, plus the date and time. Record what they tell you. Keep a file of receipts, warranties, correspondence and photographs.

7 Contact your credit or debit card company, if you used it to make the purchase, and request in writing that the retailer be "charged back". Credit card companies protect consumers from unauthorised charges, incomplete orders, defective products or false advertising.

A courteous and pleasant approach will aid your efforts. Avoid becoming confrontational or emotional.

8 Write a letter if your efforts fail to get results. Get the name of the person who will handle your complaint (preferably someone in management). Go online to the Citizens Advice Bureau Service's advice website (adviceguide.org.uk) to find tips on what to include in a letter of complaint. Send the letter by special delivery to confirm the company receives it.

Try to get retailers and service representatives to see your point of view. A good question to ask is "What would you do if you were in my situation?"

9 If the company still fails to fix the problem, report your complaint to your local Citizens Advice Bureau. To find the contact details of your nearest Citizens Advice Bureau, visit the service's website (nacab.org.uk) or look it up in the phone book.

10 Consider the small claims court as a final remedy. The small claims court is a do-it-yourself legal recourse for claims under £5,000. Fill in a claim form – obtainable from your local court or, if you live in England or Wales, online from courtservice.gov.uk. Your local Citizens Advice Bureau will give help, if needed, with filling in a claim form and pursuing the case. Hiring a lawyer should be considered only in extreme cases as your legal fees will mount quickly.

11 Let a manager or supervisor at the company in question know that you intend to go public. Most newspapers have consumer reporters who may be interested in your case. Or search out one of the television "consumer rip-off" series. Contact them with a letter detailing your grievance and asking for help in finding a solution. Companies hate bad press – even the threat of it can whip them into behaving.

6 Sell Products and Services Online

The internet has revolutionised selling for many small businesses and individuals with home businesses. You no longer need a shop built of bricks and mortar to sell your wares and you can reach many more interested buyers – your "passing trade" can be a surfer in another city or continent. Use existing sites or set up your own online shop.

Steps

Sell through existing venues

1 Go to sites such as Amazon.co.uk to sell used books, CDs and other items at a fixed price. You can list items in exchange for a percentage of the sale.

2 Post items for sale on classified ad sites. Visit a directory, such as uk.dir.yahoo.com, to find lists of sites. Some are internet-only, like adpost.com/uk, while others are internet versions of magazines such as *Exchange and Mart* (exchangeandmart.co.uk) and *Loot* (loot.com).

3 Use online auction sites like eBay.co.uk to sell collectibles, antiques, out-of-print books and anything else you find in the attic or garage (see 10 "Use Online Auction Sites").

4 Get listed in directories and on referral websites if you have a professional service for hire.

5 If you're selling financial, romantic, psychic or other advice, consider using a site like Keen.com. Customers get connected to you through the service, which charges the customer by the minute and keeps a percentage of the profits.

Set up a cybershop

1 Set up an online shop. A substantial investment is required for start-up costs, which include domain name registration, site hosting, e-commerce software, site development and maintenance, marketing, credit card transaction fees, internet access and customer services. There's also the time spent on design, taking photos of inventory and updating the site (see 157 "Hire Someone to Design and Build Your Website").

2 Design a sleek, professional, easy-to-navigate site that loads quickly at both dial-up and broadband speeds. Or, check out Amazon.co.uk, eBay.co.uk and Yahoo Shopping for starter packages allowing you to create an online shop – the bonus is that you tap into the heavy traffic of these popular sites and take advantage of search engines.

3 Include concise, informative copy and photographs to bring traffic to your site and hold attention. Update the site frequently to keep the content fresh.

What to Look For

- Existing sites
- Capital investment for e-commerce
- Website design
- URL placement

Tip

Image is everything when you sell online. Post copy that is impeccably written and free of errors. Include high-quality, well-cropped photographs of your products.

4 Register your URL on all the major search engines (including Google.com, Yahoo.com, Lycos.com and HotBot.com) to make sure your site shows up in relevant searches. Include keywords in meta tags in HTML files to increase the chances of getting hits from search engines. You may, however, find that paying for placement results in more traffic.

5 Advertise your website on heavily trafficked sites and through banner swaps (see 160 "Buy Advertising on the Web"). See Cyberatlas.internet.com for a compilation of online marketing statistics and articles.

6 Establish trust. Post your privacy policy prominently. Make sure customer-service information is clearly displayed, including third-party recommendations, and provide quick response. Set up a secure server to handle credit card transactions. Answer customer queries by phone or e-mail as promptly, effectively and courteously as you can.

7 Use discretion: Obnoxious, blinking ads and spam e-mails drive away customers.

Warning

Beware of individuals or companies that offer to sell instant access to wholesale inventories for your commerce site. Finding wholesale inventories isn't easy, and anyone who says differently is misleading you.

7 Save Money with Special Offers

The "money-off your next purchase" offers that drop through your letterbox or appear in newspapers and magazines can trim your shopping bills – if you have the time, discipline and patience actually to use them. Keep track of the money you save, then reward yourself every now and then. You deserve it!

Steps

1 Special offers are used by companies to promote their products on the safe bet that most people will never take them up. Set up an easy-to-use system to store your special offer coupons. Keep them alongside your car keys as a handy reminder to take them with you when you go shopping.

2 Keep special offer coupons only for products you would buy in any case (see 1 "Be a Smart Consumer"). Don't let irresistible savings dupe you into buying items you don't need.

3 Know prices. Brand-name products with a money-off deal often cost more than generic products at full price.

4 Look to layer savings. If a supermarket is offering a special price to promote an item and you also have a manufacturer's money-off coupon, use both. Use your supermarket loyalty card at the same time for maximum saving.

5 Scour newspapers, magazines and the internet for special offers on products that interest you.

What to Look For

- Newspaper and magazine inserts
- Manufacturers' coupons
- Loyalty cards

Tip

A web search for "special offers" will yield thousands of hits, so make your search as specific as possible.

Warning

Special offers, like produce, are perishable. Use them before they expire.

8 Negotiate

Many people hate negotiating, but with a few simple tactics, it can be rewarding and fun. The following steps relate mostly to making purchases but the overall ideas – research the market, be upbeat and positive, and know what something is worth to you – can be applied to almost any negotiation. See 1 "Be a Smart Consumer" as well.

Steps

1 Do your research in advance to find the best deals. If you're looking for consumer goods, first make a comparison of prices and features of available products. Consult *Which?* magazine or its online version, or online comparison tools like DealTime.co.uk, shopping.net or uk.shopping.yahoo.com. If you're negotiating a salary increase, know what other people in your profession are making. If you want to buy a pedigree puppy, find out what they're going for.

2 Know what an item is worth to you and set an upper limit on what you're willing to spend. It's easy during negotiations for the game to shift. A salesperson might offer a price reduction on one item as long as you buy an additional one. Keep your needs and your goal well defined and stick to your limit. This also applies to salary negotiations: securing an increase in pay may necessitate additional responsibilities.

3 Adopt a direct but lighthearted attitude. Nobody wants to deal with a sourpuss. This applies to salary negotiations as well as purchases. Your boss will deal with you more openly if you are able to state your position clearly, including why you deserve that pay rise. Practise salary negotiations with a professional (see 145 "Hire a Careers Counsellor").

4 Remain indifferent when making purchases. Hardball price negotiation requires the seller to believe that you are willing to walk away. To be convincing at this, you must indeed be willing to walk. Practise with small purchases and you'll see this is true. Remember that most consumer goods, even major purchases like cars, are not "one of a kind", "rare" or "hard to find," so don't be swayed by these claims. This tactic has limited application for salary negotiations unless you are truly ready to quit. Threatening to resign is not likely to secure your pay rise.

5 Make the seller (or your boss) want to say yes. Most people want to be deal-makers and problem-solvers. Salespeople want to sell. Your boss wants productive and loyal employees. You have a problem and you want their help. They are the important decision-makers and you will have a great deal of respect for them if they can solve this problem.

6 Hire professional help for complicated negotiations. Buying and selling houses, for example, is too complicated for most non-professionals (see 184 "Sell a House Without an Estate Agent")

What to Look For

- Know the market
- Be friendly
- Make the seller want to help

Tip

Friends and relatives are a great source of information about sensitive financial matters but be sure to conduct additional research. Stories involving money are always subject to exaggeration.

9 Buy Green

The environmental challenges of pollution, global warming and scarce resources are daunting. Can you make a difference through your daily purchases? Yes, if you're prepared to do a little research. Every pound spent on environmentally friendly products encourages manufacturers to think green.

GREEN PRODUCT	HOW IT HELPS
Kitchen	
Cloth (tea towel/dish cloth)	Saves trees and reduces the use of paper.
Cloth shopping bag	Reduces the use of paper or plastic bags.
Nontoxic kitchen cleaner	Reduces the amount of phosphates and other toxins flowing down the drain.
Energy-efficient appliance	Conserves energy and natural resources. Source of the most dramatic differences are found in energy-efficient fridges.
CFC-free fridge	Reduces the emissions of chlorofluorocarbons (CFCs), which contribute to ozone depletion and global warming.
Unbleached coffee filter	Reduces possible use of the toxic pollutant chlorine.
Bathroom	
Unbleached toilet tissue	Reduces possible use of the toxic pollutant chlorine.
Tampon without plastic applicator	Reduces plastic applicators in waterways, where they pose danger to fish and birds, which mistake them for food.
Electric razor	Reduces waste.
Nonaerosol deodorant/hairspray	Eliminates aerosol release of CFCs.
Low-flow shower head	Conserves water.
General household	
Bulk-size cleaner	Reduces waste.
Nontoxic cleaner	Reduces water, air and land pollution from polishes, detergents and other cleaning agents.
Rechargeable batteries	Reduces toxic waste found in disposable batteries.
Reusable camera/lighter	Reduces waste.
Car/transport	
Fuel-efficient vehicle	Reduces petrol consumption and air pollution.
Bicycle	Reduces pollution through zero-emission transport.
Public transport	Reduces pollution and fuel consumption
Office	
Recycled paper	Saves trees and encourages production of recycled products.
Refillable toner cartridge	Reduces toxic and excessive waste of toner cartridges.

10 Use Online Auction Sites

Imagine having a car-boot sale that millions of people visit. Online auctions allow you to do just that. Television sets, rocking chairs or designer wedding dresses – if you have it or are dying to get it, an online auction is the place to go. Yahoo.com and Amazon.co.uk have auction sites, but eBay.co.uk is widely considered to be the premier site for buyers and sellers alike. For more general auction tips, see 374 "Buy at Auction".

Steps

Buying

1 Find out the going rate for what you're shopping for. Check final bids for similar items in archived auctions. See 1 "Be a Smart Consumer" and 375 "Know What Your Collectibles Are Worth".

2 Check a seller's history for positive comments. Online auctions are self-policing with buyers and sellers offering feedback on each other. A seller's name will be followed by the number of auctions he or she has held and a satisfaction rating by the bidders.

3 Provide feedback on other sellers to encourage them to do the same for you. Take a deep breath before you fire off an inflammatory negative review – these reviews are permanent and may reflect poorly on you.

4 E-mail the seller with any questions, and if anything about the seller seems dubious, don't bid.

5 Read the item description carefully; some sellers bury negative information in confusing language or small print. If the size of an item isn't included and is important, e-mail the seller for it – photos can be deceptive.

6 Find out the cost of delivery beforehand. If it's not listed, ask the seller. Some sellers overcharge for delivery to make extra money on the deal.

7 Use proxy bids, which let you make an initial bid and set a maximum one. Your bid then gets automatically increased against competing bids, until you win the auction or someone outbids your maximum. Most sites let you know via e-mail when you've been outbid.

8 Add pennies to your offer to sneak above other bids. For example, if someone has a maximum bid of £50 and you bid £50.05, you'll beat them with only 5p.

What to Look For

- Buyer and seller history
- Item description
- Proxy bids and sniping
- Dutch auctions
- Site regulations
- E-mail communication
- Delivery and insurance

Tips

Know your limit. Avoid getting swept up in the bidding frenzy and paying more than an item is worth or that you can afford.

Be wary of fake bidders who work in league with the seller to drive up the auction price artificially. If you suspect a seller is using fake bidders, report it to the website administrator.

Both eBay.co.uk and Amazon.co.uk insure auctions from reputable sellers up to a certain amount. They also offer escrow services so buyer and seller can safely exchange large amounts of money.

Many auction sites have wonderful community features that allow you to network with other collectors. Take advantage of them.

9 Be a sniper. Bid at the very last minute before an auction ends to "snipe", or snatch away an item from another bidder. There are websites that will do the sniping for you for a fee.

10 Use a credit or debit card if possible. These cards provide protection for you as a buyer that cheques and money orders don't. Never send cash.

11 Save all e-mails related to a transaction until it is completed and you are satisfied with your purchase.

Selling

1 Buy several items from an auction site before you begin selling to build up your personal profile with positive feedback.

2 Include photos that show the complete item, plus details of unique features or flaws. Compress the image files to minimise download time for people looking at your stuff.

3 Do a search before you list an item to make sure there aren't other people auctioning the same thing. Wait to list your item until the other auction ends.

4 Use so-called Dutch auctions (in which you sell more than one of the same item) only on very popular products; otherwise you'll drive down the demand and price.

5 Know the auction site's rules. For example, most auction sites (including eBay.co.uk) prohibit the sale of explosives, live animals and human body parts.

6 Plan your auction to end at a time when lots of people use the site, such as week nights or weekend days. Run longer auctions so more people have time to stumble upon them.

7 Give bidders every reason to place a bid. Accept credit cards and offer guaranteed satisfaction. Respond promptly to questions from bidders.

8 E-mail the winning bidder promptly to arrange payment (many sites use PayPal). Ship the item as soon as the payment goes through. Print all e-mails related to a sale and file them until the transaction is completed.

9 Package items securely. Find out up to what value the delivery service automatically insures packages. Buy insurance for packages worth more than that sum.

Write (and spell-check) an attention-grabbing title and a thorough, accurate product description. Include condition, history, dimensions, distinct markings, delivery costs, and payment options. Glean keywords from other ads that people are likely to search for and write your item description accordingly.

Warning

Never provide your bank account number to sellers. If a seller asks for this information, report it to the web administrator immediately.

11 Buy Bargain Clothing

Just because your budget is limited doesn't mean you have to wear poorly made leggings and a baggy T-shirt all year round. With just a small amount of effort you can look great without spending a fortune. It's a question of establishing your own personal style and pursuing all possible sales avenues.

Steps

1 Check out charity shops like Oxfam and shops advertising "Nearly New" clothing. Look in the *Yellow Pages* to find out where these shops are located and then visit the ones that are in the most affluent areas of your town, city or county. You're bound to find one or two choice designer items in good condition in charity shops in up-market areas.

2 Scour the local newspaper for the dates and locations of jumble sales and fairs, such as those held by schools and charities such as the National Childbirth Trust. Target those held in the wealthier areas and then be first in the queue at the door well before the event starts. You'll be there with the second-hand dealers. Make a beeline for the clothes and sift through carefully and persistently, looking for timeless articles that suit your style.

3 Make yourself well-informed about the dates of department store sales and keep an eye open for closing down sales of any small boutiques in up-market areas. You will usually be buying at the end of a season, so ensure that you choose clothes that either suit your particular style, which pays no heed to fashion trends, or that you buy classic-looking clothes that will not date. Then, when you finally put them on the following summer, you will not look absurdly passé.

4 Many mail order clothing companies, such as Boden, have websites they are keen for you to use. Register with them online to receive advance news of discounted lines or special money-saving offers available only to online buyers.

5 Many catalogue companies hold regular end-of-line warehouse sales. Register with those companies that sell clothes you like and wait for the fliers to arrive with details of the date and location of the next warehouse sale.

6 Check out the street markets in your area. Market traders will always be cheaper than High Street retailers. Some traders will happen to carry stock that is just right for your look. If you find a stall you like visit it on a regular basis throughout the year.

7 Resist impulse buying. "The more you buy, the more you save" is a big, fat tempting lie. Buying and saving are two different things. If you buy something you don't need, you're not saving anything, you're wasting (see 1 "Be a Smart Consumer").

What to Look For

- Charity shops in affluent areas
- End-of-season and end-of-line sales
- Targetted online and warehouse sales

Tips

Create a look for yourself that is distinctive and not tied to a particular fashion trend. Search only for articles of clothing that suit that specific look.

Seek out market stalls with stock that you like and nurture a relationship with the stall owners. If you buy items from their stall regularly, they will try to source articles they think you will like and put them by for you when you next visit.

Make it your motto never to buy anything at full price. Always wait for the department store sales and the special discounts offered by the mail order companies.

Familiarise yourself with the factory shops in your area (see 521 "Purchase Clothes at Factory Shops").

12 Buy Wholesale

A large chunk of the money you pay for goods in any shop goes to the retailer, so it makes sense to try to buy wholesale. But how low can the prices go? Further reductions may be possible through buying larger quantities or even securing a business licence.

Steps

1 Work your network of colleagues, friends and family to find wholesale sources. Plumbers, contractors, landscape gardeners, florists, interior designers and jewellers all have access to wholesale markets and/or prices. These professionals may require that you hire them to take advantage of reduced prices, so balance these expenditures against potential savings.

2 Call wholesale suppliers and ask if they are prepared to sell to the general public. Wholesalers are listed in the *Yellow Pages* by category, such as "Builders' Merchants". They'll charge VAT and mark up prices a bit, but you can still find great bargains.

3 Join associations or professional groups that share your interests. Many groups, through their combined buying power, have access to lower prices. Magazines and websites devoted to your special interest will probably advertise groups to join.

4 Consider setting up officially as a small business or retail trader if you use a lot of something. Most wholesale suppliers will sell to you once you are set up. Establishing yourself in this way is not as difficult as it might first seem. Existing hobbies, interests or skills can be treated as a business venture. For example, if you enjoy gardening, look into setting up as a plant nursery. A few sales to friends will make you legitimate. Research legal requirements carefully and compare costs to expected savings.

5 Pay by credit card wherever possible for optimal protection as a purchaser. If you have to pay cash-on-delivery, make sure to inspect all merchandise thoroughly before you accept goods.

What to Look For

- Wholesaler contacts
- Wholesale suppliers

Tips

Some companies buy over-stocked or discontinued items and sell them in bulk quantities at wholesale or below-wholesale prices. While these can be great bargains, there's probably a reason for this – they were unpopular to begin with.

Cosmetic seconds, items that are functionally sound but have a slight blemish, can be great deals. Usually the blemish is insignificant, but be sure to check before you buy.

13 Get Out of Debt

In 2004 it was estimated that a quarter of all UK adults were in trouble with debt. Even if you feel you have your borrowing under control, it's downright silly to bend over backwards to find bargains, yet pay thousands of pounds in interest every year without thinking twice. It makes sense to pay off outstanding loans and credit card debt as quickly as possible. Some of these guidelines may sound harsh but the price you'll pay for ignoring them is even harsher.

Steps

1 Make a monthly budget and stick to it. Housing, food, utilities, car and insurance payments have to be made. Allocate an additional amount each month to paying off your debt. Many financial planners say this is the most effective way to manage your finances (see 141 "Buy Personal Finance Software").

2 Control your spending. This is the first step towards fixing money problems. Most people who spend too much are enthralled with the act of buying, not the value of the goods. Question every purchase – what will happen if you don't buy it? You might be surprised how little real value most stuff has and how easily you can do without it.

3 Keep a shopping diary listing what you buy each day and how much it costs. This may seem tedious but will track each expenditure and encourage conscious cutbacks on spending.

4 Destroy all of your credit cards except one, with the lowest possible (long-term) interest rate. Leave this card at home and use it only for emergencies. Transfer the debt on your other cards to this remaining card (see 126 "Negotiate a Better Credit Card Deal"). Carry a small amount of cash for daily expenses.

5 Maintain contact with your creditors. Avoiding phone calls and letters from your creditors will make your problems worse. They want to work with you and it's in your interest to do so too.

6 Refinance your mortgage at a lower rate. If your credit is already bad, this may not be possible. But if you can get a lower rate, you can apply your savings directly to pay off your debts, or pull extra cash out to take care of it at once (see 173 "Get a Better Mortgage Deal" and 174 "Save on Your Mortgage").

7 Investigate a home equity loan with which you can pay off other debts. The idea is to combine your debts into one payment, at the lowest possible interest rate. If you have credit card debt, you're probably paying a very high interest rate, so other loan options are worth exploring. Approach your building society or bank for information (see 185 "Release Capital from Your Home").

8 Sell valuables and use the money to pay off your debt. Ferraris, yachts and other expensive toys should be eliminated. They won't be fun anyway, if they're dragging you into financial ruin.

What to Look For

- Mortgage options
- Liquidated assets
- Cutbacks on spending
- Lower interest rates
- Lower payoff amount

Tips

Pay your bills on time. Besides imposing hefty late fees, creditors bump up interest rates for late payments. Pay parking tickets and fines swiftly to avoid late penalties.

Call the credit company if you are running into difficulties and explain your problem. You may be surprised by how helpful they are.

Never try to ignore a debt problem. Face up to it early for the best hope of success.

Warnings

Don't be tempted by a consolidation loan – a single bigger loan to pay off all your existing debts. This only means borrowing even more money, plunging you deeper into debt.

Don't apply for a zero-interest card unless you're absolutely committed to paying off your debt before the interest-free period ends. If you don't, you could get stuck with a very high rate.

14 Buy Nothing

Ownership can be a burden. Once you buy something, you have to carry it around, fix it, remember where you put it and keep it clean. Experiment with the freedom of buying nothing and embrace the refreshing philosophy of the "simple life".

Steps

1 Practice reverse snobbery. Express contempt for people who mindlessly buy things. This has two benefits: It raises the act of not buying things to a lofty moral height, from which you can denigrate others, and you get to enjoy the irony of simultaneously being a snob while making fun of other snobs.

2 Go to shopping centres and department stores and briefly let your materialistic impulses loose. Try on some sweaters and choose three or four. Add a few ties or scarves. Walk around for a few minutes enjoying your stack of loot. Then put it back on the shelf and walk out. Think about how unnecessary that stuff is. You probably already have something just like it. What a relief to not have more junk around the house.

3 Get satisfaction from money saved, not money spent. Set up a direct deposit so that 10 per cent or more of your salary goes automatically into a savings or investment account.

4 Become a scrounger. Old bicycles, furniture, building materials, vehicles, books and clothing are everywhere, once you start looking. Become skilled at resurrecting old stuff and finding uses for it. Take pride in being an eccentric recycler.

5 Look for barter opportunities. Swap your homegrown vegetables for repairs on your house, for example. With your neighbours, set up a local barter network where credits can be earned and exchanged for needed services. Because no money is exchanged when you barter, you avoid paying tax, which can mean a substantial saving.

6 Consider having a "buy nothing Christmas" this year. Make token presents for close friends and relatives, and encourage them to do the same. Live up to the maxim "It's the thought that counts".

What to Look For

- Needs versus wants
- Ways to save, not spend

Tips

Studies have shown that most children want more time from their parents, not more toys.

29 November is Buy Nothing Day, with worldwide demonstrations in support of more sensible consumption.

JY YOUR WAY INTO SOMEONE'S FAVOUR • BUY LOVE • FIND THE RIGHT RELAXATION TECHNIQUE FOR YOU • BUY HEALTHY FAST FOOD •
ING SERVICE • SELL YOURSELF ON AN ONLINE DATING SERVICE • SELL YOURSELF TO YOUR GIRLFRIEND/BOYFRIEND'S FAMILY • BUY FLC
HOOSE FILM FOR YOUR CAMERA • BUY RECHARGEABLE BATTERIES • GIVE TO A GOOD CAUSE • TAKE PART IN A CAR BOOT SALE • EMPLC
DENT DISCOUNTS • BUY FLOWERS WHOLESALE • GET A PICTURE FRAMED • EMPLOY A REMOVAL COMPANY • EMPLOY A LIFESTYLE MAN
Y FOR A HALLOWE'EN PARTY • BUY A GREAT BIRTHDAY PRESENT FOR UNDER £10 • SELECT GOOD CHAMPAGNE • BUY A DIAMOND • BUY
A GIFT LIST • BUY WEDDING GIFTS • SELECT BRIDESMAIDS' DRESSES • HIRE AN EVENTS ORGANISER • HIRE A BARTENDER FOR A PARTY
NOUNCEMENTS • SELL YOUR WEDDING DRESS • BUY AN ANNIVERSARY GIFT • ARRANGE ENTERTAINMENT FOR A PARTY • COMMISSION A
SON WHO HAS EVERYTHING • BUY A GIFT FOR PASSING EXAMS • SELECT A CHRISTMAS TURKEY • BUY A HOUSEWARMING GIFT • PURCH
AND • WRITE A MESSAGE IN THE SKY • HIRE A BIG-NAME BAND • GET INTO A PRIVATE GAMBLING ROOM IN LAS VEGAS • BUY SOMEONE A
TIMES • EMPLOY A BUTLER • BUY A FOOTBALL CLUB • BUY A PERSONAL JET • SELECT A CLASSIC CAR • ACQUIRE A BODY GUARD • BO
YHOUND TO RACE • BUY A RACEHORSE • BUY A VILLA IN TUSCANY • EMPLOY A PERSONAL CHEF • BUY A JOURNEY INTO SPACE • EMPL
TUNE • HIRE AN EXPERT WITNESS • MAKE MONEY FROM ACCIDENT COMPENSATION • DONATE YOUR BODY TO SCIENCE • MAKE MONEY
ANCIAL ADVISER • PLAN FOR RETIREMENT • COPE WITH HIGHER EDUCATION COSTS • BUY AND SELL SHARES • CHOOSE A STOCKBROKE
S INSURANCE • BUY LIFE INSURANCE • GET PRIVATE HEALTH INSURANCE • BUY PERSONAL FINANCE SOFTWARE • CHOOSE AN ACCOUN
E OUT A PATENT • MARKET YOUR INVENTION • FINANCE YOUR BUSINESS IDEA • BUY A SMALL BUSINESS • BUY A FRANCHISE • LEASE RE
BSITE • HIRE A GRAPHIC DESIGNER • ACQUIRE CONTENT FOR YOUR WEBSITE • BUY ADVERTISING ON THE WEB • SELL YOUR ART • HIRE
LISH YOUR BOOK • START A BED-AND-BREAKFAST • SELL A FAILING BUSINESS • BUY A HOT DOG STAND • SHOP FOR A MORTGAGE • GE
JSE AT AUCTION • SHOP FOR A HOUSE ONLINE • BUY A PROPERTY FOR RENOVATION AND RESALE • EVALUATE BEFORE BUYING INTO A N
A PLOT OF LAND • HAVE YOUR HOUSE DESIGNED • HIRE AN ARCHITECT • HIRE A BUILDER • GET PLANNING PERMISSION • BUY A HOLID
OAD • BUY TO LET • RENT YOUR HOME FOR A LOCATION SHOOT • FURNISH YOUR HOME • FURNISH YOUR STUDIO FLAT • BUY USED FUF
JY HOUSEHOLD APPLIANCES • BUY FLOOR-CARE APPLIANCES • BUY EXTENDED WARRANTIES ON APPLIANCES • FIND PERIOD FIXTURES
ME • SELECT PAINT, STAIN AND VARNISH • CHOOSE DECORATIVE TILES • CHOOSE A DEHUMIDIFIER • BUY A WHIRLPOOL BATH • BUY A SH
LLPAPER • BUY A WOOD-BURNING STOVE • SELECT FLOORING • SELECT CARPETING • CHOOSE KITCHEN CABINETS • CHOOSE A KITCHEI
DKE ALARMS • BUY CARBON MONOXIDE DETECTORS • BUY FIRE EXTINGUISHERS • CHOOSE AN ENTRY DOOR • BUY A GARAGE-DOOR OP
DOOR FURNITURE • BUY THE PERFECT ROSE • BUY FLOWERING BULBS • BUY FLOWERS FOR YOUR GARDEN • SELECT PEST CONTROLS
OMATIC WATERING SYSTEM • START A NEW LAWN • BUY A LAWN MOWER • BUY KOI FOR YOUR FISH POND • BUY A STORAGE SHED • HIF
DUCE • CHOOSE A PERFECT PEACH • BUY AND SELL AT FARMERS' MARKETS • SELECT KITCHEN KNIVES • DECIPHER FOOD LABELS • SE
FECT BURGER • PURCHASE A CHRISTMAS HAM • BUY ORGANIC BEEF • BUY HAGGIS • PURCHASE LOCAL HONEY • CHOOSE A CHICKEN
TRUFFLES • BUY ARTISAN BREADS • BUY ARTISAN CHEESES • PURCHASE KOSHER FOOD • BUY SENSIBLY IN SUPERMARKETS • CHOOS
ER A GREAT CUP OF COFFEE • BUY A COFFEEMAKER OR ESPRESSO MACHINE • PURCHASE PARTY BEER • CHOOSE THE RIGHT WINE • C
RM • CHOOSE AN OVULATION PREDICTOR KIT • PICK A PREGNANCY TEST KIT • CHOOSE BIRTH CONTROL • CHOOSE WHERE TO GIVE BIR
BABY CLOTHES • CHOOSE NAPPIES • BUY OR RENT A BREAST PUMP • CHOOSE A CAR SEAT • BUY CHILD-PROOFING SUPPLIES • FIND F
A GARDEN PLAY STRUCTURE • FIND A FAMILY-FRIENDLY HOTEL • ORGANISE A FUND-RAISING EVENT • BUY BRACES FOR YOUR KID • BL
MODEL • SELL USED BABY GEAR, TOYS, CLOTHES AND BOOKS • FIND A COUPLES COUNSELLOR • HIRE A FAMILY SOLICITOR • BUY OR I
CHASE A TOOTHBRUSH • BUY MOISTURISERS AND ANTIWRINKLE CREAMS • SELECT PAIN RELIEF AND COLD MEDICINES • CHOOSE A CO
DUCTS • BUY WAYS TO COUNTER HAIR LOSS • BUY A WIG OR HAIRPIECE • BUY A NEW BODY • GET A TATTOO OR BODY PIERCING • OBT/
H • SELECT SPECTACLES AND SUNGLASSES • HIRE A PERSONAL TRAINER • SIGN UP FOR A YOGA CLASS • TREAT YOURSELF TO A DAY /
N ANTIQUE MARKET • BUY AT AUCTION • KNOW WHAT YOUR COLLECTIBLES ARE WORTH • BARTER WITH DEALERS • GET AN ANTIQUE AF
NS • BUY AN ANTIQUE QUILT • BUY FILM POSTERS • LIQUIDATE YOUR BEANIE BABY COLLECTION • SCORE AUTOGRAPHS • TRADE YU-GI-I
SELL SPORTS MEMORABILIA • SELL YOUR FOOTBALL-CARD COLLECTION • CHOOSE A DESKTOP COMPUTER • SHOP FOR A USED COMP
IPUTER PERIPHERALS • CHOOSE AN INTERNET SERVICE PROVIDER • GET AN INTERNET DOMAIN NAME • NETWORK YOUR COMPUTERS •
PLAYER • BUY A VIDEO RECORDER • CHOOSE A PERSONAL DIGITAL ASSISTANT • CHOOSE A MOBILE PHONE SERVICE • GET A BETTER DI
TAL CAMERA • BUY A HOME AUTOMATION SYSTEM • BUY A STATE-OF-THE-ART SOUND SYSTEM • BUY AN AUDIO/VIDEO DISTRIBUTION SY
SYSTEM • BUY VIRTUAL-REALITY FURNITURE • BUY TWO-WAY RADIOS • BUY A MOBILE ENTERTAINMENT SYSTEM • GET A PASSPORT, QUI
L LUGGAGE • FLY FOR NEXT TO NOTHING • TAKE A TRIP ON THE TRANS-SIBERIAN EXPRESS • BUY DUTY-FREE • SHIP FOREIGN PURCHAS
AN CYCLING HOLIDAY • CHOOSE A CHEAP CRUISE • BOOK A HOTEL PACKAGE FOR THE GREEK ISLANDS • RAFT THE GRAND CANYON • E
SHAW IN RANGOON • TAKE SALSA LESSONS IN CUBA • BUY A CAMERA IN HONG KONG • BUY YOUR WAY ONTO A MOUNT EVEREST EXPE
TEAM • BUY ANKLE AND KNEE BRACES • CHOOSE RUGBY PROTECTION KIT • BUY GOLF CLUBS • SELL FOUND GOLF BALLS • BUY PORT
LOY A SCUBA INSTRUCTOR • BUY A SKATEBOARD AND PROTECTIVE GEAR • BUY SKATES • GO BUNJEE JUMPING • GO SKYDIVING • BUY
TS AND BINDINGS • BUY SKI BOOTS • BUY A BICYCLE • BUY AN ELECTRIC BICYCLE • BUY CYCLE CLOTHING • BUY A PROPERLY FITTING
• BUY A SURFBOARD • BUY FLY-FISHING GEAR • BUY ROCK-CLIMBING EQUIPMENT • BUY A CASHMERE JUMPER • PURCHASE VINTAGE
KTAIL DRESS • BUY DESIGNER CLOTHES AT A DISCOUNT • CHOOSE A BASIC WARDROBE FOR A MAN • BUY A MAN'S DRESS SHIRT • PICK
HER JACKET • BUY MATERNITY CLOTHES • GET A GREAT-FITTING BRA • CHOOSE A HIGH-PERFORMANCE SWIM SUIT • BUY PERFORMANC
TORY SHOPS • BUY A NEW CAR • BUY THE BASICS FOR YOUR CAR • BUY A USED CAR • BUY OR SELL A CAR ONLINE • BUY A HYBRID CA

BUY TIME • BUY A BOUQUET OF ROSES • BUY SOMEONE A DRINK • GET SOMEONE TO BUY YOU A DRINK • BUY YOUR WAY INTO THE BE
SCREEN • BUT FURTHER EDUCATION • ORDER EXOTIC FOOD • ORDER AT A SUSHI BAR • BUY DINNER AT A FRENCH RESTAURANT • EMPL
O SAY SORRY TO YOUR PARTNER • BUY MUSIC ONLINE • EMPLOY MUSICIANS • ORDER A GOOD BOTTLE OF WINE • BUY AN ERGONOMIC
ANER • EMPLOY AN AU PAIR • BUY A GUITAR • BUY DUCT TAPE • GET A GOOD DEAL ON A MAGAZINE SUBSCRIPTION • GET SENIOR CITIZI
FIND A VET • BUY PET FOOD • BUY A PEDIGREE DOG OR CAT • BREED YOUR PET AND SELL THE LITTER • BUY OR RENT FOR A FANCY DR
RY MADE OF PRECIOUS METALS • BUY COLOURED GEMSTONES • CHOOSE THE PERFECT WEDDING DRESS • BUY OR RENT MEN'S FORM
A PHOTOGRAPHER • HIRE A CATERER • FIND THE IDEAL CIVIL WEDDING VENUE • THE COST OF MARRYING • ORDER PERSONALISED INVITA
RKS SHOW • BUY A MOTHER'S DAY GIFT • BUY A FATHER'S DAY GIFT • SELECT AN APPROPRIATE COMING-OF-AGE GIFT • GET A GIFT FOR
RISTMAS CARDS • BUY CHRISTMAS STOCKING FILLERS • BUY CHRISTENING GIFTS • PURCHASE A PERFECT CHRISTMAS TREE • BUY A PF
PAY A RANSOM • GET HOT TICKETS • HIRE A LIMOUSINE • BUY A CRYONIC CHAMBER • RENT YOUR OWN HOARDING • TAKE OUT A FULL-I
XURY CRUISE AROUND THE WORLD • BUY A TICKET TO TRAVEL FOR A YEAR • BOOK A TRIP ON THE ORIENT-EXPRESS • OWN A VINEYARD
OSTWRITER TO WRITE YOUR MEMOIRS • COMMISSION ORIGINAL ARTWORK • IMMORTALISE YOUR SPOUSE IN A SCULPTURE • GIVE AWAY
DICAL GUINEA PIG • SELL YOUR STORY TO THE TABLOIDS • SELL YOUR SOUL TO THE DEVIL • NEGOTIATE A BETTER CREDIT CARD DEAL •
TRADE (OR NOT) • BUY ANNUITIES • BUY AND SELL MUTUAL FUNDS • BUY BONDS • SELL SHORT • INVEST IN PRECIOUS METALS • BUY SE
ND CASUAL WORK • SELL YOUR PRODUCT O   HEADHUNTER • SELL YOURSELF IN A JOB INTE
CE • LEASE INDUSTRIAL SPACE • LEASE OFFI   MENT • HIRE SOMEONE TO DESIGN AND BUILD Y
OACH • SELL ON THE CRAFT CIRCUIT • HIRE A   RY • SELL A SCREENPLAY • SELL YOUR NOVEL •
ER MORTGAGE DEAL • SAVE ON YOUR MORTO   D • OBTAIN HOUSE INSURANCE • BUY A HOUSE •
• EXCHANGE CONTRACTS ON A PROPERTY •   AN ESTATE AGENT • RELEASE CAPITAL FROM YO
• RENT A HOLIDAY HOME • BUY A FLAT • REI   COUNTRY • BUY A LOFT APARTMENT • BUY PRO
• BUY DOOR AND WINDOW LOCKS • CHOOSE   IGHT FIXTURES • BUY A PROGRAMMABLE LIGHT
BED AND MATTRESS • HIRE AN INTERIOR DES   NCORPORATE A GREATER SENSE OF SPACE INTO
BUY A TOILET • CHOOSE A TAP • BUY GLUES   MENTS • GET SELF-CLEANING WINDOWS • CHOO
OP • BUY GREEN HOUSEHOLD CLEANERS • S   SECURITY SYSTEM • BUY A HOME ALARM SYST
UY TIMBER FOR A DIY PROJECT • HOW TO SE   R, PAINTER OR ELECTRICIAN • HIRE A GARDENE
OIL IMPROVERS • BUY MULCH • BUY A COMP   BLE GARDEN • HIRE A GARDEN DESIGNER • BUY
E SURGEON • BUY BASIC GARDEN TOOLS • B   BUY AN OUTDOOR LIGHTING SYSTEM • BUY O
BS AND SPICES • STOCK YOUR KITCHEN WIT   RESH PRODUCE • SELECT MEAT • STOCK UP FC
FRESH FISH • SELECT RICE • PURCHASE PR   LTON • GET FRESH FISH DELIVERED TO YOUR DC
G OILS • SELECT OLIVE OIL • SELECT OLIVES   VINEGAR • CHOOSE PASTA • BUY TEA • BUY COF
REAL ALE • ORDER A COCKTAIL • CHOOSE A   STOCK A WINE CELLAR • STOCK YOUR BAR • D
A MIDWIFE OR DOULA • PLAN A HOME BIRT   R A NEW BABY • BUY A NEW COT • CHOOSE A PL
CHILDCARE • FIND A GREAT NANNY • FIND T   TER-SCHOOL CARE • SIGN YOUR CHILD UP FOR
BUY BOOKS, VIDEOS AND MUSIC FOR YOU   HIRE A TUTOR • ADOPT A CHILD • GET YOUR C
ELTERED HOUSING • CHOOSE A CARE HOME   PLOT • PAY FOR FUNERAL EXPENSES • GET VIAG
ITARY MTHERAPY • SEE A MENTAL-HEALTH P   BUY HOME-USE MEDICAL SUPPLIES • SELECT HA
ST IMPLANTS • GET WRINKLE-FILLER INJECT   ACTITIONERS • CHOOSE A MANICURIST • GET W
A • BOOK A MASSAGE • GET ON ANTIQUES F   SHOP AT AN ANTIQUE FAIR OR FLEA MARKET • P

**Daily
Life**

• BUY SILVERWARE • EVALUATE CARNIVAL GLASS • BUY AND SELL STAMPS • BUY ANTIQUE FURNITURE • GET CLUED UP ON CLARICE CL
S • SEIZE STAR WARS ACTION FIGURES • SELL YOUR VINYL RECORD COLLECTION • SELL TO A PAWNSHOP • BUY AND SELL COMIC BOOI
PERIPHERALS • CHOOSE A LAPTOP OR NOTEBOOK COMPUTER • SELL OR DONATE A COMPUTER • BUY PRINTER PAPER • BUY A PRINTE
E THE MEMORY IN YOUR COMPUTER • BUY COMPUTER SOFTWARE • CHOOSE A CD PLAYER • BUY BLANK CDS • BUY AN MP PLAYER • CH
I YOUR PHONE COMPANY • BUY VIDEO AND COMPUTER GAMES • CHOOSE A FILM CAMERA • CHOOSE A DIGITAL CAMCORDER • DECIDE
UY A SERIOUS TV • CHOOSE BETWEEN DIGITAL TV PROVIDERS • GET A DIGITAL VIDEO RECORDER • GET A UNIVERSAL REMOTE • BUY A F
CHASE CHEAP AIRLINE TICKETS • FIND GREAT HOTEL DEALS • HIRE THE BEST CAR FOR THE LEAST MONEY • GET TRAVEL INSURANCE •
E UNITED KONGDOM • TIP IN A FOREIGN COUNTRY • TIP PROPERLY IN THE UK • BRIBE A FOREIGN OFFICIAL • GET AN INTERRAIL PASS •
HEAP BUT FANTASTIC SAFARI • RENT A CAMEL IN CAIRO • GET SINGLE-MALT WHISKY IN SCOTLAND • BUY A SAPPHIRE IN BANGKOK • HIF
HIRE A TREKKING COMPANY IN NEPAL • RENT OR BUY A SATELLITE PHONE • BUY YOUR CHILD'S FIRST CRICKET BAT • ORDER A STRIP FC
• BUY A RACKET • BUY A HEALTH CLUB MEMBERSHIP • BUY AN AEROBIC FITNESS MACHINE • BUY SWIMMING EQUIPMENT • BUY A JET
IFTING EQUIPMENT • CHOOSE A CAR RACK • BUY SKIS • BUY CLOTHES FOR COLD-WEATHER ACTIVITIES • SELL USED SKIS • BUY A SNO
BUY THE OPTIMAL SLEEPING BAG • BUY A TENT • BUY A BACKPACK • BUY A CAMPING STOVE • BUY A KAYAK • BUY A LIFEJACKET • BL
G • SELL USED CLOTHING • ORDER CUSTOM-MADE COWBOY BOOTS • BUY CLOTHES ONLINE • FIND NON-STANDARD SIZES • BUY THE P
E • BUY A WOMAN'S SUIT • BUY A MAN'S SUIT • HIRE A TAILOR • BUY CUSTOM-TAILORED CLOTHES IN ASIA • BUY A BRIEFCASE • SHOP
OUT CLOTHES • BUY A HEART-RATE MONITOR • SELECT A WATCH • BUY KIDS' CLOTHES • CHOOSE CHILDREN'S SHOES • PURCHASE CLC
A CAR • BUY A MOTORCYCLE • BUYING AND CHANGING MOTOR OIL• WASH A CAR • WAX A CAR • BUY CAR INSURANCE • SPRING FOR A

15 Buy Happiness

As Samuel Johnson once said, "Poverty is a great enemy to human happiness". It may be true that happiness is something you can't literally buy, but money wisely spent can at least provide you with an escape from soul-destroying drudgery and give you increased access to excitement and entertainment.

Steps

1 Move slowly. Don't throw yourself, and your money, into the first hare-brained scheme that comes along. Spend time savouring the joys of contemplation.

2 Don't let laziness rule your buying decisions. Sitting in a deck chair while servants fawn over you may be fun for a short time, but it's not likely to provide long-term satisfaction. Look for goals and projects that combine fun and challenge.

3 Be wary of ventures where money and status are ends in themselves. A huge yacht is an obvious sign of wealth. But if it's not fun for you, it's no more capable of enhancing your well-being than a pedalo.

4 Surprise people. Look for activities that will stun your friends and family. If all you've ever done is sit on the couch, do something bold like getting in shape and signing up to climb Mount Everest (see 455 "Buy Your Way on to a Mount Everest Expedition").

5 Indulge in a little eccentricity. The more money you have, the wackier you're allowed to be. Buy a vintage car and drive around in a cape and goggles. Stroll to your local shops or café in your dressing gown and slippers.

6 Look for new activities with heavy technical demands, such as art photography, music dubbing, video editing, car racing or anything else that requires many hours of study and pricey equipment. You'll spend many satisfying hours shopping for supplies, learning arcane details, and talking with experts. Soon you'll feel like a member of an elite club.

7 Look for ways to include your friends and family in your new activities. You'll be happier if you can share your experiences with people close to you.

8 Avoid being pompous or superior when discussing your new acquisition or endeavour. Nothing will turn away listeners, or set you up for ridicule, more than acting as though you know everything. If you just took up sailing, for example, take joy in all the learning you can look forward to. Listen and apply yourself, and soon you'll be an expert.

What to Look For

- Fun
- Excitement
- New learning opportunities

Tips

Recognise the limitations of money. Money will get you access to things. Motivation and skill are up to you.

Don't flit from interest to interest, acquiring and discarding expensive toys as you go. This will only make you look silly without providing much satisfaction.

Drop in on worthy causes and shower them with money (see 119 "Give Away Your Fortune").

16 Buy a Better Mousetrap

Maybe you'll never build a better mousetrap, but it's easy to buy one. If you have mice or rats, get rid of them fast. You can find most of the options listed below at hardware shops. As well as the traditional cheese, peanut butter, grains and cereals or cooked bacon make appetising bait for traps. Some animals will outsmart any trap. The best approach is to look out constantly for rodent activity, seal up mouseholes and experiment with a variety of methods.

TYPE OF TRAP/FEATURES	PROS AND CONS
Live Traps Catch and release rodents unharmed, a good choice for pacifists.	Reusable and safe around children and pets. However, they require you to relocate a scared, agitated rodent. Use every caution to avoid contact.
Snap Traps Use a spring-loaded wire to trap and kill rodents.	Theoretically reusable but should probably be thrown out after a successful trapping to avoid the risk of spreading disease. Usually quick and lethal but not always; death can sometimes be slow and painful.
Glue Boards Use a shallow tray filled with glue, which attracts and holds rodents.	A single trap can catch more than one rodent. Death is very slow and some people find these unbearably creepy and cruel. On the plus side, they're non-toxic, easy to set and can't injure people.
Electronic Trap Use an electric current to dispose of rodents in a quick, non-messy way.	Not dangerous to humans but can be difficult to use in wet environments. More expensive than other traps.
Poison Rodent poisons are available in liquid, pellet or bar forms and can be effective against many pests.	Poison does not require frequent checking but also does not allow you to monitor results like a trap. Rodents can also die before they leave the building, causing short-term problems with smell.
Professional Pest Control Available from your local council or private companies – search in the Yellow Pages or on the internet.	Requires very little effort on your part but the poison is highly toxic and may require you to leave the building for a short period. Pest controllers can be expensive.
Ultrasonic Barriers Designed to ward off rodents with ultrasonic waves.	Leave no traps, corpses or poison. Evidence suggests that they're not very effective.
WARNINGS	Poison is dangerous for pets and children. You must take great care to ensure only rodents eat it. Snap traps can injure people and pets.

17 Buy Time

Have you ever stared at the microwave in frustration, thinking that 20 seconds is just too long? You might need to slow down a little. Look at the categories below and consider how many hours they consume each week. Spend a few pounds and reclaim some free time.

PRODUCTS/SERVICES	COST
Commuting	
Listen to entertaining or educational CDs in the car or on the train or tube. Make commuting time a positive part of your day.	£10–£20; free at the local lending library
Get a laptop and turn the train or tube into an office.	£550–£2,600, the higher prices for Mac users
Take a taxi or minicab and use the time to work or read a book.	Varies by distance
Around the House	
Hire a cleaner.	£6–£8 per hour
Employ an au pair.	£50 per week plus food
Buy a dishwasher	£150–£200
Employ someone to run your errands.	£25-£30 per hour
Employ electricians, plumbers or other tradespeople.	At least £50 per call-out
Employ a decorator.	£100 per day
Employ a window cleaner.	£10 to £15 per visit
Garden and exterior	
Rent power tools and equipment to speed up projects.	£20 to £200
Employ a neighbour's child to weed flowerbeds or mow the lawn.	£5 for a job
Employ a gardener.	£8–£10 per hour
Employ a landscape gardener.	£15 per hour upwards
Employ a handyman for gutters, chimneys and roofs.	£20 per hour
Employ a tree surgeon.	£20 per hour
Wardrobe	
Use a pick-up-and-deliver laundry and ironing service.	£5–6 plus cost per item
Use a dry cleaners' to do repairs.	£10–£50 per piece
Buy clothes by mail-order or online.	£3–£5 delivery charge

PRODUCTS/SERVICES	COST
Food	
Have supermarket shopping delivered to your home.	Typically £5 per delivery – check deals available
Buy ready meals.	£3–£5 per person
Order takeaways delivered to your door.	£5–£10 per meal
Eat out – and never wash up again!	Under £10–£70 per meal
Employ a personal chef four to five nights a week.	£200–£400 per week
Health	
Buy a comfortable mattress to avoid wasting time on insomnia.	£300–£400
Consult a sleep clinic to remedy sleep disorders.	Depends on treatment
Employ a personal trainer who comes to your home.	£30–£300 per hour
Buy home exercise equipment.	£100–£1,000
Finances	
Bank online.	Free
Buy a software program to streamline your bookkeeping.	£50
Have an accountant take care of your tax affairs.	£500–£1000 a year
Employ a bookkeeper.	£10 per hour
Social Events and Holidays	
Mail-order or shop online.	Delivery and handling per order
Have items gift-wrapped.	Free to £5
Employ caterers, party planners.	£100 to £5,000 and up
Employ a personal shopper.	£20 per hour and up
Employ a social secretary.	£15,000 per year

18 Buy a Bouquet of Roses

A rose is a rose, OK? *Mais non*: other than the classic lover's gift of a dozen long-stemmed roses, there are many varieties and a rainbow of colours guaranteed to put a bloom on anyone's cheek.

Steps

1 Look for closed buds on the brink of unfurling. Petal tops should show the first signs of opening, and the bud should be a little soft and springy, never hard. Then close your eyes and inhale their scent – some varieties are more fragrant than others.

2 FInd beautiful roses cheaply at a supermarket. A dozen stems may come for under £5 and be available in a variety of colours.

3 Visit a wholesale flower market (see 49 "Buy Flowers Wholesale") if there is one in your area. You'll find an enormous selection of roses at a great price. Keep an eye peeled for fabulously fragrant garden roses.

4 Be on the lookout for pavement sellers hawking medium-quality but still beautiful roses.

5 Buy lovely roses perfectly arranged from a local florist. You'll pay a premium but the flowers will be sensational.

6 Send roses to a special someone far away with a flower delivery network such as Interflora (0500 43 43 43) or Teleflorist (0800 111800). They will deliver nationwide or even worldwide. Pay with a credit card for guaranteed same-day delivery.

7 Buy roses on the internet, for example from eden4flowers.co.uk or from tesco.com/flowers.

What to Look For

- Closed buds
- Fragrance
- Pavement vendors

Tips

Put your roses in water as soon as you get them home. Submerge each stem in a bowl of lukewarm water, and snip the end off at an angle while still underwater before transferring to a vase.

Mix in the packet of flower food and be sure to add more water as the roses drink it up.

Warning

Stay away from firm, tightly closed rosebuds – they've been picked too soon, won't last long and may in fact never open.

---

19 Buy Someone a Drink

Most people contemplating buying someone a drink either think about it until (and beyond) last orders, but never get up the nerve. Or they use the scattergun technique – buying a drink for anyone they catch sitting still for two seconds and blasting away in the hope of getting lucky. The best approach is something in between.

Steps

1 Try to enjoy the process, and accept that there are risks. Top goalscorers are also the strikers who miss most chances.

2 Avoid the wolf pack. Don't travel with a group of predators and expect to meet a nice person looking for a quiet time.

3 Be yourself. It sounds simple but apparently it isn't. Most people are looking for a fun, intelligent, easy-going, reasonably reliable sort. Women aren't as impressed by flashy clothes, fast cars and sporting prowess as most men think.

What to Look For

- Money in your wallet
- Lack of a drink
- Wedding ring

4 Take your time. Don't rush up to your target, but don't wait around for hours either. If you've just arrived, have a seat and relax for a few minutes. Check to see if the person does, in fact, need a drink, or if he or she already has one. If you get an encouraging look, head over.

5 If there's a surefire pick-up line in the world, the inventor is keeping it secret. Try "Hello". Look for a wedding ring.

6 Introduce yourself. If you don't get a response, you should probably forget it.

7 Offer to buy a drink. If the person agrees, you have the basis for a conversation about drink choices.

8 If your target is part of a group, be sure to acknowledge the rest of the group and include them in the conversation. If you don't, the group may close ranks and cut you off.

Tip

Meeting a stranger is always a long shot. Consider the billions of people in the world, and then think of the few you actually enjoy being with. From a statistical perspective, you could buy millions of drinks before meeting someone you like. So forget statistics.

20 Get Someone to Buy You a Drink

Decades of sexual equality and social progress have achieved only so much. Approaching someone in a bar can still be treacherous. Is a woman being unacceptably forward if she asks a man to buy her a drink? Is a man violating some rule if he expects a woman to buy him a drink? Who cares? Just have fun and you'll be OK.

What to Look For

- Lighthearted conversation
- An escape route, if needed

Steps

1 Experiment. Walk up to your target and say, "How about buying me a drink?" You know you'll at least get a reaction, so be ready with some light conversation.

2 Don't be obnoxious. Your goal is not to get free alcohol, but to meet someone. Even if he or she thinks it's weird that you're asking for a drink, a show of personality or humour should be enough to move things along.

3 Employ the obvious back-up position, if necessary: offer to buy your target a drink.

4 Don't push too hard. Be lighthearted and casual. Your target may decline now, but there's a chance you'll bump into the person again in an hour or so.

5 Don't try to isolate your target from his or her friends. Be friendly to the whole group, and increase your chances of appearing desirable.

6 Plan an escape route. Some people think that if they buy you a drink, they're buying rights to you for the entire evening.

Tips

Don't worry about looking like an idiot. Everyone looks like one sometimes.

If you get a nasty reaction from someone, it probably says more about his or her attitude than your technique.

21 Buy Your Way into the Best Society

So you've made your millions but still lack class? Well, old chap, you can't purchase a blue-blood heritage, but you can clean up your image. You'll have to throw some money around, but be sure to do it with urbanity, style and grace. Anything vulgar and your plebeian roots will show through.

Steps

1 Read magazines like *Tatler* or the society pages of *The Times* to identify the target you are aiming at.

2 Update your image with the help of a consultant. Your hair, make-up, clothes and accessories must look classy, not gaudy.

3 Observe and emulate the manners and behaviour of the well bred. When in doubt what to do, adopt a stance of mysterious understatement.

4 Buy the highest-priced season tickets to the opera and ballet to be privy to exclusive events and openings. If necessary, enlist someone to brief you on the finer points of the events that you'll be attending.

5 Establish yourself as "clubbable". Become a member of the MCC and watch cricket from the pavilion at Lord's. Make sure you are present for the sailing at Cowes week. Turn up at Ascot suitably attired.

6 Publicly distance yourself, if necessary, from any distasteful business dealings. If you made your money by "harvesting" baby seals, for example, slip a few subtle comments to the press about "the need for change" and a "new business era" while being vague about specifics.

7 Adopt a non-controversial cause (preferably one that lends itself to gala events) and give, give, give from the bottom of your wallet. Better yet, host a fund-raising party at your country house. (First, buy a country house.)

8 See and be seen at exclusive restaurants, fashion shows and the hottest parties of the season. An image consultant will know which events are the most strategic.

9 Hire a public-relations expert to get your picture into the society pages.

10 Network, network, network. Befriend influential people and make yourself indispensable to them through generous favours and an utterly discreet nature.

11 Increase your social value by purchasing homes in desirable locations. Pieds-à-terre in Paris, New York, Sydney and San Francisco will make you popular and mysteriously unavailable during certain seasons.

12 Disdain riffraff. It's essential to choose your acquaintances wisely.

What to Look For

- Image consultant
- Cultural and charity events
- Exclusive clubs
- Public-relations opportunities

Tips

Take etiquette and image improvement courses if you lack the social graces needed to interact easily in the best society.

Develop expensive hobbies and tastes so that you'll have plenty in common with society figures. Race sailing boats. Ride horses. Collect art, wine or classic cars.

Warning

The world is full of people eager to separate you from your money. Exercise due care before you hire an image consultant. Make them sign a confidentiality agreement.

22 Buy Your Way into Someone's Favour

This sounds ugly and probably is. But, if you've exhausted all the alternatives, this might be your only choice. Carefully define your goals, then perform a cost-benefit analysis: What do you want from this person and what can you expect to achieve for a given expenditure?

Steps

1 Decide if your strategy is the best approach. A botched plan could prove embarrassing.

2 Keeping your goal in mind, start small but move quickly. Take your target to a good restaurant and pick up the bill.

3 Don't force your position right away. As with any sales job, get the person talking. Learn as much as you can about their tastes.

4 Identify valuable services that you can offer. Sometimes small favours are the most effective. If the person is a keen football supporter, a ticket for a sold-out match may mean more than another gift of twice the monetary value.

5 Behave as if you are acting out of pure friendship. The person will probably understand exactly what is going on, but no one wants to face up to the fact that their favour is being bought.

6 Choose the right moment to cash in with a specific request for some return on your investment.

7 Recognise that this needs to be a short-term project. Arranging your life around mercenary practices will result in your being surrounded by a pack of sycophants instead of friends and family.

What to Look For

- Identify your goal
- Look for alternatives
- How much will it cost?
- What favours can you provide?

Tip

If companionship is your goal, consider a dog. They're better company and more reliable than a person whose friendship can be bought.

Warning

If you find yourself doing this often, you're either a politician, a pathetic loser or both.

23 Buy Love

No, of course you can't buy love – but if you have money, using it wisely can make close relationships flourish. Using money unwisely can blight your emotional life. Here are a few pointers for the well-off.

Steps

1 Know that you face the dilemma of appearing mean if you don't throw your money around, yet unattractively brash and crushing if you do. To win love, money must be spent with taste and style.

2 Avoid showering those you love with crushingly expensive gifts at all times. Gifts must show thoughtfulness, sensitivity and imagination if you are to win affection rather than attract golddiggers.

3 Find out what those dear to you want most in the world, and give it to them if you can. It may be security, rather than diamonds.

4 Use money to create a life full of excitement, curiosity and surprises. This will make you genuinely interesting and attractive.

What to Look For

- Tasteful display of wealth
- What other people really want
- Excitment and surprises

Warning

Relationships between individuals in widely different financial circumstances are always likely to be strained.

24 Find the Right Relaxation Technique for You

Do you want to find ways to manage your stress levels yourself through the practice of a relaxation technique, such as yoga or t'ai chi, or would you rather indulge in a weekly pampering by a masseur, aromatherapist or reflexologist. The choice is yours.

RELAXATION TECHNIQUES	DESCRIPTION
Yoga	Regular practice of yoga helps restore balance and harmony among the mind, body and spirit. A typical yoga session centres on a series of *asanas*, or postures, working with the breath. The session ends with meditation and relaxation techniques, leaving you feeling relaxed and centred. For information on classes and yoga organisations, contact The British Wheel of Yoga (tel: 01529 306851; website: bwy.org.uk).
Meditation	This ancient Eastern technique can relieve stress, bring about a sense of inner peace, and improve concentration. Simply sit in a comfortable positon for 20 minutes and either follow a guided visualisation or recite a *mantra* (a meaningless word) over and again, focusing on your breathing. Once you have mastered the basics, practise meditation at home whenever you want to. For more information, contact: School of Meditation, 158 Holland Park Ave., London W11 4HU.
T'ai Chi	An ancient Chinese technique, t'ai chi is a system of controlled, meditative body movements, which like yoga, helps to bring harmony and balance between mind, body and spirit.

RELAXATION THERAPIES	DESCRIPTION
Body Massage	Massage helps relieve muscular stress, leaving your body feeling free from stress. The Swedish body massage is the most widely practised. This is a deep massage, which stimulates the circulation and helps alleviate muscular aches and pains. For a more vigorous pummelling, try a Thai massage.
Shiatsu	This Japanese therapy is a great stress reliever. Finger pressure is applied to acupuncture points, using fingers, palms, elbows and feet to reduce stress and cure specific problems.
Aromatherapy	This is a form of treatment in which essential oils are massaged into the skin, inhaled or added to your bath water. Aromatherapy is especially effective for such stress-related problems as insomnia, anxiety, depression and tiredness. For a list of qualified practitioners, contact the International Society of Professional Aromatherapists (website: ifparoma.org).
Reflexology	This is the massage of pressure points on the feet, each of which relate to a particular organ or area of the body. Through massage the practitioner can identify and repair areas of the body that are out of balance. For more information contact: The Association of Reflexologists (website: aor.org.uk).

25 Buy Healthy Fast Food

Is this really possible? To a degree, if you make careful selections. Most fast-food restaurants have responded to health concerns with revised menus, which include salads and meatless burgers. Even McDonald's recently announced a broadening of its menu to include more low-fat options. When you're out with the children or on a road trip, we've got tips for quick and healthy noshing.

Steps

1 Opt for grilled, broiled or steamed dishes instead of fried whenever possible. Chicken and turkey are leaner than minced beef. Fish is always a healthy option.

2 At a fish-and-chip shop, just order the fish. Then discard the batter and eat what's inside.

3 Pick up a salad. Leafy greens and vegetables are always great. Avoid mayonnaise-based dressings – a creamy dressing will have more calories and fat than many desserts.

4 Drink water, fruit juice, skimmed milk or unsweetened tea instead of sweet fizzy drinks.

5 Avoid ordering the largest portions on fast-food menus. If you have a big appetite, fill up with additional salad or fruit.

6 Remember that fast food doesn't have to mean burgers and fries. Choose sandwiches with lean meat or tuna, or a baked potato with a filling of tuna or beans. Baked beans are full of protein, but be aware of the high sugar content.

7 Stock up on portable "fast food" while grocery shopping: cottage cheese, low-fat yogurt, carrots and fresh fruit. Apples, bananas, grapes and oranges are the world's healthiest fast food

8 Buy low-fat crisps for relatively healthy snacking. Salt-free crisps are also increasingly available.

What to Look For

- Grilled, broiled or steamed dishes
- Low- or no-fat dressings
- Fresh vegetables
- Unsweetened drinks

Tips

A fried breakfast is not a healthy start to the day unless you have hard manual labour ahead of you – and is probably not advisable even then. Croissants may seem a more stylish breakfats, but thay are huge fat bombs.

A baked potato is a good nutritional choice. Chips, however, do not satisfy the nutritional requirements of a vegetable serving and are very high in fat.

A pizza with tomato sauce, a tuna or vegetable topping and low-fat cheese is a relatively healthy meal.

26 Buy Sunscreen

By now, most of us know that the sun can be harmful. The best protection is to shield yourself with clothing, a hat and glasses whenever possible. Since this isn't always practical, you need to have some sun protection lotion. The trick then is buying the correct stuff, having it on hand, and remembering to apply it.

Steps

1 Know the difference between a *sunscreen* and a *sunblock.* A sunscreen filters out some of the sun's more harmful radiation. Sunblock aims to reflect the light completely.

2 Check the sun protection factor (SPF) on your sunscreen. An SPF of 15 means it will take 15 times longer for you to burn with the sunscreen than without.

3 Use a product with SPF 30 or higher if you're fair-skinned, at high altitude, near the equator or outside on a hot, sunny day between 10 a.m. and 4 p.m. Especially protect your children: Over the course of their life, most of the sun's damage to their skin will happen before they're 18.

4 Make sure that your sunscreen is labelled "broad spectrum" to protect against both UVA (ultraviolet-A) and UVB (ultraviolet-B) rays. Ultraviolet radiation at high doses increases your risk of basal-cell carcinoma and malignant melanoma.

5 Know what protection you're getting. A sunscreen with SPF 15 gives you 94 to 95 per cent UVB coverage; SPF 28 bumps you up to about 96 per cent coverage.

6 Buy zinc oxide or titanium oxide (or dioxide) to protect your ears, nose and lips if you're in the sun for prolonged periods daily. These opaque sunblocks are ideal for sensitive skin. Some new products offer zinc-oxide protection that's transparent, so you can avoid the white-nosed Australian cricketer look.

7 Get water-resistant or waterproof sunscreen if you'll be swimming or sweating.

8 Look for PABA-free, fragrance-free and hypoallergenic sunscreen if you're allergic to certain skin products. Do a test patch on your skin to confirm whether a sunscreen is truly allergy-free.

9 Select a sunscreen that is non-comedogenic, which means it won't block pores, if you're prone to spots.

10 Apply sunscreen liberally 30 minutes prior to exposure. Most people need at least enough sunscreen to fill a single-shot spirit glass to cover their body. Reapply every two hours, or more often if you get wet or sweat profusely.

11 Check the current level of UV radiation – the solar UV index – to decide what factor sunscreen to apply. You can find the index for Britain and foreign holiday destinations at weatheronline.co.uk.

What to Look For

- SPF 15 or higher
- UVA and UVB protection
- Zinc oxide or titanium oxide
- Water-resistant or waterproof
- Allergy-free
- Non-comedogenic

Tips

UVB rays cause sunburns. UVA rays create wrinkles and premature ageing. Studies suggest that both rays contribute to cancerous growths.

There is no proof that sunscreen prevents skin cancer. Your safest bet is to minimise sun exposure during peak hours (10 a.m. to 4 p.m.). Wear a wide-brimmed hat, UV-blocking sunglasses and tightly woven clothes if you are outside.

Warnings

There is no such thing as "safe tanning." Tanning salons expose your skin to harmful UV rays. If you burn easily but must have that golden look, use a sunless tanning lotion or foam.

Do not use sunscreen on infants under 1 year of age; keep them covered and out of the sun instead.

27 Buy Further Education

No doubt you're a busy individual, but spare a few hours a week to develop your talents and exercise your brain. There are a rich range of options available, whether your aim is to learn a practical skill that will improve your career prospects, or simply to enrich your life with knowledge and culture.

Steps

1 Be clear about your objectives and the degree of commitment you are prepared to make. Do you need to end up with a formal qualification? How many hours a week can you study?

2 Consider home study courses, like those provided by the National Extension College (nec.ac.uk) or ICS (icslearn.co.uk). Find alternatives on the internet or under "Further Education" in the *Yellow Pages*. Expect to pay £100–£400 for a course. For this you will be sent learning materials and assigned a personal tutor to check your work and give advice.

3 Visit a good bookshop or online bookseller and look for self-teaching courses. These may consist of a book or books alone, but are likely to include other learning aids such as CD-ROMs or videos. Insist on examining a product before you buy it – many are sold in sealed packs which can disguise flimsy content. Prices vary widely depending on the product, but some are available for under £20.

4 Choose to attend evening classes if you require face-to-face teaching and a sociable environment. Find out what is available in your area by looking in *Yellow Pages*. Costs may typically be £15–£20 for a two-hour class, but you will probably have to sign up for a term, around £200.

5 Investigate the Open University as a high-class option. See if any of its wide range of courses suits you. Consider one of the short "taster" courses which allows you to see whether the Open University works for you without the commitment of a full course lasting nine months or longer. Courses cost from under £100 to well over £1,000.

6 Make sure everyone knows that you are learning. It will impress friends and employers alike.

What to Look For

- Home study courses
- Self-teaching materials
- Evening classes
- Open University

Tips

Be honest with yourself before you start. Do you really have the time and the willpower for what you are going to undertake?

If you have unpredictable claims on your time which might prevent you studying regularly, choose a home study course that allows you to work at your own speed.

Be aware that many people fail to complete evening class courses and often end up paying for hours they don't use.

28 Order Exotic Food

Despite eating Chinese takeaways, heating up Marks & Spencer's chicken tikkas and buying doner kebabs on the way home from the pub, the British are still often surprisingly ignorant about food from around the world. Many of the terms below will be familiar – but do you really know what they mean?

TERM	WHAT IT IS
CHINESE	
Szechuan	Chinese cuisine originating from the western province of Szechuan or Sechuan. Spicy and flavourful, with extensive use of hot peppers.
Peking	Cuisine originating from the north of China, where rice does not grow. Expect noodles, dumplings, pancakes and plenty of spicy meat.
Cantonese	The Chinese cuisine originating from the southern port city of Canton, this is the style of Chinese cooking with which Westerners are most familiar. Most food is stir-fried or steamed, with subtle sauces; a strong emphasis on texture and rice as a staple.
Chinese Leaves	Green vegetable usually served with garlic or oyster sauce.
Chow Mein	Stir-fried noodles.
Hot and Sour Soup	Salty soup with chillies, tofu, egg and bamboo shoots. Sometimes fiery hot.
Kung Pao	Szechuan dish of cubed beef, chicken or shrimp stir-fried with chillies, peanuts and hot sauce.
Mongolian Beef	Northern dish of spicy meat with chillies and green onions atop crispy rice noodles.
Pork Shu Mai	Pork cooked with eggs and green onions, served with thin pancakes and sweet plum sauce.
Wonton Soup	Chicken broth with dumplings and vegetables.
INDIAN	
Balti	Literally "bucket", referring to the round-bottomed wok in which the curry is cooked and served.
Biryani	Savoury basmati rice dish mixed with vegetables, chicken or lamb.
Dal	Lentils, often served over basmati rice.
Korma	Meat braised with onions and gentle spices, such as cinnamon, cumin, ginger and cardamom. Yoghurt or cream is added before it is served.
Sag Paneer	White cheese with spinach and spices.
Tandoori	Chicken or seafood marinated in yogurt and spices, and charcoal-grilled.
Tikka Masala	Chicken tandoori bathed in herb-infused, creamy tomato sauce.

TERM	WHAT IT IS
JAPANESE	
Bento	Boxed meals that include meat or fish, salad, soup, rice or noodles.
Donburi	Meat or vegetables cooked with egg and served on top of a bowl of rice with a rich, flavourful sauce.
Edamame	Steamed and salted soya beans.
Gyoza	Steamed or deep-fried pork dumplings.
Miso Soup	Fish broth with miso (soyabean paste), tofu and seaweed.
Tempura	Vegetables or seafood dipped in batter and deep-fried.
Teriyaki	Charcoal-grilled meat or fish that has been marinated in a mixture of soy sauce and rice wine (sake or mirin).
Udon	Thin wheat noodles served in a hot broth with meat or vegetables, or served cold with a light dipping sauce.
THAI	
Red Curry	Medium curry with coconut milk, chillies and other spices and herbs; usually contains peanuts as well.
Green Curry	Hot curry with coconut milk, chilies and other spices, coriander leaves and Thai basil, which gives the distinctive flavour.
Pad Thai	Traditional stir-fried rice noodles with peanuts, fresh beansprouts, cooked egg, shrimp or tofu, green onions and fresh herbs.
Po Pia	Fried spring rolls.
Pra Ram	Chicken or tofu on a bed of vegetables, topped with peanut sauce.
Satay	Chicken, beef or pork grilled on skewers and served with peanut sauce.
Gai Tom Kha	Tangy coconut milk soup with chicken, mushrooms, lemon grass and galangal – a pink Thai tuber.
MIDDLE EASTERN	
Chakchouka	Egg dish cooked with tomatoes, sweet red peppers and chilli peppers.
Couscous	Steamed semolina served with a meat or vegetable stew.
Pilaf	Rice cooked with onions and stock.
Tabbouleh	Salad of bulgur (cracked wheat), typically also including cucumber, onions, mint, lime and chilli.
Tajin	Spicy slow-cooked meat or fish stew.

29 Order at a Sushi Bar

Sushi might seem the most intimidating meal ever. Raw fish? Seaweed? To eat? Yet sushi bars are one of the fastest-growing forms of eating-out in Britain today, offering a delicious meal at an economical price. If you visit one of the bars where you take food off a conveyor belt, there are certainly no problems with ordering. But for your first visit to an establishment with a proper sushi chef, you might need some advice.

Steps

1 Ask the sushi chef to recommend the catch of the day, since sushi-grade fish is especially sensitive to seasonal changes.

2 Grasp some basic terms. Sashimi is raw fish. Nigiri is fish pressed on to rice mounds. Maki are sushi rolls wrapped in nori seaweed and sliced; temaki are hand-rolled seaweed cones containing rice and fish.

3 Keep in mind that an average person eats ten to twelve pieces in one sitting. Nigiri usually comes two pieces to the order; maki is sliced into six pieces. Begin with a few dishes and order more if people are still hungry.

4 Start with edamame (steamed and salted soybeans), marinated seaweed salad, or miso soup if you like.

5 Order one or two types of nigiri. Hamachi (yellowfin tuna), maguro (tuna), unagi (broiled eel) and sake (salmon) are popular choices. Sushi is served with wasabi (a green, sinus-clearing horseradish paste) and soy sauce. Experiment to see which condiments you prefer.

6 Ask the sushi chef to make you a surprise if you're ready for further adventures in sushi.

7 Follow up with some maki favourites: spicy tuna rolls, cucumber rolls or California rolls (cooked crab and avocado). Tobiko (crunchy fish roe) is a typical accompaniment.

8 Try uni (sea urchin) topped with a raw quail egg, if you're feeling bold.

9 Cleanse your palate between bites with a sip of green tea and some gari (pickled ginger).

10 End the meal with tamago, a slightly sweet egg omelette on a bed of rice, or a refreshing bowl of green tea ice cream.

What to Look For

- Chef's recommendations
- Nigiri, maki or temaki sushi
- Pickled ginger and green tea
- Soy sauce and wasabi

Tips

It's fine to use your fingers when eating sushi. Place the fish (not the rice) on your tongue to fully savour the flavour.

Sashimi (sliced raw fish) is technically not sushi. It's best to savour sashimi as an appetiser before you fill up on rice.

Tempura rolls, unagi, salmon skin rolls and inari – tofu stuffed with rice – are good choices for those wary of raw fish.

Some people enjoy sipping sake (hot or cold) or Japanese beer with their sushi.

Warnings

If a sushi bar smells funny or it appears less than spotless, depart immediately.

Pregnant women and people with compromised immune systems should not eat raw fish.

30 Buy Dinner at a French Restaurant

Whether you're visiting France or eating out at an elegant French restaurant in Britain, it's chic to be able to cope with the menu in the original, rather than struggling to extract a translation from a smug waiter. The following list will help you enjoy French cuisine without being made to feel *un imbécile*.

COMMON MENU ITEMS	DEFINITION
MEATS	
Terrine (teh-REEN)	Ground meat or seafood (pâté) shaped like a meat loaf.
Confit (kohn-FEE)	Meat preserve, such as goose or duck.
Tripes (tr-EEP)	Tripe – stomach lining of calves or lamb.
Ris (REE)	Sweetbreads – calf or lamb glands (not to be confused with *riz* – rice).
Foie gras (FWAH GRAH)	Goose liver pâté.
Saucisson (soh-see-SAWN)	Sausage.
Tournedos (TOOR-neh-doh)	A small, lean cut of tenderloin.
Paillard (PI-yahrd)	A medallion-shaped piece of meat, poultry or veal.
VEGETABLES	
Pommes de terre (pom duh TEHR)	Potatoes.
Haricots verts (ah-ree-koh VEHR)	Green string beans.
Mesclun (MEHS-kluhn)	Mixed baby lettuces and salad greens.
Endives (AHN-deev)	Torpedo-shaped lettuce with a bitter flavour, often served braised.
Truffes (TROOF)	Truffles – fungus with a rich, earthy flavour.
DISH TYPES	
Fricassée (FRIHK-uh-see)	Meat simmered in broth and wine topped with a white creamy sauce.
En croûte (ahn KROOT)	Meat baked in a pastry.
Roulade (roo-LAHD)	Thin meat wrapped around a savoury filling, tied with string.
À la Provençal (ah lah proh-vahn-SAHL)	Usually includes tomatoes, anchovies, garlic and olives.
À la Bordelaise (ah lah bohr-d-LAYZ)	Dishes prepared with red wine.
Gratin (gra-TAN)	Baked vegetable dish with crispy cheese or butter topping.
Forestière (foh-re-STI-air)	Cooked with bacon and mushrooms.
Ratatouille (ra-tuh-TOO-ee)	Vegetable stew with tomatoes, courgettes and aubergines.
Crêpe (KRAYP)	Thin pancakes with sweet or savoury fillings.
SAUCES	
Béchamel (bay-shah-MEHL)	White, creamy sauce.
Béarnaise (behr-NAYZ)	White wine sauce with tarragon often served with beef.
Chanterelle (shan-tuh-REHL)	Sauce seasoned with mushrooms.
Beurre blanc (burr BLAHNK)	White wine and butter sauce.
Beurre noisette (burr nwah-ZEHT)	Light brown butter sauce with a nutty flavor.
Beurre noir (burr NWAR)	Dark brown butter sauce with a deep nutty flavor.
Aïoli (ay-OH-lee)	Home-made mayonnaise flavored with garlic and herbs.

31 Employ a Dating Service

You can't buy love but you can employ an assistant to help you find some. Compare the different types of dating service that help you cast a wide net for potential matches. These companies may charge anywhere from a few pounds to thousands for their services, so be sure that love doesn't make a fool out of you. Shop around and review prices and options with several services before you sign up for one.

TYPE OF SERVICE	PROS	CONS
Online Dating Service You post your profile online and respond to other profiles for a small membership fee.	Online services can provide a large selection (potentially anyone with a computer), you get to do the choosing, and you can easily sign up for more than one site. You can quickly search your area for people with compatible interests and lifestyles.	You may not have total control over information you put online, including your photo. There is no one to screen potential dates before you meet them so there's always a chance of meeting a psycho or your old gym teacher. Your e-mail address will probably be shared with spammers.
Profile dating You fill in a form giving details of your preferences and interests. The agency puts you in contact with other subscribers in your area.	This provides a reasonably cheap way of getting in touch with individuals who, like yourself, are actively looking for a partner.	The match between you and any individual on the list of contacts you are given is likely to be very rough and ready. Expect as many misses as hits.
Singles Clubs These clubs organise socials events for people to meet other singles with similar interests.	You get to meet many people at once without the awkwardness of a date. The activities are usually fun in themselves.	You still have to manage the pitfalls of meeting a potential date in a large group, a significant hurdle for many.
Video Dating These services allow you to view videos of prospective dates, while they can view your video.	You get to see your date on video beforehand, and you get to do the choosing.	Wading through files at the dating service office can be a long process. Service is being supplanted by dating websites.
Dating Consultants Dating headhunters introduce busy singles for a hefty fee; all-inclusive service offers advice on dating behaviour, simulations and seminars.	These services can be intensive and hands-on. The consultant will follow up on each date, discussing your experience with you. You have the reassurance that the person you are meeting has been screened.	Service can run into thousands of pounds. Due to the price, this is primarily a way for busy well-off people to meet other busy well-off people.

32 Sell Yourself on an Online Dating Service

Millions of people are using online dating services to meet their Romeos or Juliets. If you want to give it a whirl, start with a compelling, yet truthful, profile of yourself. Many online dating sites allow you to post a profile for free but most will charge you £15–£20 per month to make contact with other singles.

Steps

Before you sign up

1 Make a list of the qualities you'd like to find in a partner (or date).

2 Include important lifestyle issues in your profile. Are you looking for a serious commitment that could lead to marriage and children, or a strictly sexual relationship?

3 Surf various dating sites, such as Yahoo Personals, to view other profiles, making note of the things you like and dislike. This will help you not only refine your profile, but also decide which dating site you want to use.

Signing up

1 Gather or take a few flattering photographs of yourself. Your photo will be the first thing most people see. Select ones that show you looking relaxed and friendly. Emphasise the best of what you've got. Don't post a photo of your cat or you with your ex.

2 Choose a user name that is simple and straightforward. Don't use your own name.

3 Brainstorm to come up with an appealing headline for your profile. Look at other profiles to get an idea of the headline tone that you like. You don't need to be too cute or catchy, just fun.

4 Write a concise, descriptive and amusing profile of yourself. Describe who you are, what makes you unique (and desirable) and what you're looking for. Be true to yourself but don't be over-earnest. Keep the tone upbeat, light and friendly.

5 Fill out the additional questions about height, weight, eye colour and lifestyle preferences honestly. Resist the urge to manipulate these details in your favour. You'll be found out eventually and lying isn't a great way to start a relationship. Think twice before providing specific information about your income.

6 Check your profile for spelling and grammar before you submit it.

7 Beware of the seduction of spending time online answering letters – especially to people you have no interest in meeting. Guard your time and your privacy carefully.

8 Take it nice and slow after you meet. You'll need to catch up in person after the easy intimacy of e-mail.

What to Look For

- Your personal qualities and interests
- Lifestyle issues
- Flattering photograph

Tips

Choose a website that has a large selection of singles in your area. Make sure that you can search the site geographically.

Sexual comments, innuendos or jokes will attract the wrong crowd if you're looking for a long-term, meaningful relationship.

Have a friend with a digital camera take a couple of good photos of you, if you don't already have some. Consider employing a professional photographer. It will be money well spent.

While it's good to have an idea about what you like in a partner, keep an open mind. The love of your life might be nothing like what you envisage.

Warnings

Beware of the easy but limited intimacy that can rapidly develop in e-mail. Meet the person early on to see if there's any chemistry.

If you decide to meet someone in person, meet in a public place. Don't share private information until you get to know the person better.

33 Sell Yourself to Your Girlfriend/Boyfriend's Family

Some people say – and they're probably correct – that every job in the world is a sales job. No matter what your profession, you have to sell yourself, your ideas and your skills. The same is true when you meet your sweetheart's family. In a perfect world, they would instantly recognise your refined character and sincere qualities. But do you really want to chance it?

What to Look For

- The right time
- Neutral meeting place
- A small gift
- Safe conversation

Steps

1 Wait until the time is right. Try not to meet the family too soon. Be sure you're serious about the relationship so that you can deal with them sincerely.

2 Find out whom you will be meeting. Memorise their names. Addressing people by name is absolutely vital and an easy way to make your social skills and manners visible. Know the expected form for addressing the parents ("Mr Snodgrass", "Gordon").

3 Meet at a neutral location, if possible. This should be less stressful than going to their home. A restaurant familiar to you is a good option. However, be prepared to defer to the parents' preference. If you initiate a restaurant meeting it will probably be your obligation to pay.

4 Absolutely be on time. If you're late, it will almost certainly be viewed as disrespectful to them and your partner. If there's any chance that you will be late, notify someone as soon as possible. Be sure your mobile phone is charged up and you have their number. If you can't make the appointment, and you can't notify them, plan to be either dead or on life support when they locate you.

5 Bring a small gift. Find out from your partner what would be appropriate. A bottle of wine, especially at a family dinner, is almost always a tasteful offering.

6 Dress for the occasion. Have your partner tell you exactly what to wear. Don't rely on subjective descriptions like "casual" or "formal". If your partner tells you to wear your dark suit, shut up, put on the suit and make the most of it. You've got the rest of your life to show what a slob you are.

7 Show an interest in the family. They will probably want to know about you, but try to steer the conversation to their interests and activities as well. Avoid talking endlessly about yourself.

Tips

Above all, be yourself. If you're not naturally the life of the party, don't try to be one now.

Don't put too much pressure on yourself. No one expects you to be perfect. Thoughtful and polite is good enough, no matter what else happens.

8 Tell stories that highlight the fine qualities of their son/daughter. This will elevate you to worthy status due to your ability to appreciate such valuable family traits.

9 Avoid sensitive issues. Religion, politics, foreign affairs and the behaviour of young people today are all issues likely to start trouble. If you initiate a discussion on one of these topics at a first meeting, you probably deserve to be single. On the other hand, if asked a direct question, you have no choice but to answer honestly. State your position once and avoid being drawn into an argument. Remember not to swear.

Warning

Avoid groping your girlfriend or boyfriend in public. Keep physical contact to a minimum to show the parents that you love their child for more than just her or his body.

34 Buy Flowers to Say Sorry to Your Partner

You're in the doghouse. Perhaps if you explain really, really carefully what happened, she'll understand and forgive you. Hmmm ... perhaps not. Better to just give up and apologise. Flowers may offer your best chance of success.

What to Look For

- Correct flowers
- Guaranteed delivery

Steps

1 Abandon any plans to reassert your position. Now is not the time. Your objective is to repair damage and smooth things over. If you can't do this, then you're not ready for flowers.

2 Search your brain for clues about what kind of flowers he or she likes. Of course, you've had many chances to pay attention. Don't feel guilty about it now. If you're not absolutely sure what your partner favours, get red roses or Casablanca lilies (see 18 "Buy a Bouquet of Roses").

3 Have the flowers delivered to your partner at work or in a public place, if possible. Call a florist and place the order. Expect to pay at least £30, and possibly more. Don't forget to include a card and sweet message. And don't worry about embarrassing yourself – the florist has seen worse idiots than you.

4 If you can't have flowers delivered, go to the florist yourself. Give a quick outline of the situation and ask them for a suggestion. Stay away from carnations. They have "supermarket checkout" written all over them.

5 Deliver the flowers immediately. Do not stop off for "a quick half" on the way.

6 Offer an unconditional apology. Your goal is to be finished with this incident. If you think more discussion is needed, wait for a week and bring it up when both of you are alert, stress-free and even-tempered.

Tip

Some supermarkets and roadside flower stalls sell simple bouquets for less than £5. If you're not in too much trouble, you might be able to get away with this option.

35 Buy Music Online

You've got plenty of choices when shopping for music. In addition to what's available at your local record store and online shops like Amazon.com, CDBaby.com and CDUniverse.com, there are countless music files available. Apple's got the newest kid on the block with iTunes, where you can buy any song in their vast online database for less than a pound.

Steps

1 Understand the difference between streaming and downloading. Streamed music plays while the file is being downloaded from the internet. Downloaded music gets copied directly to your computer's hard disk, allowing you to listen to it any time, move it to a portable MP3 player or burn it to a CD. In some cases, it won't be possible to save streamed music – unless you record it on an external device while it's playing.

2 Get the software you need to listen to MP3s and streaming audio. Some will already be installed on your computer; if not, they can usually be downloaded for free: Winamp and Windows Media Player are the best known MP3 players for PCs; iTunes rules for Mac users. RealOne/RealPlayer streaming software works for both platforms.

3 Visit music sites to look for the musicians you want to hear. Some popular download sites are OD2 (ondemandmusic.com), Insound.com, Streetsonline.co.uk, Vitaminic.com, Playlouder.com, Epitonic.com, eMusic.com, Listen.com, MP3.com and PressPlay.com. Popular streaming sites include MusicMatch.com and Yahoo Launch (launch.yahoo.com).

4 Check for individual songs you want to hear. Artists will invariably appear on different sites at the same time.

5 Check out an artist's official website, especially if you're looking for new or obscure music. Many artists will promote songs by letting you download them directly from their own sites. Lots of radio stations stream their broadcasts on the web for free.

6 Compare the plans and prices offered at different sites. Most offer a free trial period, and then charge a subscription fee ranging from £5 per month to £40 per year. Some also offer pay-per-download plans.

7 Find out what the subscription fee includes. Look for one that gives you plenty of downloads or unlimited streaming. For streaming sites, find one that allows you to create your own custom playlists that will play only your own selected tracks.

8 Avoid plans in which downloaded music expires or becomes unplayable when your subscription lapses, or if you move the music around. Go for a service that gives you full rights to copy the music to another computer or portable player, and to burn the songs to CDs.

What to Look For

- MP3 and streaming audio software
- Free trial periods
- Subscription pricing
- Secure formats

Tips

You may have to provide some personal information (such as your name, age and e-mail address) to get songs for free.

Check out Audible.com for downloadable audio books in MP3 format.

Warnings

The advice given here concerns the legal, paid downloading of music.

Peer-to-peer (P2P) services let you swap music directly from your computer's hard drive to those of other people on the internet. One P2P service, Napster, collapsed under legal challenges from the music industry, but many other P2P services – such as Soulseek (soulseek.com) – still exist. Use them with caution, as their legality continues to be in dispute.

Many of the download sites are based in the US, so be aware that fluctuations in currency rates will affect what you actually pay.

Some music is available directly from small-label websites, some of which will only accept payment via electronic currencies. If you hold a credit card, set up a PayPal account – it's easy to do, and it's free!

36 Employ Musicians

Whether it's a string quartet or a rocking blues band, live music can make or break an event. Choosing your musicians carefully is crucial to a successful party – you don't want your event to be memorable for the wrong reasons.

Steps

1 Start your search as early as possible. Get recommendations from friends. Look under "Musicians" and "Party Planners & Organisers" in the *Yellow Pages*. Search online, where sites such as hoptiludrop.co.uk offer live musicians in a wide range of styles. Entertainment organizers, your regional musicians union and even music schools are worth contacting.

2 Call at least three prospective bands. Ask about their availability, rates, number of musicians and instruments in the band, years of experience, song lists, references and liability insurance.

3 Ask about additional costs, such as overtime, travel or meals for band members.

4 Request a demo tape and find out if you can attend a performance to observe the band in person. Confirm that the musicians on the demo tape or onstage will be the ones at your gig.

5 Check references. Ask about promptness, reliability, performance quality, interactions with the audience and overall impressions.

6 Negotiate a fee. You may be able to reduce the number of band members or the playing time to bring down the cost.

7 Get everything in writing: the fee, deposit, cancellation and refund policies, overtime fees, the band's insurance information, number of musicians and instruments, date of event, set-up time, performance time, band's attire, equipment provided by band, equipment provided by you, specific song requests, and contact information.

8 Get two signed copies of the contract. Give one to the broker or bandleader and keep one for yourself.

9 Provide a list of favourite and unwanted songs. Most bands will have a set song list to choose from, but some will learn songs if you request, although they may charge extra.

10 Call the band or organiser the week of the event to confirm the date and time. Provide directions, information about parking and your contact information for last-minute emergencies.

What to Look For

- Availability
- Rates
- Hidden costs
- Demo tape
- Live performance
- References
- Promptness
- Reliability
- Written contract

Tips

If you want the bandleader to double as an MC, make sure you approve of his or her style, tone and humour. Provide a schedule of events, such as an anniversary couple's dance, the throwing of the wedding bouquet.

Anticipate that the band will need a break every hour. Request that they play appropriate recorded music while on break.

Reputable entertainment organisers can save you some effort. They represent a variety of bands and DJs, and can handle all the logistics for you.

Budget money to tip the band at the end of the evening.

37 Order a Good Bottle of Wine

You settle into your seat, ready for a fine meal, when suddenly a leather-bound wine list is thrust into your hands. Panic no longer. Some simple considerations will help you quickly transform the process into a less intimidating, even enjoyable task.

Steps

1 Initiate a wine discussion with your dining companions but keep it simple. Find out the type of wine people prefer and what food they plan to eat.

2 Let the group know that they should definitely feel free to ignore the traditional pairing of red wines with meat and white wines with seafood and poultry.

3 If you have a favourite, suggest it to the group. They're likely to accept your recommendation.

4 Scan the list for a wine that fits the group's preferences and is within your budget range. If you can't afford any but the wines near the bottom of the list's price range, consider choosing the house wine. It's often better than other wines the restaurant is offering at a similar price.

5 Know that a dry white wine such as a New Zealand Sauvignon Blanc or a French Muscadet is often the best choice for a drink to sip while waiting for food to arrive, and goes well with a reasonably wide range of dishes.

6 If choosing a red wine, consider a Cabernet Sauvignon or a Côtes-du-Rhone as a generally acceptable option. Know that reds from Argentina and Chile are reputed to be good value.

7 Address the waiter with, for example, "I was thinking of this Muscadet unless you have a better suggestion". If the restaurant has a sommelier – a wine expert – ask the waiter to send him or her to your table to discuss suitable pairings.

8 Check the bottle's label to confirm it's the wine you ordered. Smell and sample the wine to make sure it isn't vinegary, corky or musty (if it is, send it back). Give the server the nod to pour for the rest of the table. Sip and enjoy.

What to Look For

- Red or white
- Vineyard, grape variety and vintage
- Price

Tips

If you are drinking more than one bottle of wine with a meal, try to ensure that you order the driest wine first and the sweetest wine last.

Some waiters can provide excellent suggestions, while others are clueless. Most will at least know which wines are popular with other patrons.

Some restaurants will fax you the wine list ahead of time. Also, some finer restaurants have reserved wine lists of special or rare wines available upon request.

Red for red meats, pork and red sauces/white for poultry, fish and white sauces is a helpful guideline, but not an absolute rule. Your personal preference is equally important.

38 Buy an Ergonomic Desk Chair

If you spend most of your waking hours at your desk, you know you need a chair that works with your body to spare you from needless backaches and fatigue. Test drive several chairs at furniture, office supply and specialist back-care shops before you pick the one that's right for you. Prices vary greatly: predictably, superior materials and construction cost extra. Good deals abound online and from office furniture warehouses and office clearance specialists (see 156 "Buy Bargain Office Equipment").

FEATURE	WHAT IT DOES
Back Support	• Height adjustment: Supports the lumbar area (lower back). Look for chairs that provide mid-back and upper-back support as well. • Tilt mechanism: Maintains support as you move and recline. It's best to have your back slightly reclined while seated at your desk.
Seat Pan	• Your weight should be distributed evenly on the seat. Look for a rounded or waterfall edge at the front of the seat, which prevents the seat from catching behind the knees and cutting off circulation. Three to four fingers should fit between the seat's front edge and the back of the knees. • Seat should extend at least one inch from either side of the hips for optimum comfort. Insufficient hip room can make you sit too far forward and not get enough thigh support. • Some seats adjust for a forward or backward tilt.
Armrests	• Alleviate pressure on the back but may interfere with lower desks. Look for adjustable width and height to support various tasks, including writing and reading, to ease neck and shoulder tension and to help prevent carpal tunnel syndrome. • Should be contoured, broad, cushioned and comfortable.
Fabric	• Cloth coverings are less expensive and breathe well, but vinyl or leather upholstery is easier to keep clean. Look for a durable, permeable, ventilated material.
Height Adjustment	• Pneumatic levers or gas lifts adjust seating height while in chair. For optimal posture, thighs should be horizontal with the ground and both feet flat on the floor. The chair's height should allow wrists to be straight while typing.
Stability	• Look for a chair on wheels that swivels to avoid excess stretching and twisting of your spine. A five-point base won't tip over when you recline. • Choose hard casters for carpeting and rubber-coated ones for hard surfaces. A good chair can recline and lock into various positions.

39 Choose Film for Your Camera

Although many people are switching to digital cameras, you may well be one of the millions who still take photos using film. If so, it is vital that you buy the right product. Your primary considerations are where you'll be shooting and what you want to do with the pictures. This information allows you to choose the correct film type and speed.

Steps

1 Decide whether you want photographs or slides, colour or black-and-white. Many professional photographers prefer slides because they have rich colour saturation and minimal graininess. Black-and-white delivers striking images with stark textures.

2 Choose a film size that is appropriate for your camera. Most cameras use 35 mm (or 135) film, though cartridge-film cameras need 24 mm Advanced Photo System (APS) film. Roll-film cameras use 120 or 220; large-format, hooded view cameras use single sheets of film for each exposure.

3 Understand how film speed works. Fast speeds pick up rapid action and work well in low-light situations. Slower speeds produce richer colours and greater contrast, but you'll need bright light and a steady hand. Film speed is indicated by an ISO number (how sensitive a film is to light compared to a standard from the International Standards Organisation). The faster the film, the more sensitive.

4 Choose a slow speed (25 to 64 ASA) if you want minimal graininess and colours that punch, but only if you'll be photographing in the bright sunlight. Slow speeds are excellent for close-ups, still shots and photos you plan to enlarge. You may need a tripod to steady the camera with slow film.

5 Select a medium speed (100 to 200 ASA) if you want an all-purpose film that delivers clear colours and images outdoors, or indoors with a flash.

6 Opt for 400 speed if you'll be photographing action shots or if you'll be in low-light conditions, such as cloudy days or indoors without a flash. Zoom lenses require the use of higher-speed films (400 ASA and up).

7 Get 800-speed film if you're photographing very fast action or shots with dim light. This is ideal for a fireworks show, twilight or a candlelit dinner. Speeds above 800 (1,000 to 3,200 ASA) are considered professional speeds.

8 Buy cheap film with a well known brand name unless you plan to make significant enlargements or publish your work.

9 Store film in a cool, dry place with good ventilation, such as a refrigerator, and get it developed as soon as the roll is finished. Never expose film to heat or direct sunlight.

What to Look For

- Photographic prints or slides
- Colour or black-and-white
- Film size
- Film speed
- Lighting conditions

Tips

The techniques used at mass film developers – the people your supermarket or chemist send your film to for developing – often result in grainy pictures with dull colours. If you can, find a specialist shop that has someone monitoring the developing process – this person can make adjustments to optimise colour and contrast.

Warning

When travelling, never pack your film in your checked luggage: The powerful X-rays used to scan luggage checked into the hold may destroy the film. Keep it in a mesh bag and, at security checkpoints, ask personnel to check your film by hand if it is 800 speed or higher.

40 Buy Rechargeable Batteries

Rechargeable batteries are good for the environment and for your wallet. The initial outlay per battery may be three or four times that for throwaway batteries, but even with the added initial cost of a charger (around £20) the saving over time can be impressive. Rechargeables are now less prone than they once were to the "memory effect" – crystals that form on interior plates and shorten the life of the battery. If handled properly, a modern NiMH battery in your digital camera will last for many years.

TYPE	GOOD FOR	PROS AND CONS
Alkaline	Devices that require a low amount of energy over a long time: TV remote controls, pagers, AM/FM radios.	A long-established technology compared with nickel cadmium (NiCd) and nickel metal hydride (NiMH) cells. Energy drastically decreases after the first recharge (last far fewer cycles than NiCd and NiMH batteries). Life depends on the depth of discharge: the deeper the discharge, the fewer cycles the battery can endure. Reduced service life may offset any cost advantage over standard alkaline batteries when used in items that use a lot of power fast.
Nickel Metal Hydride (NiMH)	Energy-intense products: digital cameras, music players, mobile phones and remote-control toys.	Pack a lot of power with each recharge. Last longer between charges than NiCd batteries and are less toxic to the environment. Handle the memory effect much better than NiCd batteries. Can be recharged as many as 1,000 times. Lose charge quickly, in use or not.
Nickel Cadmium (NiCd)	Power tools and emergency lighting	Most common rechargeable batteries. Easy to use, cheap and last for 500 to 1,000 cycles. Prone to memory effect; require discharging at regular intervals to avoid this. Most problems due to overcharging or improper storage. Contain cadmium, a highly toxic heavy metal, that can damage the environment if not disposed of properly. Recycle, do not discard.
Lithium Ion (Li-Ion)	Ideal for devices requiring a reliable, high-energy power source: mobile phones, PDAs, laptops, and MP3 players.	Rechargeable, powerful and light. Do not exhibit a memory problem, so can be recharged anytime without first having to be completely discharged. Li-Ion batteries produce the same energy as NiMH but weigh approximately 20 to 35 per cent less. They are also environmentally friendly because they don't contain toxins such as cadmium or mercury.
TIPS		The energy capacity of the battery is measured in milliampere hours (mAh). The higher the mAh number, the longer the battery will hold and provide its rated charge. Digital cameras need AA batteries with at least 1,800 to 1,900 mAh. The shelf life of a battery varies depending on how you use it. An alkaline battery with 2,500 mAh might die in an hour or less if you use it in a digital camera. In a remote control it could last for several months.

41 Give to a Good Cause

With so many worthy causes vying for your money, choose one or two that are near and dear to your heart. Has a loved one suffered from breast cancer? Are you a nature or animal lover? Is education or social welfare your passion? Once you've chosen a cause, there are excellent resources available to help you choose an organisation that will make the most of your donation.

Steps

1 Know that all major charities in England and Wales are regulated by the Charity Commission. Visit the Commission's website at charity-commission.gov.uk to search their register, which gives basic information on charities' objectives and finances.

2 When you have identified a charity that interests you, visit the charity's website or call it directly. Find out as much as you can about its history, programmes and recent accomplishments.

3 Find out what percentage of the charity's annual budget is spent on its actual mission versus fund-raising and administrative costs. A charity should probably spend at least 50 per cent of its budget on its mission.

4 Evaluate the mission of the charity and its effectiveness in fulfilling its mission. For those organisations that operate in the developing world, look for partnerships between the organisation and the local population for most effective use of resources.

5 Visit philanthropyuk.org, the website of the Associated Charitable Foundations, for a clear and comprehensive guide to ways of giving to charity, including detailed information on tax relief.

6 Be aware of the Gift Aid tax scheme. By filling in a simple form saying that you wish your donation to be Gift Aid, you enable the charity to claim £28 from the Inland Revenue for every £100 you donate. If you are a higher rate taxpayer, you can still get tax relief on the donation, claiming back the difference between standard and higher rate tax.

7 Consider opening an account specifically devoted to charitable contributions – for example, a Charitable Aid Foundation (CAF) Charity Account. This will make it simple to direct money at any time you want to charities of your choice

8 Obtain an affinity card. This is a credit card that pays a certain percentage on all transactions to charity. A popular example is the Halifax Visa Charity Card.

9 Join a "payroll giving" scheme, in which a percentage of your pre-tax salary is donated to charity each month. If your employers are not party to such a scheme, encourage them to join.

10 Remember that one of the best occasions for generosity is when you die. Make a will leaving either specific sums or residual money – what is left when your affairs are wound up – to charities.

What to Look For

- Financial information about the charity
- Mission statement
- Successful programmes
- Gift Aid form
- Affinity card

Tips

An organisation need not be a charity to receive donations. Schools, cultural programmes and political groups all rely on donations of money and time.

If you want to further review the charity, ask it to provide you with a copy of its recent annual reports.

Donating shares to a charity can be especially tax effective for higher-rate taxpayers. Since the gift will be both free of capital gains tax and income tax deductible, you could donate shares worth £10,000 at an effective cost to yourself of £2,000.

42 Take Part in a Car Boot Sale

Taking part in a car boot sale can be both fun and profitable if you plan it well and go with the right attitude. So, find out when and where the next one is going to be held in your area, scour the house for unwanted goods, and pack the old estate car to the roof. Add tables, chairs, coffee and a float and you're away.

Steps

1 Find out when the next car boot sale is planned to be held in your area. All sorts of people organise them – from schools and churches to farmers with a lot of land. Check the local paper, village shop, post office and local newsagent's noticeboard for advance warning and look out for fliers distributed in local cafés.

2 Phone up the organisers and book your space. Typically, you'll be charged between £5 and £20 to take part. Those interested in buying will be charged a small fee (say 50p) to get in.

3 Dig through your garage, attic, basement and rest of the house for stuff to sell. Include everything you want to get rid of – one person's junk is another's treasure.

4 Spread the word among friends and family. Offer to sell their unwanted stuff, too, for a small commission or in return for help selling the stuff on the day. Stick one of the car boot sale fliers in your own window to alert passers-by.

5 Scrub, wash, polish and dust anything you want to sell. If an item needs a simple repair that could greatly improve the price, fix it.

6 Use masking tape and a permanent marker to mark everything with a price. "£1 or less" tables or boxes save time and attract browsers. Remember that you're trying to get rid of your stuff when you price it. You may have spent a fortune on that VCR, but you'll be lucky to get much for it now. Think cheap.

7 Pack your car with stuff. You'll probably need an estate car. Take folding tables to display items and metal rails to hang clothes. Take several picnic chairs both for yourself and browsers. It will seem like a very long day if you can't sit down at all. Take food and drink, too. There will probably be both for sale at the event but you don't want to spend most of the money you make on food and drink during the day.

8 Take a cash box with a float in it. Make sure you have plenty of small change and a pocket calculator if your maths isn't that hot. You'll also need bags and boxes, newspaper to wrap easily breakable items, and a tape measure.

9 Be cheerful, get people talking and encourage haggling. Many people are reluctant to haggle but find it's fun once they start.

What to Look For

- Adverts in local paper
- Fliers in local shops and cafés
- Volunteers to help throughout the day

Tips

Price everything cheaply. Everyone expects to get bargains at a car boot sale. You're unlikely to get more than £1 for a CD, or 50p for a paperback novel for example.

Knock down the prices even further towards the end of the day – the object is to get rid of as much as possible.

Donate whatever is left to a charity shop.

Make sure you take plenty of change. You don't want to miss a sale because you can't change a £20 note.

Warnings

Taking part in a car boot sale can be extremely tiring. Make sure you take a flask of tea or coffee and some sandwiches to keep you going, and a picnic chair to sit on when you need a rest.

Protect yourself against theft and fraud. Display small valuables within eyesight. Keep change in a zipped money belt and transfer money through the day to a locked cash box concealed within the car. Do not accept personal cheques.

43 Employ a Cleaner

Weekends are too short to spend scrubbing, vacuuming and dusting and nothing beats coming home to a clean house, especially when you didn't do it. Employ a cleaning service or individual cleaner to do your dirty work so you can go out to play.

Steps

1 Decide whether you want to use a domestic cleaning service or an individual self-employed cleaner. Using a service costs more, but offers greater reliability, and the supplies and equipment are included.

2 Ask friends for recommendations. Check local newspapers, newsagents' windows, the *Yellow Pages* and the internet.

3 Call several prospective cleaners. Confirm that they'll do the required tasks (some won't do laundry, windows or washing-up). Ask about experience, availability and rates.

4 Know that a self-employed cleaner will probably want to be paid cash-in-hand. This in principle lays you open to deep trouble with the tax authorities. But if you use the cleaner regularly and want to make the situation legal, you will have to face complexities of employment law, taxation, paid holidays and sick leave.

5 Check three references before you hold interviews, to verify the person's promptness, reliability and quality of work.

6 Meet prospective cleaners with stellar references to show them the specifics of the job and to get a sense of their personality and professionalism. Some cleaners have excellent working skills but don't speak English well. Judge how important fluent communication is likely to be.

7 Ask specific questions to test a cleaner's methods: "What do you use to clean hardwood floors?" "How would you remove these stains from the top of my stove?"

8 Find out how often the cleaner will come. Some will do periodic spring cleaning while others work to a weekly or fortnightly schedule.

9 Employ the most promising individual or team for a trial period on the understanding that if you're fully satisfied, you'll go on to use them regularly.

What to Look For

- Experience
- Availability
- Rates
- Quality references
- Promptness
- Professionalism

Tips

Individual operators usually earn more hourly than someone working for a cleaning service because there's no third party or overhead.

Writing your newly hired cleaner a list of specific requests (the china should never go in the dishwasher) can be helpful. It's even more helpful if you get it translated for people whose English isn't too good.

Warning

Keep jewellery and large amounts of cash locked up when any hired workers visit.

44 Employ an Au Pair

The au pair system gives young people a chance to live abroad and improve their foreign language skills. Those who employ them get an affordable contribution to childcare or to household chores – and often a whole heap of problems as well. Before you invite a young foreigner to live in your home, carefully weigh up the advantages and pitfalls.

Steps

1 Ask around to find out other people's experience of au pairs. Form an idea of the sex and nationality of the au pair you require.

2 Language can be a crucial issue. If you speak a foreign language, go for an au pair who speaks that tongue. German, Dutch or Scandinavian au pairs will usually speak the best English. Turkish or Slovakian au pairs may have difficulty understanding or making themselves understood.

3 Decide which room in the house the au pair is going to occupy. Be sure that you are mentally prepared for the presence of a young foreigner in your house, sharing your facilities. If you have no spare bedroom, you can't have an au pair.

4 Find out which au pair agencies provide au pairs from the part of the world you have decided upon. Contact an agency and find out their terms and conditions. Choose one that has been recommended or strikes you as well organised and professional.

5 Expect to be interviewed about your needs and preferences. The job of the agency is to match your wishes with au pairs on their books. Find out what procedures the agency has followed to screen potential au pairs – have they been personally interviewed by agency staff, for example? If you are not satisfied with their screening procedures, go to another agency.

6 Select an au pair from the list provided by the agency. You will probably not be able to interview the candidates, as most will be still in their home country. Communicate by letter or e-mail. Ask pertinent questions – for example, if you will want the au pair to do household chores, ensure that this is acceptable.

7 Ensure that the agency has checked out references provided by the au pair.

8 Recognise that the person arriving to live in your home is young, in a foreign country, and possibly living away from parents for the first time. Expect some emotional problems.

9 Agree with the au pair what his or her duties will be; usually au pairs will give 25 hours of their time each week for £50 paid in cash. You can pay extra for extra hours.

10 Lay down clear rules about behaviour. Boyfriends or girlfriends, loud music, smoking, friction about sharing the kitchen or the use of the phone are all the kind of issues that can cause trouble.

What to Look For

- Personal recommendations
- Professional agency
- Language skills

Tips

If you want an au pair to look after a boy or boys, consider employing a male au pair. Boys often build a better rapport with a young carer of their own sex.

Don't dream of letting an au pair drive your children around in your car before you have subjected him or her to a personal driving test. Possession of a driving licence does not guarantee sufficient competence.

Warnings

Don't assume that it is safe to leave your children in the sole care of an au pair until you have established by personal observation that he or she is fully competent and reliable.

Never leave an au pair in sole charge of a child under the age of three.

45 Buy a Guitar

Elvis Presley and John Lennon strummed Gibson acoustic guitars. Jimi Hendrix powered through his classics on a Fender Stratocaster, while Bruce Springsteen remains steadfastly loyal to his own boss, a well-worn Fender Telecaster. If you've just picked up a guitar, or if you're a seasoned player looking to upgrade, how do you choose a new axe?

Steps

Before you buy

1 Choose between a steel-stringed acoustic guitar for folk and blues, a nylon-stringed acoustic for classical music, or an electric or electric bass guitar for good old rock and roll, to name a few.

2 Talk to follow musicians about their instrument of choice and what they love about it.

3 Research guitar brands using price guides, guitar magazines and the internet. Some models appreciate in value as they get older.

4 Consider buying secondhand instead of new. If you know your stuff, you may be able to get more value for your pound (see 3 "Buy Products and Services Online").

At the store

1 Examine the construction. Look for a straight neck, a well-balanced body and frets that are smooth and flush.

2 Strap on the guitar and hold it in playing position. Does it feel natural? Balanced? Too heavy? Does your hand fit comfortably around the neck?

3 Tune the guitar to see how smoothly the tuning keys operate and to test the sound quality of each string.

4 Play a song. Do you like the sound? Is it easy to press down the strings? Is there any buzzing or clicking that suggests problems?

5 If you are buying an electric guitar, plug it into an amp and play. Listen for crackling or humming. Test the controls for ease of use. (Humming might be caused by a bad flex; replace it with a new one.)

6 Try out several models before you decide on one. Before you buy, ask, "What can you offer me if I buy my guitar here?" Some stores will throw in freebies (plectra, guitar straps, a set of strings) or discounted accessories (amp, effects or a mike stand). Make sure the price includes a guitar case.

7 Remember that the retail price of a guitar is often negotiable (see 8 "Negotiate"). Also, make sure you know the policy on returning goods before you buy (see 4 "Take Goods Back").

What to Look For

- Reputable brand and model
- Solid construction
- Comfortable to hold and play
- Easy tuning
- Excellent sound
- Fair price

Tips

Before buying a guitar, ask the salesperson about rent-to-own deals.

Bring along a guitarist friend when you shop, especially if you can't tune a guitar.

Avoid guitar stores without marked prices and with aggressive salespeople unless you know prices and are keen to haggle.

You can buy a beginner's guitar for £100–£200, but if you want to buy a renowned model of a popular brand, such as Gibson, Fender, Rickenbacker or Guild, expect to pay £700 or more.

46 Buy Duct Tape

Do you ever feel like the entire world is being held together with duct tape? After you read the following chart, you'll know if it's true and keep a roll on hand at all times.

USES FOR DUCT TAPE
Repair splits in car seats (or other furniture, if you must).
Car repair, including attaching side-view mirrors and bumpers.
Convert a CO_2 filter on *Apollo 13* – it allowed the astronauts to breathe during their return to Earth.
Remove warts.
Twist a long piece into rope.
Tape wires down on floor or out of the way.
Tape wires back together after splicing.
Fold in half and use as bookmark.
Repair heating ducts.
Seal boxes.
Create disc labels.
Repair leak in tyre or inner tube.
Tape annoying people to walls, floor, ceiling or bed.
Roll into a ball for cricket practice.
Mark lines on a sportsfield.
Wrap around newspaper to make a dog chew toy.
Remove fluff from clothes.
Put it on your lawn and paint it green. Say good-bye to mowing.
Retread your tennis shoes.
Wrap a fizzy drink can or bottle to keep it cold.
Stare at it and try to find new uses for it.

47 Get a Good Deal on a Magazine Subscription

The cost of magazine subscriptions can creep up on you: a monthly perhaps costing £50 a year, a weekly setting you back £150–£200 annually. Be a smart consumer and save money while you get the magazines you really want.

Steps

1 Be suspicious of pitches from websites and junk mail. There are usually hidden costs.

2 Order directly from the publisher. Check the price listed on the magazine's website and on insert cards in the magazine.

3 Call the publisher's customer service line to confirm that you have the lowest rate. Ask, "Do you have a special rate for first-time subscribers?" Such rates are often unadvertised. Ask if there is a special rate for students and/or professional educators, if applicable.

4 Make sure you notice the long-term cost. Some weekly magazines may sound cheap but cost a lot annually. Remember that just £3 per issue for a weekly adds up to £156 a year.

5 Find out the cancellation policy before you subscribe to any special offer.

6 Order a two-year subscription if you know that you'll want it. You should get a few pounds off the total cost as well as insuring against a price rise during that period.

7 Request that you be billed for the magazine; don't provide your credit card number. If they have your credit card number, some magazines will automatically renew your subscription unless you call to cancel it. Magazines encourage credit-card payments because it puts inertia on their side. People often wait months or years to cancel subscriptions they no longer want.

What to Look For

- Publisher's offers
- First-time rates
- Student or educational rates
- Cancellation policy
- Multi-year discount
- Billing arrangement

Tips

You can find a magazine's subscription phone number online and in the small print near the magazine's table of contents or masthead.

Books are often much better value than magazines. If you have a special interest, consider spending your money on in-depth books on the subject. Keep up to date with latest developments free through the internet.

48 Get Senior Citizen or Student Discounts

You can save money merely by being the right age. Senior and student discounts apply to travel, entertainment and a host of products and services. A little digging will uncover all sorts of deals in your neighbourhood, and around the world.

Steps

Senior discounts

1 Contact the Saga Group (saga.co.uk) for special deals for the over 50s. Saga offers holidays, low prices for insurance and other financial services, and private healthcare deals. Subscribe to Saga Magazine for regular updates on products.

2 Call the airlines or go online to find out about discounted flight tickets for seniors. There are many offers available.

3 Buy a Senior Railcard to get one-third off the price of most rail tickets nationwide. It will cost you £18 a year – a sum you could save with your discount on a single long-distance journey.

4 Obtain a bus pass from your local council. These offer reduced price or free travel on buses for over 60s.

5 Ask about concessions at cinemas, theatres and concert halls. These are often available at specific times.

6 Look out for local discounts at shops, restaurants and cafés.

Student discounts

1 Join the National Union of Students (NUS). The NUS card gives you access to a wide range of discounts in the UK. Check out what discounts are currently available by visiting nus.org.uk.

2 Apply for an International Student Identity Card (ISIC). It will cost you £7 a year to get student discounts on international travel, hostels, entertainment, museums and more.

3 Collect student privilege cards issued by business concerns, such as the Virgin Student Card. These will give you discounts off most products and services provided by the company and its subsidiaries.

4 Take advantage of one-off special offers such as cash payments for opening accounts with banks. Internet sites – for example, studentfreestuff.com – list current offers.

5 Look out for budget travel options for young people. For example, a Young Persons Railcard gives one third off the price of most rail tickets in the UK for £18 a year. Interrail passes for European rail travel are available at cheaper rates for under-26s.

What to Look For

- Senior Railcard
- NUS card
- International Student Identity Card
- Interrail pass

Tips

Always ask before you buy. Contact customer services in person or by phone or e-mail before making a large purchase; salespeople aren't always aware of senior or student discounts.

Carry passes or ID cards with you at all times to take advantage of discounts as you discover them.

Before you use the discount, ask the salesperson if there is a lower discount available. Better deals sometimes exist through general sales or promotions.

49 Buy Flowers Wholesale

Wholesale flower markets supply fresh-cut flowers, floral accessories and plants to florists and business operators. The markets are often open to the general public and, even if you don't get wholesale prices, you'll get big discounts. Wholesale markets are especially useful if you need to buy flowers in bulk for a wedding or party.

Steps

1 Look in the *Yellow Pages* under "Flower Wholesalers" or search the internet to find a wholesale flower market in your area.

2 Phone one of the listed wholesalers to check that the market is open to the public and find out opening hours.

3 Go to bed early and set your alarm. Flower markets open as early as 2 a.m., and the best flowers disappear quickly.

4 Survey the entire market for prices and selection before you make a purchase. Vendors closest to the entrance often charge the highest prices.

5 Check that the stems are freshly cut and the leaves and buds are firm. Don't buy from a vendor who has brown or withered flowers in the mix.

6 Make your selection. The more you purchase from a single vendor, the more likely it is that he or she will be open to negotiating a better price.

7 Fill a sink or bath with about 10 cm (4 in) of cold water when you return from the flower market. Remove the newspaper wrappings and stand the flower bunches in the water until you make the arrangements. Make fresh cuts on all stems before arranging.

What to Look For

- Wholesale market
- Freshly cut stems
- Barely open buds

Tips

Flowers sold in the wholesale market are intended for resale, so many buds are closed. If you are buying flowers for a special event, allow a day or two for the buds to open.

Retail flower markets such as the Sunday market at London's Columbia Road are another excellent source for affordable fresh flowers.

50 Get a Picture Framed

Whether it's a fine watercolour or your child's finger painting, your work of art deserves a customised frame to show off its beauty and prevent deterioration over time. A skilled framer is your partner in this process. Quality framers have years of experience with preservation framing using a variety of materials and methods, and should be able to work within any budget.

TERM	DESCRIPTION
Mat	Provides a spacer to protect paper art or photographs from direct contact with the glass. This is necessary, particularly in humid climates, to prevent the art from coming in contact with condensation or sticking to the glass and permanently damaging it. It also provides structural support for the artwork. Discuss with the framer whether the picture would benefit from double or triple matting with a straight or bevel cut. Also discuss what colour and width of mat will best highlight the look of the image.
Mounting	A picture can be hinged or stuck down. Hinging is the process of using acid-free linen tape at the top of the mat and letting it hang. A more permanent method is to mount the entire picture to the backing board, achieving a smooth, flat finish. For dry mounting, some framers use a vacuum-heat mounting press, which removes air by a vacuum suction pump before the art touches the heat plate, which seals and mounts the piece.
Backing	As with mats, the wrong backing can damage your work. Insist that your framer use a lightweight neutral-pH backing, known as conservation-quality artboard. Barrier paper can be added to this as an extra precaution for works of higher value. Your picture should then be sealed to protect it from dust, air, moisture and insects.
Glass	Conservation-quality picture framing glass is specially formulated to protect framed works of art from the damaging effects of ultraviolet light. Some types of glass filter out over 97 percent of UV light. If you think reflection may be a serious problem, choose a non-reflective glass. Consider using acrylic for pictures or posters larger than 90 by 120 cm (36 by 48 in), or for pictures and prints intended for a child's room. It is lighter, shatterproof and less expensive than normal glass.
Frame	The frame you choose should be strong enough to support the final weight of the glass, mounting and artwork. Styles are up to you.
TIPS	If you can't afford a framer, try a DIY operation. Information and equipment is available from websites such as diypictureframing.co.uk.
	Get a quote in writing that details the price of the frame, mat and labour, the design plan and the completion date.

51 Employ a Removal Company

Moving house is well known to be one of the most stressful occasions in life – even if you're not worrying that your prized possessions are going to be broken in transit or even disappear without trace. Be sure that you employ a reputable removal company for your peace of mind.

Steps

1 Look into the types of removal service available at different price levels. At the top of the range, you can expect a home visit from a representative of the firm before the move, specialist packing materials for different items, and a high level of expertise. At the bottom of the market you will get a man and a van. Decide what you are prepared to pay and choose accordingly.

2 Call several removal companies, both national and local. Ask for three references and call all of them to corroborate the remover's professionalism and reliability.

3 Ask about rates. Be aware of any conditions that will trigger additional costs, such as moves over a certain distance or goods over a certain weight. Ask what happens if goods are damaged: under what conditions is the remover responsible and for how much.

4 Understand how packing options affect the price. For example, if you pack certain goods yourself, can you save some money? Or pack everything yourself with portable containers that are delivered to your home. You pack them, and the company transports them to your new home.

5 If you are moving a long distance, inquire about tracking options so that you can find out where your belongings are. Be sure the removers can guarantee a delivery date.

6 Be sure that the cost of packing materials such as bubble wrap and boxes is included in the price.

7 Obtain a free estimate if you like what you hear. Bids will vary widely. Get several bids to find the best deal.

8 Discuss with the firm any considerations unique to your move. Point out any especially large or fragile items, and ask how they will be handled. Point out issues that affect access, such as staircases, steep driveways or small attics, and be prepared to pay more for complicated moves.

What to Look For

- Quality references
- Rates
- Insurance
- Packing options
- Tracking options
- Guaranteed service
- Written contract

Tips

If you can afford it, there are firms that will organise your entire move, not only dealing with the removal company but also with all the other hassles moving involves.

Get the driver's mobile phone number so that you can keep track of his progress.

Warning

If you entrust all your household goods to someone without having checked their references or established their bona fides, it is an open invitation to theft.

9. Get a signed contract that includes the agreed price, pick-up and delivery dates, packing services, plus policies regarding payment, insurance and guaranteed services. Make sure the contract has a customer service number in case of problems.

10. Ensure that you have an accurate inventory of the goods being moved, including details of any items already damaged. Do not make a final payment until all items have been checked off as delivered and reviewed for damage in transit.

52 Employ a Lifestyle Manager

Imagine you had someone constantly on call to sort out those time-consuming problems that clog up your life, from finding a plumber to organising a flight for your Easter holidays. That person is a lifestyle manager. At a price, they will give busy people time to live.

Steps

1. Decide what sort of service you want. Do you want a personal lifestyle manager who will meet you to discuss your needs and make useful suggestions about improving the way you live? Or do you simply want a phone number to call for occasional assistance when specific problems arise?

2. Look for lifestyle management services in your area on the internet. Compare their services and pricing structure. Do they require you to sign up for a monthly fee, or simply pay by the hour? If there is a fixed fee, do you have to pay extra if you use the service for more than a certain number of hours in a month?

3. Expect to pay around £10 an hour for a service that doesn't require the lifestyle manager to leave the office – for example, finding a plumber or a flight. You will pay £20–£25 an hour for services that require someone to come to your home – for example, to be there to let a plumber in while you are at work.

4. Know that a top-range personal lifestyle manager, who will meet you from time to time to review your lifestyle and your needs, as well as providing round-the-clock services, will probably cost around £500 a month.

What to Look For

- Personal service
- Problem-solving
- Right price

Tips

If you are going to use a personal manager, this will become a significant relationship in your life. It is essential that you find someone you like and trust.

Always check references before committing yourself to any service.

53 Find a Vet

If there's a pet in your family – or in your future – you'll need to find a trustworthy vet. Tackle this just as seriously as you would trying to find a doctor for any other loved one.

Steps

1 Quiz friends for recommendations; word-of-mouth references from impassioned pet-owners are the best way to find a good vet. Ask what it is that they like about the vet.

2 Check with speciality pet stores or breeders to find a vet who specialises in a certain pet or breed.

3 Choose a vet whose office location, days and business hours are convenient for you.

4 Call potential candidates and ask what the rate is for a basic check-up.

5 Find out what emergency services are offered during and after business hours. Does the vet carry out operations on site or will your pet need to be moved elsewhere for surgical treatment. If so, which animal hospital is the vet associated with? Is it nearby?

6 Visit the vet's clinic to make sure it is clean and orderly, and that the staff is helpful and knowledgeable.

7 Arrange to meet the vet to discuss your pet. Are you comfortable talking to this person? Is he or she responsive to your questions?

8 Make sure the vet has no plans to retire soon. You'll want a vet who's likely to stay in practice for the duration of your pet's life.

9 Choose the vet that best fits your needs and bring your pet there for an initial check-up. The vet will begin a medical file on your pet.

10 Keep the vet's phone number with your emergency numbers. Share it with pet carers when you go on holiday.

What to Look For

- Personal recommendations
- Convenient location and hours
- Affordable rates
- Good emergency services
- Clean office
- Friendly staff
- Personable vet

Tips

Ask if alternative and holistic treatments such as acupuncture, chiropractic and herbal treatments are available.

Find out what food, flea control products and medicines the vet carries for sale.

If you cannot afford the treatment your pet needs, contact an RSPCA or Blue Cross clinic. If they accept that you are a case of genuine need, they will supply cheap or free treatment.

54 Buy Pet Food

Fluffy is a beloved member of your family. As her carer, you have the job of feeding her quality food that promotes good health and helps prevent disease due to nutritional deficiencies. Products for pets are regulated by UK and European food authorities to maintain minimum health standards. But not all pet foods are equal; you need to read the small print before you buy.

Steps

1 Don't be misled by the description of the food. Know that the words "chicken flavour" on a packet means only that your pet may detect the flavour of chicken; no chicken need be in the food at all.

2 Read the actual ingredients on the tin or package. Manufacturers must list the different ingredients, with the first ingredient being the predominant one.

3 Notice that many pet foods fare made up solely of "by-product meal" or meat- and bonemeal. Meal is what's left after a product is cooked at extremely high temperatures, a procedure called *rendering*. Rendered products are cheap and highly processed.

4 Read the nutritional analysis of protein, fat, fibre and vitamins that appears on the tin or packet with the understanding that these recommended percentages represent minimum amounts.

5 Check the expiry date. An impending expiry date suggests that the food has been sitting on the shelf for a long time.

6 Select food that fits the nutritional needs of your pet. There are foods specially formulated for puppies, kittens, pregnant, lactating, mature or diabetic pets, or cats with hair balls.

7 Consult your vet for dietary recommendations. Many vets sell pet food which they consider healthy.

8 Consider buying high-quality organic pet food. Firms such as Pero, Pascoe's and Yarrah market organic pet products. You can also find vegetarian food for dogs and cats. Check out the internet for suppliers if you don't have a specialist shop locally.

9 Make changes to a pet's food gradually by mixing a bit of the new food in with the old over the course of three to five days.

10 Observe your pet after you introduce new foods. A change in coat, scratching, appetite, weight, mood, stools or other areas could suggest a problem.

What to Look For

- Ingredients
- Protein, fat, fibre and vitamin content
- Special nutritional formulas
- Organic pet foods
- Expiry date

Tips

Making cheap dog food your pet's staple is the equivalent of feeding hamburgers and fries daily to a child who loves fast food. Make sure the food provides the appropriate nutritional value.

Refrigerate unused portions of canned food. Keep dry food in a sealed container to prolong freshness.

A higher price may indicate higher-quality ingredients, but don't rely on price alone. Read the label.

Warnings

Sweets are no treat for a pet: little more than 60 g (2 oz) of unsweetened chocolate can be a lethal dose for a 12.5-kg (25-lb) dog.

Dogs and cats have different nutritional needs. Never feed a cat solely dog food, and vice versa, as this could lead to malnutrition and disease.

55 Buy a Pedigree Dog or Cat

Assuming you've already answered the all-important questions of whether or not you really want to own a dog or cat and can properly care for it, and which breed you prefer, actually buying a pedigree pet requires a bit more work.

Steps

1 Contact the Kennel Club (the-kennel-club.org.uk) or the Governing Council of the Cat Fancy (gccfcats.com) to find information on your chosen breed. Through these umbrella organizations, discover the address of clubs or societies devoted to the breed – for example, the Abyssinian Cat Club.

2 Get in touch with an appropriate cat or dog breed club and ask for details of breeders and available kittens or puppies.

3 Attend dog and cat shows, and talk to the breeders who are exhibiting. Most reputable breeders will be involved in showing their animals. Talk to them about their breeding methods. The Kennel Club and Cat Fancy websites give details of shows.

4 Look for a breeder who has a thorough knowledge of the breed, and is committed to making sure the individual animal's personality is a good fit with your family.

5 Listen to the breeder. He or she should be as interested in you and the home you will provide to the pet as you are in owning the pet. Responsible breeders are very selective in choosing homes for their puppies. Be suspicious of a breeder who doesn't ask you a lot of questions about your suitability as a pet owner.

6 Ask to see at least one parent of the puppy or kitten. See how the animal interacts with the breeder. Is it friendly or does it shy away?

7 Inspect the animal carefully. It should be fully weaned and clearly ready to leave its mother. Signs of a happy animal are an active, friendly personality; clean ears, eyes and nose; healthy gums and teeth; thick, glossy coat; and a balanced gait.

8 Make sure the breeder provides you with full documentation on the animal's pedigree and its veterinary record. The pet should have received all appropriate injections and have an identity microchip implanted.

9 Some pedigree dogs and cats are prone to congenital health problems; find out what they are before you bring home your pet so you know what to look for. For example, some dog breeds should be screened for hip dysplasia and you should receive certification that that was done.

10 Research fair prices for the breed. A good breeder will happily offer references.

What to Look For

- Reputable breeder
- Pedigree record and registration
- Documented medical history

Tips

Homes for stray dogs and cats often have pedigree animals that have been abandoned by their owners. It's worth checking with your local animal rescue society for any specific breed.

If you plan on showing or breeding your new dog or cat, tell the breeder what your intentions are and be particularly rigorous in your examination of the animal.

For a pedigree dog you'll need dog food, food and water bowls, a dog bed, an ID tag, collar, lead, travel kennel and grooming equipment. Chewing toys are essential for teething puppies.

Warning

Avoid pet shops. They don't always take good care of animals and they aren't knowledgeable about breed, lineage and care.

56 Breed Your Pet and Sell the Litter

If you have discipline, a passion for animals, and a willingness to do extensive research, breeding can be a fascinating way to earn money and a great way to be around animals. The mother and newborns will need round-the-clock care and, in most cases, cuddling. If profit is your only goal, you may become frustrated with all the work that goes into breeding pedigree pets.

Steps

1 Confirm that there's a demand for the pet you intend to breed. Animal shelters are full of unwanted cats, dogs and other pets who will be put down if homes are not found.

2 Calculate medical, food, equipment and other breeding expenses. Factor in the time and energy it will take. Will you be able to make a profit?

3 Attend shows and join clubs or associations that specialise in your pet breed to stay abreast of news and to learn breeding guidelines. Talk to other breeders and get as much information as you can.

4 Read up on the reproductive cycle, mating habits, gestation, birthing process, newborn care and weaning process of your pet.

5 Advertise your intention to breed your bird, fish or other pet before you begin the mating process. It is irresponsible to breed animals without finding prospective owners beforehand. Advertise through a breed club or association, in specialist magazines or online.

6 Select your mating pair. Make sure both animals are licensed and pedigreed, if applicable. A vet or a pet expert can help identify the sex of birds, fish, amphibians or reptiles.

7 Bring your mating pair to a vet for a pre-breeding examination. The vet will check for genetic defects, sexually transmitted diseases and other health issues.

8 Mate the pair according to your research and the vet's advice. Provide attentive care to the mother and newborns.

9 Screen potential owners thoroughly. Look for caring, responsible owners.

What to Look For

- Sufficient demand
- Total expenses, time and effort
- Breeding guidelines
- Mating, birthing and weaning processes
- Pre-breeding examination
- Responsible buyers

Tips

Though you can sell puppies and kittens in advance, don't separate them from their mother until they are at least eight weeks old.

It might be easy to breed prolific reproducers, such as rabbits, gerbils and guppies, but you'll have a hard time selling the offspring for a profit.

Warning

Breeding dogs and cats is a full-time job that requires professional knowledge and is not an easy way to make money.

Thousands of unwanted pets are put down every year. Don't add to the problem with poorly planned breeding.

...TION SITES • BUY BARGAIN CLOTHING • BUY WHOLESALE • GET OUT OF DEBT • BUY NOTHING • BUY HAPPINESS • BUY A BETTER MOU...
...Y YOUR WAY INTO SOMEONE'S FAVOUR • BUY LOVE • FIND THE RIGHT RELAXATION TECHNIQUE FOR YOU • BUY HEALTHY FAST FOOD •
...NG SERVICE • SELL YOURSELF ON AN ONLINE DATING SERVICE • SELL YOURSELF TO YOUR GIRLFRIEND/BOYFRIEND'S FAMILY • BUY FL...
...HOOSE FILM FOR YOUR CAMERA • BUY RECHARGEABLE BATTERIES • GIVE TO A GOOD CAUSE • TAKE PART IN A CAR BOOT SALE • EMPLO...
...DENT DISCOUNTS • BUY FLOWERS WHOLESALE • GET A PICTURE FRAMED • EMPLOY A REMOVAL COMPANY • EMPLOY A LIFESTYLE MA...
...FOR A HALLOWE'EN PARTY • BUY A GREAT BIRTHDAY PRESENT FOR UNDER £10 • SELECT GOOD CHAMPAGNE • BUY A DIAMOND • BUY
...A GIFT LIST • BUY WEDDING GIFTS • SELECT BRIDESMAIDS' DRESSES • HIRE AN EVENTS ORGANISER • HIRE A BARTENDER FOR A PART...
...OUNCEMENTS • SELL YOUR WEDDING DRESS • BUY AN ANNIVERSARY GIFT • ARRANGE ENTERTAINMENT FOR A PARTY • COMMISSION A...
...SON WHO HAS EVERYTHING • BUY A GIFT FOR PASSING EXAMS • SELECT A CHRISTMAS TURKEY • BUY A HOUSEWARMING GIFT • PURCH...
...ND • WRITE A MESSAGE IN THE SKY • HIRE A BIG-NAME BAND • GET INTO A PRIVATE GAMBLING ROOM IN LAS VEGAS • BUY SOMEONE A...
...*TIMES* • EMPLOY A BUTLER • BUY A FOOTBALL CLUB • BUY A PERSONAL JET • SELECT A CLASSIC CAR • ACQUIRE A BODY GUARD • BO...
...YHOUND TO RACE • BUY A RACEHORSE • BUY A VILLA IN TUSCANY • EMPLOY A PERSONAL CHEF • BUY A JOURNEY INTO SPACE • EMP...
...TUNE • HIRE AN EXPERT WITNESS • MAKE MONEY FROM ACCIDENT COMPENSATION • DONATE YOUR BODY TO SCIENCE • MAKE MONEY...
...NCIAL ADVISER • PLAN FOR RETIREMENT • COPE WITH HIGHER EDUCATION COSTS • BUY AND SELL SHARES • CHOOSE A STOCKBROKE...
...S INSURANCE • BUY LIFE INSURANCE • GET PRIVATE HEALTH INSURANCE • BUY PERSONAL FINANCE SOFTWARE • CHOOSE AN ACCOUN...
...E OUT A PATENT • MARKET YOUR INVENTION • FINANCE YOUR BUSINESS IDEA • BUY A SMALL BUSINESS • BUY A FRANCHISE • LEASE R...
...BSITE • HIRE A GRAPHIC DESIGNER • ACQUIRE CONTENT FOR YOUR WEBSITE • BUY ADVERTISING ON THE WEB • SELL YOUR ART • HIRE
...LISH YOUR BOOK • START A BED-AND-BREAKFAST • SELL A FAILING BUSINESS • BUY A HOT DOG STAND • SHOP FOR A MORTGAGE • GE...
...USE AT AUCTION • SHOP FOR A HOUSE ONLINE • BUY A PROPERTY FOR RENOVATION AND RESALE • EVALUATE BEFORE BUYING INTO A N...
...A PLOT OF LAND • HAVE YOUR HOUSE DESIGNED • HIRE AN ARCHITECT • HIRE A BUILDER • GET PLANNING PERMISSION • BUY A HOLID...
...OAD • BUY TO LET • RENT YOUR HOME FOR A LOCATION SHOOT • FURNISH YOUR HOME • FURNISH YOUR STUDIO FLAT • BUY USED FU...
...JY HOUSEHOLD APPLIANCES • BUY FLOOR-CARE APPLIANCES • BUY EXTENDED WARRANTIES ON APPLIANCES • FIND PERIOD FIXTURES
...ME • SELECT PAINT, STAIN AND VARNISH • CHOOSE DECORATIVE TILES • CHOOSE A DEHUMIDIFIER • BUY A WHIRLPOOL BATH • BUY A SH...
...LLPAPER • BUY A WOOD-BURNING STOVE • SELECT FLOORING • SELECT CARPETING • CHOOSE KITCHEN CABINETS • CHOOSE A KITCHE...
...OKE ALARMS • BUY CARBON MONOXIDE DETECTORS • BUY FIRE EXTINGUISHERS • CHOOSE AN ENTRY DOOR • BUY A GARAGE-DOOR OI...
...DOOR FURNITURE • BUY THE PERFECT ROSE • BUY FLOWERING BULBS • BUY FLOWERS FOR YOUR GARDEN • SELECT PEST CONTROLS
...OMATIC WATERING SYSTEM • START A NEW LAWN • BUY A LAWN MOWER • BUY KOI FOR YOUR FISH POND • BUY A STORAGE SHED • H...
...DUCE • CHOOSE A PERFECT PEACH • BUY AND SELL AT FARMERS' MARKETS • SELECT KITCHEN KNIVES • DECIPHER FOOD LABELS • S...
...FECT BURGER • PURCHASE A CHRISTMAS HAM • BUY ORGANIC BEEF • BUY HAGGIS • PURCHASE LOCAL HONEY • CHOOSE A CHICKEN...
...TRUFFLES • BUY ARTISAN BREADS • BUY ARTISAN CHEESES • PURCHASE KOSHER FOOD • BUY SENSIBLY IN SUPERMARKETS • CHOOS...
...ER A GREAT CUP OF COFFEE • BUY A COFFEEMAKER OR ESPRESSO MACHINE • PURCHASE PARTY BEER • CHOOSE THE RIGHT WINE • (...
...RM • CHOOSE AN OVULATION PREDICTOR KIT • PICK A PREGNANCY TEST KIT • CHOOSE BIRTH CONTROL • CHOOSE WHERE TO GIVE BI...
...BABY CLOTHES • CHOOSE NAPPIES • BUY OR RENT A BREAST PUMP • CHOOSE A CAR SEAT • BUY CHILD-PROOFING SUPPLIES • FIND
...A GARDEN PLAY STRUCTURE • FIND A FAMILY-FRIENDLY HOTEL • ORGANISE A FUND-RAISING EVENT • BUY BRACES FOR YOUR KID • E...
...A MODEL • SELL USED BABY GEAR, TOYS, CLOTHES AND BOOKS • FIND A COUPLES COUNSELLOR • HIRE A FAMILY SOLICITOR • BUY OF...
...RCHASE A TOOTHBRUSH • BUY MOISTURISERS AND ANTIWRINKLE CREAMS • SELECT PAIN RELIEF AND COLD MEDICINES • CHOOSE A CO...
...ODUCTS • BUY WAYS TO COUNTER HAIR LOSS • BUY A WIG OR HAIRPIECE • BUY A NEW BODY • GET A TATTOO OR BODY PIERCING • OB...
...TH • SELECT SPECTACLES AND SUNGLASSES • HIRE A PERSONAL TRAINER • SIGN UP FOR A YOGA CLASS • TREAT YOURSELF TO A DAY
...AN ANTIQUE MARKET • BUY AT AUCTION • KNOW WHAT YOUR COLLECTIBLES ARE WORTH • BARTER WITH DEALERS • GET AN ANTIQUE A...
...NS • BUY AN ANTIQUE QUILT • BUY FILM POSTERS • LIQUIDATE YOUR BEANIE BABY COLLECTION • SCORE AUTOGRAPHS • TRADE YU-G...
...SELL SPORTS MEMORABILIA • SELL YOUR FOOTBALL-CARD COLLECTION • CHOOSE A DESKTOP COMPUTER • SHOP FOR A USED COM...
...MPUTER PERIPHERALS • CHOOSE AN INTERNET SERVICE PROVIDER • GET AN INTERNET DOMAIN NAME • NETWORK YOUR COMPUTERS
...PLAYER • BUY A VIDEO RECORDER • CHOOSE A PERSONAL DIGITAL ASSISTANT • CHOOSE A MOBILE PHONE SERVICE • GET A BETTER I...
...TAL CAMERA • BUY A HOME AUTOMATION SYSTEM • BUY A STATE-OF-THE-ART SOUND SYSTEM • BUY AN AUDIO/VIDEO DISTRIBUTION S...
...SYSTEM • BUY VIRTUAL-REALITY FURNITURE • BUY TWO-WAY RADIOS • BUY A MOBILE ENTERTAINMENT SYSTEM • GET A PASSPORT, QU...
...AL LUGGAGE • FLY FOR NEXT TO NOTHING • TAKE A TRIP ON THE TRANS-SIBERIAN EXPRESS • BUY DUTY-FREE • SHIP FOREIGN PURCHA...
...IAN CYCLING HOLIDAY • CHOOSE A CHEAP CRUISE • BOOK A HOTEL PACKAGE FOR THE GREEK ISLANDS • RAFT THE GRAND CANYON •
...KSHAW IN RANGOON • TAKE SALSA LESSONS IN CUBA • BUY A CAMERA IN HONG KONG • BUY YOUR WAY ONTO A MOUNT EVEREST EXI...
...L TEAM • BUY ANKLE AND KNEE BRACES • CHOOSE RUGBY PROTECTION KIT • BUY GOLF CLUBS • SELL FOUND GOLF BALLS • BUY PO...
...PLOY A SCUBA INSTRUCTOR • BUY A SKATEBOARD AND PROTECTIVE GEAR • BUY SKATES • GO BUNJEE JUMPING • GO SKYDIVING • BU...
...OTS AND BINDINGS • BUY SKI BOOTS • BUY A BICYCLE • BUY AN ELECTRIC BICYCLE • BUY CYCLE CLOTHING • BUY A PROPERLY FITTIN...
...T • BUY A SURFBOARD • BUY FLY-FISHING GEAR • BUY ROCK-CLIMBING EQUIPMENT • BUY A CASHMERE JUMPER • PURCHASE VINTAG...
...CKTAIL DRESS • BUY DESIGNER CLOTHES AT A DISCOUNT • CHOOSE A BASIC WARDROBE FOR A MAN • BUY A MAN'S DRESS SHIRT • PIC...
...THER JACKET • BUY MATERNITY CLOTHES • GET A GREAT-FITTING BRA • CHOOSE A HIGH-PERFORMANCE SWIM SUIT • BUY PERFORMA...
...TORY SHOPS • BUY A NEW CAR • BUY THE BASICS FOR YOUR CAR • BUY A USED CAR • BUY OR SELL A CAR ONLINE • BUY A HYBRID C...

BUY TIME • BUY A BOUQUET OF ROSES • BUY SOMEONE A DRINK • GET SOMEONE TO BUY YOU A DRINK • BUY YOUR WAY INTO THE B
SCREEN • BUT FURTHER EDUCATION • ORDER EXOTIC FOOD • ORDER AT A SUSHI BAR • BUY DINNER AT A FRENCH RESTAURANT • EMP
O SAY SORRY TO YOUR PARTNER • BUY MUSIC ONLINE • EMPLOY MUSICIANS • ORDER A GOOD BOTTLE OF WINE • BUY AN ERGONOMIC
ANER • EMPLOY AN AU PAIR • BUY A GUITAR • BUY DUCT TAPE • GET A GOOD DEAL ON A MAGAZINE SUBSCRIPTION • GET SENIOR CITIZ
FIND A VET • BUY PET FOOD • BUY A PEDIGREE DOG OR CAT • BREED YOUR PET AND SELL THE LITTER • BUY OR RENT FOR A FANCY DR
ERY MADE OF PRECIOUS METALS • BUY COLOURED GEMSTONES • CHOOSE THE PERFECT WEDDING DRESS • BUY OR RENT MEN'S FORM
A PHOTOGRAPHER • HIRE A CATERER • FIND THE IDEAL CIVIL WEDDING VENUE • THE COST OF MARRYING • ORDER PERSONALISED INVIT
RKS SHOW • BUY A MOTHER'S DAY GIFT • BUY A FATHER'S DAY GIFT • SELECT AN APPROPRIATE COMING-OF-AGE GIFT • GET A GIFT FOI
RISTMAS CARDS • BUY CHRISTMAS STOCKING FILLERS • BUY CHRISTENING GIFTS • PURCHASE A PERFECT CHRISTMAS TREE • BUY A P
PAY A RANSOM • GET HOT TICKETS • HIRE A LIMOUSINE • BUY A CRYONIC CHAMBER • RENT YOUR OWN HOARDING • TAKE OUT A FULL-
XURY CRUISE AROUND THE WORLD • BUY A TICKET TO TRAVEL FOR A YEAR • BOOK A TRIP ON THE ORIENT-EXPRESS • OWN A VINEYARD
OSTWRITER TO WRITE YOUR MEMOIRS • COMMISSION ORIGINAL ARTWORK • IMMORTALISE YOUR SPOUSE IN A SCULPTURE • GIVE AWA
DICAL GUINEA PIG • SELL YOUR STORY TO THE TABLOIDS • SELL YOUR SOUL TO THE DEVIL • NEGOTIATE A BETTER CREDIT CARD DEAL
TRADE (OR NOT) • BUY ANNUITIES • BUY AND SELL MUTUAL FUNDS • BUY BONDS • SELL SHORT • INVEST IN PRECIOUS METALS • BUY S
ND CASUAL WORK • SELL YOUR PRODUCT O[...] [...] HEADHUNTER • SELL YOURSELF IN A JOB INTI
CE • LEASE INDUSTRIAL SPACE • LEASE OFFI[...] [...]MENT • HIRE SOMEONE TO DESIGN AND BUILD
DACH • SELL ON THE CRAFT CIRCUIT • HIRE A[...] [...]RY • SELL A SCREENPLAY • SELL YOUR NOVEL
ER MORTGAGE DEAL • SAVE ON YOUR MORT[...] [...]D • OBTAIN HOUSE INSURANCE • BUY A HOUSE
• EXCHANGE CONTRACTS ON A PROPERTY •[...] [...]AN ESTATE AGENT • RELEASE CAPITAL FROM YO
• RENT A HOLIDAY HOME • BUY A FLAT • RE[...] [...]COUNTRY • BUY A LOFT APARTMENT • BUY PR
• BUY DOOR AND WINDOW LOCKS • CHOOSE[...] [...]GHT FIXTURES • BUY A PROGRAMMABLE LIGH
BED AND MATTRESS • HIRE AN INTERIOR DES[...] [...]NCORPORATE A GREATER SENSE OF SPACE INT
BUY A TOILET • CHOOSE A TAP • BUY GLUES [...] [...]MENTS • GET SELF-CLEANING WINDOWS • CHO
OP • BUY GREEN HOUSEHOLD CLEANERS • S[...] [...] SECURITY SYSTEM • BUY A HOME ALARM SYS
UY TIMBER FOR A DIY PROJECT • HOW TO S[...] [...]R, PAINTER OR ELECTRICIAN • HIRE A GARDENE
OIL IMPROVERS • BUY MULCH • BUY A COMP[...] [...]BLE GARDEN • HIRE A GARDEN DESIGNER • BL
E SURGEON • BUY BASIC GARDEN TOOLS • B[...] [...] BUY AN OUTDOOR LIGHTING SYSTEM • BUY C
RBS AND SPICES • STOCK YOUR KITCHEN WIT[...] [...]RESH PRODUCE • SELECT MEAT • STOCK UP F
FRESH FISH • SELECT RICE • PURCHASE PR[...] [...]LTON • GET FRESH FISH DELIVERED TO YOUR D
G OILS • SELECT OLIVE OIL • SELECT OLIVES[...] [...]VINEGAR • CHOOSE PASTA • BUY TEA • BUY CO
REAL ALE • ORDER A COCKTAIL • CHOOSE A[...] [...] STOCK A WINE CELLAR • STOCK YOUR BAR •
E A MIDWIFE OR DOULA • PLAN A HOME BIRT[...] [...]R A NEW BABY • BUY A NEW COT • CHOOSE A F
CHILDCARE • FIND A GREAT NANNY • FIND T[...] [...]TER-SCHOOL CARE • SIGN YOUR CHILD UP FOI
BUY BOOKS, VIDEOS AND MUSIC FOR YOUI[...] [...]HIRE A TUTOR • ADOPT A CHILD • GET YOUR C
ELTERED HOUSING • CHOOSE A CARE HOME [...] [...]LOT • PAY FOR FUNERAL EXPENSES • GET VIAC
NTARY MTHERAPY • SEE A MENTAL-HEALTH P[...] [...]BUY HOME-USE MEDICAL SUPPLIES • SELECT H
ST IMPLANTS • GET WRINKLE-FILLER INJECT[...] [...]ACTITIONERS • CHOOSE A MANICURIST • GET W
A • BOOK A MASSAGE • GET ON ANTIQUES R[...] [...] SHOP AT AN ANTIQUE FAIR OR FLEA MARKET •
• BUY SILVERWARE • EVALUATE CARNIVAL GLASS • BUY AND SELL STAMPS • BUY ANTIQUE FURNITURE • GET CLUED UP ON CLARICE C
S • SEIZE STAR WARS ACTION FIGURES • SELL YOUR VINYL RECORD COLLECTION • SELL TO A PAWNSHOP • BUY AND SELL COMIC BOC
PERIPHERALS • CHOOSE A LAPTOP OR NOTEBOOK COMPUTER • SELL OR DONATE A COMPUTER • BUY PRINTER PAPER • BUY A PRINTI
E THE MEMORY IN YOUR COMPUTER • BUY COMPUTER SOFTWARE • CHOOSE A CD PLAYER • BUY BLANK CDS • BUY AN MP PLAYER • C
M YOUR PHONE COMPANY • BUY VIDEO AND COMPUTER GAMES • CHOOSE A FILM CAMERA • CHOOSE A DIGITAL CAMCORDER • DECIDE
BUY A SERIOUS TV • CHOOSE BETWEEN DIGITAL TV PROVIDERS • GET A DIGITAL VIDEO RECORDER • GET A UNIVERSAL REMOTE • BUY A
RCHASE CHEAP AIRLINE TICKETS • FIND GREAT HOTEL DEALS • HIRE THE BEST CAR FOR THE LEAST MONEY • GET TRAVEL INSURANCE •
E UNITED KONGDOM • TIP IN A FOREIGN COUNTRY • TIP PROPERLY IN THE UK • BRIBE A FOREIGN OFFICIAL • GET AN INTERRAIL PASS •
HEAP BUT FANTASTIC SAFARI • RENT A CAMEL IN CAIRO • GET SINGLE-MALT WHISKY IN SCOTLAND • BUY A SAPPHIRE IN BANGKOK • H
HIRE A TREKKING COMPANY IN NEPAL • RENT OR BUY A SATELLITE PHONE • BUY YOUR CHILD'S FIRST CRICKET BAT • ORDER A STRIP I
S • BUY A RACKET • BUY A HEALTH CLUB MEMBERSHIP • BUY AN AEROBIC FITNESS MACHINE • BUY SWIMMING EQUIPMENT • BUY A JE
IFTING EQUIPMENT • CHOOSE A CAR RACK • BUY SKIS • BUY CLOTHES FOR COLD-WEATHER ACTIVITIES • SELL USED SKIS • BUY A SNC
• BUY THE OPTIMAL SLEEPING BAG • BUY A TENT • BUY A BACKPACK • BUY A CAMPING STOVE • BUY A KAYAK • BUY A LIFEJACKET • E
G • SELL USED CLOTHING • ORDER CUSTOM-MADE COWBOY BOOTS • BUY CLOTHES ONLINE • FIND NON-STANDARD SIZES • BUY THE
IE • BUY A WOMAN'S SUIT • BUY A MAN'S SUIT • HIRE A TAILOR • BUY CUSTOM-TAILORED CLOTHES IN ASIA • BUY A BRIEFCASE • SHOI
OUT CLOTHES • BUY A HEART-RATE MONITOR • SELECT A WATCH • BUY KIDS' CLOTHES • CHOOSE CHILDREN'S SHOES • PURCHASE CL
A CAR • BUY A MOTORCYCLE • BUYING AND CHANGING MOTOR OIL • WASH A CAR • WAX A CAR • BUY CAR INSURANCE • SPRING FOR

Special Occasions

57 Buy or Rent for a Fancy Dress Party

Whatever masked affair you're attending – tarts and vicars, 60s' psychedelic, old school rave – it's an opportunity to show off your ingenuity and creativity while having fun doing it.

Steps

1 Search online or in the *Yellow Pages* under "Fancy Dress" for rental shops in your area. Costs vary, but expect to pay up to £60 for a full outfit on weekend hire. Don't forget VAT should be included in the price as with standard retail clothes. Theatre costume departments are also a useful source if you want to achieve a movie-quality look, but run to the £90 mark and up for the basics, and more for accessories. Check mediaeval-banquet.co.uk and fairygodmother.co.uk for starters.

2 Scour your local charity shops (see 497 "Purchase Vintage Clothing") for possible outfits and gaudy accessories or, if you're incredibly lucky, even the perfect period outfit from Victorian to Versace. This may be the cheapest option, but it will be haphazard and you'll need to scour quite a few to find what you're looking for. Pick'n'mixing from several of them might be an option, but give yourself time to do this.

3 Fulfill your favourite fantasy. If you've always wanted to be a flamenco or ballroom or ballet or Western line dancer, you'll find the right dance outfit at a dance supply store to buy – you can at least dress the part if not dance it. Look under "Dancewear" in the *Yellow Pages* and check out danceworld.ltd.uk.

What to Look For

- Costume rental shops
- *Yellow Pages* under "Fancy Dress", theatrical supplies
- Charity shops
- Party shops, party aisles in toy shops
- Inventiveness

Warning

Some rental shops may not deliver during October for Hallowe'en, so plan ahead. Even if you're buying, delivery can take two weeks to a month.

58 Buy for a Hallowe'en Party

Hallowe'en is bigger than bonfire nights these days, especially if you have young children who are less jumpy about ghouls and ghosts than loud fireworks! So first plan your party – invite your child's friends and their mums or dads to a Hallowe'en party .

Steps

1 Buy basic hallowe'en party materials as you would for a birthday party: hallowe'en party plates, cups and napkins and table covers, all available from supermarkets and party accessory shops.

2 Get your pumpkin early from garden centres, nurseries, greengrocers or the supermarket. Expect to pay up to £5 for a biggish one. Then you'll have to carve out the eyes and mouth and empty the pith and pips and place a tea light or two inside.

3 Buy bin-liners to use as effective black cloaks, white face make-up, black nail varnish and lipstick from toy shops. Witches' hats, cloaks, fake blood, false nails and monster outfits can be bought from toy shops, newsagents and supermarkets.

What to Look For

- Nice big pumpkins
- Multi-pack sweets to give out for "trick or treating", also fun cheap toy-shop trinkets like rubber bats.
- A last-minute dash around a supermarket's seasonal aisle for discounts.

Warning

If you really must go "trick or treating" make sure children are accompanied in the dark, and only go to houses that are expecting you.

59 Buy a Great Birthday Present for Under £10

Let's face it – the prime reason we spend more than we want to is last-minute desperation. But you can stay beneath the £10 mark and still give someone a birthday smile. Keep a stash of ready-wrapped, always-welcome gifts (and birthday cards) for both sexes and all ages on hand, and you'll never box yourself into a corner.

ITEM	DESCRIPTION
Gift Vouchers	Everyone knows what you paid, but, hey, that's cool – it's the thought that counts and you've shown you've thought. Children will be happy to spend a bespoke voucher in in its entirety and teenagers can tag it on to some cash for that music shop gift, i.e. CD, DVD, computer game.
Picture Frames	Perennially useful gift for adults or children on any occasion, from stationers, picture frame shops, and just about any other high street shop or off-beat boutique. Check out charity shops also for occasional bargains.
Books	Go for book offers like "3 for 2" so you always have spare pressies.
CDs, DVDs	An enormous online selection includes discounted offerings to make giving someone music or movies a snip. Or burn your own personalised CD filled with the birthday boy or girl's favourite tunes. Then do a personalised sleeve.
Candles	Keep a fragrant stash in your cupboard. Look for good-quality candles in the sales with a soothing rather than overbearing fragrance. Some cheap candles don't burn well.
Lotions, Soaps	Have a bottle or two of beautiful scented lotion or hand-made soap stored away for a pleasing, simple gift.
Vases	A beautiful vase is always welcome, especially when filled with flowers from your garden. Charity shops and occasional sales are good sources of glass, pottery, china and silverware.
Wine	Knot a colourful kitchen towel around a bottle of wine.
Mini Tool Kit	Good to tuck in the kitchen drawer or car boot. Watch the shelves until you see a deal.
WARNING	In theory, there's nothing wrong with recycling gifts you've received that would suit someone else much better. Just remember to note on the box or bag who gave it to you before you put it in storage and forget. Avoid embarrassing moments later by recycling it in a different circle of acquaintances.

60 Select Good Champagne

Champagne instantly conjures up images of festive celebrations, but there's no need to wait for a special occasion to break out the bubbly. There's plenty to choose from in the £15 – £30 price range but also bargains below £15 too. So whether you want fizz for a delicious food accompaniment, as an aperitif or party drink check out supermarket and online offers. A quick day trip to Tesco, Auchan or Carrefour in Calais will give you sound savings, but closer to home check out Oddbins.com and other shops for deals.

TERM	WHAT IT MEANS
Champagne	The only legitimate champagne, according to French law, hails from France's Champagne region.
Sparkling Wine	All other products. (California's Korbel Champagne being one exception.) Called *spumante* in Italy, *sekt* in Germany, and *vin mousseux* in France.
Méthode Champenoise	A rigorous, multi-step process. Indicates a top-quality sparkling wine was made exactly the same way as French champagne – "fermented in this very bottle".
Vintage Champagne	Made only on occasions. Wines from the declared year must compose at least 80 per cent of the cuvée (blend of still wines), with the balance coming from reserve wines from prior years. Must be aged for three years before release.
Nonvintage Champagne (NV)	These blends of usually five to seven years make up 75 to 80 per cent of those bottled. It is typically made in a definitive house style and maintained by meticulous blending. It is with this reserve that the winemaker is able to create the same style every year.
Sweetness	Determined by the winemaker during the process of fermentation with the addition of *dosage* (a secret blend of wine, sugar and sometimes brandy). Levels include *brut* (very dry), *extra brut* (extra dry, but sweeter than brut), *sec* (medium sweet), *demi-sec* (sweet, considered a dessert wine) and *doux* (very sweet, considered a dessert wine).
Rosé	Made by adding a small amount of red still wine to the cuvée, although some producers extract colour by macerating the juice with red grape skins.
Blanc de Noirs	The clearer the better and more full-flavoured. Made entirely from the red Pinot Noir and/or Meunier grapes.
Blanc de Blancs	Usually more delicate and the lightest in colour. Made entirely from chardonnay grapes.
Crémant	Made with only slightly more than half the pressure of standard sparkling wines. Has a creamier mouth-feel.
Grand Cru	The top ranking a French vineyard can receive. Means "great growth".
Premier Cru	Second highest ranking of French vineyards. Means "first growth".
Grande Marque	A French term for "great brand" and is used unofficially to refer to the best champagne houses.

61 Buy a Diamond

Diamond rings are priceless in terms of sentimental value – but affairs of the heart aside, the key to a diamond's commercial value is its rarity. A smaller stone can be worth more than a larger one provided it has more rarity factors – greater clarity and brilliance, and fewer inclusions, or internal flaws. Here's how to find the brilliant best.

Steps

1 Determine what you want or can afford to spend.

2 Establish a relationship with a jeweller who has expert gemstone knowledge. While their qualifications are worth noting, of far more importance is the feeling you get when you're in the shop. If you don't feel good about what you're looking at or who you're dealing with, leave.

3 Study styles. The traditional solitaire – a single diamond held aloft by a six-prong setting – is still the most popular. See how bezel settings, where a slim border of platinum or gold surrounds a smallish diamond, can make the gem look bigger. Take a look at three-diamond settings. A row of diamonds or a diamond surrounded by sapphires or emeralds is called an anniversary or eternity-ring style.

4 Become fluent in the four Cs of the international language of diamonds: carat weight, colour, clarity and cut.

• Diamond weights, not sizes, are measured by carats. A single carat weighs about as much as a small paper clip. Carats are divided into fractions or decimal points. Jewellers should disclose precise amounts and ranges.

• Letters represent diamond colours with D (colourless, very rare and most desirable) to Z (light yellow or brown and less desirable). Grades vary, so ask your jeweller. It's also a matter of taste. Winter-white diamonds look best with platinum, warmer shades with golds.

• Clarity grades measure *birthmarks* – internal flaws are called *inclusions,* external ones *blemishes.* Grades include FL for flawless, VSI for very slightly included and I3 for included.

• Seek out a cut that maximises brilliance, fire and sparkle.

5 Get your diamond certified after you've bought it – it's cheaper that way than purchasing a diamond already certified by an independent diamond grading organisation. A certified diamond might add an extra £200 – £400 to the cost while getting it graded afterwards might only set you back £100 – £150.

6 Be prepared to compromise: ultimately it's size versus colour versus quality (grade), so why not reduce the size (size isn't everything) to allow for an increase in grade and colour quality, according to your budget. And it's not really an issue anyway until you budge over the £500 mark.

What to Look For

• Expert advice
• Style you'll love forever
• The four Cs
• Grading report

Tips

Your jeweller can have a unique report number laser-inscribed on your diamond's outer edge. If you ever have it resized or professionally cleaned, you can make sure you're getting your own diamond back. Grading reports and identification numbers also serve insurance purposes.

Some jellewers will have free booklets that can be helpful for prospective diamond-buyers. But this is no substitute for seeking a jeweller's guidance on a one-to-one basis. Check out diamonds online, such as thediamondbuyingguide.com or debeers.com, but be wary of online claims.

Warning

Don't think of the diamonds in engagement rings as an investment. You're already paying a mark-up of 100 per cent or more when you buy retail.

62 Buy Jewellery Made of Precious Metals

Buying a silver necklace, a gold bracelet or a platinum wedding ring sounds pretty straightforward, but you'll want to understand how to choose between various precious metals. There's yellow, white and rose gold; different carat gold; real gold; pure gold—and that's before you get to the mysterious markings for silver and platinum.

Steps

1 Shop at a jewellery store that makes you feel good. Trusting the jeweller, and subsequently the advice and jewellery he or she offers, is very important.

2 Buy only from a reputable retailer who will accept returns – preferably one affiliated with a professional trade association such as The National Association of Goldsmiths. Look for a badge, logo or certificate.

3 Look for hallmarked jewellery. This means the required purity level has been independently assessed. If it is carat-marked, then it must also be stamped with a hallmark. Be more wary of jewellery-purity and marking claims from the Far East and the United States. The laws in the UK regarding hallmarking and purity levels are more stringent.

4 Check the craftsmanship. A high-quality piece should look just as good from the back as it does from the front, have no rough edges anywhere and – if it's a necklace or bracelet – come with a sturdy matching clasp.

5 Buy gold in a range of colours and levels of purity. The higher the carat rating (not to be confused with carat, the weight measurement for diamonds), the more pure gold is in a piece and the richer the colour (and softer the item).

- 24-carat gold is 100 per cent pure gold, so soft that it is not hallmarked for jewellery. 22-carat is the highest hallmarked standard.

- 18 carat is 75 per cent gold, mixed with copper or silver. It is more "lemony" in tone and is strong enough for rings.

- 14 carat is 58.3 per cent gold. Its lightly reddish hue comes from added copper alloys, which also lend it durability.

- 9 carat is 37.5 per cent gold. Less than 9-carat gold is not recognised as gold.

6 Explore the intricate designs that can be created with silver jewellery. Prized for its rich lustre, and almost as soft as gold, it's often alloyed with copper for strength.

7 Step up to platinum jewellery for the rarest, purest and heaviest precious metal. Platinum is incredibly dense but also very soft. Why buy platinum? Think of it this way: If you have a large diamond, would you rather it be secured by gold prongs or platinum ones that are twice as dense?

What to Look For

- Marked metal
- Manufacturer's marking or hallmark
- Style you'll always love
- Timeless appeal
- Flattering colour

Tips

The misleading term *solid gold* merely signifies that a piece isn't hollow; don't confuse solid gold with pure gold.

The absence of any carat markings at all may mean that a piece is less than 9 carats.

Gold-filled jewellery is 9-carat or higher gold that has been mechanically bonded to a base material. In gold-plated or electroplated items, the gold is applied electrolytically to a base material such as copper.

Warning

A titanium ring sounds cool, but if you're in an accident and your arm or hand is injured, rescue personnel will not be able to cut the ring off to save your finger.

63 Buy Coloured Gemstones

Prized for centuries for their beauty, and often used as currency, gemstones hold ageless appeal. Modern treating techniques enhance their look and improve their durability. Whatever your favourites – rubies, sapphires, emeralds or others – find a good jeweller to buy from.

Steps

1 Purchase from a jeweller whose character you trust. Since virtually all gemstones are treated, the opportunity for deception is great – you want to be dealing with someone you can depend on. If something about the experience is off-putting, leave.

2 Learn about lab-created and treated stones. Ask jewellers if a naturally mined stone has been treated – heated, bleached, coated or dyed to improve the look or durability. Some treatments can weaken a stone and lower its price.

3 Keep your eyes open for imitations, generally made of glass or plastic. Jewellers will tell you what's what.

4 Apply the four Cs to buying gemstones just as you would to purchasing diamonds (see 61 "Buy a Diamond"). Gemstones, however, don't carry letter grades for guidance; a trustworthy jeweller will show you how to be discerning.

5 Shop around. Numerous companies operate in the field of coloured gems, so prices fluctuate far more widely than those of diamonds, and it pays to watch them over time. A one-carat ruby, for instance, can vary enormously in cost – and may be just as expensive as a diamond. And gems over three carats in size leap up in price because they are rare. Colour – shade and saturation (whether the colour is dull or intense) – also greatly affects price. Clarity is also important (the gem should have few flaws or inclusions), as is a perfect, light-reflecting faceted cut.

6 Check the shop's return and refund policy before finalising your purchase.

7 Make sure your receipt details all the stone's specifications including its weight and size. Ask for a grading report, and check that the receipt specifies whether the stone is a natural gem, lab-created or treated stone.

What to Look For

- Natural versus lab-created or imitation gems
- The four Cs (cut, colour, clarity, carat)
- Detailed receipt

Tip

General trading standards would require potential purchasers to be informed if the gem has been colour-enhanced and certainly if any marks have been lasered out. Find out if the treatment is permanent or the stone requires special care.

64 Choose the Perfect Wedding Dress

You've dreamed about walking down that aisle since you were a little girl, and now the big day is approaching. Whether you're choosing a dress off the peg, having one made just for you, or restoring a hand-me-down, follow these tips and make your dream come true.

Steps

1 Start your search six to nine months ahead. Special orders can take four to six months, plus time for alterations.

2 Keep your file of photographs of dresses you like from bridal magazines, advertisements and boutique promotions handy when you shop.

3 Choose a style appropriate for the ceremony. For a formal wedding, a floor-length dress in ivory, white, cream or champagne, often worn with gloves and a train, is an elegant choice. Semiformal dresses can be also be pastels, a floor-brushing (ballerina) length, with a short veil and no train. At a less-formal or second wedding, the bride may choose a long or short dress, or even a two-piece suit. A short veil may be very stylish paired with a classic pillbox hat.

4 Flatter your figure with a dress that suits you. Take a trusted, honest sister or best friend for feedback. Try one of each basic shape—princess, ball gown, sheath and empire waist – to see which flatters you most. Check that you can walk, turn, sit and bend comfortably, as well as lift your arms and hug loved ones without splitting a seam. Comfort and confidence are vital on this day of days.

5 Shop at bridal boutiques or department stores for a wide array of styles. Try on a few designer gowns first so you recognise the quality, then choose a dress based on your budget.

6 Set a budget. Made-to-order dresses can be found from around £250 and up to well over the £1,000 threshold. A simple custom-made dress can be had for something like £750 – Jessica McClintock is well known designer label at a moderate, mid-way price – with many dresses in the lower third of that range, but you can go as high as five figures for a Vera Wang creation.

7 Ask when bridal shops are next having a sample sale. Be on the lookout for warehouse sales on discontinued styles and samples.

8 Make the deposit with a credit card. Get an itemised receipt spelling out every detail (manufacturer's and design name, number, price, colour and size) and stating that the deal is cancelled if your dress isn't ready by a specified date.

9 Budget for alterations, which can be as much as some dresses. Ask if pressing is included and if they'll store your dress until the big day. Also ask for recommendations for cleaning and storing the dress. Budget for around £50 for cleaning.

What to Look For

- Inspiration in magazines
- Figure-flattering shape
- Sales

Tips

Scout local charity shops for excellent buys. Bridal gowns have been worn only once, so providing they've been professionally cleaned, there's no problem. Designer cast-offs cost more, but you could find a real steal for under £100.

Look for quality: beads sewn on rather than glued, satin that doesn't feel so thin it might tear, a built-in petticoat or slip, and gloriously soft lace and detailing. French lace is best; the cheap stuff is stiff.

Scout online bridal sites for a wide selection of new and second-hand choices, such as 1stcallforweddings.co.uk.

You can hire wedding dresses for around £160 for the weekend but you need to order well in advance. Check out almostnewwedding-dresses.co.uk for starters.

Not particularly sentimental? See 76 "Sell Your Wedding Dress".

Warning

Falling in love with a particular dress or style does not mean that it will flatter your figure. Ask for honest advice from someone who knows what they're talking about.

65 Buy or Rent Men's Formal Wear

Men's formal wear carries its own array of decisions, styles and accessories. You may wish to invest in a morning suit or dinner jacket if your lifestyle calls for formal gatherings several times a year. If you're rarely coaxed out of your blue jeans – and especially if your waistline tends to expand and contract – a rented morning suit or dinner jacket should fit the bill. The rule of thumb is that if a lady wears a floor-length dress, the gentleman should wear formal attire, and that style is dictated by time of day and level of formality.

Steps

1 Give yourself enough lead time. Reserve rented formal wear or order a tailor-made morning suit three months prior to an event to guarantee availability.

2 Do a search for morning suits online. Many have a photo gallery to demystify the process of ordering and allow you to choose the elements, then go to a store for a fitting.

3 Look under "Wedding Services – Dressing" in the *Yellow Pages* for local hire and websites.

4 Consult with the sales person when considering the wide range of options. Jackets have a notch, peak or shoulder lapel. They can be ultra-formal full dress tails, a cutaway jacket suitable for formal events before 6 p.m., or a dinner jacket, appropriate for any formal affair. Shirt choices include a laydown, wing and cavalier collar, finished off with a bow tie, cravat or laydown tie.

5 Choose colours according to the time of day and nature of the event. Grey is traditional before 6 p.m., and black for all formal evening affairs. You may wish to consult your date for the evening, and coordinate cummerbund or waistcoat as desired.

6 Secure a knowledgeable specialist's help when gearing up for a wedding. Formal hire selection should be guided by the colour of the bride's gown and bridesmaids' dresses. Wedding-party rental specials may include a jacket, trousers, vest or cummerbund, shirt, braces, cufflinks, studs and tie from around £100 or more. Don't forget the top hat and gloves too if the occasion requires it.

7 Ask ushers who don't live locally to get professionally measured and forward the details at least three weeks before the big day. Try-ons and last-minute tweaks should happen a few days ahead.

8 If you're buying a morning suit, expect to pay at least £500 – far more for a custom-made or designer brand. Prices range according to the style, options and fabric chosen.

9 Make sure everything fits by trying on your formal wear in advance of the event. Wedding parties in particular need to find out ahead of time if all the ushers received the correct sizes.

What to Look For

- Appropriate formality for venue
- Flattering cut
- Accessories
- Timeless style if you buy

Tips

Double-check when to pick up and return formal wear and accessories if you're renting. The best man in a wedding generally takes care of collecting and delivering them.

Discounts are there to be had. Usually, if you hire five suits or over, the deal is that the groom goes free. So if you are hiring for the ushers too check first and seek an outlet that does offers on multi-hire.

If you're buying formal wear, choose a style that will fit in at weddings, gala evenings and any formal occasion. Steer towards the classics so it won't go out of style.

Warning

Have measurements taken professionally. Having your spouse or friend measure you is a recipe for disaster.

66 Getting a Gift List

Gift registries aren't just for weddings anymore. More department stores are offering customised gift lists for any celebration, be it a christening, birthday, special anniversary or retirement. By registering, you help yourself and your guests by asking for what you really want. Allow one week to set it up from scratch.

Steps

1 Pore over magazines and catalogues and collect tear sheets, colour swatches and patterns. Note brands, design names, model names, patterns and numbers.

2 Phone for an appointment and allow plenty of time when you go in to register. Bring your binder of information, photos and ideas.

3 Be sensitive about prices when choosing items. Take into consideration how many people are attending and guests' financial status. Cover a wide price range so no one feels burdened.

4 Check computerised lists periodically to make sure they're being updated regularly. Keep mailing labels from gifts as proof of purchase in case you need to return anything (see 4 "Take Goods Back").

5 Some shops give you a hand-held scanner so you can zap the items you want.

6 The gift list/celebration service offered by many department stores is free. For some department stores you may need to be a card holder to take advantage of their list. Check this out first.

7 Another great advantage of the gift list is that enables large home items, such as furniture, to be included often with free or nominal delivery charges within a certain radius of the store. This is very handy. Of course, if the store is national with branches around the country then that makes life easier too.

8 Some department stores, such as Selfridges, actually "donate" 5 per cent to your budget and allow a "personalised shopping day" with free restaurant vouchers and the like.

9 Enlist a wedding planner's assistance to help you hone your list.

10 Always check if the registry includes the actual gift or a voucher or pledge in lieu of the specific gift.

What to Look For

- Store(s) with a wide variety of merchandise
- Online registry
- Registry available at all store branches
- Smart advice

Tips

Make sure your registry can be viewed and purchased online. Also check how long after the event date you can make returns.

There are tasteful ways to let people know where you're registered, but don't do it on the wedding invitations.

All national retailers have an online store – for example, johnlewis.com and debenhams.com. Click on their "Gift List" icon.

Warning

If you register at too many different stores, you may not receive full sets of some items.

67 Buy Wedding Gifts

You've received the invitation, you know what you'll wear, now you just need to find the perfect gift. Check the couple's wedding list first, or select a more personal or unusual gift.

Steps

1 Send the personal touch. Have satin-covered down pillows monogrammed or engrave a pair of crystal champagne flutes with their names and the wedding date.

2 Plant the thought of a long and prosperous marriage with a tree or flowering rose if the couple is buying a new home.

3 Send the bride and groom on a hot-air balloon ride or a sunset cruise. A set of golf or tennis lessons is a fun wedding gift. Non-traditional gifts are especially appropriate for second marriages when all the household necessities are covered.

4 Give the bride a gift certificate for an afternoon of spa luxury. If money's no object, include her bridesmaids or maid of honour.

What to Look For

- Registry items
- Unique, memorable or personal gift

Warning

Check that any bridal registry list is up-to-date before you buy. Consider selecting an item from a category that's near completion to give the bride and groom the satisfaction of getting a full set rather than bits and pieces.

68 Select Bridesmaids' Dresses

You'll wear it again, right? More and more, today's brides are choosing a colour and fabric, then letting their bridesmaids each choose a dress that flatters her figure. If you take the more traditional route, be thoughtful and choose a dress that's both attractive and affordable.

Steps

1 Get started. Fittings should begin four to six months before the big day. You may want to take a few maids shopping with you.

2 Decide on a colour and length. Depending on the time of day, season and degree of formality, you may choose a floor-length, silk sheath for a formal wedding, or a tea-length pastel sheer for a warm afternoon ceremony. Rule of thumb: If a bride is wearing a floor-length dress, bridesmaid dresses should not be short.

3 Keep the figures of all of your bridesmaids in mind when selecting a style. A full-figured woman may not feel comfortable in a short, strapless cocktail-style dress, for example.

4 Send your bridesmaids shopping for different dresses in one designer's line, or choose any dress of a certain colour and length.

5 Less is more. Since bridesmaids usually pay for their own dresses, keep cost in mind. About £200 is a good figure, but if you can do it for less, everyone will be happier.

What to Look For

- Flexible design range
- Figure-flattering styles
- Coordination of colours, fabrics, styles
- Sane prices

Tips

Bride's and bridesmaids' dresses should complement each other and be uniform enough to look good in pictures.

Check out the *Yellow Pages* under "Wedding Services—Dressing".

69 Hire an Events Organiser

With a skilled events organiser or party planner backing you up, you can throw a company picnic for 100 people, an intimate dinner party, or a country wedding – all without breaking into a sweat. Replace panic with peace of mind and enjoy the festivities.

Steps

1 Base preliminary logistical decisions on your budget: number of guests, atmosphere, location, date and time, food (buffet, sit-down meal, cocktail party, box lunches) and degree of formality. Give yourself at least six to nine months' lead time when planning a large event.

2 List those tasks you want taken off your shoulders. Party planners will plan budgets; rent audio/visual and other equipment; scout venues; hire and manage live music; manage guest lists; arrange for decorations, parking and security; handle airline and hotel bookings for out-of-town events or guests—even hire portable toilets.

3 Remember that well-connected professionals can save you money by passing on discounts and perks they get from suppliers and banquet managers. And since they're experienced with service-provider contracts, arrange for them to handle all the negotiations, notifying you of any hitches or price increases.

4 Consult the *Yellow Pages* under "Event Organisers" or "Party Planners" and "Wedding Services – Organisers and Planners" as well as local wedding and business reference guides, and ask for referrals from trusted friends, colleagues, caterers, and local hotels and businesses for event planners, consultants or coordinators.

5 Interview likely prospects. Ask how many events they've produced, what kind, for how many, and what made these events special to find out if they're experienced in the kind of event you're throwing. See what aspects of the event they will assume control over. They should also be able to offer creative ideas to suit your budget.

6 Discuss whether you will be billed by the hour, the event or as a percentage of the total budget. Ask if package prices are available. Explain in detail what you want the coordinator to do, then ask for a quote in writing. Ask what he or she can do to reassure you that costs won't run over, at least not without your prior agreement.

7 Query the coordinator to see how he or she would handle potential catastrophes such as the caterer running out of food, the DJ not showing up, or a sudden downpour drowning out a lavish outdoor event.

What to Look For

- Well-connected
- Referrals and references
- Proven performance
- Creative
- Committed
- Calm under pressure

Tips

Your organiser should find out about local noise issues.

Hire a licensed, insured company for major events.

8 Ask if you can drop by one of their events in progress. Request contact details of previous clients and call them to ask about their experience with that particular event coordinator.

9 Spell out the project's scope in detail; describe the planner's responsibilities and delineate all payment information in a written, signed agreement.

70 Hire a Bartender for a Party

The ideal bartender keeps more than cocktails and white wine spritzers flowing. A skilled professional can interact affably while moving at warp speed to keep up with thirsty guests and avoid a bottleneck at the bar.

Steps

1 Get recommendations from friends, caterers or party planners. If your search comes up short, go online to find a nearby agency.

2 Check that the bartender has his or her own bar kit. Pros travel with their own wine opener, pour spouts, cocktail shaker, strainer, long-handled spoon, towel and knife for cutting garnishes. You provide the blender, beverages, glasses and ice.

3 Test expertise, since good bartenders know major mixed-drink recipes by heart. Ask how many years of experience the bartender has and of what kind. Bar staff used to working in pub-style establishments may not know how to make cocktails.

4 Quiz prospective bartenders on how they set up their bars and how they cope with non-stop drink demands and empty glasses and bottles. They should be in command of their work space, rubbish and empties' containers, and supply of glassware and beverages.

5 If you're planning the party yourself rather than hiring a caterer (see 72 "Hire a Caterer"), ask the bartender's advice on what to order. An experienced bartender can help you calculate how much alcohol you'll need and what types (see 307 "Stock Your Bar").

6 Avoid novices or anyone too fresh out of hotel and catering management courses. Look for a tidy appearance and attire.

What to Look For

- Recommendations
- Good people skills
- Organised
- Tidy appearance and attire

Tip

Good bartenders ask about guests' ages and tastes, and know which drinks different groups favour. A relatively sedate gathering of over-50s calls for a different approach than for a wild crowd of thirty-something revellers

71 Hire a Photographer

Professional photographers offer digital and traditional photographs and while you may be a dab hand at either for casual snaps, nothing replaces a professional photographer who can truly do justice to those special moments for those times when it really counts.

Steps

1 Start looking for a photographer as soon as you have the time and location nailed down, six months to a year in advance of the event.

2 Choose a photographer who specialises in the type of event you're holding such as weddings, family portraits, corporate head shots and more. Ask for references and get personal recommendations whenever possible. Use the *Yellow Pages* as a last resort and look under "Photographers – General". Then check their websites to get a feel for the quality and specialisms of a particular photographer.

3 Ask to see samples of their work similar to what you want. Check out their website, if they have one, for samples of their style and versatility. Look for relaxed expressions and posing, and watch out for stiff, over-formal staging. Great pictures look natural and easy.

4 Trust your instincts. Do you get a good feel from the photographer? Does he or she listen to what you really want?

5 Ask how long he or she has been in business and get a sense of their level of professionalism. You want someone who dresses and acts sharp to shoot your event.

6 Specify if you want colour or black-and-white pictures.

7 Inquire if digital photographs are an option. If so, find out if you will view the pictures as paper proofs, contact sheets or on a CD. Some photographers set up a page on their website so you can proof images online.

8 Ask how long will it take to see the proofs, if you get to keep them, how reprints and enlargements will be handled and what they cost. Enquire about bulk discounts on large orders and the possibility of ordering prints online.

9 Review the contract and button down all the details. All terms should be specified, including the deposit and cancellation and refund policies.

10 Touch base in the weeks prior to your event to finalise all the details. Give the photographer a list of people you definitely want to be photographed.

What to Look For

- Expertise in your event
- References
- Excellent photographs
- Prompt and professional
- Black-and-white, colour or digital pictures
- Website with samples
- Clearly spelled out terms

Tips

If your event will be photographed digitally, look at a printout of a sample photograph to make sure you're satisfied with the quality.

Check out the studio if you are having portraits taken. Look for a place to change clothes if you care to, as well as comfortable ambient temperature. Does it have an iron and ironing board, lighted mirror for make-up and so on. You need to be very comfortable in the studio environment in order to take a relaxed photograph – is there a nice sofa, and coffee, tea facilities and other refreshments? Are there toys and comics for the kids?

Warning

Try to get an idea about whether the photographer is intrusive, bossy or arrogant. A wedding or any other event that is dictated by the photographer can be a miserable affair for everyone.

72 Hire a Caterer

How many times have you been served a cold plate of rubber-tasting chicken at a dinner? The food can make or break any event, be it an intimate brunch, a business power lunch or a wedding banquet. That's why finding the right caterer for the occasion is crucial.

Steps

1 Start your search as soon as you have the date and event venue nailed down. Ask friends for recommendations. If you loved the food at an event, ask the host for the caterer's number. Also, your venue may have a list of preferred caterers.

2 Create a budget based on what you want or can afford to pay per head for food and beverages, and go over this with prospective caterers. High prices don't necessarily guarantee quality. Some famed caterers resort to pre-made pasta sauces, while many small operators make everything from scratch and use fresh ingredients.

3 Look at the caterer's portfolio of colour photographs. Look at the presentation in individual dishes, table designs and buffet spreads. Does the food look beautiful and delicious?

4 Get phone numbers of previous customers and ask them if they were satisfied with the caterer.

5 Ask for sample menus that fit your budget. The caterer will create a tasting for you of all the items. Besides evaluating the dishes' flavour, you can gauge a caterer's desire to please you with additional special requests. Do they use heavy oils and butter in their recipes, or would they be willing to switch to healthier options? Do they offer vegetarian dishes? A larger caterer may offer more dishes to sample, but this is not the most important criterion. Just make certain the company can handle the total number of guests, even if it has to outsource some tasks.

6 Expect to be charged a set fee per person for food. This ranges from £5 to £50 per head depending on the event, plus additional costs for beverages, furniture rental or other extras. Ask for an estimate on the rates for servers, bartenders and clearing up staff. A six-hour bash might last eight hours, and unless you arrange otherwise, the caterer must keep paying the staff until the last guest leaves.

7 Review the venue with your caterer, who will want to see the kitchen facilities and space where guests will mingle and dine. Make sure that the caterer surveys the space carefully and plans the positioning of food and beverage tables to optimise traffic flow. This is crucial to arranging serving and dining tables.

8 Determine who will provide or rent tables, chairs, centrepieces, marquee, glassware, utensils and linens. Also confirm the number of waiting staff, their dress code, taxes, tips and payment schedule. Have all agreed-upon details written into the contract.

What to Look For

- Referrals
- Tasty food
- Clear price estimate
- Organised planning

Tips

Clarify the dress code for servers and staff. The bistro look – a neat white shirt, black tie and trousers, and an apron – has overtaken the black tie look, although you can go formal if you wish.

Ask your caterer and the venue if you can bring in your own alcohol – this can save you a bundle. Buy from a discount off-licence or wine merchant store that will let you return unopened bottles.

Alternatively, take a van or estate car and drive to Calais – the savings can be in the £100s .

Determine whether you are expected to tip the caterer after the event.

Warnings

Some function halls or hotels won't allow you to bring in outside caterers, so double-check up front.

Find out if the caterer is insured. If they're not, you're taking a big risk.

You would be right to worry if a caterer doesn't ask lots of questions about what you like and hate, and about your ideas about the event. A lack of curiosity sends up a red flag that you're in for generic, impersonal service.

73 Find the Ideal Civil Wedding Venue

If you're planning a civil wedding the choice of venues is beginning to get more tuned in to today's young couples. In England you could have the thrill of a service inside the moving pod of the Millennium Wheel or the more stationary but elegant grandeur of Blenheim Palace – to name just two special wedding venues!

Steps

1 Check out the official England & Wales website for your nearest register offices and other approved sites at gro.gov.uk. Local authority services can provide you with a paper copy of the list of approved sites in England and Wales for £5.00.

2 If you want to keep it simple and inexpensive, go for the register office option. Make the ceremony more personal by selecting your own non-religious music and/or readings. Discuss what you'd like with the registrar when planning the wedding.

3 If you want to make the event more special, check out the list of approved sites. There are now a huge number of hotels and other venues throughout the UK in which you can get married. There is a venue for every taste: castles, such as Camelot Castle, Tintagel; football grounds and racecourses, such as Goodwood Racecourse, Chichester; film studios, such as Teddington Studios, Twickenham; and even London Zoo in Regents Park. Each charges a different fee, so discuss the options with your partner, decide which best suits your taste and which you can afford, and go for it.

What to Look For

- Venue for ceremony that you and your partner feel comfortable with
- Fee to be considered
- local.services@ons.gov.uk

Tip

If you wish to be married in the Church of England you or your partner will need to be living in the parish. If in doubt check with the vicar. If he agrees to marry you he will arrange for the banns to be called on three Sundays before the day of your ceremony or for a common licence to be issued. The marriage will also need to be registered by the vicar.

74 The Cost of Marrying

So you're ready to get hitched? Apart from all the huge costs of the wedding party, caterers and all the ancillary services you'll need on the big day, don't underestimate the actual cost of getting married in a church or register office (or other approved building).

Steps

1 The basic civil marriage cost is currently nudging around the £100 mark including the registrar's fee, the marriage certificate (actually only £3.50!) and all the legal niceties.

2 Don't forget the charge made by the owners of the approved premises if you are going down that route.

3 For marriage in the Church of England or Church in Wales check with the vicar of the church in which you wish to marry – but you should budget for at least £300 with no trimmings. Once you add bells, choir and organist you're looking at up to £500 for a standard church; but that can skyrocket to whatever the church wish to charge for any picturesque and fashionable place of worship.

What to Look For

- Local council's scale of fees
- Required documents
- Picture identification
- Wedding date

Tip

If you have no idea which local church you wish to get married in, start by looking under "Places of Worship" in the *Yellow Pages*.

75 Order Personalised Invitations and Announcements

Whether it's an anniversary, new baby or a wedding, invitations and announcements run the gamut from charming home-made cards to embossed, foil-stamped pieces. What you choose will depend on personal style, number of guests and your budget, as well as how much time you would like to devote to the project.

Steps

1 Start working on wedding invitations as soon as you've nailed down the time and location, at least five months ahead of time. Invitations should be posted four to six weeks before the event.

2 Send "save the date" cards three to six months ahead if you're inviting guests who need to make travel arrangements.

3 Finalise your guest list to determine how many invitations you need. Plan to print 20 to 30 extra invitations and envelopes in case of late additions to the list or botched addresses.

4 Decide what you want to spend: your budget dictates your options including paper, printing method, design and calligraphy.

5 Place your order in a stationers or printers. Pick paper and a type style that suit the mood of the event. You'll choose colour, texture and special effects like pressed flowers. Stay with standard sizes and save a bundle; otherwise envelopes have to be custom made.

6 Hire a designer to create a personalised invitation or announcement if you don't find what you want at a stationers. He or she will create a unique, fun, elegant or whimsical look to your specifications (see 158 "Hire a Graphic Designer").

7 Explore printing effects. Traditional engraving, elegant letterpress, and relatively inexpensive thermography are all classy extras. Plain offset printing with black ink is the least expensive.

8 Proofread your piece very carefully when your printer gives you a proof to check. Have a fresh pair of eyes read it too.

9 Hire a calligrapher to write the names (about £1 per name) or address the envelopes for a stunning, formal touch. A professional may charge up to £5 per envelope, including post code! Contact your local arts guild to find one.

10 Be judicious about the number of enclosures and envelopes your invitation includes. There is no rule that says you have to have an inner and outer envelope as well as one for the reply card. Save money by using just one outer envelope and enclosing a pre-stamped RSVP postcard.

What to Look For

- Order in good time
- Appropriate design
- Trustworthy stationers
- Careful proofreading
- Envelope-addressing plan

Tips

Save even more money by having only the invitations printed, and then have a custom rubber stamp made for under £15 for the return address.

Print directions and a map if needed on your own computer and slip it into the envelope. Add gift registration information on the reverse side of the directions (but not on the wedding invitations).

Order thank-you notes at the same time to match the invitations, and get enough to cover engagement and wedding gifts.

Warning

Don't post your invitation without correct postage. Take the completed envelope with all the enclosures down to the post office to be weighed.

76 Sell Your Wedding Dress

Maybe you went way over budget buying the most divine wedding dress in creation and now need some cash, or you don't have space to store it for the future. So sell the dress to recoup some of its cost.

Steps

1 Send your gown to a dry cleaner that specialises in bridal wear. Do this immediately after the wedding – perspiration or a teeny splash of champagne can yellow and set quickly. Point out and identify visible stains for treating.

2 Invest in a dust-proof heirloom box if you must store your dress even briefly. Some dry cleaners can hermetically seal it. Avoid plastic bags and hangers—they seal in humidity and can damage or stretch delicate fabrics.

3 Advertise your ad in the local press.

4 For your ad, state the colour, style and cut of dress, size and special features and condition.

5 To hit the peak times for weddings, such as the summer months, remember that brides should be thinking about selecting wedding dresses six months in advance. So winter/spring should be an optimum time for advertising. Of course not everyone can plan a wedding with military precision, so try the early months too to catch those last-minute frantic wedding dress searches.

6 Advertise your dress online. You'll need a full-length colour photograph that really shows it off to advantage and a full description right down to the beading, condition, price paid and size.

7 Give your dress to a charity shop if you don't need the cash. You will be doing a really nice deed for a bride on a budget (some say it's good luck to pass along your happiness). See 498 "Sell Used Clothing".

What to Look For

- Heirloom box
- Advertise in the local press
- Charity shop
- Online sites such as almostnewweddingdresses.co.uk are a good place to start searching. They have designer dresses such as Vera Wang and others.

Tip

See 64 "Choose the Perfect Wedding Dress".

Warning

While your dress waits to find its new owner, keep it in top-notch condition. Stuff the bodice and sleeves with white, acid-free tissue paper. If you must use a hanger, sew some straps inside the dress's waistline to hook around the hanger for extra support and avoid any stretching. Cover your dress in a white sheet and keep it in a dry, cool spot.

77 Buy an Anniversary Gift

The tradition of tying gifts to particular wedding anniversaries began in central Europe. Medieval German wives received silver wreaths on their 25th anniversary, gold ones on their 50th. Other traditions have added to the eight original gifts. (Diamonds, which originally marked the 60th anniversary, are now common gifts early in marriage.) Here's how to marry the old with the new.

YEAR	TRADITIONAL	MODERN
First	Paper	Frame a poem or love letter; artist's sketch from a wedding photograph.
Second	Cotton	Clothing, linens, gift certificate for clothing item.
Third	Leather	Briefcase, handbag, leather jacket, wallet.
Fourth	Fruit/Flowers	Plant a garden, give a fruit tree.
Fifth	Wood	Jewellery box, plant a tree.
Sixth	Iron	Wrought-iron garden gate, golf clubs.
Seventh	Wool/Copper	Jersey, cookware.
Eighth	Bronze/Pottery	Sculpture, matching coffee mugs.
Ninth	Pottery/Willow	Willow tree, wicker furniture.
Tenth	Tin/Aluminium	Metal-framed sunglasses, digital camera, tools, bicycle.
Eleventh	Steel	Kitchen knives.
Twelfth	Silk/Linen	Tablecloth, scarf, pyjamas, linens.
Thirteenth	Lace	Antique tablecloth, curtains, table runner.
Fourteenth	Ivory	Piano.
Fifteenth	Crystal	Candlesticks, wine glasses, clock.
Twentieth	China	Trip to China, new place setting.
Twenty-fifth	Silver	Airline tickets wrapped in a silver bow, tray, tie clip, goblets, antique coins.
Thirtieth	Pearl	Earrings, necklace; mother-of-pearl inlaid pocket knife.
Thirty-fifth	Coral	Trip to the tropics, coral beaded necklace.
Fortieth	Ruby	Jewellery.
Forty-fifth	Sapphire	Jewellery.
Fiftieth	Gold	Watch, clock, pen, jewellery.
Fifty-fifth	Emerald	Trip to Ireland, jewellery.
Sixtieth	Diamond	Watch, jewellery.

78 Arrange Entertainment for a Party

The crowd gasps. Breathless, all eyes are on centre stage. At your party? Sure! Finding and hiring just the right entertainer takes a knack and some time but is worth the effort.

Steps

1 Call an agency unless you have a strong personal referral (look under "Theatrical & Variety Agents" in the *Yellow Pages*). The fees are a little higher since they include commissions, but the performers are pros (ask for a publicity package), and if someone falls ill, a good agency will find a stand-in. Also look under "Party Planners & Organisers" in the *Yellow Pages* or "Corporate Entertainment" if it's an office party.

2 Work out the number of guests, their ages and the party's tone and choose appropriate entertainment.

3 Have the children's theme-party entertainer provide a goody bag, or plan a crafty activity and send the child home with a gift he or she makes for a tangible memory of the party.

4 Get a contract or letter of agreement that includes the scope and description of the act and itemises payment information, cancellation policy and penalties for defaulting (by either party).

5 Give your event a whole different flavour (and avoid cleaning up) by having it at an ice rink, bowling alley, ceramic-making studio, swimming pool or laser-tag emporium.

What to Look For

- References and referrals
- Crowd-appropriate acts
- Performed for similar age groups and crowds
- Contract or written agreement
- Sane prices
- Chance to test-drive or view acts

Tip

Review a video or watch an actual performance to make sure your choice of entertainment is appropriate.

FOR KIDS' PARTIES	FOR ADULTS' PARTIES
Caricature artists	• Acrobats
Climbing wall	• Casino night
Clowns	• Elvis impersonators
Costumed cartoon characters and caped crusaders	• Hypnotists
Interactive theatre, storyteller	• Musicians
Magician	• Psychics, palm and tarot-card readers, astrologers
Petting zoo or wildlife visitors	• Singing telegrams
Puppet shows	• Stand-up comedians
Themes: face painters, musical games, sing-alongs, jewellery making, science demonstrations	

79 Commission a Fireworks Show

A dazzling fireworks display can add a more than a memorable touch to a party, wedding or business event. For a safe and sizzling evening, leave the pyrotechnics to the pros, sit back and enjoy.

Steps

1 It's not as prohibitively expensive as you might imagine – a professionally fired-up basic back garden display might set you back around £800, and that would include insurance, VAT and all the licences and legal niceties. The display would run for seven or eight minutes with various "shells" and "cakes". Close to the £2,000 mark gets you a 20-minute pyrotechnic display. Major company pyrotechnic events run up to £60,000 and more.

2 Get referrals for several reputable, well-established fireworks providers or pyrotechnics companies experienced with similar-size shows. Make sure they are insured and ask what their policy covers. Check references diligently.

3 Sit back and let a full-service operation or event planner take over by organising necessary permits and talking to fire inspectors. If you do it yourself, you'll need to contact the fire brigade, learn about local and technical guidelines, ask for copies of relevant legal requirements and licences and review them with the technicians.

4 Check with the local authority regarding safety zones and licences. These mandatory distances between spectators and fireworks are governed by how far fireworks travel from their ignition point to the outer perimeter of flaming, falling debris. Compliance with these codes will dictate your choice of fireworks.

5 Find out if the local fire service needs to issue a permit or approve the location and facilities.

6 Give your fantasies full rein when brainstorming with pyrotechnics providers. Discuss your budget and whether you're after a particular colour scheme, theme or effects choreographed to music. Describe your audience.

7 Look at videos of past performances to get ideas. Ask for their advice; they are the pros. Take advantage of their creativity. They'll dream up tricks to maximise your extravaganza, like having effects reflect in a lake or light up a statue.

8 Find out how much pyrotechnics you'll get for your pound. Get a fully itemised, written proposal confirming the agreed-upon display and location, and listing every shell with quantities, names, sizes and descriptions.

9 Get contractual assurance that transportation of fireworks will meet local regulations, and that the fee includes cleaning up debris and waste disposal of the fireworks.

What to Look For

- Experienced pyrotechnicians
- Established company
- Creativity within your budget
- Best mix of splash and show length
- Detailed proposal
- Itemisation of responsibilities
- Professionally fired and fully insured

Tips

Discuss the optimum moment to light the fuse. Fireworks most often cap off an evening, but don't leave it too late for the weary or tipsy to enjoy it.

Most firework companies offer special DIY retail packs if you are being really budget-minded. Look under "Fireworks" in the *Yellow Pages* (next to "First Aid Training"!). Search websites such as shellscape.com and sandlingfireworks.com for starters.

Warning

Make sure all liability issues are fully taken care of. If the pyrotechnics company doesn't have an umbrella policy covering all possible contingencies, contact your insurance company and discuss a temporary policy.

80 Buy a Mother's Day Gift

Go on, say "thank you" to acknowledge the hard work and loving care that goes into motherhood, and to honour all the special mothers in your life – your sister, grandmother, spouse, friend, mother-in-law – in these unique and creative ways.

Steps

1 Offer your mum a chance to explore a new passion. If she's spoken of an unexplored interest – such as art, music, gourmet cooking, singing or golf – sign her up for lessons. Contact local community centres, teachers or clubs for references. If she's always wanted to play the drums, rent a set and locate a teacher.

2 Buy a tray of plants or flowers for her garden and plant them where she chooses; or put in a vegetable garden (see 253 "Start a Vegetable Garden").

3 Make her sigh with a fabulous spa day or a massage certificate, or book her a professional beauty treatment.

4 Get her computer hooked up to the internet, or buy her a mobile phone on contract if she says, "You never call! You never write!"

5 Plant a container with a lush mini herb garden that she can snip at will while cooking.

6 Have some favourite family photographs copied and framed for her to enjoy.

7 Take her to a local gym for a sample session of yoga, tai chi or personal training sessions. Better still, you go too.

8 Take her sewing machine in to be serviced.

9 Gather your clan and book a professional photographer to take a portrait of the whole family. Costs range widely, but expect to pay anywhere from £25 to £150 and up depending on the studio, and the number and size of prints you end up ordering (see 71 "Hire a Photographer").

10 Buy a gift certificate from a favourite shop where she usually wouldn't indulge herself.

11 Take a walk on the wild side and buy her a pair of walking boots (available from direct mail companies, such as Hawkshead, hawkshead.com).

12 Book a West End show – it's not as pricey as it sounds and if you try the internet there are bargains and special deals to be had. For example, if she likes ballet, Sadlers Wells Theatre in London has seat prices from £8 with perfectly good views.

What to Look For

- Gift that says love
- Gift that says thanks
- Gift that says you thought about it
- Unusual, not just traditional

Tip

Create a Mother's Day gift with the kids. Ask them to draw and sign portraits of Mummy or Grandma, then buy simple frames and help them prepare and wrap their gifts.

81 Buy a Father's Day Gift

Okay so it's a greetings card creation, but it's nice to get the kids to think about dad or grandpa or you to think about husband, first-time dad or good friend. It's a great chance to be creative which isn't difficult because the array of men's gifts at department stores would leave you with the impression that every male in the country is not only in need of a new tie or gadget, but a golf fanatic. On the contrary, men's passions are diverse. Try these ideas for great dad gifts.

Steps

1 Zero in on an enduring hobby or new interest, then shop for gear and accessories he doesn't have yet. Is he a science or computer buff, a car or bike fanatic, a fisherman, a cook, a gardener or basketball fan? Shop at carphonewarehouse.com for that latest mobile phone gadget, splash out on tickets for Glastonbury at £100+ each or buy a couple of tickets to a football game for slightly less.

2 Do something fun together. Plan a fishing or camping trip, or even a balloon ride. Look under "Balloons – Hot Air" in the *Yellow Pages*. Or buy tickets and popcorn, and let him choose the movie.

3 Go high-tech with gizmos and toys all men find irresistible. A Tablet PC, for instance, enables him to scribble on-screen in meetings and type up notes later on. It's a pen and paper and notebook and desktop all rolled into one for around £2,000.

4 Appeal to his practical side. Buy him jump leads for the car, a really good road map (such as from Collins.co.uk) or a Leatherman mini tool kit for his glove compartment.

5 Feed his sweet tooth with a bag of his favourite childhood sweets. Try cadbury.co.uk or thorntons.co.uk for a variety of tasty gift ideas that will tempt anyone off the Atkins Diet. Alternatively, pick up a savoury treat like smoked salmon or a 9 kg (20 lb) can of pistachios.

6 Head for a DIY store and get him a cordless drill. These are as essential to survival as food, water and the remote.

7 Birdie, don't bogie. Buy a set of monogrammed golf towels and a pack of golf balls (real or chocolate), and spring for a guest pass for a day on the green. Better yet, go with him.

8 Add a little dazzle to his wardrobe. If he likes to go out on the town, order a pair of monogrammed silver cuff links. If he's just a regular Joe, update his bedraggled wallet or briefcase.

9 Give him the world. Find a gorgeous wall map, atlas or globe at stanfords.co.uk to whet his wanderlust.

What to Look For

- Hobbies and passions
- Nostalgia
- Shared memories

Tip

Give little ones a hand with their Father's Day gifts. They can create their own hand-drawn or computer-aided greetings for Dad or send him a virtual Father's Day tie.

82 Select an Appropriate Coming-of-Age Gift

Most religions and cultures have their own unique ways of celebrating young girls' and boys' rites of passage – the coming-of-age milestones that mark their transition from children to young men and women. Below are two key coming-of-age ceremonies. Celebrate their new status in society with a special gift.

Steps

Confirmation

1 Celebrate the admission of young people into full participation in church life. Don't forget that older people can also be confirmed.

2 Monogram or inscribe a white prayer book, or engrave a silver rosary bracelet. Engrave a silver frame with the child's name and date and put a commemorative photograph or keepsake invitation inside.

3 The Catholic Church will confirm children of eight while other churches wait until they are older. Catholic girls have traditionally worn white dresses for their confirmation. Treat the celebrant in her traditional white dress to a professional portrait.

Bar and bat mitzvah

1 Say "Mazel tov!" at Jewish coming-of-age rituals. The day marks the first time the bar mitzvah boy (age 13) or bat mitzvah girl (age 12) is called to the Torah to recite a blessing over the weekly reading. The celebration that follows usually includes a festive meal at a synagogue, restaurant or banquet hall.

2 Follow the tradition of giving cash in multiples of 18. (Each letter in the Hebrew alphabet corresponds to a number, and the two letters that form *chai*, "life" in Hebrew, add up to 18.)

3 Give a gold or silver symbol on a chain – a chai, *chamsa* (Hebrew for "the hand of God," to ward off the evil eye), or Star of David. Buy a mezuzah, a small case with a prayer scroll inside, for the boy or girl's home.

4 Buy Israel bonds (israelbonds.com) or plant a tree in Israel (jnf.org).

What to Look For

- Religious or cultural significance
- Lifelong keepsakes

Tip

Gifts of cash can be set aside for college or a large purchase later.

83 Get a Gift for the Person Who Has Everything

Even if money's no object, it takes creativity to find or buy a truly memorable gift for someone who has everything. Think of his or her personal history, memories and passions and you're on track to make a lasting impact. These starting points and strategies will help you channel inspiration, no matter what the budget.

Steps

1 Tap into the universal fascination with family roots. Buy affordable software to help someone trace a family tree; Family Tree Maker is one of many good products (genealogy.com).

2 Name a Scottish whale or another beautiful creature after him or her. The Hebridean Whale and Dolphin Trust (whales.gn.apc.org), photo-identifies minke whales and lets you name the creature exclusively for its lifetime (20 to 30 years) for £150 and up. You'll receive a photograph, a certificate and a year's membership.

3 Get a fabulous wall map of an area your recipient is interested in at Stanfords (stanfords.co.uk), which has an excellent selection of exquisitely rendered maps or globes, aerial photograph and historical maps.

4 Compile family memorabilia – photographs, certificates, personal notes and family documents – into a keepsake album. Get it professionally bound. Or buy an album from an a photographic shop—ask for guidance on acid-free paper, preservation and mounting.

5 Ask a local historical society, local council responsible for parks or botanical garden in your recipient's hometown about donation options. Explain that you're looking for an item with special meaning. Maybe you can have a tree or park bench dedicated with a plaque (the likely cost is £100 and up).

6 Hire a master perfumer to create a unique scent. For around £12,000, French perfumer Oliver Creed will create one – the fee includes airfare and three nights in a top Parisian hotel.

7 Commission a local writer to write your recipient's life story and help you print a limited-edition book. Seek out local ghost writers and designers. (See 116 "Employ a Ghostwriter to Write Your Memoirs" and 158 "Hire a Graphic Designer".)

8 Hire a Master of Wine for a personal wine tasting with a group of friends. There are only a few hundred MVs so this is something special – and you'll get to taste some fabulous wines (in the £25 to £50 range). Of course, you may have to spit out like the professionals do, rather than gulp down.

What to Look For

- A moment of fame
- A nod to heritage
- Unique
- Personal
- Nostalgic

Tip

See 118 "Immortalise Your Spouse in a Sculpture".

84 Buy a Gift for Passing Exams

Getting those GCSEs or A levels or graduating from university are exuberant milestones. Receiving the announcement isn't necessarily a call for gifts, but if you choose to give one, here are some ideas to help the recipient celebrate both his or her hard-earned accomplishments as well as the opportunities that lie just ahead.

What to Look For

- Personalised
- Give meaningful message
- Help with practical needs

Steps

1 Frame the certificate. Some university graduates may appreciate a framed photo of their college (see 50 "Get a Picture Framed"). Have the graduate's initials and graduation date monogrammed on a picture frame.

2 Inscribe a classic hardcover book, dictionary or encyclopedia with a note of love and pride. You can get special stick-on 'ex-libris' imprimateurs to note the achievement.

3 Buy personalised stationery with a college graduate's newest letters after his or her name (see 75 "Order Personalised Invitations and Announcements").

4 Give money or gift certificates, always appreciated by those in a cash-poor phase. For the graduate entering the business world, select a briefcase – M&S have a very good and modern range (see 511 "Buy a Briefcase"), Montblanc pen, leather desk set or business card holder. Perhaps best of all, work your network for job leads and present a few key introductions, listed in a gift card.

5 If they haven't already got one, splurge on a special graduate with a mobile phone, personal digital assistant or even a laptop (see 412 "Choose a Personal Digital Assistant" and 397 "Choose a Laptop or Notebook Computer"). Sterling silver key chains, cuff links or a money clip are other classy options.

6 Feather the nests of both high school and college graduates with essentials like lamps, clocks, microwaves, mini fridges, basic cookware, towels and bathroom necessities. Sixth-form students will appreciate sweatshirts, hats, fleece throws and backpacks emblazoned with the insignia of their college-to-be.

7 Celebrate a new chapter in life with something fun – a bicycle, CD or DVD player, digital camera, television and video recorder combination, or audio system.

85 Select a Christmas Turkey

The only turkey present at your Christmas dinner should be the beautiful golden-brown centrepiece on the table – not the poor chef who has been sweating in the kitchen. Start browsing through cookbooks early in December to find the perfect cooking method and get going early on ordering your festive feast.

Steps

1 Buy a frozen bird weeks ahead and plan on thawing it out in the fridge for several days before roasting. If you're challenged for time, get a frozen bird already larded, stuffed and basted, or self-basted.

2 Choose a fresh turkey for noticeably tastier meat. Check to see that it is wrapped securely, then pack it in a separate bag to prevent leakage.

3 Pre-order an organic or free-range turkey that has been living the high life on feed free of hormones, antibiotics and pesticides. Free-range turkeys are allowed to wander around to their heart's content rather than being cooped up in a cage. Ask your local grocer or butcher, or go online to find a supplier in your area. A few sites to consider are meats.co.uk and deliaonline.com.

4 Purchase 450 to 680 g (1 to 1½ lb) of turkey per person. Err on the high side to make sure you have some leftovers.

5 Buy a fresh or frozen breast, boneless if you prefer, if you are catering for a small group or for a bevy of white-meat fans. Around 2 kg (4 lb) serves four very nicely.

6 Buy a precooked, ready-to-slice whole turkey and serve it cold or heat it up. These birds are available baked, honey-glazed or smoked for extra flavour. Online sources include shopping.co.uk and ivillage.co.uk.

What to Look For

- Fresh or frozen
- Free-range or organic
- Size

Tip

Check frozen birds' packaging for any signs of damage or frost buildup – clues that it might have partially thawed out, then been refrozen. Make sure it is solidly frozen, with no areas that feel soft to the touch.

Warning

Never defrost a frozen turkey at room temperature. Bacteria begin to multiply as soon as the surface warms.

86 Buy a Housewarming Gift

Celebrate a friend or relative's new digs with a thoughtful housewarming gift and help get them set up in their new house in style. Browse through 59 "Buy a Great Birthday Present for Under £10", and consider these ideas, too.

Steps

1 Bring a plant for a traditional gift. Lucky bamboo symbolises good fortune, grows in water and lasts for years.

2 Give a bottle of wine, tea bags, cappuccino mix or a bag of flavourful ready-ground coffee. Package with a pair of wine glasses, mugs or demitasse cups.

3 Feed growling stomachs with cookies, cake, pastries or a fresh fruit basket. Or bring a savoury snack of cheeses and a crusty loaf of fresh bread.

4 Buy kitchen towels or a few hand towels and bars of soap.

5 Give a loaded picnic basket to dine on in their empty house then enjoy outdoors at a later date. A couple of folding beach or garden chairs can likewise serve many purposes.

6 Bring a new tool for the tool box: A cordless screwdriver, 8-m (25-ft) measuring tape, or a socket wrench set are all essential for projects around the house.

What to Look For

- Helpful
- Useful
- Versatile

Tip

If you're handy with a hammer, good at hanging pictures or a great organiser, ask if you can lend a hand.

87 Purchase Christmas Cards

It pays to think early about buying and sending out Christmas cards. Make them yourself, have photo cards made or buy them new.

Steps

1 Buy cards cheap right after this year's Christmas is over.

2 Buy charity cards to contribute some of the money to a deserving cause. If you donate to your favourite charities throughout the year, you are likely to receive several unsolicited batches of greeting cards from them.

3 Buy cards online at sites that post either to you or directly to your recipients with personalised messages.

4 Create custom photo cards at various online sites. Mail-order them or print them out on your own computer. Or take your negative to Boots or Tesco and print out your cards blazingly fast and at a reasonable cost.

What to Look For

- Off-season prices
- Special sales
- Ways to express yourself

Tip

Keep a permanent mailing list with names and addresses. Either tuck it inside your box of greeting cards or store it on your computer. Update it each year, and you'll have no excuse not to address and send cards out early the following year.

88 Buy Christmas Stocking Fillers

The definition of stocking filler has expanded from small gifts – coin-shaped chocolate, cheap trinkets, plastic toys, nuts and oranges – to include gourmet chocolates, CDs and MP3 players, and much more.

WHO	WHAT
Babies	Bath toys; washcloths, fuzzy letter cubes, rattles or small soft toys.
Small Children	Classic wooden toys, balls (larger than 5 cm/2 in in diameter), crayon and glitter-pen sets, and stickers. Scientific wonders from a well-stocked science or toy store. Age-appropriate videos and CDs. (See 334 "Buy Books, Videos and Music for Your Children".)
Girls	Stickers, a locking diary, stretchy beaded or flower rings and bracelets and hair decorations, socks in crazy colours and designs, manicure set or nail polish, walkie-talkies, comics, books and CDs.
Boys	GameBoys, walkie-talkies, football cards, cap, socks, remote-control mini-cars, combat cards, comic books, books and CDs.
Teenagers	CDs and cases, video games, the latest computer accessory, mobile phone with a colour screen, two-way radios, shop gift vouchers.
Grandparents	Playing card sets, luggage labels, old-time movies, scarf, coin purse, pillbox, ready-to-water amaryllis bulb in a small pot, magnifying glass, compass or book-on-tape.
Women	Bars of hand-made soap, thick wool socks, film, lavender sachets, skin-softening socks and gloves to wear overnight, gift certificates for espresso drinks, CDs, plane tickets (surprise!).
Men	Universal remote, business-card holder, stainless steel travel mug, tyre gauge, glasses case, paperback, GPS device, crossword-puzzle book, socks, guidebook to a surprise destination.
Fitness Enthusiast	Pedometer or heart-rate monitor, resistance bands, dumbbells, skipping rope, workout or yoga video, running socks, instant ice packs, hip pack with pockets, electrolyte replacement drinks, energy bars.
Gardeners	New trowel or other hand tool, leather gardening gloves, all-weather gardener's hat or waistcoat, seed packets.
Home Owners	Decorative wine-bottle stoppers, small tools, kitchen towels, napkin rings, potholders, oven gloves, refrigerator magnets or coasters. See 86 "Buy a Housewarming Gift".
Chefs	A pizza cutter, wooden spoons, a stove-top milk frother, ergonomically correct kitchen tools, barbecue tools, flexible plastic cutting boards.
WARNING	Check the labels on kids' toys to see if they're age-appropriate and safe.

89 Buy Christening Gifts

Selecting a meaningful and long-lasting christening gift requires some careful thought and forward planning. Rather than think of baby gifts, choose something that will last and have even greater emotional and financial value when the baby has matured to 18 years old.

Steps

1 Give a case of vintage wines or port in keeping with a very old tradition. After 18 years the baby can crack open the bottles in your honour or auction them off for a nice profit.

2 Buy premium bonds, another traditional christening gift. You can buy as many as your budget allows and there's always the chance that the baby (or at least baby's parents) could win an occasional jackpot. Share certificates are another variation on this theme.

3 Give the baby a cash or cheque in £10 increments each year up to 18.

4 Why not donate an acre of rainforest saved forever in the baby's name for £25? Click onto worldlandtrust.org.

5 A first edition of a hardback children's novel, encyclopedia, reference work, preferably signed by the author will accrue in value each year as well.

6 Keep it personal: go for personalised gifts, such engraved silverware, framed prints or the "day-you-were-born"-style charts.

What to Look For

- Longevity and appreciation in value
- Personalised gift
- Reflection of family values
- Spirit of giving

Tip

Try the internet for gift ideas, such as baby-gifts.co.uk and ukshops.co.uk/content/Christening-Gift.html.

Warning

Perhaps you might ask the parents beforehand what would be an appropriate gift for their children. If you waltz in with an expensive computer game, they might not thank you for it.

90 Purchase a Perfect Christmas Tree

The best thing about decorating your home for Christmas is filling it with the seductive scent of pine needles. Whether you buy a cut or living tree, freshness is the key to longevity, fragrance and beauty. Here's a guide to finding – and keeping – the perfect tree.

Steps

1 Keep a live tree in a container outside during the year and move it into the living room every December.

2 Cut your own at a tree farm specialist garden centre for the ultimate evergreen. If you're buying a cut tree, check to see how fresh it is. The fragrance should be strong. Grasp a branch and pull on the pine needles; if they pull out easily, the tree has dried out already.

3 To aid water absorption, quickly put the tree in a stand with water in it and keep it filled. A six-foot tree will drink a gallon of water every two days. Leave the tree outside in water until you are ready to decorate.

What to Look For

- Fresh smell
- Pliable needles
- Needles that don't drop

Tip

Check out the British Christmas Tree Growers Association website at bcta.co.uk and look under "Christmas Goods" in the *Yellow Pages* for home-grown freshly-harvested Christmas trees.

TREE	DESCRIPTION
Balsam Fir	2- to 4-cm (¾- to 1½-in) short, flat, long-lasting needles that are rounded at the tip; dark green colour with silvery cast, fragrant, dense. Good for garlands and swags.
Blue Spruce	Dark green to powdery blue, very stiff needles, 2- to 4-cm (¾- to 1½-in) long; good form; will drop needles in a warm room; symmetrical; best among species for needle retention. Branches are stiff and will support many heavy decorations.
Douglas Fir	Good fragrance; blue to dark green, holds 2.5- to 4-cm (1- to 1½-in) needles well; needles have one of the best aromas among Christmas trees when crushed. Good, conical shape; dense.
Leyland Cypress	Foliage is dark green to grey colour; upright branches with a feathery appearance; light scent; good for people with allergies to other Christmas tree types.
Noble Fir	2.5-cm (1-in) long, bluish green needles with a silvery appearance; dense; short stiff branches; keeps well; is used to make wreaths, door swags and garlands.
Norway Spruce	Shiny, dark green needles 1.3- to 2.5-cm (½- to 1-in) long. Needle retention is poor without proper care; strong fragrance; nice conical shape. Very popular in Europe.
Scots Pine	Stiff branches; stiff, dark green needles 2.5- to 7.6-cm (1- to 3-in) long; holds needles for four weeks; open appearance offers more room for ornaments; keeps aroma throughout the season; does not drop needles when dry.
Virginia Pine	Dark green needles are 4- to 7.6-cm (1½- to 3-in) long in twisted pairs; strong branches enable it to hold heavy ornaments; strong aromatic pine scent; from specialist suppliers.
White Pine	Soft, blue-green needles, 5- to 13-cm (2- to 5-in) long in bundles of five; retains needles throughout the holiday season; very full appearance; little or no fragrance; fewer allergic reactions as compared to more fragrant trees; slender branches will support fewer and smaller decorations than a Scotch Pine.
White Spruce	Needles 1.3- to 2-cm (½- to ¾-in) long; green to bluish green needles; crushed needles have an unpleasant odour; good needle retention.

TION SITES • BUY BARGAIN CLOTHING • BUY WHOLESALE • GET OUT OF DEBT • BUY NOTHING • BUY HAPPINESS • BUY A BETTER MOUS
Y YOUR WAY INTO SOMEONE'S FAVOUR • BUY LOVE • FIND THE RIGHT RELAXATION TECHNIQUE FOR YOU • BUY HEALTHY FAST FOOD • E
NG SERVICE • SELL YOURSELF ON AN ONLINE DATING SERVICE • SELL YOURSELF TO YOUR GIRLFRIEND/BOYFRIEND'S FAMILY • BUY FLO
OOSE FILM FOR YOUR CAMERA • BUY RECHARGEABLE BATTERIES • GIVE TO A GOOD CAUSE • TAKE PART IN A CAR BOOT SALE • EMPLO
DENT DISCOUNTS • BUY FLOWERS WHOLESALE • GET A PICTURE FRAMED • EMPLOY A REMOVAL COMPANY • EMPLOY A LIFESTYLE MAN
FOR A HALLOWE'EN PARTY • BUY A GREAT BIRTHDAY PRESENT FOR UNDER £10 • SELECT GOOD CHAMPAGNE • BUY A DIAMOND • BUY
A GIFT LIST • BUY WEDDING GIFTS • SELECT BRIDESMAIDS' DRESSES • HIRE AN EVENTS ORGANISER • HIRE A BARTENDER FOR A PARTY
OUNCEMENTS • SELL YOUR WEDDING DRESS • BUY AN ANNIVERSARY GIFT • ARRANGE ENTERTAINMENT FOR A PARTY • COMMISSION A
SON WHO HAS EVERYTHING • BUY A GIFT FOR PASSING EXAMS • SELECT A CHRISTMAS TURKEY • BUY A HOUSEWARMING GIFT • PURCH
ND • WRITE A MESSAGE IN THE SKY • HIRE A BIG-NAME BAND • GET INTO A PRIVATE GAMBLING ROOM IN LAS VEGAS • BUY SOMEONE A
TIMES • EMPLOY A BUTLER • BUY A FOOTBALL CLUB • BUY A PERSONAL JET • SELECT A CLASSIC CAR • ACQUIRE A BODY GUARD • BO
YHOUND TO RACE • BUY A RACEHORSE • BUY A VILLA IN TUSCANY • EMPLOY A PERSONAL CHEF • BUY A JOURNEY INTO SPACE • EMPL
TUNE • HIRE AN EXPERT WITNESS • MAKE MONEY FROM ACCIDENT COMPENSATION • DONATE YOUR BODY TO SCIENCE • MAKE MONEY
NCIAL ADVISER • PLAN FOR RETIREMENT • COPE WITH HIGHER EDUCATION COSTS • BUY AND SELL SHARES • CHOOSE A STOCKBROKE
S INSURANCE • BUY LIFE INSURANCE • GET PRIVATE HEALTH INSURANCE • BUY PERSONAL FINANCE SOFTWARE • CHOOSE AN ACCOUN
E OUT A PATENT • MARKET YOUR INVENTION • FINANCE YOUR BUSINESS IDEA • BUY A SMALL BUSINESS • BUY A FRANCHISE • LEASE RE
SITE • HIRE A GRAPHIC DESIGNER • ACQUIRE CONTENT FOR YOUR WEBSITE • BUY ADVERTISING ON THE WEB • SELL YOUR ART • HIRE
LISH YOUR BOOK • START A BED-AND-BREAKFAST • SELL A FAILING BUSINESS • BUY A HOT DOG STAND • SHOP FOR A MORTGAGE • GE
SE AT AUCTION • SHOP FOR A HOUSE ONLINE • BUY A PROPERTY FOR RENOVATION AND RESALE • EVALUATE BEFORE BUYING INTO A N
A PLOT OF LAND • HAVE YOUR HOUSE DESIGNED • HIRE AN ARCHITECT • HIRE A BUILDER • GET PLANNING PERMISSION • BUY A HOLID
DAD • BUY TO LET • RENT YOUR HOME FOR A LOCATION SHOOT • FURNISH YOUR HOME • FURNISH YOUR STUDIO FLAT • BUY USED FUI
Y HOUSEHOLD APPLIANCES • BUY FLOOR-CARE APPLIANCES • BUY EXTENDED WARRANTIES ON APPLIANCES • FIND PERIOD FIXTURES
E • SELECT PAINT, STAIN AND VARNISH • CHOOSE DECORATIVE TILES • CHOOSE A DEHUMIDIFIER • BUY A WHIRLPOOL BATH • BUY A SH
LPAPER • BUY A WOOD-BURNING STOVE • SELECT FLOORING • SELECT CARPETING • CHOOSE KITCHEN CABINETS • CHOOSE A KITCHE
KE ALARMS • BUY CARBON MONOXIDE DETECTORS • BUY FIRE EXTINGUISHERS • CHOOSE AN ENTRY DOOR • BUY A GARAGE-DOOR OF
DOOR FURNITURE • BUY THE PERFECT ROSE • BUY FLOWERING BULBS • BUY FLOWERS FOR YOUR GARDEN • SELECT PEST CONTROLS
OMATIC WATERING SYSTEM • START A NEW LAWN • BUY A LAWN MOWER • BUY KOI FOR YOUR FISH POND • BUY A STORAGE SHED • HI
DUCE • CHOOSE A PERFECT PEACH • BUY AND SELL AT FARMERS' MARKETS • SELECT KITCHEN KNIVES • DECIPHER FOOD LABELS • SE
FECT BURGER • PURCHASE A CHRISTMAS HAM • BUY ORGANIC BEEF • BUY HAGGIS • PURCHASE LOCAL HONEY • CHOOSE A CHICKEN
TRUFFLES • BUY ARTISAN BREADS • BUY ARTISAN CHEESES • PURCHASE KOSHER FOOD • BUY SENSIBLY IN SUPERMARKETS • CHOOS
ER A GREAT CUP OF COFFEE • BUY A COFFEEMAKER OR ESPRESSO MACHINE • PURCHASE PARTY BEER • CHOOSE THE RIGHT WINE • C
RM • CHOOSE AN OVULATION PREDICTOR KIT • PICK A PREGNANCY TEST KIT • CHOOSE BIRTH CONTROL • CHOOSE WHERE TO GIVE BIF
BABY CLOTHES • CHOOSE NAPPIES • BUY OR RENT A BREAST PUMP • CHOOSE A CAR SEAT • BUY CHILD-PROOFING SUPPLIES • FIND
A GARDEN PLAY STRUCTURE • FIND A FAMILY-FRIENDLY HOTEL • ORGANISE A FUND-RAISING EVENT • BUY BRACES FOR YOUR KID • B
MODEL • SELL USED BABY GEAR, TOYS, CLOTHES AND BOOKS • FIND A COUPLES COUNSELLOR • HIRE A FAMILY SOLICITOR • BUY OR
CHASE A TOOTHBRUSH • BUY MOISTURISERS AND ANTIWRINKLE CREAMS • SELECT PAIN RELIEF AND COLD MEDICINES • CHOOSE A CC
DUCTS • BUY WAYS TO COUNTER HAIR LOSS • BUY A WIG OR HAIRPIECE • BUY A NEW BODY • GET A TATTOO OR BODY PIERCING • OBT
H • SELECT SPECTACLES AND SUNGLASSES • HIRE A PERSONAL TRAINER • SIGN UP FOR A YOGA CLASS • TREAT YOURSELF TO A DAY
N ANTIQUE MARKET • BUY AT AUCTION • KNOW WHAT YOUR COLLECTIBLES ARE WORTH • BARTER WITH DEALERS • GET AN ANTIQUE A
IS • BUY AN ANTIQUE QUILT • BUY FILM POSTERS • LIQUIDATE YOUR BEANIE BABY COLLECTION • SCORE AUTOGRAPHS • TRADE YU-GI
SELL SPORTS MEMORABILIA • SELL YOUR FOOTBALL-CARD COLLECTION • CHOOSE A DESKTOP COMPUTER • SHOP FOR A USED COMP
PUTER PERIPHERALS • CHOOSE AN INTERNET SERVICE PROVIDER • GET AN INTERNET DOMAIN NAME • NETWORK YOUR COMPUTERS •
PLAYER • BUY A VIDEO RECORDER • CHOOSE A PERSONAL DIGITAL ASSISTANT • CHOOSE A MOBILE PHONE SERVICE • GET A BETTER D
AL CAMERA • BUY A HOME AUTOMATION SYSTEM • BUY A STATE-OF-THE-ART SOUND SYSTEM • BUY AN AUDIO/VIDEO DISTRIBUTION S
SYSTEM • BUY VIRTUAL-REALITY FURNITURE • BUY TWO-WAY RADIOS • BUY A MOBILE ENTERTAINMENT SYSTEM • GET A PASSPORT, QU
L LUGGAGE • FLY FOR NEXT TO NOTHING • TAKE A TRIP ON THE TRANS-SIBERIAN EXPRESS • BUY DUTY-FREE • SHIP FOREIGN PURCHA
AN CYCLING HOLIDAY • CHOOSE A CHEAP CRUISE • BOOK A HOTEL PACKAGE FOR THE GREEK ISLANDS • RAFT THE GRAND CANYON •
SHAW IN RANGOON • TAKE SALSA LESSONS IN CUBA • BUY A CAMERA IN HONG KONG • BUY YOUR WAY ONTO A MOUNT EVEREST EXP
TEAM • BUY ANKLE AND KNEE BRACES • CHOOSE RUGBY PROTECTION KIT • BUY GOLF CLUBS • SELL FOUND GOLF BALLS • BUY POF
LOY A SCUBA INSTRUCTOR • BUY A SKATEBOARD AND PROTECTIVE GEAR • BUY SKATES • GO BUNJEE JUMPING • GO SKYDIVING • BUY
TS AND BINDINGS • BUY SKI BOOTS • BUY A BICYCLE • BUY AN ELECTRIC BICYCLE • BUY CYCLE CLOTHING • BUY A PROPERLY FITTINC
• BUY A SURFBOARD • BUY FLY-FISHING GEAR • BUY ROCK-CLIMBING EQUIPMENT • BUY A CASHMERE JUMPER • PURCHASE VINTAGE
KTAIL DRESS • BUY DESIGNER CLOTHES AT A DISCOUNT • CHOOSE A BASIC WARDROBE FOR A MAN • BUY A MAN'S DRESS SHIRT • PIC
HER JACKET • BUY MATERNITY CLOTHES • GET A GREAT-FITTING BRA • CHOOSE A HIGH-PERFORMANCE SWIM SUIT • BUY PERFORMAN
TORY SHOPS • BUY A NEW CAR • BUY THE BASICS FOR YOUR CAR • BUY A USED CAR • BUY OR SELL A CAR ONLINE • BUY A HYBRID C

BUY TIME • BUY A BOUQUET OF ROSES • BUY SOMEONE A DRINK • GET SOMEONE TO BUY YOU A DRINK • BUY YOUR WAY INTO THE BE
SCREEN • BUT FURTHER EDUCATION • ORDER EXOTIC FOOD • ORDER AT A SUSHI BAR • BUY DINNER AT A FRENCH RESTAURANT • EMPL
SAY SORRY TO YOUR PARTNER • BUY MUSIC ONLINE • EMPLOY MUSICIANS • ORDER A GOOD BOTTLE OF WINE • BUY AN ERGONOMIC
ANER • EMPLOY AN AU PAIR • BUY A GUITAR • BUY DUCT TAPE • GET A GOOD DEAL ON A MAGAZINE SUBSCRIPTION • GET SENIOR CITIZ
FIND A VET • BUY PET FOOD • BUY A PEDIGREE DOG OR CAT • BREED YOUR PET AND SELL THE LITTER • BUY OR RENT FOR A FANCY DR
RY MADE OF PRECIOUS METALS • BUY COLOURED GEMSTONES • CHOOSE THE PERFECT WEDDING DRESS • BUY OR RENT MEN'S FORM
PHOTOGRAPHER • HIRE A CATERER • FIND THE IDEAL CIVIL WEDDING VENUE • THE COST OF MARRYING • ORDER PERSONALISED INVITA
RKS SHOW • BUY A MOTHER'S DAY GIFT • BUY A FATHER'S DAY GIFT • SELECT AN APPROPRIATE COMING-OF-AGE GIFT • GET A GIFT FOR
RISTMAS CARDS • BUY CHRISTMAS STOCKING FILLERS • BUY CHRISTENING GIFTS • PURCHASE A PERFECT CHRISTMAS TREE • BUY A PI
AY A RANSOM • GET HOT TICKETS • HIRE A LIMOUSINE • BUY A CRYONIC CHAMBER • RENT YOUR OWN HOARDING • TAKE OUT A FULL-F
URY CRUISE AROUND THE WORLD • BUY A TICKET TO TRAVEL FOR A YEAR • BOOK A TRIP ON THE ORIENT-EXPRESS • OWN A VINEYARD
OSTWRITER TO WRITE YOUR MEMOIRS • COMMISSION ORIGINAL ARTWORK • IMMORTALISE YOUR SPOUSE IN A SCULPTURE • GIVE AWA
DICAL GUINEA PIG • SELL YOUR STORY TO THE TABLOIDS • SELL YOUR SOUL TO THE DEVIL • NEGOTIATE A BETTER CREDIT CARD DEAL
RADE (OR NOT) • BUY ANNUITIES • BUY AND SELL MUTUAL FUNDS • BUY BONDS • SELL SHORT • INVEST IN PRECIOUS METALS • BUY SI
ND CASUAL WORK • SELL YOUR PRODUCT O[...]HEADHUNTER • SELL YOURSELF IN A JOB INTE
CE • LEASE INDUSTRIAL SPACE • LEASE OFFI[...]MENT • HIRE SOMEONE TO DESIGN AND BUILD Y
ACH • SELL ON THE CRAFT CIRCUIT • HIRE A[...]RY • SELL A SCREENPLAY • SELL YOUR NOVEL
ER MORTGAGE DEAL • SAVE ON YOUR MORT[...]D • OBTAIN HOUSE INSURANCE • BUY A HOUSE
• EXCHANGE CONTRACTS ON A PROPERTY •[...]AN ESTATE AGENT • RELEASE CAPITAL FROM YO
• RENT A HOLIDAY HOME • BUY A FLAT • REI[...]COUNTRY • BUY A LOFT APARTMENT • BUY PR
BUY DOOR AND WINDOW LOCKS • CHOOSE[...]GHT FIXTURES • BUY A PROGRAMMABLE LIGHT
ED AND MATTRESS • HIRE AN INTERIOR DES[...]NCORPORATE A GREATER SENSE OF SPACE INT
UY A TOILET • CHOOSE A TAP • BUY GLUES[...]MENTS • GET SELF-CLEANING WINDOWS • CHO
OP • BUY GREEN HOUSEHOLD CLEANERS •[...]SECURITY SYSTEM • BUY A HOME ALARM SYS
UY TIMBER FOR A DIY PROJECT • HOW TO S[...]R, PAINTER OR ELECTRICIAN • HIRE A GARDENE
IL IMPROVERS • BUY MULCH • BUY A COMP[...]BLE GARDEN • HIRE A GARDEN DESIGNER • BU
SURGEON • BUY BASIC GARDEN TOOLS • B[...]BUY AN OUTDOOR LIGHTING SYSTEM • BUY C
BS AND SPICES • STOCK YOUR KITCHEN WIT[...]RESH PRODUCE • SELECT MEAT • STOCK UP FC
FRESH FISH • SELECT RICE • PURCHASE PR[...]LTON • GET FRESH FISH DELIVERED TO YOUR DO
G OILS • SELECT OLIVE OIL • SELECT OLIVES[...]VINEGAR • CHOOSE PASTA • BUY TEA • BUY CO
REAL ALE • ORDER A COCKTAIL • CHOOSE A[...]STOCK A WINE CELLAR • STOCK YOUR BAR •
A MIDWIFE OR DOULA • PLAN A HOME BIRTH[...]R A NEW BABY • BUY A NEW COT • CHOOSE A P
CHILDCARE • FIND A GREAT NANNY • FIND T[...]TER-SCHOOL CARE • SIGN YOUR CHILD UP FOF
BUY BOOKS, VIDEOS AND MUSIC FOR YOUR[...]HIRE A TUTOR • ADOPT A CHILD • GET YOUR C
LTERED HOUSING • CHOOSE A CARE HOME[...]PLOT • PAY FOR FUNERAL EXPENSES • GET VIAG
TARY MTHERAPY • SEE A MENTAL-HEALTH P[...]BUY HOME-USE MEDICAL SUPPLIES • SELECT H
ST IMPLANTS • GET WRINKLE-FILLER INJECT[...]ACTITIONERS • CHOOSE A MANICURIST • GET W
A • BOOK A MASSAGE • GET ON ANTIQUES R[...]SHOP AT AN ANTIQUE FAIR OR FLEA MARKET •

Splurges &
Rare Events

• BUY SILVERWARE • EVALUATE CARNIVAL GLASS • BUY AND SELL STAMPS • BUY ANTIQUE FURNITURE • GET CLUED UP ON CLARICE C
S • SEIZE STAR WARS ACTION FIGURES • SELL YOUR VINYL RECORD COLLECTION • SELL TO A PAWNSHOP • BUY AND SELL COMIC BOC
PERIPHERALS • CHOOSE A LAPTOP OR NOTEBOOK COMPUTER • SELL OR DONATE A COMPUTER • BUY PRINTER PAPER • BUY A PRINTE
THE MEMORY IN YOUR COMPUTER • BUY COMPUTER SOFTWARE • CHOOSE A CD PLAYER • BUY BLANK CDS • BUY AN MP PLAYER • C
YOUR PHONE COMPANY • BUY VIDEO AND COMPUTER GAMES • CHOOSE A FILM CAMERA • CHOOSE A DIGITAL CAMCORDER • DECIDE
UY A SERIOUS TV • CHOOSE BETWEEN DIGITAL TV PROVIDERS • GET A DIGITAL VIDEO RECORDER • GET A UNIVERSAL REMOTE • BUY A
CHASE CHEAP AIRLINE TICKETS • FIND GREAT HOTEL DEALS • HIRE THE BEST CAR FOR THE LEAST MONEY • GET TRAVEL INSURANCE •
E UNITED KONGDOM • TIP IN A FOREIGN COUNTRY • TIP PROPERLY IN THE UK • BRIBE A FOREIGN OFFICIAL • GET AN INTERRAIL PASS •
HEAP BUT FANTASTIC SAFARI • RENT A CAMEL IN CAIRO • GET SINGLE-MALT WHISKY IN SCOTLAND • BUY A SAPPHIRE IN BANGKOK • HI
HIRE A TREKKING COMPANY IN NEPAL • RENT OR BUY A SATELLITE PHONE • BUY YOUR CHILD'S FIRST CRICKET BAT • ORDER A STRIP F
• BUY A RACKET • BUY A HEALTH CLUB MEMBERSHIP • BUY AN AEROBIC FITNESS MACHINE • BUY SWIMMING EQUIPMENT • BUY A JE
FTING EQUIPMENT • CHOOSE A CAR RACK • BUY SKIS • BUY CLOTHES FOR COLD-WEATHER ACTIVITIES • SELL USED SKIS • BUY A SNC
BUY THE OPTIMAL SLEEPING BAG • BUY A TENT • BUY A BACKPACK • BUY A CAMPING STOVE • BUY A KAYAK • BUY A LIFEJACKET • B
G • SELL USED CLOTHING • ORDER CUSTOM-MADE COWBOY BOOTS • BUY CLOTHES ONLINE • FIND NON-STANDARD SIZES • BUY THE
E • BUY A WOMAN'S SUIT • BUY A MAN'S SUIT • HIRE A TAILOR • BUY CUSTOM-TAILORED CLOTHES IN ASIA • BUY A BRIEFCASE • SHOF
OUT CLOTHES • BUY A HEART-RATE MONITOR • SELECT A WATCH • BUY KIDS' CLOTHES • CHOOSE CHILDREN'S SHOES • PURCHASE CL
A CAR • BUY A MOTORCYCLE • BUYING AND CHANGING MOTOR OIL• WASH A CAR • WAX A CAR • BUY CAR INSURANCE • SPRING FOR

91 Buy a Private Island

It used to be that only the rich and famous owned carphones and private atolls, but now everyone's got a mobile phone and islands can be purchased for less than a luxury car. It's no big deal at all – search for an island on the internet, contact its broker, fill out the paperwork, and voilà! Your own fantasy island.

Steps

1 Decide on location. In general, the colder the climate, the cheaper the island. A misty, rocky isle in northern Europe can be had for under £30,000, whereas a small tropical island might be seen as a snip at £500,000. Keep in mind that although you can buy an island, you can't rule it – every island for sale is part of a sovereign state, and you're subject to that country's laws.

2 Investigate what islands are on the market by searching websites such as Private Islands Online (privateislandsonline.com) or Vladi Private Islands (vladi-private-islands.de). Contact the owner or broker of each island and ask lots of questions: How isolated and accessible is it? Can it be developed? How are necessities supplied? What is the status of existing facilities and infrastructure for food and water, electricity and fuel?

3 Enquire about renting the island before you decide to buy it. You test-drive a car, so why not take the island for a spin? Many owners rent their island properties for part of a year, with prices ranging from around £600 for three days (Turneffe, Belize) to £4,750 a day (Little Whole Cay, Bahamas). A brief stay may show that your Robinson Crusoe fantasy isn't as romantic as it seemed.

4 Before finalising the purchase, check the ownership policy and political stability of the nation that governs the island. Make sure the government keeps a registry of deeds and guarantees unrestricted ownership. You don't want to lose your investment to a banana republic.

What to Look For

- Type and location of island
- Online island brokers
- Livability factors
- Rental options
- Stable government

Tip

An island broker can also arrange for a manager to safeguard your island while you're away.

Warning

Make sure that someone on the mainland knows where your island is and how long you intend to stay – it's not uncommon to be stranded on your own island.

Beware of global warming! If your island is a low-lying atoll, it may be scheduled to disappear beneath the waves in 50 years, taking your investment with it.

92 Write a Message in the Sky

If you're looking for an unusual way to make a *huge* impression on your special someone, the sky's the limit. Hot-air balloons offer an airborne banner to carry a message of love in letters the height of a house. And you can go for an intimate cruise in them as well.

Steps

1 Look for a service offering luxury balloon flights in the *Yellow Pages* or on the internet.

2 Ask the balloon company if they will fit banners with your personal message on the side of one of their balloons. Most companies

What to Look For

- Balloon flight service
- Simple, effective message

will. For example, Skypower (skypower.co.uk) will have a banner made to your specification for £800 – twice that to cover both sides of the balloon.

3   Compose a touching message for optimum impact, but keep it simple. If you're proposing, this task shouldn't be too difficult. There's nothing wrong with "I love you". Add some artwork ideas – hearts and Cupids rarely go amiss.

4   Book a champagne flight for two on the personalised balloon. This will cost another £600. Drift across the English countryside in blissful intimacy, sipping the fizzy stuff, while the banners above your head advertise your sentiments to the world.

93 Hire a Big-Name Band

So, your boss wants to book the hottest band in the land to impress the shareholders? Be prepared to cough up some serious cash if you're lucky or clever enough to break through to the appropriate agent and swing the deal.

Steps

1   Find out who represents the band or artist you want to hire. Plunge into the world of entertainment agencies on the internet. Some sites list agents (for example, singers-uk.org). Get on the phone and talk to people until you find the name and contact details you need.

2   Budget in excess of £100,000 for a one-time performance by a really big-name band. Costs include transport for the band and crew, accommodation and security.

3   Contact the agency or management company that represents the band you'd like to hire. If you're lucky enough to reach the band's agent or manager *and* find that the band is available when you need it, be prepared to discuss all relevant details including the nature of the event, date and time, venue, transport, security, publicity, insurance and cost.

4   Write up what the industry calls a *firm offer* based on details discussed in your phone conversation. The document (which can be considered legal) should be a one-page outline that summarises everything you would provide the band, as well as a deadline of no more than one week for the agent to respond to your offer. Fax the document directly to the agent.

5   Wait for the agent to review the terms of your offer with the artist and hope that it will be accepted.

6   Put your dancing shoes on.

Warning

Don't rely on a balloon flight to celebrate a birthday or other anniversary. Balloons are dependent on the weather and you may well not be able to make a flight on your day of choice.

What to Look For

- Entertainment agency websites
- Band's agent or management company

Tip

You have a much better chance of hiring a band that was famous in the 70s or 80s and is now struggling to find gigs. So why not get real and go for a blast from the past?

Warning

Even a verbal agreement may be legally binding. Be very clear about what you plan to do.

94 Get Into a Private Gambling Room in Las Vegas

The world's richest gamblers gravitate to a "high roller" room in Las Vegas and other private gaming tables at the world's top casinos. Because their credit line and bets are so huge, major casinos maintain a full-time staff just to lure these loaded leviathans.

Steps

1 Arrive with a massive bankroll. Becoming a *bona fide* "high roller" takes much more than betting big. The top gamblers – and there are only about 500 worldwide – need to have a credit line of £3 million to £4 million.

2 Make a name for yourself. Getting into the top flight of gambling is by invitation only. If you're worthy, then you won't even need to ask – the casinos will already know who you are and invite you and your family to stay and play as long as you like. Private jet transport, luxury accommodation, gourmet cuisine, free show tickets, expensive gifts, fine wines, butlers and chauffeurs are all on the house.

3 Gamble big – very big – around £100,000 per bet. Australian billionaire Kerry Packer, the world's highest-stakes gambler, bets up to £250,000 per hand while playing seven blackjack hands at a time. His losses once amounted to £13 million in a weekend. Do you still think you can swim with these sharks?

4 Master baccarat, the richest game in the casino and the one most often played in the private room. These are often no-limit games as maximum bets cramp a high roller's style.

What to Look For

- Seven-figure credit line
- Minimum £100,000 bets
- No-limit baccarat experience

Tips

If you're really trying to achieve world status as a gambler, play at Bellagio (bellagiolasvegas.com), which caters specifically to the richest of the rich.

About 85 per cent of the world's biggest gamblers are Asian, and 15 per cent are women.

Warning

Gambling can be addictive. Never gamble what you can't afford to lose.

95 Buy Someone a Star

It sounds romantic, doesn't it? Naming a star after your sweetheart, knowing that people will gaze upon it for eternity. As long as you're aware that official astronomical organisations will never recognise your star's name (and will laugh if you ask), it's your money to burn.

Steps

1 Be aware that no matter what claims a company makes, the star name you purchase and have registered has absolutely no validity among the scientific community, and will not be recognised by anyone else on the planet. Yes, it may be copyrighted, but you can copyright your grocery list. Sorry.

2 Search online for star-naming websites, such as International Star Registry (international-star-registry.org) or Star Listings (starlistings.co.uk). Pay from about £25 to £100 and you'll get a package that includes an official-looking parchment certificate with your star's name on it, a dedication date and telescopic

What to Look For

- Online star-naming companies
- Your star (look hard)

Tips

There is nothing to prevent a star-naming company from selling the same star to different people.

Do not embarrass yourself by asking an astronomer to point the telescope towards your star.

coordinates of the star and a chart with your star circled in red. You may also get an informative booklet with details of the constellations. As usual, you pay more for more in the package.

3 Conduct your own star search. Finding your star will probably be impossible without a telescope. Worse, the coordinates given by star-naming companies are often inaccurate. Most people who buy a star never actually see it.

4 Save your money. If you really want to name a star after someone, find a nice, twinkling star together (make sure it's not a planet or satellite), plot it on a star chart, name it, and print a certificate on fancy paper. It will be just as valid as the certificate from any commercial star-registry service.

Warning

Only the International Astronomical Union can officially name celestial bodies, and it names stars using catalogue numbers, not people's names. No private company has ever been given the authority to name stars.

96 Pay a Ransom

Many rebel factions and terrorist groups in unstable regions of the world consider kidnapping and extortion a customary means of earning revenue to support their cause. Organised crime also poses a potential threat, particularly to wealthy families. It is an unfortunate fact that very few kidnappings end with the safe release of the victim without a ransom being paid. If you're at risk, here's what to do.

Steps

1 Purchase a kidnap/ransom and extortion insurance policy to protect you, your family and your employees if you live, work or travel in a high-risk zone. Many insurance companies offer plans to cover a ransom, payment to informants, and other expenses such as medical and psychiatric care. Search online to find appropriate cover.

2 Insure your business as well as yourself: Both personal and corporate assets are at risk when kidnappers attempt to extort ransom money.

3 Call in local police to investigate in the event of extortion or a kidnapping. They will be able to add another layer of security and surveillance to the investigation process.

4 Contact specially trained experts, familiar with the local laws and the dynamics of kidnapping, to swiftly mobilise international resources. An expert may work with a private detective to analyse notes, set up a drop site for the demanded money, and protect the premises and the threatened individuals.

5 Check your policy in advance: If you have purchased kidnap or extortion insurance, a private detective and trained crisis-management experts may be covered.

What to Look For

- Kidnap/ransom and extortion insurance
- Police
- Trained experts
- Private detective

Tips

If you travel frequently to high-risk regions – Colombia, for example, which has a bad kidnapping record – insurance coverage could save your life.

Insurance companies can also assist with employee training to minimise losses due to kidnap or ransom.

Warning

Ransom demands are growing each year. Today, the average ransom demand in kidnappings is in excess of £400,000. In many cases, much more is demanded.

97 Get Hot Tickets

We feel your pain: Hot Chilli Peppers are in town and you can't find front-row tickets anywhere. Fret not, because those hard-to-get tickets – West End musicals, top Premiership games, Stones concerts, Formula One grand prixs, Wimbledon finals – are almost always available if you're willing to invest the time and the money. Here's how to dance the hot ticket tango.

Steps

1 Start with the least expensive ticket source, and move up from there if you have to. Call the venue directly or search one of the prime online ticketing sources, such as ticketmaster.co.uk or firstcalltickets.com. Or try lastminute.com. You might get lucky.

2 See if anybody in your town is trying to unload his or her choice seats at a reasonable price. Get today's local paper and look under "Tickets" in the classifieds section. Local online classifieds are a good source as well. If you are in London, visit the *Evening Standard* website at thisislondon.co.uk.

3 A bid on eBay.co.uk is another possible way to go, but it's not without risk (see 10 "Use Online Auction Sites") and is likely to be quite expensive.

4 Check out online concierge services, a route few people know about – for example, conciergedesk.co.uk. They will take the hassle of searching for tickets off your hands.

5 Arrive at the event early if you're desperate, with plenty of cash in hand to buy tickets from a tout – essentially a tax-free ticket broker *sans* office. If the price is too high, wait until the show is about to start. Touts still holding tickets at the last minute will usually unload them at very reduced rates.

What to Look For

- Primary ticket providers
- Local newspaper or online ads
- Online ticket brokers
- Online concierge services
- Touts

Tips

If you're staying at a hotel, ask the staff to help you with finding hard-to-get tickets. Be sure to tip well for the service.

Although it's illegal in most circumstances to resell tickets at higher than their face value, it's not illegal to purchase them.

Warning

Beware of counterfeit tickets, particularly from touts. It's very tough to distinguish the fakes from the real thing.

98 Hire a Limousine

So you drive an old Ford Escort. That's OK. As long as you have some money saved up for a night on the town, you can still play millionaire by hiring a limousine. In fact, due to fierce competition, you can ride in just about any type of stretch limo for a lot less than you'd expect.

Steps

1 Assess your finances. A standard stretch limousine (six to eight passengers) will set you back about £60 per hour; a larger version (eight to ten passengers) costs slightly more – about £70 per hour. Both usually have an hourly minimum of four to five hours (although this is often negotiable). For speciality limos such as a Mercedes, a Hummer or a superstretch (up to 24 passengers), expect to pay several thousand pounds for an outing.

2 Research, research, research. Be sure the limo operator is licensed and insured. Decide what type of limo you want and for how long, based on the event and the number of people in your party. List the amenities you're looking for, whether it's a bar, stereo, TV and DVD player, video-gaming system, intercom, sunroof, Jacuzzi, or all of that and a bag of crisps. Prices may or may not be posted online. You'll need to do some phone work to get the best deal.

3 Find out the year and make of the limo you'll be hiring, its condition, and the complimentary amenities before you give a deposit. Make sure the deposit is refundable if the limo doesn't meet with your satisfaction. Many limo companies will advertise one type of car and show up at your door with something entirely different. Most list photos of their limos on their websites. If quality is a top priority, plan a visit to the limo company and reserve the exact limo that suits your needs.

4 Employ a quality driver. This is crucial – a bad driver can ruin your evening. Make sure the drivers are experienced, professional and know the area. If possible, fax an itinerary to the company beforehand so the driver knows where he or she is going and what to expect. When the driver shows up, be sure to communicate any special needs you may have.

5 Be sure to ask whose responsibility it is to stock the limo with any necessary party treats ahead of time. Some companies will provide everything you need; others expect you to bring your own. Sometimes you can negotiate a lower rate if you offer to stock the bar yourself.

6 Find out if a tip for the driver is included in the rate; regardless, you'll be expected to give your driver something, so try to keep it separate if you can.

What to Look For

- Licensed operator
- Desired amenities
- Late-model limo
- Experienced, professional driver
- Ample party supplies

Tips

Make sure your limo is ample enough to fit everyone comfortably. If you have six passengers, get a car that accommodates eight.

If you want high-quality drinks, negotiate for them up front, or plan to bring your own.

Ask if smoking (or other activities) is allowed. Even if it's not, most drivers will look the other way if the price is right.

If it's truly a special occasion, don't be cheap. Like most things in life, you get what you pay for: Most upmarket limo companies have superior drivers, vehicles and accoutrements.

Try to clear everything with your driver in advance. He or she is your captain for the evening and can be your best friend or your worst nightmare.

Warning

Make sure the limo company and their drivers are properly licensed and insured when making your reservation. This will ensure you are dealing with a reputable company.

99 Buy a Cryonic Chamber

You may think that cryonic freezing – preserving deceased humans in the hope that they may be revived in the future through new medical technologies – is for weirdos and megalomaniacs. But since you can't take your money with you, why not place a bet on a long shot?

Steps

1 Visit alcor.org, the website of the US-based Alcor Life Extension Foundation, the world's largest provider of cryonics services. Also contact Alcor UK, a group of British cryonics enthusiasts, to discuss your options (020 7232 0558).

2 Choose between three modes of cryonic supension (all Alcor services are priced in US dollars): neuro-suspension, preserving the head only, will cost UK applicants $65,000; whole body suspension costs $135,000; neuro-suspension plus whole body suspension is $165,000.

3 Complete the membership application and pay the $150 sign-up fee and $398 for annual dues. Sign Alcor's legal membership documents in the presence of two witnesses.

4 Die. There is no legal precedent anywhere in the world allowing a cryonic procedure to take place before death.

What to Look For

- Alcor website
- Alcor UK
- Cryonic suspension type
- Membership fees and dues

Tip

Alcor have special arrangements with UK undertakers to shift your body to their American facility for cryonic treatment as quickly as possible after death.

100 Rent Your Own Hoarding

In Los Angeles, it's common for the almost-famous to rent a hoarding simply to advertise their silicone-and-plastic-enhanced selves. That may not be the British way, but you still might want thousands of motorists to take note of a cause dear to your heart.

Steps

1 Know that hoardings are sized by "sheets". The smallest is 6 sheets (1.2 m by 1.8 m/4 ft by 5 ft), while the standard large size is 48 sheets (3.1m by 6.2 m/10 ft by 20 ft).

2 Communicate your message in eight words or less. If the hoarding is near fast-moving traffic, the lettering should be at least 3 m (9 ft 9 in) high.

3 Know that the cost will depend on the size of the hoarding and its location. Roadside hoardings are normally rented out for two months at a time. You can rent a number of specific hoarding sites chosen by you (known as line-by-line rental) or a block of hoardings across a given area (campaign rental).

4 To mount a truly professional campaign, employ a creative agency and an outdoor buying specialist. Otherwise contact the media company that owns the hoarding (the owner's name is usually marked on a lower corner).

What to Look For

- Clear objective and message
- Suitable size
- Heavy traffic location

Tip

Contact the Outdoor Advertising Association of Great Britain (oaa,org.uk) for further useful information.

Warning

Tests show that hoardings motivate very few people to contact you unless you are giving away a gift or money.

101 Take Out a Full-Page Ad in *The Times*

Placing an advertisement in print media to promote a cause or a product is fairly easy, especially now that most daily newspapers are desperate for advertising revenue. Even if you want to go for something as grandiose as a full-page ad in *The Times,* all you need is plenty of spare cash to splurge.

Steps

1 Decide whether you want to handle placing the advertisement yourself. The alternative is to employ an advertising agency. They will take care of everything on your behalf, but obviously you will pay for the service. Know that it is perfectly possible to handle the process yourself, as the following steps show.

2 Decide where and when you would like your ad to appear. You can choose between *The Times* and *The Sunday Times,* and also between the different sections of these newspapers – main news, business, sport, and so on. Your choice will depend on your message and your target audience. Be aware that the choice will affect the price. The main news section is the most expensive for advertising. Specific placings within sections of the newspaper will also be more expensive than others.

3 Call *The Times*'s switchboard at 020 7782 5000 and tell the operator that you want to place a full-page ad. They will put you through to the advertising sales department.

4 Explain your wishes. Ask for details of the cost of different placings and other options. Be aware that a colour ad is more expensive than black-and-white. Expect to be quoted a price of around £25,000 for a full-page black-and-white ad in the main news section and over £40,000 for a colour ad.

5 Agree a date, placing and price. The advertising department will then book your space on their system.

6 Supply your financial details so the newspaper can bill you for pre-payment. This is a requirement for new clients.

7 Create the ad in accordance with the production specs provided by the newspaper's advertising department. You could do this yourself or, preferably, have a professional do it (see 158 "Hire a Graphic Designer"). Supply the ad in the electronic form specified by *The Times*.

What to Look For

- Advertising agency
- Choice of section
- Varying prices
- Production specs
- Pre-payment

Tip

If you make a bulk order, such as six ads through a week, the price per ad will drop significantly.

Warning

The Times will not run ads that offend against the rules laid down by the Advertising Standards Authority or that it feels are out of keeping with the tone of the newspaper. If the newspaper suspects that your advertisement could contain material that is excessively violent or sexual, or that could be misleading or inaccurate, they will ask to examine the text and images. They may ask for changes in wording or in the choice of pictures, or even refuse the ad altogether.

102 Employ a Butler

The traditional Jeeves-style manservant may have lost ground in recent years to "personal lifestyle managers", but fully trained butlers remain much in demand. Locating the right person for your butlering needs takes some time, energy and money, but you'll be thankful when your household runs like a well-oiled machine.

Steps

1 Be very clear what you expect your potential butler to do before you begin the search and interviewing process. Tasks include arranging dinner parties, looking after your yacht, making travel arrangements, maintaining the household budget, looking after visitors, doing the laundry, getting the children off to school, tending the garden and directing other workers in the household. Many butlers double as a personal assistant, handling correspondence and coordinating your calendar.

2 Estimate the time it will take to accomplish those duties. Could you hire a part-time butler or simply a personal assistant? Determine this in advance to find the appropriate person for the job and your budget.

3 Decide whether or not you want your butler to be an in-house resident. This will be determined by how much living space you have and how many hours of work you require. It's very important for the butler to fit in with your family or household. Reputable agencies coordinate extensive interviews between you and butler candidates before the butler is placed.

4 Analyse the costs. As well as the butler's salary, which may be in excess of £50,000, there are a host of hidden costs. These will probably include a search fee to the recruitment agency (a percentage of the butler's first annual gross salary); all the butler's travel-related expenses, including airline tickets, taxis or car rentals (one assumes you will have a second home abroad); employer's tax and national insurance; and a generous Christmas present to reward loyal service.

5 Contact a specialist organisation such as the Guild of Professional English Butlers (guildof butlers.com) or the Butler Bureau (butlerbureau.com), or a general domestic staff recruitment agency such as SLM (slmrecruitment.co.uk).

6 Search for a butler via local and national newspapers if you decide not to use an agency. Consider placing a personal ad in *The Times*, still the butler's favourite read.

What to Look For

- Expected duties and their duration
- Hidden costs
- Butlers' Guild or Butler Bureau
- Recruitment agency
- *The Times*

Tip

Recruitment agencies usually offer a free consultation without obligation.

Warning

If you don't want your butler to live in your house, it will still be your responsibility to pay for his accommodation and travel to and from your home, as well as any other work-related transport.

103 Buy a Football Club

Perhaps you're a football fan who dreams of owning the local team and propelling it to glory. Or you're rich and bored and fancy an exciting way of gambling with your money. Whatever tempts you to buy into football, make sure you can afford it. You may not need the £140 million Roman Abramovich paid for Chelsea, but it won't be cheap.

Steps

1 Make a fortune. To purchase a controlling share (51 per cent) of a professional football club, a prospective owner needs a net worth of millions of pounds. Even then, you'll almost certainly need to form a partnership with other potential buyers.

2 Look for teams that might be ripe for a takeover or available at a knock-down price. Gordon Gibb, a 26-year-old Scot, bought Bradford City for £1 in 2002 (although he was taking on £37 million in debts and had to pump around £2 million of his own money into the club almost immediately). If you want at all costs to buy your local team, wait for the right moment when the current ownership is vulnerable.

3 Consider the development potential of the club in relation to its debts. It may not be attracting enough support to cover the players' inflated wages, but at the same time have exploitable assets worth millions.

4 Establish whether the club owns its ground. If so, is it in a prime location? You could raise investment backing for your purchase bid by promising to sell off the ground for development and relocate the club to a remote suburb. If this promise becomes known, expect hate mail from the fans.

5 Arrange to meet the team's owners or creditors. Most football club negotiations are done at the dinner table or over drinks.

6 Employ a good PR firm to boost your image once the deal is done. Announce how much money you intend to put into the club and paint a rosy picture of your ambitions for the future. Meanwhile, quietly put a cap on wages and sell a couple of overpriced players to raise ready cash.

What to Look For

- Partial or full ownership
- Underachieving teams
- Informal negotiations

Warning

As the chairman, you'll find your reputation will be linked directly to your team's performance. Win the championship and you're a saint; sink to relegation and you're the fans' worst enemy.

104 Buy a Personal Jet

Ever since Bill Lear revolutionised the private aircraft market with the introduction of his Learjet 23 in 1964, corporate chief executives and wealthy travellers have been flying in style on their own jets. The business jet has become so common that most passengers are middle management types. In fact, it's now a buyer's market.

Steps

1 Do a cost-benefit analysis before you pay for a private jet. Aviation experts suggest that 350 to 400 hours of flight time a year usually justifies full ownership of a jet. Otherwise, you should consider fractional ownership or other ways of bagging a seat on a private flight when you need it (see Tips).

2 Consider the hidden costs. Along with a price tag that ranges from over £2 million to £30 million and up for a new private jet, take into account necessities such as insurance, fuel, catering and pilots – who are in short supply. Aircraft management companies will take care of these needs for about £70,000 to £150,000 a year, depending on the size and use of the jet.

3 Determine the size and flying range you'll need. Light jets (around £2.5 million to £6 million) can take five to eight passengers roughly 3,000 km (1,875 miles); mid-size executive jets (£6 million to £12 million) can take up to nine passengers from 3,000 to 5,000 km (1,875 to 3,125 miles); and large executive jets (£12 million to over £30 million) can carry twelve passengers around 6,500 km (over 4,000 miles). See the chart below for some specific models.

4 When you're ready to buy, contact private jet manufacturers and ask for aircraft specifications and pricing. Next, shop online via private jet dealers such as CharterAuction.com, which sells new and used jets, including repossessed aircraft at large discounts.

Tips

Consider fractional ownership: You purchase a share in a jet plane from a management company, then pay a monthly fee and hourly operations costs. On as little as four hours' notice, the management company sends out whichever jet is most conveniently located.

Alternatively, consider schemes through which you buy the right to a fixed number of hours a year on a fleet of jets – 100 hours is typical.

Warning

A used private jet may not be a great deal, because it may not comply with current stringent regulations. It could require several hundred thousand pounds and many months of repair time to bring the ageing jet up to standard.

AIRCRAFT	PRICE (millions)	RANGE (km/nautical miles)	SPEED (Mach)	LENGTH (m/ft)	CAPACITY (passengers)
Learjet 45	£6.5	3,889/2,100	.81	17.7/58	Up to 9
Boeing Business Jet	£32	11,482/6,200	.82	33.5/110	Up to 25
Cessna Citation X	£12	6,297/3,400	.92	22/72	Up to 10
Gulfstream V	£25	12,038/6,500	.87	29.3/96	Up to 19
Dassault Falcon 2000	£12	5,556/3,000	.85	20.1/66	Up to 12

105 Select a Classic Car

If you have the money, and you want to display it with taste and style, what could be better for your image than driving around in a car that's a design classic dripping with class? The question is, do you know the models to choose?

Steps

1 Try a car that's redolent of London in the Swinging '60s. There never has been a car more instantly recognisible or acclaimed then the Jaguar E-Type. As all models are now at least two decades old, buy one worked over by experts – for example, consider a purchase from the E-Type Centre (e-type.co.uk). Know that you'll turn every head in the street as you drive by.

2 Consider a Morgan Plus Eight. Here is a car built today that looks like a vehicle a racy Spitfire pilot might have driven to Biggin Hill in the Battle of Britain. Morgans are so equisitely handcrafted that you'll have to join a waiting list to buy a new one. You can be sure that you have a car with exclusivity as part of its appeal.

3 Look at a Triumph TR6 if you want to experience the days when driving was for fun. Definitely for the young (at heart), these small, nippy open-top 1970s sports cars are low on comfort but high on thrills – and always catch the eye. Check the internet for dealers; there is a healthy market in used TR6s.

4 Drive a car that Marilyn Monroe once owned. A late 1950s to early 1960s Ford Thunderbird is a car that makes you think you've stepped into an old Hollywood movie. Don't expect high performance, but you'll make an impression. Search the internet for used models. You may have to go to an American dealer.

What to Look For

- Classic car
- Dealer websites
- Spares and servicing
- Restoration service

Tip

If you can't afford to buy a classic car in pristine condition, consider buying up a semi-wreck and having it reconditioned. This is not cheap, but it can be cheaper.

Warning

Be aware that classic cars are unlikely to be fully reliable and may be short on comfort and/or safety features. Ensure that spares and specialist servicing are available in your area.

106 Acquire a Bodyguard

There are two reasons for hiring a bodyguard: You need protection or you want to look like someone who needs protection. If you're in the second group, simply locate a large guy with a suit, shades and one of those little ear radios. If you really need protection, read on.

Steps

1 Educate yourself about the range of available services. Bodyguards are more than big guys in suits. Top security professionals are likely to have specialised driving skills, weapons training, risk avoidance skills and medical training.

2 Look online for security services in the UK. The International Bodyguard Association–UK (ibauk.com) is one organisation that will discuss your security needs and provide trained bodyguards.

3 If you still feel unsafe, consider a new line of work – or new friends.

What to Look For

- Specific skills of security personnel
- Proper training

Tip

A good security company will offer training and advice for clients, to help understand potential risks and enhance your security.

107 Book a Luxury Cruise Around the World

Magellan led the first world cruise, and since then it's been the ultimate way to explore in luxurious comfort. Essentially you're a full-time passenger along a cruise line's entire seasonal route, staying on while most other passengers disembark after travelling a segment. On a typical three-to-four-month voyage, you may visit more than 50 seaports in dozens of countries.

Steps

1 Examine the chart opposite for examples of the kind of cruises currently on offer. Visit cruise ship company's websites to gather more details. Most world cruises depart from the United Kingdom in the winter and sail to tropical regions.

2 Decide how much you're willing to spend. At the bottom of the range, you can sail around the world for three months for as little as £9,000–£10,000, exploiting discounts and travelling in a shared inside cabin. If you want to travel in style, though, the price will be much, much higher – expect to pay in excess of £100,000 for a luxury suite on the *QE2*.

3 Check online brokers offering cruise bargains. Examples of such websites include cruisedeals.co.uk and cruiseplanners.co.uk. You will find others if you search around. Unlike virtually every other type of cruise, world cruises are rarely available at a discount at the last minute, but you never know your luck.

4 Book as far in advance as possible, at least six to eight months, to earn 30 per cent or more discount for early reservation and early payment. Cruise companies also offer loyalty discounts for repeat travel.

5 Plan carefully. Cruise cancellation penalties can be severe – typically a 100 per cent loss if you cancel 74 days or less prior to sailing. Trip cancellation and worldwide medical insurance are strongly recommended (see 434 "Get Travel Insurance").

6 Pack appropriately. The *QE2,* for example, hosts more than 50 formal evenings during its world cruise (see 65 "Buy or Rent Men's Formal Wear").

What to Look For

- Price level
- Early booking
- Travel cancellation insurance

Tip

Freighter travel offers the best world cruise value, with fares typically being from £50 to £100 a day lower than conventional cruise ship rates. The majority of freighter cruises range in duration from about 30 to 75 days (see 445 "Choose a Cheap Cruise").

COMPANY/ SHIP	DEPARTURE/ ARRIVAL	TRIP LENGTH	PORTS OF CALL
Cunard *Queen Elizabeth 2* (cunard.com)	Southampton	121 nights	New York, Caribbean, Acapulco, Los Angeles, Honolulu, Papeete, Moorea, Auckland, Sydney, Padang, Manila, Nagasaki, Osaka, Taipei, Hong Kong, Laem Chabang, Singapore, Colombo, Mumbai, Dubai, Cairo, Naples, Barcelona.
Fred Olsen *Black Watch* (fredolsen.co.uk)	Southampton	102 nights	Malaga, Valletta, Alexandria, Salalah, Mumbai, Cochin, Phuket, Singapore, Ho Chi Minh City, Cairns, Brisbane, Sydney, Noumea, Papeete, Balboa, Aruba, Bridgetown, Azores, La Coruña.
P&O *Aurora* (pocruises.com)	Southampton	80 nights	Madeira, Barbados, Aruba, Acapulco, San Francisco, Honolulu, Pago Pago, Auckland, Sydney, Brisbane, Darwin, Manila, Hong Kong, Singapore, Mumbai, Cairo, Athens, Lisbon
P&O *Adonia* (pocruises.com)	Southampton	100 nights	Majorca, Athens, Cairo, Salalah, Mumbai, Goa, Colombo, Phuket, Penang, Singapore, Laem Chabang, Vung Tao, Hong Kong, Manila, Kota Kinabalu, Brisbane, Sydney, Singapore, Kuala Lumpur, Maldives, Seychelles, Madagascar, Port Elizabeth, Cape Town, Dakar, Madeira

108 Buy a Ticket to Travel for a Year

Many people dream of taking a year out to see the world, whether it's before they settle down or after they retire. There are plenty of 12-month round-the-world flight deals that cater for this desire, but you need to choose the right one to meet your needs and itinerary.

Steps

1 Decide what places you really must see and where you want to spend time. Using an atlas, string your key places together to form a first sketch of a desired itinerary.

2 Work out how much you can afford to pay for an air ticket. Ensure that you take into account the other costs of a year's travel, including accommodation.

3 Look into different flight deals. Visit some of the many websites brokering round-the-world tickets, such as westernair.co.uk or travelbag.co.uk. They will present you with a range of options.

4 Know that tickets specify the maximum number of kilometres you can travel and the number of stopovers you can make. The more kilometres and stopovers, the higher the price. Expect to pay between £800 and £2,000 for a 12-month economy class ticket. For business or first class you will pay much more.

5 Try to book your ideal itinerary. You will probably find that you need to make changes and compromises to fit in with available routes – that flight from Djakarta to Sydney is just not available, or only by a circuitous route that will cost a hefty supplement.

6 Check the flexibility of the ticket. Do you have the option of changing your route once you are travelling? Can you easily change the dates of particular departures? Is backtracking allowed? Some tickets do not let you fly twice into the same airport. When you are satisfied, fix your route and book.

What to Look For

- Ideal itinerary
- Suitable price
- Websites advertising round-the-world deals
- Distance and number of stopovers
- Flexibility

Tips

Consider the right time to start your trip. Twelve-month tickets are cheaper if you start your journey outside the summer high season. But research weather conditions along your route to ensure you avoid the monsoon or other extreme weather.

Don't do all your travelling by air. Plan to make some stages of the journey overland for the view and the experience. There is no difficulty with flying in to one airport and out of another.

109 Book a Trip on the Orient-Express

Since 1883, when this fabled train made its inaugural journey between Paris and Istanbul, the Orient-Express has been synonymous with decadence, scandal and adventure. If you've always wanted to experience the romantic era of deluxe rail travel, here's your ticket to ride.

Steps

1 Choose which area you want to tour. The Orient-Express company operates privately owned, custom-built trains in the UK, continental Europe and southeast Asia.

2 Choose a route. Some routes are only one-way, some offer a return option, and some are Grand Tours ending up where you started. Meals, tea and coffee are included, as are hotel

What to Look For

- Destination
- Route
- Glamour
- Intrigue

Tip

The butler did it.

accommodation and guided tours during stopovers. Fares are per person and based on double occupancy of a compartment. Private compartments are available for an additional fee.

3 Book your trip at Orient-Express.com or through a travel agent. If you've chosen a one-way Orient-Express route, it's usually a good idea to have a travel agent arrange your holiday around the railway ride, including airline flights and hotel accommodation after the rail trip is ended.

Warning

It is the passenger's responsibility to ensure that he or she complies with visa and vaccination requirements.

ROUTE	LENGTH OF TRIP	PRICES
Venice Simplon Orient-Express		
London–Paris–Venice (and vice versa)	2 days/1 night	£1,310 (£1,900 return)
London–Paris–Venice–Rome	3 days/2 nights	£1,475
Venice–Rome	1 day	£325
Venice–Vienna–London	5 days/4 nights	£1,465
Venice–Prague–Paris–London	5 days/4 nights	£1,600
Paris–Budapest–Bucharest–Istanbul (and vice versa)	6 days/5 nights	£3,615
British Trains		
Grand Tour of Great Britain: London–York–Edinburgh–Oban–Chester–Bath–Wells–London	7 days/6 nights	£2,850
Northern Belle	Day trips and weekend outings	£170 to £595
British Pullman	Day trips	£150 to £270
Eastern & Oriental Express (Singapore, Malaysia and Thailand)		
Singapore–Bangkok (and vice versa)	3 days/2 nights	£960 to £1,930
Singapore–Bangkok–Chiang Mai	7 days/6 nights	£1,140 to £2,210
Bangkok–Chiang Mai	2 days/1 night	£560 to £1,020
Bangkok–Chiang Mai–River Kwai–Bangkok	3 days/2 nights	£780 to £1,580
Singapore–Bangkok–Chiang Mai–River Kwai–Bangkok	8 days/7 nights	£1,590 to £3,220

All prices are per person, double occupancy of a cabin, for 2004. Prices for the Eastern & Oriental Express vary according to the standard of occupation. The low figure is a standard Pullman compartment, the high figure for the Presidential suite.

110 Own a Vineyard

There are many ways to make a fortune, but buying a vineyard in the UK is not likely to be one of them. Although global warming has recently helped turn parts of England and Wales into wine-producing areas for the first time in over 1,000 years, making a living at the business in Britain requires skill, dedication and a dose of luck.

Steps

1 Research what's involved with winemaking. Buy all the books you can on the subject and study them carefully. Become fully informed on growing vines, grape varieties, every aspect of the production process and the wine market.

2 Take stock of your assets and your determination. Producing quality wines year after year takes expertise in microbiology, agronomy, marketing, enology and machine repair, or the time and money to hire experts. Winemaking is hard work regardless of whether it turns a profit and requires 100 per cent determination and dedication.

3 Decide whether you want to buy an existing operation. There are about 380 vineyards in the UK, so each year a number come up for sale. Know that buying an existing vineyard gives you vines, equipment and facilities already in place, and established distribution and sales networks. It also limits your own choices – you mostly have to go along with the grape varieties and methods you acquire – and may land you with a business that is not going well, hence the sale.

4 Consider creating a vineyard from scratch. You will be able to build the business you want. However, you will need the expertise to buy the right land for the vines you are to grow and you will have to survive without an income for five to seven years while you wait for the first saleable vintage.

5 Do your sums with utmost care. If you are buying an existing vineyard, scrutinise the books. Work out realistically how much profit you expect to make on what volume of sales. Then halve that figure. If you think you can survive on the halved estimate, you are probably looking at a going concern.

6 Consider whether there is potential for growth. You may feel that too big an operation would overstretch you, but experience shows it is easier to make a vineyard survive as a business if it grows in scale.

7 Decide whether you have the expertise to handle all aspects of the business. If not, factor in the cost of experts or consultants you will have to employ.

What to Look For

- Expertise in winemaking
- Existing business or site for new vineyard
- Reasonable profit margin
- Room for expansion
- Ancillary money-making activities

Tips

To grow grapes successfully in Britain you will need a sheltered, south-facing slope with well-drained soil.

Know what grape varities are appropriate to British conditions. The EU has drawn up a list of six grape varieties "recommended" for the UK, plus 12 others "authorised" and 18 others "provisionally authorised".

8 Investigate all the possible ways of making money through side-line activities. Could you set up a restaurant or shop attached to the vineyard, or run tours of the vineyard for visitors? If so, will you employ staff or do all the work yourself?

9 Join the UK Vineyards Association to meet other people in the same business. Exchange information and share grumbles.

10 Know that you will be heavily dependent on the weather. A poor harvest through wet overcast conditions can cut your income drastically. Pray for warmth and sunshine.

Warning

Expect sales to plummet due to numerous uncontrollable variables: poor weather, disease, infestation, the economy – the list goes on.

111 Buy a Greyhound to Race

Greyhound racing is a vibrant sport to follow, and what could give it more excitement than racing your own animal? Buying and racing a greyhound is neither prohibitively expensive nor difficult to do.

Steps

1 Go to your local stadium and watch some races. Decide what kind of race you want your greyhound to excel in. Are you looking for a sprinter quick out of the traps with good early pace, or a stayer who will win 800 m (½ mile) "marathons"?

2 Take some other fundamental decisions. Do you want to be sole owner or are you going to form a syndicate with friends or family to buy the greyhound? What is your budget?

3 Know that the cheapest option is to buy an untrained puppy, available from £300 to £1,000, depending on breeding. However, be aware that buying a puppy is a risky option for a beginner. You will be a poor judge of breeding. Many puppies never make it to race.

4 Contact the racing manager at your local stadium. He will put you in touch with trainers attached to the track. The trainers will have greyhounds for sale or will look for a suitable animal once you have explained your budget and other preferences.

5 Be aware that the price of a decent racing greyhound begins at around £1,500. The top dogs in the country change hands for in excess of £20,000, but £5,000 buys a classy greyhound.

6 Take into account the cost of keeping a greyhound in training. Expect to pay around £5 a day, plus vet's bills, which can be substantial.

What to Look For

- Sprinter or stayer
- Local trainer
- Training costs
- Retired Greyhound Trust

Tip

Bitches are cheaper than dogs. This is because bitches are forbidden to race for ten weeks after they come into season, an event that occurs about every six months. However, the enforced rest can improve performance, and bitches can be used for breeding after retirement.

Warning

You are responsible for the welfare of the animal when its racing days are over. Either care for it as a pet or find a suitable home. Contact the Retired Greyhound Trust (retiredgreyhound.co.uk) for advice.

112 Buy a Racehorse

Fantasising about seeing your colours on the next Red Rum? Eager for the excitement of a gamble? Owning a racehorse is an exhilarating, rewarding pursuit if you know how to play the game. And it need not be beyond your purse, as long as you know what you are doing.

Steps

1 Decide whether you want to opt for sole ownership or some form of co-ownership. A sole owner will probably need to find at least £5,000 to £10,000 to buy a half-way decent racehorse, and more than that annually for its upkeep.

2 If you opt for co-ownership with friends or family, choose between the different options. A syndicate of up to twelve people can share ownership of a racehorse. Up to 20 people can form a racing partnership, in which two members are registered as the official owners.

3 Consider all the costs before you take the plunge. Expect to spend around £12,000 annually to keep a horse in training. Costs include training expenses, veterinary charges and food, including dietary supplements to keep your horse in top racing condition.

4 Be clear about what kind of horse you want to own. Are you interested in flat racing or National Hunt racing, for example?

5 Decide if you have the knowledge to buy your own horse or if you need help. Unless you know a great deal about buying racehorses, employ a trainer or a bloodstock agent, who will offer advice and recommend horses that meet your budget. The British Horseracing Board (britishhorseracing.com) has a directory of trainers. The Federation of Bloodstock Agents has names of reputable agents.

6 Choose a trainer with great care. He or she will be the key person in the success or failure of your racing enterprise. Some trainers interested in serving private syndicates have websites you can visit. Ensure you meet a number of trainers face to face before committing yourself. Ask how easily you will have access to your horse at the stables – there is not much point in owning a horse and not being allowed to see it when you want.

7 Be aware that racing is a strictly regulated sport. You will need to cope with bureaucratic procedures. Register your horse with the Jockey Club. Apply for colours – the same brightly coloured racing silks must be worn every time a jockey rides your horse.

What to Look For

- Bloodstock agent and trainer
- Total cost of ownership
- Sole ownership versus co-ownership
- Registration of horse and racing colours

Tips

Draw up a written agreement for co-owners of the racehorse, even if they are friends or family. Specify how much each person is to contribute each month, and deal with issues such as what happens if someone fails to pay on time.

Consider sponsorship as an aid to financing racehorse ownership. Add the logo of a company to your colours and recoup some cash even without winning races.

Contact the British Horseracing Board for details of ownership seminars.

8 Consider joining a professionally-managed racing club or syndicate. These advertise in the *Racing Post* or on websites. Shop around, contacting numerous syndicates or clubs before you invest. Joining an existing set-up is the most practical entry to racehorse ownership if you don't have a lot of money or time to cope with regulations. A managed syndicate will typically require you to invest a lump sum of £1,000 or more up front and then make a monthly payment of £100 to £150. This could give you a part share in two or three horses – and in their winnings.

VENUE	DETAILS
Yearling Race or Training Race	• Yearling sales take place at races from August to October. Training sales are held at Newmarket in October. • All horses running are for sale. Prices can be very high. Yearlings will probably average £10,000, but top horses sell for over £1 million.
Bloodstock Auction	• Horses usually grouped by type being sold: yearlings, horses in training, point-to-point, or breeding stock. • Horses are listed in auction sales catalogues, with family tree and date of birth (if horse is a yearling). • Employ a bloodstock agent or trainer to help.
Private Purchase	• Easiest way to purchase a horse. • Horse sold to you directly from a stud at negotiated price. • Lets you get the best possible advice from trainer or bloodstock agent before you buy.
WARNING	When you buy a racehorse at a yearling race or auction, be prepared to pay for, insure, transport and house the horse immediately after the race or at the auction's fall of hammer.

113 Buy a Villa in Tuscany

So you want to become one of the lucky people who owns a romantic villa in "Chiantishire". Well, thousands of Brits have done it, but that doesn't mean that it's altogether simple. Buying any home is a complicated process, but buying one in a foreign country is a recipe for disaster unless you do your homework.

Steps

1 Decide exactly where in Tuscany you want to buy your villa based on careful research over the course of many trips to the region. The most common complaint among foreign home-owners about buying a Tuscan villa is that they didn't do enough research and regret the location they chose. Where are the local airports and stations? Is the area accessible in harsh winters? What are the locals like? Make sure that you love the locality and your neighbours just as much as the house.

2 Work out the exact type of villa you want and how much property you're willing to take on. Consider how much land you want to maintain, who will maintain it while you're away, and how much living space you need to be comfortable.

3 If your estate agent asks you to, sign the *Proposta irrevocabile d'acquisto,* once you've found your dream villa and you're ready to make an offer. Although this means *irrevocable proposal of purchase,* it's not a binding document and doesn't mean you've reserved the villa even though there's been an offer price and a written acceptance by the seller. This piece of paper is only enforceable between the seller and the estate agent.

4 Sign the *compremesso,* the first of two binding contracts you enter with the seller once you've agreed on a price. The *compremesso* is basically a proof of intention to buy the villa and is binding in a court of law. It includes information such as the seller and the buyer, description of the property to be sold, the price, and the date of the final contract, or *rogito.* Once you and the seller have signed the *compremesso,* you are committed by law to the transfer of the property. You may still withdraw, but at the risk of losing your deposit.

5 Obtain a *codice fiscale,* or tax code, which you need in order to pay tax on the building. The *codice fiscale* works just like a National Insurance number and is easy to apply for.

6 Autograph the *rogito,* pop the cork and let the *vino* flow! This final contract is a legally binding document that requires the presence of a *notaio,* or notary public, to oversee the signing of the *rogito* (describes the property and land) and collect tax on the property. The *rogito* also includes the date of the sale, name of the seller, the new buyer (that's you), and the declared value of the property.

What to Look For

- Location, location, location
- Desired type and size of villa
- *Proposta irrevocabile d'acquisto* (purchase proposal)
- *Compremesso* (preliminary contract)
- *Codice fiscale* (tax code)
- *Rogito* (final contract)
- *Notaio* (notary public)

Tip

If you don't speak Italian, you can have a *scrittura privata,* or simplified version of the contract, read aloud by the notary and directly interpreted by a representative.

Warning

Within the time limit that is stipulated in the *proposta irrevocabile d'acquisto,* if the estate agent is approached by another buyer who makes a better offer for the same property, the agent can make another "irrevocable proposal to buy" for the same property without your knowledge, even though doing that isn't considered respectable.

114 Employ a Personal Chef

A personal chef can be a godsend to those with a full and busy life. You could hire one to help you eat better or lose weight, to avoid doing food shopping, or simply to save time spent cooking. But the best part is the quality of the food – there's always some gourmet snack in the freezer just waiting to be reheated.

Steps

1 Know the difference between a personal chef and a private chef. The former serves several clients, usually one per day, and often provides multiple meals that are stored and frozen for the week. The latter is usually a live-in employee who prepares up to three meals per day.

2 Determine what your weekly budget is for your personal chef. He or she may typically charge around £125 a day, to which you need to add VAT, the cost of ingredients and travel expenses. Prices vary widely depending on the region and level of service that is desired.

3 Decide exactly what you'd like your chef to do. Some stock the freezer with a number of meals for the week. Others bring their own pots, pans and utensils while preparing your dishes on-site.

4 Begin your search online or in your local newspaper. Visit websites such as home-cooking.co.uk for the contact details of personal chefs in your area.

5 Be sure that your chef not only meets your culinary requirements but also has a disposition that fits well with you and your family, since he or she will become a regular in your home. And don't hesitate to ask for references.

6 Tell your personal chef what your likes and dislikes are as well as any individual dietary requirements, and specific requests so that he or she can plan your menu accordingly. Have your chef submit menus for your approval, and ask if packaging, labelling and storing frozen dishes are all features included in the agreed-upon price.

What to Look For

- Rates and services
- Packaged meals
- Cooking equipment
- Websites listing personal chefs
- References
- Menu requests

Tip

As well as regular home cooking, personal chefs will prepare food for dinner parties, usually including themed meals.

Warning

Make sure that your personal chef is fully insured in the unfortunate event that he or she causes injury to you or your family.

115 Buy a Journey into Space

American businessman Dennis Tito opened a new era in April 2001 when he became the world's first space tourist, paying for a round trip to an orbiting space station. You could join the elite group of humans who have left the Earth's atmosphere – currently less than 500 people have had that experience. All you need is time and loads of money.

Steps

1 Understand what is involved in travel to space. You will need to train as an astronaut or cosmonaut does. This will require roughly six months of your time, to be spent at the Gagarin Cosmonaut Training Centre at Star City, Russia.

2 Consider whether you are fit enough for the severe physical demands of training and the flight itself – you will need to pass rigorous medical tests.

3 Look on the internet for a travel company offering space trips. Space Adventures Ltd (spaceadventures.com) are the prime organisers of space tourism, but check out other companies such as Incredible Adventures (incredible-adventures.com).

4 Expect to pay around £12 million for training, launch from the Baikonur Cosmodrome aboard a Russian Soyuz space vehicle, a two-day flight to the International Space Station (ISS), about 100 orbits on board the ISS, and the trip back to Earth.

5 Consider other options if £12 million is unfortunately a little beyond your budget. The same space travel companies will offer an experience of zero gravity through a parabolic freefall flight in an aircraft for about £3,500. For a flight to the edge of space on board a modified Russian MiG-25 supersonic fighter, expect to pay around £7,500.

6 Bide your time if you don't have the money for space travel at present. Astronaut Buzz Aldrin, the second man to walk on the Moon, is confident that "space hotels" will be orbiting the Earth with a regular complement of holidaymakers on board within 20 years. So prices are likely to fall.

What to Look For

- Space travel agency
- Cosmonaut training programme
- Soyuz flight and space station orbits
- Zero-gravity flight
- Flight to edge of space

Tip

If £12 million seems a bit steep for an eight-day holiday, reassure yourself with the thought that the holiday involves travelling 4–5 million km (around 3 million miles) – so it works out at about £3 a kilometre.

Warning

Space travel is very unsafe by the standards we are used to in everyday life on Earth – compared, say, with air travel or motoring. Two Space Shuttles have been lost, for example, in little over 100 missions. Space travel is for risk-takers only.

116 Employ a Ghostwriter to Write Your Memoirs

Everyone tells you to write a book about your life because it would make a phenomenal story. You would, but your writing skills aren't up to it. Time to hire a ghostwriter to weave your stories, diaries and research into a bestseller with your name on the cover.

Steps

1 Find a ghostwriter. Search the author database of the Society of Authors (societyofauthors.org). Look in the classified ads of publications such as *The Bookseller*. Or try contacting literary agents, listed in the *Writers' and Artists' Yearbook*.

2 Get an estimate of the costs as well as how long the project will take. Your ghostwriter will charge either a fixed fee, or per 1,000 words (typically £100–£200 per thousand), or a fee plus a royalty on future sales (if the writer thinks your memoirs are publishable). The writer will charge more if he or she has to carry out research.

3 Be sure to check the credentials of the ghostwriter you're considering and ask for references. Legitimate freelancers will be happy to provide this information. Scrutinise samples of the ghostwriter's published material and check to see if it meets the quality and style that you're looking for. Talk with previous employers.

4 Realise that as you investigate ghostwriters, they will also be evaluating whether they can work with you and whether writing your memoirs is even worth the effort. If you can't relate well to a ghostwriter during initial meetings or conversations, you may be better off parting ways.

5 Make clear at the outset if you want the ghostwriter's help to create a book proposal and pitch it to an agent or a publishing house. It's usually not the ghostwriter's job to get your memoirs published – just to write them (see 164 "Hire a Literary Agent").

6 Ask your writer to send you an outline of contents and a sample chapter so you can be sure that he or she has a good grasp of the project before you sign a contract. Ghostwriters may expect a partial fee for an outline and sample text.

7 Establish in the contract if you want sole authorship (where the ghostwriter receives no credit or mention at all). This is crucial for avoiding future misunderstandings and lawsuits.

8 Have a publisher, acquisitions editor or lawyer examine the contract for you on *your* behalf before you sign it. Remember, what is not in the contract is as important as what is in it.

9 Give your ghostwiter all the materials that you possess on the subject, and as many interviews as needed once the contract is signed.

What to Look For

- Authors' database
- Time and cost estimates
- Credentials and references
- Compatibility
- Outline and sample chapter
- Contract

Tips

Bringing in a ghostwriter during the early stages of a project often shortens the process.

Ghostwriters not only write, they also edit, collaborate and research on behalf of the client. Sometimes they write nothing at all and simply coach.

To help you develop your storytelling skills, see if your ghostwriter is willing to coach you in the areas where you're weakest. It may cost you more, but you'll learn faster with this type of constructive criticism.

Warning

The ghostwriter may expect phone, postage and other minimal petty-cash expenses to be paid by you.

117 Commission Original Artwork

Although there are many artists who produce commissioned art – from family portraits to custom-made wedding rings – finding just the right artist for the job is the most important and the hardest step.

Steps

1 Determine what media you're interested in (painting, sculpture, film) and the project's budget before you begin searching for an artist (see 118 "Immortalise Your Spouse in a Sculpture"). You'll find out quickly whether you can afford a well-known and established artist or a less expensive, emerging one.

2 Search for an artist through art agencies, art dealers and galleries, the internet and personal references. Beyond aesthetic considerations, look for an artist who will listen to your ideas, follow your direction and clearly understand what you want the finished piece to look like.

3 Once you've identified an artist who is willing and able to work with you, set a date to hold a planning session and begin to write down as many ideas and detailed descriptions about the commissioned piece as possible.

4 Create an agenda for the meeting that will ultimately become a creative brief. Include as many details as possible in your discussion. What is the piece for? How large will it be? What format? Are there specifications that need to be met? This will help guide you and the artist through the meeting and ensure that you express all your ideas and concerns. The more successfully you and the artist communicate with each other, the more closely your expectations will be met.

5 Be sure to have a commission contract drawn up and signed before further work is done. This legally binding contract should include details regarding the following: preliminary designs, payment schedule, completion date, insurance, shipping and installation, termination agreements, ownership and copyright, alterations and maintenance, contact information, and the state in which the work is produced.

6 Schedule a review of preliminary sketches as the artist begins the project. A commissioned artist must be open and willing to follow your direction. At the same time, you're paying for his or her talent and vision. Don't consistently squelch his or her creativity merely to stay in control of the process. This is a collaborative process, not a win-or-lose proposition.

7 Review the sketches thoroughly at each review stage in the process and be honest in your assessments. Carefully examine the finished piece and give it your final approval. Remember to get the artist's certificate of authenticity and any other documentation that he or she may provide.

What to Look For

- Art agencies
- Art dealers and galleries
- Commission contract
- Preliminary sketches
- Artist's certificate of authenticity

Tips

Depending on the complexity of the work and the budget, you may ask the artist for a second, more refined series of sketches to solidify a direction or narrow the choices. The artist should not begin work on the final piece until he or she is completely clear on every aspect of the project.

If the subject can be studied in person, allow the artist to do so as much as he or she likes. This will help the artist capture nuances and contours that photographs are rarely able to convey.

Warning

If the commission is extensive, complicated and/or involves several artists, you should probably hire a professional art consultant to manage the project.

118 Immortalise Your Spouse in a Sculpture

Now here's a gift for the person who thinks he or she has everything. Nothing says "I love you" like a timeless, original, full-size bronze likeness of your beloved. The result is certain to be a conversation piece like no other. But first you need to take some action.

Steps

1 Take the time to interview as many scupltors as possible; commissioning the right artist is critical. The interviewing process will allow you and your spouse to see the differences in style and technique, and also help define what you're looking for. You may even look into hiring an outside consultant, who has far more resources, to find the perfect sculptor for the job.

2 Contact your artist of choice by e-mail or telephone to discuss your initial ideas, requirements, completion date and price. The size, materials, weight, base and a horde of other factors will affect the final price. If the price is too steep, consider emerging artists; they may not charge as much but may still produce excellent work.

3 Make an initial appointment with the artist, which usually lasts for about an hour, and ask your spouse to attend. Specify to the artist exactly what you want the sculpture to look like, including posture and attitude. The artist will take photos and measurements of your spouse, discuss the angle and mood, and may even create a mask of your spouse's head to work with.

4 Draw up a formal commission contract, which the artist will probably supply. The first payment – commonly one-third of the total fee – is usually due upon signing the contract. Details such as size, materials, base, completion date, schedule of payments and sitting sessions should be stipulated.

5 Pay the second instalment before the artist creates the mould. At this point discuss colour, if that's an option, and decide how the piece will be mounted. The artist will then rework the piece with wax for the fine details, finalise the patination (colouring of the bronze), then put it on its base.

6 Return to the studio when the piece is being finalised for any final touch-ups. Most sculptures take four or five sittings to perfect. The sculpture is not complete until you and the artist are completely satisfied with the likeness and mood of the piece.

What to Look For

- Sculptor
- Commission contract
- Payment schedule
- Size, materials and base
- Preliminary sitting
- Patination
- Subsequent sittings

Tips

Many sculptors are willing to travel, so if you find one with a phenomenal reputation but outside your local area, ask if the artist will come to you for the project.

In addition to bronze, take a look at stone, onyx and the many resin castings available.

119 Give Away Your Fortune

Giving away a lot of money isn't as easy as it seems. In fact, most wealthy philanthropists probably had an easier time acquiring their fortune than giving it away. Deciding who gets what is the tough part. Once you've made that decision, the following information may make the ways in which you

VEHICLE	WAYS TO GIVE	BENEFITS OF GIVING
Property	If you own property that is fully paid off and has appreciated in value, you can donate it to a charity as an outright gift. It can sometimes be the simplest solution, with many tax benefits.	• You get to deduct the fair market value of your charitable gift against tax, avoid all capital gains taxes, and remove that asset from your taxable estate. • If you make a gift of property to your children or other individuals, the gift will be liable to inheritance tax if you die within seven years.
Cash	The simplest way to give away your fortune is to make a cash gift to an individual or worthy cause. The tax implications are much simpler as well.	• You can deduct a cash gift to charity from your taxable income. Under the Gift Aid scheme, you can give the charity the benefit of the standard rate tax relief, while keeping higher rate tax relief for yourself. • Again, inheritance tax applies if you die within seven years of making a large cash gift to family or friends. The maximum gift allowable is £3,000 a year.
Shares	If the shares or unit trusts you purchased over a year ago are now worth more than you paid for them, you can donate them to charity on advantageous terms.	• You will avoid the capital gains tax on the appreciation of the assets and get income tax relief on the sum donated. Your income tax deduction is based on the appreciated shares' full fair market value when you donate the shares.
Trust	Setting up a trust is recognised as a highly tax-effective way of passing on your wealth to your children or other relatives. A charitable trust is a similar vehicle for donating to charity. Consult a financial adviser if you want to adopt this option.	• Trusts give you more control over the provision of money to your eventual inheritors or to charities than would be the case with an outright gift, while also providing potential for maximising tax relief.

donate your fortune a bit easier, particularly in the tax arena. Always seek the advice of a lawyer, tax professional and/or investment professional when making plans for a large donation (see 127 "Choose a Financial Adviser").

VEHICLE	WAYS TO GIVE	BENEFITS OF GIVING
Bequests	Charitable bequests are easy to make since there are no complex rules. You can name a beneficiary in your will in two ways. Either you make a specific bequest of a cash sum or property to a cause, or you bequeath the remainder of your estate after other specific bequests and administrative costs have been paid. The latter is called a residuary bequest.	All charitable bequests are free of inheritance tax. You can also leave money to a charitable trust, if you have one, free of tax.
Art Bequest	When you die, leave a work of art or other item of historical or aesthetic interest or value to a museum or similar institution. It is important to ensure that the museum actually wants your bequest.	Leaving an art object to a museum or gallery is more efficient in terms of inheritance tax than bequeathing the value of the object in cash. The fact of your generosity will also be publicised in information that accompanies the work on display.
Endowments	An endowment guarantees a perpetual flow of money to any cause you wish to support. The endowment capital sum, or principal, can never be touched but spins off interest to provide funding to support medical research or the arts, provide athletic or academic scholarships, finance scientific research or fund a non-profit foundation. The institution that benefits from the endowment has a responsibility to invest the money wisely, maintain the long-term value of the fund, and direct the resulting funds precisely as the donor requests.	Have yourself, your spouse, your dog, your best friend, or your hero remembered with a financial award (the Bob Smith Literary Prize), a scholarship (the Bob Smith Scholarship Fund), or a facility of some kind (the Bob Smith Library). You get to say exactly how you wish the funds to be used. While institutions clearly prefer broad discretion in directing the funds, you can be as specific as you want.
WARNING	Without a will, you are powerless over how your assets are distributed after your death (see 344 "Write a Living Will").	

120 Hire an Expert Witness

If you're in serious trouble with the law, you'll not only need the best lawyer you can afford, you may also need to hire expert witnesses to testify on your behalf. If you're representing yourself (never a smart move) or want to be more involved in your lawyer's selection of expert witnesses, the following steps may be helpful.

Steps

1 Decide on the type of expert you need. Does the case involve medical issues? Advanced technology? An expert witness referral service such as Expert Witness (expertwitness.co.uk) can pair you up with the right person. Or try contacting the Expert Witness Institute (ewi.org.uk).

2 Contract the expert as a consultant and then determine whether or not you want him or her to testify at trial. Realise that as long as the expert is a consultant, his or her work is confidential.

3 Know that when the expert's name is disclosed as a potential witness in the matter, his or her prior work becomes subject to examination. Be sure that your expert's track record will stand up to close scrutiny.

4 Expect to pay expert witnesses on an hourly basis. The wide range of rates from under £50 to over £500 an hour is determined by your needs.

5 Decide just how much information you want to give the witness about the case, and explain in detail the exact issue or issues that you'll need addressed. An aggressive expert who asks to review any and all case materials could easily become party to facts that are potentially damaging to your case.

6 Provide the expert with the expected trial or deposition dates as early as possible and define the time commitment needed.

7 Let your expert know that you expect nothing but honest answers both before and during the trial.

What to Look For

- A good lawyer
- Expert witness referral service
- Appropriate expert
- Appropriate fee
- Time commitment

Warning

Avoid experts who want to direct the case or who seem to be tailoring their answers to fit what they think you want. These experts often lack credibility.

121 Make Money from Accident Compensation

Every year thousands of people turn misfortune into cash by going to court to seek compensation for various kinds of injury. The rise of "no-win-no-fee" lawyers has taken most of the financial risk out of legal action. Adopt the right approach and that stumble over a cracked paving stone could land you in the money.

Steps

1 Decide whether you are in a position to make a claim for accident compensation. Ask yourself whether you have suffered any kind of injury in the last three years in an incident that was not your fault. If so, was someone else to blame through their negligence or incompetence?

2 Consider all forms of injury. Whiplash as a result of a car crash is obvious, but what about that occasion when you twisted your ankle stepping into a pothole? This could be negligence on the part of those responsible for keeping roads free of potholes. Do not forget accidents at work – potentially your employer's responsibility. Medical negligence, involving failure by a doctor or dentist to provide you with the best treatment, can also lead to a successful compensation claim.

3 Look for a specialist solicitor to assess your legal position. Look in the *Yellow Pages* under "Solicitors" or "Compensation Claims", or search on the internet. You will find dozens of national and local organisations specialising in accident compensation. Some are groups of solicitors, others management companies that put you in touch with solicitors.

4 Make some phone calls and visit some websites. The National Accident Helpline (0800 376 0146) or the Accident Compensation Information Service (accident-compensation-information.co.uk) are possible starting points among many.

5 Know that you are looking for a service that is absolutely free and without risk. Conditional fee arrangements ("no-win no-fee") are almost universal. Be aware that this only means you do not pay the solicitor if you lose your case. You may still have to pay him if you win – for example, a percentage of your compensation. And you may be liable for the other side's expenses if you lose. Know that you do not need to accept any such costs or risks. Find a service that takes no payment from you even if you win, and that guarantees to pay all costs if you lose. Shun all others.

6 Follow through the procedure laid down by the solicitors or compensation company to assess the validity of your claim. Be aware that if one refuses to take up your case, another might take a different view.

7 Expect compensation to vary depending on the impact of the injury on your earnings and the degree of suffering you have experienced. Typical payments range from £2,000 to £20,000.

What to Look For

- No-fault injury
- Accident compensation service
- No payment if you win
- No costs if you lose
- Compensation award

Tip

Many people have legal expenses cover as part of their home or car insurance. Check your policies. If you have this cover, you don't need a "no-win no-fees" solicitor.

Warning

"No-win no-fee" arrangements are not permitted in Northern Ireland.

122 Donate Your Body to Science

If you're just dying to get into medical school, you can always enrol later in life. Donating your body to science is the ultimate rare event, a once-in-a-lifetime opportunity to benefit medical teaching and research – since the study of human anatomy does require a body.

Steps

1 Arrange the donation of your body to a local medical school or university. If you are in the London area, contact the London Anatomy Office (020 8846 1216), which coordinates donations to the many medical schools and similar institutions in the capital. In other parts of Britain, contact a local medical school or university direct.

2 Expect to receive a registration package that explains in detail what procedures will be followed if you donate your body. Read it carefully.

3 Sign a consent form stating your desire to donate your body, and put a copy of it with your will and other personal documents. Cancel your decision at any time by notifying the medical school or university in writing.

4 Arrange for the medical school or university to be notified when you die, so that your body can be properly transported and prepared. When your corpse is delivered to the medical institution, it will be embalmed and refrigerated until it is needed for study.

5 Check with the school to see what its policies and procedures are regarding your body after it has been studied. Most institutions will either return the body to your family for burial or respectfully cremate your remains at their expense and give your ashes to your loved ones.

6 Don't expect to get paid for your donation. By law, medical schools are not permitted to purchase anyone's body.

7 Rest in peace? Perhaps not. Your spouse, adult children, siblings, parents or guardians can refuse to hand over your body to the medical school after your death, despite your express wishes. For this reason, it is vital to inform your next of kin of your decision and win their agreement to implement it.

What to Look For

- London Anatomy Office
- Medical school or university
- Consent form
- Final disposition policy

Warning

Her Majesty's Inspector of Anatomy oversees the treatment of donated bodies, but nothing can guarantee that your body is handled exactly as you wish once you are dead. If stories of bodies kept in refrigerated vans make your blood run cold, don't donate.

123 Make Money as a Medical Guinea Pig

There are many good reasons to rent your body to science. You can help advance medical research, benefit future generations – and make some cash. Clinical trials can be financially rewarding, although you need to give careful thought to your personal safety.

Steps

1 Know that the best money for medical research volunteers comes from pharmaceutical companies wanting to test new products on human subjects. Visit volunteer recruitment websites of drug companies such as Richmond Pharmacology (trials4us.co.uk) or GlaxoSmithKline (ukclinicaltrials.gsk.co.uk) to form an idea of what opportunities are available.

2 Consider becoming a member of BioTrax (biotrax.co.uk), an organisation that provides members with information on current medical research projects looking for volunteers.

3 Look out for advertisements in newspapers or on the radio seeking volunteers for research. Talk to your friends and colleagues about your interest in being a guinea pig – most volunteers hear about research projects through word-of-mouth.

4 Be clear about your own medical condition. Some tests require "healthy subjects". Do you qualify? There is no point in putting yourself or the research organisation to pointless trouble by turning up for drug trials and then failing a medical because you are a heavy drinker. Other tests may require you to be suffering from a specific condition, such as asthma, or to have a specific family medical history. The more specific the requirements, the more desperate the researchers will be to have you, and the more money you'll make.

5 Be clear about what you will be required to do before you sign up as a volunteer. An experiment will usually involve multiple visits to the research location and possibly overnight stays. Be sure that this fits in with your other commitments.

6 Find out as much as you can about the experiment you are getting involved in. Know that research on human subjects is strictly regulated, reducing serious risks to a minimum. But be aware that the drugs you are being administered may not have been authorised by regulatory authorities as safe for use – hence the tests on you and other volunteers. If you are worried, sign up only for experiments with products that have already been cleared as safe for clinical use.

7 Sign a consent form once you've found an experiment that works for you. This states the procedure and duration of the experiment, possible risks or side effects, and how much you'll be paid.

8 Know that payments vary widely, but look for around £20–£25 an hour for some experiments, or £600–£700 for a full weekend.

What to Look For

- Type of experiment
- Requirements
- Time commitment
- Consent form

Tips

Know that there are many research programmes also requiring volunteers that do not involve drug-testing. These can range from sleep-deprivation experiments to experiments with diet and nutrition and various forms of psychological testing. For most such programmes, however, you will only be paid expenses or a minimal fee.

You are allowed to leave an experiment at any time if you feel sick or are in pain, but you would be unwise to do so if the best medical advice is to continue.

Warning

Researchers are suspicious of "professional" volunteers who take part in projects repeatedly as a source of income. They may attempt to trace your volunteering history and will be especially keen to ensure that you are not involved in two test programmes simultaneously.

124 Sell Your Story to the Tabloids

Have you been intimate with a famous football star? Did a politician's dog chase your cat? Was a TV personality at a party you attended where illegal substances were consumed? You could be on to money if the tabloids want to buy your story – but you need to handle the situation with care if you expect to profit.

Steps

1. Bring yourself into contact with the rich and famous. If you don't cross paths with celebrities, your story is unlikely to be in high demand.

2. Collect and save those photos, text messages, e-mails, letters and tapes. A story not backed up by solid evidence will be no more than rumour. Your evidence is what you really have to sell.

3. If your story is a minor one – an amusing brush with someone well known – contact newspapers direct. Phone and say you have a story. Try to extract some offer of money by proposing an exclusive. Don't be surprised if a journalist asks you what you look like and says he will pay for the story if you pose in a short skirt for an accompanying photograph. If that kind of thing offends you, don't get involved with the tabloids.

4. If you have a major story involving real dirt on a top celebrity, employ an agent. Search for Max Clifford or similar on the internet. An agent will not only negotiate the best price with a newspaper, but also look after you when you momentarily become a well-known personality.

5. Be aware that you are likely to become the object of hostile scrutiny and personal attack on the part of tabloid rivals of the newspaper to which you have sold your exclusive. Are you sure that your life will bear close examination? If you have any skeletons in the cupboard, they are likely to turn up on the front page of a rival tabloid.

6. Look for ways of exploiting the situation beyond the immediate payment for a story. Becoming a minor celebrity yourself could be a stepping stone to TV appearances, a deal to write a book, and so on. What you make of this will depend on your talents.

What to Look For

- Contact with celebrities
- Supporting evidence
- An agent
- Payment

Tip

Be careful who you tell about your story until it is sold. Resist the temptation to tell all your friends. You don't want one of them to have gone public with the story before you do.

Warnings

If you go ahead with an aggressive story, you could face legal proceedings initiated by powerful people with top-class lawyers.

A kiss-and-tell is widely considered a low way to make money. Think about your spiritual well-being as well as your bank balance.

125 Sell Your Soul to the Devil

The quickest way to sell your soul to the Devil is to join the Church of Satan (it takes a few hours). Established by Anton Szandor LaVey in San Francisco in 1966, the church teaches its members to take pride in having the strength and dedication to implement the tools of Satan and the wisdom to recognise the Unseen in our society.

Steps

1 Find a cold room that has not received sunlight for three days and large piece of natural parchment paper that also has been in total darkness for three days.

2 Draw a large pentagram on the parchment paper and place it on the floor in order to protect yourself. Stay inside the pentagram from beginning to end. Treading outside it will make any mistake permanent.

3 Saturate the air with incense of your choice, and conduct the ritual in solitude to maintain full powers of concentration.

4 Take a vial of goat's blood (not sheep's blood, ever!) and scatter drops within the pentagram – but not outside it, and not on your feet. After the scattering you must not tread on the blood, otherwise you will carry it with you outside the pentagram.

5 Memorise and utter the Church of Satan Invocation: "In the name of all the Lords of the Abyss, I call out to the Powers of Darkness. Come to my aid for I am helpless before my adversaries. I am thy servant. Thy will is as my own. I am ever dutiful in serving thee. Come forth from thy dark abodes and answer to your names. Hear my plea!"

6 Send $100 (about £70, depending on the exchange rate) to the Church of Satan (churchofsatan.com). In 16 weeks, you'll receive an embossed crimson card declaring you a member of the church. This card is your means for identifying yourself as a genuine member of the Church of Satan to other members.

What to Look For

- Cold, dark room
- Parchment
- Incense
- Goat's blood
- Church of Satan invocation
- Lifetime membership fee

Tip

Since Satanism is a philosophy that holds individualism as one of its main values, the Church of Satan doesn't expect all its members to agree on everything – or even to get along with each other.

Warning

Once you complete the ritual, the adamantine Gates of Hell are thrown open. Boldly stride within and learn about the "Feared Religion", or slink away in fear and ignorance. The choice is yours.

TION SITES • BUY BARGAIN CLOTHING • BUY WHOLESALE • GET OUT OF DEBT • BUY NOTHING • BUY HAPPINESS • BUY A BETTER MOUS
Y YOUR WAY INTO SOMEONE'S FAVOUR • BUY LOVE • FIND THE RIGHT RELAXATION TECHNIQUE FOR YOU • BUY HEALTHY FAST FOOD •
NG SERVICE • SELL YOURSELF ON AN ONLINE DATING SERVICE • SELL YOURSELF TO YOUR GIRLFRIEND/BOYFRIEND'S FAMILY • BUY FLO
OOSE FILM FOR YOUR CAMERA • BUY RECHARGEABLE BATTERIES • GIVE TO A GOOD CAUSE • TAKE PART IN A CAR BOOT SALE • EMPLO
DENT DISCOUNTS • BUY FLOWERS WHOLESALE • GET A PICTURE FRAMED • EMPLOY A REMOVAL COMPANY • EMPLOY A LIFESTYLE MAN
FOR A HALLOWE'EN PARTY • BUY A GREAT BIRTHDAY PRESENT FOR UNDER £10 • SELECT GOOD CHAMPAGNE • BUY A DIAMOND • BUY
A GIFT LIST • BUY WEDDING GIFTS • SELECT BRIDESMAIDS' DRESSES • HIRE AN EVENTS ORGANISER • HIRE A BARTENDER FOR A PARTY
OUNCEMENTS • SELL YOUR WEDDING DRESS • BUY AN ANNIVERSARY GIFT • ARRANGE ENTERTAINMENT FOR A PARTY • COMMISSION A
SON WHO HAS EVERYTHING • BUY A GIFT FOR PASSING EXAMS • SELECT A CHRISTMAS TURKEY • BUY A HOUSEWARMING GIFT • PURCH
ND • WRITE A MESSAGE IN THE SKY • HIRE A BIG-NAME BAND • GET INTO A PRIVATE GAMBLING ROOM IN LAS VEGAS • BUY SOMEONE A
TIMES • EMPLOY A BUTLER • BUY A FOOTBALL CLUB • BUY A PERSONAL JET • SELECT A CLASSIC CAR • ACQUIRE A BODY GUARD • BO
YHOUND TO RACE • BUY A RACEHORSE • BUY A VILLA IN TUSCANY • EMPLOY A PERSONAL CHEF • BUY A JOURNEY INTO SPACE • EMPL
TUNE • HIRE AN EXPERT WITNESS • MAKE MONEY FROM ACCIDENT COMPENSATION • DONATE YOUR BODY TO SCIENCE • MAKE MONEY
NCIAL ADVISER • PLAN FOR RETIREMENT • COPE WITH HIGHER EDUCATION COSTS • BUY AND SELL SHARES • CHOOSE A STOCKBROKE
S INSURANCE • BUY LIFE INSURANCE • GET PRIVATE HEALTH INSURANCE • BUY PERSONAL FINANCE SOFTWARE • CHOOSE AN ACCOUN
E OUT A PATENT • MARKET YOUR INVENTION • FINANCE YOUR BUSINESS IDEA • BUY A SMALL BUSINESS • BUY A FRANCHISE • LEASE R
SITE • HIRE A GRAPHIC DESIGNER • ACQUIRE CONTENT FOR YOUR WEBSITE • BUY ADVERTISING ON THE WEB • SELL YOUR ART • HIRE
LISH YOUR BOOK • START A BED-AND-BREAKFAST • SELL A FAILING BUSINESS • BUY A HOT DOG STAND • SHOP FOR A MORTGAGE • GE
SE AT AUCTION • SHOP FOR A HOUSE ONLINE • BUY A PROPERTY FOR RENOVATION AND RESALE • EVALUATE BEFORE BUYING INTO A N
A PLOT OF LAND • HAVE YOUR HOUSE DESIGNED • HIRE AN ARCHITECT • HIRE A BUILDER • GET PLANNING PERMISSION • BUY A HOLID
OAD • BUY TO LET • RENT YOUR HOME FOR A LOCATION SHOOT • FURNISH YOUR HOME • FURNISH YOUR STUDIO FLAT • BUY USED FU
Y HOUSEHOLD APPLIANCES • BUY FLOOR-CARE APPLIANCES • BUY EXTENDED WARRANTIES ON APPLIANCES • FIND PERIOD FIXTURES
E • SELECT PAINT, STAIN AND VARNISH • CHOOSE DECORATIVE TILES • CHOOSE A DEHUMIDIFIER • BUY A WHIRLPOOL BATH • BUY A SH
LPAPER • BUY A WOOD-BURNING STOVE • SELECT FLOORING • SELECT CARPETING • CHOOSE KITCHEN CABINETS • CHOOSE A KITCHE
OKE ALARMS • BUY CARBON MONOXIDE DETECTORS • BUY FIRE EXTINGUISHERS • CHOOSE AN ENTRY DOOR • BUY A GARAGE-DOOR O
DOOR FURNITURE • BUY THE PERFECT ROSE • BUY FLOWERING BULBS • BUY FLOWERS FOR YOUR GARDEN • SELECT PEST CONTROLS
OMATIC WATERING SYSTEM • START A NEW LAWN • BUY A LAWN MOWER • BUY KOI FOR YOUR FISH POND • BUY A STORAGE SHED • H
DUCE • CHOOSE A PERFECT PEACH • BUY AND SELL AT FARMERS' MARKETS • SELECT KITCHEN KNIVES • DECIPHER FOOD LABELS • SI
FECT BURGER • PURCHASE A CHRISTMAS HAM • BUY ORGANIC BEEF • BUY HAGGIS • PURCHASE LOCAL HONEY • CHOOSE A CHICKEN
TRUFFLES • BUY ARTISAN BREADS • BUY ARTISAN CHEESES • PURCHASE KOSHER FOOD • BUY SENSIBLY IN SUPERMARKETS • CHOOS
ER A GREAT CUP OF COFFEE • BUY A COFFEEMAKER OR ESPRESSO MACHINE • PURCHASE PARTY BEER • CHOOSE THE RIGHT WINE • •
RM • CHOOSE AN OVULATION PREDICTOR KIT • PICK A PREGNANCY TEST KIT • CHOOSE BIRTH CONTROL • CHOOSE WHERE TO GIVE BI
BABY CLOTHES • CHOOSE NAPPIES • BUY OR RENT A BREAST PUMP • CHOOSE A CAR SEAT • BUY CHILD-PROOFING SUPPLIES • FIND
A GARDEN PLAY STRUCTURE • FIND A FAMILY-FRIENDLY HOTEL • ORGANISE A FUND-RAISING EVENT • BUY BRACES FOR YOUR KID • E
A MODEL • SELL USED BABY GEAR, TOYS, CLOTHES AND BOOKS • FIND A COUPLES COUNSELLOR • HIRE A FAMILY SOLICITOR • BUY OF
CHASE A TOOTHBRUSH • BUY MOISTURISERS AND ANTIWRINKLE CREAMS • SELECT PAIN RELIEF AND COLD MEDICINES • CHOOSE A C
DUCTS • BUY WAYS TO COUNTER HAIR LOSS • BUY A WIG OR HAIRPIECE • BUY A NEW BODY • GET A TATTOO OR BODY PIERCING • OB
TH • SELECT SPECTACLES AND SUNGLASSES • HIRE A PERSONAL TRAINER • SIGN UP FOR A YOGA CLASS • TREAT YOURSELF TO A DAY
N ANTIQUE MARKET • BUY AT AUCTION • KNOW WHAT YOUR COLLECTIBLES ARE WORTH • BARTER WITH DEALERS • GET AN ANTIQUE A
NS • BUY AN ANTIQUE QUILT • BUY FILM POSTERS • LIQUIDATE YOUR BEANIE BABY COLLECTION • SCORE AUTOGRAPHS • TRADE YU-G
SELL SPORTS MEMORABILIA • SELL YOUR FOOTBALL-CARD COLLECTION • CHOOSE A DESKTOP COMPUTER • SHOP FOR A USED COM
MPUTER PERIPHERALS • CHOOSE AN INTERNET SERVICE PROVIDER • GET AN INTERNET DOMAIN NAME • NETWORK YOUR COMPUTERS
PLAYER • BUY A VIDEO RECORDER • CHOOSE A PERSONAL DIGITAL ASSISTANT • CHOOSE A MOBILE PHONE SERVICE • GET A BETTER
TAL CAMERA • BUY A HOME AUTOMATION SYSTEM • BUY A STATE-OF-THE-ART SOUND SYSTEM • BUY AN AUDIO/VIDEO DISTRIBUTION S
SYSTEM • BUY VIRTUAL-REALITY FURNITURE • BUY TWO-WAY RADIOS • BUY A MOBILE ENTERTAINMENT SYSTEM • GET A PASSPORT, Q
AL LUGGAGE • FLY FOR NEXT TO NOTHING • TAKE A TRIP ON THE TRANS-SIBERIAN EXPRESS • BUY DUTY-FREE • SHIP FOREIGN PURCHA
HAN CYCLING HOLIDAY • CHOOSE A CHEAP CRUISE • BOOK A HOTEL PACKAGE FOR THE GREEK ISLANDS • RAFT THE GRAND CANYON •
KSHAW IN RANGOON • TAKE SALSA LESSONS IN CUBA • BUY A CAMERA IN HONG KONG • BUY YOUR WAY ONTO A MOUNT EVEREST EX
L TEAM • BUY ANKLE AND KNEE BRACES • CHOOSE RUGBY PROTECTION KIT • BUY GOLF CLUBS • SELL FOUND GOLF BALLS • BUY PO
PLOY A SCUBA INSTRUCTOR • BUY A SKATEBOARD AND PROTECTIVE GEAR • BUY SKATES • GO BUNJEE JUMPING • GO SKYDIVING • BU
OTS AND BINDINGS • BUY SKI BOOTS • BUY A BICYCLE • BUY AN ELECTRIC BICYCLE • BUY CYCLE CLOTHING • BUY A PROPERLY FITTIN
F • BUY A SURFBOARD • BUY FLY-FISHING GEAR • BUY ROCK-CLIMBING EQUIPMENT • BUY A CASHMERE JUMPER • PURCHASE VINTAG
CKTAIL DRESS • BUY DESIGNER CLOTHES AT A DISCOUNT • CHOOSE A BASIC WARDROBE FOR A MAN • BUY A MAN'S DRESS SHIRT • PI
THER JACKET • BUY MATERNITY CLOTHES • GET A GREAT-FITTING BRA • CHOOSE A HIGH-PERFORMANCE SWIM SUIT • BUY PERFORMA
TORY SHOPS • BUY A NEW CAR • BUY THE BASICS FOR YOUR CAR • BUY A USED CAR • BUY OR SELL A CAR ONLINE • BUY A HYBRID C

BUY TIME • BUY A BOUQUET OF ROSES • BUY SOMEONE A DRINK • GET SOMEONE TO BUY YOU A DRINK • BUY YOUR WAY INTO THE BI
SCREEN • BUT FURTHER EDUCATION • ORDER EXOTIC FOOD • ORDER AT A SUSHI BAR • BUY DINNER AT A FRENCH RESTAURANT • EMPL
O SAY SORRY TO YOUR PARTNER • BUY MUSIC ONLINE • EMPLOY MUSICIANS • ORDER A GOOD BOTTLE OF WINE • BUY AN ERGONOMIC
ANER • EMPLOY AN AU PAIR • BUY A GUITAR • BUY DUCT TAPE • GET A GOOD DEAL ON A MAGAZINE SUBSCRIPTION • GET SENIOR CITIZ
FIND A VET • BUY PET FOOD • BUY A PEDIGREE DOG OR CAT • BREED YOUR PET AND SELL THE LITTER • BUY OR RENT FOR A FANCY DR
RY MADE OF PRECIOUS METALS • BUY COLOURED GEMSTONES • CHOOSE THE PERFECT WEDDING DRESS • BUY OR RENT MEN'S FORM
PHOTOGRAPHER • HIRE A CATERER • FIND THE IDEAL CIVIL WEDDING VENUE • THE COST OF MARRYING • ORDER PERSONALISED INVIT
RKS SHOW • BUY A MOTHER'S DAY GIFT • BUY A FATHER'S DAY GIFT • SELECT AN APPROPRIATE COMING-OF-AGE GIFT • GET A GIFT FOR
RISTMAS CARDS • BUY CHRISTMAS STOCKING FILLERS • BUY CHRISTENING GIFTS • PURCHASE A PERFECT CHRISTMAS TREE • BUY A P
PAY A RANSOM • GET HOT TICKETS • HIRE A LIMOUSINE • BUY A CRYONIC CHAMBER • RENT YOUR OWN HOARDING • TAKE OUT A FULL-
URY CRUISE AROUND THE WORLD • BUY A TICKET TO TRAVEL FOR A YEAR • BOOK A TRIP ON THE ORIENT-EXPRESS • OWN A VINEYARD
OSTWRITER TO WRITE YOUR MEMOIRS • COMMISSION ORIGINAL ARTWORK • IMMORTALISE YOUR SPOUSE IN A SCULPTURE • GIVE AWA
DICAL GUINEA PIG • SELL YOUR STORY TO THE TABLOIDS • SELL YOUR SOUL TO THE DEVIL • NEGOTIATE A BETTER CREDIT CARD DEAL
RADE (OR NOT) • BUY ANNUITIES • BUY AND SELL MUTUAL FUNDS • BUY BONDS • SELL SHORT • INVEST IN PRECIOUS METALS • BUY S
ND CASUAL WORK • SELL YOUR PRODUCT O   A HEADHUNTER • SELL YOURSELF IN A JOB INTE
CE • LEASE INDUSTRIAL SPACE • LEASE OFFI   MENT • HIRE SOMEONE TO DESIGN AND BUILD '
ACH • SELL ON THE CRAFT CIRCUIT • HIRE A   RY • SELL A SCREENPLAY • SELL YOUR NOVEL
ER MORTGAGE DEAL • SAVE ON YOUR MORTG   D • OBTAIN HOUSE INSURANCE • BUY A HOUSE
• EXCHANGE CONTRACTS ON A PROPERTY •   AN ESTATE AGENT • RELEASE CAPITAL FROM YC
• RENT A HOLIDAY HOME • BUY A FLAT • REN   COUNTRY • BUY A LOFT APARTMENT • BUY PR
• BUY DOOR AND WINDOW LOCKS • CHOOSE   GHT FIXTURES • BUY A PROGRAMMABLE LIGH
ED AND MATTRESS • HIRE AN INTERIOR DES   NCORPORATE A GREATER SENSE OF SPACE INT
UY A TOILET • CHOOSE A TAP • BUY GLUES   MENTS • GET SELF-CLEANING WINDOWS • CHO
OP • BUY GREEN HOUSEHOLD CLEANERS • S   SECURITY SYSTEM • BUY A HOME ALARM SYS
UY TIMBER FOR A DIY PROJECT • HOW TO S   R, PAINTER OR ELECTRICIAN • HIRE A GARDENE
OIL IMPROVERS • BUY MULCH • BUY A COMP   BLE GARDEN • HIRE A GARDEN DESIGNER • BL
SURGEON • BUY BASIC GARDEN TOOLS • B   BUY AN OUTDOOR LIGHTING SYSTEM • BUY C
BS AND SPICES • STOCK YOUR KITCHEN WIT   RESH PRODUCE • SELECT MEAT • STOCK UP F
FRESH FISH • SELECT RICE • PURCHASE PR   LTON • GET FRESH FISH DELIVERED TO YOUR D
G OILS • SELECT OLIVE OIL • SELECT OLIVES   INEGAR • CHOOSE PASTA • BUY TEA • BUY CO
REAL ALE • ORDER A COCKTAIL • CHOOSE A   STOCK A WINE CELLAR • STOCK YOUR BAR •
A MIDWIFE OR DOULA • PLAN A HOME BIRT   R A NEW BABY • BUY A NEW COT • CHOOSE A F
CHILDCARE • FIND A GREAT NANNY • FIND T   TER-SCHOOL CARE • SIGN YOUR CHILD UP FOI
• BUY BOOKS, VIDEOS AND MUSIC FOR YOU   HIRE A TUTOR • ADOPT A CHILD • GET YOUR C
LTERED HOUSING • CHOOSE A CARE HOME   LOT • PAY FOR FUNERAL EXPENSES • GET VIAC
TARY MTHERAPY • SEE A MENTAL-HEALTH P   BUY HOME-USE MEDICAL SUPPLIES • SELECT H
ST IMPLANTS • GET WRINKLE-FILLER INJECT   ACTITIONERS • CHOOSE A MANICURIST • GET V
A • BOOK A MASSAGE • GET ON ANTIQUES R   SHOP AT AN ANTIQUE FAIR OR FLEA MARKET •

Personal Finance

• BUY SILVERWARE • EVALUATE CARNIVAL GLASS • BUY AND SELL STAMPS • BUY ANTIQUE FURNITURE • GET CLUED UP ON CLARICE C
S • SEIZE STAR WARS ACTION FIGURES • SELL YOUR VINYL RECORD COLLECTION • SELL TO A PAWNSHOP • BUY AND SELL COMIC BOC
PERIPHERALS • CHOOSE A LAPTOP OR NOTEBOOK COMPUTER • SELL OR DONATE A COMPUTER • BUY PRINTER PAPER • BUY A PRINT
E THE MEMORY IN YOUR COMPUTER • BUY COMPUTER SOFTWARE • CHOOSE A CD PLAYER • BUY BLANK CDS • BUY AN MP PLAYER • C
YOUR PHONE COMPANY • BUY VIDEO AND COMPUTER GAMES • CHOOSE A FILM CAMERA • CHOOSE A DIGITAL CAMCORDER • DECIDE
UY A SERIOUS TV • CHOOSE BETWEEN DIGITAL TV PROVIDERS • GET A DIGITAL VIDEO RECORDER • GET A UNIVERSAL REMOTE • BUY A
CHASE CHEAP AIRLINE TICKETS • FIND GREAT HOTEL DEALS • HIRE THE BEST CAR FOR THE LEAST MONEY • GET TRAVEL INSURANCE •
E UNITED KONGDOM • TIP IN A FOREIGN COUNTRY • TIP PROPERLY IN THE UK • BRIBE A FOREIGN OFFICIAL • GET AN INTERRAIL PASS •
HEAP BUT FANTASTIC SAFARI • RENT A CAMEL IN CAIRO • GET SINGLE-MALT WHISKY IN SCOTLAND • BUY A SAPPHIRE IN BANGKOK • H
HIRE A TREKKING COMPANY IN NEPAL • RENT OR BUY A SATELLITE PHONE • BUY YOUR CHILD'S FIRST CRICKET BAT • ORDER A STRIP
• BUY A RACKET • BUY A HEALTH CLUB MEMBERSHIP • BUY AN AEROBIC FITNESS MACHINE • BUY SWIMMING EQUIPMENT • BUY A JE
IFTING EQUIPMENT • CHOOSE A CAR RACK • BUY SKIS • BUY CLOTHES FOR COLD-WEATHER ACTIVITIES • SELL USED SKIS • BUY A SN
• BUY THE OPTIMAL SLEEPING BAG • BUY A TENT • BUY A BACKPACK • BUY A CAMPING STOVE • BUY A KAYAK • BUY A LIFEJACKET • E
G • SELL USED CLOTHING • ORDER CUSTOM-MADE COWBOY BOOTS • BUY CLOTHES ONLINE • FIND NON-STANDARD SIZES • BUY THE
E • BUY A WOMAN'S SUIT • BUY A MAN'S SUIT • HIRE A TAILOR • BUY CUSTOM-TAILORED CLOTHES IN ASIA • BUY A BRIEFCASE • SHO
OUT CLOTHES • BUY A HEART-RATE MONITOR • SELECT A WATCH • BUY KIDS' CLOTHES • CHOOSE CHILDREN'S SHOES • PURCHASE C
A CAR • BUY A MOTORCYCLE • BUYING AND CHANGING MOTOR OIL• WASH A CAR • WAX A CAR • BUY CAR INSURANCE • SPRING FOR

126 Negotiate a Better Credit Card Deal

That plastic card in your wallet isn't the only thing flexible about your credit – your card's interest rate and annual fee are, too. Credit card offers range all across the board. That's great news for you as a consumer, because with a little effort you can get a better deal.

Steps

1 Find out which cards have lower rates than your current card. Call your credit card company and indicate that you are thinking of cancelling your account and moving to another card with a much lower rate. Ask for a rate that matches the other card.

2 Negotiate a reduction in your annual fee. Finance charges are not the only cost of holding a credit card. The annual fee can add up to much more than your monthly finance charges. Call your credit card company and negotiate hard to reduce or even eliminate this fee. Again, threatening to close your account usually gets their attention. Don't bother trying this with cards that are co-branded with airlines or hotels to offer rewards; these cards will never have their fee dropped.

3 Go to a site such as creditcardexpert.co.uk to compare rates, but make sure you pay attention to all the details of the agreement. Note whether there is a grace period and how long it is; how long the introductory rate is in place; what the late fee is; whether the rate applies to new purchases, balance transfers, cash advances or only some transactions; and whether the introductory rate automatically increases if a payment is late.

4 Cite your history as a customer. If you've been with a company for a while, play up your loyalty. Calculate your debt-to-income ratio by dividing your net monthly income by your monthly debt obligations. If the figure is higher than 0.36 then you may be refused credit; if you have a low figure, however, then you may be able to secure a very low rate elsewhere – and you should tell your current card company that.

5 Arrange for a balance transfer to your new card from your old card once you line up a better rate elsewhere. Read the fine print about balance transfer interest rates: they can often be higher than the interest on purchases.

6 Factor in the perks. Many cards that give added benefits, like airline miles or cash rebates, often charge annual fees and have higher interest rates. If you use your card substantially, these benefits add up and may be sufficiently valuable to compensate for the amount of the fees. Do the sums to see if you will come out ahead on benefits.

7 If you pay off your balance in any one month, forget interest rates and maximise other benefits. Let's face it, if you don't carry a balance, who cares what the rate is? Go for the added benefits like miles, loyalty points, cash rebates or low or no annual fees.

What to Look For

- Lowest interest rate
- Rate and fee details
- More competitive cards
- Added benefits

Tips

If you have a good history with your credit card company, try asking for both a larger credit line *and* lower interest.

If you're looking for rock-bottom rates, check out teaser cards that offer zero per cent interest for a set period of time. Be aware, though, that the rate may apply only to balance transfers, and it will inevitably rise.

Since credit card companies make more money out of customers who don't pay their balances in full, you may actually be in a better negotiating position if you've had a history of on-time payments but don't pay off the balance each month.

127 Choose a Financial Adviser

Are you on the lookout for someone to advise you on financial issues that go beyond basic investing? The right person may be a financial adviser. Advisers come in all types. Some focus on investments; others work in planning insurance, budgeting, estate and related issues. But as with almost anything in the world of money, *caveat emptor.*

Steps

1 Be clear on what your life goals and objectives are when searching for a suitable adviser. Do you want a comfortable retirement, a university education for your children, a holiday home, capital to finance a career change or something else?

2 Decide whether you need the resources of a full-service national firm or if a local office will be sufficient. National firms have big-name investment researchers and analysts on board to generate their own opinions. Generally, the more services available, the higher the overhead a firm has to cover and the higher the fees charged to its clients. In many cases, access to research information more than makes up for the added fees, but be sure you'll actually take advantage of them before you pay for them.

3 Ask friends and colleagues for recommendations and references. Try to interview at least three advisers. Find someone who understands the debt (mortgage, car loans, etc.) side of your equation and will take that into account when creating your plan.

4 Check the adviser's credentials. Certified financial advisers will have a Financial Planning Certificate (or equivalent), and may well have other qualifications for more specialist fields such as trusts and pensions. They will also be registered with watchdogs set up by the Financial Services Act. Contact the Society of Financial Advisers (sofa.org) or IFA Promotion websites like money.msn.co.uk and unbiased.co.uk for a list of advisers.

5 Get a feel for the adviser's philosophy. Some advisers are highly aggressive when it comes to investing, while others are more conservative. But it's your money, and any decent adviser should be able to map out a plan that fits your needs and comfort level.

6 Make certain you know exactly how the adviser will be compensated. Some charge a flat fee for setting up a financial plan; other advisers sell products on a commission basis. Be sure to negotiate if you like the adviser but the fee seems high.

7 Ask the adviser for references, especially from clients whose needs are similar to yours. If the adviser balks or talks about confidentiality, find someone else.

8 Establish how and how often your adviser will be in contact with you. Will it involve phone calls, e-mail updates or quarterly reports? And if your finances take a downturn, will your adviser call with feedback and reassurance, or will you have to pursue him or her?

What to Look For

- Financial objectives
- Specific services
- Credentials and references
- Compatible philosophy
- Compensation basis

Tips

If an adviser is part of a large firm, ask if you'll be handed over to someone else for things like taxes and insurance. Some people prefer one adviser who'll handle all their financial dealings.

Tied and direct sales advisers are "tied" to one company, whose products they sell, while independent advisers can recommend products from any company.

Financial advisers who are paid on a commission may try to steer you to invest in products that will yield them the best compensation rather than those that are in your best interests. Fee-based advisers are generally preferred for their objectivity.

Ask about the charges for phone consultations and questions. It may seem like a quick question to you, but that 15-minute phone call may result in a large bill.

Warning

Make sure your investment pot is large enough to warrant getting an adviser. If you have only £1,000 to invest and an adviser is going to charge you £200, you'd be better off learning what you need to do on your own.

128 Plan For Your Retirement

With life expectancy in the UK ever on the increase, it's going to be increasingly difficult to fund the traditional "old age" pension that we were brought up to believe would support us post-retirement. In fact, retirement may eventually become a luxury that few can afford.

Steps

1 Start planning for retirement early. Think about where you want to live, and how much money you will need to fund your lifestyle. Factor in all the basic expenses such as food, clothes, car, council tax, etc., as well as luxuries such as holidays and meals out. Your retirement could last for 20 or 30 years, so you need to look a long way ahead when preparing your budget.

2 If you are going to have the comfortable old age you assumed would be your reward for years of toil and tax paying, you need to start saving now, because it is not going to come on a plate. The government is keen to help you, and will provide concessions, chipping in the tax that you have paid (or would pay) on the money you've saved. These contributions form a pension fund, which is invested over the years until your retirement.

3 If your company offers a pension scheme, this will probably be worth signing up to. Such plans are usually good value for money because the employer also makes monthly contributions. It should be noted though that "final salary" schemes, in which the pension is based on your income at the time of retirement, are now increasingly hard to find: the occupational schemes in public services such as the police, fire brigade, civil service and teaching are just about the best on offer anywhere.

4 Consider too the new "stakeholder" pensions, which are supported by the government and are most suited to medium- or high-income earners, and also the self-empoyed, who have in the past received a very poor deal from pension schemes.

5 Be aware that any pension plan that involves investing on the stock market will never be completely reliable. A pension plan that has performed very well for years can suddenly dip, and if this happens just before you are due to retire, the lump sum you had envisaged may suddenly be much smaller than anticipated.

6 Be prepared to be versatile, looking at other ways of making money either for your old age or during it. The website money.guardian.co.uk has plenty of useful ideas. Here are some involving property.

- Buying a flat or house and then renting it out could provide a steady income, and one that is likely to increase year on year. There could be gaps between tenants, however, so this should not be your only source of income. You can sell the property at any time (tenancy agreements permitting), and so release the equity, providing a lump sum. And if the property price has gone

What to Look For

- Eligibility date
- Contribution limits
- Investment options
- Company matching
- Vesting period
- Borrowing privileges

Tips

While stocks can give solid long-term gains, they may be volatile over the short term. If you've got a long time until your retirement, you can afford to be more aggressive in your investment choices. If you're closer to retirement, consider less volatile investments, like bonds or cash.

Seek out specialist advice on remortgaging your home, as many high street financial advisers will not have all the details of these schemes.

up during your ownership, then you will make a nice profit, although there will be Capital Gains Tax to pay. During these days of stock market uncertainty and company pensions that fail to materialise, having an investment that you can see may feel very reassuring.

- Renting out a room in your home can also bump up your retirement income. The Rent-a-Room scheme allows rent of up to £4,250 a year per household free of tax. The room must be furnished, and the rent could be just for the room or also for meals, cleaning and laundry.

- If you have a large family home, with two or more free bedrooms, consider offering bed and breakfast. You will have to pay tax on the profit, of course, assuming you earn above your personal threshold, but at least the house will be earning some money, and you get to stay somewhere that would otherwise be too large for you.

7 Consider investing in bonds, which do not provide a guaranteed income but are a more reliable investment than shares. One choice is a bond ISA, whose tax-free status means that each £1,000 invested may earn up to £30 a year. Distribution bonds (a mix of bonds and shares) and with-profits bonds, which guarantee the safety of your capital, are other options to check out. Finally, there are "high income" bonds, which guarantee a regular income of up to 10 per cent a year for three years, but do not guarantee the capital itself. Poor stock market performance could therefore mean that you lose your savings.

8 Remember that you can release some of the capital tied up in your home by remortgaging it. A product called a "lifestyle mortgage" allows you to remortgage up to 50–60 per cent of your home. Unlike most mortgages, however, you do not have to pay monthly interest on this loan. Instead, the interest, which should be set at a fixed rate, is "rolled up" and added to the amount of the mortgage. When you (and your partner, if applicable) need to move into care, or die, the mortgage company will redeem the total debt from the sale of the house, leaving the remainder of the equity in your estate. Alternatively, you could enter into a "home reversion plan", by "selling" some or all of your property to an insurance company for a cash sum of 35–60 per cent of its value. You then continue to live at home either rent-free or for a nominal sum. When you move into care or die, the insurance company takes the agreed percentage of the sale proceeds. Lifestyle mortgages are regulated by the Financial Services Authority. Home reversion schemes are currently unregulated but will become regulated in the near future.

Warnings

Not all investment schemes are appropriate for everyone. Remortgaging, for example, may not be advisable for people on benefits or who have short leaseholds.

Most equity release schemes involve legal and valuation fees which could be as high as £1,000. (Some companies will reimburse these fees if you follow through with the loan.)

129 Cope with Higher Education Costs

The funding of university education has become one of the hottest political issues in Britain and no one can be sure what twists and turns lie ahead. But one thing looks certain: higher education is set to be far more expensive in the future. Are you ready to cope?

Steps

Parents

1 Know that some financial analysts predict that fees for a university education in England and Wales, currently set to be capped at £3,000, will soon rise to an average of £10,000 a year. Fees for top universities are expected to rise much higher.

2 Be aware that you also have to take account of a student's living costs for a period of three or four years – probably a sum of around £7,000 a year is to be expected.

3 Know that, unless you are on a low income, you will probably be responsible for most of these costs.

4 Estimate how much money you will need to fund your children's higher education. Base a first calculation on fees and maintenance costs at current prices. Then take inflation into account. Work out how long it will be before each child is at university, then apply a notional inflation rate – say 4 per cent a year – to your figures. Look at the sum you arrive at, and sit down for a while to recover.

5 Reject despair. Consider how you can prepare to save enough money to cope with these costs when they arrive. Realise that the first rule is to start early. If possible, begin investing for your child's university education as soon as he or she is born.

6 Exploit the wonders of compound interest. Even if you pay quite a small sum regularly into a modest but safe building society account, compound interest will work in your favour to build up a substantial fund over 18 years.

7 Consider a stock market investment, especially if your children are still young (see 130 "Buy and Sell Shares). Although short-term fluctuations can make shares a risky investment, there is good evidence that over longer periods the market outperforms other investments. Choose unit trusts or investment trusts to spread the risk.

What to Look For

- Calculation of future costs
- Early saving
- Student loan

Tips

Start your child saving early. Open a tax-free account in the child's name at a building society and encourage relations to give money as birthday presents. Know that if a parent puts money into their child's account, the Inland Revenue may insist that tax is paid on the interest – it's too obvious a vehicle for tax avoidance.

Be aware that all figures for the future cost of higher education are speculative. Err on the side of pessimism. If fees turn out to be less than expected, you have a nest-egg to use for other purposes.

8 Know that, starting at birth, financial analysts suggest that you should find a sum of around £1,000 invested each year will be enough to pay one child's way through university.

9 Monitor long-term investments regularly to check whether they are delivering what you need.

Students

1 Know that most students are now leaving university with debts in excess of £11,000, while their probable starting salary in their first job is around £14,000 a year.

2 Know that student loans, established to replace student grants and provided through the Student Loans Company (SLC), offer the best terms for student borrowing. Visit the SLC website (slc.co.uk) for further information.

3 Apply for a student loan once you expect to be accepted for a university course. Apply to your Local Education Authority (LEA) if you are in England and Wales; the Student Awards Agency if you are in Scotland; your Education and Library Board in Northern Ireland. They will decide how much loan you are entitled to. The amount will depend on various factors, including your parents' income, your location (London loans are higher) and the course you intend to follow.

4 Be aware that your student loan is unlikely to meet all your costs at university. Students discover that on average they face a shortfall of £3,000 to £4,000 a year – before the anticipated rise in university fees. Many cover this shortfall by further borrowing.

5 Take sensible measures to control your spending in your student years (see 13 "Get Out of Debt"). Take advantage of interest-free overdrafts from banks keen to have your custom. Look out for low-interest offers on credit cards (see 126 "Negotiate a Better Credit Card Deal").

6 Seek out part-time work that fits in with your commitment to your course. Find out if there is work you can turn into full-time employment for part of those long university holidays.

7 Know that you will be required to start repaying your student loan in the first April after leaving university, as long as you are earning over £10,000 a year.

Warning

Credit cards can offer good short-term deals for students in debt, but the overuse of credit cards for pain-free spending beyond your means is a sure route to financial disaster. Paying cash is an effective way to remind yourself of the realities of life.

130 Buy and Sell Shares

Shares are a lot like sex at secondary school: everyone pretends to know everything, few actually know anything and nobody ever lets on about what they don't know. Here's what to look for, and how to build a stock portfolio that's right for you.

Steps

1 Understand how shares operate. Shares are a form of equity investing, because when you buy shares in a company you actually get partial ownership of that company. When a company does well, its value increases, and so does the value of the shares.

2 Get to know the stock exchanges. Shares are traded on three major exchanges in the UK: the London Stock Exchange, which includes some of the biggest companies in the world, the Alternative Investment Market (AIM), which handles new companies, and Techmark, the London Stock Exchange market for innovative technology companies. Nasdaq Europe (formerly EASDAQ) is an electronic exchange. Each exchange trades the shares of different companies, so once you choose a company to invest in, find out which exchange it is traded on in order to monitor it.

3 Familiarise yourself with different types of shares. *Growth shares* are shares in relatively inexpensive companies that have a good chance to increase in value. *Income shares* have less growth potential but consistently produce high dividends. Other types include *value shares,* which are a variant of growth shares; *cyclical shares,* which are tied to economic ups and downs; and *international shares,* which are stocks in foreign companies that may or may not be traded on UK exchanges.

4 Match your shares to your needs and temperament: invest in risky shares only if you have the stomach and the time to ride out market fluctuations.

5 Clarify your investment goals. Do you need to stockpile funds for your retirement? Are you looking to purchase a house within two years? Are you looking for investments that produce income? Or do you want a combination of all of these? As a general rule, the longer the investment time frame, the more calculated risks you can afford to take.

6 Determine how shares fit into your overall portfolio. Shares, like all investments, should take up a limited portion of your assets according to your master financial plan. Construct an asset

What to Look For:

- Types of shares and companies
- Solid products or services
- Good financials
- Undervalued shares (low price-earnings ratio)
- Technical analysis

Tip

Diversify for greater safety. When buying several shares, mix things up. Buy shares from different industries, and balance risky shares with more reliable (blue-chip) choices.

allocation for your entire investment portfolio, decide how much of it should go to shares and stick to that percentage. As shares gain and lose value, you may need to buy or sell to maintain your planned mix.

7 Start with simple parameters. Pick companies that you know and products that you're familiar with. Do you use them? Are they good?

8 Understand the underlying fundamentals of the companies whose shares you buy. These include the markets they are in, their balance sheet (which shows assets and liabilities) and their competitors. Another indicator is the company's past and present earnings and how that relates to the number of shares the company has outstanding (known as *earnings per share*). This is a closely watched number among professional investors.

9 Review stock analyses from research firms that sell subscriptions to their reports. Local libraries typically carry recent issues.

10 Calculate the stock's price-earnings (P/E) ratio. This ratio divides the price per share of the stock by its earnings per share. This shows you how expensive a share price is when compared with the company's actual earnings. As a rule, the higher the P/E, the more the potential of the company may already be priced into the stock.

11 Get professional help. The most traditional avenue is through a stockbroking firm, where you can get first-hand advice from a stockbroker. But you'll pay a commission for any transaction (which, depending on the broker, can be substantial). See 131 "Choose a Stockbroker".

12 Look at online brokerages and discount houses. The commissions are low, the trades are quick and the research resources are often extensive, but you won't get any hand-holding.

Warnings

Never buy on so-called tips. Not only can the information be suspect, but tips can often circulate long after action has occurred. Trading on an old tip is like buying an umbrella after the rain has stopped.

The dot.com era has taught investors to be cautious when following analysts' recommendations. Investment banks that publish reports on companies may also do other banking or consultation work with the company. And while this may not be a conflict of interest at every bank, it has certainly raised eyebrows in recent years. The bottom line is that overly bullish recommendations need to coincide with your own independent research.

131 Choose a Stockbroker

Plenty of investors buy stocks on their own. But if you prefer not to fly solo, it pays to know what sort of broker best fits your needs. You may want someone who will actively plan your investments, or you may prefer someone who's available only if you need advice.

Steps

1 Determine the services you're looking for and your investment goals. Brokers offer varying degrees of services: some may focus purely on investing, while others may place a greater emphasis on investor education and financial planning. See 127 "Choose a Financial Adviser", too.

2 Compare "execution only" firms and advisory firms. "Execution only" brokers make securities purchases and sales at a lower commission, but offer little or no advice; advisory brokers will work with you on an investment strategy, but you'll pay more.

3 Ask friends and colleagues for recommendations. Try to interview at least three candidates before making a choice.

4 Meet the prospective brokers in their offices and enquire about their investment philosophy and how they handle clients. Ask for details about any special training or designations they may have. Ask how long they've been in business, and if they've ever been disciplined (see Tip).

5 Discuss compensation. Find out what the fee structures and minimum purchase requirements are. Ask about any special commission they might get for certain brands of mutual funds.

6 Find out how often your broker checks in with clients. If you want to hear from a broker only every few weeks, don't choose someone who prefers to strategise at every shift of the market.

7 Ask a broker for referrals to clients whose background and goals match your own. If the broker balks, look for someone else.

What to Look For

- Services you need
- Similar philosophy
- Credentials
- Appropriate fee structure
- Track record with clients

Tip

The Financial Services Authority (fsa.gov.uk) is a good source of information on stockbrokers.

Warning

Follow your gut feeling when meeting potential brokers. Like all salespeople, brokers run the gamut from ultra-pushy and aggressive to more relaxed. Work with someone whose style you feel comfortable with.

132 Day-Trade (or Not)

For a while, it seemed that everyone was day-trading. And even though it sounds simple – buy a fast-moving stock and ride out its short-term price movement – it's a strategy that's fraught with risks. Not even professional money managers do it that often. But if sky-diving is your style, at least be prepared before you take this leap.

Steps

1 Put day-trading in context with your entire financial picture. Individual equities are an asset class like any others. Construct an asset allocation for your entire investment portfolio, and

What to Look For

- Online order execution
- High-speed internet connection

decide how much of it should be allocated to day-traded shares. Talk to a financial adviser; most will recommend allocating only a small portion of your assets to day-trading.

2 Learn what to look for. Some traders monitor price movement in the hopes of catching an upturn; others keep an eye out for quarterly or annual reports that may impact on short-term prices.

3 Do your homework on shares. Trade in a small number of securities and understand the fundamentals of their business. Stock prices are affected by many factors, so understand what drives the price for your specific stock. Get to know the companies well, and watch them like a hawk.

4 Know the pace and the risks. Day-trading goes against the very core values of long-term investing. Rather than holding stocks for the long run, day-traders opt for a hit-and-run approach, often buying and selling shares the same day.

5 Sign up for online order execution, which is critical for speedy buys and sells. Most firms that offer this service charge a monthly fee for access, plus a per-trade charge.

6 Get broadband or another high-speed connection for your computer. Since day-trading truly trades on speed, you must have real-time access to data, which can cost anywhere from £15 to £35 a month for the service. Although you don't have to have a special software package, buying one can help you to spot trends. Ask if you can operate from your broker's office, if access to the right equipment is something you currently lack. Some firms may be willing to set you up in return for a commitment to make a certain number of trades per week.

7 Set aside enough time. Successful day-trading requires constant attention. If you have a job or some other time-consuming responsibility, that sort of focus may be hard to come by. If you are serious, treat day-trading as a job.

8 Choose one to three trading techniques that you'll use and stick to them, such as watching for a three- to five-day pullback on a particular share's price after an event or trading technique. Don't go beyond your comfort zone or knowledge base.

9 Start cautiously. Try day-trading just one or two stocks using only a modest investment. Watch them closely, and see what drives their price movements. You'll gain experience, and it's a cheap education if things go badly.

10 Keep a journal detailing the trades you've made, what cycles you see in the market, when you were successful and when you failed. Review your journal every few weeks to spot trends and to learn from your mistakes.

Tip

Use stop-loss orders – where you specify a price for a share to be sold automatically – to limit the downside risks of day-trading.

Warning

Be sure you are familiar with the rules of day trading, such as how much money you need to start out with. These rules are updated at regular intervals, and you need to stay abreast of changes.

133 Buy Annuities

Annuities can prove to be a valuable element in funding your retirement plans. An annuity is basically a contract for which you make an up-front payment. In return, the company selling the annuity promises to pay you regular payments in the future. But you must know how annuities function and what their key features are.

Steps

1 Start shopping. Insurance companies, banks, stockbroking firms, mutual fund companies and even non-profit making organisations all sell annuities.

2 Learn the two basic kinds of annuities and how they differ.

   • A *fixed annuity* guarantees you a certain future payment. This is a good option only for very, very conservative investors. The rate of return on your money is low, and annuities use actuarial tables based on a person living to be 100.

   • With a *variable annuity*, you choose where to invest your money, and the size of your payment depends on the performance of that invested capital. You can choose to invest in shares, mutual funds, money markets and other options.

3 Put money into the annuity during the accumulation period; receive payments during the payout period. Choose between immediate or deferred payouts.

4 Check out the tax implications: you don't pay any tax on the annuity as long as you don't withdraw any money. Once the payout begins, the money you receive is taxed as ordinary income.

5 Note that with designated pension plans, you can take a lump sum out on retirement, leaving the rest of the money in the fund. Once you reach the age of 75, however, that money must be invested in an annuity. The company from which you buy the annuity will then pay you a certain amount per annum, based on expected interest rates and using mortality tables.

6 Choose a beneficiary. Should you die before the payout period – or at some point during the payout period itself – your beneficiary gets a death benefit (either all the money in the account or a predetermined minimum).

7 Be clear on what the other fees are, such as any mortality and expense risks charges and administrative fees. And always get a complete list of all fees and charges attached to any annuity.

8 Work with your tax adviser when considering an annuity. For all the tax advantages of annuities, you may do better in the long run with a pension plan where you work.

What to Look For

• Fixed versus variable annuities
• Accumulation and payout periods
• Death benefit
• Surrender charges
• Other fees and expenses

Tips

If you're considering a variable annuity connected with a mutual fund, ask about the fund's performance, just as you would with any mutual fund.

Studies show that variable annuities make sense only for people with a longer time frame. It can take 5 to 15 years before the tax benefits outweigh the often higher fees imposed by variable annuities.

Ask about a "free look" period to assess communication and record keeping. Many companies let you own an annuity for up to ten days. Then, if you're dissatisfied in any way, it will return all your money without any surrender charges.

Warning

Independent ratings on annuities are hard to come by. Get advice from your financial adviser before choosing an annuity.

134 Buy and Sell Mutual Funds

If you want to acquire a broad range of investments with just one purchase, mutual funds are the way to go. They're easy to buy, just as simple to sell and rich in benefits and features. You will have to do your homework to identify which ones best fit your needs.

Steps

1 Get to know the basic make-up of mutual funds. Mutual funds are a portfolio that can contain a variety of securities, including shares, bonds and certificates of deposit. Most funds have a specific focus or concentration.

2 Identify your investment goals. Specific objectives will help you to determine the sort of mutual fund that best fits your needs. Do you need to save in order to send your child to university? Buy a holiday home? Fund your retirement?

3 Determine how mutual funds fit into your overall portfolio. Like all investments, only a portion of your assets should be allocated to mutual funds (according to your plan). Determine that percentage and stick to it. Most mutual funds consist of shares, which have more inherent risk than other investments. Younger people, for example, may hold a larger percentage of their assets in mutual funds, as their investing timeline is usually longer.

4 Evaluate your tolerance for risk and tailor your investments accordingly. If you're risk averse but you buy the most aggressive fund on the market, you're likely to be in for some sleepless nights.

5 Start your search. Most financial magazines have annual issues that rate mutual funds according to performance, risk and other parameters. Websites such as moneydemon.co.uk and money-extra.co.uk have fund evaluation tools.

6 Investigate performance – in particular, a fund's long-term performance. For instance, Fidelity's well-known Magellan Fund has a ten-year average rate of return of 9.15 per cent. Also, some companies rate mutual funds against others in their own class.

7 Check out a fund's expenses. Mutual fund costs are ultimately subtracted from proceeds to investors and are usually expressed as an expense ratio. Magellan has an expense ratio of less than 1 per cent.

8 Get a sense of a fund's volatility. Compare one year's performance to the next. A stable fund will perform relatively consistently from year to year, while a fund with greater risk may go through highs and lows like a roller coaster.

9 Buy the fund through a financial adviser (you may have to pay a one-time fee) or the fund family itself, or use an online broker.

What to Look For

- Type of fund
- Investment goals and time frame
- Long-term fund performance
- Low expenses
- Volatility

Tips

See who's managing a fund and how long he or she has been there. The current manager may not be responsible for all those juicy past performance numbers.

Check out portfolio turnover. Every time the fund sells a share, it generates a taxable return. The more a fund changes its mix, the greater your tax liability will be.

Tracker funds are an excellent first step into mutual funds. These are passively managed funds that are designed to mimic the return of the market as a whole. While actively managed funds try to beat the market (sometimes they do, sometimes not), tracker funds strive for a reliable market rate return. They also have much lower management fees.

Warning

Avoid funds that charge a "load". This is a one-time fee – often as much as 8 per cent – just to buy into the fund. You can find plenty of no-load funds that perform admirably.

135 Buy Bonds

While shares are a form of ownership in a company, bonds are more of a pure loan. In effect, you lend money to a company or the government with the guarantee that you'll get it back over time, in exchange for getting paid interest. In that sense, buying bonds can provide a nice mix with shares and other investments. And you can do it yourself, although it's wiser to work with a financial adviser to be sure the bonds fit with your particular investment strategy.

Steps

1 Ask your financial adviser what types of bonds are available and who sells them. Companies issue *corporate bonds* to pay for various activities. These usually offer the highest rate of return (known as the yield). The UK government issues *treasury* or *government bonds*, known as gilts. They pay income at a fixed rate and usually have a redemption date when they will be redeemed for a fixed sum (though some, such as war loans, have no redemption date).

2 Find out when the bond matures and how the interest payment is structured. A short-dated bond matures in five years or less; a medium-dated bond in 5 to 15 years; a long-dated bond in 15 years or more. Interest, which is paid gross, can be paid monthly, quarterly or annually.

3 Select a bond that works for your income needs; for example, if you have to make a tuition payment monthly, get a bond that pays interest monthly.

4 Pay close attention to a bond's rating to determine how safe that bond is. A higher rating generally means a secure bond. And the higher the rating, the lower the interest rate; junk bonds are risky but offer a much higher return (if the companies actually survive to pay back your loan). You may find a corporate bond with a lower rating and fairly good rate of return. The hard part is assessing how stable a company will be over the life of the bond so you can get your money back.

5 Know what "call" indicates. A bond's issuer, whether a company or the government, retains the option to retire bonds early if it is in their interest to do so. This means that when interest rates go down, a bond issuer has the option of paying it off before the maturity date so that it can issue new bonds at a lower rate. You, as the investor, have your cash back, but you're faced with a lower rate of return if you reinvest the money.

6 Understand that bonds generate income through a series of prearranged payments to bondholders. But you can also make money because of interest-rate movement. For example, if you own a bond that yields 7 per cent interest and interest rates go down, any new bonds being issued will pay less than the one you own. That makes your bond a more valuable commodity.

What to Look For

- Corporate bonds or gilts
- Term to maturity
- Yield
- Rating

Tips

Shop and compare. Not all sellers may offer every available bond, nor will two sellers necessarily quote the same price for a bond. Waiting for the market to shift may also work to your advantage, but be aware that the same bond may not be available next week.

Diversify. As with shares, it's better to mix up the sorts of bonds you own. Diversity of type, yield and maturity offers greater safety.

Issuers are developing all sorts of innovative bonds to meet specific needs, so keep abreast of developments to make sure you buy the bonds that are right for you.

7　Be very aware of the risks involved. Interest-rate movement can also work against bonds. If interest rates go up, the bond you're holding becomes less valuable than new bonds that get issued. In addition to call provisions, companies can also go bankrupt and default on their bonds (think Enron), leaving bondholders with no interest or principal payments during the bankruptcy, and new bonds or a combination of shares and bonds once the company exits bankruptcy protection.

8　Buy the bonds from an advisory stockbroker (often charging a sizable commission – be sure to ask), from an "execution only" stockbroker (which costs less) or online. Just pick the bonds you want and place an order. You can buy and sell gilts through a stockbroker or, at a lower price, through the Bank of England postal service.

9　Consider bond funds. Many financial institutions offer bond funds, which pool money from many investors to buy funds of differing types and maturities. You're still buying bonds, with all the inherent risks, but the risks are spread among the investors.

136　Sell Short

You might want to think of selling short as the flip side of the traditional stock market strategy. Rather than hoping your shares do well, you're betting on them to do poorly. If it seems risky, you're right – you're essentially swimming against the tide. There's money to be made, but it's critical to know the ins and outs of this aggressive system.

Steps

˙1　Set up a margin account at a stockbrokers. You need to put up collateral, such as cash or shares, and the stockbrokers will lend you up to 50 per cent of their value.

2　Use the margin account to borrow shares of stocks from other accounts with your broker's help. You then sell them. If the price of the shares goes down, you buy the shares again at the lower price, return them to the accounts you borrowed from, and keep the difference. That's the practical definition of "shorting a stock".

3　Know the sorts of conditions that work. Selling short can be an effective strategy if the market as a whole is dropping. It can also be useful with a stock whose company has been hit by bad news or other developments that cause the stock to decrease in value.

4　Try short-selling on a very limited basis. You'll get a feel for how it works – and how it can hurt.

Warning

If you're buying a small number of bonds at £1,000 each, the cost of the trade may be so high as to wipe out any yield you'd earn. Look carefully at the commission and the annual percentage rate (APR) to make sure it's worth proceeding.

What to Look For

- Margin account
- Market downturns
- At-risk shares

Warning

Selling short can leave you having to pay a huge tab if things go against you. For example, if you short shares at £5 a share and instead it goes up to £15, you're on the hook for £10 for every share you shorted.

137 Invest in Precious Metals

Experienced investors have long known that gold, silver and platinum can be a solid investment choice. Precious metals are stable in times of worldwide uncertainty, or when the economy is bad. Used correctly, they can be an effective component of a diversified investment portfolio, but remember, they are an investment like any other, and have an element of risk (albeit more modest). It's essential to achieve the proper mix of investments.

Steps

1 Be familiar with the five principal ways to invest in gold and precious metals: tangible coins and bars; certificates; precious metals mutual funds; shares in mining companies; and gold and metals futures.

2 Go with coins or bars if you're interested primarily in safety and diversity.

3 Break down tangible precious metals into its subcategories: bullion and numismatics. Gold bullion (or bars) is pure or almost pure gold. Numismatics are minted coins, which often commemorate special occasions.

4 Search for both online and brick-and-mortar precious metals dealers. Find out how long the dealer has been in business, whether he or she specialises in one segment of the market and who the typical client is.

5 Shop around. The mark-up on coins and bars will vary. One popular choice for coins is the 1 troy ounce size, as they are easy to buy, sell and store.

6 Educate yourself about the numismatics market. The design and condition of a coin can affect its price as much as the precious metal content itself.

7 Choose certificates if you would rather not store anything. A certificate represents ownership of a certain quantity of a specific precious metal.

8 Consider stocks and funds for additional choices. Precious metals funds, because they are diversified and managed, are the most stable. Stocks are less stable, because you're buying into only one company.

9 For a higher risk/higher potential return alternative, consider precious metals futures if you feel confident of your ability to predict whether the value of metals will increase or decline. Futures are a contract to buy or sell metals at a particular price at a specific point in time. Doing well with them depends solely on what happens to the value of those metals during the contract term.

What to Look For

- Coins or bars
- Certificates
- Mutual funds
- Futures

Tips

Because of their volatility, precious metals should represent only a small portion of your portfolio – 10 per cent at the most.

The most conservative way to go into precious metals is through a mutual fund. It's professionally managed, diversified and is particularly well suited to new investors.

Warning

The drawback to precious metals is that they increase in value only when the price per ounce goes up. By contrast, shares and bonds can pay dividends and offer other income sources. If conditions for gold are poor, your stash can sit for years doing virtually nothing.

138 Buy Serious Illness Insurance

Here's a sobering thought: you're far more likely to suffer an injury and lose time from work than you are to be killed outright. Even the most systematic and aggressive savings programme can be drained if you're unable to work for a year or more. That makes serious illness insurance – which provides an income if you become very ill or are injured and unable to work – an absolute must.

Steps

1 Learn about the elements of a serious or critical illness plan. The *benefits period* is how long the policy will continue to provide you an income. The *elimination period* is the time between when you become ill or are injured and when you start getting benefits. Most policies provide benefits to age 65, but offering only two years of benefits is not unheard of. Be clear on what type of coverage you have.

2 Find out if your employer offers a serious illness plan. It's not common, but it is out there.

3 Make sure your plan provides enough coverage. Most serious illness plans replace only 50 per cent of gross earnings.

4 Know what is covered. Many serious illness policies have strict guidelines for which illnesses and disabilities are covered and which are not. For example, mental disabilities and incapacitation are grey areas. Read the fine print.

5 Calculate your financial needs. If you were laid up for a year, how much money would you and your family need to live? Be sure to factor in future expenses, like university education. Bring your financial picture into focus and compare that to the coverage. Being underinsured can be a big financial risk.

6 Shop around for an illness plan if your employer doesn't offer one. Contact agents and search online sites that give rate quotes. Large insurance providers all offer illness packages.

7 Supplement your company's plan with individual long-term serious illness coverage if your employer's programme won't cover all of your family's expenses.

8 Tinker with your policy so you get adequate coverage without paying too much. The less you settle for in monthly benefits, the lower your premium.

What to Look For

- Employer-provided coverage
- Adequate coverage
- Supplemental individual coverage to fill in the gap
- Affordable premium

Tips

If you can afford only limited coverage, try to protect yourself with as much savings as possible.

If the coverage is too expensive, increase the elimination period, say from 60 days to 90 days, to cut your costs.

You can buy optional riders that provide for cost of living and future earnings increases. If you are in your 20s or 30s, this may be a good addition to consider.

139 Buy Life Insurance

Having too little life insurance can be devastating to your family should you make an early exit. Having too much is an utter waste of money. That makes knowing how much you need – and what type of coverage is best for you – a critical decision.

Steps

1 Determine if you need life insurance. If no one, such as a spouse or a child, depends on your income, then it's pointless for you to insure yourself. Life insurance is protection against lost income – no more, no less. Similarly, if you are well off financially, your family may not need an influx of cash when you die.

2 Calculate how much coverage you'll need. Determine how much your beneficiaries need to live on, and for how long. Losing a loved one is difficult emotionally and financially, and many dependants will want a period in which they won't have to worry about money. While two years is the average cushion, some people may want to make sure their beneficiaries are set for life. Calculate all expenses for the covered period, including big money items like college and mortgages, as well as living expenses like clothes and food. Then subtract the amount of money you think your beneficiaries will make from salaries and investments (remember, they may not go back to work right away). By subtracting all estimated expenses from the income you estimate your beneficiaries will earn, you get a basic idea of how much insurance coverage you need.

3 Choose what type of coverage best meets your needs. Think of insurance in terms of decreasing responsibility as you get older. When you are younger and have children and a mortgage, you need protection. As you get older, your children have left home and you probably have few or no payments left on your mortgage, so you need less protection.

- *Term* (fixed length) life insurance is the simplest way to go – you pay the premium and are covered for a specific benefit for the period during which you want coverage. When you stop paying, you stop being covered. Term life insurance is a much cheaper option, but be aware that it is not a form of saving. You can choose between various options, including level term, in which benefits remain the same throughout the period that the policy is in place, decreasing term, where your prospective payout falls over the years, and increasing term.

- *Mortgage* life policies pay off your mortgage if you die. Most mortgage deals are conditional upon taking out such insurance.

- *Whole life* insurance, as its name implies, is life insurance that lasts until you die or decide to cash it in. The premiums are understandably far more costly than term insurance, since the

What to Look For

- Sufficient coverage
- Reasonable premiums
- Death benefit
- Term versus whole life policy
- Universal or variable life
- Cash value

Tips

Know the terminology. A *premium* is the money you pay to keep the policy in force. The *death benefit* is the payment dictated by the policy to be made upon your death. The *beneficiary* is the person or persons who will receive the death benefit.

The cost of term life insurance has been falling, so it may be worth replacing an existing term policy you have. Check current rates for term life insurance at comparison sites such as insurancesite.eu.com.

Evaluate whether it makes sense to get an insurance policy on someone else, such as your spouse or business partner, whose death would cause real hardship for you. Insurance policies can be purchased for just about anyone.

insurer is certain to have to pay out at some point. Unlike term insurance, it can be viewed as a form of saving. Be aware, though, that if you want to cash in the policy early, you may have to pay a surrender charge.

4 Check the ratings. Insurers run the gamut from shaky upstarts to household-name institutions. Most companies are rated for financial strength and claims-paying ability by independent rating agencies.

Borrow against your life insurance

1 Your insurer may allow you to borrow from the cash value of the policy, especially if you have whole life insurance. Do this only as an absolute last resort. If you own a home, consider an equity loan before borrowing from your cash value. With an equity loan, your interest is deductible and you will most often get a better rate than the insurance company is willing to offer (see 185 "Release Capital from Your Home").

2 Contact your insurance company if you have no other options and find out how large your cash value is and how much you can borrow. The amount available to you depends on how much cash has accumulated in the policy. That, in turn, depends on how long the policy's been around, how much you've paid into it, and other factors. For example, if you have a £300,000 policy with a cash value of £50,000, your borrowing capability will be based on the £50,000 cash value.

3 Understand that when you borrow against your cash value, you must pay interest on the amount you borrow. The interest you pay does not go into your cash value, as many people think. Instead it goes back into the pockets of the insurance company.

4 Carefully check the terms and conditions of the loan. Some insurance companies restrict how much of your cash value you can borrow, and have special payback terms. Make certain that the interest rates are lower than what other loan sources, such as home equity loans, are offering.

5 Withdraw the money. There is no restriction on how you can use the money. You don't ever have to pay it back, as long as you're willing to have a reduced death benefit for your beneficiaries when you do pass away. But, you'll also pay interest on it for the rest of your life. On top of that, any interest you owe on that loan will also be deducted from the payout.

Warnings

If you borrow from a policy that is characterised as a modified endowment contract, you could create a taxable event under certain circumstances.

If you stop paying premiums after eight or ten years when the cash value has risen enough, and take a loan against it, you may actually have to continue paying annual premiums. Find out in advance if you have this type of vanishing premium policy and under what circumstances you'd have to start paying premiums again.

140 Get Private Health Insurance

Private medical insurance is not the growth area it once was. The cost of policies has escalated rapidly – premiums rose by about 70 per cent between 1998 and 2003 – while the National Health Service has been slowly getting its act together. But private insurance is still a passport to privileged treatment, and with a little research you can find a scheme that fits your budget and your needs.

Steps

1 Get a job with private medical cover as one of the perks. Search for your own insurance only if you're self-employed, or if your company doesn't offer it.

2 Be aware that it is no use waiting for your health to deteriorate before seeking private medical insurance. No company will cover you for a condition from which you are currently suffering, and they are very unlikely to cover you for any recurrent condition from which you have suffered in the previous five years.

3 Contact the Association of British Insurers (ABI) for information on the basics of private medical insurance and directions on how to proceed. Visit their website at abi.org.uk or phone 020 7600 3333. Surf for other websites offering information and links, such as health-insurance-uk.org.

4 Decide whether you want to consult an independent adviser before approaching health insurance companies. This is generally recommended unless you're very confident of your ability to steer through the complexities of the medical insurance scene. You will find many independent advisers on the internet.

5 Know that the cost of your insurance will be determined by two factors. One is your age. Insurance for a 65-year-old will cost twice as much as for a 45-year-old. The other is the nature of the cover your require. Naturally, the more comprehensive the coverage, the more it will cost.

6 Before committing yourself to any scheme, look carefully at what it covers and what it doesn't. Know that private medical insurance is primarily designed to cover treatable acute conditions requiring hospital stays and surgery – heart disease, for example, or cancer. Pay extra if you want a policy that will cover out-patient consultations or alternative therapies.

7 Be aware that policies never cover long-term incurable illnesses, accident and emergency, cosmetic surgery, HIV/AIDS, or conditions considered self-inflicted.

What to Look For

- Employer-provided coverage
- Independent advisers
- Medical insurance company
- Suitable policy
- Right price
- Restrictions
- Critical illness policy

Tips

Be sure that you really need private medical insurance. Consider relying on the NHS – believed by many to be improving rapidly – but on occasion paying for private treatment.

Consider taking out a critical illness policy as well as private medical insurance. A critical illness policy gives you a lump sum payment to cope with the consequences of a stroke, cancer or other life-changing illnesses.

Most standard private medical insurance does not cover "hazardous activities". If, for example, you ride a horse or play ice hockey, get separate specialist medical insurance for these activities.

8 Find out what restrictions there are on the hospitals where you can receive treatment. Note, for example, that BUPA Heartbeat, one of the most popular schemes, offers three levels of hospital access: the cheapest restricts you to local BUPA-approved hospitals; the next level gives you access to both private and NHS hospitals nationwide; and the third throws in access to the Cromwell Hospital and Health Clinic in London. Choose what you can afford.

9 Ask about other ways of reducing the cost of a policy. There may be an excess option, which cuts premiums in return for your agreeing to forego a small part of any claim. Some schemes allow you to cut premiums by agreeing to accept NHS treatment if it is available quickly – say within six to twelve weeks.

10 Know that the insurer will almost certainly expect you to make a declaration of your medical history. Give all the information fully and correctly or at some future date they may not pay for your treatment.

11 Be sure you understand and are happy with all details of an agreement before you take out a policy. Be aware that you have a cooling-off period – usually 14 days – during which you may change your mind and withdraw from the agreement if you have second thoughts.

12 Understand that, once you are insured, you should obtain written authorisation from the insurer before you go ahead with any treatment. The insurer will send a claim form to be filled in by you and by your GP or specialist.

13 Be aware that most bills will be paid direct by the insurer, but some bills may be presented to you. In those cases you will have to claim the money back from the insurer.

14 Expect premiums to rise regularly, not only because of inflation, but also because you are getting older and therefore more likely to make a claim.

Warnings

Always check the small print carefully before signing up for private medical insurance. Pay special attention to the list of exclusions – the medical procedures or conditions not covered by the policy. If these include the conditions or procedures you are most likely to require, don't sign.

Keep up the monthly or annual premium payments. If you fall behind, you may find the insurance will not pay up when you need it.

Do not be confused into thinking that a hospital cash plan is a substitute for private medical insurance. Such schemes are cheap, but they provide only small cash payments if you are hospitalised.

141 Buy Personal Finance Software

Some people just aren't cut out to work with a broker or a financial planner. But they still have finances to manage. Whether you need unbiased financial advice or an efficient way to track your money, don't overlook financial software.

Steps

1 Decide what you need in a software program. Basic programs include cheque book balancing, online banking, investment tracking and organising data for use in tax preparation software. More advanced programs, geared toward small businesses, are capable of double-entry bookkeeping, tracking accounts payable and receivable, tax strategies, printing invoices and more. Many have online bill payment or can print cheques from your printer, which is helpful when you're knee-deep in monthly bills.

2 Visit local computer software shops or check out sites that sell personal finance software, such as Amazon.com, to compile a list of available titles. Also check out sites that rate software, such as PCMagazine.com. With a list of brand names and application titles, turn to the manufacturer websites – such as Intuit.com, which manufactures Quicken – to gather more detailed information about hardware required to operate the software, level of complexity and pricing. Some websites even offer a free trial or demo.

3 Ask around among friends and colleagues to see if they use the program and, if so, whether they like it.

4 Make sure the application is not too complex for you. Some are geared towards novices, while others are better suited to experienced users. Match the program's level to your own.

5 Choose a program that offers regular upgrades. This is particularly important with tax software, as the government has no doubt changed several tax laws since you started reading this book.

6 Look for internet connectivity. Some financial programs let you download share prices, analysis, bank statements and other data. Others enable you to share data online between two or more users.

What to Look For

- Functions you need
- Ease of use
- Upgrades
- Internet connectivity

Tips

No matter which program you buy, use it regularly. The software is useful only if you keep your records up to date with it.

Check with your bank to see if it offers online banking and bill payment through desktop software. To save money and retain customers, many banks offer these services only through their own website.

Also consider web-based financial services. Some sites offer financial management and electronic bill payment, and all you need is online access. These services usually have fewer features, but if your needs are simple, this could be the way to go.

142 Choose an Accountant

You don't want to fill in your income tax return? Join the queue. Trying to keep up with ongoing changes in the tax laws is reason enough to want to work with an accountant. Not all accountants are the same, however, so it's important to know what you want and how to get it.

Steps

1 Make sure you really need an accountant. If your return is straightforward and simple, spending money on professional tax preparation may be a waste. You might only need the help you can get from a software program (see 141 "Buy Personal Finance Software").

2 Choose a tax adviser if your return isn't too complex. Independent people offering financial services may be perfectly suitable, and their costs will be much lower than an accountant's.

3 Hire a qualified accountant if your return is more involved and you need that one-to-one relationship.

4 Make certain you and your accountant are a good fit philosophically. If you're conservative, steer clear of an accountant who wants to aggressively bend the rules on your deductions. You'll simply end up convinced that April is the cruellest month.

5 Check references to learn how responsive a particular accountant is. An accountant who is slow to respond can end up costing you money in late fees and penalties.

6 Save money on fees by giving your accountant organised files and receipts. The cleaner your records are, the less time an accountant has to spend in organising them (and the less likely it is that you'll miss a valuable deduction).

7 Review your tax return carefully before filing it, even if a professional prepared it. Accountants are human, but their mistakes can ultimately cost you money.

What to Look For

- Accountancy firm or individual tax adviser
- Suitable training
- Similar philosophy

Tips

If you're unsure whether an accountant is worth the money, bear in mind that you may get back more in tax savings than your accountant charges. After all, it's an accountant 's job to stay current on any changes that can work in your favour. And the fee is tax-deductible.

Know who's going to prepare your return. In some accountancy firms, subordinates do the actual preparation and company principals only look over the final product.

BUY TIME • BUY A BOUQUET OF ROSES • BUY SOMEONE A DRINK • GET SOMEONE TO BUY YOU A DRINK • BUY YOUR WAY INTO THE BE
SCREEN • BUT FURTHER EDUCATION • ORDER EXOTIC FOOD • ORDER AT A SUSHI BAR • BUY DINNER AT A FRENCH RESTAURANT • EMPL
SAY SORRY TO YOUR PARTNER • BUY MUSIC ONLINE • EMPLOY MUSICIANS • ORDER A GOOD BOTTLE OF WINE • BUY AN ERGONOMIC
ANER • EMPLOY AN AU PAIR • BUY A GUITAR • BUY DUCT TAPE • GET A GOOD DEAL ON A MAGAZINE SUBSCRIPTION • GET SENIOR CITIZ
FIND A VET • BUY PET FOOD • BUY A PEDIGREE DOG OR CAT • BREED YOUR PET AND SELL THE LITTER • BUY OR RENT FOR A FANCY DR
RY MADE OF PRECIOUS METALS • BUY COLOURED GEMSTONES • CHOOSE THE PERFECT WEDDING DRESS • BUY OR RENT MEN'S FORM
PHOTOGRAPHER • HIRE A CATERER • FIND THE IDEAL CIVIL WEDDING VENUE • THE COST OF MARRYING • ORDER PERSONALISED INVIT
RKS SHOW • BUY A MOTHER'S DAY GIFT • BUY A FATHER'S DAY GIFT • SELECT AN APPROPRIATE COMING-OF-AGE GIFT • GET A GIFT FOR
RISTMAS CARDS • BUY CHRISTMAS STOCKING FILLERS • BUY CHRISTENING GIFTS • PURCHASE A PERFECT CHRISTMAS TREE • BUY A P
AY A RANSOM • GET HOT TICKETS • HIRE A LIMOUSINE • BUY A CRYONIC CHAMBER • RENT YOUR OWN HOARDING • TAKE OUT A FULL-
URY CRUISE AROUND THE WORLD • BUY A TICKET TO TRAVEL FOR A YEAR • BOOK A TRIP ON THE ORIENT-EXPRESS • OWN A VINEYARD
OSTWRITER TO WRITE YOUR MEMOIRS • COMMISSION ORIGINAL ARTWORK • IMMORTALISE YOUR SPOUSE IN A SCULPTURE • GIVE AWA
DICAL GUINEA PIG • SELL YOUR STORY TO THE TABLOIDS • SELL YOUR SOUL TO THE DEVIL • NEGOTIATE A BETTER CREDIT CARD DEAL
RADE (OR NOT) • BUY ANNUITIES • BUY AND SELL MUTUAL FUNDS • BUY BONDS • SELL SHORT • INVEST IN PRECIOUS METALS • BUY S
ND CASUAL WORK • SELL YOUR PRODUCT O... ...A HEADHUNTER • SELL YOURSELF IN A JOB INTE
CE • LEASE INDUSTRIAL SPACE • LEASE OFFI... ...MENT • HIRE SOMEONE TO DESIGN AND BUILD
ACH • SELL ON THE CRAFT CIRCUIT • HIRE A... ...RY • SELL A SCREENPLAY • SELL YOUR NOVEL
ER MORTGAGE DEAL • SAVE ON YOUR MORT... ...D • OBTAIN HOUSE INSURANCE • BUY A HOUSE
• EXCHANGE CONTRACTS ON A PROPERTY •... ...AN ESTATE AGENT • RELEASE CAPITAL FROM YO
• RENT A HOLIDAY HOME • BUY A FLAT • RE... ...COUNTRY • BUY A LOFT APARTMENT • BUY PR
BUY DOOR AND WINDOW LOCKS • CHOOSE... ...GHT FIXTURES • BUY A PROGRAMMABLE LIGHT
ED AND MATTRESS • HIRE AN INTERIOR DES... ...NCORPORATE A GREATER SENSE OF SPACE INTO
UY A TOILET • CHOOSE A TAP • BUY GLUES... ...MENTS • GET SELF-CLEANING WINDOWS • CHO
OP • BUY GREEN HOUSEHOLD CLEANERS • S... ...Y SECURITY SYSTEM • BUY A HOME ALARM SYS
UY TIMBER FOR A DIY PROJECT • HOW TO S... ...R, PAINTER OR ELECTRICIAN • HIRE A GARDENE
IL IMPROVERS • BUY MULCH • BUY A COMP... ...BLE GARDEN • HIRE A GARDEN DESIGNER • BU
SURGEON • BUY BASIC GARDEN TOOLS • B... ...• BUY AN OUTDOOR LIGHTING SYSTEM • BUY C
BS AND SPICES • STOCK YOUR KITCHEN WI... ...RESH PRODUCE • SELECT MEAT • STOCK UP F
FRESH FISH • SELECT RICE • PURCHASE PR... ...LTON • GET FRESH FISH DELIVERED TO YOUR D
G OILS • SELECT OLIVE OIL • SELECT OLIVE... ...VINEGAR • CHOOSE PASTA • BUY TEA • BUY CO
REAL ALE • ORDER A COCKTAIL • CHOOSE A... ...STOCK A WINE CELLAR • STOCK YOUR BAR •
A MIDWIFE OR DOULA • PLAN A HOME BIRT... ...R A NEW BABY • BUY A NEW COT • CHOOSE A F
CHILDCARE • FIND A GREAT NANNY • FIND T... ...TER-SCHOOL CARE • SIGN YOUR CHILD UP FOR
BUY BOOKS, VIDEOS AND MUSIC FOR YOU... ...HIRE A TUTOR • ADOPT A CHILD • GET YOUR C
LTERED HOUSING • CHOOSE A CARE HOME... ...PLOT • PAY FOR FUNERAL EXPENSES • GET VIA
TARY MTHERAPY • SEE A MENTAL-HEALTH P... ...UY HOME-USE MEDICAL SUPPLIES • SELECT H
ST IMPLANTS • GET WRINKLE-FILLER INJECT... ...ACTITIONERS • CHOOSE A MANICURIST • GET W
A • BOOK A MASSAGE • GET ON ANTIQUES R... ...SHOP AT AN ANTIQUE FAIR OR FLEA MARKET •
• BUY SILVERWARE • EVALUATE CARNIVAL GLASS • BUY AND SELL STAMPS • BUY ANTIQUE FURNITURE • GET CLUED UP ON CLARICE C
S • SEIZE STAR WARS ACTION FIGURES • SELL YOUR VINYL RECORD COLLECTION • SELL TO A PAWNSHOP • BUY AND SELL COMIC BOC
PERIPHERALS • CHOOSE A LAPTOP OR NOTEBOOK COMPUTER • SELL OR DONATE A COMPUTER • BUY PRINTER PAPER • BUY A PRINTI
THE MEMORY IN YOUR COMPUTER • BUY COMPUTER SOFTWARE • CHOOSE A CD PLAYER • BUY BLANK CDS • BUY AN MP PLAYER • C
YOUR PHONE COMPANY • BUY VIDEO AND COMPUTER GAMES • CHOOSE A FILM CAMERA • CHOOSE A DIGITAL CAMCORDER • DECIDE
UY A SERIOUS TV • CHOOSE BETWEEN DIGITAL TV PROVIDERS • GET A DIGITAL VIDEO RECORDER • GET A UNIVERSAL REMOTE • BUY A
CHASE CHEAP AIRLINE TICKETS • FIND GREAT HOTEL DEALS • HIRE THE BEST CAR FOR THE LEAST MONEY • GET TRAVEL INSURANCE •
E UNITED KONGDOM • TIP IN A FOREIGN COUNTRY • TIP PROPERLY IN THE UK • BRIBE A FOREIGN OFFICIAL • GET AN INTERRAIL PASS •
HEAP BUT FANTASTIC SAFARI • RENT A CAMEL IN CAIRO • GET SINGLE-MALT WHISKY IN SCOTLAND • BUY A SAPPHIRE IN BANGKOK • H
HIRE A TREKKING COMPANY IN NEPAL • RENT OR BUY A SATELLITE PHONE • BUY YOUR CHILD'S FIRST CRICKET BAT • ORDER A STRIP I
• BUY A RACKET • BUY A HEALTH CLUB MEMBERSHIP • BUY AN AEROBIC FITNESS MACHINE • BUY SWIMMING EQUIPMENT • BUY A JE
FTING EQUIPMENT • CHOOSE A CAR RACK • BUY SKIS • BUY CLOTHES FOR COLD-WEATHER ACTIVITIES • SELL USED SKIS • BUY A SN
BUY THE OPTIMAL SLEEPING BAG • BUY A TENT • BUY A BACKPACK • BUY A CAMPING STOVE • BUY A KAYAK • BUY A LIFEJACKET • B
• SELL USED CLOTHING • ORDER CUSTOM-MADE COWBOY BOOTS • BUY CLOTHES ONLINE • FIND NON-STANDARD SIZES • BUY THE
E • BUY A WOMAN'S SUIT • BUY A MAN'S SUIT • HIRE A TAILOR • BUY CUSTOM-TAILORED CLOTHES IN ASIA • BUY A BRIEFCASE • SHOL
UT CLOTHES • BUY A HEART-RATE MONITOR • SELECT A WATCH • BUY KIDS' CLOTHES • CHOOSE CHILDREN'S SHOES • PURCHASE CI
CAR • BUY A MOTORCYCLE • BUYING AND CHANGING MOTOR OIL• WASH A CAR • WAX A CAR • BUY CAR INSURANCE • SPRING FOR

Careers

143 Find Casual Work

Each year, millions of people in Britain – many of them students or low-paid workers – take on temporary casual employment. The jobs on offer are usually unskilled and require little or no training. So here are some ideas if you're looking for a holiday job – or simply to earn a little extra cash.

Steps

1 What kinds of work will suit you best? If you have existing skills, interests or qualifications, put them to good use.

2 Try the internet. You'll find plenty of websites devoted to placing casual labourers. If you're taking a year out between school and university, try gapwork.com, which may even be able to find you work overseas.

3 Look for advertisements in your local press or Job Centre.

4 Many small retail businesses advertise vacancies by posting notices in their windows.

5 Target seasonal industries. Every Christmas, the Royal Mail takes on tens of thousands of additional temporary staff. (Ask at your local post office or look on royalmail.com.) Similarly, during the summer, many farms are reliant on temporary workers for fruit and vegetable picking – most of these will advertise in the local press.

What to Look For

- Review your skills, interests and qualifications
- Scour the internet and local press
- Think about seasonal industries

Tip

Even if a business isn't advertising for casual staff, you've nothing to lose by asking. Leave them your name and telephone number in case something comes up.

Warning

Avoid subscribing to agencies that charge for the privilege of finding you work – the employer should pay any such fees to the agent.

144 Sell Your Product on TV

The rapid growth of digital television has seen a wild proliferation of new TV channels. One of the fastest television growth markets is home shopping – there are well over 30 broadcasting in the UK alone. Selling a product on TV might be a bit of a long shot, but it's one that can pay off big time if you hit the jackpot – just ask George Foreman!

Steps

1 Think about the benefits your product offers. Can it easily be demonstrated on television? Does it solve a problem? Is it topical or timely in some way? Watch QVC or other home shopping channels to see if this approach would work for your product.

2 Take a look on QVC.com and click on the Frequently Asked Questions section, then on Vendor Information. Make a note of other home shopping websites advertised on TV.

3 Different shopping networks have different approaches to accepting new products. Some will make decisions based on your own sales material, others may require person-to-person hard sell.

What to Look For

- A unique product
- A demonstrable product

Tips

Products most likely to succeed on home shopping channels are usually unique, of limited availability and can be easily demonstrated on television.

4 Create the right impression when approaching home shopping channels with your ideas. Use smart-looking headed notepaper and have a professionally designed brochure made up.

5 Even if you get an initial thumbs-up, it may be weeks or months before you get to the second round of evaluation. Before you meet company representatives ensure that you can actually produce sufficient quantities of your product to meet reasonable levels of demand. Since most home shopping channels earn a percentage of profits on items sold you may have to work hard to convince them.

6 Consider hiring a professional to sell your product on air. Live TV can be a nerve-wracking experience for a novice.

7 Be prepared, if necessary, to pay to get your product on the air.

It's well known that by far the highest proportion of TV home shoppers are women over the age of 40. You may be in trouble if your product doesn't appeal to that group.

145 Hire a Careers Counsellor

Has your career reached a turning point? Are you miserable in your job or looking for strategic routes to climb the corporate ladder? Careers counsellors are effective at providing assistance to people whose careers are in transition.

Steps

1 Ask job centres and specialist agencies for recommendations and call them.

2 Find out what the fees are and what services are offered. Will you be taking any self-assessment tests? Will the counsellor help you polish your job-hunting skills and build up your network? Do you need to work on communicating more effectively to be more successful in your current job?

3 Find out if the counsellor specialises in a particular industry. It will probably be pointless to hire someone unfamiliar with your field.

4 Ask for credentials. Unlike doctors or lawyers, anyone can set themselves up as a careers counsellor. How many years of experience does yours have? What kind of clients has he or she worked with? Has the counsellor published any books? Ask for and call references.

5 Take self-assessment tests and personality inventories as your counsellor directs. Fill out questionnaires that will help identify and clarify your values. Your counsellor will show you how the results relate to your career and how to maximise your strengths.

6 Follow your counsellor's guidance and explore career options, develop strategies, gather information, hone your communication skills and much more. For more general personal help consider hiring a life coach (see 162 "Hire a Life Coach").

What to Look For

- Suitable services
- Sound credentials
- Proven track record
- Good rapport

Tip

The internet is a good source of information on careers counselling.

Look in one of the major online book stores for careers advisory guides.

Warning

Beware! Just like the field of personal finance, careers counselling attracts more than its fair share of rogues and charlatans.

146 Hire a Headhunter

Running a business can monopolise more time than you have to recruit new talent – particularly if you're a one-man band. Hire a headhunter to fill key positions and bring in qualified personnel.

Steps

1 Investigate the cost. Headhunters may charge you as much as 40 per cent of your new employee's first-year salary, although 20 to 30 per cent is more the norm.

2 Understand how employment agencies charge. Most will only charge a fee if they find someone suitable. A retained search firm will charge a fee based on a percentage of the new employee's salary, but will do a lot more background work to narrow the list of qualified candidates. Most top headhunters will work in this way, and many will want a fee if you fill the position with them or without them.

3 Find a headhunter with extensive experience in your particular industry or functional area to get the type of candidate you're looking to hire.

4 Verify their success rates. Some top headhunters may still only be able to achieve success rates of over 75 per cent, depending on the industry they specialise in or the type of position they are trying to fill.

5 Ask questions about the process they use for identifying potential candidates, whether any personality or skill-based assessments are performed, and if references are routinely verified.

6 Check the firm's references. Asking past clients about the firm's performance is an excellent way to gauge how they'll approach your hiring needs – reputation is everything in the headhunting business, so always do your homework.

7 Ask who'll be doing the actual search: a principal member of the headhunting firm or a lower-level staff member. Find out how long a typical recruitment search takes.

8 Ask if there are any companies that can't be approached. Many headhunters won't poach from other clients, which will limit the pool of candidates they bring to you. Similarly, provide a list of companies you do want them to approach. There will be a very good chance that you know your competition better than the headhunter, so be prepared to share your knowledge.

9 Be as detailed as possible in your job requirement description. A recipe for failure is to tell a headhunter, "We need a really smart person to head up sales." A more successful description is, "We need a candidate who has served in a board-level capacity with a high-profile multinational, handling international distribution of enterprise software to value-added resellers throughout Europe."

What to Look For

- Fee for service
- Expertise in your field
- Familiarity with a functional area
- Proven track record
- Solid references
- Restrictions on recruiting

Tips

Good searches can take up to six months.

Be very specific about the type of company from which you want your poached staff to be found.

147 Sell Yourself in a Job Interview

How do you make someone want to hire you? Simple: put yourself in the shoes of the interviewer and focus on his or her needs and you'll become an irresistible applicant.

Steps

1 In the days before the interview, find out as much as you can about the company: How is it performing? What is its mission statement and who are its customers? What are the interviewer's priorities and responsibilities? The more you know, the more you'll be able to ask informed questions about the job.

2 Study the description of the job for which you have applied. Be clear about what is expected and if you have the background and skills to do it.

3 Take an inventory of your strengths and practise discussing how they complement the requirements of the job. It may help to write down specific examples that demonstrate these strengths and enable you to speak fluidly and intelligently about them.

4 Make a winning first impression at the interview. Be prompt, make eye contact and give a firm handshake. Dress one notch above what's expected for the position you're interviewing for.

5 Look for common ground between you and the interviewer to establish a positive rapport and to stand out from the crowd. You may share the same school or university, or have mutual friends. Be careful not to overplay this and look desperate.

6 Turn what could be seen as potential weaknesses into strengths. You might say: "I haven't worked in promotions but I coordinated getting the word out for my son's school carnival and we had twice as many people attend this year." Be calm and confident.

7 Use specific examples to describe why you're a perfect match for the job. Ask probing questions to demonstrate a genuine interest in the position. In the process, interview the interviewer to find out why the position is open. Get a sense of the company turnover rate, and how it keeps its employees happy. Don't forget that you're trying to find out if you want to work for that company as much as they're trying to find out if they want you.

8 Demonstrate that you are a problem-solver. Identify an issue the company is facing or a problem you might potentially encounter in that job and discuss how you'd solve it.

9 Make the interviewer feel good about hiring you. Be enthusiastic, responsive, truthful and friendly.

10 Follow up with a thank-you note that reiterates your qualifications and mentions specific topics covered in the interview to trigger the person's memory about your interview.

What to Look For

* Research the company
* Practise, practise, practise
* Strengths tied to job requirements
* Confidence
* Strategic thank-you notes

Tips

By focussing your attention on the interviewer's needs, you'll take your mind off your nervousness. The interviewer will hopefully see a confident applicant.

Always bring an extra copy of your CV.

If practical, a few days before your interview, hang around outside the building while the employees are leaving, making a note of the way they dress and behave.

Warning

Questions about religion, race, gender, marital status and sexual preference may contravene some laws. Interview questions should focus on the job, not your personal life.

148 Take Out a Patent

If you want to protect an invention, your safest bet is to get a patent. This is granted by the government to the inventor, giving the right for a limited period – up to 20 years – to prevent others making, using or selling that invention without permission from the inventor. Getting a patent sorted out can be a long and costly business, but it could pay off big-time if your idea is a hit.

What to Look For

- Patience
- Similar patents
- A patent agent

Steps

1 If you're thinking of applying for a patent in the UK you should not publicly disclose the invention before you file an application. This could be classified as "prior publication" of your invention and may invalidate a patent – even if later granted.

2 To patent your idea you need to register it with the Patent Office – a government department that deals with patents, copyright and trademarks. They have a particularly easy-to-follow website at patent.gov.uk.

3 A number of specialist invention promotion firms exist in the UK, some of which advertise on TV. If you plan to go down this route, ensure that they sign a confidentiality agreement before disclosing any details. Interview them rigorously: ask for success rates and evidence that they are qualified to deal with your invention.

4 A UK patent is granted on the basis of a legal document known as a "specification". Unless you have prior experience with patents, consider hiring a registered patent agent to assist with this process.

5 To file an application your specification should contain:

• Description: This must explain your invention. Begin with a summary, before describing in detail its significant features and the problem it aims to solve.

• Drawings: These should be of professional quality, at least good enough to provide photocopies. (A full list of requirements can be found on patent.gov.uk/howtoapply/drawings.htm.)

• Claims: This is where you have to describe your invention in detail. It deals with technical fact, and shouldn't refer to any commercial issues.

• The Abstract: This is a brief summary, published by the Patent Office about 18 months after it has been filed.

6 File your specification – along with Patents Form 1/77 – at the Patent Office. There is no cost for this application, although, if an agent is doing this on your behalf, they will charge a fee.

7 Although the patent lasts for 20 years, renewal fees have to be paid annually from the fifth year. The fee increases on an annual basis: to renew for the fifth year costs £50; renewal during the final (20th) year of the patent costs £400.

Tip

Developing a prototype of your invention may not be required for your patent application. That said, a prototype can point out flaws in your concept or design that would be good to know before you go to the trouble of patenting a process that doesn't perform as expected.

Warning

If you go to a patent agent, make sure that they are registered with the Chartered Institute of Patent Agents (CIPA). Take a look on their website (cipa.org.uk).

149 Market Your Invention

"If a man write a better book, preach a better sermon, or make a better mousetrap than his neighbour, though he build his house in the woods, the world will make a beaten path to his door." That just goes to show what the eminent Ralph Waldo Emerson knew about business! Even the most brilliant invention ever devised will remain obscure if potential customers don't know about it. Here are some ways to get the word out about your invention.

Steps

1 Fine-tune your prototype to resolve any lingering design issues. You'll need a flawless version to sign up licensees and investors or show potential clients.

2 Decide if you intend to retain full control of the concept or if you will license it to an established business.

3 Consult a lawyer early on in the process. It's essential to protect your intellectual property when dealing with potential licensees.

4 Draw up a marketing plan. This is absolutely central to gaining attention for your invention. Define your customers and pinpoint your competition. Even if you want to sell your idea outright, a sound marketing plan will make your pitch that much more comprehensive.

5 See 148 "Take Out a Patent".

6 Budget sufficient funds to get the word out – from trips and trade shows to print and television advertising. Hire professionals to help craft the message (see 157 "Hire Someone to Design and Build Your Website" and 158 "Hire a Graphic Designer"). Identify and attend trade shows and research any event where potential customers or buyers might be found.

7 Set your price. Research your competition so you get a sense of what the market will bear. If you want to sell the product outright to someone else or license it in some way, call in a consultant to determine a fair market value.

8 Consult your lawyer to understand what kinds of licensing deals you can make. Cover derivative work, where a licensee makes a new product that extends your original concept.

9 Write and issue a press release. Contact your local newspaper with a request to profile your invention, and e-mail the editor of trade publications that might be read by your target audience. Send out a press kit with information about your product, your background and the key benefits to newspapers, magazines and television stations in your area. Get the word out to everyone you can think of.

What to Look For

- Produce a working prototype
- Protect your intellectual property
- Marketing plan
- Legal advice
- Financial backing

Tips

Be wary of companies purporting to market your invention. As the inventor, save the money and do a better job of it yourself.

Talk about your invention at local groups or the chamber of commerce. You never know where your potential backers might be.

Find a financial angel. These are private investors who will fund business ideas, back inventions and provide you with manufacturing capital. Ask your accountant or lawyer for referrals, and look into angel organisations. Read 150 "Finance Your Business Idea".

150 Finance Your Business Idea

A great business idea without money is like a brand-new car with no fuel: both are nice to look at but don't go anywhere. Fortunately, there's a wide range of sources you can call upon to drum up money to get your new venture moving.

Steps

1 Write a comprehensive business plan. This document outlines your idea, including how you plan to develop it and – most important of all – how you see it making money. Consult a wide variety of books, or type "business plan" into a search engine for more sources to help you write a business plan.

2 Build a convincing business model for your company. This will have detailed financial data describing every aspect of your business, including costs for sourcing or manufacturing your product, projected sales, marketing expenses, as well as general and administrative overheads.

3 Determine how much money you are going to need. Include start-up funds and sufficient capital to keep the business afloat until your revenue covers your expenses. Add up all of your anticipated expenses during start-up: salaries, building leases and equipment purchases, furniture, office supplies, telephone service and business card printing (see 158 "Hire a Graphic Designer"). The more specific your list of expenses, the lower your chances of running out of money.

4 Seek out help from those who have done it before. Consider offering them shares in your company for their assistance (but not before you decide if you want to retain full ownership).

5 Decide on the legal status of your company. A small company can easily start business as a sole trader or partnership. If you want to limit the potential for personal damage should things go wrong, set up a limited liability company. A good accountant should be able to help you out here.

6 Seek professional advice when determining the deal you are prepared to give to investors. Decisions may include whether to take money as debt or to give up equity, the rights and privileges (if any) that come with being an investor and, most important for them, how investors get paid.

7 Decide what kind of investors you want. Many companies want powerful executives or financiers as investors, but find them meddling and impatient. Friends and family can be an excellent source of friendly money, but investing in start-ups is risky, and relationships can go sour if people start losing money.

What to Look For

- Comprehensive business plan
- Overall funding needs
- Appropriate lending institutions
- Sources of collateral
- Alternative sources of capital

Tips

When it comes to business financing, investigate all possibilities. Often, you can combine funding from various sources to create a suitable package.

8 Use your savings. Any lenders or investors will expect you to fund your business to the best of your financial ability and self-financing is always the best way to retain control.

9 Go to a bank or building society with which you already have a relationship, and ask about a business loan. You're likely to get a better reception from an institution you have a proven track record with than from a new lender. Consider internet banks when looking for the lowest available interest rates.

10 Turn to suppliers you plan to use and ask whether they would be willing to provide products or services up front, as a means of reducing your start-up costs. In return you could offer them full payment plus interest within a specified amount of time. Working this way lowers or even eliminates your need for external financing.

11 Ask potential suppliers if they would help finance your company, either by providing extended payment terms or extending a loan. As vendors have the most to gain when it comes to landing a significant contract, some may be willing to give you some starting help in return for a guarantee of business.

12 Put up collateral. Depending on the size of the loan, you might offer your house or other type of property.

13 Tap into your own assets. Many entrepreneurs have valuable assets they can borrow against to start their business. Home equity is the most obvious choice, with the added bonus that interest payments are tax deductible. Some insurance policies may also be borrowed against. Entrepreneurs have to gauge the degree to which they leverage their personal assets against the risks of start-up businesses.

14 Consider using a credit card. It's relatively easy and quick to get needed funds from your credit cards through cash advances, although the interest rates are much higher than those from other sources.

15 The following UK government websites may provide useful information for start-up business:

- businesslink.co.uk
- enterprisezone.org.uk
- britishchambers.org.uk
- btgplc.com
- bvca.co.uk
- companies-house.gov.uk
- dti.gov.uk
- inlandrevenue.gov.uk/home.htm
- hmce.gov.uk

Warning

Although investors provide what seems to be free money, they will also want to own a portion of your business in return. Many venture capitalists and angel investors will only consider business opportunities where they are able to own 20 to 50 per cent of the company.

151 Buy a Small Business

If you have your heart set on working for yourself, buying an existing business might be just the ticket – or it can be a nightmare if you're not prepared. Know what you want and investigate your options aggressively. First, read 150 "Finance Your Business Idea". Then, do your research – the more you learn, the better your chances of success.

Steps

1 Analyse why you want to buy a business. Are you looking for greater independence or the possibility of increased income?

2 Consider your background. It's more likely you'll do well if you choose a business you're familiar with. Are you interested in a specific product, or an operation that's service-oriented?

3 Contact local business brokers to identify companies that are in trouble, and thus may be ripe for a takeover.

4 If you find a business that takes your fancy, perform a complete financial review of its affairs. This should typically include the company's past income statements, balance sheets, and statements of cash flow, as well as its projected finances looking forward. Carefully study liabilities; as the new owner you will be inheriting the company's debt as well as its business. It's a good idea to work closely with an accountant familiar with businesses in the same field.

5 Get a credit report on the company to evaluate its track record and to double-check the accuracy of its reported numbers. Credit ratings on millions of individuals in the UK are held by two main companies: Equifax (equifax.co.uk) or Experian (experian.co.uk).

6 Ask for a due diligence package, which should include past tax returns, any significant contracts the company has signed (including office or store leases) and any employee or contractor agreements. It will also include legal documents, such as filings, articles of incorporation and any past or pending lawsuits the company is involved in. Work closely with a lawyer to evaluate these and other documents.

7 Ask why the business is for sale. Is the current owner retiring, or hoping to pass off some ongoing problem – or worse, a fatally flawed business or location – to an unsuspecting buyer?

8 Focus on the problems. It's easy to be blinded by the appeal of a business, but pay just as much attention to the flaws. Are they correctable or likely to be a constant headache?

What to Look For

- An appealing business
- Credit report
- Detailed financial records
- Outside financing
- A fair price

Tips

Look for a business that has real growth potential. For instance, a pizzeria that currently operates limited hours might boom if it stayed open longer.

Once you buy the business, give yourself a chance to become comfortable with it. A drop off in income during the first few months of ownership shouldn't be a cause for panic.

9 Observe the business. If you're considering buying a restaurant, for example, watch the customer traffic for a week to see if it measures up to the revenue the current owner claims. Talk to customers to get their honest take on the product or services.

10 Use a business broker or consultant if you feel you need some help locating potential businesses for sale or determining if the asking price is reasonable.

11 Prepare a comprehensive business plan if you need to raise capital. Banks and other lenders will want to see detailed plans of how you envisage future growth. Calculate what you can afford to invest. Read 150 "Finance Your Business Idea".

12 Determine a valuation for the business. Most industries have a standard method and concentrate on a multiple of the previous year's revenue (the exact multiple will depend on the industry). If the business has a lot of capital equipment (a manufacturer, for example), the market value of the equipment is taken into account. Fast-growing businesses in a hot market are usually valued higher, as future potential is factored into the selling price.

13 Justify the purchase price to yourself. Once you've determined a valuation, or come to an understanding on price, run your own analysis to see if it fits your needs. Calculate a break-even on the business. If you're 10 years from retirement, does it make sense to buy a high-priced business that won't show decent returns for 15 years?

14 Ask if the current owner will consider financing part or all of the sale. That can mean a low down payment and an attractive payment schedule for you.

15 Consider proposing that the current owner stays on for a period after you have bought the business – this can be a major boost if he or she is a real asset. Many owners stay on as consultants to smooth the transition. This can be an effective way to smooth over problems that may crop up during a transition of ownership.

Warning

Be wary of any business with incomplete or confusing financial records. That may hint at a poorly run operation or an owner who's not eager to share all the facts. If something seems fishy, it usually is.

152 Buy a Franchise

If you want to go out on your own, but not necessarily start a business from scratch, buying a franchise may be an option to consider. You can own your business, and get support and guidance as you start out. Franchises also have a track record you can investigate. The odds of success are much greater with an established company rather than with a start-up, but the downside is that franchise fees, royalties and other issues can drive up overall costs of doing business.

Steps

1 Identify your skills and interest to target an appropriate franchise. If you have a design background, a sign-making franchise would match your skill set. If you don't even like to put petrol in the car, stay away from an oil-change franchise.

2 Be aware that effectively you'll still have a boss. Even though it's your business, franchises have tight rules and regulations, and may well have strong views on how the business should be run. Although it's a business partnership, the franchisor is ultimately in control.

3 Determine how much cash you have to invest up front in such a venture. Some franchises may be out of your league simply based on the required down payment. Setting up a McDonald's, for example, may cost over three-quarters of a million pounds.

4 Choose between a larger franchise that carries more brand-name value and a smaller operation that offers more personal, hands-on support and responsiveness if you run into problems.

5 Investigate how long the business has been around. Many franchises have surprisingly short life spans. Think of all the ice cream kiosks and sandwich shops that have come and gone over the past decade. Assess whether a franchise is riding out a short-term fad or is part of a trend – like Dunkin' Donuts – that's here to stay.

6 See 150 "Finance Your Business Idea" and run your own detailed financial model. Don't rely on the numbers the franchisor gives you. Create a detailed analysis of sales, cost of sales and goods, overhead and franchise fees. Determine how much you have to invest up front, and how much you will take home at the end of the day. Check out the royalties: the going royalty for a franchise is anywhere between 3 and 10 per cent of your gross turnover. If you need further help, consult an accountant or financial planner with expertise in franchises.

7 Ask what the company expectations are: some franchisors demand quick success translated into specific sales numbers, while others will give you time to grow.

What to Look For

- Suitable business and approach
- Franchise history
- Ongoing support
- Adequate training
- Terms of royalties
- Supplies and equipment

Tips

The British Franchise Association (BFA) hold seminars for existing or would-be franchisees (british-franchise.org).

Useful information can be found on the Which Franchise website (whichfranchise.com).

8 Find out how you will be supported. Will the franchise help with advertising, book-keeping and personnel matters? Ask how much training the parent company offers and what it involves.

9 There is no specific legislation in the UK covering franchises. However, in order to become a franchisee you will have to enter into a legal agreement with the franchisor – this is widely known as "The Franchise Agreement".

10 Seriously consider hiring a lawyer to review these documents. He or she may also be able to help negotiate a better deal with the franchisor. You will need someone with extensive experience of franchises, rather than a general practice lawyer.

11 Put your financial affairs in order. Most franchises will want to see evidence of your financial security or business experience before selling you a franchise.

12 Talk to other franchises. Pick their brains for every tiny bit of information and feedback you can get. Track down franchisees who have left the company to understand what went wrong for them. Their story could be yours a few years down the line.

13 Ask your banker, lawyer or accountant if they've heard anything – either positive or negative – about the franchise. If it's an existing retail business, informally canvass opinion from customers, old and new.

14 Find out about supplies and equipment. Some franchises require that you buy almost everything you need from them. Although you may benefit from economies of scale, you should be sure that the rates are reasonable and competitive with other sources, and not an underhand way of clawing further profit from franchisees.

15 Ask what the franchise fee covers. Some investments pay for all start-up costs, while others don't include training and marketing, to keep the stated up-front cost low.

16 Find out if additional capital investments will be needed down the line in order to be profitable, or if the start-up costs are the only major investment.

17 Hire a general manager or operations supervisor with industry experience in order to give yourself the best chance of success.

153 Lease Retail Space

If you're selling a product, you may need a space from which to sell your wares. Find a location that's accessible to your customers and suited to the needs of your business.

Steps

1 Make sure that any space you're considering is big enough for both your current needs and future growth. Be realistic and don't over-commit yourself.

2 Do your homework beforehand. Investigate traffic patterns; tour the building. Find out who the previous tenant was, and why the business left. Learn what kinds of marketing the location does in support of its tenants.

3 Weigh the benefits of guaranteed foot traffic at a shopping-centre location against premium rent. Some shopping centres require that all tenants stay open during centre hours, and pay for common area usage as well as the shop's own space and upkeep. Shops may also be asked to pay a percentage of sales to the owner of the shopping centre.

4 Identify your closest competitors. Also check out neighbouring businesses with an eye for complementary products or services. Is there an established cluster economy? If you are locating in a shopping centre, check the lease agreement for any guaranteed protection against competition (shopping centres may rent only to a set number of similar stores at any given time).

5 Evaluate whether the physical location fits in with your product line. Do you need a large, bright space or would a charming, cosy nook be more appropriate?

6 Investigate any restrictions on signage. Signs are vitally important to retail businesses, yet many landlords decide on what a shop can and cannot do. The rules may be even stricter in a shopping centre, which closely monitors its physical appearance.

7 Negotiate the terms of your lease aggressively. Never accept wording that's confusing or that leaves you wondering who is liable for what. Ask for the right of first refusal on adjacent space in case you need to expand. Negotiate for free improvements and other incentives before signing your lease.

8 Hire a lawyer who not only specialises in lease negotiations, but knows your area and, preferably, has dealt with your kind of business before. A lease negotiation can sometimes cover tens, if not hundreds, of terms, and you want someone in your corner who's seen it all before.

9 Know who's responsible for the maintenance of the heating, air-conditioning and other systems, as well as keeping up the car park and building exterior. This can be critical in some older buildings.

What to Look For

- Sufficient space
- Room to grow
- A fair lease

Tips

If negotiation isn't in your blood, have a lawyer handle the transaction.

If you're unsure of whether your business can make it in a particular location, one option is to lease a stall or kiosk for a short period. You won't be able to stock much merchandise, but you will get a feel for the amount of traffic, interest in your goods, and demographics of the shoppers there.

Investigate liability insurance carefully. Since the general public will be walking through your shop, be sure that you have adequate coverage in case an accident happens on the premises.

Warnings

Some landlords charge a percentage of sales in addition to the monthly lease payment. For such an arrangement to be worth it, get guarantees on foot traffic and low penalties for leaving your lease early.

Think twice about renting space just because it's cheap. You'll quickly find out just why it's so inexpensive – that location may have a track record for failed businesses, or the layout discourages foot traffic.

154 Lease Industrial Space

Finding and renting industrial space is different from renting office space or an apartment and requires specific information to ensure you get the space you want at an affordable rate. Here's a list of things to bear in mind.

Steps

1 Determine the type of space you'll need. Have a good grasp about requirements for phone, broadband data service, gas, water and electricity. You'll want enough power to provide adequate lighting and operate necessary equipment. Take all of your needs into consideration when looking at space: storage for both your raw materials and finished products, a production area or assembly line, ceiling height, column spacing, loading bay or drive-in access, signage, offices and toilets. Think about proximity to main roads for access, as well as public transport, parking requirements and, possibly, rail access.

2 Try to develop a preliminary layout that takes into account all aspects of your operations. The layout should include utility connections for each piece of equipment. With this information, you can determine what type and how much space you'll need.

3 Take a drive through industrial zoned areas where you might want to locate. Look for "space available" signs with names and phone numbers to call for information. Interview brokers with signs advertising promising properties and ask to be taken on a tour of suitable spaces at terms you could afford.

4 Request a copy of the lease form for the space for your and your lawyer's review.

5 If necessary, be prepared to provide a viable business plan and financial statement for the landlord to review before he or she decides whether or not to accept your lease offer. Then make a written offer.

6 If you choose to use a broker, remember that commissions are generally paid by the landlord, so using a broker shouldn't cost you anything. But also remember that a landlord's broker may not represent your best interests. In such cases, you can work with your own broker, who can take you on a tour of available properties. Be sure to confirm whom the broker represents.

7 Prepare to negotiate all of the lease terms, not just lease rates. Industrial leases can be long and complex. Make sure the terms of the lease protect the interests of both you and the landlord, and yet are not unreasonable for the tenant.

What to Look For

- Appropriate zoning
- Suitable location
- Functional space
- Adequate space
- Affordable lease rates and terms

Tips

Many of Britain's towns and cities have specially designed small business centres. These are usually large office blocks or old factories that have been converted into small units. They may offer free shared services, such as provision of a staffed reception area, telephone answering or secretarial facilities.

For hi-tech small businesses, similar arrangements may be found in "science parks".

Are customers, clients or suppliers going to visit you in your office? If so, think about the appearance of your space, and perhaps even the surrounding area: they may have an impact on your image or credibility, especially if you work in a visual field such as art, architecture or design.

155 Lease Office Space

Leasing space for your company affects profit, employee satisfaction and ability to grow. Plan ahead, know what you're looking for, and be ready to shop aggressively.

Steps

1 Gauge what your space requirements are now and what they may be in years to come. A general rule of thumb is to allot 16 to 23 sq m (175 to 250 sq ft) of usable space per person.

2 Contact a commercial estate agent for help in finding suitable rental space. Agents should have inside knowledge on what space is coming on the market soon and can advise you on which properties are the best. Some firms specialise exclusively in office space leases.

3 Discuss improvements you want to have made before you think about moving in. Tenant improvements are subject to serious negotiation, particularly if vacancies are high.

4 Examine parking carefully. Will you have a number of parking spots set aside for your employees, or will they have to compete for street parking?

5 Reduce your costs considerably by sharing space with another firm, including office equipment, reception areas, meeting rooms and toilets. But know that sharing space brings less privacy.

6 Check out business centres in which entrepreneurs have access to low-cost office space. You may benefit from sharing expertise as well as office space. Check out businesslink.co.uk for more advice on the subject.

7 Consider all-inclusive executive office suites. Although the rate may be a bit higher, many suites come furnished and have access to office equipment and conference rooms. This can reduce up-front costs for physical space and equipment to almost nothing. Many also provide a receptionist.

8 Read a prospective lease exhaustively. Review your monthly payment, the length of the lease, what the landlord is responsible for, any provisions for getting out of the lease early and other standard clauses such as annual rent increases tied to inflation. Ask if the lease includes maintenance. Don't forget telephone lines, cable service, broadband internet connections and other communication needs.

9 Review occupancy date, options regarding expansion, extension of the lease term, termination, contraction, and first right of refusal on adjoining space, as well as security, reception area, amenities (lunch rooms, toilets, snack vending), access to conference rooms and what is the expected response time when a problem arises.

What to Look For

- Current and future space needs
- Commercial estate agent
- Price
- Infrastructure
- Sharing or sub-letting
- Business centres

Tips

Don't be afraid to negotiate the terms of your lease. With rental rates dropping, landlords may be hungry to rent their space as best they can.

Large businesses often go through cycles of lay-offs; you may be able to find a company with extra office space it would be willing to sublet at a bargain price.

Are customers, clients or suppliers going to visit you in your office? If so, think about the appearance of your space, and perhaps even the surrounding area: they may have an impact on your image or credibility, especially if you work in a visual field such as art, architecture or design.

10 Find out about any restrictions on signage. Signs are vitally important to retail businesses, yet many landlords retain the power to decide on what a store can and cannot do.

11 Leases can be long and complex. If you don't feel up to the job, retain the services of a lawyer who not only specialises in lease negotiations but knows your area and, preferably, has dealt with your kind of business before. Make sure the terms of the lease protect the interests of both you and the landlord, and yet are not unreasonable for the tenant.

156 Buy Liquidated Office Equipment

Stock your office on the cheap with discontinued equipment, and damaged and surplus furniture. Desks, workstations and computers can all be bought for a fraction of what you would pay for new. But if you see something you like, act now – it could be gone tomorrow.

Steps

1 Start by doing an internet search. You may be surprised at the number of companies offering used office equipment. Key words such as "liquidated office stock" and "office surplus" should lead you to some great suppliers.

2 Get quotes on items that you're interested in, and then compare with prices found in new office supply stores or catalogues.

3 Watch the classified ads in your local paper for notices of upcoming office furniture liquidations. *Exchange and Mart* and *Loot* may also be able to point you towards some bargains.

4 Check auction sites such as eBay (ebay.co.uk).

5 Read the public auction notices in the business section of your newspaper; you can get significant savings on used and discontinued furniture and equipment from bankruptcies.

6 Contact the purchasing department at your local council to learn of upcoming equipment sales. Some companies regularly sell off used office paraphernalia they no longer need.

7 Examine the equipment or furniture to see if it's damaged in any way. Even the slightest knock may peel more off the price.

What to Look For

- Internet-based companies
- Council sales
- Comparative price quotes
- Public auctions

Tips

Office equipment, such as desks, tables and chairs, is notoriously expensive when bought new. Consequently, second-hand prices for such items may still be higher than brand new "home office" alternatives bought from stores like MFI or IKEA.

157 Hire Someone to Design and Build Your Website

Everyone has a website these days (you *do,* don't you?). Some are for fun, while others are pure business. If you're planning a new site, you need to decide its function before you can create its form. Then, if you don't want to build it yourself – or know better than to try – you'll be better prepared to hire someone to do it for you.

Steps

1 Decide if the website will be for personal use or a business tool. Do you want a purely informational site for prospective clients? Or will it be interactive, so that visitors can buy a product or service online?

2 Ask friends and business associates if they can recommend a suitable website designer. Identify at least three contenders to compare their styles, prices and technical expertise.

3 Review the designers' own websites to see samples of their own work. Ideally, look at examples of sites that are similar to your business.

4 Ask designers to describe their approach to building a site. Some concentrate purely on getting information to visitors, while others focus more on design aesthetics or technical issues. Find out whether the individual is a designer or a programmer at heart. Technical experts typically don't have the design talent needed to make a site look great as well as work seamlessly. Likewise, a designer may not be as up-to-date on the latest web technology or know how to engineer the site in the best way. A company with several experts may be the wisest way to get all of the expertise you need.

5 Find out what specifics they would recommend for your site, including how many pages you'll need, how the content is best arranged, how to apply technical solutions to problems and other issues. Compare these recommendations in order to gauge how experienced the designer is. Pay attention to how well they communicate and if you could establish a good rapport.

6 Bring along a list of websites you like and why. Discuss with prospective designers to get feedback and be confident that they understand what you want your site to look like.

7 Discuss their fee structure. Does the cost include web hosting, registering a domain name, or updating the web site? (This is often a hidden cost, since many sites need to be updated by a trained programmer or designer.) Ask whether you will be able to maintain the site yourself.

8 Set up a schedule that details what each phase will accomplish, what materials they need to get from you, and an overall timeline for the whole project. Fees will be tied to the schedule.

What to Look For

- An experienced designer
- Previous work
- Technical skills
- Design expertise
- Appropriate fees
- Site management

Tips

Your website is a part of your brand image, so you'll want to match yours to your company identity. A graphics design company may want a flashy, whistles-and-bells home page; an undertaker might opt for something a bit more restrained.

Don't be afraid to keep shopping if a designer seems too expensive or doesn't come up with the sort of website you have in mind. There are plenty of designers out there.

158 Hire a Graphic Designer

A designer's job is to communicate your vision in printed materials or on the internet. Graphic artists bring together a variety of visual skills – typography, colour, illustration, photography – to deliver a message to your customers on a business card, logo, brochure, website, poster, invitation, book or even a T-shirt. If you don't know Helvetica from a hole in the ground, it's time to find yourself a designer.

Steps

1 Decide what you need. Does your new company need business cards? Would a logo help establish your presence in the market-place? Do you need to tap into a new pool of customers? Have you got a product or service that nobody knows about? Effective graphic design lets people know who you are and what you do.

2 Ask friends and colleagues for recommendations – this is always the best approach. Similarly, ask printers if they can recommend a designer with whom they've worked. Look at the designers' websites to see if their style is suited to what you're looking for.

3 Review the designers' portfolios. Get a sense of how similar your business is to the type and size of the clients they typically work with. When you see something particularly interesting or good, ask them about their brief for that particular job and how they arrived at their solution.

4 If you like their work, discuss the project you need done. Expect the designer to ask you lots of questions about the project and your business.

5 Ask for a quote. Some designers will price small jobs on the spot. Others will send you a quote later, which should include a ballpark estimate for printing. Design fees are in addition to illustration, photography and printing costs, but the designer manages all of those elements.

6 Budget according to size and complexity of the design. It goes without saying that black-and-white or two-colour work will be cheaper than full-colour. Logos are the most time-intensive and tend to command higher prices. Actual fees are usually based on the amount of work and the size of the client. A new corporate identity for Joe's Pizza Place will be vastly cheaper than one for British Telecom.

7 Hire the designer. Make sure the contract has all the details of the job, including a printing estimate and schedule, before you sign it.

8 Meet and review sketches to determine if the designer is going in the right direction. He or she will take your feedback and refine the concept. You'll meet several times during the process to keep tightening up the design until it's complete and printed.

What to Look For

- Good recommendations
- Clear idea of what you want
- Someone you can work with well

Tips

For website work, also see 157 "Hire Someone to Design Your Website". Some graphic artists work in both print design and web design.

Designers tend to specialise in different areas, such as corporate identities, which involves designing a logo and applying it to business cards, stationery, brochures and the company's website. Others specialise in environmental graphics, signage, exhibit design or product package design, while still others are strictly book designers.

Start collecting materials that you like: business cards or logos, brochures and other printed pieces with a style that catches your eye.

Warning

Check final proofs with the utmost care: If there's a "typo" – an error in the typography – and you've signed off on the job, you'll be charged for fixing the error. Always check phone numbers, e-mail address, web URLs and postcodes very carefully.

159 Acquire Content for Your Website

Unlike many other business tasks, getting material for your website can be an easy and inexpensive matter. And finding the right content may make your site a real eye-catcher. Whether you're trying to boost traffic or provide information, you'll find a wealth of sources.

Steps

1 Set up a Frequently Asked Questions (FAQ) section on your site and establish message boards where visitors can share your information. Develop a newsletter and archive it at the site. Work up other proprietary material, such as booklets and articles.

2 Build in links to other sites. This connects your visitors to other sources of information and can build your traffic as well if the sites link back to yours.

3 Check out websites that offer articles, reports and other items for reprinting, as long as the source is credited. Be careful not to use copyrighted materials without permission.

4 Contact authors of articles in trade journals and specialist newsletters and ask if they would submit an article for your site in return for publicising their business. Offering to post a photo of the author and a short blurb about their firm may be enough to entice experts to provide good material you can use.

5 Most of the material the government distributes is copyright free. Check out some of these sites:

- businesslink.co.uk
- enterprisezone.org.uk
- companies-house.gov.uk
- dti.gov.uk
- inlandrevenue.gov.uk
- hmce.gov.uk.

6 Buy it outright if necessary. For special reports, research and stock photos. The prices you pay will vary according to size or quantity of the material and whether royalties are involved.

7 Run advertisements in online classifieds looking for writers. Remember, content can be submitted from anywhere.

8 Don't go overboard – content overkill can drive a visitor away by making a site too complex to navigate and too slow to load.

9 Consider a syndication service. If you have the budget, a number of web businesses offer a wide range of information for use on your website. Try uclick.com for comics and cartoons.

10 Be vigilant about copyright issues. If you have any doubts, contact the person or website whose content you want to use. They will probably want appropriate credit, and even payment.

What to Look For

- Free content
- Modestly priced content
- Copyright issues

Tips

Don't be shy about offering links. Most other websites will be pleased to hook up.

Surf the internet. There are countless websites that offer free content.

160 Buy Advertising on the Web

Internet-based advertising may be critical to the growth of your web-site or business. But promoting yourself on the internet is like any other form of advertising. You need to think about your target audience and set clear objectives about what you want the ads to do. Here's how to get started.

Steps

1 Find out where to buy online ads. An advertising network – one of about 100 firms that sell space across a number of online sites with a single purchase – is the easiest place. Other options include advertising agencies, national newspaper sites, e-mail newsletters, search engines and sites that specialise in reaching a technology audience.

2 Determine who your target audience is and where they are most likely to spend time when online. Those are the sites where you want to be seen. It is worth spending more to reach the people who will actually become customers.

3 Judge the effectiveness of each type of advert. Banners – the advertising boxes that appear on a web page – are the most common, but have become less and less effective. So-called "interstitial" adverts pop up on a page or interrupt between pages, but can be much more expensive to produce and place. The key is targeting a specific audience, such as parents, home owners or dog lovers.

4 Hire an advertising agency or designer (see 158 "Hire a Graphic Designer") who specialises in web advertising to design an advert for you. Pay careful attention to the wording, message and how your company or service is branded. Make sure it is consistent with your overall marketing, so that you reach the appropriate audience and they don't click off your site once they find you.

5 Shop aggressively. The market is competitive, so look around for the best prices and a deal that meets your needs. Advertising sales people will expect you to negotiate prices.

6 Choose the price structure that works for you: if you choose per impression, you may pay a CPM (cost per thousand) each time your banner appears. Per click-through, you'll pay for each hit your advert gets. Per lead, you may pay each time you get an online registration or a request for a catalogue. Per sale, you pay each time someone buys something you've advertised. Rates are highly variable.

7 Review your results and make adjustments as necessary. Changes can usually be completed and integrated within days. Check to see if you met your goals once the campaign is done. If not, give consider revamping your campaign or choosing another form of advertising.

What to Look For

- Type of advertisement
- Price structure
- Appropriate placement
- Cost-effective results

Tips

Consider the issue of timing. Make sure your adverts will appear when your target audience is most likely to see them.

Try a test campaign first to see what results your advert brings. If you find a winner, broaden your campaign.

161 Sell Your Art

Some artists may recoil at the notion of selling their work, but it's the best way to lose that "starving artist" label. Approaching your work as a saleable commodity as much as an artistic creation can ultimately boost your visibility and, hopefully, your sales. Put your creativity to work and get the word out in as many ways as possible.

Steps

1 Network. Join a museum or artists' group to meet other artists as well as potential customers. Ask other artists questions about how they are selling and distributing their work.

2 Develop a marketing plan to attract new business.

3 Blow your own trumpet. Send out press releases and propose article profiles to local newspapers and national publications to heighten awareness of you and your work. Articles that feature you and show photographs of your work are guaranteed to garner attention and potential clients.

4 Create a website to introduce people to your work (see 157 "Hire Someone to Design and Build Your Website"). Then gather addresses and send out periodic mailings featuring new work. Or, save time and money by sending out e-mail updates with links to new work posted on your website. Include links to any articles or sites that have caught your eye.

5 Enter competitions. Use any honours and awards you receive to net publicity and greater exposure for your work.

6 Ask the owners of coffee bars, shops and restaurants if they'd be interested in displaying your art. Offer a small commission from any resulting sales. Also consider buying a stall at local art fairs and shows (see 163 "Sell on the Craft Circuit").

7 Look for galleries that feature art complementary to yours. Offer diversity – a gallery that has 20 artists doing seascapes may not be on the lookout for another.

8 Sell yourself to the gallery owner. Be able to discuss your work convincingly and clearly, including how it's created and why it will appeal to his or her customers.

9 Be prepared to pay a hefty commission for gallery visibility. Some may take as high as a 50 per cent cut of the retail price.

10 Push for a public showing of your work at galleries, with an opening night reception. Send out invitations to clients, friends, family and high-profile community members.

11 List your work on auction sites such as eBay (ebay.co.uk) to appeal to consumers who don't have the time or inclination to pay gallery prices. Set a reserve price that ensures that you'll get a decent return on your time and effort.

What to Look For

- Networking
- Visibility
- Galleries and alternative venues

Tips

To boost your visibility, have an open-studio sale. Invite everyone you know – most particularly gallery owners – to come and see your work for themselves.

Devote time to putting down your brushes and putting on your marketing hat. That can spark creative thinking on ways to sell your work more effectively.

Warning

If you show at a gallery, beware of hidden costs. Insurance and any additional framing, presentation or marketing costs may be passed along to the artist. Check with gallery owners.

162 Hire a Life Coach

A life coach – sometimes called a personal or executive coach – can be a boon to your professional and personal development. A coach can help you identify your personal and professional goals, then direct you in how to achieve them given your own strengths, personality and ambition. He or she is more of a personal problem solver, there to help you figure out what it is you want out of life, and how to get it.

Steps

1 Ask friends or colleagues for referrals to coaches with whom they've worked. Try to get a recommendation from someone with circumstances similar to yours.

2 Request a list of referrals from coaches you've identified, so that you can speak to individuals they've counselled to get a sense of who is in the best position to help you.

3 Interview at least three coaches before making your selection. Although anyone can set up as a life coach, ascertain whether they have credentials that you personally value. For example, some may have greater confidence in a life coach who is also a published author, or holds a post-graduate degree or counselling qualifications.

4 Ask the candidates to talk about their background and about what makes them a successful coach. Decide whether your personalities are compatible. Be sure you'll feel comfortable asking for help and taking direction from any potential coach. Is their approach hands-on and proactive, or is it so laid-back that you'll get feedback only when you seek it?

5 Schedule how long and how often you'll meet. Will face-to-face meetings will be augmented by phone calls, e-mails and other communication? Will there be any limits on this? How long should you commit to working together?

6 Develop realistic time frames to accomplish the goals you've set.

7 Find out what kind and how much homework will be expected. Will that fit your style and timeframe?

8 Get a quote on how much the coach charges. Near the top end of the scale, costs can reach £1,000 a month or more. Some will provide face-to-face counselling while others may be more phone- and e-mail-based.

9 Listen to your gut reaction. No matter how highly recommended a coach is, how many years they've been coaching or what famous clients they have, if you're not comfortable working with them, it won't be worth it.

What to Look For

- Recommendations from friends and colleagues
- Professional credentials
- Style of approach
- Amount and kind of feedback
- Service fees

Tip

Find out if a coach offers any alternatives to his or her regular service. Some, for instance, offer lower group rates or may provide problem-solving help as and when required.

163 Sell on the Craft Circuit

Selling crafts may seem like a small and simple business, but nothing could be further from the truth. From simple home-made pottery to exotic hand-crafted jewellery, the craft circuit now means big business, providing an excellent livelihood for creative souls all over the UK.

Steps

1 Get to know the different types of craft fairs. Some are sales events tied to a specific season, such as Christmas. Others are recurring events – flea markets or street fairs – that take place every week.

2 Identify those fairs best suited to your work. Some restrict entrance to artisans who have previously applied for and received permission to participate, while others simply require payment of an entrance fee. There are a number of useful internet sites – such The Internet Craft Fair (www.craft-fair.uk) – that list forthcoming fairs across the country.

3 Be aware that entrance to some fairs may be based on the quality or reputation of your work.

4 Talk to fellow artisans and discover for yourself which shows are worth participating in and which are not. Research major events in your region and on the internet. Many will advertise in local newspapers or magazines.

5 Attend fairs that will attract your targeted audience. Some fairs attract buyers from gift shops looking to make large wholesale purchases, while others attract customers shopping for things for their home. Determine what type of buyer is attracted to each show, and if it coincides with your target market.

6 Apply to craft shows as far in advance as possible. The most favourable locations generally go to the earliest to sign up, and the best shows have long waiting lists. Your wait will be in direct proportion to how many other vendors are in your particular category of work. Your application should reflect any awards you've won, as well as years of experience, to increase your chances of being accepted. If asked for your preference, request a corner location in the middle of the floor – this usually gets more traffic than mid-aisle booths.

7 Have professional photos taken of your work to include with your application. Keep a variety of colour and black-and-white prints, as well as slides available to send when requested. Set up a website so that customers can view your work online. See 161 "Sell Your Art".

8 Do a cost-benefit analysis on the entrance fee versus expected revenue. Some of the more exclusive fairs may charge vendors considerable amounts of money to participate. Don't forget to

What to Look For

- Recurring and seasonal fairs
- Satisfied vendors
- Vendor requirements

Tips

Craft experts will tell you how important it is to keep introducing new products. This will keep you from becoming boring to repeat customers.

Whenever possible, try to bring along help to relieve the boredom, help you serve customers and provide a break if you need one.

include all expenses, including travel, hotels and moving your merchandise to and from the show. Can you can bring in enough cash from your sales to make the effort worth it?

9   Jump-start your craft fair experience by exhibiting in local shopping centres, which are generally easier to get into and run all the year round. You'll get a feel for what customers like in your area and have a chance to polish your sales skills, which will be invaluable if you move into larger shows.

10 Do your homework for specific shows and plan your inventory carefully to know what will appeal to the people walking the aisles. You want to have a variety of products to appeal to a broad range of customers, but you need to balance that against the cost of transporting and displaying the items.

11 Price your merchandise according to what others of your skill and ability are charging, as well as the size of the piece, the amount of time you invested creating it, cost of materials and business overheads. Some fairs are very upmarket while others are more mass market – your merchandise should be priced appropriately.

12 If appropriate to your craft, consider buying or renting a booth. Outside shows generally require a covered area in order to protect your work from both sun and rain. You'll also need a table or display unit, tablecloths or covers, a chair and storage boxes to pack and transport your work safely, and a space to store it between fairs.

13 If your products are moderately expensive, consider providing your customers with facilities to pay by credit card. Sometimes banks are reluctant to allow part-time or home-based businesses to hold merchant accounts, so you may have to be persistent. As an alternative, consider using online financial services such as PayPal (www.paypal.com).

14 Do plenty of preparation before the fair and distribute handouts with prices, product lines and contact details. Increasingly important, create or update your website (see 157 "Hire Someone to Design and Build Your Website").

15 Many people don't buy at the fair, but delay making their buying decisions until they've reached home. Make sure that they know how to get hold of you after the event.

16 Start locally to see how your merchandise moves before you branch out to fairs outside your area.

17 Be prepared to travel if you do well and want to continue to grow. Making the most of the craft circuit may mean travelling to fairs a long way outside your area to find a new base of prospective customers.

Interacting with customers is critical to your success. Let buyers know how long a particular item took to create and what inspired you. Describe any unusual techniques you've adopted. An effective, eye-catching sign can be critical to attracting customers to your wares.

164 Hire a Literary Agent

Many publishing houses won't even glance at a book proposal unless it has come in through an agent. Agents with valuable connections can distribute your work and will also have the know-how and experience to negotiate the best deal. They can also be a very useful source of guidance and advice. But it's essential to find a suitable match.

Steps

1 If you have friends or colleagues in the publishing world, ask them for references. Find out with whom they're working and if they're satisfied.

2 Find books similar to ones you want to write and make note of the name of the literary agent who represented the author (they are often thanked in the acknowledgments).

3 Visit agency websites for information on genres in which they specialise, clients they represent, method of communication and any guidelines for submissions. Check if you can send in a full manuscript. Most agents don't read unsolicited manuscripts and many won't read unsolicited proposals.

4 Consider both large and small agencies. The bigger ones may have greater resources; the smaller operations may give you more personalised service. If you're taken on by a larger firm, find out who will be your personal agent; the agency may have a famous name, but a newcomer, junior associate or assistant may actually handle your account.

5 Have any agent outline exactly what he or she will do for you, and what the speciality is. Some agents will help you land magazine assignments – others will work only on book projects.

6 Find out how long the prospect has actually worked as an agent. If the person is relatively new to the field, ask what he or she did before, to gauge what publishing connections can be brought to the table. An agent's greatest asset is his or her relationships with editors.

7 Get a sense of how aggressive an agent might be. Some will go to the ends of the earth to sell your project. Some won't go any further than the end of their desks. Ask to talk to past clients to find out which category this particular agent falls into.

8 Ask about commissions. Agents may charge up to 15 per cent commission on anything they sell on your behalf, and some may also charge for incidentals like photocopies and postage. And since agents only earn a fee when they have generated income for you, they have a strong incentive to work on your behalf.

9 Request a written contract that confirms everything you and your new agent have agreed to.

What to Look For

- Client/agent matching services
- Large versus small agencies
- Type of clients
- Aggressive personality
- Commission

Tips

Wherever possible, get a personal referral. Agents, like publishers, rarely look at unsolicited materials.

Anyone considering going the self-publishing route won't need an agent at the start. However, if the book does well, publishers may come calling, and you'll need an agent then to represent your interests. See 167 "Sell Your Novel".

Given that the UK book publishing market is almost entirely centred around London, be wary of hiring a literary agent based away from the capital.

Warning

Never work with an agent who charges to read a book. That's simply a rip-off!

165 Pitch a Magazine Story

Many of the articles you read in magazines will have started with a writer pitching an idea to an editor. The field of freelance writing has a few land mines, particularly for first-timers, so you'll need to watch your step.

Steps

1 Find out if the magazines you'd like to write for accept freelance submissions. Although increasingly rare, some publications are still exclusively staff-produced.

2 Match your idea to the publication. Identify magazines that would publish the kind of idea you have in mind. Read back issues of the magazine(s) or check the online archives to get a feel for the readership, the topics covered and the tone of the articles. Be certain that the magazine hasn't covered your idea already. Also, look closely at the length of the articles and see if it fits in with your style.

3 Both *The Writer's Handbook* (panmacmillan.com) or *The Artists' and Writers' Yearbook* (acblack.com) will provide you with names and contact addresses for many of Britain's magazine publishers. However, don't feel obliged to stick with the UK market – e-mail really has created a global village.

4 Review editorial calendars, which are often featured on magazine websites. These may give advertisers, readers and writers an idea of what may be coming up in future issues. Keep upcoming topics in mind when you're pitching your ideas, and be sure to mention the particular issue to which you think your idea will be particularly well suited.

5 Think at least three months ahead – the minimum timeframe in which most magazines work. That means you'll need to pitch Mother's Day ideas in December or January and back-to-school subjects no later than May or June.

6 Avoid the biggest rookie mistake: sending a finished, unsolicited manuscript. Instead, find out how the magazine accepts article ideas. Ask to see a copy of its writers' guidelines and follow them to the letter.

7 Pinpoint the best editor for your idea, or call the magazine and ask which editor is best to contact, and how he or she prefers submissions (via e-mail or conventional mail).

8 Craft a one-page query letter. Identify the specific audience that may find the article interesting. And cite any statistics or research that supports your proposal.

9 Include photocopies of actual articles you've had published with your query letter. If the magazine is of general interest, submit a variety of cuttings; if it focuses on a particular topic, include cuttings that show your expertise in that area.

What to Look For

- A fresh idea
- A suitable magazine
- Editorial calendars
- Writers' guidelines
- Contract details

Tips

Pay rates will vary with the magazine, the scope of the story and your experience. As a rule, the smaller the magazine or your portfolio, the lower the rate. Most magazines offer a rate per thousand words.

If you have photography skills, ask about taking your own pictures as a way to boost your fee.

Think about sending in several good ideas in one enquiry letter. You may boost your chances and get more than one assignment.

166 Sell a Screenplay

Think you've got the next *My Big Fat Greek Wedding* on your hard drive? We've all probably felt that at one time or another. Sadly, not all of us know what to do once the last page rolls off the printer. Here are some pointers on selling your screenplay.

Steps

1 Contact production companies and film studios to find out who receives unsolicited screenplays. Find out if material needs to come through an agent. If so, take the plunge and get one; it may even help with those studios that don't insist on this.

2 Get a personal contact to hand-deliver your script. Even if it's the father of a friend's friend, any type of personal connection is better than an unsolicited submission. Work your address book; you'd be surprised how many contacts you have.

3 Write a logline, which is a three- to four-sentence description of your plot line. Many producers make preliminary decisions based on a logline, so make sure it has a killer punch.

4 Draft a synopsis, which is often requested as a second-round qualifier by a studio executive or agent. This one-page summary expands on the logline, complete with character descriptions and plot twists.

5 Make sure your screenplay is long enough but not too long. The general rule of thumb is 100 to 140 pages.

6 Check that everything's spelled correctly. Typos can sink even the most readable story. Consider hiring an editor if you want to be sure your copy flows well and is free of gaffes.

7 Send a clean, crisp copy of the screenplay. If you don't have a decent printer, get your script run out at a photocopying shop.

8 Keep your first page simple but informative: the title, your name and whatever contact information may be relevant.

9 Don't bother with arty or colourful covers. Like CVs printed on coloured paper, a script that's dolled up suggests something that doesn't warrant any attention otherwise.

10 Apply for consideration to screenwriting contests. Ben Affleck and Matt Damon's Project Greenlight (projectgreenlight.com) searches for aspiring screenwriters and directors, and Kevin Spacey's TriggerStreet (triggerstreet.com) provides a forum for screenwriters. Being chosen for participation in one of these events could move you to the front of the screenwriters' line.

11 Remember that – for now, at least – you're a writer, not a director. Keep ideas about lighting and camera angles to yourself.

What to Look For

- Studio contacts
- A sharp-looking script
- A compelling story

Tips

Check out scriptwriting software. It can help you with dialogue, action and overall format.

The script must be able to stand on its own. Any letter you include to justify its merits will probably give a studio enough reasons to reject it.

Send your script to as many studios as you can. The more you hit, the better your chances of a sale.

Pay rates will vary. In most circumstances, a newcomer will command far less than an established professional.

167 Sell Your Novel

Conventional wisdom holds that you have only a couple of minutes to convince an editor that your novel is worth buying. That makes every second critical to presenting your work in the best light. Don't forget that everyone from Philip Pullman to J.K. Rowling started out this way.

Steps

1 Pay a professional editor to review your book and polish it. Editors can be a big help when it comes to identifying flaws in a plot or stilted dialogue.

2 Make sure your manuscript is clean, free of mistakes and neatly bound. Although non-fiction books may be bought on the basis of a proposal, outline and – in some cases – a sample chapter, fiction is only purchased after reading the entire manuscript.

3 Get an agent. Most publishing houses won't even look at a manuscript unless it comes via an agent (see 164 "Hire a Literary Agent").

4 Choose publishing houses that specialise in the genre of book you've written. If you think you're the next Danielle Steel, don't pitch your romance novel to a house that deals exclusively in history. Do send your material to as many houses that seem a reasonable fit.

5 Write a solid covering letter to accompany your manuscript. This is absolutely critical to getting an editor's attention. Start the letter with a "hook" – something unique or provocative about the book. This makes the editor want to read the novel itself. Also include:

- Why you chose this particular editor. That shows you've done your homework.

- Any information about prior publishing experience you have. If you have none, however, don't let on that you're a beginner.

- A brief summary of the novel – making sure that it's no longer than three paragraphs – with an estimated word count.

- A description of the audience you think will read your novel, such as suspense fans, sci-fi junkies or teenagers.

6 Post the manuscript to as many publishers as you think are potential buyers – unless your agent agrees to market your work. Tell the publisher if you are submitting to other publishers or if they are the only one.

7 Wait. Depending on the size of the publishing house, it can take several months before you hear anything. Hold off e-mailing or phoning to ask about the status of the book. That's a sure way to turn off an editor.

8 Turn over any offers to your agent. He or she is more objective and will work to get you higher advance payments, which in turn means higher percentages for the agent.

What to Look For

- An agent
- Suitable publishing houses
- Covering letter and summary
- Patience

Tips

Check out either *The Writers' And Artists' Yearbook* (acblack.com) or the *Writer's Handbook* (panmacmillan.com). Both are excellent sources of names and contacts in the British publishing world.

Get a personal introduction to a publisher. Even if the connection is personal ("his children and my children go to school together"), if it seems appropriate, use it.

Include a self-addressed, stamped envelope in the overall package so that an editor can send back your manuscript.

Try not to get discouraged. Most great books have been through the rejection meat grinder before getting published.

Once you have exhausted all the possibilities at traditional houses, look into the idea of self-publishing (see 168 "Self-Publish Your Book").

168 Self-Publish Your Book

Self-publishing can be a smart choice for writers. It's cost-effective, relatively fast, pays much better than standard royalty contracts, and lets you maintain control over the publishing process. But there are drawbacks to consider.

Steps

1 Decide what your goal is. Some writers want to print just enough copies of their prized project for colleagues and friends; others think they have a book that will sell to a larger audience.

2 Examine competing titles to make sure you're not covering the same ground. Find out what sales of those books have been to see if it's really worth your while to tackle a similar topic.

3 Determine the format you'd like to publish in: hardback, paperback, or ebook – which is essentially an electronic file and requires no paper printing.

4 Check out print-on-demand publishers. If all you want to do is get a book published, these vanity presses will do the job for a price. Some vanity houses will print just a few copies for a few hundred pounds. Print-on-demand is ideal for very short runs (25 to 500 copies). Instead of printing on traditional, ink-based offset printing equipment, pages are reproduced using what amounts to a sophisticated copier. A digital file from a page layout program links directly to a high-speed copier and then the pages are machine-bound. Some shops offer perfect binding so it looks just like a printed book. Look at sources like Trafford.com, Xlibris.com and Iuniverse.com.

5 Print your book directly from your completed files using a direct-to-press printer. Instead of producing a different piece of film for each colour of each page, the files are transferred directly to the printing plate. You'll eliminate all the film costs, and save time too.

6 Shop aggressively if you really want your book to sell. If you're an established writer considering self-publishing, look around. You can either choose to have a print-on-demand company, such as those mentioned above, handle all the layout, printing and production activities, or go to a local offset printer and oversee each of those steps in the process personally.

7 Ask potential suppliers to send you samples of their recently printed books. Don't be shocked by the results: the quality will vary considerably with regard to the quality of paper used, cover design, layout and whether it was run on a sheet-fed press or a web press. Ask questions about how individual pieces were produced.

What to Look For

- An affordable publishing house
- Good-quality work
- Print run minimum
- Print-on-demand option
- Distribution capability
- Decent royalty structure

8 View competitors' books to determine what size and format you'd like your book to take. Find out if there are standard sizes with which you should work in order to reduce costs, or whether a different format will help your book stand out. Format sizes can affect which print-on-demand publisher you can work with.

9 Familiarise yourself with printing costs. These will vary, but you can expect to spend more than £1 per book for a minimum print run of several thousand copies. You may also be charged extra for layout help, editing, design of a book cover, and for photos. Typical fees are £2 to £5 per page for editing, £2 to £5 for production, £500 to £5,000 and beyond for design, plus £2 per 300-page book for printing. (Note: these figures are only rough guidelines, and will vary according to the specific project.)

10 Hire a designer with book experience (see 158 "Hire a Graphic Designer"). He or she will design the type and flow the pages. That same person may also be able to produce a spectacular jacket – although there are designers that specialise in this area. This will boost your costs – in some cases by a considerable amount – but the difference in creating a quality product will be significant.

11 Total up your costs, including printing, graphic design, artwork, photography, copy editing and other expenses. A traditional publishing house would normally absorb these costs, but then again, you would lose control of the project.

12 Request an International Standard Book Number (ISBN), which is the standard code for identifying your book, at www.isbn.org.

13 Find out how and by whom your book will be distributed. Some print-on-demand companies will handle it in-house. If you do it yourself, you'll need to have the books shipped to you, to contact book chains about stocking your book, potentially visit each bookstore individually, and handle any mail orders on your own. Some book shops will accept a limited number of your books on consignment, which means you leave them and if they sell, you get paid; if they don't, you pick them up in a couple of months. Some companies have extensive book-shop distribution; others focus more on online sales, which will have bearing on the types of activities you'll need to perform to be successful.

14 Be prepared to sell yourself. Any real marketing of the book will have to come from you. Self-publishing will inevitably also mean self-promotion, or hiring a publicist to do it for you.

Tips

In general, the more copies you print, the lower the unit cost. On the other hand, you don't want a garage forever packed to the rafters with your books.

Self-publishing has its risks but also its rewards. Most publishing companies pay authors a royalty of between 5 and 10 per cent of sales; self-publishers can increase that to 50 per cent or more.

169 Start a Bed-and-Breakfast

For many people, running a bed-and-breakfast (B&B) may seem like a dream job. This is a business, however, that you'll need to go into with your eyes wide open. If you're not a people person committed to working long hours, seven days a week, then running a B&B may be more like your worst nightmare. Do some homework to ensure your plan is a realistic one.

Steps

1 Most B&Bs are owner-occupied properties run by a husband and wife partnership. Consider how having paying guests wandering around your house day and night will impact on your day-to-day life and relationship.

2 Evaluate whether you have the right personality. Being outgoing and friendly is part of the job whether or not you feel like it. Interview B&B owners and learn about their lives – and whether that's the life you really want.

3 Honestly assess your own strengths and weaknesses. As a small businessman, there will plenty of new skills that you will need to acquire, but if you perpetually kick off projects and then quickly lose interest, then running a B&B (or any other business, for that matter) may not be for you.

4 Decide where you'd like to live and work. Locations close to tourist attractions are generally the most popular, although out-of-the-way accommodation can be just as popular if there is something distinctive and alluring about the place or its surrounding area. It's a good idea to consult the local Planning Department to ensure that there are no major changes in the pipeline that might adversely affect your business.

5 The easiest way to start a B&B is by buying an existing business. If, however, you plan to start from scratch you will need planning permission from your local council. Be aware that, unlike renting a room out in your house, the Inland Revenue views B&Bs as a formal business arrangement. Most B&Bs have the legal status of sole trader or partnership.

6 Draw up a business plan. Work your numbers carefully. The profit margin for many B&Bs is modest at best. You may need financial assistance to get your B&B off the ground (see 150 "Finance Your Business Idea").

7 Determine how many guests you can and want to accommodate. Some B&Bs limit themselves to just a few guests, others may take in 20 or more.

8 Survey local competitors' prices. You'll want to be competitive with others in the area. But don't be scared of competition – in fact, B&Bs often do better in areas where there are plenty of other B&Bs in operation.

What to Look For

- Current business skills
- Location
- Planning regulations
- Comprehensive business plan
- Financing
- Insurance
- Marketing
- Location

9 Develop an effective yet realistic marketing plan and budget. How will people hear about your B&B? Effective advertising can be expensive and high-income customers may be difficult to reach. Free ink makes for terrific marketing, and it's cheaper than advertising, so explore getting editorial coverage in local papers, regional publications and national travel magazines. For larger B&B businesses a good PR consultant may be worth the cost if you can get the right coverage.

10 Ensure that your B&B is adequately insured. In addition to the standard buildings and contents insurance that nearly all home-owners take out, you will need public liability cover, for civil actions that may be brought against you by guests who have been injured on your premises. Other possible coverage may be employee liability and cancellation insurance, covering you if guests with reservations pull out.

11 Compile a list of contact information for past guests – preferably e-mail addresses – so that they can be contacted in future. Make sure you are listed in all relevant B&B guides and directories, and both printed publications and online resources. Put up a website to attract customers from outside the area (see 157 "Hire Someone to Design and Build Your Website").

12 You can keep your overheads low in the early years by doing the cooking and cleaning yourself. As you become more successful you might consider hiring experienced staff to keep things running smoothly: a housecleaner, cook, dishwasher, bartender, waiter and gardener may be helpful additions during the peak season.

13 Consider subscribing to a reservation service agency in order to reach a broader market, reduce your workload and even turn over the financial dealings to the experts.

14 Set guest policies and house rules regarding check-in and -out schedules, cancellations and late arrivals, as well as whether pets, children and smoking are permitted.

15 Cater to your guests by making their experience as wonderful as possible. Serve excellent food and – if licensed – build a good wine list. Make sure the rooms are clean and inviting. It's the little things that will keep guests coming back time and time again.

16 Network with fellow B&B owners, visitors' bureaus, tourism offices and chambers of commerce to increase awareness of your business.

Tips

Most B&B guests are looking for personal attention and charm when they make a reservation. Be sure you deliver that in order to win loyal customers.

B&Bs in new buildings are rare. Guests frequently want old-world charm, not the latest construction.

If you're renovating, be sure to set aside plenty of space for your own private living space. At the end of the day, you'll always want to retreat into your own rooms for much-needed privacy.

170 Sell a Failing Business

Businesses may flourish, and businesses may flounder. Companies go through good times and bad. When the bad times are bad enough, they can force the owner to put the business on the block. Here are some special considerations to ensure that you and the buyer both get a fair deal.

Steps

1 Accept that you probably won't get a top price for a business which has gone bust. The best you may be able to expect is a "fire sale" price. Recognise that the market for a struggling business is small. You may be limited to buyers with experience in turnarounds.

2 Consider bringing in a consultant or business appraiser who can help you determine a fair market value. Emotional involvement may restrict your ability to come up with a reasonable price tag. Produce comparable valuations of similar properties in your area.

3 Consider using a broker to sell the business. An experienced broker can put you in contact with far more buyers than you would be likely to find on your own.

4 Disclose your business's problems, as a well-prepared buyer will uncover them, anyway. But if there is a personal reason for a recent fall-off in business – such as the owner's ill health – be sure to state it up front. If the business's troubles are a recent phenomenon, you may be able to get more money than if the decline has been consistent and long-term. Be forthcoming, even if you aren't asked directly. Failing to disclose significant problems may provide grounds for fraud when later discovered.

5 Present facts and figures about your business at its prime to show prospective buyers what kind of money the business once generated, and could in the future. Amount of customer traffic, average transaction amount, and weekly or monthly receipts are all useful information.

6 Clear any pending litigation and sizeable debt before you go on the market. Nothing can kill a business sale faster than a lawsuit or large debts.

7 Establish trust with potential buyers by being up-front about the challenges your business faces.

8 Be patient. It may take a buyer time to create a plan to restore the business to profitability.

9 Separate assets from the business entity, such as equipment, technology or property. Sell them or license them if you can't get a buyer for the whole company. Licensing technology your company has developed may provide an ongoing source of income, even if you can't divest the rest of the business's assets.

What to Look For

- A reasonable price
- A business broker
- Trust with a buyer

Tips

Emphasise the opportunity in the business. Possibilities – rather than just problems – may sway some buyers.

Choose a broker carefully. Some won't hustle to sell a business that shows poor prospects.

Warning

Try not to shut the business down in the hope of selling to someone who will re-open it. Once a business has closed, the only real assets for sale are the property and equipment. You'll get far less from the sale if yours is not a "going concern".

171 Buy a Hot Dog Stand

No matter if they're frankfurters or bratwurst, the wiener is a winner. Owning a hot dog stand may especially appeal to the entrepreneur who can't stomach a desk job. But there's a good deal more involved than boiling the water and slathering on the mustard.

Steps

1 There is no national legislation covering street trading in the UK. Instead, the *Local Government (Miscellaneous Provisions) Act 1982* allows local councils to decide who can trade, what they can sell, and where they carry out their business.

2 Before you can start your business you must apply to your local council for street trading consent. The specific regulations differ from council to council.

3 If you intend to sell food on the streets you will be expected to register with the council's Food and Safety Office. They ensure that you comply with legal standards of hygiene and safety. (They also have the power to close you down and even prosecute if you break the law.)

4 Before you start trading, sign up for a course on food handling. Some councils may even insist on this before granting you a trading permit.

5 Build a financial model for your hot dog stand. Spy on other vendors in the area to see how many hot dogs they sell, and how much food they throw out at the end of the day. Separate your variable costs, which will increase with each sale – hot dogs, napkins and condiments, etc. – and your fixed costs, which you have to pay even if you sell nothing, such as equipment, permits and fuel. From this you will be able to calculate the number of sales you have to make to break even. Can you do it?

6 Find a location. Your council will advise you of areas in which you are allowed to trade. Identify a busy street with few existing food options, or a large business with hungry employees. Factor in the tastes and demographics of the neighbourhood when deciding what you plan to sell.

7 Buy the necessary equipment – the cart, coolers, food-handling gear, cooking equipment – from a restaurant supply store. Also, look into leasing equipment, which requires less capital up front.

8 Buy your supplies (see 274 "Select Meat"). Shop around for the best prices and tastiest product. Check out restaurant supply stores and bulk warehouses. Don't overlook your local grocery shop, particularly if your stocking needs are modest.

9 Research stock level requirements. Food businesses lose tremendous amounts of money due to bad ordering and spoilage. Plan your inventory to have a minimal amount on hand at any time.

What to Look For

- Local regulations
- Health codes
- Good location
- Clean, functional equipment
- Great-tasting food

Tips

Be consistent. If you feature a certain hot dog or brand of drink, stay with it. Customers like that kind of predictability.

Don't skimp on condiments. Offer everything from mustard to jalapeños. If there are regional tastes where you live, make sure you cover them as well.

CTION SITES • BUY BARGAIN CLOTHING • BUY WHOLESALE • GET OUT OF DEBT • BUY NOTHING • BUY HAPPINESS • BUY A BETTER MOU
UY YOUR WAY INTO SOMEONE'S FAVOUR • BUY LOVE • FIND THE RIGHT RELAXATION TECHNIQUE FOR YOU • BUY HEALTHY FAST FOOD •
TING SERVICE • SELL YOURSELF ON AN ONLINE DATING SERVICE • SELL YOURSELF TO YOUR GIRLFRIEND/BOYFRIEND'S FAMILY • BUY FL
HOOSE FILM FOR YOUR CAMERA • BUY RECHARGEABLE BATTERIES • GIVE TO A GOOD CAUSE • TAKE PART IN A CAR BOOT SALE • EMPL
JDENT DISCOUNTS • BUY FLOWERS WHOLESALE • GET A PICTURE FRAMED • EMPLOY A REMOVAL COMPANY • EMPLOY A LIFESTYLE MA
Y FOR A HALLOWE'EN PARTY • BUY A GREAT BIRTHDAY PRESENT FOR UNDER £10 • SELECT GOOD CHAMPAGNE • BUY A DIAMOND • BUY
T A GIFT LIST • BUY WEDDING GIFTS • SELECT BRIDESMAIDS' DRESSES • HIRE AN EVENTS ORGANISER • HIRE A BARTENDER FOR A PART
NOUNCEMENTS • SELL YOUR WEDDING DRESS • BUY AN ANNIVERSARY GIFT • ARRANGE ENTERTAINMENT FOR A PARTY • COMMISSION A
RSON WHO HAS EVERYTHING • BUY A GIFT FOR PASSING EXAMS • SELECT A CHRISTMAS TURKEY • BUY A HOUSEWARMING GIFT • PURC
AND • WRITE A MESSAGE IN THE SKY • HIRE A BIG-NAME BAND • GET INTO A PRIVATE GAMBLING ROOM IN LAS VEGAS • BUY SOMEONE
E TIMES • EMPLOY A BUTLER • BUY A FOOTBALL CLUB • BUY A PERSONAL JET • SELECT A CLASSIC CAR • ACQUIRE A BODY GUARD • BO
EYHOUND TO RACE • BUY A RACEHORSE • BUY A VILLA IN TUSCANY • EMPLOY A PERSONAL CHEF • BUY A JOURNEY INTO SPACE • EMF
RTUNE • HIRE AN EXPERT WITNESS • MAKE MONEY FROM ACCIDENT COMPENSATION • DONATE YOUR BODY TO SCIENCE • MAKE MONE\
ANCIAL ADVISER • PLAN FOR RETIREMENT • COPE WITH HIGHER EDUCATION COSTS • BUY AND SELL SHARES • CHOOSE A STOCKBROK
SS INSURANCE • BUY LIFE INSURANCE • GET PRIVATE HEALTH INSURANCE • BUY PERSONAL FINANCE SOFTWARE • CHOOSE AN ACCOUM
LE OUT A PATENT • MARKET YOUR INVENTION • FINANCE YOUR BUSINESS IDEA • BUY A SMALL BUSINESS • BUY A FRANCHISE • LEASE P
BSITE • HIRE A GRAPHIC DESIGNER • ACQUIRE CONTENT FOR YOUR WEBSITE • BUY ADVERTISING ON THE WEB • SELL YOUR ART • HIRE
BLISH YOUR BOOK • START A BED-AND-BREAKFAST • SELL A FAILING BUSINESS • BUY A HOT DOG STAND • SHOP FOR A MORTGAGE • G
USE AT AUCTION • SHOP FOR A HOUSE ONLINE • BUY A PROPERTY FOR RENOVATION AND RESALE • EVALUATE BEFORE BUYING INTO A
Y A PLOT OF LAND • HAVE YOUR HOUSE DESIGNED • HIRE AN ARCHITECT • HIRE A BUILDER • GET PLANNING PERMISSION • BUY A HOLI
ROAD • BUY TO LET • RENT YOUR HOME FOR A LOCATION SHOOT • FURNISH YOUR HOME • FURNISH YOUR STUDIO FLAT • BUY USED FU
JY HOUSEHOLD APPLIANCES • BUY FLOOR-CARE APPLIANCES • BUY EXTENDED WARRANTIES ON APPLIANCES • FIND PERIOD FIXTURES
ME • SELECT PAINT, STAIN AND VARNISH • CHOOSE DECORATIVE TILES • CHOOSE A DEHUMIDIFIER • BUY A WHIRLPOOL BATH • BUY A S
LLPAPER • BUY A WOOD-BURNING STOVE • SELECT FLOORING • SELECT CARPETING • CHOOSE KITCHEN CABINETS • CHOOSE A KITCHI
OKE ALARMS • BUY CARBON MONOXIDE DETECTORS • BUY FIRE EXTINGUISHERS • CHOOSE AN ENTRY DOOR • BUY A GARAGE-DOOR C
TDOOR FURNITURE • BUY THE PERFECT ROSE • BUY FLOWERING BULBS • BUY FLOWERS FOR YOUR GARDEN • SELECT PEST CONTROL
TOMATIC WATERING SYSTEM • START A NEW LAWN • BUY A LAWN MOWER • BUY KOI FOR YOUR FISH POND • BUY A STORAGE SHED • H
ODUCE • CHOOSE A PERFECT PEACH • BUY AND SELL AT FARMERS' MARKETS • SELECT KITCHEN KNIVES • DECIPHER FOOD LABELS • S
RFECT BURGER • PURCHASE A CHRISTMAS HAM • BUY ORGANIC BEEF • BUY HAGGIS • PURCHASE LOCAL HONEY • CHOOSE A CHICKEN
T TRUFFLES • BUY ARTISAN BREADS • BUY ARTISAN CHEESES • PURCHASE KOSHER FOOD • BUY SENSIBLY IN SUPERMARKETS • CHOO
DER A GREAT CUP OF COFFEE • BUY A COFFEEMAKER OR ESPRESSO MACHINE • PURCHASE PARTY BEER • CHOOSE THE RIGHT WINE •
RM • CHOOSE AN OVULATION PREDICTOR KIT • PICK A PREGNANCY TEST KIT • CHOOSE BIRTH CONTROL • CHOOSE WHERE TO GIVE B
Y BABY CLOTHES • CHOOSE NAPPIES • BUY OR RENT A BREAST PUMP • CHOOSE A CAR SEAT • BUY CHILD-PROOFING SUPPLIES • FIND
Y A GARDEN PLAY STRUCTURE • FIND A FAMILY-FRIENDLY HOTEL • ORGANISE A FUND-RAISING EVENT • BUY BRACES FOR YOUR KID •
A MODEL • SELL USED BABY GEAR, TOYS, CLOTHES AND BOOKS • FIND A COUPLES COUNSELLOR • HIRE A FAMILY SOLICITOR • BUY OF
RCHASE A TOOTHBRUSH • BUY MOISTURISERS AND ANTIWRINKLE CREAMS • SELECT PAIN RELIEF AND COLD MEDICINES • CHOOSE A C
ODUCTS • BUY WAYS TO COUNTER HAIR LOSS • BUY A WIG OR HAIRPIECE • BUY A NEW BODY • GET A TATTOO OR BODY PIERCING • OE
TH • SELECT SPECTACLES AND SUNGLASSES • HIRE A PERSONAL TRAINER • SIGN UP FOR A YOGA CLASS • TREAT YOURSELF TO A DAY
AN ANTIQUE MARKET • BUY AT AUCTION • KNOW WHAT YOUR COLLECTIBLES ARE WORTH • BARTER WITH DEALERS • GET AN ANTIQUE
NS • BUY AN ANTIQUE QUILT • BUY FILM POSTERS • LIQUIDATE YOUR BEANIE BABY COLLECTION • SCORE AUTOGRAPHS • TRADE YU-C
O SELL SPORTS MEMORABILIA • SELL YOUR FOOTBALL-CARD COLLECTION • CHOOSE A DESKTOP COMPUTER • SHOP FOR A USED COM
MPUTER PERIPHERALS • CHOOSE AN INTERNET SERVICE PROVIDER • GET AN INTERNET DOMAIN NAME • NETWORK YOUR COMPUTERS
PLAYER • BUY A VIDEO RECORDER • CHOOSE A PERSONAL DIGITAL ASSISTANT • CHOOSE A MOBILE PHONE SERVICE • GET A BETTER
TAL CAMERA • BUY A HOME AUTOMATION SYSTEM • BUY A STATE-OF-THE-ART SOUND SYSTEM • BUY AN AUDIO/VIDEO DISTRIBUTION
SYSTEM • BUY VIRTUAL-REALITY FURNITURE • BUY TWO-WAY RADIOS • BUY A MOBILE ENTERTAINMENT SYSTEM • GET A PASSPORT, Q
AL LUGGAGE • FLY FOR NEXT TO NOTHING • TAKE A TRIP ON THE TRANS-SIBERIAN EXPRESS • BUY DUTY-FREE • SHIP FOREIGN PURCH
IAN CYCLING HOLIDAY • CHOOSE A CHEAP CRUISE • BOOK A HOTEL PACKAGE FOR THE GREEK ISLANDS • RAFT THE GRAND CANYON
KSHAW IN RANGOON • TAKE SALSA LESSONS IN CUBA • BUY A CAMERA IN HONG KONG • BUY YOUR WAY ONTO A MOUNT EVEREST EX
L TEAM • BUY ANKLE AND KNEE BRACES • CHOOSE RUGBY PROTECTION KIT • BUY GOLF CLUBS • SELL FOUND GOLF BALLS • BUY PC
PLOY A SCUBA INSTRUCTOR • BUY A SKATEBOARD AND PROTECTIVE GEAR • BUY SKATES • GO BUNJEE JUMPING • GO SKYDIVING • BU
OTS AND BINDINGS • BUY SKI BOOTS • BUY A BICYCLE • BUY AN ELECTRIC BICYCLE • BUY CYCLE CLOTHING • BUY A PROPERLY FITTIN
T • BUY A SURFBOARD • BUY FLY-FISHING GEAR • BUY ROCK-CLIMBING EQUIPMENT • BUY A CASHMERE JUMPER • PURCHASE VINTAC
CKTAIL DRESS • BUY DESIGNER CLOTHES AT A DISCOUNT • CHOOSE A BASIC WARDROBE FOR A MAN • BUY A MAN'S DRESS SHIRT • P
THER JACKET • BUY MATERNITY CLOTHES • GET A GREAT-FITTING BRA • CHOOSE A HIGH-PERFORMANCE SWIM SUIT • BUY PERFORMA
TORY SHOPS • BUY A NEW CAR • BUY THE BASICS FOR YOUR CAR • BUY A USED CAR • BUY OR SELL A CAR ONLINE • BUY A HYBRID

Property

172 Shop for a Mortgage

Unless you have a stash of cash, you'll need to get a mortgage to buy a home. In recent years, interest rates have been at their lowest level for decades, enabling many more people to own houses or trade up to more expensive properties. Engage a mortgage broker to shop around for you, or dive in yourself.

Steps

1 Find a mortgage lender. Traditionally it was only building societies that arranged such loans, but now mortgages are widely available from banks and other financial institutions. First you should decide which type of mortgage you want. Mortgages broadly fall into one of three categories:

Repayment

The most common type of loan. The buyer pays off a proportion of the loan each month and then pays interest on the remainder. All of the money goes to the lender. Some repayment mortgages are *flexible*, allowing over- or underpayments to be made according to circumstances.

Interest Only

Also known as *endowment* mortgages, these are more risky. The buyer pays only a monthly interest charge to the lender while at the same time paying into an independent scheme intended to pay off the full amount of the loan at the end of the period. The buyer must make up for any shortfall in value – which is likely with low interest rates and poor-performing money markets.

Current Account

This puts your mortgage, saving and cheque accounts into one large loan, which can be paid into or drawn from at will. Most experts agree that this is the most economical way of running a mortgage, providing you are disciplined with your money.

2 Calculate how much you can afford to pay every month and choose your terms. Terms may be for 15, 20, 25 or 30 years. Obviously, a 15-year programme lets you buy the house outright in half the time, but the monthly payment is higher.

3 Mortgages can have a fixed or variable interest rate. If you take out a fixed-rate mortgage you could lose out if interest rates fall; a variable-rate mortgage means that your monthly payments will depend on movements in interest rate.

4 Shop around for a mortgage lender. Start by contacting your bank or an existing mortgage lender – you may be given preferential conditions.

What to Look For

- Interest rates and terms
- Affordable monthly payment
- Low or no loan fees

Tips

Shop aggressively. Mortgage lending is very competitive, so don't be shy about asking for better terms.

Go over mortgage costs carefully. Different lenders will often call the same cost by different names.

Be aggressive. If one lender has a lower cost on one particular item, use that as leverage to reduce another lender's charges.

If you are a first-time home buyer, you may qualify for a lower deposit or interest rate. Check with a range of mortgage lenders to see what is available.

5 If you don't want to scour the market yourself, look for a mortgage broker who will have access to most lenders and can quickly compare rates to find you the best deal. ALWAYS ensure that a mortgage broker is completely independent.

6 Shop online. Many online lenders offer exceptionally low rates and quick turnaround.

7 Fill out a mortgage application form. If you are using a broker, he or she will do this on your behalf – all you'll have to do is sign on the dotted line. Mortgages are signed in respect of a property, so although you may get an agreement in principle from a lender, the mortgage will only be formally approved when the lender has approved the property you intend to buy.

8 Following approval, the mortgage lender will notify you in writing. This should take less than 14 days.

9 Once you have signed the mortgage agreement, the lender will make a payment to your solicitor – this will then be paid to the vendor's solicitor once the contracts have been exchanged.

173 Get a Better Mortgage Deal

Gone are the days when anyone wanting to buy their own home would be forced to beg from their building society. The mortgage world is now a competitive business with lenders doing all in their power to undercut one another. So if your current mortgage rate is too high, take steps to get yourself a better deal.

Steps

1 Check your current policy for any early payment penalty clause. If one exists – common in fixed-rate repayment mortgages – the cost must be factored into any potential savings that might be made by moving.

2 If you have an endowment mortgage, seek advice in making any changes – with money markets volatile since the mid-1990s, most endowment policies will not pay for their loans without topping-up. (Many who took out endowment mortgages from the late 1980s are known to have been misled. If you were not actively told that your policy might not cover the final payment of your home you may be entitled to some kind of refund.)

3 Look at the deals on offer from the banks and high-street building societies. Some may offer financial inducements or low interest rates to entice new customers.

4 Alternatively, contact a mortgage broker. He or she will know the best deals that apply in your circumstances. Be aware that there is usually a charge for this service (although some may obtain their fees from the mortgage lender).

Warning

Remember that if you default on your mortgage payments the lender may have the right to repossess your home. If this happens it will be auctioned and bring a considerably lower price than if you were to sell it on the open market.

What to Look For

- Lower interest charges
- Low loan fees

Tip

f you replace an endowment mortgage, it may be worth continuing to pay into the endowment fund and view it as a savings plan.

174 Save on Your Mortgage

A home mortgage is the biggest ongoing debt most people will ever face. You can find ways of reducing the overall cost of this debt without going through the hassle of searching for a new mortgage. In particular, paying off your mortgage more quickly is one of the most powerful money strategies you can employ.

Steps

1 Find out whether your mortgage policy allows you to pay off more of the debt whenever you want. If not, you may need to look for a different, more flexible mortgage deal.

2 If your policy is sufficiently flexible, pay off your mortgage early by adding more to your monthly payment. Calculate whatever you can afford, and simply add that each month. For example, by paying an extra £100 a month on a 25-year, £70,000 mortgage at an interest rate of 5 per cent, you slice eight years off the life of the mortgage, and you save over £18,000 in interest. Not bad!

3 Alternatively, make a lump sum repayment each time that you have enough cash saved. This will have a similar effect to increasing monthly payments.

4 Consider an "offset" mortgage in which your mortgage is linked to a savings account. The bank or building society will deduct the money you have invested in the savings account from your mortgage debt when calculating your monthly interest payments. So if you have a £70,000 mortgage and £10,000 in the savings account, you will only pay interest on £60,000. You can use this method to reduce your monthly payments, or keep the payments level and use the excess payment to pay off part of your debt.

5 Check regularly with your lender whether they have better mortgage deals on offer than the one you are signed up for. Most lenders have fixed-rate loans available that keep the interest low for a set period. In principle, you can take a continuous series of fixed-rate loans to keep payments low permanently, although watch out for the effect of fees charged each time you switch to a new deal – they can eat up any benefit from lower payments.

6 Change to another mortgage provider if you think there is real advantage in it. Typically it's not worth doing unless you can secure a rate at least 1 per cent lower (see 173 "Get a Better Mortgage Deal").

What to Look For

- Affordable extra payments
- Refinancing

Tips

Every extra pound you pay off goes directly towards reducing the principal that you owe on your home.

See 172 "Shop for a Mortgage" and 173 "Get a Better Mortgage Deal".

Warning

If you alter your policy so that you can make higher monthly payments, ensure that there are no penalty clauses for changing back – for many mortgage holders, a sudden rise in interest rates may mean that agreed monthly payments suddenly become hard to meet.

175 Get a Mortgage You Can Afford

A home is the single largest purchase most of us are ever likely to make. With interest rates historically low, and competition for custom among mortgage lenders high, many people are taking out mortgages that in a harsher financial climate they would struggle to afford.

Steps

1 Look at the chart below. The column on the left represents the interest rate; the row along the top represents size of mortgage.

2 If you are putting down a 20 per cent deposit on a house costing £250,000, look in the £200,000 column at the current interest rate to find your monthly payment. Look at how that payment changes if the interest rate goes up.

3 For amounts not listed, look in the £100,000 column and multiply by the appropriate factor: for a £180,000 mortgage multiply the mortgage payment by 1.80.

What to Look For

- Current interest rates
- Changes in the financial climate

Warning

Note that the figures below do not include other possible required payments, such as insurance.

RATE	£50,000	£100,000	£150,000	£200,000	£250,000	£300,000
3%	£237.10	£474.21	£711.31	£948.42	£1,185.52	£1,422.63
3.25%	£243.65	£487.31	£730.97	£974.63	£1,218.29	£1,461.94
3.5%	£250.31	£500.62	£750.93	£1,001.24	£1,251.55	£1,501.87
3.75%	£257.06	£514.13	£771.19	£1,028.26	£1,285.32	£1,542.39
4%	£263.91	£527.83	£791.75	£1,055.67	£1,319.59	£1,583.51
4.25%	£270.86	£541.73	£812.60	£1,083.47	£1,354.34	£1,625.21
4.5%	£277.91	£555.83	£833.74	£1,111.66	£1,389.58	£1,667.49
4.75%	£285.05	£570.11	£855.17	£1,140.23	£1,425.29	£1,710.35
5%	£292.29	£584.59	£876.88	£1,169.18	£1,461.47	£1,753.77
5.25%	£299.62	£599.24	£898.87	£1,198.49	£1,498.11	£1,753.77
5.5%	£307.04	£614.08	£921.13	£1,228.17	£1,535.21	£1,842.26
5.75%	£315.55	£629.10	£943.65	£1,258.21	£1,572.76	£1,887.31
6%	£322.15	£644.30	£966.45	£1,288.6	£1,610.75	£1,932.90
6.25%	£329.83	£659.66	£989.50	£1,319.33	£1,649.17	£1,979.00
6.5%	£337.60	£675.20	£1,012.81	£1,350.41	£1,688.01	£2,025.62
6.75%	£345.45	£690.91	£1,036.36	£1,381.82	£1,727.27	£2,072.73
7%	£353.38	£706.77	£1,060.16	£1,413.55	£1,766.94	£2,120.33
7.25%	£361.40	£722.80	£1084.21	£1,445.61	£1,807.01	£2,168.42
7.5%	£369.49	£738.99	£1,108.48	£1,477.98	£1,847.47	£2,216.97
7.75%	£377.66	£755.32	£1,132.99	£1,510.65	£1,888.32	£2,265.98
8%	£385.90	£771.81	£1,157.72	£1,543.63	£1,929.54	£2,315.44
8.25%	£394.22	£788.45	£1,182.67	£1,576.9	£1,971.12	£2,365.35
8.5%	£402.61	£805.22	£1,207.84	£1,610.45	£2,013.06	£2,415.68
8.75%	£411.07	£822.14	£1,233.21	£1,644.28	£2,055.35	£2,466.43

176 Obtain House Insurance

If you own a home, insurance is an absolute must. Not only is it essential to protect your investment, no mortgage lender will fund a loan without some form of buildings insurance.

Steps

1 As a home owner you can expect to pay two types of insurance. Building insurance covers your home, and contents insurance covers everything you own inside the building. Some insurers will give you discount if you take out a policy that covers both. (Some will go even further if you add car or life insurance to the deal.)

2 For buildings insurance, estimate how much it would cost to rebuild your home. Many home owners mistakenly look at how much their home is worth. Insurance companies use guidelines for estimating replacement costs and the resulting premiums for total replacement policies.

3 Compare different providers. Premiums differ depending on where you live, the value of your home, and other factors such as how long you've lived there and whether there have been past claims at that address.

4 Consider internet insurers. A relatively new breed of insurer, these companies have lower operating overheads than those found on the high street and are able to pass the savings on to the buyer.

5 Find out what steps you can take to lower your premium cost, such as installing a security system. Some insurance providers will also offer lower rates for existing customers, so turn to your car insurer for a home owner's quote first.

6 You can save money by raising or lowering the contribution that you have to pay towards each claim (the "excess"). A policy that you agree to pay the first £100 of any claim will be much higher than one in which you agree to pay the first £1,000.

7 An insurance broker should be able to find you the best deal on offer, but you may have to pay a fee for the service. (Be aware that some seemingly independent brokers have "favoured" insurers which often – by some mysterious coincidence – offer them the highest commission!)

8 Understand exactly what is covered in your policy. On "new for old" policies (where stolen or damaged goods are replaced) be sure to ask how the insurer defines replacement cost.

9 Ask about "valuables" – most insurers will require objects of above a certain value to be listed separately. There may be a value limit on any single item.

10 Some contents policies will also cover items lost or damaged outside the home, such as cameras or personal music players.

What to Look For

- Rebuilding costs
- Coverage for contents
- Valuables

Tip

For items not covered by a standard policy, such as artworks or antiques, you should be able to buy add-on coverage.

Warning

If you work from home – or have a paying hobby – you may be wise to take out separate business insurance. Failure to do this may affect your other policies should you make a claim.

177 Buy a House

Unlike in many parts of Europe, for most Britons home ownership is one of life's fundamental aspirations, and something that most of us achieve at some point. However, it also requires homework, legwork and considerable effort on your part to ensure that the process goes as smoothly as possible. Here's how to make your dream a reality, and avoid some of the nightmare pitfalls that the process sometimes throws up.

Steps

1 Decide if it makes sense for you to buy a house or keep renting. If your job keeps you on the move, it may not be worth it. Depending on the state of the property market, you may need to stay put for several years to recoup various fees involved. If your desire to own a home is based on wanting to create stability, keeping control over your living situation, building equity and investing in your future, go for it.

2 Work out how much you can afford to pay for your new home. Consider your deposit, stamp duty, estate agent's fee, mortgage, and buildings and contents insurance. As a rule of thumb, an individual can expect to obtain a mortgage of between three and four times his or her annual income; a couple can expect offers of two or three times their joint income. Add the size of your deposit – how much of your own money you want to make available – to work out how much you can afford to pay for a house.

3 Mortgage lenders may consider your credit rating when deciding whether or not to offer you a loan, so strengthen your credit: pay off credit cards, resolve any credit disputes and cancel unused cards. Mortgage lenders take into account both how you use the credit you have available and whether your available credit is too high for your income.

4 If in doubt about your credit rating, contact a credit agency and request a personal credit report. Contact either Equifax (equifax.co.uk) or Experion (experion.co.uk). Reports only cost £2, so it's good value for money.

5 Think about what kind of home you want. Do you want a newer home that requires little or no refurbishing? Would you prefer an older home with character that might require some repair work? One floor or two? Are you interested in a flat, a terrace, a semi-detached, townhouse or a detached building in the country?

6 Decide where you want to live. Think about how long it will take to commute to work, evaluate local schools, and look at the resale value of the homes in the area. Scout out what's available in the vicinity. Look at prices, home design, proximity to shops, schools and other amenities.

(continued)

What to Look For

- A suitable house
- A good location
- An affordable mortgage
- Appraisal
- Survey
- Understand the fees involved

Tips

Be patient. Finding a home that fits your family's needs can take some time.

Home values fluctuate with the ups and downs of the economy.

Buying a home is likely to be the biggest single investment you'll ever make. Choose wisely.

7 Visit the area to gauge what's on the market.

8 Find a mortgage lender – usually a bank or building society – and arrange to be pre-approved for a mortgage. A dedicated mortgage broker may be able to find a deal more suited to your needs – but you will be charged for the service. (See 172 "Shop for a Mortgage".)

9 Be ready to hand over a substantial down payment. Many mortgage lenders will require a deposit of at least 5 per cent of the purchase price.

10 Register with an estate agent. Have the details of properties that fall within your brief sent to you. Visit any properties that interest you: the more homes you look at, the better idea you will have of your likes and dislikes. This will help you filter out future choices.

11 Look for an estate agent who will search for suitable properties, represent your interests and negotiate on your behalf. A buyer's representative can evaluate the properties you view, do a market analysis to determine its value in the marketplace, select an appropriate price to begin negotiations and advise you in writing the contract.

12 Be aware that you don't have to buy through an estate agent. Many people prefer to save money by selling privately, advertising in newspapers or magazines.

13 Go into exhaustive detail when describing to your agent what you want in a home: the number of bathrooms and bedrooms, attached garage, land and anything else that may be important, like good light or a big enough garden for the kids. If your agent shows you homes that aren't what you want, find another one who listens more attentively.

14 Don't be bullied by an estate agent. When the property market is hot it's easy to feel under pressure to make a quick decision. DON'T. Buying a house is a serious investment – maybe the most important you'll ever make – so make sure that you get what you are looking for, not what somebody else thinks you should have.

15 Shop aggressively. Look at as many homes as possible to get a sense of what's available. Don't rush into buying if you don't have to.

16 Look beyond the property itself to the neighbourhood and the condition of nearby homes to make sure you aren't buying the only gem in sight. The area in which your home is located is sometimes a bigger consideration than the home itself, as it has a major impact on its value.

Tips

Find out your credit rating early on to assess how strong your mortgage application is.

Always factor in your removal costs when deciding how much you can spend on a home.

Warning

Get a firm estimate of how much you can expect to pay in legal costs and stamp duties. These can provide a nasty surprise if unexpected.

17 Visit properties you're seriously interested in at different times of the day to check traffic and congestion, available parking, noise levels and general activities.

18 Most of us will have to sell our current homes in order to afford a new one (see 183 "Sell a House"). If so, any offer to buy that you make will be contingent on that sale. Such offers are more risky and less desirable for the seller, as the sale can't be completed until the buyer's house is sold. It will certainly figure in your bargaining position. Consequently, you may need to put your current house on the market at the same time as looking for a new one.

19 Try not to fall in love with one particular property. It's great to find exactly what you need, but if you get your heart set on one home, you may end up paying more than it's worth because you're emotionally invested. The deal may also fall apart.

20 When you've found your ideal home work out how much you want to offer. Unless the property is in a particularly hot area, or the market is buzzing, it's usual to open with a bid of at least 10 per cent below the asking price. But note that sometimes (especially in Scotland) offers over the asking price are specifically requested.

21 Any mortgage lender will insist that you have the prospective property surveyed. This can be a simple valuation survey, so that the mortgage lender is happy that the property is worth what you are paying for it, or a full structural survey. Where possible, you should always go for the latter.

22 IMPORTANT NOTE: Even if you are paying for the property in cash you should still have it surveyed.

23 Hire a solicitor specialising in buying and selling property. They will perform on your behalf the necessary searches to prove that the property is registered in the name of the vendor. If you choose not to hire a solicitor you must do this for yourself – although it is possible, it is also time-consuming and arguably not worth the money you'll save.

24 Agree a date on which you can take possession of the property.

25 At a time advised by your solicitor, you will have to transfer your deposit from your bank account to your solicitor's account. Your mortgage lender will do the same. This money will be paid to the vendor's solicitor who will then exchange contracts.

26 Once your solicitor has exchanged contracts with the vendor you can move in.

178 Buy a House at Auction

"Sold to the highest bidder!" Buying a home through an auction can mean incredible deals. In most cases, the seller is a mortgage lender who repossessed the property when the former owner was unable to keep up payments on the mortgage. Despite the sad circumstances, competition for these homes can be keen.

Steps

1 See 374 "Buy at Auction" and 177 "Buy a House" for more detailed information.

2 Scour the internet for specialist property auction sites – all of the established auctioneers will have an online presence. (You can enter something like "PROPERTY AUCTIONS IN THE UK" into any web search engine.)

3 To get the best out of property auctions you can't be too specific about where you want to live. If you have your heart set on a particular neighbourhood, then the chances of something suitable coming up at auction will be slim.

4 Make sure you have the finance in place beforehand. You are unlikely to get an agreement for a mortgage on a property bought at auction. (Although, if you're able, you could buy using a loan – with a substantially higher interest rate – and then get a mortgage to pay off the loan once you had purchased the property (see 172 "Shop for a Mortgage").

5 Order a catalogue for any upcoming auctions that interest you. (There is usually a substantial charge for these.)

6 Note the details of any property that interests you. It will be listed with its "reserve price" – the lowest price at which the vendor will allow the property to be sold.

7 Visit the property. If you intend bidding, have a professional survey done beforehand. This will reveal any major structural problems, and give you an estimate of its actual market value.

8 Before the auction, decide on the maximum figure you would be prepared to pay. Don't go above it – it's easy to get carried away in a bidding war.

9 At the auction, place bids by raising your hand. Some auction houses will allow bidding via the telephone or the internet.

10 Understand that when the gavel comes down, if your bid is the highest you are deemed to have made a legally binding contract. There's no backing out now!

What to Look For

- Pre-approved mortgage
- Inspection reports
- Free and clear title

Tip

Some auctioneers will set a reserve that guarantees a minimum price will be received. This means that even if you're the winning bidder, you may not get the house if your highest bid isn't over the reserve price.

Warning

If a property you buy at auction turns out to be a lemon, you have very little come-back. This route is for risk-takers only!

179 Shop For a House Online

The internet offers myriad opportunities for house hunting, especially if you are looking to move into a new area. In most cases, though, the internet will be used simply to look at houses on offer, and find out about local amenities – the practicalities and legalities remain the same as for buying any other type of property.

Steps

1 See 177 "Buy a House" for many of the basic steps common to buying any kind of property.

2 Decide on a location. Property web pages usually give you the choice of searching by county, town or postcode. The internet provides numerous opportunities to suss out a new area before even visiting. Draw up a list of amenities that you require from any location you envisage living in, and type them into a search engine along with the name of the area – for example "Health Clubs in Hastings UK".

3 Decide on the property type and age of the home, or other specific features, such as number of bedrooms, bathrooms, garages or size of garden.

4 Surf the internet for sites that offer listings – such as Fish4.co.uk – or the web pages of estate agents operating in the area in which you are interested. You should obtain good results by entering "estate agents" alongside the town name into a search engine.

5 Find out if there is a weekly property guide to your area, and if it is accessible via a website.

6 Contact the agent listed if you see a home that fits your criteria. Ask for further information, such as more photographs and the home's history. In such cases the estate agent will send out their standard information sheet on the property; they will also almost certainly ask you to register with them, so they can send you details of similar properties should they arise.

7 Set up an appointment to meet the estate agent if you are still interested.

8 Look out for individuals selling their own homes on the internet. As they are saving money by not using an estate agent they may accept lower bids.

What to Look For

- Property websites
- Online estate agents
- Individual sales

Tip

Request e-mail updates on available houses and additional information about the community in which you are interested.

180 Buy a Property For Renovation and Resale

It just needs a little tender love and care, right? If you're willing to put some elbow grease into it, buying a property to renovate and sell on can be a profitable endeavour. But there is a level of risk involved and a substantial commitment of time and effort on your part – not to mention long periods of time when you may be living in chaos and sawdust. But if you're still up for the challenge, it can be a rewarding experience.

Steps

1 Decide on the geographic area in which you want a property. Whether you intend to live in a home or not will impact on where you'll want to buy. Remember that your ideal place to live may not be the best place to invest in property.

2 Be prepared for an extensive search. Many such properties – particularly those in especially bad shape – don't command much attention, so you may have to hunt around. Drive through desirable areas to spot "For Sale" signs.

3 Keep in mind that "location, location, location" is still the mantra of any property purchases, whether for a single family home or a renovation-to-sell job. Steer away from properties in areas where the market profile is going downhill – you'll have trouble recouping your investment no matter how beautiful the structure. Find out if the asking price is comparable with the prices of other homes in the area.

4 Make sure the property is in an area of appreciating house values. That way, your house will be worth even more when your repairs are completed, rather than less because of worsening market conditions in the area. Try to meet some of the neighbours who might give you some information on what's been going on.

5 Look in the classified ads and on estate agents' books for magic phrases, such as "in need of repair" or "some modernisation necessary".

6 Buying at auction – if you have the finances in place – is where many run-down bargains can be found. Scour the internet for specialist property auction sites – all of the established auctioneers will have an online presence (see 178 "Buy a House at Auction").

7 Keep a special eye out for properties that need only cosmetic improvements. Houses that could use new paint, carpeting or flooring are the least expensive and offer the fastest potential turnaround. Larger problems, such as faulty foundations are often prohibitively expensive and may undermine eventual profit, depending on what you got the house for and how much you think you can sell it for.

What to Look For

- Decent location
- Profit potential
- Reasonable repair requirements
- Surveys

Tips

Be patient. Unlike the many television home make-over shows that can give the impression that renovations happen within a weekend or two, it can take a long time to find and much longer to spruce up, particularly if you're also holding down a full-time job.

When selling, timing is often as important as the state of a house. If you sell during a hot market, the appreciation in price can help offset the cost of your improvements.

Don't be taken aback by properties that have been on the market for a long time. It's not unusual for some houses to be up for sale for a year or more, depending on market conditions.

8 Watch for vacant homes that have not been kept up by the owner. These forgotten houses can often have the most motivated seller you could hope to find.

9 If you find an appealing property with seemingly reasonable repair needs, have the home professionally inspected. Specify that the final sale is contingent on a satisfactory full structural survey.

10 If possible, accompany the surveyor when he or she goes through the house for a blow-by-blow account. Then review the report in detail to see what's wrong. You may also need to get additional inspections. Be sure that the surveyor generates a narrative report rather than a checklist.

11 Get a formal appraisal of the home's value and how much it should sell for after it is restored to good condition.

12 Set your target purchase price. Professionals would generally suggest bidding at least 30 per cent below the property's potential renovated value.

13 Get several bids from contractors of how much it will cost to fix what needs to be fixed (see 242 "Hire a Builder, Plumber, Painter or Electrician"). Be sure to check zoning requirements and include permit fees. To make the effort worthwhile, the house's value should increase at least £2 for every pound you spend on improvements. Calculate the potential value of the house after renovations and be sure that it isn't higher than comparable houses in the area. Be realistic about repair costs.

14 If you intend doing much of the repair work yourself, be realistic about your skills, free time and overall commitment. You'll face a lot of problems on the way, so make sure you have the drive to overcome them.

15 Try to make your agreement to buy the property contingent on your obtaining a satisfactory bid for the cost of renovation. That way, if the bids you receive are simply too expensive, you can still back out of the deal. Keep in mind that contingencies of any kind could make it hard to negotiate a lower price or even make a deal in a seller's market when competition among buyers can be intense.

16 Make sure you have your finances in place. Some – but by no means all – mortgage lenders will make loans available for a large-scale renovation projects (see 172 "Shop for a Mortgage"). Alternatively, consider using an existing property to raise the finances (see 185 "Release Capital from Your Home").

17 Make whatever repairs and renovations are necessary and then sell the property (see 183 "Sell a House"). It's as easy as that!

Warnings

As a general rule of thumb, improvements that are invisible to the average home buyer or merely bring the home in line with expected minimum standards WON'T add to the resale value. If you make the wrong kind of improvements – such as converting two bedrooms into a master suite when you only had two bedrooms to begin with – you won't see much of a return on your investment.

Another potential pitfall is over-improving the home compared to other homes in the neighbourhood. If in doubt, think average!

181 Evaluate Before Buying into a New Area

Property experts always say that the three most important things to consider when evaluating a property are "location, location and location". That's because a home in a fashionable area with convenient shopping and good schools nearby will hold its value far better than an identical home in a less popular area. Of course, it will also be much more pleasant to live in. Ask these questions to determine the quality of the neighbourhood you're considering, and to evaluate other local factors that go into making a house a good home – and a good investment.

What to Look For

- Visual clues
- Noise levels
- Issues of planning and development
- Local amenities
- Cultural offerings

Steps

1 How well do the local residents look after their property? This will give you a strong indication of the types of people living in the neighbourhood.

2 Try to find out the ratio of owners to renters in the area. Home owners are more likely to make an effort to keep their property in good order than those renting.

3 Are the local roads and pavements well-maintained? This may indicate how well the local council manage their funds, or their particular leanings.

4 If you are a parent, consider things from the perspective of your child. What is the quality of local schools? Are they close by, or will you have to arrange transport. Is the traffic heavy? If so, is it safe for children? Are there local parks?

5 Pay a visit to the area at night. How does it feel? Does it change in character? Is it noisy? Even the friendliest of areas can take on an aura of menace after nightfall.

6 Is it safe? Check how much crime there is in the area with the local police station. Remember, though, that gentrification is rife in some parts of bigger cities – neighbourhoods that a few years ago were crime-ridden, no-go areas may suddenly have become property hotspots.

7 Check for local amenities. Are hospitals, fire and police stations close enough for your needs?

8 Is the area on a flight path? If so, how frequently do aircraft fly overhead?

9 Are main roads or train stations so close that they may cause noise pollution problems?

10 Check for cultural amenities. Does the area have any theatres, cinemas, music venues or sports facilities that you might want?

11 Check for local development issues. Ensure that the property or area that interests you won't soon become a major building site, or that the park at the foot of that beautiful garden won't soon be razed to make way for an industrial park.

Tip

Look on the internet by entering the name of your desired area – along with such words as "problems", "developments" or "entertainment" – in one of the popular search engines such as Google.

182 Exchange Contracts on a Property

When all the terms of the contract have been met and agreed, the solicitors of both parties will finally be able to transfer ownership of the property. This is an absolute necessity for the completion of a sale to take place.

Steps

1 Review all your mortgage documents. Before you sign anything, make absolutely certain that you are getting the mortgage you thought you were.

2 Make sure all surveys and inspections have been satisfactorily performed, all agreed work completed, and all clearances for completed work provided. You must do this prior to the signing of any documents.

3 If possible, do a walk through of the property prior to the signing of any documents. Make sure all agreed work has been completed to your own satisfaction.

4 Agree on a date in which contracts can be exchanged and you can move into the property.

5 Before you move in, contact the utility companies – telephone, water, gas and electricity – to ensure that you will have a service from that date.

6 Make arrangements to take possession of the keys once the transaction has been recorded.

What to Look For

- Documentation
- Walk through
- Completion date
- Moving date

Tips

Be sure to read all the paperwork you will be signing, and follow up to make sure that these steps have been taken.

Once the home is in your name, get the locks changed and a new set of keys made.

183 Sell a House

Like buying a home, selling one is a significant project. Even if you plan to use an estate agent, it's in your best interest to understand all the various elements that contribute to a successful sale. The more you know, the more cash you'll be able to pocket in the end. Think of your preparation as money in the bank.

Steps

Get prepared

1 Decide if you want to use an estate agent or not. A selling agent generally receives 1.5 to 2.5 per cent of the sale price. In return, he or she should work aggressively to sell your home and list it where it will reach the maximum number of potential buyers. On the other hand, you may be able to save many thousands of pounds by handling the marketing and sale of your home on your own. Read 184 "Sell a House Without an Estate Agent" and pay particular attention to the time involved.

What to Look For

- A suitable agent
- Realistic asking price
- An aggressive marketing plan

Tips

Research how fast homes are selling in your area. That will give you an idea of how long you may have to wait to sell your home.

(continued)

2 Get recommendations from satisfied friends and acquaintances and interview several agents who specialise in your geographic area. Get a feel for their approach and how they'll go about marketing your home. Ask them to outline their strategy for making your home as attractive as possible.

3 Review current listings in your area to get a feel for what your home might be worth. Look for estate agents who sell properties like yours – they will be more knowledgeable about that market and attract more suitable buyers. Look at the window displays of prospective estate agents.

4 Your agent should get comparative prices on nearby homes and do a market analysis, taking into account the size, location, condition and other elements to price it accurately. Understand how the agent established the asking price.

5 Find out where the details of the house will be listed and – increasingly important – if it will have an online presence. Also ensure that your agent will be producing a professional-looking fact sheet to help market the house.

6 Make sure that any agent you consider belongs to a professional body, such as the National Association of Estate Agents (NAEA). The NAEA sets certain standards for its members.

7 A good agent should know the local area well, and be able to show you examples of similar properties they've sold recently. Agents use comparisons to make their valuations, which can be difficult if your home is in some way unusual – all the more reason to use an agent who has recently sold a property like yours.

8 Interview at least three prospective estate agents before making a choice. Go with the agent that makes you feel most confident – not necessarily the one with the highest quote.

Get ready to show

1 Perform any needed repairs on the interior and exterior of your home and fix, paint or otherwise repair anything that may hinder a sale.

2 Increase kerb appeal. Try to ensure that your home makes the best first impression possible. Clean the windows, cut the grass and weed the flowerbeds.

3 Remove any extra furniture, wall hangings or ornaments that might distract potential buyers. Remember the phrase "less is more". Give any walls that need it a fresh coat of neutral paint.

4 Place a "For Sale" sign in your front garden and have fact sheets readily available.

If you're buying another home, you can make that purchase contingent on the successful sale of your current home.

Beware of estate agents who suggest they can get an unreasonably high sales price. An agent might use a high listing price to get your business, and then seek a lower price later.

Be aware that VAT is payable on estate agent's fees.

5   Keep your house neat and tidy. Prospective buyers may often appear with as little as half an hour's notice. If you've handed over your keys while you are at work you may not even have the opportunity to tidy up.

6   Consider boarding your pets while the house is being shown. Not everyone loves them, and they may distract, irritate or scare potential buyers.

Make the deal

1   Establish your flexibility. Decide ahead of time how much, if any, you're willing to trim from the asking price to make a sale. Alternatively, in a competitive market, be prepared to deal with multiple offers.

2   Get yourself psyched up for some hard-nosed business. Depending on market conditions, you shouldn't expect any would-be buyer to offer the full asking price the first time around. In a buyer's market, you'll need to determine what is most important to you – price, moving date, keeping the appliances – and get the best deal possible. That said, the first offer is frequently the best offer, so don't be unreasonable. In a seller's market, expect to get close to your asking price or over in a very short period of time. But be careful: pricing your home too high could keep it on the market for longer than you wanted – and you may end up having to drop the price later anyway to improve your chances of a sale.

3   Weigh the pros and cons of multiple offers, if you're lucky enough to have them. Consider the offering price, how solid the buyer's financing is, whether the sale is contingent on the sale of the buyer's house. It might be preferable to accept a slightly lower offer from a first-time buyer than a higher offer from some- one in a long "chain". Only you can decide. Your estate agent should be able to advise you on such matters.

4   Reduce the asking price if your home doesn't attract any offers at all even though several people have been round to see it. Start with a 5 per cent drop and see if that boosts interest.

184 Sell a House Without an Estate Agent

If the notion of handing over a fat commission cheque to an estate agent irks you, consider selling your house on your own. Before you go down this path, factor in everything that's involved: you'll not only put out that sign on your lawn, but be taking phone calls, scheduling appointments, buying classified ads and conducting negotiations. All on your own.

Steps

1 Read 183 "Sell a House" for the basic rundown.

2 Consider whether it makes sense financially to go to the trouble and expense of marketing and selling your house yourself, based on the commission you're saving. On a £250,000 home that could mean a saving of around £6,000.

3 Understand that you will, of course, incur additional marketing expenses that you wouldn't otherwise have, such as newspaper listings, flyers, signs and websites, but these will cost a small proportion of an estate agent's fee.

4 For many would-be DIY sellers, time may be more of a critical factor than saving money. Be aware that serving as your own agent means that you'll need to be available at all times to take telephone calls from potential buyers, schedule viewings, and be at the house when they want to visit. If your free time doesn't allow for this level of flexibility, using an estate agent may make more sense.

5 Set a fair price for your home. Study the sale prices of comparable homes in your neighbourhood. (You can get this information from a local estate agent or newspaper.) Before you set the asking price, take into account solicitors fees, other selling expenses, and the amount of cash you want after the sale. Your home will sell faster if it is priced appropriately.

6 Use internet directory sites such as Fish4 (fish4.co.uk) to find out how actual sale prices compare to asking prices – use this as a guide for your "bottom line".

7 See "Get Ready to Show" steps under 183 "Sell a House". Clean your house thoroughly and get rid of all clutter. Pay particular attention to the front of your home and the main entrance.

8 Prepare a professional-looking, letter-size fact sheet that contains at least one full-colour photo of the front of the house (and, if appropriate, some of the inside rooms), a complete list of saleable features and amenities, council tax banding and your contact information.

What to Look For

- Clean, attractive property
- Time to prepare, show and negotiate
- Appropriate asking price
- Widespread advertising
- Final negotiations

Tips

One way to smooth any prospective problems before they crop up is to only consider offers from buyers who are pre-qualified for a mortgage.

Take the time to thoroughly understand contracts. Ensure that you discuss anything you don't fully understand with a solicitor.

8 Get the word out. Place an ad in the property section of your local newspaper. Put up signs advertising your property for sale on your front lawn or in a front window. Post flyers. Consider setting up a website.

9 Use a solicitor to handle the contractual side of the deal. (See "Make the Deal" steps under 183 "Sell a House".)

185 Release Capital from Your Home

Many UK home owners may be are unaware that it may be possible to raise immediate cash based on the value of their property – or, in the case of mortgage-payers, on the equity they hold in that property.

Steps

1 Understand that a home equity loan is based on the equity in your house. To work out your equity, take the current value of your home minus any money you still owe in loans or mortgages. If you own a home or you're a mortgage payer, the equity can be used to help you get a loan. If your home is worth £250,000, and your mortgage balance is £100,000, you have an available equity of £150,000.

2 The most straightforward way in which you can raise money against equity is to re-mortgage your property. This will only be possible if you own the property already. Most lenders will treat you in the same way as any other mortgage seeker, the amount they will lend you will depend on your personal circumstances (see 172 "Shop for a Mortgage").

3 If your mortgage is small relative to the market value of your home – a common occurrence in areas of the country that have seen property prices boom – you may be able to raise cash by taking out a secured loan. The lender will agree a loan value and fixed interest rate, and take your equity as security.

4 Consider a home reversion plan. Popular among the retired, this entails "selling" a percentage of your home to a finance company for a fixed sum or a monthly income: the proviso is that you retain the right to live there for the rest of your life. When your home is eventually sold on your death – or on your moving into care – the finance company takes the agreed percentage of the proceeds of the sale. If house prices have gone up, the company reaps the benefit of the increase.

5 A home income plan (sometimes known as a mortgage annuity scheme) is a form of secured loan. In this case, with the cash you release you buy an annuity, which provides you with a regular guaranteed income. This is not good choice when interest rates are low.

What to Look For

- Maximum loan available on your home
- Low interest rate to start
- Inexpensive or free set-up

Tips

Although equity release schemes are most popular among the over-60s, an increasing number of younger homeowners are following this route to pay for home improvements, a new car or their children's education.

Warnings

If you take out a secured loan you may put your home at risk. You will, however, benefit from a lower interest rate than would be offered with an unsecured loan.

Most equity release schemes involve legal and valuation fees – this could be as much as £1,000. (Some companies will reimburse these fees if you follow through with the loan, however.)

186 Buy a Plot of Land

Have you fantasised about living in a remote part of the countryside? Can you simply not find the house you want from what's available on the market? Buying a plot of land on which to build your dream home has its own set of considerations. But the most important one of all is still location.

Steps

1 Check local newspapers in your targeted area for plots for sale. Some rural estate agents specialise in land sales, and may be able to help you find one that's good value and suitable for the kind of home you want to put on it.

2 Consider the location carefully, as well as proximity to shopping districts and parks, quality of the schools, traffic and congestion, public transport and the crime rate. Look at the lay of the land.

3 Features such as steep drop-offs, drainage problems or poor access roads may increase costs. Find out if utilities such as gas, electricity, sewerage and water are available, especially if you are buying a plot off the beaten path, and how much it will cost to access them.

4 Define in general terms the type of structure you'd like to build, including square footage, number of floors, number and types of rooms, architectural style, as well as any specific features you want, such as a swimming pool or tennis court. Depending on the size and design of your home, a particular plot may or may not work.

5 Consult a local architect. He or she will not only have a good idea of the land on the market, but will know what may or may not be deemed acceptable by the local Planning Department. Whatever you plan to do with the land once you've bought it will have to be agreed by the local council. (See 188 "Hire an Architect" and 190 "Get Planning Permission".)

6 Investigate what the future holds for neighbouring properties. Will other houses be built? How many? Are they residential or could commercial buildings be put in? How will this affect traffic? Is there a possibility of additional buildings or roads being added in the future? How will your view be impacted? Look into potential environmental disputes such as water rights or endangered species habitats that could affect your property's value or ability to be sold or developed.

7 Hire a surveyor to map out the specifics of the property.

8 Find out if your plot of land faces any natural phenomena, such as flooding. You may need to have an engineer conduct a survey to spot potential sliding problems.

9 See 177 "Buy a House" for specific information on legal and financial requirements.

What to Look For

- Location
- Utilities and services
- Lie of the land
- Ideal structure
- Surveyor
- Financing

Tips

Speak to local builders to learn more about housing developments they are building and plots that are still available. If you can find a builder (see 189 "Hire a Builder") who owns land that interests you, you will generally simplify the process of buying land and building a home, which can be done in one single transaction.

Visit the plot several times at different times of the day to get a complete feel for sun and shade patterns, as well as traffic and parking issues.

187 Have Your House Designed

Having trouble finding an existing house that you want to buy? Why not consider having your dream house built to your own specification.

Steps

1 Determine the size of your budget. Don't forget to account for the cost of buying a plot of land (see 186 "Buy a Plot of Land").

2 Draw up a detailed, prioritised list of what you want your home to include: size and style of living areas, number of bedrooms and bathrooms, office and library space and garage size. Think carefully about the "must-have" and the "would-be-nice" features. Don't forget to include outdoor features such as a swimming pool or tennis courts.

3 Ask yourself how you want to use the house now and in the future. Do you like to entertain? Do you want a casual open-plan design or formal dining and living rooms? Is your home eventually likely to need to accommodate ageing parents, returning adult children or grandchildren? Do you need a separate entrance for live-in staff?

4 Think seriously about hiring an architect to design the house for you. This will not only give you a unique building but enable you to include features that match your requirements *exactly*. Architects are also usually local experts in such matters as planning requirements and costing. Remember, the tighter the brief you give your architect, the better the match will be (see 188 "Hire an Architect").

5 Alternatively, you could consider cutting (or reducing altogether) an architect's fees by purchasing ready-made house plans. These are widely available from specialist companies. Some architects may offer plans for sale online – some sites may even let you specify exactly what features you want, such as a certain size of kitchen or number of bedrooms.

6 A third alternative is to buy a "kit home". Companies operating in this area of the market may provide a total service, from helping acquire planning permission to erecting the building.

7 Before you go ahead with any work, evaluate the plan for overall size, traffic patterns (movement throughout the building), exterior materials, efficient use of space and materials, and well-planned work and storage areas.

8 If you are working with ready-made plans, hire an architect to make any desired modifications, and provide new drawings.

9 Find a building contractor and project manager. (This won't be necessary if you have an architect, or have bought a kit home.) (See 189 "Hire a Builder".)

What to Look For

- Plans that suit your needs
- Kit home specialists
- Architect to design from scratch or modify plans
- Plot requirements

Tip

Chances are good that plans will need to be adapted to meet your family's specific needs, so don't be afraid to make modifications with the help of an architect.

188 Hire an Architect

Architects go beyond strict functionality to create spaces that actually enrich the quality of life. They think holistically to create a home that truly works with the land it sits on. Chemistry is key when choosing an architect since you'll not only be spending a lot of time together, but sharing a great deal of personal information during the process.

Steps

1 Visit riba.org, the website of the Royal Institute of British Architects. Every practising British architect must have passed their RIBA examinations, otherwise he or she is not legally entitled to trade as architect.

2 If you're tearing down anything more structurally significant than plasterboard internal walls, or if the job involves any plans or new construction, hire as an architect.

3 Ask friends and colleagues for recommendations. Try to identify someone with a project similar to yours, and visit the job site or finished home if possible. Find out if there are any issues about which you should be aware.

4 The RIBA website contains a regional directory of all practising architects from which you can make a short list. Make sure that you interview several candidates. Review their academic and professional credentials and awards. You're assessing whether the architect listens to your ideas and is able to offer plausible, creative but financially achievable solutions to your requests. Above all, you need to "click" personally with your architect.

5 Bring an architect into the picture when you know essentially what you want, but before you decide on a course of action. As trained problem solvers, architects should be able to provide solutions at the front end of the process on all aspects of design and cost-effective use of building materials. Architects are also familiar with all building codes and other legal requirements. They also understand the importance of intangible elements such as natural light.

6 Work up a sketch or provide photos of buildings you like from magazines and other sources. The architect must be able to accommodate your lifestyle and specific space requirements.

7 Make sure you understand how his or her fees are structured. Your job may be priced as a fixed figure, a percentage of total construction costs, or on an hourly time and materials basis. You'll pay more for overtime and making changes to the plans; you'll also be asked for a retainer before work begins.

8 Make sure all elements of the contract are clearly spelled out in writing before you allow work to begin. The contract should include a detailed description of the job, estimated budget and schedule of completion.

What to Look For

- An experienced architect
- Personalities that mesh
- Projects similar to yours

Tip

Be sure to ask about any issues that are important to you, such as solar power or energy-efficient materials.

Warning

Discuss what mechanisms are in place to stay within budget and what protection you have if actual costs exceed the budget.

189 Hire a Builder

The right builder is essential to the success of any kind of large-scale home improvement project. But finding one may also be rather easier said than done.

Steps

1 Read 242 "Hire a Builder, Plumber, Painter or Electrician" for background information.

2 Try to interview at least three or four builders. Ask an architect for recommendations. If an estate agent assisted your purchase of the property, consider asking him or her for recommendations. Also consult friends and neighbours. If you see builders at work on a house near your home, ask the owners what they think of the quality of the work.

3 Use an architect (see 188 "Hire an Architect") if drawing up plans for a new home or if undertaking major renovation work.

4 Get at least two competitive bids for every job. Compare the bids to make certain they cover the same scope of work, use the same quality of materials, provide the same warranties, and have the same completion date. Make sure that all the builders see the building site and are quoting based on that site, including any excavation or other site-specific costs.

5 Ask for references from each party. Check the references. (Be sure to do this when the builder is not present.) Ask if the builder has undertaken any projects similar to yours. If so, do your best to check them out.

6 If necessary, retain a solicitor with experience in construction cases to draft or review the contract. Be sure that the payment schedule for the builder is clear and understandable.

7 Make absolutely certain that the contract clearly specifies the start and completion dates. Consider requesting some type of late fee or penalty if the completion is delayed beyond a certain grace period (notwithstanding circumstances beyond the builder's control, such as inclement weather).

8 Execute the approved contract.

9 Make any required deposit payment, and be sure to write your cheques according to the schedule (not earlier and not later).

10 Consider hiring an independent project manager to oversee the work being done, and to make periodic checks that the project is on-schedule and on-budget.

What to Look For

- Good references
- Similar projects

Tips

Remember that you'll be working closely with the builder – be sure to select someone with whom you can establish a comfortable relationship.

Don't assume that the most expensive builder is the best, or the least expensive the worst. Prices quoted may well vary based on factors such as schedule, efficiency, overhead and distance from the job.

Warnings

Though recommendations from an estate agent can be a good way to find a builder, be advised that the agent may have a prior business relationship with the builder and that it may factor into the recommendation.

Be very wary if any of your chosen contractors asks for full payment up front. A deposit of 10 per cent is fair.

190 Get Planning Permission

If you're erecting a new building or considering a renovation project of any size, there's a good chance that you'll have to request formal planning permission from your local council for the work to go ahead. This is usually a fairly straightforward – if sometimes frustrating and time-consuming – matter. Here's how you do it.

Steps

1 As a rule of thumb, the types of work listed below will require formal planning permission:

• Additions or extensions to buildings that exceed "permitted development rights". If, for example, you want to add a porch to your house you only require planning permission if it exceeds 3 sq m (30 sq ft) in size.

• You want to divide off a part of your house for use as a separate home.

• You want to build a separate house in your garden, or on land that you own.

• Your proposed work goes against the terms of previously granted planning permission.

• The work might obstruct road users or impinge upon the rights of your neighbours.

(NOTE: this list is by no means intended to be exhaustive.)

2 You do not generally need planning permission to perform repairs, external decoration (unless in a listed property – for which many different regulations will apply) or installation of a satellite dish.

3 For major projects, your architect will usually apply for planning permission on your behalf (see 188 "Hire an Architect").

4 Call your local Planning Department. They will be able to advise you immediately as to whether you need permission to undertake your intended work, and whether it needs to be "full" or "outline".

5 Request an application form. Complete and return, along with any accompanying details, such as architectural drawings. There will also be a fee, which differs from council to council.

6 Be aware that it could take anything up to three months before your application is considered.

7 If it is refused, the Planning Department is legally obliged to give you the reasons. Discuss them with the Planning Officer to see what what would be necessary for them to be passed.

8 As a last resort, you have the right to appeal to the Secretary of State for Transport, Local Government and the Regions.

What to Look For

- Outline or full planning permission
- Architectural drawings
- Appropriate paperwork
- Application fee

Warning

If your work goes ahead without planning permission your local council has the right to demand that you apply after the event; if permission is then refused, you will have to undo the work you've had done – at worst this could even mean the demolition of your home.

191 Buy a Holiday Home

Buying a holiday home – that haven away from it all – is an enticing thought, but the process is subject to the same considerations as any other financial decision you might make. Know what you're looking for, shop aggressively and pay attention to the numbers to ensure you walk away with the best deal possible.

What to Look For

- Mortgage pre-qualification
- Price
- Location

Steps

1 Consider where you've taken holidays in the past. Or if you're looking in a new geographic region, rent a home there first to make sure you love the area.

2 Decide whether this is a place where you'd like to spend every holiday. If you're not sure, then it may not be wise to buy.

3 Get your finances in place. Make sure you can really afford it. If you have a mortgage on your main home you may not be eligible for one for your holiday home. One solution – assuming that both partners of a couple are working – is for one partner to take out a mortgage on the main home and the other to take out a mortgage on the holiday home. (See 172 "Shop for a Mortgage" and 173 "Get a Better Mortgage Deal".)

4 If you have sufficient equity, you may be able to use your main home to finance your holiday home (see 185 "Release Capital From Your Home").

5 Select the type of holiday home that best suits your needs.

6 Consider other aspects. For example, is proximity to water important? As a rule, the closer you are to desirable attractions in any area, the more you're going to pay for that convenience.

7 Check local estate agents and newspapers to get a feel for the value of properties in the area. The process is then the same for buying any other property.

8 View various homes in different settings. Get a sense of how location, size of the homes and other factors affect price Determine whether the holiday property you are considering buying is priced fairly.

9 Consider ongoing maintenance. How will you keep the house up if you're not there all the time, particularly if it's subject to a wide variety of weather conditions? Factor in the cost of hiring a local individual or service to look after the property in your absence.

10 Consider renting out the property at times when it is not being used. In some desirable areas, rental charges may well cover your mortgage and maintenance costs.

11 Review 177 "Buy a House" for the rest of the house-buying process.

Tips

Shop for lower prices during the off-season.

If you're seeking a time-share, look on the internet for people selling their weeks independently.

Most experts agree that you should buy a holiday home for pleasure rather than purely as an investment.

192 Rent a Holiday Home

Would your family enjoy a week in a cosy beach cottage? Or is your ideal getaway an apartment overlooking the golf course? As always, begin by deciding what you want, whether it's a house, villa, chalet, hotel or cabana. There's plenty to choose from out there!

Steps

1 Plan ahead – up to a year in advance. If you frequently take holidays in a particular spot, set time aside to check out the rental market and get a jump on next year's reservations.

2 Find out when the peak rental season is. Save some money by taking holidays off-season, but be aware that the weather, and snow or water conditions, may not be as agreeable. Conversely, it is likely to be far less busy.

3 Check local classified ads and websites to see what's available.

4 Tour the properties for a first-hand look. If you can't go in person, make sure you can see clear photos of the home and facilities.

5 Inquire about other amenities that may be important to you, such as pool, beachfront or lake access, hot tub, kitchen or laundry facilities.

6 Read any lease or rental agreement completely before signing. Be clear about all elements of the contract, including the security and cleaning deposits, liability issues and extra costs, such as pool or laundry fees.

What to Look For

- Sufficient space
- Affordability
- Convenient location
- Amenities and activities

Tip

Travel abroad on the cheap by swapping houses with someone from another country. Search the internet for international agencies.

Warning

Don't get saddled with a hefty cleaning fee. Before you sign the contract, ask if cleaning is included or if you'll need to hire a service.

193 Buy a Flat

If your lifestyle choice doesn't include mowing the lawn, think about buying a flat. Popular choices for both first-time home buyers, older people who are ready to down-size, or trendy urban types, flats and apartments are typically smaller and less expensive than a single family home, and – at the top end of the scale – can include attractive amenities such as pools and fitness facilities, or lobby security. But it's important that you consider both the pluses and the minuses.

Steps

1 Think about how long you're going to stay in one place. Buying a flat is no different than buying a single-family home – unless the housing market is hot you may need to live there at least a couple of years to recoup the costs.

2 Give some thought to what you want. If you're not interested in the pool or sauna, understand that an apartment's price and ongoing monthly service fees will reflect their use regardless of

What to Look For

- Amenities of interest
- Good reputation
- Good construction
- Service charge

Tip

Count how many common walls you may have with neighbours for a feel for how much noise you may hear (or transmit).

your interest in swimming or sweating. Make a note of features that are important to you, such as parking, security, proximity to public transport, laundry facilities, acceptable pet policies, and number of bedrooms and bathrooms.

3 Visit various apartment communities and multi-unit buildings so you know what's available where you live. Try to get a sense of prevailing prices.

4 Think about the cities or areas where you'd like to live. Consider commuting times and the types of amenities you'd like your local neighbourhood to offer.

5 Get pre-qualified for a mortgage (see 172 "Shop for a Mortgage").

6 Register with estate agents in your chosen area. The more you approach, and the more specific your brief, the better the matches you'll be offered.

7 Keep a file of clipped newspaper adverts, computer printouts and notes. Go through your file and call for appointments to see your choice. Make note of any additional information you get.

8 See 177 "Buy a House" – most of the basic steps are equally applicable when buying a flat.

9 Inspect flats carefully.

10 Find out if the building has a good reputation. Ask the current residents how often repairs and maintenance are required, and how good the soundproofing is between units.

11 Check out parking, storage, security and other amenities.

12 Ask if there is a home owners association. Find out what the hot issues are and if members are fighting tooth and nail. You may want to keep looking – nobody wants to live where neighbours are at each other's throats.

13 Talk to other members and find out if there are any restrictive rulings. For instance, some buildings may even dictate what sort of Christmas lighting you can put up. Ask for the same information as you would for buying a house.

14 Budget in service charge payments – these will probably include costs of cleaning, repair, and periodic maintenance, such as painting and replacement of communal carpets.

15 Make an offer and close on the deal. See 177 "Buy a House" for more specifics.

Drive by any prospective buildings to get a feel for the area.

The internet can provide useful information on prospective areas.

194 Rent a Flat or House

The rental markets in many areas are cyclical: a few boom years with renters scrambling for any available studio followed by a glut in availability. In either scenario, the most desirable rental units are snapped up the quickest. Do your homework, then hit the streets.

Steps

Conduct the search

1 Work out how much you can afford. Be sure to include utilities. A good rule of thumb is no more than 30 per cent of your net monthly income.

2 Think about the cities or areas where you'd like to live. Consider commuting times and the types of amenities you'd like your local neighbourhood to offer.

3 Write down what features are important to you, such as parking, security, proximity to public transport, laundry facilities, acceptable pet policies, and number of bedrooms and bathrooms.

4 Scan the "flats to let" listings in the local newspaper where you want to live; ask friends and work colleagues to keep an eye out for vacancies; check online services; look out for rental signs in targeted areas.

5 Sign up with an agency service if you are new to the area, can't get around, don't have time to go through the classifieds or want fewer choices to consider. Depending on the market, this service may be free (paid for by landlords) or cost you a percentage of your rent when you land the flat.

6 Consider sharing if you're looking for cheaper space. Be clear what qualities you desire in a room-mate, as well as types of people or habits you'd prefer to avoid, such as smokers.

Case the joint

1 Inspect the property carefully. If there's any damage, you not only want to ask that it be fixed, but don't want to be blamed for it later. Make sure such problem areas are addressed in a lease, either by your agreeing to live with it, or the landlord agreeing to fix it by a certain date.

2 Check out common walls (any walls shared with an adjoining flat). The more walls in common, the greater the chance of noise from next door. Also consider a common entrance in terms of how much privacy you may want.

3 Ask about amenities such as enclosed parking or a garage, a garden, storage, laundry facilities or concierge services.

What to Look For

- Sufficient space
- Privacy
- Any prior damage

Tips

Drive by any prospective buildings to get a feel for the area.

The internet can provide useful information on prospective areas.

Negotiate the deal

1 If you find a flat you love but it is a stretch financially, ask if there are responsibilities you can take on to lower your rent, such as cutting the lawn or sweeping common areas.

2 Examine your lease in detail: How much notice is required prior to moving, how large a deposit you have to make, how much cleaning is required upon leaving to get your deposit back, and other provisions. Some agreements require first and last months' rent plus a security deposit – a significant chunk of change. Is the lease month to month, or a six- or twelve-month period?

3 Find out what kinds of cosmetic changes you can make, such as painting walls, or structural changes, such as adding shelving.

195 Buy a Place in the Country

Fed up with the pace of the Big City? How about stepping back and taking in the country air?

Steps

1 Leaving the rat-race behind is one of *the* great romantic dreams, but don't get carried away with the moment – make sure that you act with a clear head.

2 Consider the practicalities. What about your career? Can you commute to your existing job? Can you work from home? If not, do you have the financial resources to support yourself while you seek alternative employment.

3 Think about your lifestyle. Most towns and cities have a wealth of amenities – music venues, restaurants, theatres, cinemas, health clubs – that are lacking in more isolated areas: if you enjoy a busy social life, the peace and quiet may be appealing, but will you miss it in the long term?

4 How practical are you? Be aware that you may have to deal with practical problems on your own – there might not be a handy local plumber to fix a burst pipe for you.

5 Locate the area of the country that interests you. Follow steps in 177 "Buy a House".

6 There are plenty of monthly magazines – such as *Country Life* – that detail rural properties for sale.

7 Consider a fall-back plan for if it all goes horribly wrong. Begin by renting a country property, and letting your city home for the same amount of time.

What to Look For

● Working from a rural setting
● Renting and letting to begin

Warning

Be aware that the desire to get away from it all may be symptomatic of a deeper underlying problem – if you're specifically running from something, the problem is almost certain to catch up with you eventually.

196 Buy a Loft Apartment

For some time, the hippest of urban dwellers have sought out old factory conversions or newly built loft-style apartments. For some, they make an ideal place in which to live and work; others just like the feel of open-plan living.

Steps

1 See 177 "Buy a House".

2 Investigate what kind of loft space you can get for your budget. Lofts are generally wide open spaces, with high ceilings. The cheapest will need a fair amount of work to be livable.

3 Although the vogue for apartments was started by poverty-stricken artists in New York, it's now a lifestyle for those with means. Even a modest-sized loft apartment in some of London's most fashionable areas will easily exceed the million-pound mark – especially those overlooking the River Thames.

4 Keep your eyes peeled and your ears close to the ground. Loft apartments are very fashionable and suitable buildings are usually snapped up by property developers with great speed.

5 Look for undeveloped buildings in former industrialised areas, such as old dockside warehouses. Look beyond an ugly exterior – it's the vast expanse inside that should interest you. For smaller conversions, look into buying former public houses or schools.

6 Look for estate agents and – if relevant – architects that have specialised in loft apartments.

What to Look For

- Location
- Undeveloped buildings

Tip

When buying a "shell" – a bare unit – remember to budget for necessary work, such as installing a kitchen and bathroom facilities.

197 Buy a Property Abroad

Once upon a time, buying a house abroad was only for the rich. But with house prices in much of mainland Europe substantially lower than in the UK, it has become possible for those of more modest means.

Steps

Deciding To Do It

1 Think it through. SERIOUSLY.

2 Decide where you want to live, and try to imagine your day-to-day life in a new country.

3 Many people contemplate such a move after returning from their holidays. Be aware that a great time spent as a tourist is usually a rather different experience than being a permanent resident.

What to Look For

- Language
- Legal issues
- Experiences of others

4 Find out if it's really possible to make such a move. Does the country in which you want to live have entry regulations? Australia, for instance, has a points system based on personal factors, such as education or career. Others may take your wealth into consideration.

5 Scour the internet in search of people who have already made the move. Learn from their experiences.

6 Consider practical issues. Can you speak the native tongue? Will you be able to work? Is there a demand for your profession? Will your children be able to resume school without major disruption?

7 Contact the embassy for the country in question. Many of those that are actively seeking to recruit will produce useful information packs. At the very least they will be able to advise you of any unique pitfalls.

The Process

8 Overseas property seekers often are looking for sea and sun, so the coastline tends to be the most popular – and expensive.

9 Apply the same rules as if purchasing in the UK. Don't act on a whim. Do plenty of research. Start off by taking a holiday in the area you're considering. Are there enough facilities for what you require? Or do tourist attractions out-number the local amenities? The best source of knowledge is those who have done it before: there is no shortage of "ex-pats" with stories from which you can learn.

10 Unless you're conversant with the local language, conduct your enquiries through a reputable third party. In London and the south east there are many reputable estate agents who are expert in dealing with overseas properties. Use established companies and beware of anyone who gives you the hard sell.

11 Make sure you have a good lawyer with an excellent command of English and the native tongue to deal with the endless stream of rules and regulations. (In Spain, for instance, you can inherit debts from a previous vendor.)

12 Make sure you have the finances in place before you put in an offer. You may find it difficult to get a mortgage in the UK to pay for a foreign home. Mortgaging and renting out a British home is a popular solution.

13 Start a direct debit from a native bank account to pay your regular utility bills. (Be aware that some foreign banks are considerably less lenient towards late payers than the UK.) Pay up in time.

14 Be aware that if you intend to remain resident in Britain, and wish to rent out your overseas property when it's empty, you could find yourself with income tax demands from both countries.

Warning

Think before committing yourself wholesale to a new way of life. Instead of selling up, why not rent out your home until you're satisfied that you want to make the permanent move?

If acting independently, you MUST make sure that you understand your obligations under local legislation. Wherever you happen to be in the world, when dealing with the law, ignorance is never an adequate defence.

198 Buy to Let

With mortgage rates enjoying a record low, why not consider buying a second property with the intention of renting it out. Buying to let gives you an asset that will (probably) increase in value as well as bringing in an additional monthly income.

Steps

1 Assess your financial requirements and goals. Do you need a steady stream of income from your rental or do you plan to sell it for a profit in a couple of years? If it's the latter, look for lower priced property that you can fix up as you rent it out.

2 Consider your finances. Even if you already have a mortgage, some building societies will give you a second mortgage for such projects. Common among couples is for each partner to carry a separate mortgage.

3 Consider being a resident landlord by purchasing a multi-unit property and living in one flat. In many cases, the income from the other unit(s) will cover your mortgage payment, allowing you to effectively live for free. Being on-site has some other significant advantages, including ensuring that the property is well-maintained.

4 Decide if you want to do maintenance yourself. If you have the skills, equipment and temperament to deal with upset tenants and a blocked toilet in the early hours of the morning, fine. If that's not your scene, you live far away from your new property, or you are short on free time, it may be worth paying a letting agent to deal with business on your behalf – but expect to pay up to 20 per cent of your potential rent in fees.

5 As a landlord, you will have a legal responsibility to provide accommodation that comes up to environmental health standards. You may have to spend money on a newly purchased property to get it up to scratch.

6 Choose the kind of property you want. Single-family houses are generally less expensive than properties containing a number of flats because of pure size, but generate less income. Flats, on the other hand, can require more upkeep.

7 Get your finances in place. If you have a mortgage on your main home you may not be eligible for one for your second home. If both partners of a couple are working, one solution is for one partner to take out a mortgage on the main home and the other to take out a mortgage on the investment home. (See 172 "Shop for a Mortgage" and 173 "Get a Better Mortgage Deal".)

8 If you need a mortgage, make sure you are pre-approved before you start looking.

What to Look For

- Income produced meets financial goals
- Suitable property
- Appealing location
- Vacancy rates
- Area rental rates

Tips

Check to see whether the value of other area properties have increased or decreased in the past five years. Try to buy in an area that's on the way up.

Pay attention to when improvements were made to a property, which aids in the estimate of the building's value. Recent renovations are worth more than upgrades done a decade or more ago.

Be on the lookout for any hazards common to older properties, such as asbestos, lead-based paint and electrical systems that are not up to code. Budget in reconciling these problems.

9 Register with as many estate agent as possible operating in the area that interests you.

10 Choose property where people will want to live, close to shops, parks and decent schools, and in a well-kept area.

11 Consider what improvements, if any, will be necessary before you can start renting out.

12 Plan on spending plenty of time and money advertising for and interviewing potential renters. Have a contingency plan in place if a unit remains vacant for a few months.

13 Determine what a competitive rental rate is for your property by asking rental agents what they would expect to charge or by looking at rents being advertised in the same area.

14 Make certain that whatever income you derive covers the costs of owning the property, plus a profit.

15 See 177 "Buy a House" – most of the basic steps are equally applicable when buying a flat.

Some cities offer low interest financing to property owners needing to make renovations. Look into such programmes if you know you'll need to have the property painted, windows replaced or similar exterior repairs made.

Discuss any tax benefits with a tax specialist. There may be local tax incentives for renovating your property as well as advantageous approaches to declaring your expenses.

199 Rent Your Home for a Location Shoot

Lights, camera, cheque! Getting your home in a movie or on TV can be fun and pull in some extra cash to boot. But there are issues to bear in mind, not only to increase the chances of making your home a star, but to protect it in the process.

Steps

1 Submit your home as a possible location with film studios, production companies and advertising firms. All of these will maintain lists of properties available for shooting purposes.

2 Ask what the rate is. Depending on how long the production crew will be in your home and the scope of the project, pay will range from several hundred pounds per day for a modest setting, to many thousands of pounds for something more exotic. If the location is in a television series, they could come back on a regular basis.

3 Expect your home to be taken over by people setting up shop in all parts of the house, including the bathrooms. Find out whether you should remove your furniture or make any changes before they come in or whether the production crews will do this. Ask if they plan to make any temporary changes and what they'll be.

4 Ask for a written policy outlining what the company does in case anything is damaged. The contract should include a provision to "return the house back to its original state", which may involve repainting or carpet cleaning, and the time frame for doing so.

What to Look For

- Studio and production company property lists
- A contract

Warnings

Don't expect to make huge amounts of money renting out your house. Consider that while the production crew is filming, you'll more than likely have to pay to live somewhere else.

Production companies use trucks to haul cameras, and tracks and cranes that need off-site parking locations, which could significantly inconvenience you and your neighbours.

UY TIME • BUY A BOUQUET OF ROSES • BUY SOMEONE A DRINK • GET SOMEONE TO BUY YOU A DRINK • BUY YOUR WAY INTO THE BES
REEN • BUT FURTHER EDUCATION • ORDER EXOTIC FOOD • ORDER AT A SUSHI BAR • BUY DINNER AT A FRENCH RESTAURANT • EMPLOY
RRY TO YOUR PARTNER • BUY MUSIC ONLINE • EMPLOY MUSICIANS • ORDER A GOOD BOTTLE OF WINE • BUY AN ERGONOMIC DESK CH
R • EMPLOY AN AU PAIR • BUY A GUITAR • BUY DUCT TAPE • GET A GOOD DEAL ON A MAGAZINE SUBSCRIPTION • GET SENIOR CITIZEN
BUY PET FOOD • BUY A PEDIGREE DOG OR CAT • BREED YOUR PET AND SELL THE LITTER • BUY OR RENT FOR A FANCY DRESS PARTY
PRECIOUS METALS • BUY COLOURED GEMSTONES • CHOOSE THE PERFECT WEDDING DRESS • BUY OR RENT MEN'S FORMAL WEAR • G
PHER • HIRE A CATERER • FIND THE IDEAL CIVIL WEDDING VENUE • THE COST OF MARRYING • ORDER PERSONALISED INVITATIONS AND
KS SHOW • BUY A MOTHER'S DAY GIFT • BUY A FATHER'S DAY GIFT • SELECT AN APPROPRIATE COMING-OF-AGE GIFT • GET A GIFT FOR T
ARDS • BUY CHRISTMAS STOCKING FILLERS • BUY CHRISTENING GIFTS • PURCHASE A PERFECT CHRISTMAS TREE • BUY A PRIVATE ISLA
ET HOT TICKETS • HIRE A LIMOUSINE • BUY A CRYONIC CHAMBER • RENT YOUR OWN HOARDING • TAKE OUT A FULL-PAGE AD IN *THE TI*
ROUND THE WORLD • BUY A TICKET TO TRAVEL FOR A YEAR • BOOK A TRIP ON THE ORIENT-EXPRESS • OWN A VINEYARD • BUY A GREY
ITE YOUR MEMOIRS • COMMISSION ORIGINAL ARTWORK • IMMORTALISE YOUR SPOUSE IN A SCULPTURE • GIVE AWAY YOUR FORTUNE
ELL YOUR STORY TO THE TABLOIDS • SELL YOUR SOUL TO THE DEVIL • NEGOTIATE A BETTER CREDIT CARD DEAL • CHOOSE A FINANCIA
NNUITIES • BUY AND SELL MUTUAL FUNDS • BUY BONDS • SELL SHORT • INVEST IN PRECIOUS METALS • BUY SERIOUS ILLNESS INSURA
YOUR PRODUCT ON TV • HIRE A CAREER COU   URSELF IN A JOB INTERVIEW • TAKE OUT A PATEN
LEASE OFFICE SPACE • BUY LIQUIDATED OFF   N AND BUILD YOUR WEBSITE • HIRE A GRAPHIC
RE A LITERARY AGENT • PITCH A MAGAZINE S   OVEL • SELF-PUBLISH YOUR BOOK • START A E
GAGE • GET A MORTGAGE YOU CAN AFFORD   E • BUY A HOUSE AT AUCTION • SHOP FOR A H
SELL A HOUSE • SELL A HOUSE WITHOUT A   YOUR HOME • BUY A PLOT OF LAND • HAVE YO
T A FLAT OR HOUSE • BUY A PLACE IN THE C   ROPERTY ABROAD • BUY TO LET • RENT YOUR
RIENTAL CARPET • BUY LAMPS AND LIGHT FI   SYSTEM • BUY HOUSEHOLD APPLIANCES • BU
R • HIRE A FENG SHUI CONSULTANT • INCOR   YOUR HOME • SELECT PAINT, STAIN AND VARNIS
D ADHESIVES • CHOOSE WINDOW TREATMEN   OSE WALLPAPER • BUY A WOOD-BURNING STOV
HOME TOOL KIT • BUY A VIDEO SECURITY SY   Y SMOKE ALARMS • BUY CARBON MONOXIDE D
• HIRE A BUILDER, PLUMBER, PAINTER OR E   DOOR FURNITURE • BUY THE PERFECT ROSE •
FERTILISER • START A VEGETABLE GARDEN •   MATIC WATERING SYSTEM • START A NEW LAWI
EES • BUY A SPA POOL • BUY AN OUTDOOR   E • CHOOSE A PERFECT PEACH • BUY AND SEL
IP A KITCHEN • CHOOSE FRESH PRODUCE •   T BURGER • PURCHASE A CHRISTMAS HAM • E
ER • BUY A REAL STILTON • GET FRESH FISH   UFFLES • BUY ARTISAN BREADS • BUY ARTISAN
NTS • PURCHASE VINEGAR • CHOOSE PASTA   T CUP OF COFFEE • BUY A COFFEEMAKER OR E
S FUNCTION • STOCK A WINE CELLAR • STO   AN OVULATION PREDICTOR KIT • PICK A PREGN
R UP FOR A NEW BABY • BUY A NEW COT • C   S • CHOOSE NAPPIES • BUY OR RENT A BREAST
GOOD AFTER-SCHOOL CARE • SIGN YOUR C   LAY STRUCTURE • FIND A FAMILY-FRIENDLY HOT
GAME SYSTEM • HIRE A TUTOR • ADOPT A C   • SELL USED BABY GEAR, TOYS, CLOTHES AND
Y A CEMETERY PLOT • PAY FOR FUNERAL EX   HBRUSH • BUY MOISTURISERS AND ANTIWRINK
HAIR • BUY HOME-USE MEDICAL SUPPLIES •   S TO COUNTER HAIR LOSS • BUY A WIG OR HAI
TIC PRACTITIONERS • CHOOSE A MANICURIS   ES AND SUNGLASSES • HIRE A PERSONAL TRA
SHOP AT AN ANTIQUE FAIR OR FLEA MARKE   UY AT AUCTION • KNOW WHAT YOUR COLLECT
QUE FURNITURE • GET CLUED UP ON CLARICE CLIFF • BUY COINS • BUY AN ANTIQUE QUILT • BUY FILM POSTERS • LIQUIDATE YOUR BE
TO A PAWNSHOP • BUY AND SELL COMIC BOOKS • BUY AND SELL SPORTS MEMORABILIA • SELL YOUR FOOTBALL-CARD COLLECTION
TER • BUY PRINTER PAPER • BUY A PRINTER • BUY COMPUTER PERIPHERALS • CHOOSE AN INTERNET SERVICE PROVIDER • GET AN INT
BUY BLANK CDS • BUY AN MP PLAYER • CHOOSE A DVD PLAYER • BUY A VIDEO RECORDER • CHOOSE A PERSONAL DIGITAL ASSISTANT
OSE A DIGITAL CAMCORDER • DECIDE ON A DIGITAL CAMERA • BUY A HOME AUTOMATION SYSTEM • BUY A STATE-OF-THE-ART SOUND
A UNIVERSAL REMOTE • BUY A HOME CINEMA SYSTEM • BUY VIRTUAL-REALITY FURNITURE • BUY TWO-WAY RADIOS • BUY A MOBILE
EAST MONEY • GET TRAVEL INSURANCE • PICK THE IDEAL LUGGAGE • FLY FOR NEXT TO NOTHING • TAKE A TRIP ON THE TRANS-SIBER
FOREIGN OFFICIAL • GET AN INTERRAIL PASS • TAKE AN ITALIAN CYCLING HOLIDAY • CHOOSE A CHEAP CRUISE • BOOK A HOTEL PACK
COTLAND • BUY A SAPPHIRE IN BANGKOK • HIRE A RICKSHAW IN RANGOON • TAKE SALSA LESSONS IN CUBA • BUY A CAMERA IN HONG
FIRST CRICKET BAT • ORDER A STRIP FOR A FOOTBALL TEAM • BUY ANKLE AND KNEE BRACES • CHOOSE RUGBY PROTECTION KIT • E
UY SWIMMING EQUIPMENT • BUY A JETSKI • EMPLOY A SCUBA INSTRUCTOR • BUY A SKATEBOARD AND PROTECTIVE GEAR • BUY SKA
ES • SELL USED SKIS • BUY A SNOWBOARD, BOOTS AND BINDINGS • BUY SKI BOOTS • BUY A BICYCLE • BUY AN ELECTRIC BICYCLE •
KAYAK • BUY A LIFEJACKET • BUY A WET SUIT • BUY A SURFBOARD • BUY FLY-FISHING GEAR • BUY ROCK-CLIMBING EQUIPMENT • BL
NON-STANDARD SIZES • BUY THE PERFECT COCKTAIL DRESS • BUY DESIGNER CLOTHES AT A DISCOUNT • CHOOSE A BASIC WARDRO
ASIA • BUY A BRIEFCASE • SHOP FOR A LEATHER JACKET • BUY MATERNITY CLOTHES • GET A GREAT-FITTING BRA • CHOOSE A HIGH-
SE CHILDREN'S SHOES • PURCHASE CLOTHES AT FACTORY SHOPS • BUY A NEW CAR • BUY THE BASICS FOR YOUR CAR • BUY A USEI
UY CAR INSURANCE • SPRING FOR A NEW PAINT JOB • BUYING AND CHANGING A BATTERY • BUY THE RIGHT FUEL • BUY FUEL TREATI

Home & Garden

200 Furnish Your Home

Today's home is where you go to relax and refresh yourself, attend to the details of your life and share the company of others. An extension of your personality and lifestyle, a carefully furnished home is a true haven. Shop with style, versatility and easy care in mind to ensure that your space will be functional as well as attractive.

Steps

1 Window-shop first. Visit a variety of shops, and pore over catalogues before making a choice you'll live with every day.

2 Make a style file. Collect photos not just of interiors, but also of patterns, graphics and shapes you like. Carry a swatch envelope with fabric samples, paint-colour chips and other colour samples. Found a peach nail polish that's just the right shade for a rug? Brush some on a piece of paper.

3 Assess your lifestyle. Do you give elegant dinner parties or invite friends over for supper? Do you need a sofa long enough for a nap? Your furnishings should accommodate your activities.

4 Measure rooms carefully, then sketch floor plans, rooms and furniture arrangements on graph paper. Even better, make cutouts of furniture you can move around. Or, look for room-layout software. Keep traffic flow in mind: You don't need a straight route through each room, but avoid obstacle courses.

5 Prowl auctions, car boot sales and your family's houses for used furniture (see 202 "Buy Used Furniture"). Buy new pieces that complement old favourites. Before you discard an older piece, consider refinishing or painting to help it blend with your new furniture. Make sure it suits your needs for appearance, comfort, function and durability.

6 Pick colours that work for the long term. Don't tie yourself to this season's "in" colours, but realise they may dominate choices in many furniture products. Neutral upholstery is easy to work with, but pass on all-white if you have kids or pets.

7 Opt for practical, easy-to-live-with fabrics. Save bright, trendy patterns for replaceable slipcovers. If you have a cat, avoid open-weave fabrics and leather, and look for upholstery that's more likely to stand up to claws.

8 Buy the best quality you can afford when choosing a major piece such as a sofa. It's likely to get constant use and it needs to last. If your budget allows, invest in features such as a hardwood frame and hand-tied springs. Stain-resistant fabrics may cost more up front, but they'll quickly earn their keep.

9 Don't feel restricted to the styles of the samples in the shop. You can order many pieces in different woods, finishes and fabrics, and each one creates a different look. Leg, skirt and cushion options can customise your choice.

What to Look For

- Versatility
- Four-point test: appearance, comfort, function, durability
- Practical colours and fabrics
- Quality
- Free delivery

Tips

Take advantage of free decorating advice. Many furniture shops have in-house experts ready to help.

Measure doorways and stairways to be sure furniture can reach its intended spot. Always carry a tape measure when shopping (shop-tag dimensions can be wrong).

It's important to size your furnishings to the room. A large, high-ceilinged room needs large, even oversize furniture. Standard pieces will look lost.

Keep your eyes peeled. Glean ideas from friends' homes, house tours, TV and films, and home decor books and magazines.

10 Shop at places that have earned a reputation for excellent quality and good customer service. Free delivery – including unpacking and placing in the room – is a plus.

11 Don't buy all the furnishings you need at once, even if you can afford to. Choose a few good pieces and enjoy adding to the ensemble gradually while giving yourself room to change your mind and allow your taste to expand and develop.

Consider a sofa divided into sections, especially if you anticipate moving often. You can rearrange the pieces to adapt to different room dimensions.

201 Furnish Your Studio Flat

Small is beautiful – and even comfortable if you're a shrewd decorator. Furnishings must work harder; clever storage is essential. With a little imagination and ingenuity, one-room living won't drive you up the wall.

Steps

1 Create rooms within the room to better manage the space. Hang fabric, blinds or curtains from ceiling rods or tracks, and define zones with area rugs. Partition areas with a folding screen or use chests and shelves on casters. Low bookshelves can cordon off a space while providing necessary storage.

2 Give a dramatic bed or sofa a starring role. Even when space is compact, you need a few large-scale focal points.

3 Put multipurpose pieces to work. Use a trunk, chest or ottoman as a coffee table and storage unit; configure wood storage cubes to any height or width; treat a tailored daybed as extra seating.

4 Buy high-quality, versatile furnishings you can use later in a larger home. Today's TV table on wheels is tomorrow's entertaining trolley. A sectional sofa will become separate chairs. A beautiful storage cupboard is useful in almost any room.

5 Keep the scale light to avoid overwhelming your space. Choose see-through and reflective furniture with glass or plastic shelves and tabletops, as well as tubular or wire legs.

6 Maximise storage by building a window seat or platform bed over drawers. Install an efficient system in your bedroom cupboard and you may not need a chest of drawers. Create storage space on the walls, doors and even the ceiling using shelves, bins and hooks. Collect baskets, hatboxes and funky vintage suitcases for stackable storage that can double as side tables and bedside tables.

7 Enhance room volume with mirrors. Lean a tall mirror against a wall to expand perspective. Hang a group of small mirrors across from a window to bounce light around.

What to Look For

- Mobile room dividers
- One great focal point
- Multipurpose furniture
- Inventive storage

Tips

Use paint and loose covers to unify secondhand or mis-matched items. Paint pieces the same colour as walls for a light, airy look.

Arrange furniture on the diagonal to make the room look wider.

202 Buy Used Furniture

No longer just for student rooms, vintage furniture is now chic. Thank trends such as the country look and eclectic decorating, as well as rising interest in comfortable weekend homes. Shop for versatility and timeless design, and each piece will last for years.

Steps

1 Carry a list of what you're looking for, noting the ideal and maximum dimensions for each piece. Remember to measure the clearance of doorways and stairs. Keep a tape measure with you. You never know when you'll see something.

2 Visit second-hand, charity and house clearance shops regularly. Ask them to call you when something you want comes in.

3 Attend auctions and get on the mailing list. Older furniture is often well constructed, but use auction previews to inspect for damage. Sit on a chair to test for comfort, loose joints or wobbly legs. Open doors and drawers to check for any sticking, broken parts or damaged or missing hardware. See 374 "Buy at Auction" and 375 "Know What Your Collectibles Are Worth".

4 Shop at flea markets, car boot sales and estate sales. While the best selection is on the first day, the best deals are on the last half day – sellers don't want to transport furniture home or store it over the winter. See 372 "'Shop at an Antique Fair or Flea Market".

5 Think versatility. Value design above finish or upholstery, which can be changed. How would a piece work if you shortened its legs or removed its drawers? If it's not an antique, imagine how paint or a loose cover can create a fresh personality.

6 Add repair costs to an item's selling price if you don't know how to refinish or refurbish yourself. Steam-cleaning stained fabric is affordable, but reupholstering can eat up any savings unless the piece is top quality and will hold its value.

7 Drive a vehicle roomy enough to get your furniture home from the flea market or car boot sale. Shops in a permanent location usually allow a few days' grace for pickup, but most items are auctioned on the spot. The auctioneer might help you arrange for professional delivery, but that boosts your purchase price.

8 Request an exchange or money-back guarantee in case you find that a piece is badly damaged or just doesn't fit.

What to Look For

- Sturdy construction
- End-of-sale bargains
- Versatile design
- Minimal need for repair

Tips

Mention your used-furniture needs to friends. You might be able to swap pieces so both find happy new homes.

It's easy to replace door and drawer hardware on vintage (not antique) pieces.

See 381 "Buy Antique Furniture".

203 Buy Door and Window Locks

"Locks only keep honest people out", the saying goes, but high-quality door and window hardware make your house or flat less attractive to burglars. If you survey your home as a potential target and don't try to cut corners, you'll find security devices you can trust.

Steps

1 Ask your local police for a home security inspection. Or, ask a locksmith to evaluate your home, explain all security options, and install professional-quality devices. Call members of the Master Locksmiths Association (locksmiths.co.uk).

2 Replace hollow-core entry doors with solid hardwood at least 4.5 cm (1¾ in) thick, steel-clad or insulated fibreglass doors. The frame should not have gaps wide enough for a crow bar.

3 Install exterior doors with hinges on the inside. Burglars can pop out exterior hinges and remove a locked door. Install a 180-degree peephole rather than a door chain. Make sure you can't put a hand through your letterbox and reach the lock.

4 Upgrade Yale locks (thieves can jemmy their latches with a credit card) to ones with hardened steel pins or a dead bolt. If you like the convenience of a Yale lock, add a mortice lock above it.

5 Invest in good-quality mortice locks (under £50), which withstand kicking, prying, wrenching, hammering, sawing and drilling. A single-cylinder mortice lock is key-operated from the outside; a double-cylinder is key-operated from both sides. If your door has a glass pane or is near a window, install a double-cylinder model so a burglar can't break the glass and unlock the door. Keep a key for emergencies near the door, not in the lock.

6 Shop for mortice locks that have a steel bolt with a 2.5 cm (1 in) throw (the bolt extends that far into the door frame), striking plates secured with 6 to 7.5 cm (2½ to 3 in) screws, five- or six-pin cylinders and a free-spinning solid-metal cylinder collar. Screws must be long enough to penetrate the framing around the door.

7 Install a steel door pin near each hinge to secure swing-out doors, preventing the door from being pried out.

8 Secure sash windows with a nail or bolt. Drill the hole through both sashes at a downward angle to prevent a burglar from jiggling the pin loose. Keyed sash stops are also available.

9 Install retractable window grilles for worry-free ventilation on basement and ground-floor windows.

10 Prevent sliding doors from being lifted off their tracks by using vertical bolts or antilift plates between the doors and their top tracks. Heavy-duty keyed locks mount on the inside edge of the frame.

What to Look For

- Police or locksmith's advice
- Solid door and sturdy frame
- Upgraded Yale locks
- Dead bolts
- Sliding- and swinging-door locks
- Window-sash stops
- Window grilles

Tips

Basement and back doors, as well as the interior door to an attached garage, should have the same level of security as entry doors.

Give only car keys – no house keys – to mechanics and parking valets. Most high-security lock keys can only be copied with your permission at dealers and locksmiths.

When you move to a new home, change its locks – or at least the cylinders. You never know who has keys to the old hardware.

Look for locks that conform to BS3621 (thief resistant) as an extra guarantee of quality.

Warning

While security is important, make sure that safety is not compromised. Keep all necessary keys near to each lock (though not visible) so that doors and windows are readily unlocked in case of fire.

204 Choose an Oriental Carpet

Oriental carpets bring a richness to a room not easily matched by any other floor covering. For thousands of years, Asian artisans have woven rugs in distinctive patterns from individually knotted strands. Careful shopping involves knowledge and scrutiny of pattern, material and craftsmanship.

Steps

1 Measure your space carefully so you know what size of carpet will fit. For stair runners, measure and count the number of risers.

2 Bring a photograph of the room where the carpet will go so you can choose the colours and pattern. Patterns include geometric, floral, pictorial and decorative.

3 Opt for wool for warmth, softness and resilience. Consider less-rugged but sensuous silk for luxury, low-traffic areas and warm climates. If a carpet is labelled as *art silk,* it's actually rayon.

4 Ask what the country of origin is. Traditionally, Persia (now Iran) produced the finest carpets. Genuine Oriental carpets come from Afghanistan, China, India, Iran, Nepal, Pakistan, Tibet, Turkey, Azerbaijan, Armenia, Romania, Albania, Morocco and Egypt. True Oriental carpets are not made in Western countries. Also find out in what area of the country the rugs were woven or by what people. For example, while Turkish rugs run the gamut in quality, the city of Hereke is known for its exceptional silk carpets.

5 Inspect the rug carefully. Turn it over to examine its colour and weave. Artificially aged (called washed and painted) rugs are usually lighter on the back than on the front. This contradicts normal fading, in which the back would never be exposed to daylight, and the face of the rug might fade. Washed and painted isn't necessarily a bad thing; just know that you are not getting a naturally aged rug.

6 Check knot count. A higher count creates more detail and usually adds durability, but the count can vary by design and country of origin. A higher knot count usually equals a higher price per square metre.

7 Test for colourfastness by rubbing a damp cloth over a dark area of the rug. If the colour comes off, keep shopping.

8 Ask the salesperson to "do a little better". Bargaining is expected. Price will depend on the carpet's country of origin, quality, age and condition.

9 Arrange to take the carpet home as a trial run on approval. Get a due-back date in writing.

10 Insist on a receipt with a detailed description, including age, country of origin, and materials, such as silk or wool. Based on this, many shops will accept the carpet as a trade-in later.

What to Look For

- Suitable colour and pattern
- Wool or silk
- Country of origin
- Naturally or artificially aged
- High knot count
- Price based on quality, origin, age and condition
- Trial at home
- Trade-in and trade-up policies

Tips

Find a reputable shop with knowledgeable salespeople. Beware of perpetual going-out-of-business sales and travelling hotel-room sales.

Avoid shops with no price tags on rugs and buy only from reputable auction houses.

Wilton, Karistan and Couristan brand carpets are made by machine in Oriental rug designs, but they are not considered Oriental rugs. No genuine Oriental rugs are made of nylon or polypropylene.

Buy abroad to get extraordinary deals. Be prepared to bargain. See 439 "Ship Foreign Purchases to the United Kingdom".

Warning

Discounts exceeding 20 per cent usually indicate the original price has been inflated.

205 Buy Lamps and Light Fixtures

Just as jewellery accessorises a dress, decorative light fixtures accessorise a room and create a mood. More than beauty, however, effective lighting adds safety, comfort and drama. Use illumination from three sources of light: general (or ambient), task and accent.

Steps

1 Choose lighting according to its application. General, or ambient, lighting brightens an entire room indirectly; task lighting helps you read, sew, cook or do paperwork under focused illumination; accent lighting spotlights decorative objects.

2 Experiment with different bulbs to achieve the brightness, warmth of tone or clarity of light you're looking for. Warm incandescent, colour-true halogen or super-efficient compact fluorescent bulbs are now on the market. The latter type lasts up to ten times longer but uses only one-fifth of the energy – for example, a 20-watt compact fluorescent is as bright as a 100-watt incandescent bulb.

3 Use recessed lights, floor lamps and soffit uplights for entertaining and watching television instead of a harsh, single ceiling light. Add table lamps for reading or sewing, and track lights to accent art and architectural features.

4 Create dining-room intimacy with a low pendant or a candle-style chandelier (both on dimmer switches). Use twin lamps on a sideboard for soft background light.

5 Cook up an efficiently lit kitchen. Under-cabinet lights brighten worktops so you don't work in your own shadow. Halogen bulbs render food colours accurately. Position recessed, track and pendant lights to illuminate work areas. Install low-voltage strip lights inside cabinets with glass doors.

6 Furnish the bedroom with general and task lighting for a relaxing atmosphere. Flank the bed with mounted sconces or swing-arm lamps to free up bedside table surfaces. Recessed lights are inconspicuous and ideal for low-ceiling rooms.

7 Focus on function in the home office. To avoid eyestrain, use at least 100 watts of incandescent or 40 watts of fluorescent task lighting for reading, writing and computer work. Supplement table and floor lamps with uplights and wall lights that spotlight plants or bookshelves.

8 Shop for style and construction as well as price. Fixtures sold at lighting showrooms may cost more, but usually are higher quality, and lighting consultants can offer design advice. Custom finishes, blown-glass shades and halogen bulbs also add to the cost of fixtures.

What to Look For

- General, task and accent lighting
- Several light sources
- Focus on room function
- Suitable bulbs

Tips

Use dimmers to adjust the brightness of almost any fixture to suit different moods.

Arrange lamps at the correct height. When you're sitting, the bottom of a table lamp's shade should be at eye level, 97 to 107 cm (38 to 42 in) above the floor.

The height of standing lamps may be flexible – they can beam light up to add a soft glow to a dim corner or focus down with a shade for reading.

Lamps can be customised with new shades. You can also change the adapters on track lighting to accommodate many types of hanging fixtures.

206 Buy a Programmable Lighting System

Imagine being able to call out "Let there be light!" and have all the lamps in your house respond immediately. Sophisticated whole-house lighting systems are now available to both create moods and offer increased convenience and security. Costs range from £150 for simple functions to several thousand pounds for full-house systems.

Steps

1 Focus on wireless systems if you're retrofitting this technology to an existing home. Wireless systems use infrared or radio frequency (RF) signals instead of behind-the-walls wiring. For new construction, install wireless or hardwired systems.

2 Decide what to connect. Integrate lighting devices with entertainment – lights dim and shades lower automatically when you start a film. Or link safety and security devices: As alarm sensors are tripped, they activate flashing lights; if fire alarms sound, the whole house lights up.

3 Place control pads in convenient locations. With some hardware variations, each system's central control unit connects to wall-mounted keypads, from which you command lights and devices. Install keypads at entry doors, bedsides or wherever they're desired. Keypads hold up to nine buttons, linked to receivers in outlets, sockets and wall switches.

4 Programme lighting scenes: custom, dimmable lighting combinations designed for the moods or activities you enjoy in each room. Different light levels work better for entertaining, reading, dining and watching TV. In addition, there are sleep, holiday and emergency modes. Once you've programmed key settings, they can be stored for easy access.

5 Control your environment. Timers and remote controls are favourites to access your system. Some feature an in-car option. As you reach your driveway, you can turn on interior and exterior lights. Others allow you to connect to the central control – and the home itself – through a computer or web-enabled personal digital assistant to access your system from almost anywhere.

6 Find dealers and installers through manufacturer websites. Look for manufacturer-trained personnel especially for hardwired systems. Programmable lighting sources include GE Lighting (gelighting.com), Lutron (lutron.com) and others. These firms also offer design and programming, integration with other electrical systems, and user training.

What to Look For

- Wireless or hardwired systems
- Functions beyond lighting
- Lighting scenes
- Helpful extensions
- Trained dealers and installers

Tip

Before buying, check the method of programming. Some systems must be programmed by professional installers, some you set up with a personal computer, and others you program from the keypads themselves.

207 Buy Household Appliances

The best appliances are the ones that do the job well and also save time and energy. Would a jumbo oven (or two) or a fridge-door ice dispenser make your life easier? Prioritise your architectural and space needs and budget and then consider style.

APPLIANCE	PRICE RANGE	DESIGN OPTIONS AND FEATURES
Refrigerator and Freezer	£90 to £3,000	Built-in models fit flush with cabinets. Ice and water dispenser; water filter. Trim-kit option disguises front panel as cabinet. Spillproof shelves. Separate temperature and humidity controls. Energy Star label. Colour, stainless-steel or glass doors.
Cooker	£500 to £7,000	Built-in or freestanding. Spillproof elements or glass hob. Warming drawer. Gas rings with electric oven. Infinite heat source (provides continuous heat front-to-rear, left-to-right for easy movement of large cookware). Infinitely adjustable heat electronic controls. Built-in grill or griddle. Large oven window. Agas and Rayburns can run your hot water and heating.
Hob	£60 to £800	Glass or electric (coil, radiant, halogen or induction). Various widths. Glass smooth-top surface. Flexible element configuration. Digital displays. Hot-ring indicator. Sealed gas rings. Electric bridge to small rings for larger cooking area and keep-warm elements. Very low and very high commercial-grade models.
Wall Oven	£250 to £850	Single or double oven. Thermal, fan or speed-cook system. Enamel or stainless-steel finish. Delay start. Larger interior. Glass door; side-opening door. Steam option (for baking). Temperature probe.
Microwave	£40 to £750	Countertop, built-in or mounted under the counter models. Dial or electronic controls. Programmable settings. Microwave-convection combo. For grilling, a quartz grill gives a more even finish than a radiant grill.
Dishwasher	£190 to £700	Smart loading pattern to fit maximum number of dishes safely. Dish drawers available for small loads. Extra sound insulation. Dual spray heads. Delay start. Trim option to disguise front. Stainless-steel interior. Slimline models for small spaces. Energy Star label.
Washing Machine	£150 to £1,200	Front loader; freestanding, stacking or combination. Dial or electronic controls. Load sensors. Favourite cycle settings. Built-in water heater. High-efficiency (Energy Star–rated) models. Quiet operation. Stainless-steel interior. Extra-large capacity.
Tumble Dryer	£90 to £800	Front loader; freestanding, stacking or combination. Extra-large capacity. Variety of cycles. Moisture sensor. Extended tumbling. Quiet operation. Adjustable end-of-cycle alert sound. Electronic controls. Removable drying racks. Stainless-steel interior. Condensor or vented.

208 Buy Floor-Care Appliances

Could you eat off your floors? Although you probably wouldn't want to even if they were squeaky-clean, regular cleaning will increase the life of your floors and help you breathe more easily by removing allergens. Because no single appliance cleans all floors – carpet, wood, tile, linoleum or vinyl – look for one that fits your particular needs with features that make the job easier.

Steps

1 Know what kind of vacuum power to look for. Cleaning effectiveness is determined by suction, not horsepower. Instead of motor sizes, compare the airflow, expressed in the form of air watts.

2 Buy a full-size vacuum for overall performance. Uprights (£60 to £300) require less bending, but they're heavy to hoist up stairs. Look at light and self-propelled models. Features like carpet-pile selectors, bag-change signals, attachments, and retractable or extra-long cords add convenience. Bagless models are very popular, but try before you buy to see if they are for you.

3 Choose a cylinder vacuum (£20 to £350) if most of your cleaning is on bare floors, on stairs and in furniture-crowded rooms. Cylinders with a powered head have a separate motor that turns a brush to deep-clean carpet. Look for different cleaning attachments and an easy-to-empty dirt container.

4 Clean floors quickly with a cordless electric sweeper (about £50). Some use suction only; others add a brush to loosen dirt. You can also tackle stairs and small messes with a handheld-only vacuum known as a dustbuster (£30 to £55).

5 Banish allergens with a high-efficiency particulate air (HEPA) vacuum filter system. These workhorses remove 99 per cent of the dust, pollen and mites captured with a specially sealed bag or filter. (Bagless vacuums also can be HEPA models.)

6 Sanitise hard-surface floors and relieve allergies with steam cleaners (£250 to £500), which turn tap water into 120°C steam that loosens dirt and grease from tile, hardwood, laminate and vinyl flooring. A cleaning cloth traps dirt and protects surfaces.

7 Deep-clean carpets when needed with a do-it-yourself wet-cleaner machine. Note: for Oriental rugs and non-colourfast fabrics, dry shampooers are safer.

What to Look For

- Manoeuvrable uprights
- Powerful cylinder vacuums
- Electric sweepers
- Handheld dustbusters
- Safe deep-cleaners
- Sanitising steam cleaners

Tips

Make sure that any attachments are easy to use, the bag or dirt container is easy to empty and the unit is easy to manoeuvre.

Bag or bagless? Bagless vacuums confine allergens, but emptying the dust container puts some of it back in the environment. They do save you the job of buying and changing bags.

Occasionally turn rugs over and vacuum the back side to remove gritty dirt.

Warning

If you have pets, seal and discard vacuum cleaner bags at least once a week. Be aware that fleas can continue to develop inside vacuum cleaner bags and re-infest the house.

209 Buy Extended Warranties on Appliances

An extended warranty or service contract is like an insurance policy –
your investment pays off only when the worst happens. But do you
really need one? These days, the majority of brand-name appliances
are well-built and will last their normal life span with few or no
repairs, rendering extended warranties unnecessary. If you do choose
to get one, make sure you do your homework.

Steps

1 Research the brand's repair history via independent consumer
   agencies, such as the Consumers' Association (which.net). Most
   appliances include a one-year warranty – five years for major
   parts – and you should have few problems during that time.

2 Consider who is offering the warranty. You'll get the best
   service from the manufacturer, who is most concerned with
   your satisfaction. Second choice is a dealer's warranty. Be
   cautious about third-party warranties sold by the dealer but
   independently serviced. Should that company disappear, you
   might be out of luck. Dealer warranties and third-party warranties
   often earn a commission for the seller.

3 Read the actual contract, not just the brochure that markets it.
   Understand what is covered and excluded. Compare the extended warranty to the original equipment warranty to make sure the
   extended one isn't just repeating coverage offered in the original
   warranty. Find out what you have to pay before the policy pays
   out and if you must get estimates or second opinions before
   repair. Ask what the standard minimum repair charge is.

4 Ask questions. What maintenance must you perform to validate
   the contract? Can you renew it annually? Do you get reimbursed
   for expenses such as for clothes ruined by a faulty washer or
   dryer, or food lost if the freezer fails?

What to Look For

- Brand and model repair
  history
- Preferred manufacturer
  coverage
- Thorough contract
- Terms that fit your needs

Tips

Can't decide at purchase
time? Return the registration
card; many manufacturers
will contact you with an
extended-warranty offer
when the original warranty
nears expiration.

Many credit-card companies
automatically extend a manufacturer's warranty by one
year when you use their
card.

Warning

Warranties can often set you
back more than half the cost
of replacing the insured item.

210 Find Period Fixtures

From doorknob to dado, finding appropriate fixtures is key to the restoration of a period home. Booming interest in vintage decor has spread from purists to home owners who wish to retain the original spirit of their home. Do your research and pay attention to the details.

Steps

1 Contact your local library, historical society and similar organisations for photographs, artefacts and other research materials from nearby houses of the same period as yours. Those buildings probably share similar features that may remain even if your house's are gone.

2 Visit museums and historic sites until you learn to recognize the proportions and details of pieces appropriate to your house's period. Browse vintage books and magazines.

3 Subscribe to magazines that focus on restoring and decorating older homes. Their advertising is your direct route to period-sensitive new products, such as cabinets inspired by the Victorian or Arts and Crafts eras.

4 Join appropriate groups such as the National Association of Decorative and Fine Arts Societies (nadfas.org.uk) or the Victorian Society (victorian-society.org.uk) who can give advice and share information relevant to your home.

5 Join historic preservation organisations to meet like-minded home owners who have faced similar shopping challenges.

6 Attend interior shows to identify craftspeople and repair shops you can hire to duplicate or re-create custom items.

7 Shop at auctions and antique shops for early chandeliers, sconces and ceiling-light fixtures. Take a magnet with you to determine the metal finishes. It will stick to steel or iron but not bronze or copper.

8 Find period-looking knobs, pulls, latches, hinges, house numbers and other hardware from many catalogue sources and at specialist shops.

9 Play detective in your own home to find traces of old paint and wallpaper, covered-up flooring and structural clues partially hidden by previous renovation work. Explore your loft and basement for dismantled house parts. Be careful when dealing with lead-based paint and avoid contact with asbestos insulation.

10 Explore salvage yards for vintage plumbing fixtures. Sinks and baths are easy to find, and most are in remarkably good shape. If they're not, porcelain reglazing services can repair marks and scratches to make surfaces look good as new.

11 Work with a salvage yard or woodworking shop to locate period-style wainscoting, doors, windows and mantelpieces.

What to Look For

- Historical accuracy
- Period-inspired design
- Licensed reproductions
- Usable antiques

Tips

Need a fresh background for your period finds? Several paint companies have created well-researched historic palettes of appropriate hues.

To replace or supplement damaged tiles or wallpaper, contact firms that specialise in matching existing materials. If they can't find more, they may reproduce your originals.

Examine flea-market buys carefully for repairs and signs of wear. Beware of reproductions being advertised as antiques. Get written documentation of an item's age and provenance.

Warning

Update wiring on old lamps and light fixtures for safe operation.

211 Buy a Bed and Mattress

Do you really have a bad back – or just a bad bed? Buying a new mattress set can be confusing and expensive – a kingsize can cost £300 or £3,000. Most of us spend one-third of our lives in bed, though, so it's worth it to find one that's just right for your body.

Steps

1 Look at construction, not price. A £400 mattress and fully sprung bed base may be as good as a £700 set. In more expensive pocket-spring mattresses, each spring rests in its own fabric pocket and responds independently to the weight above. In less expensive continuous-spring mattresses, a single length of wire forms the springs.

2 Test mattress support by lying beside your sleeping partner; you shouldn't roll towards each other and one person shouldn't feel motion as the other leaves the bed.

3 Consider coil count and the gauge of the wire in the coils as indicators of firmness (and often quality). Generally, the more coils, the firmer the mattress, although thicker wires can compensate for fewer coils. Lower gauge means the wire is thicker.

4 Consider a waterbed – helpful for some back problems – or an airbed, where electronically controlled air pockets adjust firmness for each person. Make sure your floor can accommodate a waterbed's weight.

5 Check out latex rubber and viscoelastic mattresses (£250 to £500). The dense foam is energy absorbing, heat sensitive and self-adjusts to body mass and temperature. Allergy and dust-mite resistant, this mattress doesn't need to be turned.

6 Take a test nap on a polyurethane foam mattress (£100 to £300). They also self-adjust and come in various thicknesses and firmnesses.

MATTRESS	DIMENSIONS
Standard Single	75 by 200 cm (30 by 80 in).
Single Extra-long	90 by 215 cm (35 by 85 in).
Standard Double	135 by 200 cm (53 by 80 in).
Queen	150 by 200 cm (60 by 80 in).
King	180 by 200 cm (71 by 80 in).
Super King	215 by 200 cm (85 by 80 in).

What to Look For

- Correct dimensions
- Sleeping support
- Quality and firmness
- Top comfort

Tips

Before investing in a new bed, try it out: ask to sleep on a friend's bed for a night.

Choose a bed 10 to 15 cm (4 to 6 in) longer than the tallest person sleeping in it.

Why buy a mattress and bed base set? A new mattress on an old bed base will last only one-third as long as it should.

If a large bed base spring won't fit up your stairs, ask about one which comes in two pieces.

Warnings

When you're in the shop for a mattress sale, be on guard for the salesperson's nudge towards fancier models. What's more, you'll find the same mattress labelled differently at different shops. This makes comparison shopping practically impossible.

If you buy a super thick mattress, your old sheets may no longer fit.

212 Hire an Interior Designer

You don't have to be rich to hire an interior designer. In fact, professional advice can stretch your budget and help you avoid mistakes, saving money in the long run. Let a designer find just what you need – or didn't know you needed – to bring your dream home to life.

Steps

1 Collect magazine clippings of the style, colour, fabrics and furnishings you like and decide which existing furnishings you wish to keep. Sketch a simple floor plan.

2 Visit show houses and model homes or read local publications to find designers whose work you like. Ask in local interior design shops for recommendations or look on the web.

3 Interview each designer to assess compatibility – you'll need to work well together. Review portfolios and ask for references.

4 Determine each designer's fees. He or she might charge for a consultation, a flat project fee, an hourly fee, a percentage of the project cost, or cost plus (wholesale plus markup). Fees vary widely by location, reputation and experience.

5 Set the project's scope and budget. Ask about ways to save money to cut the overall cost of the job. Maybe you can do some of the painting yourself. Find out if you can spread out a big project and do just one or two rooms at a time.

6 Sign a contract before work begins. Clarify what services the designer will provide, when he or she will be on site, whether the designer or someone else will oversee the work, all budget details, how you will be billed, and the projected time frame. Clarify in your contract how cost overruns will be handled.

What to Look For

- Compatibility
- Relevant experience
- Fees to match your budget
- A clear contract

Tips

If all you need is basic advice on furnishings and colour or pattern schemes, try in-house decorators at furniture showrooms and upmarket paint or wallpaper shops.

Finding an interior designer is like finding a hairdresser: at first you must show or explain the style you're after, but later he or she will understand what makes you happy.

213 Hire a Feng Shui Consultant

Feng Shui literally means "wind and water" in Chinese. This ancient philosophy is based on principles rooted in an extraordinary sensitivity to nature. Feng shui maintains that a balanced environment positively affects the health and success of those who live there. How do you find a good consultant? Read these tips.

Steps

1 Study the principles behind both Eastern and Western feng shui methods to understand the various theories. Delve into books, browse the internet or take short courses to gain knowledge.

What to Look For

- Classical versus Western approach
- Training and professionalism
- Trustworthy practices
- Acceptable fees and results

2 Focus on classical feng shui for assessments based on ancient disciplines such as yin and yang, Flying Stars, Five Elements and the I Ching, which relies on astronomy, mathematics and Oriental astrology. Consultations require thorough readings of the living environment, people, time and energy.

3 Consider practices such as Black Hat and Eight Life Aspirations. They are complementary mixtures of ancient and modern practice developed over the last 20 years.

4 Ascertain credentials; ask for and call references. When and where was the consultant trained? How many consultations has he or she done? What affiliations does he or she hold? Try to get a sense of how well you would work together.

5 Find out how the consultant works. Ask which feng shui tradition is he or she a practitioner of? How are fees structured? What consultation services are included – for example, is there a report or follow-up? Are repeat visits necessary?

Tip

Some consultants sell cures or other products. Don't feel pressured to purchase these; in fact, hard-sell techniques contradict a professional approach.

Warning

Some consultants may be only slightly better informed than you, having only attended a one-day workshop.

214 Incorporate a Greater Sense of Space into Your Home

Most people undertake major changes because their home no longer fits their needs. They like the location but need more – or a different – living space. Solutions can be simple or radical, expensive or relatively modest to achieve.

What to Look For

- Lifestyle needs
- Same-space adaptability
- Indoor-outdoor living

Steps

1 Analyse whether your home does what you need it to do. What activities does your family enjoy? Which rooms or spaces work for you and which don't?

2 Evaluate your home's natural setting. Do you want better visual access to any landscape features? Do you enjoy great views only at certain times of the day or year? Would you like greater access to the outdoors?

3 Investigate building another room in the garden. This could be a home office, a garden room for relaxing or a self-contained living area for a teenager. If the room is at the end of the garden, the walk to and from it become part of your everyday living space.

4 Knock two rooms into one. First check with a structural engineer about the load-bearing capacity of the different walls. An architect at this stage may be able to suggest imaginative ideas to make the most of your space (see 188 "Hire an Architect").

5 Open up the house to the elements. Add French windows on to the patio, make a section of roof out of glass, enlarge a window on to the garden. All give a sense of space and allow the outdoors inside.

Tip

Shop around and ask for recommendations for architects. A good architect not only comes up with innovative ideas, but can make sure a large project runs to schedule and on budget.

Warning

Investigate whether or not you need planning permission. The local planning department can give useful advice about what is likely to be accepted if they are involved at an early stage.

215 Select Paint, Stain and Varnish

What's the easiest way to update a room? Paint! How do you protect wood against the elements (or your child)? Stain or varnish! If you're drowning in a sea of options at the paint shop, your enthusiasm may wane. Relax. Your ideal finish starts here.

Steps

1 Choose the right paint for the indoor room you are painting. Indoor paints can be divided into water-based and oil-based paints. Each is available in numerous different finishes. Water-based paints are fast to dry and it is often possible to apply more than one coat in a day, but they do not flow as well as oil-based, and brush marks are more likely to be visible. Oil-based paints usually need to be left overnight before another coat can be applied, but give a very smooth finish and are very hard wearing.

2 Decide how much sheen you want. Matt paint minimises irregularities, but its dull finish can trap dirt. Satin or eggshell finishes resist dirt and stains on high-contact walls. Gloss is a popular choice for woodwork. Specially formulated wipe-clean and hard-wearing paints are available for areas such as kitchens and hallways that get hard use.

3 Choose a colour. You can buy tiny tester pots of different colours and finishes to try out on your walls – this is a great idea as many colours look different in the context and lighting of a room than on a colour chart. Most interior paints can be custom-mixed in a machine, available widely in DIY shops. You simply choose the exact shade you want, check it is available in the finish you prefer, and ask the store to mix the quantity you need.

4 Select a primer, if necessary, and an undercoat. A primer is used on bare surfaces and forms a good base for receiving other paints. An undercoat helps the top coat to go on smoothly, providing a smooth and even surface. Different primers are available for different surfaces, such as wood, plaster, laminate, and so on.

5 Buy exterior paints that are blended for colour retention, mildew resistance and flexibility during temperature changes. They also come in a huge variety of finishes. Prepare the surface to be painted well, washing it down with a fungicidal wash, and sanding down any flaking areas to sound paintwork.

6 Highlight wood grain or harmonise different varieties of wood with wood stain. On floors and other areas that receive a lot of use, you can varnish over the stain to make the finish harder wearing. Always test the stain and varnish on a small section of prepared wood. Apply one or two coats of stain and then, if you are using varnish, add this on top. Try different combinations to see which depth of colour and finish you prefer before coating the whole area. It's much easier to add another coat to deepen colour than to try and remove stain or varnish.

What to Look For

- Water- or oil-based paint
- Suitable sheens
- Easy-clean finishes
- Durable exterior formulas
- Even-tone stains
- Protective varnishes
- Appropriate primer and undercoat

Tips

More expensive paint contains more of the pigments and binders that help the paint flow better, are easier to apply, hide better, and produce uniform colour and sheen. Top-quality paint can last twice as long. Because of all this, your overall project cost is less if you buy better quality paint.

Seal wood knots on bare wood with knotting sealant, otherwise the knot will, over time, "bleed" through the paint finish.

Tint primer to match finish coat for better coverage.

If you are painting over an existing coat of paint, remember that oil-based paints will cover water-based, but water-based paints will not generally cover oil-based.

The most popular times to paint are in late spring and early autumn, avoiding extremes of heat and cold.

7 Buy a high-quality paintbrush to make the job go faster and smoother. Premium brushes have hardwood handles and flagged or split-bristle tips that hold more paint. Use natural-bristle brushes with oil-based paints. Nylon or polyester bristle brushes are better for water-based paints. Buy a 7.5 to 10 cm (3- to 4-in) wide wall brush for broad, flat surfaces; a 7.5 cm (3-in), straight-edge trim brush for doors, wainscoting, and window frames; an angled-bristle sash brush for edging and painting windows. Single-use foam applicators are fine for touch-ups but deteriorate during big jobs. Rollers are quick to use and give a good finish, especially on hard-to-reach areas such as the top of a high hallway, and often give good coverage with exterior paint.

8 Buy the right brush cleaner at the same time as you buy your paints, stains and varnishes, following the guidelines on the tin. Brushes left improperly cleaned will perform poorly the next time you use them.

216 Choose Decorative Tiles

Decorative tiles make any room or small space memorable. These durable, practical works of art add personality for anything from a couple of pounds to £30 each. The hard part of choosing accent, border, mural and mosaic tiles is narrowing it down to your favourites.

Steps

1 Imagine what colours or designs will reinforce your room's decorative theme – you'll have thousands of options. Handmade artisan tiles offer rich glazes, strong textures and whimsical pictorial designs, but cost more than mass-produced tiles.

2 Contact kitchen design shops, interior designers and ceramic supply shops to find a tile artist in your area.

3 Mix field tiles and accent tiles for a striking and less-expensive effect. Repeated across a large area, plain or solid-colour field tiles are sold by the area; accent tiles, which are added to trim or decorate field tiles, are priced per piece based on size, design, glaze and how they're made.

4 Use border tiles to emphasise a horizontal plane, frame a mirror or window, define where different surfaces meet or cap an area of related field tiles.

5 Repeat a wallpaper, china or fabric motif with a tile mural. Mass-produced murals using stock decals cost less.

6 Re-create old-world texture and detail with mosaics, now available preassembled on mesh backings for easy installation. Glass and metal are the hot materials in this category. Their reflective and translucent qualities wake up bland kitchens and bathrooms.

Warning

Wear a face mask while applying varnish: follow the instructions on the label.

What to Look For

- Colour and design
- Artisan or handmade options
- Function plus decoration
- Easy installation

Tips

Install pricey tiles strategically for budget-conscious impact at eye level or in locations where the design attracts notice.

Ask an interior designer for advice if you're unsure about mixing tile shapes and proportions.

217 Choose a Dehumidifier

High levels of humidity can cause condensation on walls and windows, and may aggravate arthritis, rheumatism and asthma. A dehumidifier reduces levels of humidity, and some models can pump the excess moisture from the room. Your surroundings end up warmer, drier and cleaner, and all for a running cost of about 2p an hour.

Steps

1 Look at where you need a dehumidifier. In the home or in a caravan or motorhome, the size and noise levels will be important, whereas for an outside workshop or garage, price might be a higher consideration.

2 Choose one that is suitable for the space you need to dry out. Dehumidifiers are made for single rooms and six-bedroom houses, with all capacities inbetween. Price is generally dictated by the area to be dehumidified, with machines for small areas starting at around £120 and the larger ones around £300. There are, however, additional features that also affect price.

3 Go for an adjustable humidistat. You can then choose how much moisture you want to be removed from the air, and the machine will switch itself off once that level has been reached. This saves money and reduces noise. These are often combined with timers so you can choose when you want the dehumidifier to run – during the day if it is near a bedroom for example.

4 Select a dehumidifier with a specialist filter if you want to remove pollen from the air – this is ideal for hayfever sufferers. All dehumidifiers have dust filters to remove mould spores and dust mites up to a point, but if you pay more you often get more effective filtration.

5 Look for a machine that can pump the water it has collected out of the room. This is ideal for places such as cellars that may need constant drying out, or if you are leaving a machine on when you are away, in a holiday home, for example. Machines not fitted with a pump simply collect water in a tank, indicate how full the tank is, and can be emptied manually.

6 Find out about internal defrosting systems if you are planning to use the dehumidifier in an unheated place such as a garage in winter. Most dehumidifiers stop working if their condensation coil freezes, but those fitted with an internal defrosting system keep going for longer.

What to Look For

- Right size for your chosen location
- Adjustability
- Extra filtration for cleaner air
- Pump or manually emptied tank
- Internal defrosting option

Tip

Look for safety features such as a child lock if you want your unit to be tamperproof.

Warning

Choose a dehumidifier that uses CFC-free refrigerants.

218 Buy a Whirlpool Bath

Up to your neck in hot water with all this confusion about jets and pumps? Not to worry. Once you choose between an air-jet bathtub and a whirlpool system, your cares will bubble away.

Steps

1 Choose a bath system. In air-jet baths, air is propelled through dozens of small holes for an all-over bubbling action. In whirlpool baths, air and water is forced through four to eight large jets for a vigorous massaging action. These powerful jets open, close and swivel to adjust pressure and flow. Smaller jets may cycle along the backrest or target the feet or neck.

2 Figure out where the bath will go. Easiest to install are 1.5 m (5 ft) long models that slide into your existing bath alcove. Recess-mount baths fit between walls, which butt against the bath rim. Deck-mount baths drop into the floor or a platform, requiring a tiled surround. Corner baths maximise floor space.

3 Make sure your water heater is large enough to fill about two-thirds of your bath with warm water. Whirlpool baths vary in size, holding 95 to 560 litres (25 to 150 gallons) of water.

4 Test size, back support and comfort in showroom models. To accommodate short and tall people, compromise on a bath about 1.7 m (5½ ft) long by 84 to 107 cm (33 to 42 in) wide. Before buying a giant bath for two, think how often you'll share it, since you'll be paying to heat a lot of water.

5 Weigh your bath options. Enamelled cast iron is durable but heavy – make sure your floor can support it. As for lightweight plastic, moulded acrylic resists stains better than sprayed-on gel-coated fibreglass baths. Easy-care enamelled steel baths come in just a few sizes and shapes.

6 Make sure you have access to the components. All mechanical baths require maintenance access via an apron or a panel in the bath surround. Whirlpool baths may require a large opening to reach pipes; air-jet systems need access to the motor only.

7 Pay attention to the details: look for protected jets, and sensors that cut the motor if the water is low, so the motor won't burn out. Built-in grab bars and slip-resistant floors add safety. Units with internal water heaters maintain a consistent temperature.

8 Determine if you want a self-cleaning system. Because whirlpool baths recirculate water, their systems need frequent cleaning. Some air-jet systems automatically purge bacteria-causing residue after each use.

9 Consider your budget. Whirlpool and air-jet baths sell for anywhere from less than £800 to more than £15,000, depending on system, size, materials used and other options.

What to Look For

- Air-jet versus whirlpool
- Number and location of jets
- Size and shape
- Preferred material
- Safe and hygienic system

Tips

Jacuzzi is the best-known whirlpool brand, not a generic term.

Because air-jet baths don't recirculate, users can add aromatherapy salts or oils. In whirlpool tubs, these products can leave residue in the pipes.

Ask if the motor must go next to the tub. Installing the motor up to 4.5 m (15 ft) away will reduce noise and vibration.

Opt for a 2-horsepower variable-flow pump over a 1-horsepower one for more power and less energy consumption.

See 263 "Buy a Spa Pool".

Warnings

Keep young children away from tubs unless there is constant adult supervision. The suction action may catch long hair, causing the person's head to be trapped under water.

The tub must be connected to the ring main by a qualified electrician.

219 Buy a Shower

Today's showers feature multiple sprays, antiscald valves, and artistic styles and finishes. Height-adjustable models fit any budget, and other options raise the price from £30 to upwards of £300.

Steps

1 Choose a handheld nozzle (£50 and up) with a controlled spray to bathe children, wash pets or help those who need to shower sitting down. Some mount on a vertical slide bar for versatility.

2 Pamper yourself with a unit that offers adjustable force and aerated, massaging, and drenching rain-shower spray patterns.

3 Select a finish to match your taps. Non-tarnishing surfaces mean easier upkeep but cost more.

4 Shop around for a model that enables you to select the flow that you want. Choosing a low-flow (economy) option can knock pounds off your electricity bill, and help with your water bill too if your water is metered.

5 Protect against scalding with pressure-balance and maximum temperature controls.

What to Look For

- Spray patterns
- Practical finish
- Water-saving features
- Safety options

Tips

If you have hard water, look for self-cleaning spray holes that shed mineral build-up.

Compensate for low pressure with a model designed to concentrate water flow.

220 Buy a Toilet

Although it's one of the most used fixtures in the bathroom, most of us never think about what makes one toilet different from another – until it's time to buy one. Models range from very basic equipment to a truly royal flush.

Steps

1 Choose from traditional two-piece toilets that have cistern and bowl bolted together, low-profile one-piece toilets, and easy-to-clean wall-mounted tankless ones.

2 Pick your throne with comfort and space in mind. Narrow spaces favour round bowls, but elongated bowls provide another 5 cm (2 in) of support. Seat heights range from 25 cm (10 in) for kids to the standard 35 to 38 cm (14 to 15 in) for adults and the wheelchair-accessible 43 cm (17 in).

3 Choose a flush action. All new toilets use 6 litres (1.6 gallons) of water to flush. Affordable gravity-fed toilets run water from the tank into the bowl to create a siphon that drains waste. Pressure-assisted toilets use compressed air to propel water and expel waste with noisy turbolike force.

4 Look for extras like a built-in pump to boost water pressure, and a 7.5 cm (3 in) flush valve and 5 cm (2 in) trapway to clear the bowl quicker.

What to Look For

- Easy-to-clean design
- Comfortable height
- Efficient flushing action

Tips

Treat yourself to heated seats, deodoriser fans and bidet-style spray-and-dry devices. Self-closing lids reduce noise and arguments.

Most toilets bolt to the floor 30 cm (12 in) from the wall, but some require 25 or 35 cm (10 or 14 in).

Dual flush options will minimise water consumption.

221 Choose a Tap

A well-made, well-designed kitchen or bath tap combines function and style, and makes life easier. Better valve mechanisms and tougher finishes boost durability and looks. See what's on tap these days.

Steps

1 Make sure you choose taps that match the existing hole or holes on your sink or bath, otherwise you'll have to drill more holes or cover unused holes with a plate – which is likely to spoil the overall effect.

2 Get a handle – or two – on design. Separate taps let you adjust water temperature more precisely with independent hot and cold controls. They are usually a pillar shape, with a metal top with a handle at the top for turning the tap on and off, or the tap body can be covered with a metal or plastic head that you grab and turn to control the water. Large wing levers and cross-shaped handles are popular styles. The large wing levers enable you use one lever to switch the water on and to adjust the temperature, ideal for those who find turning traditional taps hard. Choose a style to complement your bathroom suite and the age and style of your house.

3 Mixer taps are available for both kitchen and bathroom, and mix the hot and cold water supply as it comes out of the single spout. You need almost equal pressure in your hot and cold water supplies for these taps to work, so check your pressure first. In the bath, a hand-held shower attachment can be fitted to the tap; the water is diverted via the shower by pressing a knob or turning a lever.

4 Start with the finish if style is important. Chrome-finish taps are the least expensive and often carry long warranties against scratches. Colourful plastic or enamel coatings are vulnerable to chips, scratches and damage from solvents. Stainless steel costs 25 to 40 per cent more than coated taps. Explore finishes such as brushed chrome, satin nickel and oil-rubbed bronze for vintage appeal. Brushed or satin finishes disguise scratches, too.

5 Choose a spout. Beyond the standard, straight-spout taps, you'll find high-arching goosenecks, handy for filling tall pots. Do you need to direct the water accurately into two or three bowls in your kitchen sink?

6 Remember that the simpler the design, the less there is to break or wear out. Whichever you choose, look for a lifetime warranty on the valve as well as the finish.

What to Look For

- Practical handles and controls
- Durable, appealing finish
- Lifetime warranty
- Special options and accessories

Tips

You don't have to pay top money for good quality. Many taps share the same basic parts – and even finishes – across several price lines.

For a streamlined, modern look, choose a wall-mounted tap, often used with ceramic bowls.

Try out taps before you buy: are they easy to handle, especially with wet, soapy hands? Will they be easy to clean?

Warning

Before carrying out any work on taps, turn off the water supply.

When it comes to do-it-yourself projects or crafts, choosing the appropriate glue or adhesive will provide stability and strength. It gets a little sticky: glues are based on natural polymers, such as starch and protein from flour, milk and animal parts, while adhesives come from synthesised polymers.

FOR WOOD	DESCRIPTION	USES, PROS AND CONS
Contact Adhesive	Liquid in tubes, or tubs (500 ml, £8.50)	Used for craft projects. Bonds laminates, wallboards, plywood and hardboard panels, and leather goods Once tacky, it bonds on contact and permanently. Use in well-ventilated area.
Hot-Melt Glue	Sticks (1 kg for £5.50) used in electric glue gun	Excellent adhesive for crafts and household repairs. Fast-setting; needs little clamping.
Resin Wood Adhesive	Bottle (1 litre, £7.50)	Use on any interior wood. Waterproof.
Waterproof Adhesive (synthetic resin, Cascamite)	Powder or liquid mixed with water just before use (125 g, £3)	For use on outdoor woodwork, including boat building.
White Glue (polyvinylacetate or PVA)	Creamy white standby we all know and love (1 litre, £12)	Used for craft projects. Sets in an hour. Dries clear and won't stain. Interior use as not moisture- or heat-resistant. For all soft-woods and hardwoods. Tends to run.
Exterior PVA	Plastic bottle (1 litre, £4)	Waterproof, dries clear.
Flooring PVA	Plastic bottle (1 litre, £5.50)	Bonds wood and laminate flooring. Dries clear. Low shrinkage.
Mitre Glue	Plastic bottle (200 ml, £7)	Bonds mitres; for cornice and profile mitres, trims, picture frames, MDF skirting and architrave, worktop end trims.
Polyurethane Glue	Gel (310 ml, £6)	Used for woodworking. Multipurpose but expensive. Bonds wood to concrete, fibre-glass, metal, masonry and timber. Sets in up to 30 minutes. Fills gaps.

FOR OTHER MATERIALS	DESCRIPTION	USES, PROS AND CONS
Acrylic Resin	Two-part adhesive	For interior or exterior use. Sets in less than a minute without clamping. Good at filling gaps. Waterproof; cleans up with acetone.
Contact Cement (rubber-based)	Bottles or cans (500 ml, £4)	Used to bond wood or to bond plastic laminate to counters and tabletops; also bonds rigid PVC, leather, cork, rubber, stone, metals and dense fabrics. Apply with paintbrush or roller. Once tacky, bonds on contact and permanently.
Cyanoacrylate (instant glue, Super Glue)	Single glue tube (20 g, £1.50)	Used to repair ceramics, eyeglasses and more. Bonds instantly with drop or two. Use with caution; can seal eyelids, skin together.
Epoxy	Two-part catalyst and hardener; often sold in two-tube syringe set (25 ml, £2)	Excellent for china repairs. Bonds dissimilar materials. Strong and waterproof. Cleans up with acetone. Full strength in 24 hours.
Gap-Filler Adhesive (solvent- or non-solvent based, Gripfill brand)	Thick; tubes or caulking-gun cartridges (350 ml, £2)	Bonds batons, skirting, carpet gripper to most porous and non-porous masonry, metal and timber.
Wall-Covering Adhesives	Wheat or premixed polymer-base (various prices)	Mix powdered type to make clear adhesive for paper that is not prepasted; use vinyl-over-vinyl adhesive to adhere new over existing wall covering.
Glue Sticks	Chapstick-like tubes in various sizes	Great for paper and light fabrics where see-through isn't an issue. Can be lumpy.
Adhesive "Gun"	Spray in form of aerosol (£7) or canister (£10) for use with "gun" (£20)	Produces fine strands of adhesive that form a web pattern. Suitable for bonding furniture, shopfitting, laminating, woodworking.
Spray Adhesive (3M Spray Mount)	Aerosol spray (various sizes under £15)	Permanent or repositionable adhesives good for paper, scrap books, photo albums. Messy to use; toxic fumes.
WARNINGS	Glues and adhesives are often toxic. Be sure to use in a well-ventilated area, or wear a respirator. Keep all adhesives and glues away from children.	

223 Choose Window Treatments

Change a room's mood, maximise privacy and frame your view – all with the right window treatments. A wide range of styles, fabrics and materials add function and flair to any room.

TREATMENT	MATERIALS	WHERE AND WHY TO USE
Blinds • Horizontal	Metal, plastic, wood	Achieve contemporary, linear look where wall space is minimal. Durable and easy to clean; control light and privacy with quick lift or tilt.
• Vertical	Aluminum, vinyl or reinforced fabric.	Practical and minimal treatment diffuses glare through large windows, or sliding or French doors. Overlapping panels rotate for light control.
• Roller	Vinyl, canvas or bonded fabric.	Inexpensive, versatile. Create consistent exterior view under varied curtains. Provide moderate to blackout privacy. Variety of fabrics, trims.
• Roman	Choice of fabric determines appearance.	Controlled by cords and pulleys; boast casual, unfussy lines. Panels lift, stack and almost disappear when blind is raised. Add some insulation.
Curtains	Fabric in many colours, patterns, fabrics and textures from lace to velvet; effects from flowing or gauzy to fun, formal and elegant.	Suit many decorating styles; heading treatments (how curtain hangs from rod) direct look. Fabric adds visual warmth; optional lining insulates. Couple with gauzy inner curtains for different quality of light, or lightweight lining to protect fabric from fading.
Swags	Soft or sheer fabric.	Simple, no-sew treatment. Drape over another treatment or use alone to soften window frame without reducing light. Portable.
Shutters	Wood or polymer panels or louvres; fabric, glass or metal inserts.	Add traditional or cottage charm to many window styles. Install to play up architectural elements or when there is no room to extend treatment beyond window frame. Shutters adjust easily for light and privacy. Measure precisely to fit frame dimensions.
Cornices and Valances	Anything from wood to silk-flower garland.	Top window with shelf, panel or decorative accent that suits treatment below or stands alone. Can hide curtain headings or make window and ceiling look taller.

224 Get Self-Cleaning Windows

If you could banish one home maintenance chore, would it be washing windows? Wishes do come true: a new type of glass actually breaks down and loosens dirt, minimising spots and streaks with very little help from you.

Steps

1 Determine whether self-cleaning windows are right for your area. They work better in wet regions than dry ones because they require water to wash away dirt and grime.

2 Understand the chemical make-up of the glass:

   • The sun's ultraviolet light activates a durable, transparent titanium dioxide coating that is chemically fused to the glass. Even on cloudy days, the resulting *photocatalytic action* oxidises organic dirt and loosens it from the surface.

   • Normal glass panes are *hydrophobic* (water repellent): raindrops slide down, leaving behind dirt streaks and evaporated spots. Self-cleaning glass is *hydrophilic*: it forces water to spread out evenly in a sheet, washing away dirt loosened by the photocatalytic action. The sheeting action allows the window to dry quickly with minimal spotting and streaking. At night, the glass remains hydrophilic but loses its photocatalytic action.

3 Research self-cleaning glass through glass contractors and DIY stores. The main manufacturer now offering self-cleaning glass is Pilkington (activglass.com).

4 Do a cost-benefit analysis. Windows equipped with self-cleaning glass cost 10 to 20 per cent more than windows with ordinary glass. Factor in the elbow grease and window-cleaning fluid, and you may have yourself a deal.

5 Plan when and where to install self-cleaning windows. When you're buying new or replacement windows, upgrade to self-cleaning glass particularly where access is difficult or dangerous: huge plate-glass or second-storey windows, skylights, conservatories and glass roofs.

6 Consider combining self-cleaning glass with low-emissivity (insulating) and solar-control glazing to save energy costs as well as cleaning time.

What to Look For

- Appropriate climate
- Cost-effectiveness for your situation
- Low-emissivity and solar control glazing

Tip

During dry spells, you'll need to give a light spray with the hose to rinse the exterior of self-cleaning windows. Also, the glass won't shed any inorganic matter – paint spatters, for example.

225 Choose Wallpaper

You've decided to be adventurous and wallpaper your walls, but the choices are overwhelming. What look are you after? How do you find the best wallpaper to meet your decorating style, needs and budget?

Steps

1 Chart a decorating course based on your furniture, carpet, curtains, art and collections. Decide which colours, motifs or other elements you want to enhance or unify.

2 Measure your room and sketch a detailed floor plan, including doors, windows and other permanent features. Plot wall height minus skirting boards and coving, then measure the length of each wall segment. Round up measurements to the nearest 10 cm. To find the area, multiply room height by circumference, then subtract openings you won't be papering. (It's always better to buy too much than too little and be stuck in the middle of your project.)

3 Take your notes, along with paint, carpet and fabric samples, to wallpaper dealers, DIY centres or interior decor shops. Borrow sample books to see how the paper looks in your home.

4 Take the stress out of blending paper and border designs with manufacturer's swatch books. Pick bold patterns for large rooms full of activity or for rooms used briefly or only occasionally – a hall or formal dining room. Select neutral, smaller patterns for a family room, bedroom or home office.

5 Diminish architectural flaws. Stripes accentuate crooked walls. Choose a forgiving floral or intricate pattern to disguise cracked or uneven walls or mask an awkward room shape. Apply liner paper first over bricks, concrete blocks or panelling.

6 Pay attention to the repeat (the vertical distance between the start of the pattern and the start of its first repeat). Large repeats require that you cut longer pieces to match patterns when hanging. If walls are fragmented – in a kitchen, say – opt for a smaller repeat.

7 Choose vinyl or vinyl-coated paper for a kitchen, bathroom, child's room or anywhere you need a durable, easy-to-clean surface. Vinyls tend to cost less than papers.

8 Choose paper wallpaper for a living room, dining room or other light-use area. More delicate than vinyl, paper adheres well but can tear when wet. Prices vary for machine-printed, decorator hand-blocked and silk-screened types.

9 Place your order. Paper is priced by the single roll; most borders are sold in various lengths. Using your measurements, a salesperson will calculate how much to order. Buy all the rolls you need at once to assure uniform run or dye-lot numbers.

What to Look For

- Detailed floor plan
- Coordinated patterns
- Pattern repeat
- Durability and cleanability

Tips

Wallpaper displays can be daunting, but you'll often find books sorted by style or room via a coloured-dot or other marking system. Some books contain only borders.

Buy an extra roll to repair damaged areas in the future. Use trimmings to line drawers and decorate lamp shades or storage boxes.

Warnings

Make sure the adhesion method required is suitable for your skill level. Many papers arrive prepasted – just wetting them makes them stick – but you must paste some papers (often imported or designer brands) before hanging. Some borders and wall decals are self-sticking.

If you do not have solid wallpapering skills, hire a professional to do the work for you. You'll save money (no botched up rooms to redo), frustration and time.

226 Buy a Wood-Burning Stove

Beyond their romantic glow and homely crackle, modern wood-burning stoves produce low-cost heat, and burn cleanly and efficiently, producing minimal ash and smoke. You pick the technology and choose the ideal-size stove to match your heating needs. Buy the most efficient stove you can afford. It'll pay for itself in the long run.

Steps

1 Evaluate your home's floor plan to determine where you should install a wood-burning stove. Some stoves can heat an entire house, powering radiators and heating hot water; others work best as heaters for the most-used areas. A stove placed in one room will heat adjacent rooms if there's good airflow at the ceiling and floor.

2 Show a dealer a sketch of your home, the area that needs heat, and a description of the insulation surrounding that area. The dealer will help you calculate the proper stove size, expressed in kilowatts (kW). You'll waste money if you buy too big a stove, and it will use more fuel than necessary and make the area too hot to be comfortable.

3 Talk to one or more professional chimney sweeps about the brands you're interested in, and get their recommendations. You'll need to have your chimney lined and insulated if it is not already – a stove burns more efficiently than an open fire and so tar can build up in the chimney

4 Understand how your stove burns most efficiently. Keep the doors shut to enable the wood to give off the maximum heat. Use only well-seasoned wood (seasoned for about two years), and always burn it on a bed of wood ash – you do not need to remove the cold ashes every day. The stove radiates heat directly from the front, but also heats by convection, in which heat from around the stove is directed back into the room.

5 Consider if you would like to burn fuel other than wood. It is possible to adapt a wood-burning stove to burn other solid fuels such as coal. This involves buying a kit that enables air to circulate under the base of the fire.

6 Check out the huge range of designs available, with single and double doors, flat top or canopy, double-sided access for a stove in the centre of the room, and various finishes and decorative details. Leading brands include Vermont Castings (Vermontcastings.com), Yeoman (yeoman-stoves.co.uk) and Morso (Morsostoves.co.uk). Prices range from £200 to over £1,000.

What to Look For

- Best location
- Desired heat output
- Decorator details
- Convenient features

Tip

Look for standard features including self-cleaning glass, hidden hinges and reversible flues, as well as optional accessories such as spark guards.

Warnings

Your home's air will become very dry when heated with a wood stove. Combat this with a humidifier or by placing a kettle of water on the stove.

Dirty chimneys can cause catastrophic chimney fires. Hire a chimney sweep for regular cleanings.

227 Select Flooring

The materials you choose for flooring anchor each room's style and function. All materials aren't suitable for all situations, though. Think about wear and tear, for example: tiles are great in kitchens as areas can be replaced. Prices are a guide for materials only; variable installation costs can balance total price.

MATERIAL; PRICE; FORMAT; FEATURES		
Solid Wood From £40 per sq m Strips, planks, parquet; unfinished or prefinished. Many species, styles; natural character; can be refinished several times (long life). Adds to home's value. Can be laid over many existing floors. Not ideal for bathrooms or shower rooms.	**Laminate** From £15 per sq m Planks and tiles. Realistic look-alike for wood and stone; durable and stain-resistant; easy to install. Hollow sound; surface cannot be refinished. Makers of some brands discourage bathroom installation.	**Cork** From £30 per sq m Sheets and tiles, unfinished or prefinished. Natural insulator; long-wearing and self-healing; environmentally friendly; hypoallergenic; comfortable. Shades vary. Hard to clean and can stain easily unless sealed.
Engineered Wood £25 per sq m Strips and planks, usually prefinished. Easier and less expensive to install than some solid wood; laminated construction adds stability. May be professionally refinished at least once.	**Vinyl** £10 to £30 per sq m Sheets and tiles. Many colours and patterns; water-resistant in sheet form; resilient. Hard-wearing, warm underfoot, low maintenance, hygienic and fire resistant. Lower grades can tear, dent and discolour; not environmentally friendly.	**Ceramic** £10 to £40 per sq m Tiles. Many styles and colours, including mosaic; easy to clean; impervious to moisture and stains (glazed tile). Ideal for showers and wet rooms Cold; noisy; requires perfect surface underneath; grout needs periodic sealing.
Concrete Variable; existing surface can be used Solid surface; variable texture; can paint or varnish. Hard, stable, gives an "industrial" look ideal in some urban settings and lofts. Unforgiving if breakables dropped; cold.	**Linoleum** £25 to £40 up per sq m Sheets and tiles. Wide colour range goes all the way through; durable; self-healing; environmentally friendly; antistatic. Can rot if water seeps underneath.	**Stone** £20 to £50 and up per sq m Slabs and tiles. Natural material; earthy look and texture; durable; adds value to home. Can be brittle, slippery; seal porous types against stains; check floor can bear weight.

TIP Reclaimed wood and stone are available from reclamation yards. Old wooden dance floors and flooring from squash courts are desirable as well as old pine or elm floorboards and old flagstones. Before buying, check there is enough from the same source to meet your needs.

228 Select Carpeting

Wall-to-wall carpet can make or break the way your living spaces look. Carpeting is warm, quiet and comfortable, and offers more colours and textures than any other flooring. Compare fibre and pile to make sure the look you love is also durable and easy to keep clean.

Steps

1 Pick pile length and type. In cut-pile carpets, the yarn stands up straight from the backing. In loop-pile construction, the yarn loops over and returns to the backing. Level (same-height) and multilevel loops are casual and durable. Cut-and-loop or sculptured carpets combine both types, and both hide footprints and trap soil.

2 Narrow your texture choices. Saxony and velvet styles boast smooth, uniform surfaces suitable for formal rooms, although they show footprints and vacuum marks. Frieze types have an extreme amount of twist (see Step 3), making them durable in high-activity spaces. Berbers weave fat yarns into a nubbly, sometimes multicoloured texture. Shag pile carpets have a luxurious, decorative feel but are not for heavy-traffic areas.

3 Compare the pros and cons of each type of carpet fibre keeping in mind your preferences for resilience, stain resistance, wear and cleanability. Understand twist's role in quality and performance. During carpet construction, fine strands – filaments – are spun into a tightly twisted yarn and heat-set for shape. Higher (tighter) twist creates stronger yarn and more durable carpet.

4 Consider nylon (£7 to £25 per sq m), the most popular synthetic fibre. Hard-wearing nylon provides brilliant colours and hides soil and traffic well. Thanks to its resilience, wear resistance and cleanability, nylon works almost anywhere.

5 Look to polypropylene carpeting (£5 to £18 per sq m) when you need high stain, static and mildew resistance, but resilience isn't a priority.

6 Choose polyester (£5 to £13 per sq m) for its soft feel and colour clarity. Less durable than nylon, polyester stands up moderately well to wear and stains, but its cleanability is only fair. Best for use in low-traffic areas.

7 Pay a premium for wool (£17 to £45 or more per sq m), the oldest carpet fibre. Naturally soft and hard-wearing, wool has excellent resilience but low stain resistance (unless it's treated); it wears and cleans well compared with all other fibres.

8 Check density by folding back the carpet and examining its backing. Carpet with more yarn tufts per square inch is more crush resistant. The less backing you see, the denser the carpet. Combine a dense pile with with a heavier weight and you'll have a long-lasting carpet.

What to Look For

- Suitable pile and texture
- Fibre pros and cons
- High twist, density and face weight
- Quality carpet underlay

Tips

A firm and resilient underlay acts as a shock absorber and extends the life of any carpet, regardless of its quality. Use a thick backing when installing over concrete.

Remember to budget for the cost of installation – ask for a quote before buying.

If you're sensitive to new-carpet fumes, seek out a green label certifying reduced volatile organic compounds; ask that the carpet be aired before installation.

Have a remnant's cut edges bound to create a room-size rug you can take with you when you move.

See 204 "Choose an Oriental Carpet".

229 Choose Kitchen Cabinets

Picking out cabinets for your new or revamped kitchen is not an open and shut matter. The choices for door style, wood, finish and handles are endless. Cabinets can add up to 70 per cent of a kitchen's cost, so research your options for the best return on your investment.

Steps

1 Analyse your kitchen layout and your family's lifestyle and cooking habits. Plot what you need to store and display, as well as accessories that will simplify and organise your kitchen activities.

2 Get professional guidance – from an architect, a kitchen designer, at a shop or on the internet – to narrow your style and component choices and make the most of your space.

3 Choose stock cabinets when controlling costs is your priority. Mass-produced in standard sizes, stock cabinets leave room in your budget for upgrades elsewhere. You'll find fewer finish options but many popular styles, woods and accessories.

4 Go for custom-made units if you need to fit exact dimensions. Top-quality materials and craftsmanship increase both the cost and delivery time. Semi-custom cabinets are also made to order, but their set widths may require inserts for a perfect fit.

5 Select the wood you want and desired finish. Maple, oak and cherry are favourite hardwoods. Signs of quality cabinets are grain that matches from piece to piece and high-quality finishes.

6 Investigate manufactured finishes such as laminate or thermofoil. Both are easy to clean, but also less durable. Ask about typical repairs and what the guarantee covers. Examine a showroom sample that has been in use for a while to see how it wears.

7 Weigh up cost over quality, remembering that some parts of the kitchen have much harder use than others. For the highest quality, insist on construction that can support heavy cookware and withstand countless openings, bumps and spills. Doors with fitted mortised corners are sturdier than noninterlocking butt joints.

8 Peek inside cabinets. Most stock and semicustom units use solid wood only for the exposed frame, doors and drawers. Even top-quality cabinets may contain veneer-covered plywood inside. Both are less likely to warp than solid wood, and can be stained or painted.

9 Look for drawers that extend completely and are equipped with self-closing glides. Well-made drawers have dovetailed or dowelled joints rather than stapled ones and a strong bottom that's glued into grooves.

What to Look For

- Stock, semi-custom or custom-made options
- Wood and finish choices
- Sturdy construction
- Furniture-quality details

Tips

Look at other kitchens to fine tune your layout ideas and get a sense of the colour and wood you like.

If your old cabinets are in good shape but dated, look into painting them, ensuring that you prepare the surface well to get a good paint finish. Alternatively, replace the doors and drawer fronts, leaving the existing carcasses, and upgrade later.

If you love the look of an expensive hardwood, keep in mind that less expensive woods can be stained to look like your choice. For example, you can order a cherry finish on pine.

Self-assembly cabinets are not of the highest quality but are great for an instant makeover, and can save you up to 40 per cent.

230 Choose a Kitchen Worktop

Worktops have an enormous impact on the look and feel of your kitchen. The many choices available offer varying cost, weight, durability, upkeep and aesthetics. Consider customising each work zone with the most appropriate surface. Install luxury materials only where you need them to save money.

MATERIAL/PRICE	PROS	CONS
Laminate £33 and up	Easy to install; many colours, patterns and textures; resists stains and impact; inexpensive.	Has visible seams; you can't cut on it; difficult to repair if scratched. Not advised for wet environments.
Ceramic Tile £15 and up	Easy to install and repair; wide range of design options; glazes fight off moisture, scratches, heat, stains.	Grout between tiles can stain or mildew; sharp impact can crack tiles; can be tough to clean grout.
Wood £65 and up	Includes ash, walnut, birch, cherry, maple, oak and beech. User-friendly surface; easy on knife edges; takes on character; can be renewed by sanding and oiling.	Vulnerable to water, cuts and burns; requires thorough cleaning when exposed to raw meat or fish; needs regular treatment with mineral oil or beeswax.
Solid Laminate £400	Sold as Corian brand; dozens of colours and stonelike patterns; near-invisible seams blend with integral sinks and edge; very hardwearing.	Requires professional installation; expensive.
Engineered Stone £130 and up	Granite look but more uniform; never needs sealing; resists stains, heat, scratches.	Requires professional installation and repair. Stone heavy; poor impact resistance compared with real granite; visible seams.
Granite £160	Toughest and least porous material; highly scratch- and stain-resistant if sealed. Gorgeous natural colours, patterns.	Requires professional installation and repair, periodic sealing; expensive to buy and install; visible seams; heavy.
Marble £120 and up	Traditional, old-world look; cool, nonstick surface ideal for baking.	Porous and prone to stains, scratches, discoloration; needs regular sealing and professional installation.
Limestone £400 and up	Heat-, impact- and stain-resistant; limited colour palette; requires periodic sealing and polishing.	Softer than granite and marble; soapstone and slate alternatives have rustic character.
Slate £150 and up	Once sealed resists stains, burns, scratches; shades vary from quarry to quarry.	Heavy; needs periodic sealing. Requires professional installation.
Stainless Steel £150 to £250	Commercial look; resists heat; sanitary and easy to clean.	Requires professional installation; shows scratches and fingerprints.
TIP	All prices are per sq m. Ask for a quote for installation.	

231 Buy Green Household Cleaners

Synthetic and solvent-laden, today's cleaners, brighteners and bleaches fight dirt with less effort than ever before. But many of these products get their strength from chemicals that pollute your household air and water runoff and threaten your health during normal use. You can be clean and green, though, if you're alert to product contents.

Steps

1 Read labels and packaging to determine each product's ingredients. Environmentally friendly cleaners contain nontoxic, biodegradable ingredients and non-petroleum based surfactants. They don't create fumes or leave residues and are never tested on animals. Don't be fooled by the terms *natural* or *nontoxic*. These are not regulated and can be used as the manufacturer wishes.

2 Keep household products in their original containers so that safety information and directions for use always remain with the product.

3 Choose cleaners that do not contain toxic ingredients. Formaldehyde and ammonia irritate the skin, eyes and lungs. Benzene is classified as a carcinogen. Caustic soda fumes almost instantly corrode respiratory passages. Even minimal exposure to bleach and hydrochloric and sulphuric acids cause coughs or headaches; further contact can easily damage lungs.

4 Reduce allergies and skin or eye irritation by buying products without artificial fragrances and colours. Many of these additives do not degrade in the environment and may have toxic effects on fish and mammals.

5 Shop green at farmers' markets and natural food shops. Look for the natural products aisle in your supermarket. Check online at sites such as Greenpeace (greenpeace.org.uk/Products/Toxics).

6 Make your own cleaner recipes from lemon juice, borax, baking soda and white vinegar. Label these mixtures so they're not mistaken for a beverage.

What to Look For

- Clear labelling
- No toxic ingredients
- No artificial colours and fragrances

Tips

Use any cleaner in a well-ventilated area.

Practise prevention first. Wipe spills quickly to avoid stains. Line the oven bottom to catch spills. Use screens over drains and don't pour grease down them.

See 9 "Buy Green".

Warnings

Reject any product that does not list ingredients and anything labelled with Caution, Warning, Danger or Poison.

Some common household cleaners are extremely dangerous when combined: Never mix chlorine bleach and ammonia – the result is toxic chloramine gas.

Install childproof locks on your supplies cupboard.

232 Stock Your Home Tool Kit

With a basic set of tools, you can often take care of small jobs around the house yourself. Buy the best quality tools you can afford and gradually add more until you have a full home tool kit. Look for brands that offer lifetime guarantees.

TOOL	WHAT TO LOOK FOR
Claw Hammer	Comfortable but forceful size (16 oz) with curved claw can prise out nails without gouging plaster (£7 or more). Drop-forged, steel head. Also useful for general carpentry work.
Screwdrivers	Buy a kit with multiples or individually (£10 for a set). Get a standard (slotted) head, a Phillips and a Pozidriv head (both +-shaped) in several different sizes.
Putty Knives	Get stiffer blades for scraping; flexible ones for applying putty and filler and for mixing materials (£3 to £6). Different widths available.
Tape Measure	Retractable, spring-loaded metal tape; 5 m (16 ft) long (£5).
Spirit Levels	Use a 20 cm (9-in) torpedo level (£7 and up) for installing appliances, hanging pictures or doing basic carpentry. Keep a larger level on hand for major projects. A longer level is more accurate.
Insulated Electricians' Pliers	15 to 20 cm (6 to 8 in) long (from £9) with serrated, straight jaws. Locking pliers can grab with tremendous force. Look for sets with multiple types.
Set of Spanners	Available in imperial and metric sizes. Ring spanners are potentially stronger than open-ended ones (£15).
Trimming Knife	Sold as Stanley knife. Cuts cardboard, carpets and more. Replaceable, retractable blades.
Junior Hacksaw	15 cm (6 in) long hacksaw (£4) is quiet, portable and safe. Use for sawing metal. Can be used in confined spaces.
Electrical Mains Tester	Use to test for presence of electrical current. Buy CE approved (£2).
Electric Drill	Drills holes and drives screws quickly and easily. Get variable-speed, reversible model with keyless chuck to hold bits in place (from about £15). Cordless rechargeable drills cost more but let you work anywhere. Get one with enough power to get the job done – 9.6–12 v is sufficient for most household jobs.
Set of Paint Brushes	Various sizes are useful from 2.5 to 7.5 cm (1 to 3 in). Prices can range from £10 for a set of five brushes to £30 for a single brush.
Combination Square	30 cm (12 in) long (£5). Can be used as a steel rule, try square, mitre square and level.

233 Buy a Video Security System

Somewhere between a baby monitor and commercial video surveillance, installing a video security system in your home offers peace of mind beyond what mechanical locks and wireless sensors can provide. Answer the front door without opening it, or watch your children play in their rooms or the garden – all from the TV screen or anywhere in the world via the internet.

Steps

1 Plan which areas you want to have monitored. Exterior doors are a logical spot, as well as landscaped areas where intruders can lurk. Inside the house, consider monitors for rooms occupied by children or elderly family members.

2 Monitor entries with a video door phone system. Most include a weatherproof camera with an infrared lens for night vision. Look for cameras that tilt or pan to show a broader area than a door peephole can. Many systems have two-way microphones.

3 Consider extra features such as motion sensors, dome (overhead) cameras and a device that automatically takes time- and date-stamped snapshots when a visitor presses the doorbell – creating a record of who comes while you're not home.

4 Decide how you'll view images. Basic systems (from about £180) include four cameras and a black-and-white monitor; upgrade (£300 plus) to get larger and/or colour monitors, which can display up four cameras on one screen, and more cameras.

5 Link the system to one or more televisions so you can see who's at the door without leaving your couch. Connect a VCR to record what the camera sees; network with a personal computer to view images from one or more cameras at the same time. An internet connection lets you view the images from any web-enabled device. Password systems let you open your front door remotely to let in guests or repairmen.

6 Create an intercom system with closed-circuit TV access by adding web cams and monitors. Each system – wired or wireless – has a few transmission limitations. Some only receive signals within a limited distance. Signals generally travel farther when they're in the line of sight instead of travelling through walls.

7 Choose auxiliary indoor cameras according to their purpose. In a baby's room, for example, look for an infrared lens and a directional microphone that activates the camera only when the baby coos or cries.

What to Look For

- Video door phone with adjustable lens
- Optional security features
- Connection to TV, VCR or internet
- Auxiliary indoor cameras

Tips

View monitor reception in person to make sure the image is acceptable. If you buy online, check the return policy first.

Make sure outdoor cameras have weatherproof housings and will operate in cold temperatures.

You can conceal miniature wireless cameras as small as 5 cm (2 in) tall almost anywhere. Distance and barriers, however, will restrict their ability to transmit.

See 419 "Buy a Home Automation System".

234 Buy a Home Alarm System

Each year more than 800,000 UK homes are burgled. Most of them have no alarm system. Electronic security devices provide affordable peace of mind, often act as a deterrent, and recognise and react instantly to unauthorised entry.

Steps

1 Survey your home and determine how many windows and doors you want integrated into the system.

2 Contact the National Security Inspectorate (nsi.org.uk) or your local police crime prevention officer for names of security system companies. Ask each company for an inspection, a recommendation and a quote in writing.

3 Decide whether you want to contract with a 24-hour central monitoring service for a monthly fee. If your system detects a break-in, it alerts security professionals to contact local police. Less expensive dialler accessories can link sensors to your phone lines and call preselected numbers if security is breached.

4 Consider your family's lifestyle. Do people or pets sometimes roam the house at night? Select appropriate sensors and locations.

5 Choose a system with a control panel that can monitor all the zones in your home. Each window or door integrated into the system is considered a zone. A basic system (about £50 without monitoring) can control four zones, but many can be expanded.

6 Determine locations for the control panel and keypads. The control panel commands the system and the keypads allow you to programme the system and turn it or its components on and off. A typical setup puts one keypad near the front door and another keypad – and perhaps a panic button – close to the bedrooms.

7 Look for systems that connect to lighting controls, smoke and carbon monoxide sensors, and flood detectors (see 419 "Buy a Home Automation System").

8 Choose a user-friendly code that everyone in the family can remember in an emergency. Try the keypad to check that it's easy to use.

9 Realise that it's difficult to retrofit a hardwired security system. With a wired system, you'll have to drill holes in walls so wires can be routed. If you want to avoid this expense and inconvenience, choose a wireless system.

What to Look For

- Sensor, control panel and keypad locations
- Some form of system monitoring
- Reputable security firm
- Hardwired or wireless system
- Add-on alarm options
- User-friendly system

Tips

The monitoring service you choose may be limited based on what system you buy. Choose the service before the system.

With a key-chain remote, you can disarm the security system, turn on lights and unlock the door – all from your car in the driveway.

Check that your system has a battery for back-up power.

Ask how often you have to perform maintenance tests.

Warnings

More and more false alarms are forcing police to change their priorities on answering alarm calls. Contact your local police to find out what their policy is.

If any alarm or security system representatives come to your home, ask to see company identification to make sure they are legitimate.

235 Buy Smoke Alarms

Your home most likely has at least one smoke alarm, but is it enough? Smoke alarms provide an early warning that can save lives, but different fires call for different alarm types.

Steps

1 Protect your home right now with easy-to-install battery-powered alarms. Some use lithium batteries which last ten years.

2 Look at using mains smoke alarms. These can also be interlinked so that a fire in one room will set off all the alarms in the house. This is useful if there is a fire smouldering downstairs, for example, once you have gone to bed. Ensure that a mains smoke alarm is backed up with a battery in case of power cuts.

3 Detect fast-flaming fires fed by paper, electricity and flammable fluids with ionisation alarms (£20 to £40), which use a harmless amount of radioactive material.

4 Get photoelectric alarms (£20 to £800), which have sensors and light beams that react quickly to slow-smouldering fires such as bedding and upholstery fires, which often kill from smoke inhalation.

5 Play it safe. For full protection, buy dual-detection alarms (from £25), which combine both fire-sensing technologies. Because these run on batteries, hybrid units work independently and are not wired to other alarms.

6 Buy alarms with a hush button that silences the alarm while you clear away smoke. Buttons big enough to push with a broom handle are easiest to activate.

What to Look For

- Battery or mains power
- Ionisation, photoelectric or hybrid type
- Large hush button

Tips

Choose a smoke alarm that conforms to the British Standard BS5466 Part 1; it should carry the kitemark.

Vacuum your smoke alarm at least once a year to ensure that dust isn't impairing the sensor.

Warning

Many fires occur in homes with smoke alarms that have been disconnected because cooking fumes set them off. To avoid this, get a kitchen alarm with a hush button.

236 Buy Carbon Monoxide Detectors

Called "the silent killer," odourless, tasteless carbon monoxide (CO) gas results from faulty gas appliances or flues. A CO detector is your only means of protection.

Steps

1 Shop for a CO detector. There are only three types; they're all affordable (£30 to £50) and easy to install:

• A biometric CO detector has a gel cell of synthetic haemoglobin that absorbs CO. The combination battery and sensor module must be replaced every two to three years, but the detector should last about ten years. After an alarm, the sensor should clear itself within 2 to 48 hours when left in fresh air. If it is not cleared, it will sound again when put back in the detector. Sensors that don't clear must be replaced.

What to Look For

- Electric or battery power
- Digital display
- Indicator light

Tips

Whichever type of alarm you choose, buy the freshest one available. Open the package to find the date of manufacture stamped on the back.

- A semiconductor detector is a plug-in device with an electronic sensor, and lasts from five to ten years.

- An electrochemical detector responds differently to different levels of CO exposure. Its self-powered battery doesn't need to be replaced, and the detector will last for at least five years.

2 Look for the Peak CO Memory feature on more expensive models. These displays remember the highest level of CO registered over a given time, which helps emergency personnel determine the severity of the problem, and can tell you if the detector sensed high CO levels while you were away.

3 Buy a detector with special light features if someone in your family is hard of hearing. During an alarm, an indicator light flashes as the horn sounds. Although many alarms have a liquid crystal display (LCD), it's easier to read a light-emitting diode (LED) display in dim light.

4 Listen for a continuous siren that indicates a full alarm. A repetition of loud pulsating beeps means there is some CO buildup; a chirp every minute alerts you to an alarm or battery problem.

You may be entitled to a free safety check on your gas appliances to monitor CO levels. Check with your gas supplier.

Look for carbon monoxide detectors that meet British Safety Standards BS 7860 or BS EN 50291 and that carry the kitemark.

Warning

Always use CORGI registered installers to fit new gas appliances, and have your gas appliances serviced once a year.

237 Buy Fire Extinguishers

You never want to have to use them, but it's wise to own several fire extinguishers. Used correctly, they'll reduce flame and smoke damage and may save your home – or your life. But not all fires are alike and using the wrong type of extinguisher will actually make things worse.

Steps

1 Look for colour coding that tells you what substance each sort of extinguisher contains. The different substances are best suited for particular sorts of fires. There are four types of extinguisher:

- Water, indicated by red. Use for wood or paper fires. Never use on electrical, fat, or oil fires.

- Dry powder, indicated by blue. Use on petrol, oil, gas, paint, furniture, wood, solvents and electrical equipment.

- Foam, indicated by cream. Use on paper, wood, textiles, fabric and flammable liquids. Do not use on electrical or chip pan fires.

- Carbon dioxide, indicated by black. Use on oil and petrol fires.

2 Buy the most suitable extinguisher for each room. The most useful at home are the dry powder and foam ones. Keep one in the garage, and another near the boiler. Choose ones you can carry easily and fix them in an accessible place.

What to Look For

- Correct sort of extinguisher
- Manageable size and weight

Tips

Make sure you and other family members understand how to operate your home's fire extinguishers.

Have the extinguisher serviced annually, or as the manufacturer recommends.

Warning

Only tackle fires in the early stages. If in doubt, call the fire brigade and ensure you and your family leave the building.

238 Choose an Entry Door

In homes as in personal relationships, nothing beats a great first impression. A high-quality door sets a welcoming tone and raises the perceived value of your home as well as providing added security.

Steps

1 Complement your home's architecture with an appropriate door style – mouldings and raised panels for a traditional house, sleek lines for contemporary style, ornate carving for a Victorian.

2 Simplify installation with a prehung door, already framed and weather-stripped. Door-replacement kits include steel frame inserts, but are available in fewer sizes than prehung doors.

3 Get out your measuring tape and select the size you need. A standard single door is 76 to 91 cm (30 to 36 in) wide and 198 to 213 cm (78 to 84 in) long. Special sizes outside these standard measurements can be commissioned. Keep in mind that changing your existing door size will require costly structural work.

4 Choose a wood door for natural warmth and beauty, and for the most appropriate look in an old house, but expect it to require maintenance. Wood doors used to warp and crack over time, but today's engineered-wood cores, laminated construction and vapour barriers help keep doors weathertight.

5 Buy a steel door for strength and security. Most new models feature heavy galvanised steel around a wood or steel frame, with a dense polyurethane foam core that insulates almost five times better than wood. Choose standard steel, steel embossed with wood grain or vinyl-clad steel.

6 Select a PVCu door for the look of wood without its upkeep. These models are both tough and energy-efficient. PVCu is available in different colours and finishes, it won't rust and resists shrinking and swelling. GRP is a fibreglass alternative that has good insulation properties.

7 Brighten your foyer with a glass door panel, transom or sidelights. Frosted, bevelled and leaded patterns range from simple to ornate, private to unobstructed. For security and noise reduction, order laminated glass.

8 Complement your door's style and scale with solid brass or bronze handle sets and locks. Pick tarnish-free metal finishes with lifetime guarantees if the door is exposed to weather.

9 Invest in quality materials that will last for decades. Prices vary between manufacturers and according to style, size, material and options. A 91 by 203 cm (36-by-80-inch) wood door can cost £200 up into the thousands, depending on the type of wood, construction, finish and glazing. Panelled single PVCu doors start at about £300.

What to Look For

- Appropriate style
- Easy installation
- Suitable size and scale
- Durable materials
- Decorative glass inserts
- High-quality door furniture
- Energy saving features

Tips

Save energy with features such as compression weather-stripping, a thermal-break threshold, an extended sill plate, a triple bottom sweep and a moisture-resistant bottom rail.

To decide what colour, take a picture of your home from across the street. Print several black-and-white copies and use coloured pencils to plan different door styles. Or, take a picture with a digital camera, then try out different colours in any graphic editing program.

Order wood and veneer doors prefinished. Finishes applied on site (paint, varnish and polyurethane) are difficult to maintain on solid-wood doors.

239 Buy a Garage-Door Opener

Yes, you could operate a garage door manually, but why would you? Each year more and more of us buy a remote opener. Beyond dependability, compare cost, safety, security and noise – important for garages that contain workshops or have bedrooms or offices overhead.

Steps

1 Look at the different mechanisms for operating the garage doors. Most fit to existing doors, whether they be single up-and-over doors, double doors, or sectional doors. Choose from the mechanisms suited to your doors. Some doors, such as vertically tracked canopy or dual track non-protruding garage doors will need a canopy arm (about £50) to be fitted in addition to the opener.

2 Assess how noisy the openers are likely to be and how much this matters to you. If the garage is away from the living areas of the house, the noise may not affect you, but if it is below a bedroom or office, you may want to select a quieter mechanism, which will cost more. Some of the most popular mechanisms are chain drives (from £150), which used a metal chain on a metal drive, but these are noisy. Others have plastic casing or operate by a belt mechanism; both of these systems are quieter.

3 Look at upgrading your door if space is an issue. Sectional doors and roller doors do not open outwards, so allow close parking either side of the door. This may be useful if you have several cars or a large vehicle such as a people carrier.

4 Check how powerful a motor you need. Some older style garage doors are particularly heavy and so require a more powerful motor to be effective.

5 Take safety concerns into account. An automatic reverse feature stops and reverses the door if it touches something – a child playing underneath, for example. You can buy a separate unit (from £25) to fit to the garage wall that projects an invisible beam to detect obstructions, and reverses the door if it detects anything. For heightened security, get an opener that operates a light that goes on as you drive into the garage and allows you time to unlock and unload your car and leave the garage before it switches off.

6 Buy an opener at a shop or from a dealer and put it in yourself, or ask for a quote for the unit to be professionally installed. Most openers include two remotes. A wireless outdoor keypad comes in handy if you forget the remote or its battery is dead. An indoor keypad adds convenience.

What to Look For

- Quiet, dependable action
- Power and speed
- Automatic reverse
- Wireless keypads

Tips

Look for a model with magnetic stop sensors for precise opening and closing.

Mechanisms with fewer parts require less maintenance.

240 Buy Timber for a DIY Project

A successful do-it-yourself project starts with good wood. At first you may think there's a secret timber yard code when you confront the many types and dimensions of wood. But once you take time to learn how the industry prepares its timber and determines sizes, it's easy to choose and order the wood best suited for your purpose – and maybe save money, too.

Steps

1 Using a plan or sketch of your project, take a cutting list of all the pieces you need in each length to a timber yard or builders' merchants. Some DIY stores also offer a good selection, quality wood and considerable expertise, though prices may be higher.

2 Choose softwood or hardwood. Most construction wood is softwood and is milled from fast-growing evergreens – pine, fir, cedar, redwood. Hardwood comes from dense-grained deciduous trees such as maple, cherry and oak. Used for fine woodworking, it's available in more thicknesses and in random widths and lengths.

3 Decipher timber sizes. Timber is sold rough-sawn or planed (known as PAR, or planed all round). Sawmills cut wood into standard sizes and this rough-sawn timber is measured as it is cut from the tree, before drying and shrinkage, so measurements may not be exactly accurate. Planed timber is smaller by about 5 mm (³⁄₁₆ in) in all dimensions than the sawn timber.

4 Buy precut wood for popular uses – stair treads, window sills, shelving and pieces such as spindles and furniture legs. These save time but cost more.

5 Choose the thickness and width of timber that you need, and then specify the length. Thickness ranges from 12 mm (½ in) up to 75 mm (3 in), and width from 25 mm (1 in) to 225 mm (9 in). Not all widths and thicknesses are available together, and some sizes are available sawn or planed, other just sawn or just planed. When you have an idea of what you need, go and ask at a local timber yard what they can supply or suggest and you can adjust your list accordingly. Standard lengths start at 1.8 m (6 ft) up to 6 m (20 ft). A timber yard can often cut your wood to the length you need.

6 Select pine or fir for rough-cut projects and framing. Pick hardwood for fine furniture and projects that will get a clear finish. Pine cuts easily and takes paint and varnish well. In hardwoods, ash and poplar are typically painted because they stain unevenly. Stain maple and oak to highlight their grain. Walnut is strong and stains nicely; beech looks great varnished or stained but is hard on saws.

What to Look For

- Timber yard, builders' merchants or DIY shop
- Wood choice
- Precut wood
- No defects
- Moisture content

Tips

The only way to ensure that you get high-quality wood is to pick out the boards yourself – or at least approve their selection.

Timber prices vary by season, region, availability and demand.

Once you've calculated how much wood your project requires, get 10 per cent extra to allow for mistakes and to match grain. Don't buy more than that. Wood can warp if it's not stored in ideal conditions.

7   Inspect for defects. Knots are a cosmetic flaw (unless they're large or about to pop out), but splits often get wider. To check for warping, lift one end of a board and sight down its edge to see if it bends in either direction. To check for bowing or arching, lay the wood on a level surface. A seriously bowed, cupped or crooked board is seldom workable, although minor bows will flatten out as you nail.

8   Check moisture content, or seasoning. Timber is kiln-dried or air-dried. Kiln-dried wood has about 8 per cent moisture content; air-dried, 15 to 25 per cent. For indoor furniture, kiln-dried timber is preferable because the wood shouldn't dry out any further.

9   Choose plywood for its strength and stability, the result of gluing several thin layers of wood together at right angles. Plywood used for sheathing, subfloors and rough carpentry typically has a veneer of Douglas fir, graded on each side. If both sides will show in your finished project, buy A-A or A-B grade. Plywood comes in 2440 by 1220 mm (4 by 8 ft) panels 6 mm, 9 mm, 12 mm, 15 mm, 18 mm and 25 mm thick. It can be interior or exterior grade.

10 Use hardwood-veneer plywood for furniture and cabinet making. It also comes in 2440 by 1220 mm (4 by 8 ft) sheets, but most dealers will sell a partial sheet. Thicknesses vary from 1.5 mm to 50 mm. Be sure to ask for *cabinet-grade plywood,* which is typically 9-ply birch coming from Denmark and other sources, and available through plywood distributors. Use cabinet-grade plywood for built-in projects, combined with more costly solid woods for exposed areas. You can get plywood with a veneer of virtually any kind of wood.

11 Shop for suitable timber for building decks, picnic tables and play structures. Heartwood grades of redwood and cedar are naturally rot- and insect-resistant; prices vary widely by season and location. Consider composite (wood-plastic) wood for durable, splinter-free decking. Engineered timber products come from small-diameter and fast-growing plantation trees. They use wood fibre more efficiently than conventional timber, reducing pressure on old-growth forests and resulting in stronger struc-tures. Choose exterior plywood – made with waterproof glue, and also known as marine ply – for other outdoor projects.

Warning

Ask for FSC certified wood. All forest products carrying the Forest Stewardship Council (FSC) label have been independently certified as supporting environmentally appropriate, socially beneficial, and economically viable management of the world's forests.

241 Select Roofing

Protect your largest investment – your home – with a roof that looks great and lasts a long time. Compare the materials' pros and cons to decide which one meets your needs and budget. Contact the National Federation of Roofing Contractors (nfrc.co.uk) for a licenced contractor to help you calculate your roof's area and installation costs. Keep in mind that a more expensive roof should carry a longer warranty.

Steps

General

1 Narrow down your choice of materials to what will be suitable for your roof. If you are working on a pitched roof, you have a choice of the numerous types of tiles, slates and shingles. Asphalt and bitumen are traditional choices for a flat roof.

2 Consult your local planning officer if you are planning to change the roofing material. Replacing like with like is unlikely to need planning approval, but using a different type of tile or selecting a heavier or lighter material to replace the existing roof may need approval under building regulations.

3 Ask an architect or structural engineer to advise you on your final choice of roofing to check that your home can carry the added weight.

4 Consider installing solar panels on part of your roof. You may be able to generate your own energy, heat your own water and reduce your electricity bills.

Pitched roofs

1 Look at the many types of tiles suitable for a pitched roof. Tiles come in a number of materials:

- Clay tiles can be hand-made, machine-made and large format and come in many subtly different finishes. They are also widely available secondhand. Most hand- or machine-made tiles are plain, with a coverage rate of about 60 tiles per sq m. Each tile overlaps two others, so the weight is increased. Clay tiles are a relatively expensive roofing material as they are labour-intensive to lay. Second-hand clay tiles are more expensive than new, and you need to ensure you have enough matching tiles to finish a roof. Large-format clay tiles are similar to those of concrete and are laid at about ten per sq m, so are considerably cheaper. They are long-lasting and need little maintenance.

- Concrete tiles can be interlocking or plain. The interlocking tiles are laid at about ten per sq m and make a very cost-effective choice. Plain concrete tiles, like plain clay tiles are laid at about ten per sq m. They are long-lasting and need little maintenance.

What to Look For

- Building regulations
- Professional advice
- Choice of materials

Tips

Investigate how much battening is needed on a pitched roof for the tiles you choose. This adds to cost and labour.

Get the right insulation products and ventilation. You need to retain heat while allowing moist air to escape. A huge choice is available depending on roofing material and type of roof.

If you are totally replacing a roof, consider if you need a dormer window or skylight. Even if you are not thinking of converting your attic space at the moment, it is far cheaper to have the window fitted along with a new roof, than to undertake the work separately.

Roofing is outside work so your project may be subject to weather-related delays. Spring and summer are the best times to do roofing work.

- Slate tiles can be natural or man-made. Natural tiles are traditionally from Wales, Cumbria, Scotland or Cornwall. There are also many imported types, from China, Spain, the USA and Canada, among other places. Man-made slates come in various materials including fibre-cement, resin-based, and concrete. Natural slate tiles can be new or second-hand and are pricier than man-made ones. Slate is a relatively expensive roofing material but is long-lasting.

  - Shingles and shakes are typically made of cedar. They look natural and weather well and evenly. They are reasonably inexpensive as roofing and are environmentally friendly, but require some ongoing maintenance.

2 Thatch is another alternative for a pitched roof, although you are likely to be simply replacing an old thatched roof. Thatching is time-consuming, but the end result is beautiful and long lasting if well maintained. It is expensive to insure because of the risk of fire.

Flat roofs

1 Select from several products available for flat roofs. Take advice on suitability for your roof from the dealer as flat roof coverings poorly installed are notoriously leaky, and leaks are virtually impossible to fix long term. Asphalt and bitumen are the main choices. Mastic asphalt is a waterproof mixture incorporating bitumen, and comes in different grades for different purposes. Bituminous membranes are relatively easy to lay by a variety of methods. Both make cheap roofing material.

2 Investigate sheeting. Corrugated steel is an inexpensive and hardwearing choice for outbuildings or where the look of the roof is not that important. Terned stainless steel is strong and recyclable, but more expensive and is ideal for modern roofs, where crisp, clear lines are desired.

Warning

Roofing is a highly skilled task, and many people are killed or injured annually in falls from roofs. Do not undertake it yourself unless you have the proper knowledge and training, and ensure any roofing contractor you hire has full insurance.

When you're hiring a home improvement professional, you're buying that person's ability to bring your concept to life. It is of critical importance to find a trustworthy, licenced professional for any work that includes carpentry, concrete, insulation, plumbing, painting, flooring and tiling.

What to Look For

- Satisfied past clients
- Relevant experience
- Personal attention
- Low but realistic bid
- Detailed contract

Steps

General Builder

1 Talk to people you trust who have hired builders. Gather leads from a local architects, or, if you know an estate agent from when you bought your property, ask them (bearing in mind that some estate agents have business relationships with builders). If you have an old property that requires specialist building work, look for builders working on similar properties in your area and contact them. Seek advice from groups such as the Federation of Master Builders (fmb.org.uk) and the National Home Improvement Advisory Service (nhias.org).

2 Identify several builders. Describe your project and ask if they've handled comparable jobs in the past year. Check their availability for your intended time frame. Discuss your budget. Narrow the field to those available builders who impressed you most. Good communication is essential, so consider whether you can form a good working relationship with them.

3 Ask for names and numbers of current and former customers. Interview them about each builder's strengths and weaknesses, and ask how the job went. Was the quality of the work and materials what was expected? Was the project completed on time and within budget? During work, did the builder keep them informed? Were there any unexplained absences? Did the crew and subcontractors treat the property and family respectfully? Would they hire him or her again? Ask a customer from four or five years ago how the job held up.

4 Solicit competitive bids from at least three builders, making sure that they see the site and factor in any site-specific costs. They will use the architect's blueprints to make an accurate bid, or ask them about designing plans for you (see 188 "Hire an Architect"). If there are significant differences between bids, ask why. A low bid won't end up costing the least if you soon have to replace poor-quality materials or shoddy workmanship.

5 Discuss the builder's guarantee. If something seems amiss, go elsewhere.

6 Ask for the payment schedule. Execute a written contract specifying the work to be done, estimated start and finish dates, total cost and payment schedule. Include penalties for unacceptable delay. A detailed contract protects both you and the builder. Accept informal letters of agreement for jobs costing £500 or less.

Builders' Tips

Review sample bids and contracts and compare them to those you receive to see if the contractor puts schedule details and product selections in writing.

Call a builder's suppliers and subcontractors to make sure he or she pays their bills on time.

Plumber

1 Follow the steps for builders.

2 Confirm that the bid includes removal of any fixtures that need replacing, such as an old bath.

3 Ask what their minimum and hourly charge is. Also ask if 24-hour emergency service is available, and about additional costs.

4 Contact the Institute of Plumbing (plumbers.org.uk) for recommendations, and if your plumbing work involves a gas central heating system, make sure the plumber is CORGI registered.

Painter

1 Follow the steps for builders.

2 Have the painter inspect the site before submitting a bid. Make sure multiple quotes cover the same specifications – all preparation including lead paint removal, areas to paint, number of coats, and paint brands and colours.

3 Discuss the painter's preferred methods of paint application – spraying or hand painting – as well as paint removal: torching, sanding, or using chemicals.

4 Make sure your contract holds the painter responsible for cleaning paint spatters from all surfaces (windows, floors, and so on) and that both your property and adjacent property (such as your neighbour's car) is protected.

5 Clear a room of furniture and all movable items before the painter starts. Anything you cannot remove, pile in the middle and cover thoroughly with a dust sheet.

Electrician

1 Follow the steps for builders.

2 Tell the electrician what you need to be done. Electrical contractors don't necessarily handle all kinds of jobs. If you are having an extension or extensive work undertaken, ask for advice on any electrical devices that might be useful to fit at the same time, from extra sockets to a mains surge protector. You don't need to take the advice, but it is often easier to do all the necessary work at once rather than go back and try to add items afterwards.

3 Hire an electrician affiliated with the National Inspection Council for Electrical Installation Contracting (niceic.org.uk).

Plumbers' Tips

Shop around and buy your own fixtures to save the plumber's mark-up (see 221 "Choose a Tap").

Painters' Tips

If you're hiring a painter to do stencilling or other decorative techniques, confirm that he or she has relevant experience.

Find out if your painter belongs to the Painting and Decorating Association (paintingdecorating association.co.uk).

Warnings

Make sure the builder provides you with a certificate of insurance before you make any payments or work begins.

Be wary of builders who ask for more than 30 per cent up front. A more reasonable figure is 10 per cent.

243 Hire a Gardener

If you just don't have the time, skill or patience to cultivate your dream garden, hire a gardener to transform your patch into an oasis. Or you can just hire someone for the basic upkeep – mowing the lawn, raking leaves and taking away debris – and take care of the more creative work yourself.

Steps

1 Decide if you'd like garden help on a regular or occasional basis. Typically, a standard-size suburban garden requires at least several hours of work each week during the growing season.

2 Ask neighbours and friends for recommendations. Ask why they like their gardener and what special skills that person might have. Or ask for names at a local nursery.

3 Schedule tasks seasonally. Some tasks like cutting the grass and weeding need to be done weekly; others like fertilising happen a few times a year; and still others, such as pruning and planting bulbs, are required annually. Gardening services can give you estimates that run from an hourly rate to a seasonal fee. If all you need is someone to mow the lawn and clean up debris, a weekly service should suffice.

4 Tell the gardener how you want your garden treated and what materials can and can't be used. If you want the weeding done by hand instead of with a weedkiller, for instance, make this clear.

5 Choose a gardener whose gardening style matches yours. If you like a natural look, then don't hire someone who tries to turn every shrub into a poodle.

6 Determine the gardener's skill level if you need special services, such as sprinkler maintenance or repair.

7 Decide if you or the gardener will choose, buy or put in plants. The gardener will usually bill you separately for plants and other supplies such as fertiliser or soil additives.

8 Make sure you agree on work schedule details, such as what happens on rainy days, public holidays and annual leave.

What to Look For

- Recommendations
- Jobs required
- Matching styles
- Type of garden
- Skill level

Tips

Keep tabs on what your gardener is doing, or you may end up paying for regular chemical spraying or herbicide lawn applications that do more harm than good.

Remember a good gardener on special occasions with a gift or bonus.

Warning

Be wary of gardening businesses that stop by your house and tell you what problems your garden has and how they will fix them. A reputable business won't do this.

244 Buy Outdoor Furniture

When the weather turns warm and inviting, you want to spend your time outside. Create enticing outdoor rooms with furniture that not only reflects your style, but stands up to the elements and your family's activities. Different materials require different care.

Steps

1 Match the furniture to your style, just as you would do indoors. Many styles are available, including traditional English cottage, Italian piazza, French café and modern.

2 Be realistic about your price range. A teak table, for instance, can range from £250 to £1,500 and up.

3 Look at different materials and how they suit your garden and your style. (See chart below.)

4 Look for made-for-outdoors seat cushions that resist mildew, sun fading and tearing; filling should be a polyester material that does not absorb water and dries quickly.

5 Try out the furniture before buying. Make sure chairs and benches are comfortable to sit in.

6 Get a large enough table for your needs and space. A 1.2-m (4-ft) round table seats five people comfortably.

7 Add a comfortable seat or two, such as a pair of reclining chairs for lounging.

8 Include a classy-looking umbrella for protection against sun and rain, and to string lights in for evening parties.

What to Look For

- Style
- Price
- Material
- Comfort
- Appropriate table size
- Umbrella

Tips

Count on your furniture lasting for many years as long as you take care of it, using wood preservatives if required.

Buy teak only from sources that use sustainable harvesting methods. This information should be indicated clearly in the description of the furniture. This ensures that the wood was grown on a plantation, not harvested from depleted natural sites.

MATERIAL	FEATURES
Plastic resin	Inexpensive, ubiquitous. Sheds rain. Store indoors during cold winters.
Cedar	Moderately priced. Durable, naturally rot- and insect-resistant. Weathers to grey; can be finished or painted.
Teak	Classic look, available in wide range of quality and prices. Turns silver-grey if untreated; to retain original colour, keep indoors or refinish frequently.
Wicker	Nice for porches or patios – works well indoors or outdoors. Move indoors during the winter. Needs cushions for comfort. Squeaks.
Aluminum	Lightweight, rustproof, usually most expensive of metal furniture. Powder-coated finish is resistant to moisture and bad weather.
Wrought Iron	Heavy and strong, needs cushions for comfort. Epoxy primer provides best rust resistance.

245 Buy the Perfect Rose

A rose is a rose is a rose, until you come face to face with the thousands of different varieties on the market. Choose a rose to please your nose and eyes, but also make sure it suits the site you have in mind in your garden – whether you're seeking a climber for an arbour or fence, a shrub rose for a flower garden, or a rose for ground cover.

Steps

1 Shop for bare-root roses from late autumn to early spring. Dormant, leafless roses sold with roots bare of soil offer the broadest selection. Planting at the bare-root stage gets plants off to a great start and is the least expensive way to buy roses.

2 Look for the best selection of bare-root roses in mail-order catalogues, on the internet, or at specialist nurseries, if you live close enough to visit. If you are buying your roses without seeing them, ensure you can get your money back if they are dead on arrival.

3 Buy container-grown roses all year round. These mature plants are more expensive, but will give the garden an established look much more quickly.

4 See and smell rose varieties at nurseries starting in April. Or visit local rose gardens to see established plants in bloom, and make a note of your favourite varieties.

5 Choose a rose that suits your conditions. In general roses do not like shade, waterlogged soil, or overcrowding. They prefer a slightly acid soil, but some will grow on alkaline soils if enough organic matter is added. Talk to a local expert from the Royal National Rose Society (rnrs.org).

6 Decide on the type of rose you want based on where you will plant it in the garden. Hybrid tea roses – the most familiar type, they flower over a long period of time with long stems and big buds for cut flowers – grow as upright shrubs. Other types of roses are designed to grow as climbers (such as 'Cécile Brünner') or ground cover.

7 Save money by choosing older rose varieties (meaning those that have been available for some time). New varieties come out every year, generally at higher prices.

8 Look into old garden rose varieties for their fragrance and nostalgic qualities. They tend to be expensive. These types include moss, cabbage and rugosa. Some have one very short but spectacular blooming season.

9 Read catalogue descriptions or nursery labels to make sure the rose you buy is disease resistant. The most common diseases, powdery mildew and black spot, affect the leaves, reduce the plant's beauty and life and are costly and time-consuming to treat. If you keep your roses well fed and healthy, they are less likely to succumb to disease.

What to Look For

- Bare-root plants
- Container-grown plants
- Fragrance
- Older varieties
- Traditional and old garden varieties
- Disease resistance

Tips

Bare-root roses usually come packed in damp sawdust or wood shavings inside a plastic bag. Look for healthy roots – white and firm, not brown and slimy looking.

Make sure container-grown plants are not root-bound, with circling roots crowding out of the container.

Look for rose-planting advice at websites of the major rose growers.

246 Buy Flowering Bulbs

Classic spring-blooming bulbs include daffodils and tulips, but other seasons also boast impressive performers, such as summer's lilies and gladioli. None are for procrastinators – or for limited thinkers who can't imagine the glory that comes from a knobbly brown sphere five or six months after you plant it.

Steps

1 Shop for bulbs at nurseries or garden centres during the planting season. The earlier in the season you buy, the better the selection. Order bulbs by mail or online ahead of the season (June and July for autumn planting), when many catalogue companies offer discounts. Mail-order sources will take your order early, and then send the bulbs to you at planting time.

2 Buy and plant spring-flowering bulbs, such as crocuses, daffodils, hyacinths and tulips, in the autumn (September to November).

3 Buy and plant summer-flowering bulbs, such as gladioli, lilies and alliums, in the spring (generally February to April).

4 Search the web for online sources, such as Broadleigh Bulbs (broadleighbulbs.co.uk) and Heritage Bulbs (heritagebulbs.com).

5 Note that bulbs are graded by size, with different sizes for top grades of various types of bulbs. For best results choose top-size bulbs. If you are planting a big area, you can save money by buying smaller sizes. Choose bulbs that are firm to the touch and do not have any mould on them.

6 Save money by buying prepackaged bags of bulbs, or spend more and buy individual bulbs in special varieties.

7 Plant enough bulbs for a showy display. You can group tulips close together, as long as they aren't touching (which promotes rot). Space other bulbs about two or three times their diameter apart. You can fit about seven tulip bulbs in a pot that's 30 cm (12 in) across.

8 Extend the flowering season by planting bulbs with different blooming times. Tulips and daffodils, among others, are labelled as early, mid- or late season.

9 Look for spring-flowering bulbs that can be forced in the autumn. These include hyacinths and certain narcissus, usually labelled for forcing.

What to Look For

- Flowering and planting seasons
- Wide range of flowering times
- Firm bulbs with no mould
- Bulk deals

Tips

Don't remove the papery coating on bulbs that have them, such as tulips, but don't worry if it slips off.

In the right climates, many bulbs will bloom year after year. Others – particularly tulips in warm climates – are one-year performers.

247 Buy Flowers for Your Garden

A flower garden can offer a romantic and fragrant feast for the senses, a renewable source for fresh cut flowers, or simple colour to brighten a patio or deck. The key is understanding what annuals and perennials are, knowing your planting seasons, and matching a plant's light and water requirements to what your garden offers.

Steps

Annuals

1 Remember that annuals are plants that grow, bloom, set seed and then die in one growing season, typically from spring to autumn. Popular examples are petunias, marigolds and zinnias. Annuals (also often called bedding plants) generally produce a fantastic show for a fairly small outlay, but need to be replaced every season.

2 Choose annuals that don't mind the cold, such as pansies, for winter, spring and autumn displays.

3 Select annuals that don't like the frost, such as marigolds and busy Lizzies, for flowering from late spring into autumn.

4 Purchase seeds from catalogues or nursery racks. Starting from seed is less expensive than buying seedlings but takes longer and is more labour intensive. Seed-starting kits are available at garden centres or from online dealers. Some annuals grow better when sown as seeds directly in the ground; others, such as begonias and petunias, take a discouragingly long time to grow from seed.

5 Buy seedlings sold in trays or as tiny individual plants (known as plugs) at nurseries. Choose vigorous specimens. Examine them for healthy green leaves just coming out, and avoid seedlings with many yellow leaves. Select plants with mostly unopened flowers. Avoid any that are root-bound, with wads of brown roots coming out the bottom of the container.

6 Give a plant what it needs in terms of sun or shade. Most annuals prefer full sun. A few, such as busy Lizzies and begonias, do well in shade.

Perennials

1 Choose perennials if you want plants that live for several years or more. Some die back to the ground in winter and reappear in the spring. Some may remain green all year in mild areas.

2 Shop for perennials nearly all year round, generally in nursery containers or small pots. Starting perennials from seed takes time, and some seeds germinate only with special care, so this is an advanced project that needs time for experimentation. During

What to Look For

- Annuals sold as seedlings in small packs
- Perennials sold in small pots or large containers
- Vigorous growth, no signs of being root-bound

Tips

Easy-to-grow annuals include busy Lizzies, marigolds, zinnias and sunflowers.

Save money by sowing nasturtium, sunflower, cosmos and California poppy seeds directly in the garden in spring. Make sure to keep them moist until they're established.

For a quick colourful effect in summer, look for sales on annuals potted in large containers.

Warning

Many summer-flowering annuals are sold as seedlings or small plants long before it is safe to plant them out. Whether your seedlings are bought or home-grown, wait until all frosts are over before planting out.

late autumn, winter and early spring, many perennials, such as phlox, display no top growth, so it looks like you're buying a pot full of soil.

3 Try to plant most perennials in early spring or early autumn. The earlier in the growing season, the smaller the container and the less expensive the plant will be. Perennials in 10-cm (4-in) pots may look small, but they are actually easier to establish in the garden than larger plants.

4 Local nurseries and garden centres may offer limited variety. Check out specialist perennial dealers with mail-order or direct-mail catalogues; specialities include day lilies, pelargoniums, ferns, irises and salvias.

5 Look for signs of vigour in a nursery plant: healthy green leaves just coming out, either right by the soil or on a shoot. Avoid plants with yellow, limp leaves or those that are root-bound.

6 Buy perennials in bloom if you want to be sure of the colour.

Fail-safe perennials for sunny spots include yarrow, rudbeckia, day lily, and Shasta daisy. For shade, try bleeding heart, hellebore, hosta, and Japanese anemone.

You can increase your supply of perennials by dividing and transplanting existing plantings. The best timing depends on the type of plant, but generally you'd do this in autumn and spring.

SEASON	ANNUALS	PERENNIALS
Early Spring	• Plant frost-hardy types: stock, Iceland poppy, pansy, snapdragon, larkspur, calendula. • Look for short, stocky plants in four- or six-packs; choose plants with or without flower buds, but with few or no open flowers.	• In bloom: campanula, columbine, doronicum, pulmonaria. • Look for medium-sized containers; at this time of year, some plants don't show above soil in pot.
Mid-spring to Mid-summer	• Plant tender types: busy Lizzie, petunia, marigold, salvia, lobelia. • Look for individually potted plants, good for quickly assembled patio displays.	• In bloom: delphinium, penstemon, day lily, peony, Shasta daisy. • Look for medium-sized containers; plants should have leaves and some will have flowers; cut off dead flower stems.
Late Summer to Early Autumn	• Plant selected late-flowering types: salvia, zinnia.	• In bloom: echinacea, hosta, phlox, rudbeckia. • Look for healthy plants; it's OK if they aren't blooming – they will next year.
Autumn	• Plant frost-hardy types such as pansy, calendula. • Start with seedlings or small pots early in the autumn, and buy larger pots as the season progresses.	• In bloom: chrysanthemum, Michaelmas daisy. • Watch for sales at nurseries.

248 Select Pest Controls

In the dog-eat-dog, aphid-eat-rose world of gardening, it's just about impossible to eliminate all pests. Here are a few tips to keep pests under control in ways that are safe for you and the environment.

Steps

1 Match plants to the right location. A plant under stress because it's in the wrong place will be vulnerable to pests. Poor soil that drains slowly can lead to disease problems. Some plants need good air circulation to keep problems at bay – powdery mildew will plague roses planted where air circulates poorly.

2 Seek out lists of pest-resistant plants for your area.

3 Know the good bugs from the bad. Go to the library or search online to find gardening resources on pests, identifying good insects, such as ladybirds, that eat bad ones, such as aphids. Top sources are organic gardening books or organisations.

4 Investigate which pests are causing damage to your garden. Some signs are easy to spot: a silvery trail indicates a slug or snail, for example. Fluffy white patches on branches may indicate woolly aphids.

5 Increase the diversity in your garden by growing a wide variety of flowers, shrubs and trees. This provides both food and a haven for birds and beneficial insects that will dine on harmful insects.

6 Cage the trunks of new trees to prevent grazing by squirrels, rabbits or deer.

7 Experiment with low-tech control methods. Use the hose to spray aphids off roses in the morning so the leaves have all day to dry. Put a wet, rolled-up newspaper among dahlias at night, and in the morning shake out all the earwigs into soapy water. Use insecticidal soaps for aphids.

8 Buy yellow sticky traps to control whiteflies around tomatoes, or other pests such as aphids, leafhoppers, leaf miners and wasps. The bugs are attracted to the colour and get stuck. You can buy a pack of five traps for less than £5.

9 Use the widely available biological control *Bacillus thuringiensis* (Bt). This affects caterpillars that eat plants to which Bt has been applied. There are different strains of Bt for different caterpillars.

What to Look For

- Ways to encourage good insects
- Low-tech solutions
- Biological controls

Tips

Expect a little plant damage. It's inevitable, and you'll live a happier, less stressful life if you accept this.

Invest in an insect identification book with a garden emphasis. This will help you learn which bugs help and which ones damage plants.

Integrated Pest Management (IPM) is a system for dealing with pests in ways that use chemicals as the last resort.

249 Buy Soil Improvers

Improve heavy (clay) or sandy soil with organic material such as compost. Improvers can help soil drain more effectively or retain water better, but don't provide as many nutrients as fertiliser does.

Steps

1 Get soil improvers for a flower or vegetable garden before planting in spring, or whenever you're doing much planting.

2 Choose from an array of improvers, such as ground bark, sand or grit, and mushroom compost. A good all-purpose choice is composted manure, which is manure that has been heaped up for a year or two.

3 Before planting a bed, add a 5 to 7.5 cm (2 or 3 in) layer of soil improver, and dig it in to a depth of 15 cm (6 in). In autumn in milder areas, you can spread it on the surface and leave it for the worms to work in.

4 For small areas, buy soil improvers by the bag. For larger areas, buy in bulk at a garden or building supply centre or, for manure, direct from a farm or stables. You can have the supplier deliver bulk material, or pick it up yourself.

What to Look For

- Type of improver
- Bags for small areas
- Bulk for larger areas

Tips

Products sold as potting mixes are not intended for use as soil improvers. Fill containers directly from the bag for growing bulbs, flowers and other plants.

Choose composted material rather than fresh manure to guard against diseases that may be passed to humans through contact with animal faeces.

250 Buy Mulch

Mulch is a blanket for your soil, holding water in, keeping weeds at bay and making the garden easier to care for. There's a wide variety of mulching material available; here's how to weed through the choices.

Steps

1 Choose an organic mulch, including coarse bark chips and compost, for your planting beds. What you choose is a matter of taste.

2 Work out how much coverage you need. This is often a matter of trial and error. Smaller quantities are sold by the bag, often by weight or in terms of litres. Follow the guidelines on the bag. Larger quantities are sold by the ton. If you over order and have space, you can always keep any surplus for next year.

3 Layer organic mulches (compost) to a depth of 2.5 to 5 cm (1 to 2 in) around flowers, vegetables and shrubs; coarser mulches (shredded bark) can be applied 7.5 cm (3 in) deep. Apply inorganic mulch such as stones of various sizes as a ground cover or for areas where soil improvement isn't a consideration. Apply in layers of 2.5 to 7.5 cm (1 to 3 in). Other inorganic mulches such as plastic sheeting or fleece just need to be bought to cover the area required with enough to dig in at the sides.

4 Save money by buying material in bulk.

What to Look For

- Organic or inorganic mulch
- Bags or bulk

Tips

Keep mulch 15 cm (6 in) away from the trunks of shrubs and trees. This prevents excessive moisture from damaging the plants.

Various types of plastic sheeting are available as mulch for vegetable gardens and other spaces where looks aren't much of a consideration. They can also be used under stone or bark mulch to control weeds.

251 **Buy a Compost Bin**

Turn kitchen scraps and garden debris into black gold – compost! This nutrient-rich organic matter is like giving your garden a boost of Popeye's spinach and can even decrease plant disease. Compost is made of vegetable kitchen waste and decomposed plant parts. Even woody stems can be added, though they should be shredded first. There are many ways to make compost and various products to help with the process.

Steps

1 Make compost by combining green material, such as grass clippings, with brown material, such as dried leaves, stems and even shredded newspaper. Buy a covered bucket to keep kitchen scraps in until you take them to the compost heap.

2 Jump-start the process with a system that makes it easy to turn compost to speed decomposition.

3 You can choose a tumbler attached to a metal frame, which allows the bin to be turned. This process usually takes five weeks. Most tumbling composters cost from £40 up.

4 Save your back with a three-bin system. One bin holds new material; as that decomposes you turn it into the next bin to mix and aerate it, then into the third bin for finishing. Three-bin systems can cost up to £200.

5 Buy a worm bin to produce even better compost with less mess and no odours. Red worms, which multiply quickly, immediately get to work, breaking down kitchen scraps and bedding material such as newspaper into compost within six months. Available from catalogues such as the Organic Gardening Catalogue (hdra.org.uk/catalog.htm), a worm bin costs about £150.

6 Buy a compost activator to speed up the decomposition process. Various organic and non-organic products are available, and some specialise in breaking down heaps with a lot of grass clippings, or producing leaf mould

What to Look For

- Tumbler
- Three-bin composter
- Worm-bin compost system

Tips

Weeds can be composted only in hot systems (which the tumbler creates).

Find out if your local council offers free or discounted composting systems.

Warning

Discourage rats by making sure there are no animal by-products or cooked food in your compost heap.

Do not compost weeds that have gone to seed or any roots of perennial weeds. These may all survive the composting process and you will spread them over your garden with the compost.

252 Buy Fertiliser

Plants grow best in fertile soil, and that means you must often help out nature by adding fertiliser. If you grow plants in containers, you have no choice: healthy plant growth demands regular feeding. First you'll need a quick chemistry lesson.

Steps

1 Understand that plants require a basic diet of three main nutrients: nitrogen (N), phosphorus (P) and potassium or potash (K). Secondary nutrients, such as calcium, are necessary to a lesser degree.

2 Read a fertiliser label to determine its ingredients. The percentages of the three main nutrients – N, P and K – are listed, often in an abbreviated form, such as 6-2-4. You'll also see any trace elements included in the mixture.

3 Use a combination of N-P-K suited to the plants you're treating. All-purpose fertilizer (5-5-5 or 10-10-10) is good for general garden use, including flower and vegetable gardens. High-nitrogen lawn food (29-3-4, for instance) is designed to encourage quick green growth.

4 Consider specialised fertilisers for plants with special needs. For instance, azalea food is formulated for plants requiring acidic soil conditions.

5 Decide whether you want a chemical fertiliser or an organic fertiliser, derived from plant and animal sources such as seaweed, chicken manure or fish, blood and bone. Chemical fertilisers generally provide more nitrogen and work more quickly; they can also burn plants more readily if directions are not followed carefully.

6 Choose a dry fertiliser to sprinkle on the ground for established areas of the garden containing trees, shrubs and flowers. The instructions will tell you if you have to work the fertiliser into the soil and water it in. Dry fertilisers also work well in a vegetable garden, where you can mix them into the soil before planting.

7 Use a liquid fertiliser for container plants (mix with water in a watering can for small applications) or if you want to spray the garden with fertiliser; some labels point out the value of applying liquid food to foliage.

8 Consider slow-release fertilisers to apply nutrients over a long season. The soil must stay moist for the fertiliser to work. These are particularly useful in containers.

9 Always follow directions carefully. Excessive fertilising is expensive and unnecessary and can hurt your plants and the environment.

What to Look For

- N-P-K percentages
- Specialist plant foods
- Organic or chemical fertilisers
- Dry or liquid fertilisers
- Slow-release fertilisers

Tips

Test your soil to determine its nutrient levels. Kits are available at gardening centres and nurseries.

Feed plants according to the instructions on the packet. Applying too much fertiliser is wasteful and can actually harm plants instead of helping them.

253 Start a Vegetable Garden

Eating fresh-picked peas or vine-ripened tomatoes is a life-altering experience. But where do you start? How do you choose from racks of seeds, catalogue after catalogue and rows upon rows of nursery seedlings? Successful small-scale vegetable gardeners know what and when to plant, and how to start the crops.

Steps

1 Grow only those vegetables you enjoy eating. Give priority to those prized for incredible flavour when eaten fresh from the garden: sweet corn, beans and peas, tomatoes and young spinach, among others.

2 Prepare a plot of flat ground that gets full sun nearly all day. Break up and turn the soil and add compost or other organic material (See 249 "Buy Soil Improvers"). A full day of blazing sunshine is especially important if you grow vegetables in the cool weather of early spring, early autumn or winter.

3 Work out how much growing space you have and plant accordingly. Lettuce, for example, can be grown in a solid mat, but tomatoes need to be spaced about 60 cm (2 ft) apart. Growing requirements are given on seed packets, in catalogues, and on nursery labels, as well as in books on growing vegetables.

4 Choose crops that require less room if you have a small garden or grow vegetables in a container. Lettuce is a great pot plant, and 'Patio' or 'Tumbler' tomatoes will grow well in a hanging basket. Plants that climb, such as runner beans, can be trained up a trellis or wigwam to take up less room horizontally. Tuck herbs and parsley into flower beds.

5 Some seedlings will withstand frost and even grow through winter, while others need a good, warm summer (and often some greenhouse or cloche protection) to ripen fully. Common vegetables that withstand varying degrees of cold include broccoli, brussels sprouts, cabbage, carrots, cauliflower, leeks, spinach and turnips. Crops that need sunny, frost-free conditions include beans, courgette, lettuce, peas, potatoes, radishes and sweet corn. Different varieties are available for different conditions, but cucumbers, aubergines, melons, peppers and tomatoes will need a spell under glass to start early or ripen fully.

6 Sow some seeds directly in the ground as they grow best that way: beans, carrots, chard, lettuce, peas, pumpkins, sweet corn and turnips. Starting your own seeds is, of course, much less expensive than buying seedlings in trays, packs and pots.

What to Look For

- Sunny spot and good soil
- Seed packets marked with current year
- Vigorous seedlings

Tips

Shop for all kinds of seeds in early spring to mid-spring – when selection is best – even if you don't plant them right away.

Keep extra seeds in an envelope in a dry, cool place, such as a plastic storage box in the garage. Many vegetable seeds can still sprout after a year or more in storage.

7   Start with nursery seedlings of certain other crops unless you are an experienced vegetable grower. These plants tend to do better when set out in the garden as seedlings: broccoli, brussels sprouts, cabbage, cauliflower and leeks. Onions can be bought as onion "sets".

8   Buy seeds at nurseries or by mail order starting just after the New Year, when the selection is freshest. Look for seed packets marked as having been packed for the current year.

9   Buy vegetables online and from mail-order seed companies for a far greater selection than you'll find at local nurseries. The Organic Gardening Catalogue (OrganicCatalog.com), Mr Fothergill's (mr-fothergills.co.uk), Suttons (suttons-seeds.co.uk) and Thompson and Morgan (thompson-morgan.com) are just a few long-established sources.

10 Shop for seedlings when your soil is prepared and you are ready to plant. Keep them moist and don't let them sit around for more than three days. Buy healthy and vigorous seedlings. They should stand up straight and be stocky, not lanky, with no yellow leaves or holes.

11 Save money and get more involved with your garden by starting seeds indoors in winter and transplanting them outdoors in spring.

12 Sow seeds of colourful radishes or giant pumpkins to introduce children to the satisfaction and fun of growing their own food. Or lean three stakes together, tie them together at the top, and train runner beans up the stakes to make a bean teepee.

Warning

Be ready to protect young seedlings outdoors from the occasional frost by laying horticultural fleece over them at night.

WHEN TO PLANT	SOW SEEDS	SET OUT SEEDLINGS
Early to Mid-Spring	Lettuce, spinach, turnips, peas, radishes, carrots, chard.	Onions, lettuce, broccoli, cabbage, celery, cauliflower, brussels sprouts, potatoes, kale.
Late Spring	Beans, courgette, melons, pumpkins, radishes, sweet corn.	Courgette, tomatoes, aubergine, onions.
Late Summer	Lettuce, spinach, cabbages, carrots, radishes, peas.	Broccoli, cabbage, kale, cauliflower.

254 Hire a Garden Designer

Maybe you need a plan for your whole garden, or perhaps you just want a classy border. Do you have special challenges such as complex drainage systems or retaining walls? It's time to call on the services of a professional designer or landscape architect.

Steps

1 Call nurseries and garden centres that offer design services or ask for recommendations. Ask friends and neighbours with beautiful gardens who did their work; a well-conceived, well-laid-out and beautiful garden is its own recommendation. Contact professional designers and design firms.

2 Look into employing a landscape architect – especially if your project is large, complex, or involves structures and landscaping. This is a professional with qualifications in the field, who is trained to work with contractors, draw architectural plans and be familiar with any relevant planning regulations.

3 Ask to see a portfolio of the designer's work. View actual gardens he or she has designed.

4 Determine your budget. Landscaping projects can bloom into many thousands of pounds depending on construction requirements.

5 Decide what the scope of work will be, both beforehand and in consultation with the designer or landscaper. You can ask the designer to draw up complete plans or to suggest plants and landscaping ideas for only some parts of the garden.

6 Find out how you will be billed: by the hour, a flat fee for a plan (a modest plan may range from £200 to £1,500), as a percentage of the project's total cost, or for the whole project. Ask what the fee schedule is. How involved will the designer be during construction and planting? Will the designer supervise installation or will it be turned over to a contractor?

7 Start early in the year. The winter season is the best time to consult with a designer. You'll be ready to go when spring weather arrives.

What to Look For

- Recommendations
- Skill
- Budget
- Scope of work

Tips

If you are an experienced gardener, save money after your professional draws up the plan by buying and planting your own landscaping.

Contact local colleges with horticulture or landscaping courses. Students working toward degrees or other qualifications may offer garden design services for much less. However, be aware that they're still learning.

Many landscape contractors also offer design services.

See 190 "Get Planning Permission" and 188 "Hire an Architect".

255 Buy an Automatic Watering System

Depending on your climate, an automatic watering system for some or all of your garden is either a nice luxury or a near necessity. While a well-designed system can save you time, energy and water, it can also be expensive. A full system is complex to plan and install, and is best left to the experts, but there are various simpler systems that you can set up yourself.

Steps

1 Decide how much of your garden needs irrigation beyond normal rainfall. Lawns are probably the biggest drinkers. Vegetables and flowers need constant moisture during the growing season. Shrubs and trees with deeper roots can get by with less frequent watering.

2 Sketch the whole area, indicating planted spaces and your watering needs.

3 Make sure you understand the automatic timer. You'll be the one adjusting and changing it with the seasons. The timer is attached to the tap and the hose and allows many (often up to 16) watering sessions a day. Timers cost £30 and up. Many can be attached to a moisture sensor in the soil (from £10), which will monitor water levels and ensure the irrigation is not turned on straight after a shower of rain, for example.

4 Look at water distributors, which are hubs that distribute water to different zones of the garden to meet different watering needs. Costing from £45, these can also be controlled by your automatic timer.

5 Consider various solutions to take the water to exactly where it is needed. Soaker hoses are porous hoses that are laid at the base of the plants. A drip irrigation system kit, starting at £20 or so, is easy to install and uses underground emitters that drip slowly or above ground emitters that drip, mist or spray at a low-pressure rate. Both types of hose be attached to a timer to regulate the times and frequency of watering.

6 Use drip lines and emitters to water container plants, especially if you are often away from home during the growing season. You'll find inexpensive kits designed for just this purpose.

What to Look For

- Low-tech soaker hoses
- Drip kit
- Smart timer

Tips

Check sprinkler heads and emitters at the beginning of every spring to make sure they are not clogged.

Warning

Overwatering can do as much damage as under-watering, especially for vegetables. Ensure your system can be adjusted.

256 Start a New Lawn

A lush lawn serves as both a verdant welcome to visitors and a soft playground for kids. You've got two basic choices for making a lawn. Laying turf – rolls of grass plus roots and soil – offers instant lawn gratification, but is pricier. Sowing seeds saves money if you're willing to keep everyone off the area, nurse along the seedlings and wait.

Steps

Getting ready

1 Measure the lawn area to determine how many square metres of coverage you need.

2 Make your lawn where it gets at least six hours of sun a day, spring to autumn – even mixes designed for shade need some sun to grow. If your garden doesn't have enough sun, consider other ground-cover choices, including gravel.

3 Find out which grasses are best for your lawn by talking to experts at a local nursery. The most common mix for a hard-wearing surface is perennial ryegrass with red fescue, smooth-stalked meadow grass and browntop or highland bent. Consider drought-resistant varieties if you live where water is scarce – lawns are typically a garden's main water user. Other mixtures are available for high-quality lawns or shady areas.

4 Decide if you want to plant seed or turf. Sow grass seed in spring or autumn (or summer if you have a good watering system). Lay turf at any time of year, but not in very dry weather.

5 Prepare the ground thoroughly for seed or turf. Weed carefully, then dig in compost or a mix of topsoil and compost to a depth of 15 cm (6 in). Rake out stones and smooth the soil. Use a roller to tamp down the soil for optimal germination and root growth.

Starting with seeds

1 Determine the amount of seed mix you need. This varies depending on the mix, so check the packet. Seed is often sold in 1 kg (2.2 lb) packs (from around £7 per pack). This is enough to cover 28 sq m (300 sq ft).

2 Use a seed spreader to distribute your seeds evenly at the required rate – this is much more accurate than scattering by hand. Fill it with half the seeds and walk up and down the lawn area, then fill it with the other half and walk at right angles to your original path to give even coverage. Rake over lightly and keep the area moist until the grass is a few centimetres high.

Rolling out turf

1 Purchase turf directly from turf farms (find sources in the Yellow Pages under "Turf and Soil Supplies") or from a local garden centre. Turf costs from £2 per sq m; check if delivery is included.

What to Look For

- Well-prepared soil
- Appropriate grass variety for your conditions
- Healthy turf

Tips

A seed spreader can be hired at a local garden centre or DIY store.

Keep newly seeded areas constantly wet until the seedlings emerge, then switch to twice-weekly watering. Water newly laid turf twice weekly. Make sure the soil stays moist between waterings.

2 Make sure the delivered turf is in good, healthy shape: moist roots, no yellow or brown grass, turf hanging together firmly.

3 Have turf delivered the morning you plan to lay it so that it doesn't dry out. If you don't lay it right away, water it just enough to keep roots moist. Start laying along a straight edge and butt up the pieces closely without overlapping. Cut any curves in once you have finished. Keep moist until the turf has rooted into the soil below.

257 Buy a Lawn Mower

Weekly chore or blissful escape? Maybe it depends on what's going on in your house while you mow the lawn. Which mower you choose depends on lawn size and type, budget and the features you need.

Steps

1 Choose between two basic mower types: rotary and cylinder. Cylinder mowers cut with spinning blades passing over a fixed blade. Rotary mowers cut with a circulating blade underneath a sturdy housing of metal, plastic or fibreglass. Rotary mowers can either move on wheels or hover on a cushion of air. Both rotary and cylinder mowers are available in petrol or electric models.

2 Consider a manual cylinder or electric rotary mower for a lawn that is 100 sq m (1,000 sq ft) or less.

3 If you want a power mower, decide if you want a cylinder or rotary type. Cylinder mowers can cut the grass shorter (down to putting green height) and give a nice clean look. Rotary types are generally less expensive, easy to operate and to sharpen.

4 Choose between petrol and electric. Petrol mowers pollute and are noisy. With quieter, electric mowers, find out if the cord length, typically 30 m (100 ft), is long enough for your lawn – you may need to buy an outdoor extension lead. For cordless models, check to see how long the battery is good for – you'll want it to last through one mowing at least.

5 Choose between push or self-propelled (motor turns wheels, good for slopes) mowers. Front-propelled types are easy to operate. For a very large lawn, hop on board a ride-on mower that cuts a larger width.

6 Keep these considerations in mind: Is the mower too heavy for you? Is it manoeuvrable enough, especially if you mow around trees? How easy is it to raise or lower the cutting height? How easy to start the motor? Is there a blade shut-off switch? Where do you put your long, cool drink?

What to Look For

- Cylinder or rotary mower
- Hand or power operated
- Cutting width

Tips

Collect grass clippings, discharge them to the side, or leave them on the lawn – these are the options that different mowers offer.

With cylinder mowers, remember to keep blades sharp, which is best done professionally.

258 Buy Koi for Your Fish Pond

Koi, Japanese-bred ornamental carp, are prized for their beauty and magnificent colouring. You should be committed to caring for the fish before investing in them, as koi can live for 20 years or longer, reaching lengths of 90 cm (3 ft) and more. Many koi owners cherish their pets with a passion.

Steps

1 Read up on koi, how they live and what care they require, before you buy. Search online for koi websites and clubs in your area. Call local nurseries for a referral to a local fish expert.

2 Prepare your pond before you buy the fish. It should be filtered and can be as shallow as 45 cm (18 in), although koi stay healthier in deeper water. Moving water (a waterfall, for example) will help oxygenate the water, but make sure the pond is big enough so that the koi can retreat to a quiet corner.

3 Shop for healthy fish. Visit a specialist shop and look for specimens with clear eyes, erect fins and no missing scales.

4 Note that fish are priced according to their size, shape, colour pattern and availability. Young koi 7.5 to 10 cm (3 to 4 in) long may cost less than £10, but older fish 56 to 61 cm (22 to 24 in) long can easily cost £500 and more (and several thousand is not out of the question for large, rare koi). Butterfly koi, named for their long, flowing fins, are more expensive than ordinary koi.

5 Buy koi during cool weather if possible; it's easier to move them at that time as their metabolisms have slowed for the winter. Koi do fine in cold water, but it's best to avoid widely fluctuating temperatures. In deep ponds, koi can survive even when the water is frozen over.

6 Feed your fish koi pellets, sold at fish and pet shops and by online pet suppliers, once or twice a day.

7 Plan to brush up on chemistry (water quality) and fish anatomy if you are serious about koi. For health information, check out sites such as Planet Koi (koicarp.demon.co.uk).

What to Look For

- Koi clubs, websites, books, magazines
- Well-prepared pond
- Healthy fish

Tip

Protect your fish from herons and other predators by providing hiding places in the pond (spaces under rocks) or a pond cover.

259 Buy a Storage Shed

For people without a garage to store their garden necessities, a pre-fabricated shed can be a lifesaver. Sheds and shed kits for every budget are available at DIY and garden centres, and online at sites such as Garden sheds.com. Choose a size and material that works with your space, and you can keep your tools, bags of compost, lawn mower and assorted junk out of sight and safe from the elements.

Steps

1 Decide how much storage space you need. A lean-to shed 1.8 m (6 ft) long and 0.9 to 1.2 m (3 to 4 ft) wide is big enough for tools and might cost £100 or so. If you'll be storing a lawn mower and more, look for a freestanding shed measuring 1.8 by 2.4 m (6 by 8 ft), which will cost £400 or more.

2 Consider the material not only for looks but for what you need to store. Wood is long lasting, the most attractive in a garden setting, readily available and weathers to a grey colour, or you can paint or stain it with wood preservative to keep it brown, or paint it a different colour. Plastic is a less-expensive and even longer-lasting alternative. Metal sheds heat up quickly to high temperatures in the summer, so they're not recommended for storing petrol or other volatile liquids and fertilisers.

3 Decide if you need a wide entrance for comfortable access for a wheelbarrow and other equipment – sheds with double doors start at around £500.

4 Choose a combination greenhouse and storage shed to maximise the space. One measuring 2.4 by 3 m (8 by 10 ft) can accommodate both tools and plants, with special shelves for setting seedlings out.

5 Take advantage of features to help you work: windows and skylights for natural light, benches for work space, ramps for easier wheeled entry.

6 Visualise how the shed will look in your garden. Even a small one can seem large. Landscaping around it with shrubs and trees can make it blend into the garden.

What to Look For

- Appropriate size
- Type of material
- Special features

Tips

DIY enthusiasts can pick up a shed kit or buy plans and build one on their own.

If you're willing to pay twice the money for the convenience, you can have a pre-built shed delivered and installed by one of the large DIY shops.

Consider turning your shed into a potting shed in springtime. You can pot up seedlings or sit down with a cup of tea while you plan your next harvest.

260 Hire a Tree Surgeon

Tree pruning is dangerous and requires real skill to avoid harming not only yourself, but your tree. If it has pest or disease problems that may compromise its health or if it has suffered storm damage, hire a tree surgeon. If your trees require annual pruning or pest control, you'll want to find someone on an ongoing basis.

Steps

1 Check with neighbours or local parks and nurseries for recommendations of reputable tree surgeons. A tree surgeon is trained to plant, maintain, prune and fell trees.

2 Contact the Arboricultural Association (trees.org.uk) for a tree surgeon in your area.

3 Ask for proof of insurance. A reputable tree surgeon will have personal and property damage insurance as well as workers' compensation insurance.

4 Check with your council to see if you need a permit for tree removal.

5 Ask for references to find out where the tree service has done work similar to what you are requesting. Call or better yet pay a visit to see how it looks.

6 Get more than one estimate.

What to Look For

- Recommendations and references
- Professional certification
- Insurance
- Estimates

Tips

Make sure any pruning estimate specifies which branches will be cut and removed.

Tree topping – cutting off the top – may improve a view, but could damage the tree, ultimately turning it into a hazard, in danger of falling on houses, fences or cars in its path.

261 Buy Basic Garden Tools

There's a tool for every garden purpose – an onion hoe, a bulb dibber, a watering can for seedlings. Stock your shed with well-built, high-quality essentials – the classic tools you'll use year after year.

Steps

1 Check for a comfortable, balanced weight. Too heavy a tool will wear you out quickly, as will a poorly balanced tool. Too light, and you will have to compensate with your own energy.

2 Feel the handle. High-quality wood should be smooth, with an even, straight grain. Longer handles provide more leverage.

3 Make sure the head's on straight. Carbon steel is the highest quality. Consider stainless-steel tools if you're willing to pay the price. They're durable, rust-resistant and easy to clean.

4 Look closely at the point where the head joins the handle. The strongest connections are forged sockets or steel strapped,

What to Look For

- Good feel and balance
- High-quality handles and blades
- Durable, strong materials
- Tools that meet your needs

Tips

Short-handled tools may make tall people stoop, but shorter people may find them more comfortable. Try both short and long handles to see which kind you like.

riveted with several rivets. Less-expensive tools often employ an all-in-one metal sleeve that extends from the head and wraps around the handle.

5 Test for sharpness. A tool's edge will hold up better if the steel is tempered, heat-treated or solid-forged.

6 Buy your tools at hardware shops and nurseries, or shop online.

Keep your tools in good shape by cleaning off soil after every use; scrape with a wooden spoon or a stiff brush. Wipe the heads with linseed-oiled cloth at the beginning and end of every season.

ESSENTIAL TOOLS	WHAT THEY DO	PRICE
Spade	Spades have flat blades and are mainly for digging holes and turning over soil.	£15 to £60
Digging Fork	Flat tines break up the soil and loosen compost; good for preparing vegetable beds.	£15 to £50
Hand Fork and Trowel	Useful hand tools for weeding, transplanting, digging small holes and working in containers.	£10 to £30 for both
Hoe	Use to cut off weeds at surface level, in paths and around established plants. Not for heavy-duty ground-breaking (instead use a pick).	£10 to £35
Edger	Look for a low-tech, easy-to-use blade that can cut a neat edge between grass and pathway.	£10 to £30
Leaf Rake	Springy and flexible, cleans up leaves from lawn and paths. Expandable model helps you clean up debris between and under shrubs at its narrowest setting and rakes up loads of leaves when fully expanded.	£10 to £15
Garden Rake	Sturdy, spiked teeth make the garden rake indispensable for levelling and smoothing beds. Must be tough.	£15 to £25
Secateurs	For cleaner, more precise cuts, look for secateurs with bypass blades, which slip past each other when closed and cut the branch cleanly. Use on branches of 2.5 cm (1 in) and smaller diameter. (Avoid anvil blades, which strike one another and crush the stem of the plant you're pruning.)	£10 to £40 and up
Loppers	Long-handled shears with more leverage for cutting branches up to 5 cm (2 in) thick. Use a pole pruner with extensions for high branches.	£12 to £40
Pruning Saw	Carry a fold-up model in your pocket. The protected blade stays sharp, and the tool is small enough so you can get into the middle of a shrub to cut a branch.	£10 to £20

262 Buy Shrubs and Trees

Whether you're transforming a stark, brand new garden into a lush refuge or just filling in some bare spots in an established landscape, you first need to know a bit about how plants are sold and when and how to buy them. Here's an introduction to what you'll encounter at your local nursery, as well as online and in mail-order catalogues.

Steps

1 Learn the basics about shrubs and trees, called *woody plants,* as opposed to soft-tissued annual and perennial plants, vegetables, ferns and so on. Shrubs and trees form the foundation of any garden, whether blooming or not.

2 Distinguish between deciduous and evergreen plants. The former lose their leaves every year in the autumn. This category includes most oaks, maples and birches. Many magnolias, camellias, rhododendrons and other evergreens keep their leaves year-round. Evergreens with needles and cones (pines, spruces and firs) are called *conifers.*

3 Understand the conditions in your garden. Test the soil with a home tester kit (available in garden centres) to see whether it is acid, alkaline or neutral; this will affect your choice of trees and shrubs. Is it heavy clay, free-draining sand, or something in between? Look at how much sun reaches the areas you wish to plant. There are shrubs and trees for sun, partial shade, and full shade, but you need to match the plants to the conditions.

4 Select plants that will flourish in your conditions. Look for this information on nursery labels, in garden books, on websites, or from experts at nurseries. Look in local gardens and parks to see what is popular and flourishing – you need not restrict your choice to these plants, but they tell you what is likely to thrive.

5 Start shopping in early spring or early autumn, just ahead of the two best planting seasons. Autumn is an excellent planting time except in the coldest areas.

6 Shop for plants while they are performing (in flower or displaying autumn foliage) if you're looking for specific colours, as long as the timing is not poor for planting (for example, in the heat of the summer).

7 Select plants grown in containers all year round. Deciduous trees will not have their leaves in winter and early spring, but this is a good time to see if the plant is a balanced shape with an even branch structure. Prices will depend not only on the plant's maturity, but on market factors including scarcity, difficulty of growing

What to Look For

- Container-grown plants year-round
- Root-balled shrubs and trees in large sizes
- Bare-root plants in winter and spring

Tips

The younger and smaller the plant, the lower the cost, and the faster it will become established, but the longer you'll have to wait for it to become large.

Mail-order and online catalogues offer great selections and good value, and prices may be half the nursery's, but postage and packing costs (10 to 25 per cent of the total order price) can offset the savings.

Mail-order container sizes tend to be smaller than those you find at local nurseries. The catalogue listing should indicate container size.

DIY shops and even supermarkets offer bargains. Shop frequently so you can buy when new stocks come in.

and transport costs. The range can be huge: but generally, the longer the plant has been cared for and grown on by the nursery, the more it costs. Some mature shrubs and trees in containers can cost hundreds of pounds.

8 Check out container-grown plants for signs of healthy, vigorous growth: new growth, no yellow leaves, compact shape, no leggy branches.

9 Inspect the roots to make sure they're not constricted (root-bound), which retards development after planting. Look for tell-tale roots poking through the container's drainage holes or emerging above the soil. If you're not sure, ask a sales assistant to help you gently pull the tree or shrub out of the pot so you can take a look.

10 Shop for root-balled plants mainly in spring and summer. These plants have been grown in fields, then dug up and wrapped in hessian. This growing method is used for large specimens, and is often the best way to buy trees. Cut away the hessian once the plant is sitting in the hole, and ask someone to let you know if the trunk is upright before you fill the hole.

11 Shop for bare-root trees and shrubs in winter and early spring while they are dormant. Mail-order and online suppliers often specialise in bare-root plants because of the ease of posting them. Bare-root is usually the least expensive way to buy deciduous plants, especially roses and fruit trees, and is also a good way to get plants started (see 245 "Buy the Perfect Rose"). Bare-root plants are small – only 60 to 90 cm (2 or 3 ft) high – and the roots, stripped of soil, are protected in moist wood chips or sawdust and packed in a plastic bag.

12 Look for bare-root plants without broken branches. Avoid trees with crossing branches that form an X and rub against each other.

13 Avoid bare-root plants that are beginning to leaf out – a sign that the plant is breaking out of dormancy and will have greater demands for water and light.

14 Prune bare-root trees or shrubs before transplanting if the nursery has not already done so. Both tops and roots need to be cut back a bit to keep them in balance (this is best done by someone with expertise).

15 Get bare-root plants into the ground as soon as possible so they don't dry out. Before planting, bury the root mass in a pile of damp ground bark or other organic matter to protect it.

Become acquainted with the delivery patterns of local nurseries and garden centres. For the best selection, shop on Thursday or Friday before the weekend shoppers descend.

Warning

Avoid trees or shrubs that have been sitting around, particularly in a supermarket or other nontraditional plant source. High temperatures and artificial or insufficient light may have stressed these plants.

263 Buy a Spa Pool

What could possibly be better than climbing into steaming hot water at the end of the day and gazing over your garden while your cares soak away? Before you peel those clothes off, however, you'll need to make several decisions about your spa or hot tub – chiefly regarding its size, cost, safety features and installation.

Steps

1 Decide where to place the spa. Take privacy, accessibility and aesthetics into consideration. Don't put the tub under overhanging trees or bushes that drop a lot of leaves.

2 Make sure the site can withstand up to 1,400 kg (3,000 lb), the average weight of a spa full of water. You'll want the strength and security of a concrete base.

3 Choose the size of a spa according to how many people will use it. The rule of thumb is to multiply 285 litre (75 gal) of water by the number of people for the total water capacity.

4 Determine your budget. Two-person spas start at about £3,000 and six-person spas start at £5,000. Ask for an estimate of monthly operating costs. Full insulation will save energy.

5 Consider what material you want. Today most spas are made of acrylic, which is easier to take care of and longer lasting than fibreglass. Spas made out of wood, most commonly redwood, are handsome but are likely to require more cleaning and upkeep, and they don't offer contoured seating as acrylic does.

6 Try before you buy. A good company will let you test spas in the showroom. (You'll want to dress for the occasion.) Pay attention to the jets' noise level, how easy it is to use the control, and the seating arrangement (especially with premoulded seats). Can you move around comfortably? Do you want a flexible seating arrangement?

7 Look for features and amenities to add to your pleasure and reduce any worries. Covers that lock with a key keep children safe and also help keep the tub clean. Thermostats keep the temperature under control. Safety switches, such as automatic shutoffs, are available.

8 Get the specifics about the dealer's delivery and installation service. Do you want the tub left in the driveway or brought right to its new location? Installation may add 5 to 10 per cent to the cost, but you may find it worthwhile, especially given electrical and plumbing factors.

What to Look For

- Location
- Size
- Budget
- Materials
- Comfort
- Safety features
- Installation help

Tips

These days the terms *hot tub* and *spa* are used interchangeably for the typical acrylic tub, usually equipped with jets to circulate the water.

Look for a spa with a skim filter – located on the side of the pool just at the water's surface – instead of an underwater filter, which can catch hair and clothing when it pulls in water.

Warning

Planning permission is not usually needed for a spa, but it's advisable to check with your local planning officer to check the regulations in your area.

264 Buy an Outdoor Lighting System

Outdoor lighting can create dramatic moods as well as illuminate steps and walkways for nighttime safety. It's also a project most home owners feel comfortable tackling. Low-voltage lighting is safe, easy to install and relatively inexpensive, with individual lights starting at £10 or even less at DIY or garden centres.

Steps

1 Decide what purpose the lighting system will serve. Do you want to highlight trees or statues dramatically, or brighten a path or entrance? Do you want creative or functional lighting, or both?

2 Choose the style of fixture you want to use. Path lights can be hidden or visible, in styles that range from flower shapes (such as tulips) to traditional lanterns, while spotlights on trees or artwork may consist of bulbs only. You can have lights fitted into the risers of steps, or have walk-on lights fitted into decking.

3 Choose the materials and finish for fixtures. Materials include aluminium, wood and copper. Black and verdigris finishes help the fixtures blend into the garden. Or match the finish to your home's colour and style.

4 Consider dramatic touches such as highlighting the form of a tree by placing a light at its base (uplighting), great for illuminating trees with interesting shapes, such as Japanese maples or oaks, and statues and water fountains. A lamp positioned above a gate or arch can spill its light on the ground like moonlight.

5 Choose a low-voltage system designed for outdoor use. You can install or move such a system easily, because the wires are buried only a few centimetres underground, and it uses 12 volts (transformers reduce the current).

6 Select the bulb wattage you want to use. Common choices range in brightness from 4 to 50 watts, typically from 18 to 24 watts. You decide how bright a bulb you want for its specific use – lighting the steps may be more important than lighting a tree.

7 Determine the size of transformer needed. Multiply the bulb wattage times the number of bulbs you need. Buy a transformer with the wattage that most closely matches this total. Don't go over that amount; if necessary, divide the bulbs into two groups and use two transformers. An automatic timer allows you to set lights to go on and off at specific times.

8 Arrange lights in a line, a T-shape or a circle, but remember that the further the last bulb is from the transformer, the dimmer its light will be.

9 Consider a motion-sensor light for safety; it turns on the light for a few minutes whenever it detects motion.

10 Check with a hardware shop or an electrician for additional information.

What to Look For

- Style of lantern
- Bulb wattage
- Transformer load

Tips

For the most effective lighting, place fewer lights close together (within a 3-m or 10-ft area) rather than more lights further apart.

For an exotic look, light ponds underwater with waterproof fixtures.

A solar lighting system is a good alternative wherever electricity is hard to come by or expensive, and sunshine is plentiful.

Consult a professional lighting designer or landscape architect for extensive lighting schemes.

BUY TIME • BUY A BOUQUET OF ROSES • BUY SOMEONE A DRINK • GET SOMEONE TO BUY YOU A DRINK • BUY YOUR WAY INTO THE BE
SCREEN • BUT FURTHER EDUCATION • ORDER EXOTIC FOOD • ORDER AT A SUSHI BAR • BUY DINNER AT A FRENCH RESTAURANT • EMPL
SAY SORRY TO YOUR PARTNER • BUY MUSIC ONLINE • EMPLOY MUSICIANS • ORDER A GOOD BOTTLE OF WINE • BUY AN ERGONOMIC
ANER • EMPLOY AN AU PAIR • BUY A GUITAR • BUY DUCT TAPE • GET A GOOD DEAL ON A MAGAZINE SUBSCRIPTION • GET SENIOR CITIZE
FIND A VET • BUY PET FOOD • BUY A PEDIGREE DOG OR CAT • BREED YOUR PET AND SELL THE LITTER • BUY OR RENT FOR A FANCY DRE
RY MADE OF PRECIOUS METALS • BUY COLOURED GEMSTONES • CHOOSE THE PERFECT WEDDING DRESS • BUY OR RENT MEN'S FORM
PHOTOGRAPHER • HIRE A CATERER • FIND THE IDEAL CIVIL WEDDING VENUE • THE COST OF MARRYING • ORDER PERSONALISED INVITA
RKS SHOW • BUY A MOTHER'S DAY GIFT • BUY A FATHER'S DAY GIFT • SELECT AN APPROPRIATE COMING-OF-AGE GIFT • GET A GIFT FOR
ISTMAS CARDS • BUY CHRISTMAS STOCKING FILLERS • BUY CHRISTENING GIFTS • PURCHASE A PERFECT CHRISTMAS TREE • BUY A PF
AY A RANSOM • GET HOT TICKETS • HIRE A LIMOUSINE • BUY A CRYONIC CHAMBER • RENT YOUR OWN HOARDING • TAKE OUT A FULL-F
URY CRUISE AROUND THE WORLD • BUY A TICKET TO TRAVEL FOR A YEAR • BOOK A TRIP ON THE ORIENT-EXPRESS • OWN A VINEYARD
OSTWRITER TO WRITE YOUR MEMOIRS • COMMISSION ORIGINAL ARTWORK • IMMORTALISE YOUR SPOUSE IN A SCULPTURE • GIVE AWAY
DICAL GUINEA PIG • SELL YOUR STORY TO THE TABLOIDS • SELL YOUR SOUL TO THE DEVIL • NEGOTIATE A BETTER CREDIT CARD DEAL •
RADE (OR NOT) • BUY ANNUITIES • BUY AND SELL MUTUAL FUNDS • BUY BONDS • SELL SHORT • INVEST IN PRECIOUS METALS • BUY SE
ND CASUAL WORK • SELL YOUR PRODUCT O[...] A HEADHUNTER • SELL YOURSELF IN A JOB INTE
CE • LEASE INDUSTRIAL SPACE • LEASE OFFI[...]MENT • HIRE SOMEONE TO DESIGN AND BUILD Y
ACH • SELL ON THE CRAFT CIRCUIT • HIRE A[...]RY • SELL A SCREENPLAY • SELL YOUR NOVEL •
R MORTGAGE DEAL • SAVE ON YOUR MORT[...]D • OBTAIN HOUSE INSURANCE • BUY A HOUSE •
EXCHANGE CONTRACTS ON A PROPERTY •[...]AN ESTATE AGENT • RELEASE CAPITAL FROM YO
RENT A HOLIDAY HOME • BUY A FLAT • RE[...]COUNTRY • BUY A LOFT APARTMENT • BUY PRO
BUY DOOR AND WINDOW LOCKS • CHOOSE[...]GHT FIXTURES • BUY A PROGRAMMABLE LIGHT
ED AND MATTRESS • HIRE AN INTERIOR DES[...]NCORPORATE A GREATER SENSE OF SPACE INTO
UY A TOILET • CHOOSE A TAP • BUY GLUES[...]MENTS • GET SELF-CLEANING WINDOWS • CHOO
OP • BUY GREEN HOUSEHOLD CLEANERS • S[...]SECURITY SYSTEM • BUY A HOME ALARM SYST
UY TIMBER FOR A DIY PROJECT • HOW TO S[...]R, PAINTER OR ELECTRICIAN • HIRE A GARDENE
IL IMPROVERS • BUY MULCH • BUY A COMP[...]BLE GARDEN • HIRE A GARDEN DESIGNER • BUY
SURGEON • BUY BASIC GARDEN TOOLS • B[...]BUY AN OUTDOOR LIGHTING SYSTEM • BUY O
BS AND SPICES • STOCK YOUR KITCHEN WIT[...]RESH PRODUCE • SELECT MEAT • STOCK UP FC
FRESH FISH • SELECT RICE • PURCHASE PR[...]LTON • GET FRESH FISH DELIVERED TO YOUR DC
G OILS • SELECT OLIVE OIL • SELECT OLIVES[...]INEGAR • CHOOSE PASTA • BUY TEA • BUY COF
REAL ALE • ORDER A COCKTAIL • CHOOSE A[...]STOCK A WINE CELLAR • STOCK YOUR BAR • D
A MIDWIFE OR DOULA • PLAN A HOME BIRTH[...]R A NEW BABY • BUY A NEW COT • CHOOSE A PI
CHILDCARE • FIND A GREAT NANNY • FIND T[...]TER-SCHOOL CARE • SIGN YOUR CHILD UP FOR
BUY BOOKS, VIDEOS AND MUSIC FOR YOUR[...]HIRE A TUTOR • ADOPT A CHILD • GET YOUR C
LTERED HOUSING • CHOOSE A CARE HOME[...]PLOT • PAY FOR FUNERAL EXPENSES • GET VIAG
TARY MTHERAPY • SEE A MENTAL-HEALTH P[...]BUY HOME-USE MEDICAL SUPPLIES • SELECT HA
T IMPLANTS • GET WRINKLE-FILLER INJECTI[...]ACTITIONERS • CHOOSE A MANICURIST • GET W
A • BOOK A MASSAGE • GET ON ANTIQUES R[...]SHOP AT AN ANTIQUE FAIR OR FLEA MARKET •

Food
& Drink

BUY SILVERWARE • EVALUATE CARNIVAL GLASS • BUY AND SELL STAMPS • BUY ANTIQUE FURNITURE • GET CLUED UP ON CLARICE C
SEIZE STAR WARS ACTION FIGURES • SELL YOUR VINYL RECORD COLLECTION • SELL TO A PAWNSHOP • BUY AND SELL COMIC BOO
PERIPHERALS • CHOOSE A LAPTOP OR NOTEBOOK COMPUTER • SELL OR DONATE A COMPUTER • BUY PRINTER PAPER • BUY A PRINTE
THE MEMORY IN YOUR COMPUTER • BUY COMPUTER SOFTWARE • CHOOSE A CD PLAYER • BUY BLANK CDS • BUY AN MP PLAYER • C
YOUR PHONE COMPANY • BUY VIDEO AND COMPUTER GAMES • CHOOSE A FILM CAMERA • CHOOSE A DIGITAL CAMCORDER • DECIDE
UY A SERIOUS TV • CHOOSE BETWEEN DIGITAL TV PROVIDERS • GET A DIGITAL VIDEO RECORDER • GET A UNIVERSAL REMOTE • BUY A
HASE CHEAP AIRLINE TICKETS • FIND GREAT HOTEL DEALS • HIRE THE BEST CAR FOR THE LEAST MONEY • GET TRAVEL INSURANCE •
UNITED KONGDOM • TIP IN A FOREIGN COUNTRY • TIP PROPERLY IN THE UK • BRIBE A FOREIGN OFFICIAL • GET AN INTERRAIL PASS •
EAP BUT FANTASTIC SAFARI • RENT A CAMEL IN CAIRO • GET SINGLE-MALT WHISKY IN SCOTLAND • BUY A SAPPHIRE IN BANGKOK • HI
HIRE A TREKKING COMPANY IN NEPAL • RENT OR BUY A SATELLITE PHONE • BUY YOUR CHILD'S FIRST CRICKET BAT • ORDER A STRIP F
BUY A RACKET • BUY A HEALTH CLUB MEMBERSHIP • BUY AN AEROBIC FITNESS MACHINE • BUY SWIMMING EQUIPMENT • BUY A JE
TING EQUIPMENT • CHOOSE A CAR RACK • BUY SKIS • BUY CLOTHES FOR COLD-WEATHER ACTIVITIES • SELL USED SKIS • BUY A SNC
BUY THE OPTIMAL SLEEPING BAG • BUY A TENT • BUY A BACKPACK • BUY A CAMPING STOVE • BUY A KAYAK • BUY A LIFEJACKET • B
SELL USED CLOTHING • ORDER CUSTOM-MADE COWBOY BOOTS • BUY CLOTHES ONLINE • FIND NON-STANDARD SIZES • BUY THE
E • BUY A WOMAN'S SUIT • BUY A MAN'S SUIT • HIRE A TAILOR • BUY CUSTOM-TAILORED CLOTHES IN ASIA • BUY A BRIEFCASE • SHOP
UT CLOTHES • BUY A HEART-RATE MONITOR • SELECT A WATCH • BUY KIDS' CLOTHES • CHOOSE CHILDREN'S SHOES • PURCHASE CL
CAR • BUY A MOTORCYCLE • BUYING AND CHANGING MOTOR OIL • WASH A CAR • WAX A CAR • BUY CAR INSURANCE • SPRING FOR

265 Buy Organic Produce

Buying organic food is a good idea – for both your own health and the environment – but it's more important with some produce than with others. Strawberries, for instance, tend to soak up toxins from pesticides, while grapefruit is protected by its thick skin. Many supermarkets and farmers' markets have a broad selection of organic foods.

Tips

Farms must meet strict growing laws and practices to be able to call their produce organic.

Research organic suppliers that will deliver seasonal goodies to your home.

Warning

Always wash your fruits and vegetables. Even organic produce can carry residual pesticides or waste from animals that share the fields.

MORE LIKELY TO BE CONTAMINATED Important to Buy Organic		LESS LIKELY TO BE CONTAMINATED Buy Organic When Available; Conventionally Grown Is OK	
Apples	Peaches	Asparagus	Grapefruit
Apricots	Peppers	Aubergines	Kiwi Fruit
Celery	Red raspberries	Avocados	Mangoes
Cherries	Spinach	Bananas	Okra
Grapes	Strawberries	Blueberries	Onions
Green beans		Broccoli	Papayas
Nectarines		Brussels sprouts	Pineapples
		Cabbage	Plums
		Cauliflower	Radishes
			Watermelons

266 Choose a Perfect Peach

Although in this country peaches are often grown under glass, they are best when left to ripen in the sun, then plucked, juicy and succulent, from a tree and eaten on the spot. If you don't grow your own, keep these tips in mind when shopping for ripe peaches.

What to Look For

- Fragrance
- Unblemished skin
- Flavour
- Varieties

Tip

Keep peaches at the top of your shopping bag and handle with care. Ripe peaches blemish and tear easily.

Steps

1 Smell the peach. Is it perfumey and sweet-scented?

2 Inspect the peach's surface. The skin shouldn't be bruised in any way; it should have a soft, downy covering of white fuzz; and it should be streaked with both pink and yellow.

3 Taste both white and yellow peaches. Most say the flavour of white peaches is the most spectacular, but your definition of perfection will depend on your own taste buds.

4 Eat that exquisite peach as soon as you get it home. Or savour peaches throughout the year, by making jam or chutney.

267 Buy and Sell at Farmers' Markets

You can't find fresher food unless you grow it yourself. Farmers' markets are a fabulous place to hunt down fresh produce, artisan breads and cheeses, nuts, oils and preserves. Plus, you're supporting small farms. For a listing of farmers' markets, contact the National Association of Farmers' Markets (farmersmarkets.net).

Steps

Selling

1 Go to the market and look around the stalls. You'll want to find out the prices and stock of any direct competitors.

2 Ask the market manager about setting up a stand. Some markets require potential sellers to fill out an application form and purchase a permanent space; others rent stalls for a nominal week-to-week fee.

3 Ask about the market's shoppers to determine how much merchandise to bring. You can also quiz experienced vendors and the market manager to get their recommendation on how much of your gooseberry jam you can expect to spread around.

4 Make your stall inviting with colourful tablecloths and umbrellas for shade or shelter. Only put out ten to twelve of each type of produce in a way that shoppers can pick out the ones they want without toppling piles. Keep your supply cool to stay fresh.

5 Give out samples of your wares. Free food attracts a crowd; tasty food makes a sale.

Buying

1 Don't make a shopping list for the farmers' market as you would for the greengrocer's. Instead, shop with your eyes and nose, smelling and squeezing produce to find the season's best. Taste samples to choose between offerings.

2 Make the full rounds of the market before you part with any cash. Find out who has the best crop of tomatoes or the choicest summer strawberries.

3 Be daring and buy something you've never tried before. Ask the stallholder how to prepare it; many will share recipes.

4 Don't succumb to temptation and overbuy. The reason to shop at a farmers' market is to get fresh, ripe food. If it hides in your refrigerator and goes bad, you might as well go to a supermarket.

What to Look For

- Competition's stock and prices
- Market managers
- Inventory to sell
- Sights and smells
- New ingredients
- The right amount

Tips

Bring lots of cash. Most sellers do not take cheques or credit cards – or if they do, you may pay more for that just-picked flavour.

Bring a large bag to take produce home. These markets don't usually pack your goods in paper or plastic.

268 Select Kitchen Knives

Any way you slice it, knives are the most important tool in the kitchen. A sharp blade and sturdy handle will help you slice and chop more efficiently. Invest in quality knives such as Sabatier to take your culinary clout to the next level.

Steps

1 Look for knives made from one piece of metal, meaning that the metal blade extends down into the handle. They'll be more durable and sturdy.

2 Get a handle on materials. Do you like the sleek feel of synthetic materials, the cool grip of metal or the warmth of wood? Hold the knives as if you were chopping to get a feel for their weight and balance.

3 Invest in an all-purpose 20 or 25 cm (8 or 10 in) chef's knife, considered the workhorse of the kitchen, and a 5 cm (2 in) paring knife. Individual knives run between £15 and £60.

4 Add a 15 cm (6 in) chopping knife and a 10 cm (4 in) boning knife, and a serrated bread knife to complete your collection.

5 Opt for an eight- or ten-piece knife set if you can afford it (they run from £200 to £450). The set comes with all the crucial pieces along with extras like a meat slicer, kitchen scissors or a sharpener.

What to Look For

- Solid metal blades
- Metal or wood handles
- Chef and paring knife
- Additional knives
- Knife sets

Tips

A sharp blade prevents accidents because it slices easily and effectively. A dull blade can cause clumsy slips that nick your hand or fingers. .

Swipe blades on a steel or stone before each use.

Dry blades completely to avoid bacteria growth if you use a knife block.

269 Decipher Food Labels

Food labels are a table of contents for prepared foods such as breads, cereals, canned and frozen foods, and those fizzy drinks we guzzle to excess. Requirements vary for each person, depending on age, weight and activity level. Read on to be an educated consumer and a healthy eater.

Steps

1 Read the ingredients. Items appear in descending order from largest to smallest amount. For example, if water is listed first on a bottle of juice, it is the primary ingredient.

2 Differentiate between the nutrition information for an average-sized serving and per 100 g (3½ oz).

3 Examine *Energy*, which gives the number of calories provided. (The guideline daily amounts for men and women are 2,500 and 2,000 calories respectively.) Look at *Fat*, which is broken down into saturated and unsaturated fats. Saturated fats are solid at room temperature, come from animal products and contribute to heart disease; unsaturated fats, which may be broken down

What to Look For

- Order of ingredients
- Serving size
- Saturated fats
- Cholesterol and sodium
- Calorie-free, fat-free and sugar-free

Tip

If you're looking for low-fat foods, a good test is to divide a serving's total number of calories by its total grams of fat. You should end up with roughly 3 g of fat per 100 calories.

further into mono-unsaturated and polyunsaturated fats, are less associated with heart problems because they don't raise cholesterol levels as saturated fats do. (The guideline daily amounts of total fat for men and woman are 95 g/3⅓ oz and 70 g/2½ oz respectively.)

4   Stay on top of cholesterol and sodium content, especially if you have high cholesterol, heart disease or other health concerns.

5   Be sceptical of the terms *light or lite,* which can refer to the colour or texture of a food. However, the term *free* indicates minuscule amounts of fats, cholesterol, sugar, sodium or calories.

270 Select Herbs and Spices

Herbs are fragrant and tender leaves of plants that don't have woody stems, such as chives, basil and parsley. Spices come from the bark, seeds, fruit, roots or stems of various plants and trees – for example, from cinnamon bark, saffron strands or cayenne pepper. Used well, both herbs and spices enhance flavour, but they can easily overpower a dish in too-large amounts.

Steps

1   Grow your own herbs, or buy fresh herbs only as you need them. (Mint and basil should almost always be bought fresh – there's really no substitute.) Submerge stems in a small glass of water (as you would a bouquet of flowers) to keep them fresh for up to ten days.

2   Choose fresh herbs that have a clean fragrance and a bright colour without any browning or wilting.

3   Stock up on dried herbs to have to hand for impromptu cooking: oregano, thyme and tarragon (see 271 "Stock Your Kitchen with Staples").

4   Look at the colour of dried herbs. They should retain some of their original colour and not be too brown.

5   Smell spices before buying them. They should be aromatic and pungent.

6   Buy dried herbs and spices from a busy shop with a high turnover so you know they haven't been sitting on the shelves for six months.

7   Browse farmers' markets for fresh seasonal herbs. You may find vendors selling bunches of dried herbs, sometimes with more exotic offerings than the supermarket. See 294 "Buy Ethnic Ingredients" and 267 "Buy and Sell at Farmers' Markets".

What to Look For

- Fresh herbs
- Dried herbs
- Clean scent
- Bright colour
- Aromatic smell
- High turnover
- Farmers' markets

Tips

The more airtight your storage container, the longer your spices will last. Date spices when you buy them and don't keep them for more than six months, after which their flavour fades.

Grind whole spices, like cumin and mustard, at home in a clean coffee grinder.

271 Stock Your Kitchen with Staples

Have you ever opened your fridge and in a fit of self-pity groaned, "There's nothing to eat!"? If you fill your kitchen cupboards and refrigerator with the basics below, you can throw together a pretty good dinner. Create a simple and savoury white bean soup from canned cannellini beans, garlic and chicken stock. Or throw together cooked penne with leftover cheese, milk and a pinch of dried mustard, cover with breadcrumbs and pop it under the grill for a real treat.

DRY GOODS

- Baking powder
- Beans, canned: cannellini, kidney, chickpeas
- Beans, dried: black, butter, pinto, black-eyed, red lentils, brown lentils, split peas
- Chocolate: bittersweet, unsweetened, semisweet; cocoa powder
- Coffee, ground
- Cornflour
- Cream of tartar
- Dried fruits: apricots, raisins, currants, sultanas, cherries
- Flour: self-raising and plain
- Garlic
- Gelatin, powdered, unflavoured

- Honey
- Oils: virgin and/or extra-virgin olive oil and sunflower
- Onions
- Pasta, dried: angel hair (capellini), spaghetti, linguine, fettuccine, macaroni, penne and rigatoni
- Peanut butter
- Polenta, dry
- Rice: arborio, basmati, long grain
- Shallots
- Soy sauce
- Spirits: Cognac or brandy, Grand Marnier, port, Calvados
- Stock cubes: low-salt chicken and beef

- Sugar: granulated, caster, brown, icing
- Syrups: treacle, golden syrup
- Tabasco sauce
- Tea: black and herbal
- Tinned tomatoes: chopped, whole and puréed
- Vanilla extract
- Vinegar: sherry, red, white and rice wine, cider, balsamic, malt
- Wines: dry sherry, Madeira, Marsala, dry Burgundy, dry Chardonnay
- Worcester sauce

HERBS AND SPICES

- Allspice: ground or whole
- Aniseed
- Basil
- Bay leaves
- Caraway seeds
- Cardamom, seeds and ground
- Cayenne pepper
- Celery seeds
- Chili powder
- Cinnamon: ground and sticks

- Cloves: ground and whole
- Cumin: seeds and ground
- Curry powder
- Dill
- Fennel
- Ginger: ground and crystallised
- Marjoram
- Mustard: seed and powdered
- Nutmeg: whole and ground
- Oregano

- Paprika
- Peppercorns, whole: black, white, green
- Poppy seeds
- Sage
- Sea salt
- Sesame seeds
- Thyme
- Turmeric

REFRIGERATOR

- Butter, unsalted
- Capers
- Cheese: Parmesan, cream, cheddar
- Eggs
- Ketchup

- Mayonnaise
- Milk
- Mustard: Dijon and whole-grain
- Preserves: marmalades and jams
- Sesame oil
- Tomato purée tube

FREEZER

- Breadcrumbs
- Chicken and/or beef broth
- Coffee beans, whole
- Frozen blueberries, raspberries
- Nuts: almonds, pecans, peanuts, pine nuts, pistachios, walnuts

272 Equip a Kitchen

It can take years to assemble the perfect array of nifty gadgets, trophy appliances and disaster-proof cookware. Equipping a kitchen is a truly personal undertaking. Depending on whether you intend to become a gourmet cook or pastry chef, you'll need different pieces of equipment. Here are the basics for a broad range of cooking interests. See also 207 "Buy Household Appliances".

LARGE APPLIANCES

- Dishwasher
- Gas or electric cooker (*gas cookers* are best overall for well-regulated heat, *gas ovens* for roasting and baking bread, and *electric* and *convection ovens* for baking)
- Refrigerator and freezer
- Optional: microwave, barbecue

SMALL APPLIANCES

- Coffeemaker
- Blender
- Electric hand mixer
- Food processor
- Knife set
- Standing mixer
- Kettle
- Toaster
- Optional: pressure cooker, espresso machine, rice cooker, ice cream maker

POTS AND PANS

- 2 or 3 saucepans
- 2 or 3 frying pans
- Nonstick omelette pan
- Roasting tin
- Stockpot
- Griddle pan
- Optional: wok, fish poacher, *bain-marie*, steamer

BAKING DISHES AND EQUIPMENT

- 3 or 4 flexible rubber spatulas
- 3 or 4 long-handled wooden spoons
- 8 to 12 ovenproof ramekins
- Casserole dishes
- Flour sifter
- Baking tray
- Measuring jugs
- Measuring spoons
- Pastry brush
- Rolling pin
- Sauce and balloon whisks
- Soufflé dish
- Cake tin with removable bottom
- Stacking mixing bowls
- Wire rack
- Optional: pastry cutters, icing bag with decorating tips, palette knife for icing cakes, 3 cake tins (square and round), 2 fluted flan tins

GADGETS AND TOOLS

- 2 large wooden cutting boards
- Baster
- Bottle opener
- Can opener
- Citrus zester
- Coffee grinder
- Colander
- Four-sided grater
- Funnel
- Garlic press
- Juicer
- Kitchen scales
- Lemon squeezer
- Long-handled fork or carving fork
- Meat thermometer
- Metal skewers for kebabs or trussing meats
- Metal spatulas
- Nutmeg grater
- Pepper grinder
- Potato masher
- Salad spinner

- Slotted spoons
- Soup ladle
- Strainers
- Tongs
- Vegetable peeler
- Wine opener
- Optional: pasta maker, spice grinder

273 Choose Fresh Produce

There's nothing like eating the season's first crop of fruits and vegetables – biting into sweet, fleshy strawberries at the beginning of summer or tasting autumn's crispy Cox apples. Choosing the freshest produce possible is mostly a matter of eating in season – something we supermarket shoppers have lost sight of.

SPRING	WHAT TO LOOK FOR	HOW TO STORE	THE DISH
Asparagus	Spears should be firm and bright green (except white or purple asparagus).	Refrigerate in open plastic bag.	Steamed asparagus with butter.
Carrots	Bright green tops, crisp, deep orange colour.	Store in closed plastic bag with tops removed.	Glaze with honey and whisky.
Cauliflower	Tightly packed florets without discoloration.	Store in closed plastic bag in refrigerator.	Blanch and cook with cream and parmesan.
Rhubarb	Crisp stalks in red, pink, green or speckled colour.	Remove leaves. Chill up to four days.	With custard in rhubarb fool.
Spinach	Bright green leaves (flat or crinkled).	Wrap stalks in damp paper towel and refrigerate in salad crisper.	Use in salads, wilted in pasta or as side dish.

SUMMER	WHAT TO LOOK FOR	HOW TO STORE	THE DISH
Apricots	Colour should be uniform.	Store at room temperature, or in refrigerator if fully ripe.	Apricot and almond tart.
Artichokes	Should be tightly closed, feel firm and heavy, with no discoloration.	Keep in a closed plastic or brown bag in the refrigerator.	Steamed with fresh caper-lemon aioli for dipping.
Aubergine	Shiny skin with firm, even texture. Small to medium are younger and sweeter.	Store in salad crisper	Marinate in balsamic and olive oil and grill.
Avocados	Squeeze gently for softness (for immediate use); will ripen uncut at home. Too soft means going bad.	Store at room temperature.	Mashed in guacamole or diced with mangoes and red onions for fish topping.
Beetroot	Fresh and unwilted leaves. Use beetroot quickly, before sugars turn to starch.	Store in open plastic bags in refrigerator.	Roast beetroot, slice and layer with goat cheese.
Broad Beans	Slightly fuzzy to the touch. Unblemished pods.	Best cooked and eaten immediately.	Purée for crostini.

SUMMER	WHAT TO LOOK FOR	HOW TO STORE	THE DISH
Cherries	Shiny, firm, not squishy. Deep scarlet.	Refrigerate. Don't wash until you're about to eat.	In trifle with kirsch, custard and sponge.
Cucumbers	Firm skins, not limp or shrivelled. Indoor have smooth skin; ridge have wrinkled skin.	Store in refrigerator away from apples and tomatoes for up to one week.	Dice and add with garlic and lemon juice to plain yogurt for vegetable dip.
Figs	Best when ripe and soft, almost shrivelled. No mould.	Store in paper towel-lined closed plastic bag in the refrigerator for two to three days.	Stuff with goat's cheese, wrap with pancetta (Italian bacon) and grill.
Garden Peas	Pods filled but not bursting.	Refrigerate in open plastic bag.	In salad, as side dish or in risotto.
Green Beans	Crisp and bright.	Store in salad crisper.	Add to pasta and salads.
Melons	Cantaloupes: tan skin (not green). Honeydews: creamy yellow skin. All, except watermelons, smell sweet at stem end. Shouldn't hear seeds rattling when shaken.	Store unripened at room temperature. Store ripe in refrigerator.	Slice and enjoy.
Nectarines	Avoid fruit with green tinge. Flesh gives slightly to pressure.	Keep at room temperature.	Cut in half and grill, then fill pit with mascarpone.
Onions	Sweet summer onions should be firm.	Store in a cool, dry place.	Caramelise for sweet pizza topping.
Potatoes	Avoid sprouts. Small have better flavour.	Keep in cool, dark place.	Roast with sea salt, herbs and olive oil.
Radishes	Firm and smooth. Small radishes tend to be milder.	Refrigerate in open plastic bag.	Shave over spinach salad with goat cheese.
Raspberries	Smell for aroma. Check underside of carton to make sure it isn't berry-stained or mouldy.	Store at room temperature if using same day. Store in refrigerator on paper towel-lined plate.	Best eaten fresh or in compote with ice cream.
Strawberries	Full red berries with some shine. No trace of mould.	Use as soon as possible; store in salad crisper.	Slice in spinach salad.

SUMMER	WHAT TO LOOK FOR	HOW TO STORE	THE DISH
Summer Squash	Not too scratched or limp; look for juice coming out of stem to tell if truly fresh.	Keep in salad crisper or at room temperature.	Slice and grill with olive oil and salt.
Sweetcorn	Silk should look fresh with unwilted leaves. Kernels should be plump, filled out.	Store in salad crisper. Cook as soon as possible.	Barbecue, then shave off kernels to toss in tomato salad.
Tomatoes	Firm but not hard, aromatic, full colour. Cracking on skin doesn't matter.	Store at room temperature out of sun.	Slice and layer with buffalo mozzarella and fresh basil, sprinkle with olive oil.

AUTUMN	WHAT TO LOOK FOR	HOW TO STORE	THE DISH
Apples	No bruising or mushy, soft skin. Should be firm – best test is taste.	Refrigerate or keep at room temperature.	Bramleys for cooking. Cox's Orange Pippin, Gala, Fuji, Braeburn or Granny Smith for eating.
Broccoli	Completely green with no yellowing; should smell sweet, not like cabbage.	Refrigerate in open plastic bag.	Braise in chicken stock with dried red-pepper flakes.
Fennel	Smooth white bulbs, firm to touch.	Keep stalk attached.	Slice thin and marinate in olive oil and lemon.
Hard-shelled Squash	Butternut or pumpkin; no soft spots.	Store in cool, dark place.	Roasted for side dishes or puréed in soups.
Pears	Colour and texture varies; best when firm with some give at stem end.	Room temperature or in salad crisper.	On gorgonzola crostini.
Persimmons	Hachiya: squishy when ripe. Fuyu: firm and orange.	Keep at room temperature.	Bake in biscuits and bread pudding.
Plums	Uniform colour and some spring when pressed.	Store in refrigerator.	Slice in fruit compote or use as pie filling.
Rocket	Deep green; avoid yellow leaves.	Paper towel-lined open plastic bags in refrigerator.	Use in salads, wilted in pastas or to make pesto.
Sweet Peppers	Firm and crisp with glossy skins.	Store at room temperature.	Roast and purée for pasta sauce.

AUTUMN	WHAT TO LOOK FOR	HOW TO STORE	THE DISH
Sweet Potatoes	Firm, smooth skin with no soft spots.	Store in cool, dark place.	Roast with coarse salt and olive oil.

WINTER	WHAT TO LOOK FOR	HOW TO STORE	THE DISH
Brussels Sprouts	Buy on stalk. Avoid yellow or brown leaves.	Store in a cool, dry place.	Slice thinly and sauté in olive oil with pancetta.
Cabbage	Firm, somewhat shiny, bright colour.	Store in salad crisper.	Use in soups, or as wrapping for meat fillings.
Celeriac	Look for fresh tops; trim off hairy stems and skin.	Store in open plastic bag lined with damp paper towel.	Grate and toss with mustard-caper dressing.
Citrus	Should feel heavy.	In salad crisper for up to two weeks.	Enjoy alone; use juice in salad dressings, or slice in salads.
Greens: Chard, Kale, Perpetual Spinach	Rich, dark leaves with no yellowing.	Store in damp towel-lined open plastic bag.	Cook in soups, or braise with olive oil, garlic and chilli pepper.
Jerusalem Artichoke	Firm, knobbly tubers.	Store in cool, dark place.	Use in soups, baked, boiled with butter or a sauce, and roasted.
Leeks	White stalk; fresh, well-hydrated top.	Store in salad crisper.	Slice for gratins or sauté with pancetta and peas for pasta.
Parsnips	Whiter means fresher.	Store in salad crisper.	Roast with other root vegetables.
Pomegranates	Should feel heavy; with a few cracks.	Store at room temperature.	Crush kernels and add the juice to champagne for apéritif.
Swedes	Smooth, firm skin.	Store in cool, dark place.	Cook in soup or roast with other root vegetables and herbs.
Turnips	Leaves fresh and unwilted; keep for some time.	Wash when ready to use; store at room temperature.	Add to last 40 minutes of stew simmering.

There are really only two types of meat: tough and tender. Tough cuts of meat come from parts of the animal, such as the legs and neck, where strong muscles develop. These cuts require long slow moist cooking methods, such as stewing, to become tender. Tender cuts come from parts of the animal that are under less stress. These cuts should be cooked quickly to retain their texture and seal in flavour. Look for high-quality cuts of whatever type of meat you are buying.

Steps

1 Choose free-range or corn-fed chicken (see 280 "Choose a Chicken"). Free-range chickens have been allowed to wander about and forage for food outside the coop for at least part of the day and they have not been fed growth promoters. As a result, they mature more slowly than intensively farmed chickens and have more flavour. You do not have to buy a whole chicken, your butcher will sell you any cut – breast, thigh or leg. Alternatively, you can buy free-range pre-packed cuts at any supermarket. Buy with the skin still on.

2 For a special occasion buy free-range French chickens or cuts. The French Poulet de Bresse and the Poulet Noir are particularly tasty.

3 Choose beef with minimal outer fat. The fat should be creamy in colour, and bones should be soft-looking with a reddish colour. The meat should be firm, fine-textured and a light cherry red. Buy organic beef to be safe (see 277 "Buy Organic Beef"). Cook it to an internal temperature of 54°C (130°F) for rare and 60°C (140°F) for medium.

4 Look for lamb that's been butchered at five to seven months or younger. It has a more delicate flavour and texture than older lamb or mutton, which takes on a rich gamey flavour. Meat from high-quality young lambs is fine-textured, firm and lean. It's pink in colour, and the cross sections of bones are red, moist and porous. The external fat should be firm, white and not too thick. In the supermarket buy prepacked cuts that carry the tractor symbol, indicating that it meets British Farm Association Standards. Cook lamb to an internal temperature of 57°C (135°F) for legs and 60°C (140°F) for ribs.

5 Select pork that's pinkish-white to pink in colour (loin meat is whiter than shoulder meat) and firm to the touch. Well-marbled pork produces tenderer results. Buy outdoor-reared pork for the best flavour. Look for the tractor symbol to ensure that it meets British Farm Association Standards. Cook pork to an internal temperature of 65°C (150°F).

6 Ask for prime-quality veal, with almost white to very light pink, firm, velvety and moist flesh. Veal is butchered young, so most of its meat is tender. Bones should be bright red, small and fairly soft to the touch. The fat covering the meat should be slight

Tips

Large cuts of meat will generally keep in the refrigerator for four to five days.

Names for cuts of meat vary considerably around the country, so if you are in any doubt as to the cut you need, ask your butcher for advice. The chart opposite is not an exhaustive list of all the names used.

See 277 "Buy Organic Beef".

Warning

Avoid beef with yellowish or grey fat, absolutely no marbling, a deep red colour, two-tone coloration, coarse texture or excessive moisture. You'll be able to tell excess moisture by a mushy or wet-looking piece of meat, or if the packaging is filled with condensation.

MEAT CUT	TOUGH OR TENDER	HOW TO PREPARE
Beef		
Brisket	Tough	Braise
Rib	Tender	Grill
Rib eye	Tender	Grill
Loin or sirloin	Tender	Grill, pan-fry
Fillet (centre cut fillet is Chateaubriand; near the end of the fillet is filet mignon and tournedos)	Tough	Marinate and grill
Flank	Tender	Sear, then braise and roast
Roasts	Tough	Roast
Skirt and plate (can include short ribs)	Tender	Grill steaks; braise ribs
Steaks (T-bone, porterhouse, sirloin)	Tough	Grill
Stewing meat	Tender	Braise, stew
Chops	Tough	Grill, roast, sauté, pan-fry
Shoulder and chuck	Tough	Braise
Rump and round	Tough	Braise
Lamb		
Chops	Tender	Grill, roast, sauté, pan-fry
Rack of lamb (ribs)	Tender	Grill, roast
Shank (leg)	Tough	Braise, stew
Shoulder	Tough	Braise, roast, stew
Stewing meat	Tough	Braise, stew
Pork		
Loin (centre cut, sirloin roasts, chops, cutlets, crown roast and tenderloin)	Tender	Grill, roast, sauté, pan-fry
Steaks	Tender	Braise
Ribs (spare ribs, baby back ribs)	Tough	Braise or stew
Roasts	Tough	Braise
Shoulder	Tough	Braise, roast, stew
Veal		
Loin or saddle (loin chop)	Tender	Roasted
Round roast (top round and sirloin tip)	Tender	Roasted
Rump	Tender	Boned and roasted
Sirloin	Tender	Boned and roasted

275 Stock Up for the Perfect Burger

The ultimate barbecuer's pride and joy, the humble hamburger is raised to lofty heights by choosing your minced beef well. When it comes to burgers, fat is our friend – health concerns notwithstanding, feisty butchers everywhere say it imparts flavour, and it helps the hamburger stay together.

Steps

1 Order minced beef from your butcher for the freshest meat possible. Specify the cut of meat, such as sirloin, brisket and so on. The cut determines the price you pay.

2 Look for meat that's red to red-brown (sometimes the top layer of the meat will oxidise and turn slightly brown). The meat shouldn't be grey or green-grey in colour and should be cold to the touch.

3 Go for the fat. The higher the fat content, the cheaper the beef.

4 Choose chuck if you want less fat. It usually contains 15 to 20 per cent, so it's still moist and full of flavour, but not as dry as minced sirloin or as juicy as ordinary minced beef.

5 Wrap meat in a plastic bag and buy at the end of your shopping trip so it stays cool for as long as possible.

What to Look For

- As fresh as possible
- Desired cut
- Red to red-brown meat
- Minced to order
- Fat content

Warning

Refrigerate at 4°C (40°F) or below and use within two days. Don't leave out for more than four hours – including time spent in the shopping trolley or car, and on your worktop – it could develop bacteria.

276 Purchase a Christmas Ham

Ham can take on myriad flavours, including honey, whisky, pepper and apple. No mere pork leg, ham is either soaked in a mix of salt, water and sugar or dry-cured with salt, herbs and sugar, then aged for several weeks and smoked. Dry-cured hams require 48 hours of soaking to remove the salt, hours of poaching and finally baking.

Steps

1 Tally up your guest list. A bone-in ham will provide three to four servings per pound, while a boneless ham will yield four to five. Factor in extra for leftovers; there's nothing like a honey-baked-ham sandwich or fried ham and eggs.

2 Order in advance. Ask your butcher or grocer's meat department how and when you should place an order for Christmas ham.

3 Browse websites and gourmet catalogues, but make sure that you allow extra time and money for delivery. F C Phipps (britainsbestbutcher.co.uk), which is based in Lincolnshire, send hams and other high-quality produce around the country. Fortnum and Mason (fortnumandmason.com) also offer an online service.

What to Look For

- Flavoured hams
- Number of servings
- Butcher or quality grocer's
- Websites
- Catalogues

Tip

Premium hams have less water added to the meat to plump it up.

Warning

To kill potentially harmful trichinosis, heat the inside of an uncooked ham to at least 68°C (155°F).

277 Buy Organic Beef

The hottest trend among the carnivore cognoscenti is organic beef. Certified organic cows are reared without the routine use of drugs, antibiotics and wormers, which is widespread in intensive cattle farming. Organic farming means that the animals are kept in more natural, free-range conditions and eat a more natural diet. The beef is consequently leaner and filled with heart-friendly omega-3 fatty acids. Converts to organic beef say that it even tastes better.

Steps

1 Buy meat from farmers that are certified organic by the Soil Association (soilassociation.org). Check the website for their online Organic Directory.

2 Ask your local butcher if he or she supplies organic beef. Larger supermarkets might also stock it.

3 Shop online. There are a number of companies that will deliver to your door.

What to Look For

- Certified organic produce
- Organic butchers
- Supermarkets with organic section
- Online organic suppliers

278 Buy Haggis

Even if you've never been to Scotland, you can still experience traditional Scottish fare with haggis. Haggis is made from minced meat (usually from a sheep), oatmeal, onions, and herbs and spices, stuffed inside a sheep's stomach. The stomach is then sewn up with thread. Haggis comes fresh or in tins, but, if you can, buy the fresh variety. Almost a contradiction in terms, vegetarian haggis is also very popular.

Steps

1 Ask your butcher if he or she sells haggis. In Scotland many butchers make their own haggis, but this happens less often south of the border.

2 Try supermarkets and up-market department stores with food halls. McSweens, a particularly popular brand, makes vegetarian haggis as well.

3 Get haggis delivered to your door. Shop on the internet at sites such as scottishhaggis.co.uk and angus.co.uk.

4 Organise the trimmings. Haggis is traditionally served with "neeps and tatties" (mashed swede or turnip and mashed potatoes), accompanied by a dram or more of malt whisky.

What to Look For

- Butcher or supermarket
- Delicatessen

Tip

Haggis is traditional fare for Burns Night on 25 January, when Scots celebrate the life and work of the poet Robert Burns, most famous for writing *Auld Lang Syne*.

279 Purchase Local Honey

Bees work hard for the honey. They may travel as far as 55,000 miles and visit more than two million flowers to gather enough nectar to make just a jar of honey. Honey's flavour comes from the source (thyme, heather, clover, eucalyptus or sunflower, to name a few), not the bee.

Steps

1 Look in the *Yellow Pages* under Beekeepers & Bee Farmers, or search on the internet. Beekeepers are the best source for locally produced honey. If they don't sell honey themselves, they'll know where to find it.

2 Shop at farmers' markets and country fairs to find various local varieties of the sweet nectar.

3 Browse the shelves of gourmet food shops to find a wide variety of honey flavours, colours and textures.

What to Look For

- Beekeepers
- Farmers' markets or fairs
- Gourmet food shops

Tip

If your honey crystallises, place the opened jar in a pan of hot water over a low heat for 15 minutes. Stir to dissolve the sugar granules.

280 Choose a Chicken

Fly away from flavourless plastic-wrapped frozen birds and head for the free range. Uncaged, organic chickens are more tasty and more healthy. Be aware that, whether you buy your bird whole for roasting or cut into legs, thighs, wings and breasts, removing the skin before cooking decreases the fat by 25 to 30 per cent, but decreases the flavour as well.

TYPE OF BIRD	CHARACTERISTICS	BEST USE
Broilers	Intensively farmed chickens stuffed with antibiotics.	The standard chicken avoided by gourmets and the health-conscious. Bland in flavour, serves well enough in curries or other strong sauces.
Capons	Castrated cock allowed to grow old and fat in comfort.	Capons' meat is mild and their size makes them perfect for a special occasion. Favoured by some for Christmas dinner. Order ahead from a butcher. Expect to pay slightly more than for other birds.
Free-range roasters	More flavour than broilers but sell at a premium because of higher cost of rearing.	A bird for roasting should be big-breasted, with plenty of meat. A free-range bird should be cooked to celebrate its own flavour. Sprinkle sea salt on the skin and baste with lashings of butter.
Corn-fed chicken	Fed on a diet of maize, which makes their flesh yellowish.	The diet gives these chickens a somewhat "gamey" flavour, like pheasant. Appeals to people who don't like their food to be bland.

281 Select Fresh Fish

Everyone agrees that freshness is more important when choosing fish than is the case with any other foodstuff. Most fish cooks would recommend buying whatever is freshest at the fishmongers', rather than insisting on a particular fish you have set your heart on. But how do you know a fresh fish from a stale one? Follow these tips.

Steps

1 Buy your fish from a reputable fishmonger who knows his business. Cultivate a relationship with the fishmonger and ask his advice on the best fish to buy.

2 Survey the range of fish on the fishmongers' slab. Do you get the impression that some of the fish look fresher than others? if so, can you rationalise your first impression? Most regular fish buyers develop an instinctive sense of what looks best.

3 Examine the fish you fancy in detail. First use your eyes. Does the fish look bright and shiny? Are its eyes clear and bright? These are signs of a fresh fish. If the fish has no shine and its eyes are dull or red, it has probably been out of water too long.

4 Smell the fish. Does it have that unpleasant odour people describe as "fishy"? If so, it is not fresh. A fish should have a clean smell with a tang of the sea about it.

5 Feel the fish with your fingers (or have the fishmonger do it for you). Is its flesh firm? If the fish's body dents too easily under the pressure of your fingers, this is a bad sign.

6 Now the clincher. Examine the gills by lifting up the small flap that covers them (the gills are on each side of the fish where the head joins the body). If the gills are pink or red, you have a fresh fish. Brown gills indicate lack of freshness.

7 Ask the fishmonger's advice on how best to cook the fish that you have chosen.

What to Look For

- Good fishmonger
- Bright, shiny fish
- Clear, bright eyes
- Fresh smell
- Firm flesh
- Pink or red gills

Tips

When possible, buy whole fish (some fish are of course too big for this to apply). Fillets are hard to test for freshness and in any case lose their freshness more quickly than whole fish through the contact of the flesh with the air. If you want fillets, have the fishmonger fillet your whole fish after you buy it.

Fish kept in your fridge will deteriorate fast. Preferably cook your fish the day that you buy it, or at worst the following day, if you want freshness and flavour.

Rice, a staple of diets around the world, is grown in beautiful marshy tiers across Asia and India, while wild rice is found in the American Midwest, and black rice comes from China. Texas has started to cultivate basmati rice, called Texmati, although purists swear by Indian basmati. Review this chart to help you put the many varieties of this precious grain to good use.

RICE	DESCRIPTION	COOKING METHOD	BEST USE
Arborio	Short-grain, polished white kernels with bland taste and soft texture.	Don't rinse; simmer 1 part rice to 2 parts liquid for 20 minutes; add the liquid gradually while stirring.	Risotto.
Basmati	Aromatic long-grain.	Rinse and simmer 1 part rice to 1½ parts liquid for 20 to 25 minutes.	Side dish with saffron, curries or Indian flavours.
Black Rice	Short-grain black rice, fragrant and nutty.	Simmer 1 part rice to 2 parts liquid for 45 minutes.	Delicious as side dish or as bed for fish dish.
Brown Rice	Long-grain with nutty flavour and firm texture.	Simmer 1 part rice in 2 parts liquid, adding a little butter to keep grains separate, for 35 to 50 minutes.	Casseroles, pilaf and salads.
Lundberg Royal	Aromatic long-grain.	Rinse and simmer 1 part rice to 1½ parts liquid for 20 to 25 minutes.	Side dish for meat and fish dishes.
Sushi Rice	Polished rice shorter than arborio; can be sweet, waxy or sticky.	Soak overnight and simmer 1 part rice to 1 part water, or following rice cooker's instructions.	Dim sum, sushi and dessert puddings
Wehani	Aromatic California long-grain hybrid that turns russet when cooked.	Rinse and simmer 1 part rice to 1½ parts liquid for 20 to 25 minutes.	Side dish or rice salads.
Wild Rice	Not rice at all, but the seed of native grass found in the American Midwest and California. Earthy and nutty, with firm to chewy texture.	Boil 1 part rice to 3 parts water, 45 to 60 minutes.	Delicious with nuts and dried fruits for stuffing, and in salads and side dishes.
TIP	Try out the colourful rices that are making their way onto shop shelves, but remember that their colour will leach during the cooking process and can taint other ingredients in a dish when cooked together.		

283 Purchase Premium Salt and Pepper

The most versatile spicing and flavouring agents are anything but bland. Used well, salt and pepper greatly enhance the flavour and overall outcome of your cooking. Most of today's table salt is mined from large deposits left by dried salt lakes. Common black pepper is made from ground dried, unripened berries of the pepper plant.

Steps

Salt

1 Swap your ordinary table salt for sea salt, which is made from evaporated seawater. Many chefs prefer sea salt because of its coarse texture, lack of additives and less astringent flavour. Use it for finishing dishes just before serving.

2 Experiment with out-of-the-ordinary salts. Try black salt, a mineral compound with a sulphur taste that dissipates, in Indian masalas or seafood dishes. Hawaiian pink salt, made from sea salt which is coloured with the iron oxide in Hawaiian "red clay", is tasty sprinkled over exotic mahimahi on the barbecue.

Pepper

1 Start with premium whole black peppercorns. Invest in a pepper mill to grind pepper at home. Hand-grinding your pepper will keep it fresh longer, as ground pepper loses its flavour very quickly. Throw out that powdery pepper that makes you sneeze.

2 Broaden your taste horizons with white or green peppercorns. Mild white peppercorns are best for light-coloured sauces, and green peppercorns, with their fresh and pungent flavour, are often used in brines and marinades.

3 Put pink peppercorns on your shopping list. Pungent and slightly sweet, they appear in up-market grocers or delicatessens either freeze-dried or packed in brine. They are often used along with white and black peppercorns for a splash of colour and as a dusting over finished dishes.

4 Look for gourmet mixes of whole black, white, pink and green peppercorns.

What to Look For

- Sea salt
- Black or pink salt
- Whole black peppercorns
- Pepper mill
- White or green peppercorns
- Pink peppercorns
- Peppercorn mixtures

Tips

Whole peppercorns stored in a cool dry place will last about a year; however, pink peppercorns only last about six months.

It's good etiquette to taste a dish before you add salt and pepper – you'll be giving the chef a chance before seasoning his or her creation.

Warning

Ask your doctor about regulating your salt intake if you are at risk of heart problems or high blood pressure.

284 Buy a Real Stilton

For a blue cheese to be a real Stilton, it has to be made either in Derbyshire, Leicestershire or Nottinghamshire, and according to a strict code. Stilton only ever comes in the traditional cylindrical shape and must be allowed to form its own crust. The distinctive blue veins are made by the insertion of stainless steel needles, which allows air to enter the body of the cheese. Curiously, Stilton has never been made in the village of Stilton, Cambridgeshire.

Steps

1 Shop around and do a taste test – good cheese shops and delis will encourage you to sample their wares. The taste and texture of Stilton varies according to age. When a cheese is about nine weeks' old and if it passes inspection, it is ready to be sold. At this time it will be quite crumbly, with a slight acidic taste. If left for another five or six weeks, the flavour will be more rounded and mellow, and the texture smoother, almost buttery.

2 Try White Stilton. It's like its blue cousin except that no mould spores are added, and it's sold when about four weeks' old.

3 Shop online. Try cheese specialists such as Neal's Yard Dairy (nealsyarddairy.co.uk).

What to Look For

- Cylindrical shape
- Distinctive blue veins
- Good cheese shop or delicatessen

Tips

Serve Stilton on a cheese-board at room temperature

Port is Stilton's traditional alcoholic partner, although it goes well with many wines.

Unlike most cheeses, Stilton freezes well, wrapped in cling film.

285 Get Fresh Fish Delivered to Your Door

Eat healthily and safely without harming the environment - order fresh or smoked fish from Atlantic waters one day and present a whole succulent, eco-friendly salmon to guests at your dinner table the next.

Steps

1 Search the internet. There are a number of high-quality fish suppliers that will deliver fish to your door. The Fish Society (fishsociety.co.uk) supplies nearly 200 premium quality fish, ranging from barracuda fillets (£15.90 for 375 g/13 oz) to organic smoked salmon certified by the Soil Association (£4.40 for 100 g/3 oz). All the fish is frozen and high-tech packaging systems keep it frozen until you transfer it to your freezer at home.

2 Check out the Marine Conservation Society's *Good Fish Guide* (mcsuk.org) for guidance on which fish to buy.

3 For the best-flavoured and textured smoked fish in particular contact Scottish fish merchants, such as the Hand-made Fish company (handmadefish.co.uk) in Shetland, which offers fresh, wild seine-net and line-caught sea fish and organic farmed fish smoked in pure Scottish hardwoods and malt whisky barrel staves. Alternatively, the Minola Smokery in Abergavenny (minola-smokery.com) offers high-quality fish smoked on split Welsh oak logs in iron smoke pots, using only natural convection.

What to Look For

- Organic farmed fish
- Line-caught sea fish

Tip

Look for companies that follow an environmentally sensitive code of practice and support the Marine Stewardship Council, which works to promote sustainable farming.

286 Sniff out Truffles

We have dogs to thank for giving us the chance to savour these highly prized fungi. Truffles grow underground, and trained dogs track them by scent. Pigs have an even better sense of smell but they are unreliable hunters as they tend to make off with the booty themselves. Fresh truffles are a delicacy and very expensive, but everyone deserves to try them at least once in their lives.

Steps

1 Hunt out fresh truffles at up-market grocers, delicatessens or department stores with food halls.

2 Search the internet for suppliers, although you may be sent to sites for the chocolate variety of truffles, which is something completely different.

3 Keep a look out for the Black Périgord truffle from central France and the White Piedmont truffle from Italy; these are the most prized truffles of all.

4 Try truffles thinly sliced in pasta and risotto dishes, or in a salad with potatoes.

What to Look For

- Up-market grocers or delicatessen
- Department stores with food halls
- Black Périgord and White Piedmont truffles

Tip

Truffles are considered by some to be an aphrodisiac.

287 Buy Artisan Breads

Handcrafted loaves of crunchy, hearty artisan breads are a world away from factory-made assembly line breads. These breads range in flavour from sweet and mild to pungent and rustic. Each loaf has its own distinct shape, texture and taste.

Steps

1 Read the ingredients. You'll easily recognise the short list of often organic, unbleached wheat flour, water, salt and yeast. If the bread is made with a sourdough starter, you may not see yeast.

2 Look for golden, ridged and crusty loaves. This is the telltale crust of bread baked in an artisan's wood-fired oven or hearth, which radiates high-temperature heat around the entire loaf.

3 Tap the crust. Listen for a hollow sound that means the bread is not dense and doughy. Inside, look for uneven webbed texture with lots of nooks and crannies of different shapes and sizes. This provides the unmistakable "mouth feel" of artisan bread.

4 Taste some samples. How the bread feels is secondary to the wonderful range of flavours available.

5 Eat promptly. Artisan loaves don't stay fresh as long as chemically preserved commercial breads do. Freeze stale portions to make bread pudding, croutons or breadcrumbs.

What to Look For

- Flour, water, salt and yeast
- Golden crust
- Hollow sound
- Good texture
- Distinct taste

Tip

Look for the many shapes and sizes of artisan breads, such as baguettes, pugliese, bâtarde, ciabatta, focaccia, raisin-walnut bread and handcrafted bagels.

288 Buy Artisan Cheeses

Instead of buying a waxy yellow block of cheese that has very little or no taste, why not indulge in handcrafted, high-flavour cheeses? Some of the most popular cheeses, such as Cheddar and Stilton, are made in Britain, but there are some wonderful cooking and tasting cheeses produced in Europe, in particular France and Italy, that deserve to be better known. Explore texture and taste, fresh to aged, as well as a variety of milk sources.

TYPE OF CHEESE	TEXTURE; TASTE; ANIMAL'S MILK	SUGGESTED USE
Fresh Cheeses		
Feta (Greece)	Soft, crumbly; traditionally salty, tangy; sheep, goat or cow, originally from ewe's milk.	Crumble on Greek salad or bake in filo pastry.
Ricotta (Italy)	Unripened firm mass of moist cheese; unsalted, milky; cow or sheep.	Ravioli or cannelloni filling.
Mozzarella di Bufala (Italy)	Moist, milky, delicate and stringy; sweet, fresh and nutty (not like mass-produced mozzarella used on pizza); buffalo.	Caprese salad (layers of mozzarella, ripe tomato, basil, extra-virgin olive oil and salt).
Chèvre (France: Loire)	Soft, but not completely smooth; nutty, tangy and aromatic; goat.	Spread on crostini as appetiser; serve lightly breaded and baked, with green salad.
Crescenza (Italy: Lombardy)	Wet and soft; rich, clean acidity; cow.	Sprinkle with herbs and spread on crusty bread.
Paneer (India)	Slightly firm, pale yellow; mild; cow or goat.	Deep-fried, barbecued in a tandoori, simmered with spinach.
Halloumi (Cyprus)	Firm; tangy, salty; cow, goat or sheep.	Skewered with crispy vegetables and barbecued.
Natural Rind		
Crottin de Chavignol (France: Loire)	Deeply wrinkled, almost brittle interior; distinctly goaty, intense and sharp; goat.	Best enjoyed on cheese board.
Perail (France)	Thin, crusty rind with pale ivory interior; moist, young, milky and nutty; sheep.	Best enjoyed on cheese board.
Chèvrefeuille (France: Perigord)	Shiny white interior; herb-infused, often wrapped in chestnut leaves; goat.	Best enjoyed on cheese board.
Soft-white Rind		
Brie (France)	Slightly dry, edible white rind, with creamy, golden interior; buttery and rich; cow.	Best enjoyed at end of meal.
Camembert (France: Normandy)	Supple, creamy and smooth interior; buttery and rich; cow.	Best enjoyed at end of meal.

TYPE OF CHEESE	TEXTURE; TASTE; ANIMAL'S MILK	SUGGESTED USE
Semisoft		
Reblochon (France)	Dark golden rind with creamy-soft interior; delicate flavour; cow.	Delicious paired with fruit for dessert.
Gouda and Edam (Holland)	Yellow or red wax rind, semisoft interior; mellow and savoury; cow.	Perfect paired with dark beer.
Taleggio (Italy: Lombardy)	Pale yellow with wax coating or thin mould; rich, buttery and runny when aged; cow.	Thinly sliced on salads.
Blue		
Stilton (England) (see 284 Buy a Real Stilton)	Slightly crumbly pale-yellow interior with blue-green veins and crusty brown rind; rich and creamy, slightly pungent and sharp; cow.	Best on cheese board or at end of meal.
Gorgonzola (Italy)	Ivory-coloured interior predominantly streaked with blue vein; savoury, creamy and salty; cow.	Pair with pears and walnuts on salads or sprinkle on thin-crust pizza.
Roquefort (France)	Creamy white interior with round blue veins and white rind; pungent, strong, salty; sheep.	Creamy salad dressings or at end of meal with slightly sweet dessert wine.
Hard		
Parmesan (Italy)	Brittle and granular; salty, nutty and sharp; cow.	Thinly sliced on grilled asparagus or grated into pastas, soups and sauces.
Cheddar (England)	Firm, dry and brittle; ranging from mild and sweet to tangy and sharp; cow.	With crisp apples on cheese board.
Pecorino (Italy)	Smooth to brittle and granular; salty, fruity and nutty; sheep; Romano type is aged 8 to 12 months, Sardo 1 to 12 months and Toscano 1 to 3 months.	Shave all three on pastas or salads.
Manchego (Spain)	Firm, smooth and golden; mellow, nutty and peppery; sheep.	Best served on cheese board.
Gruyère (Switzerland)	Golden rind and firm, golden interior; sweet, nutty and rich; cow.	Grated as topping for gratins.
WARNINGS	Cheeses that have passed their prime may smell strongly of ammonia.	
	Pregnant women shouldn't eat unpasteurised cheeses because of the harmful bacteria they may carry, which can cause foetal distress or miscarriage.	

289 Purchase Kosher Food

Keeping kosher means far more than not eating bacon. The Jewish dietary laws, called *kashruth,* require that food be grown, harvested and cooked in adherence with the kosher way. For instance, strict butchering laws demand that the animal be killed swiftly and humanely in a prescribed way that immediately cuts off blood pressure to the brain. Non-Jews also benefit. For example, vegetarians can be assured that an item designated *pareve* will not be made with any meat products.

Steps

1 Shop at a certified kosher butcher, grocer or bakery. These are easier to find in some cities than others.

2 Check if your supermarket stocks any kosher products.

3 Ask other members of the Jewish community and the synagogue for advice on where to shop.

4 Shop online and have foods delivered. Waitrose, through ocado.com, stocks a range of kosher foods. If you're willing to shop further afield, buy Jewish food from Israel at a-zara.com and have it delivered to your home.

5 If you're looking for a kosher meal while travelling, search for restaurants in databases like mail-jewish.org/krestquery.html. Kosher food is more readily available in the United States, particularly in the major cities such as Chicago, Los Angeles and New York. Disneyland and Disney World also have many kosher products available.

What to Look For

- Kosher shops
- Recommendations
- Mainstream products
- Symbols
- Websites
- Urban areas
- Kosher restaurants

Tip

You can often specify a kosher meal on an airline.

290 Buy Sensibly in Supermarkets

Do you routinely come back from your weekly or fortnightly big supermarket shop with a host of items you know you'll never use or a pile of fruit it's impossible to get through before some of it has become shrivelled or mouldy? You need to wise up in your approach to supermarket shopping to reduce waste and save money into the bargain.

Steps

1 Before you set off make a list of all that you need. Take a pencil with you and tick off each item as you select it. Do not be tempted to buy anything that is not on your list – no matter how attractively packaged or cheap – unless you see something you usually buy and use but have simply forgotten to put on your list.

2 Buy only a minimum of fresh fruit and vegetables at the supermarket. Supermarkets display their perfect-looking fruit and vegetables just inside the entrance because they have a huge mark-up on them. You can buy perfectly good fruit and veg from street markets more cheaply. It may not look quite so pristine but it will taste just as good once you've peeled the skin off.

3 Do not buy perishables in bulk: cuts of meat, dairy products, fish and bread all have a very limited shelf life, whether in the supermarket fridge or your own.

4 Check the sell-by dates on persishable goods. Goods with the closest sell-by date will invariably be at the front of the shelf at eye level. Search back through the shelf or look on the top shelf, and you'll find packs with more distant dates on them, which have arrived more recently.

5 Be selective in taking advantage of "two for one" offers. Such offers are only a bargain if you and your family are happy to consume the product before the sell-by date. That second packet of sausages might simply take up space in the fridge for a week before being consigned to the bin.

6 Buy supermarket own-brand products. Many, such as cornflakes or pasta, are exactly the same as the branded variety in taste and quality but are considerably cheaper.

7 Stock up on non-perishables. For basic store-cupboard items you can't beat the supermarket for value for money. Canned products, such as baked beans and chopped tomatoes, are good for about a year, so buy in bulk, taking advantage of any "buy six for the price of five" offers. Purchase basic household items, such as toilet paper and washing powder, in quantity: twelve toilet rolls in a pack will be cheaper per roll than two.

8 Buy your alcohol at the supermarket unless there is a wine warehouse nearby. Wine, beer and spirits are all generally cheaper at the supermarket than at the off-licence. Take advantage of any special offers, such as 10 per cent off if you buy six bottles of wine or a case of beer.

What to Look For

- Discounts on bulk purchases of non-perishables
- Sell-by dates
- Strategic placement of high-margin goods

Tips

See 265 "Buy Organic Produce" to find out how to get boxes of seasonal fruits and vegetables delivered to your door.

Paper products, nappies, party supplies and cleaning products are all prime for bulk buying because they're much costlier in small quantities and they never go off.

If you go to the same supermarket regularly ask about their loyalty card, such as the Nectar card offered by Sainsbury and the Clubcard offered by Tesco.

Warnings

Watch out for extra items being thrown into the trolley by accompanying children. They will often be tempted by attractive packaging or branded goods, which are expensive and you do not wish them to consume!

Do not feel you have to fill your trolley. There's no shame in heading for the check-out with a half-empty trolley if you've bought all that you needed.

291 Choose Cooking Oils

Some oils have a low smoking point, meaning they'll burn at lower temperatures. Others, like vegetable oil, can reach high temperatures without smoking, so they're great for deep-frying and sautéing. After you decide which oil is best for your cooking method, consider how much flavour you'd like to add to your dish. Grapeseed oil will lend the least amount of flavour to your deep-fried foods, while peanut oil imbues foods with a rich, nutty, roasted taste. (See 269 "Decipher Food Labels" and 292 "Select Olive Oil".)

OIL	RECOMMENDED USE	FLAVOUR LEVEL	SMOKING POINT
Corn	Pan-frying, deep-frying	High	High
Grapeseed	Deep-frying, pan-frying, sautéing	Low	Very High
Peanut	Stir-frying, wok cooking, deep-frying	High	High
Safflower	Deep-frying, pan-frying, sautéing, baking	Low to medium	High
Sesame	Wok cooking, dressings, finishing flavour	High	Low
Sunflower	Deep-frying, pan-frying, sautéing	Low to medium	High
Vegetable	Deep-frying, pan-frying, sautéing, baking	Low	High

292 Select Olive Oil

In Mediterranean countries, such as Italy, Spain and Greece, olive groves can be seen on nearly every countryside property, and families meet in collectives to press and bottle the combined fruits of their labour. As with wine, the characteristics of olive oil depend on the soil and climate where the trees are grown, the type of olives pressed (see 293 Select Olives) and the method of pressing.

Steps

1 Look at the colour. Green oils, made from early-harvested olives, are fruity, peppery and ripe. Yellow-gold oils taste buttery and smooth. You'll benefit from the increased polyphenols and other antioxidants in green oil, but it's mostly a matter of preference.

2 Ask to taste olive oils at an up-market grocer or delicatessen to find a flavour you like.

3 Choose extra-virgin olive oil, obtained from the first cold pressing of the olives, for most of your cooking needs. For frying, use virgin olive oil, which will impart less flavour, is less expensive and won't burn as easily as extra-virgin olive oil.

What to Look For

- Colour
- Taste
- Extra-virgin and virgin
- Filtered and unfiltered
- Price
- Websites and catalogues

Tips

Avoid light olive oil; it's diluted and flavourless, and the term *light* is meaningless. It has the same number of calories as other olive oils, about 125 per tablespoon.

4 Find a filtered olive oil for sautéing and roasting, and an unfiltered olive oil for salad dressings and to drizzle on soups or pastas.

5 Cruise the web for olive oils from all over Europe.

6 Store oils in a cool, dark place. Olive oils are a fresh food and can go rancid. Life span can be as little as three months for an unfiltered, late-harvest olive oil bottled in clear glass, to four years for an early-harvest, filtered oil packaged in a well-sealed tin or dark bottle and properly stored.

Make your own infused olive oils by simply putting herbs or lemon zest in a bottle and fill with a mild-flavoured olive oil.

293 Select Olives

Cultivated in arid grape-growing regions, olives vary greatly in colour and flavour, depending on how ripe they are when picked and the method of processing. Olives can be a part of a charcuterie board and enliven innumerable cooked dishes. They're also a natural finger-food pairing with a glass of wine.

SOURCE	VARIETY	CHARACTERISTICS	FLAVOUR
Italy	Calabrese	Dull green and cracked.	Similar to Sicilian type, but mellower.
	Gaeta	Dark, small and wilted.	Earthy and milky-oily, with herbal note.
	Ligurian	Dark brown to black.	Deep and flavourful.
	Sicilian	Cracked and green.	Sharp and bitter with flavourful punch.
France	Lucques	Small and dark.	Flavourful and distinct.
	Niçoise	Shiny, small, dense pit.	Provençal herbal flavour.
	Picholine	Medium green.	Bright, salty and crisp.
Greece	Kalamata	Fleshy, dark and shiny.	Rich and salty.
	Nafplion	Dark green.	Fruity and dense.
Lebanon	Lebanese Black	Smooth, medium-size, glossy brown and black.	Pleasant, intense earthy taste.
Morocco	Moroccan	Black dry-cured, salt-cured or oil-cured.	Earthy and acidic.
Spain	Gordal	Large, green.	Pleasantly meaty texture.

294 Buy Ethnic Ingredients

Why do Indian dhals and Thai curries taste so much better at ethnic restaurants? Because of the quality and authenticity of the ingredients. If you want to re-create the flavours of your favourite cuisine, buy authentic condiments, grains and spices. The real thing makes all the difference in the world.

INGREDIENT	SOURCE	COMMON USES	WHERE TO FIND
Banana Leaves	Mexico, Thailand	Wrap around seasoned fish or meat, and grill or steam.	Grocer's frozen section; Asian markets.
Cardamom	Africa, India	Used in chai tea. The world's second most expensive spice after saffron, black cardamom is used to spice meat or rice, while green cardamom is often used in desserts.	Premium black and green: Indian grocer; ordinary whole and ground green: supermarket's spice aisle.
Chilli Paste	Thailand, China	A spicy condiment in Thai soups and noodle dishes.	Supermarket's Asian ingredients aisle; Chinese markets.
Coconut Milk	Africa, Thailand, Philippines	Used in lemongrass and chicken soup, coconut rice and to braise shrimp. Low-fat coconut milk also available.	Supermarket's Asian ingredients aisle, or with canned foods.
Cumin	Africa, India, Middle East, Mexico	White (or ordinary) cumin, or black, which is smaller and sweeter. Whole seeds provide better flavour. Roast in a skillet and grind in a spice grinder or clean coffee grinder. Part of typical curry blend.	Indian grocer; supermarket spice aisles.
Dhal	India	*Chana* is split and husked chickpeas with a sweet aroma and flavour. *Masoor* is tiny pink lentils, but red or brown lentils may be substituted. *Toor* is pale yellow husked and split Indian lentils; don't buy the oily variety, which is treated with castor oil.	Yellow, pink, red and brown lentils widely available in larger grocer; *chana* and *toor dhal* found at Indian markets.
Fish Sauce, Thai Fish Oil	China, Thailand, Philippines, Vietnam	Used extensively in Southeast Asian soups, dressing or sauces. Made from salted, fermented fish.	Asian ingredients aisle or sold as *nam pla* (Thai) or *nuoc nam* (Vietnamese) at Asian markets.
Five-Spice Powder	China	An aromatic blend consisting of cinnamon, fennel seed, cloves, star anise and Szechuan peppercorns. Used as marinade or spice for meats and fish.	Supermarket spice aisle or Asian markets.

INGREDIENT	SOURCE	COMMON USES	WHERE TO FIND
Garam Masala	India	Widely used Indian spice blend contains cardamom, cumin, cinnamon, cloves and black pepper. Add to soups, curries and lentil dishes.	Indian markets or supermarket's spice aisle.
Hoisin Sauce	China	Sweet, syrupy sauce used in marinades and sauces for meat, poultry and seafood dishes. Refrigerate bottled hoisin.	Supermarkets and Asian markets.
Kaffir Lime Leaves	Thailand, Burma, Laos	Aromatic essential for Thai soups and curries. Refrigerate leaves stored in a plastic bag for weeks, or freeze them for two to three months.	Asian markets.
Lemongrass	Thailand	Crucial for Thai soups and curries. Lemongrass has all the bright flavour of lemon without the bite. Look for stalks with plump bases.	With supermarket's fresh herbs or bottled in supermarket's spice aisle; at Asian markets.
Oyster Sauce	China	A syrupy dark-brown sauce consisting of oysters, brine and soy sauce cooked until thick and concentrated. Popular condiment and seasoning for vegetable stir-fries and fried rice.	Supermarkets and Asian markets.
Tahini	Middle East	A ground sesame-seed paste used in hummus and baba ghanoush.	Supermarket (with peanut butter, oils or ethnic ingredients).
Tamarind	India, Middle East	Seed pod of tamarind tree. Extremely sour pulp is popular in marinades, curries and chutneys.	Found in Indian markets and some Asian markets, as well as supermarkets.
Turmeric	Africa, India, Indonesia, Thailand	Fresh turmeric is used in Thai yellow curries. Dried turmeric is found in many Indian dishes, from lentils to vegetables and meats.	Fresh turmeric at Asian markets; dried turmeric at Indian markets and in supermarket's spice aisle.
Udon Noodles	Japan	A thick wheat noodle used in vegetable and meat broth soups.	Fresh or dried in Asian markets.
Wasabi	Japan	A sharp, spicy condiment for sushi. Also called *Japanese horseradish*.	Asian markets in both paste and powder.
TIP		Shop at ethnic grocery stores and farmers' markets for the freshest ingredients. See 267 "Buy and Sell at Farmers' Markets".	

295 Purchase Vinegar

From mildly acidic to mouth-puckeringly pungent, there's a vast array of vinegars: cider, wine, sherry, rice and balsamic, to name a few. Most varieties cost just £1.50 to £6.50 for 500 ml, but aged balsamic vinegar can get pricey – £50 to £160 for about 75 ml.

Steps

1 Stock your larder with workhorse vinegars such as cider, wine, sherry, malt and balsamic vinegar (see 271 "Stock Your Kitchen with Staples").

2 Shop at a large grocer's or supermarket for a variety of cooking vinegars and less expensive balsamic vinegars.

3 Find a selection of fruit and herb-infused vinegars, and high-quality aged balsamic vinegars by shopping at gourmet food shops and delicatessens.

4 Browse Asian markets for a variety of rice-wine vinegars, sometimes blended with sake vinegar for a nice edge.

5 Let your taste buds convince you of the value of aged balsamic vinegar from Italy. Made from Trebbiano grapes, it gets its sweet rich flavour from ageing 5 to 20 years in wood barrels. Just a tiny bit imparts incredible flavour.

What to Look For

- Versatile vinegars
- Grocer or supermarket
- Delicatessens
- Asian markets
- Aged balsamic vinegar

Tips

For a dessert treat, roast ripe strawberries with a drizzle of balsamic vinegar. The vinegar caramelises the berries into a syrupy liquid, delicious over vanilla ice cream.

Mix together equal parts of salt and white vinegar to remove coffee and tea stains from cups and mugs.

296 Choose Pasta

Holding a place of honour on any athlete's dinner table, pasta makes a quick, delicious meal that you can serve with an endless list of healthy toppings.

Steps

1 Find fresh pastas in a range of flavours in your grocer's refrigerator section or at a local farmers' market or Italian delicatessen.

2 Enjoy high-quality artisanal pastas. Sold at Italian delis or gourmet markets, these pastas are dried over several days.

3 Choose from a variety of surface textures as well as shapes. Sauces stick more to ridged pastas.

4 Stash several boxes of dried pasta in the cupboard for super fast meals. It's typically made with durum wheat or semolina flour, giving it a firmer texture, but may have less flavour due to its fast, high-temperature drying process (60 to 71°C/140 to 160°F).

5 Try your hand at cranking out homemade pasta, using plain flour. Knead the dough with beetroot, lemons, saffron and spinach to infuse flavour.

What to Look For

- Fresh
- Artisanal
- Textured
- Boxed
- Homemade

Tip

The size of the vegetable or meat chunks in your sauce should roughly match the pasta size.

Warning

Store fresh pasta in the refrigerator – it can go rancid.

297 Buy Tea

Tea has moved beyond the white-gloved pinky-high afternoon tea party scene. With one-half to one-third less caffeine than coffee, it's steeped with cancer-fighting antioxidants and is the beverage of choice for much of the world. Look for loose and bagged tea in grocer's shops, tea shops and supermarkets, ranging from £3 to £25 or more for 100 g (quarter of a pound). Here are the teas you are most likely to encounter; many more regional varieties exist.

TEA	VARIETY	COUNTRY	CHARACTERISTICS
Black Tea	Assam	India	Rich, dark and malty. A good alternative for morning coffee drinkers.
	Ceylon	Sri Lanka	Less flowery than Darjeeling. Rich enough to be a morning wake-up cuppa.
	Chai	India	Prepared tea drink of brewed black tea with cinnamon, nutmeg and cardamom, mixed with milk.
	Darjeeling	India	One of the clearest-brewing black teas; delicate and floral. Often called the champagne of teas because of its high quality.
	Earl Grey	China, India, Sri Lanka	Slightly bitter orange; scented with bergamot oil.
	English Breakfast	China, India, Sri Lanka	Full-bodied blend of black teas.
Oolong Tea	Baochong	China (Taiwan)	Floral and elegant.
	Formosa Oolong	China (Taiwan)	Between black and green tea, fruity without being sweet.
Green Tea	Anemone	China	Green peony blossoms yield a fragrant, sweet and nutty brew.
	Jasmine	China	Jasmine-blossom scent.
	Pearl Tea	China (Taiwan)	Strong, dark.
	Sencha	Japan	Herbal yellow-green tea with slightly rich flavour.
White Tea	Silver Needle	China	Delicate and light.
	White Peony	China	Deeper-coloured than silver-needle tea; smooth flavour and subtle fragrance.

298 Buy Coffee

Coffee is one of our favourite legal addictions – the rich scent, full-bodied flavour and jolt of caffeine that everyone from postmen to poets relies on to kick start their morning. Follow this guide to find a daily grind that suits you best.

Steps

1 Select a grind that is suitable for your brewing method or coffee-maker (see 300 "Buy a Coffeemaker or Espresso Machine"). Whole beans retain their flavour better during storage but you will need to have a coffee grinder in your home.

2 Experiment with different roasting techniques. Coffee beans are roasted to remove moisture and add flavour, and different roasts produce different flavours. French roast results in a full-flavoured, dark bean. Italian roast is usually medium dark. Anything lighter is usually identified simply as medium or light roast.

3 Decipher labels. Estate beans are grown and processed on a single farm. Some brands achieve a consistent flavour by blending beans from various sources. Flavoured coffees are infused with liquid agents, such as chocolate, vanilla or nuts, but typically don't start with the highest-quality beans.

4 Buy coffee from a knowledgeable source. Premium roasters, like winemakers, are very proud of their blends. Beans weighing 450 g (1 lb) from a gourmet shop range from £5 to £20 but are of unbeatable quality. Bettys and Taylors of Harrogate run a mail-order service at bettysbypost.com.

5 Turn your coffee drinking into an entertaining research project by studying the general characteristics of different coffee producing regions. Coffee comes from many countries and coffee-growing regions. While it's true that soil and geography matter, any bean can be roasted in different ways, resulting in many possible flavour and blend combinations. Also, pay attention to prices, which are subject to fluctuation. For example, strong demand for Kenyan beans may drive the price up while similar beans from another region may be available for much less.

- Arabian: Often called *mocha,* this coffee is one of the most ancient, with a medium to full body, rich flavour and dry aftertaste, and chocolate tones.

- Brazilian: A medium to moderately dark roast that goes down sweet and smooth.

- Colombian: Full-bodied, fruity and acidic, with a dark roast.

- Costa Rican: Dry and medium-bodied, with a dark roast.

- Ethiopian: Sweet, medium-bodied and fruity, with a dark roast.

- Hawaiian: Delicate, dry, slightly sweet and subtle, with a medium to moderately dark roast.

What to Look For

- Suitable grind
- The right roast
- Estate beans
- Blends
- Speciality coffee beans
- Coffee beans grown in different regions

Tips

"Fair-trade coffee" is a new term and describes the effort to raise the incomes of coffee growers in developing countries.

Organic coffees are increasingly available.

- Kenyan: Dry and acidic, with a moderately dark to dark roast.

- Sumatran: Full-bodied and slightly fermented, with a dark roast.

- Light roast: Many areas produce beans suitable for light roasting, although Central American coffees frequently show up in light roasts.

- Decaffeinated: You would be hard pushed to tell the difference in flavour between decaffeinated coffee and the real, pulse-racing thing. It's usually available as medium roast only.

299 Order a Great Cup of Coffee

A "tall, skinny single" might sound like a supermodel, but it's actually just a cup of coffee. Brush up on the latest latte lingo and in no time you'll be speaking like an experienced coffee connoisseur, whether you stick to a straight-up cup of black coffee or dabble in flavoured and foamed concoctions.

TERM	TRANSLATION
Filter	Brewed coffee.
Espresso	Powerful brew resulting from steam forced through packed ground coffee. Look for rich brown "crema" on top.
Café au Lait	Equal parts brewed coffee and hot milk.
Café Latte	Espresso with steamed milk.
Cappuccino	Latte with milk foam on top.
Café Macchiato	Espresso with a hint of milk foam.
Café con Panna	Espresso topped with whipped cream.
Cafe Americano	Espresso with a dash of hot water.
Half-caff	Espresso made with half caffeinated and half decaffeinated beans.
Mocha Latte	Latte with cocoa, topped with whipped cream.
Skinny	Any coffee drink with low-fat milk instead of whole milk.
Single, Double, Triple or Quad	The number of espresso shots (one, two, three or four) in a drink.
Short, Tall, Grande	Small, medium, large cups (respectively).
Vanilla, Caramel, Hazelnut	Flavoured syrups that can be added to a coffee drink.
Irish Coffee	Coffee with a shot of Irish whiskey, double cream and three sugar cubes.

300 Buy a Coffeemaker or Espresso Machine

Brewing the perfect cup can start your morning off right, while downing a burned cup can make you walk sideways for hours. What type of machine is right for you depends on how rich you like your coffee, how much kitchen worktop space you have and how much you consume.

Steps

1 Consider how much coffee you drink to determine whether you want a 4-cup or as big as a 12-cup machine. The price of coffeemakers varies greatly – anywhere from £50 for a basic model to £650 for one that grinds your beans, makes both filter coffee and espresso, froths the milk and has a timer.

2 Want the best flavour? Go for an espresso pot, which makes black espresso on your cooker hob (without foam or froth), or a cafetiere, which makes thick and sometimes grainy coffee by hand. Filter coffeemakers are becoming more refined as well.

3 Determine if you have the space and cash for a big, gleaming piston-style espresso machine, or should you buy a compact and economical Krups espresso maker? Espresso machines can run from £65 to £350, and start at around £650 for professional and stainless-steel piston types.

What to Look For

- Cup size
- Timer
- Two-in-one machine
- Flavour
- Pro and basic models
- Space savers

Tip

A good cup of coffee or espresso has as much to do with the quality of water and beans, and the fineness of the grind, as it does with the machine. If the espresso is • too fine, you won't get a topping of rich, brown "crema" in your cup.

301 Purchase Party Beer

Getting in your supplies for a celebratory bash needn't break the bank or be a hard slog. With planning, you can buy just the right amount of beer and not have to carry it all the way home with you.

Steps

1 Locate an off-licence or drinks warehouse in your area that sells tins or bottles by the case, and find out what's available. Do this at least one week in advance, in case they need to make a special order.

2 Decide how much beer you need – you know how much your friends are likely to drink – and whether you want just lager or bitter and lager. Cases usually consist of 24 bottles or cans, but they do vary in size, from 275 ml to 500 ml, according to the make of beer. The alcohol content can vary, too. Belgian beers tend to have the highest alcoholic content.

3 Order online through sites such as Majestic (majestic.co.uk), which offers free delivery and chiller bin loan.

4 Get your supplies home. Some shops will deliver for you; otherwise, get some heavy-lifters to help you hoist everything to the party.

What to Look For

- Off licence or drinks warehouse
- Type of beer
- Alcohol percentage
- Delivery

Tip

Some suppliers will lend glasses free of charge.

302 Choose the Right Wine

Whether you want to celebrate a special occasion with a fantasic meal out with a quality wine, you want to give someone a wonderful birthday bottle, or simply that you want to complement a particular dish with the right wine, you need first-hand experience to get it right.

Steps

1 Educate yourself about wine. Contact the Wine and Spirit Education Trust (wset.co.uk) and ask about their courses. The Trust develops and manages vocational qualifications for the wine and spirit and related industries. They offer courses from a Level 1 Foundation certificate up to degree level. You can attend on a day release scheme as a full-time student or at evening classes. All classes involve wine-tasting sessions.

2 Decide whether you want to choose a wine to accompany food or to drink on its own. If it is a present, consider the tastes of the recipient: does he/she generally prefer white or red wine, dry or sweet, full-bodied or light?

3 Decide how much money you are willing to pay. Excellent wines can set you back at least £25 but there are some good wines to be had for £10 to £20. Ask the owner of your off-licence for advice within your price range.

What to Look For

- WSET courses in your area
- Friendly off-licence owner
- Wine within your price range

Tips

Read about the different wine regions and grape varieties – subscribe to *Decanter* magazine for all the latest wine news.

Experiment with a range of wines, building up a personal taste on which to draw.

303 Choose a Real Ale

You don't have to wear sandals and a cardigan to be a real ale aficionado; today fans of real ale are as diverse as the beer itself. Real ale is now available in most supermarkets but there's a large number that still have a relatively low profile. Before you down that next pint, research the many varieties out there. Of course, it's a tough job, but someone has to do it.

Steps

1 Join the Campaign for Real Ale (CAMRA) to increase your knowledge of real ale and discover new ones to try. Visit its website (camra.org.uk).

2 Read up on the different real ales in the Good Beer Guide, arguably the best place to find good pubs and good beer. Compiled by volunteers from CAMRA, it gives up-to-date information on beers and breweries around the country.

3 Keep in mind that some specialist beers contain slightly more alcohol than major beer brands.

What to Look For

- Type of beer
- Beers and pubs recommended by CAMRA
- Alcohol content

304 Order a Cocktail

Whether you prefer yours shaken, not stirred, classic cocktails from the 1920s, '30s and '40s have made a comeback. Order up a dry martini or a sidecar next time you're out on the town and enjoy.

Steps

1 Familiarise yourself with the vocabulary. *Neat* means served with no ice and not mixed; *on the rocks* means poured over ice. *Shaken* means the ingredients are poured into a shaker with ice, mixed vigorously and poured into a glass. In a *stirred* drink, the ice and ingredients are put in a mixing glass and stirred for ten seconds before they're poured into a glass. Drinks served *straight up* have no ice.

2 Name your brand. If you don't designate what type of alcohol you want in your cocktail, you'll get the least expensive brands. You can designate top-shelf brands, such as Grey Goose vodka or Bombay Sapphire gin. For example, order a Grey Goose Greyhound or a Grey Goose and grapefruit juice for a top-shelf, and more expensive, cocktail.

What to Look For

- Correct terminology
- Seasonal or speciality drinks

Warning

It's never easier to drink too much than when you're drinking cocktails.

TERM	DESCRIPTION
Aperitif	A beverage, usually alcohol-based, drunk prior to a meal to stimulate the appetite.
Collins	A drink made with a base spirit, lime or lemon juice, simple syrup and club soda. Always served in Collins glasses, usually garnished with fresh fruit.
Fizz	A drink made with a base spirit, lime or lemon juice, simple syrup and club soda. Served straight up in a wine goblet.
Highball	A simple mixed drink consisting of two ingredients (such as gin and tonic water) combined directly in the serving glass, typically a highball glass.
Liqueur	An alcoholic beverage, sometimes called a cordial, made from a spirit, a sweetening agent such as sugar or honey (or both) and additional flavourings.
Rickey	A drink made with a base spirit, fresh lime juice and club soda. Traditionally served over ice in a highball glass, garnished with a wedge of lime.
Sour	A drink composed of a base spirit, lemon juice, and simple syrup. Served straight up in a Sour glass, garnished with a maraschino cherry and an orange wheel.
Spirit	An alcoholic beverage made by distilling a fermented mash of grains or fruits to a potency of at least 40 per cent alcohol by volume. Examples include brandy, gin, rum, tequila, vodka and whisky.
Toddy	A drink made with a base spirit, hot water and various spices. Served in Irish Coffee glasses, often garnished with a lemon twist or cinnamon stick.

305 Choose a Restaurant for a Business Function

When you're wining and dining clients at a business lunch or dinner, match the venue and food to the style of your business function. Is it a brainstorming lunch with colleagues, a yearly review with an employee or a dinner with an important client? Pick the right venue and menu, and get the job done right.

Steps

1 Set your budget. Most businesses have a cap on event expenditures. Look at the price range of each restaurant that's in the running, and factor in beverages and tip.

2 Get the restaurants to send you a menu so that you can evaluate your options. Choose one that serves a variety of choices or traditional favourites (chicken, meat, fish and vegetarian dishes), where all of your guests will find something they enjoy.

3 Visit the restaurants where you're considering holding the event. Look for appropriate space to mingle before the meal starts (for evening affairs), take the noise level into consideration, inspect the toilets, read the wine list and check out the seating arrangements.

4 Note how far the restaurant is from your office and work out how everyone will get there. Is there a car park? Convenience is key if you need to maximise available time, particularly for lunch.

5 Make a reservation. Request a special area of the restaurant, or better yet, ask for a private room or banqueting hall if you have a large group.

6 Consider setting up seating ahead of time. Decide who sits where. Pair dining partners strategically, facilitate access between key people, and show respect to the top dogs.

7 Decide whether you'll have a set menu meal served or have guests order off the à la carte menu. If you're putting together a special menu, you may want to ask clients or business colleagues if they have any food allergies or dietary restrictions.

What to Look For

- Price
- Food
- Amenities
- Location
- Parking
- Reservations
- Private rooms
- Menu

Tip

Never order for everyone in the group, unless it's a set menu meal you've set up prior to the event. Otherwise, let everyone order for himself or herself.

306 Stock a Wine Cellar

Wines can be collected like rare books and enjoyed after they've acquired some age, or enjoyed immediately. If you're starting a wine collection, formulate a strategy based on how much you drink, what type of wine you enjoy and how much you're prepared to spend.

Steps

1 Start with a small inventory of 50 to 100 bottles, including two cases (12 bottles each) of wine for ageing and a case of your favourite drinking wine, either white or red.

2 Taste, taste, taste! Tasting wines will help you discover your personal preference. Avoid buying wines just because they received a high rating from professionals or friends. See if you like them before you make an investment.

3 Balance your inventory. Indulge in one or two wines you particularly enjoy, and mix in bottles of other varietals and regions to suit guests' palates.

4 Save by stocking up on ageing wines in their youth when prices are lower. Talk to a reputable wine merchant and get suggestions on particular wines that would benefit from ageing. Bordeaux, Barolo and Brunello usually take up to ten years of ageing and can be purchased for a song (£10 to £15 a bottle) in their infancy. Some whites, such as grand cru and premier cru white Burgundy, high-quality white Bordeaux, German Riesling, Sauternes and Gewürztraminer, can benefit from ageing as well.

5 Add several bottles of aperitifs and dessert wines. Dry sherry, champagne and sparkling wine suit late-afternoon sipping. Sauternes, vintage port and late-harvest Rieslings offer an after-dinner treat. See 60 "Select Good Champagne".

6 Draw the line on buying more than a case of wine if it's a new vintage or blend with no proven track record for ageing; the merchant won't be able to give you an accurate estimate of how long to hold onto it before drinking.

7 Know what you own and be able to find it quickly. Make a database of your cellar's inventory. Give each wine a location number and listing, and include the wine's name, vintage, producer, appellation, vineyard name, region, country, type (red, white, rosé, sparkling and so forth), quantity owned, price paid per bottle, value (latest estimated worth), and size of bottle (half-bottle, magnum and so on).

8 Keep the temperature of your wine cupboard, refrigerator or cellar between 10 and 18°C (50 and 65°F) for reds, and 7 to 15°C (45 to 60°F) for whites, or as directed by the vintner or wine merchant.

What to Look For

- Taste
- Balance inventory
- Deals
- Ageing-worthy whites
- Aperitif and dessert wines
- Track record
- Cellar log
- Storage temperature

Tips

Buy half-bottles of champagne and dessert wine if you're not likely to finish them off in one sitting – they don't keep well.

Nice, everyday white wines include Sauvignon Blanc, simple white Burgundy, Chardonnay and Pinot Grigio; everyday reds include Zinfandel, Pinot Noir, Barbera, Beaujolais, Merlot and simple Bordeaux.

Red wines particularly benefit from a few years of ageing: Bordeaux, grand cru or premier cru Burgundy, big Italian reds like Barbaresco and Brunello di Montalcino, Rioja, Cabernet Sauvignon and Côte Rôtie.

Warning

Wines left to age for too long can go rancid, causing the wine to slowly turn to vinegar.

307 Stock Your Bar

Shaken, stirred, on the rocks or straight up with a twist, the cocktails you mix and serve will depend on your mood and the event (casual get-together or elegant soirée). With a few recipes and a fully stocked bar, you can become the mixologist of the moment, from lemon drops to bourbon on the rocks.

ALCOHOL

Essentials	Extras
Amaretto	Apricot brandy
Anisette	Chambord
Bourbon	Crème de cacao
Brandy	Crème de cassis
Gin	Crème de menthe
Grand Marnier	Midori
Irish cream liqueur	Peach schnapps
Kahlúa	Peppermint schnapps
Rum, dark or spiced	Sambuca
Scotch whisky	
Tequila	
Triple sec	
Vermouth, sweet and dry	
Vodka	
Whiskey, Canadian and Irish	

MIXERS

Essentials	Extras
Bitters	Grenadine
Coffee	Ice cream
Cola	Lemonade
Cranberry juice	Lime cordial
Ginger ale	Milk
Grapefruit juice	Single cream
Lemon juice (fresh)	Sweet-and-sour mix
Lime juice (fresh)	
Orange juice	
Pineapple juice	
Soda water	
Sugar	
Tabasco	
Tomato juice	
Tonic	
Water	
Worcester sauce	

GARNISHES

Essentials	Extras
Celery	Crystallised sugar
Cocktail onions	Maraschino cherries
Cocoa powder	Mint (fresh)
Horseradish	Pineapple
Lemons	Raspberries
Limes	Strawberries
Martini olives	Whipped cream
Nutmeg	
Oranges	
Pepper	
Salt, coarse and fine	

GADGETS

Essentials	Extras
Bar towels	Coasters
Blender	Cocktail picks
Bottle opener	Cocktail napkins
Cocktail shaker	Cocktail umbrellas
Corkscrew	Stirrers
Glasses (highball, cocktail, martini, margarita)	
Ice bucket and tongs	
Jigger	
Lemon squeezer and zester	
Margarita jug	
Strainer	

Family Affairs

308 Donate Sperm

For those gentlemen who want to take a hands-on approach to helping someone conceive, these tips will help the process go swimmingly. Donating sperm is not a route to riches, though: the most you'll receive is £15 plus reasonable expenses for each sample you give.

Steps

1 Make sure that you are eligible to be a sperm donor. The HFEA (Human Fertilisation & Embryology Authority – hfea.gov.uk), which regulates fertility services in the UK, stipulates that donors must be between the ages of 18 and 45, healthy and free from sexually transmitted infections and certain genetic defects.

2 Contact the HFEA for a free copy of their Directory of Clinics or download it from their website. All licensed clinics are regulated and inspected by the HFEA. They must offer proper screening, which involves the sperm being frozen and quarantined for at least six months before it can be used for treatment, so that any infections, such as HIV, can be detected.

3 Find a clinic in your area that recruits sperm donors. Before being accepted as a donor, you will be offered counselling to help you understand the implications of sperm donation, although you do not have to accept this offer. You must also give written consent for your sperm to be used and stored. Your personal details (name and date of birth), as well as non-identifying information such as eye and hair colour, will be retained by the clinic and also recorded in the HFEA's confidential information register.

4 Know your rights. Under existing regulations sperm donors remain anonymous, although a planned change in the law will mean that children born after 1 April 2005 as a result of sperm donation will be able to find out the identity of the donor when they reach 18. Anyone donating sperm before April 2005 will remain anonymous. Men who donate sperm through HFEA-licensed clinics are not regarded as the legal parents of any children born as a result of their donation.

What to Look For

- Clinics holding an operating licence from the HFEA.

Tip

Donors are usually "retired" after ten successful births.

Warning

Web-based fresh sperm donation services are unlicensed by the HFEA, which means that there is no guarantee that donated sperm is properly screened. These services also cannot guarantee that a donor will not be regarded as the legal parent of a child born as a result of sperm donation.

309 Choose an Ovulation Predictor Kit

You've made that big decision – you want to get pregnant. Many couples conceive within a year simply by no longer using birth control. Help pinpoint the 24- to 48-hour stretch in your cycle when you are most fertile (right before you ovulate) with an ovulation predictor kit.

Steps

1 Buy a box of test sticks. They work by detecting the surge of luteinizing hormone present in your urine, which in turn triggers ovulation within 24 hours. Each box contains five to seven sticks, since it may take several days for the luteinizing hormone to build up to a detectible amount. An average kit is good for one cycle, checking once a day. Popular brands are the Clear Plan Home Ovulation Test and First Response.

2 Reusable electronic test kits are not yet available over the counter in the UK, although they can be bought on the internet. These have been found to be more sensitive than standard ovulation test kits in consumer trials in the US. The Clear Plan Easy Fertility Monitor utilises disposable test sticks that you place into the unit, which analyses and stores the data for you.

Tip

The tests are convenient and easy to use if you follow the directions. Some even come with a free pregnancy test as an added bonus.

310 Pick a Pregnancy Test Kit

Think you might be expecting? A home predictor kit will provide a prompt – and private – answer. These kits detect with 97 per cent accuracy whether the "pregnancy" hormone, human chorionic gonadotropin (hGC), is present in a woman's urine. Most tests work in much the same way, but vary in sensitivity.

Steps

1 Buy an early-response kit to test on or before the first day of your missed period; Clear Blue is one of the most popular brands. However, no test will pick up all pregnancies that early. You can expect a more reliable result a few days or even a week later, when the rapidly increasing hormone level is easier to detect.

2 Read the instructions. Some tests have you pass the stick through the urine stream, while with others you collect urine in a cup, then dip the stick. Many kits allow both and take five minutes or less – but they're the longest minutes of your life!

3 Make sure the result is easy to understand. Any line that appears on the absorbent wick inside the test stick should be strong and clear. If it's not, you'll need to wait a day or two and test again. Twin-packs are cheaper than buying two single kits individually.

What to Look For

- Accuracy
- Ease of use
- Clear, easy-to-understand results

Warning

It's possible to get a false negative result when you're actually pregnant (positive). If your period does not start within a week, test yourself again. If pregnancy symptoms persist despite a second negative test, see your doctor.

311 Choose Birth Control

Not ready for a visit from the stork? While only abstinence is 100 per cent effective at preventing pregnancy, most types of birth control are very reliable when used correctly. You'll need to discuss the options with your health care provider, but these guidelines will help you narrow your choices to find a method that works for you and your lifestyle.

TYPE (BRAND)	HOW IT WORKS	FEATURES
Male Condom	Blocks the sperm from reaching the egg. 86 to 98 per cent effective.	Only latex and polyurethane condoms are proven to help protect against STDs, including HIV. Buy at a chemist's. Can be used only once.
Female Condom (Femidom)	Keeps sperm from entering the body. Made of polyurethane, is packaged with a lubricant. 79 to 95 per cent effective.	Protects against STDs, including HIV. Can be inserted up to 24 hours prior to sexual intercourse. Buy at a chemist's. Visible, noisy, may be difficult to insert and remove.
Oral Contraceptives	Taken daily, the Pill's hormones (oestrogen and progestogen) block the release of eggs from the ovaries. 95 to 99.9 per cent effective.	Lightens menstrual flow and protects against pelvic inflammatory disease (PID), ovarian cancer and endometrial cancer. Does not protect against STDs or HIV. May add to risk of heart disease, including high blood pressure, blood clots and blockage of the arteries. Women who are over age 35 and smoke, or have a history of blood clots or breast or endometrial cancer, may be advised not to take the Pill. Requires a prescription.
Mini-pill	Only has progestogen, unlike the Pill, which also has oestrogen. Taken daily, prevents sperm from reaching the egg. Prevents a fertilised egg from implanting. 95 to 99.9 per cent effective.	Can decrease period flow and protect against PID, and ovarian and endometrial cancer. OK for breastfeeding women. Good option for women who can't take oestrogen or who have a risk of blood clots. Does not protect against STDs or HIV. Requires a prescription.
Copper T IUD	T-shaped intrauterine device placed inside the uterus. Releases a small amount of a hormone that blocks pregnancy. Contains copper, which stops sperm. If fertilisation does occur, IUD prevents implantation. 99 per cent effective.	Can stay in the uterus for up to 10 years. Does not protect against STDs or HIV. Requires visit to a health care provider for insertion and removal.
Progestasert IUD	Plastic T-shaped intrauterine device placed inside the uterus. Contains progesterone, which prevents sperm from reaching the egg. 98 per cent effective.	Can stay in the uterus for one year. Requires fitting and follow-up visits with health care provider.

TYPE (BRAND)	HOW IT WORKS	FEATURES
Intrauterine System (Mirena)	T-shaped device placed inside the uterus. Releases hormone that blocks pregnancy. 99 per cent effective.	Stays in the uterus for up to five years. Does not protect against STDs or HIV. Not all health care providers insert the IUS. Requires follow-up with health care provider.
Injections (Depo-Provera)	Shots of the hormone progestogen in the buttocks or arm every three months. 99.7 per cent effective.	Does not require daily use. Does not protect against STDs or HIV. Requires follow-up with health care provider.
Diaphragm or Cervical Cap	Diaphragm blocks sperm from reaching the egg; inserted inside vagina before intercourse. 80 to 94 per cent effective. Cervical cap is 80 to 90 per cent effective for women who have not given birth, 60 to 80 per cent for women who have.	Spermicides with nonoxynol-9 (available at chemists) will help protect from the STDs gonorrhoea and chlamydia. Some women can be sensitive to nonoxynol-9 and need to use spermicides that do not contain it. Requires health care provider to establish the correct size and fit in the first instance.
Patch (Ortho Evra)	A patch worn on the skin that releases progestogen and oestrogen into the bloodstream. 99 per cent effective.	Does not require daily use. Appears to be less effective in women who weigh more than 90 kg (14 st). Does not protect against STDs or HIV. Requires a prescription.
Surgical Sterilisation	Tubal ligation or "tube tying" prevents eggs from leaving the fallopian tubes. Male vasectomy prevents sperm from entering ejaculate. 99 to 99.5 per cent effective.	Requires surgery.
Nonsurgical Sterilisation (still under trial in the UK and not yet available)	A thin tube is used to thread a tiny spring-like device through the vagina and uterus into each fallopian tube and to cause scar tissue to grow and eventually plug the tubes. 100 per cent effective when successfully implanted.	In the US, where nonsurgical sterilisation is available, it has been shown that the scar tissue takes about three months to grow, so women are advised to use another form of birth control during this time. Follow-up visits are also required.

312 Choose Where to Give Birth

Picking where to give birth can be an anxiety-inducing job. If you know you want to give birth in hospital, you may not be able to choose which hospital you go to, although in some areas there is a choice of NHS maternity units available. You need to look at all the options available and find out as much as possible about each. In the process you are likely to find out more about your own preferences and priorities for the birth of your child.

What to Look For

- Recommendations
- Desired facilities
- Statistics on types of births in different units

Steps

1 Ask your GP what is on offer in your area. Home births are encouraged in some areas (see 314 "Plan a Home Birth"), though not in others, sometimes due to staff shortages. There are two main types of NHS maternity units. In large hospitals, a specialist maternity unit is led by a consultant obstetrician. In smaller or "cottage" hospitals, units may be staffed by midwives and GPs; these units usually deal only with straightforward births and have to transfer more complicated cases to a larger hospital.

2 Look at private alternatives in the form of independent midwives and doulas (see 313 "Hire a Midwife or Doula") or private hospitals. Few private hospitals offer maternity services (most are in London) and they are not covered under private healthcare schemes (such as BUPA). A private birth may cost up to around £7,000.

3 Visit any hospitals or arrange to meet any private individuals under consideration. You need to look at the facilities on offer; factors influencing your decision might include space; whether there are quieter rooms if you have had a birth with complications; whether there is a birthing pool. Familiarise yourself with the surroundings. If you have a birth plan, take it along and discuss it with a midwife; find out what could happen if things don't go according to plan.

4 Check statistics on maternity units, including the number of births they handle a year, what pain relief they offer, the rate of interventions (caesarians, ventouse and forceps deliveries), and so on. Bear in mind that larger hospitals almost inevitably have a higher intervention rate because complicated births are referred to them; it is also argued that larger hospitals tend to be quicker to intervene.

5 Book in with the maternity unit (or private hospital or individual of your choice) when you have made your decision. You can sometimes book a couple of options to secure them and make your final choice nearer the time.

Tips

Geographic location is likely to be a major factor in your decision.

Consult drfoster.co.uk or birthchoiceuk.com for statistics on different maternity units in the UK and for advice on making your decision.

313 Hire a Midwife or Doula

Being pregnant is a life-altering transition. Your questions and concerns will grow along with the new life in your tummy. Many women are finding the answers and reassurance they need with indpendent midwives and doulas.

Steps

Finding an independent midwife

1 Decide if you want an independent midwife to provide pre-natal care and attend your birth. Indpendent midwives are self-employed and give you continuity of care throughout your pregnancy and birth. Such midwives generally approach birth with a holistic, natural, no-intervention-unless-necessary policy; they can deliver babies at home as well as in hospitals.

2 Find an independent midwife in your area by contacting the Indpendent Midwives Association (independentmidwives.org.uk).

3 Arrange to meet a few of the independent midwives who operate locally. Find out their attitudes to birth and what they specialise in – many have experience in home births following a difficult previous birth. Some can loan equipment such as a birthing pool for home births. It is crucial to check their qualifications (all midwives, independent and within the NHS, are strictly regulated), and the exact service they provide. Also see who you feel most comfortable with – you need to feel you can build a strong and trusting relationship.

4 Make your choice. Costs vary, but the fee may be around £2,500.

Finding a doula

1 Hire a doula if you want a well-trained person to assist you during pregnancy and birth. A doula supports the mother (or couple) physically and emotionally during the birth, but does not provide medical support: that remains the role of the midwife and medical staff. A doula will help with positioning, massage and other pain-management techniques. A post-natal doula provides emotional and practical support in the home in the early days and weeks after the birth, enabling the mother to recover fully, establish breastfeeding and enjoy time with her new baby and other siblings. A birthing doula may charge a fee of £250–500, while a post-natal doula is likely to charge an hourly rate for help.

2 Arrange to meet doulas who operate in your area. Contact Doula UK (doula.org.uk) for a list of local doulas, or contact the NCT (nct-online.org) or La Leche League (laleche.org.uk) for further advice and information.

3 Interview your choices carefully, following the same guidelines as for an independent midwife. Look for someone you trust to back up your choices while making you feel comfortable and secure.

What to Look For

- Shared views about pregnancy and birth
- Personalised care
- References

Tips

Studies have shown that healthy women with no pregnancy complications are in equally good hands with an NHS doctor or midwife. Other studies find that women who use independent midwives and doulas have shorter labours with fewer complications.

If you go into hospital to deliver your baby, your independent midwife will accompany you, but the hospital consultant team are likely to assume responsibility.

314 Plan a Home Birth

If you plan to have a natural birth and like the idea of giving birth in the comfort of your home, then a home birth may well be the best option for you. Get the all-clear from your GP, and start planning.

Steps

1 Discuss the range of birth options with your GP (see 312 "Choose Where to Give Birth"). He or she will be able to let you know if it is possible to have a home birth in your area, and whether it is advisable in your case.

2 If your doctor is happy to endorse your wish for a home birth, ask him or her for the contact details of the local NHS home birth team of midwives. They will usually be based at your nearest cottage or large hospital.

3 Make an appointment to meet the home birth team. They cannot guarantee which of them it will be that eventually attends your home birth. However, they hope that you will have met each one of them during your periodic routine check-ups, so that the midwife who does attend the birth will not be a stranger to you. If you want one-to-one care with the same midwife throughout your pregnancy and birth, search out an independent midwife (see 313 "Hire a Midwife or Doula").

4 Go to the periodic informal information sessions that the midwives arrange at the hospital. These allow you to get to know the midwives and to discuss any concerns you have about your pregnancy or birth. You will also be able to exchange views and information with other women at a similar phase in their pregnancy who have also chosen to have a home birth.

5 Sign up with a local pre-natal yoga class. Here you will do yoga postures expressly selected to help prepare your body for the birth and also be shown the best positions to adopt to minimise pain during labour. Contact the Active Birth Centre in London (tel: 020 72816760; website: activebirthcentre.com) for details of their yoga for pregnancy classes (£12–£20 per class) and a list of active birth teachers practising throughout the UK.

6 Consider using complementary medicines, such as homeopathy and aromatherapy, at the birth. Find a practitioner in your area and make an appointment to see him or her. They will be able to advise which remedies are appropriate to reduce pain during labour and to help repair the body after the birth.

7 Decide if you want a water birth. Advocates claim that giving birth in water aids relaxation and reduces the pain of labour. If the idea appeals, contact a company that hires out birthing pools, such as Splashdown Waterbirth Services (tel: 0870 4444403). Prices range from £220 to £265 for four-week hire, depending on the type of pool. Have the pool delivered two weeks before your baby is due.

What to Look For

- Locally based team of home birth midwives
- Shared views of pregnancy, labour and delivery
- Pre-natal yoga classes
- Natural forms of pain relief
- Companies hiring out birthing pools

Tip

Ask your midwife to recommend a company that hires out TENS machines. A TENS machine is a portable, non-invasive machine that you can use to reduce pain during labour. It gives out little pulses of electrical energy, which are transmitted through your skin via pads you attach to your back. This causes your body to release endorphins. It costs about £30 to hire one for a month.

Warning

If you have an underlying condition that might shift your pregnancy into a higher-risk category (diabetes, high blood pressure, epilepsy), or a history of birth complications, your GP will insist on a hospital birth.

315 Hire a Child Therapist

You know it's not just a phase that your child is going to grow out of. However, you don't have to go it alone: seek the professional assistance of a therapist. You'll need to devote a great deal of time and care to finding the right person. It's important that you and your child hit it off with the therapist; otherwise, little will be accomplished.

Steps

1 Identify your child's needs. Really listen to your child's teachers and understand that he or she may behave differently at home. Try to grasp the full dimension of what's going on.

2 Get personal referrals from people you trust. Check with your family doctor and school teachers, and other parents who've undertaken a similar search.

3 Contact your doctor if you suspect your child has special needs that should be addressed. For attention deficit disorder, contact ADDISS, the Attention Deficit Disorder Information and Support Service (addiss.co.uk). If learning disabilities are suspected, talk to your child's head teacher and request a learning assessment.

4 Contact several therapists to ask about their approach. Ask about their qualifications (see 352 "Hire a Mental Health Professional").

5 Find out about fees and office hours. If you have private health insurance, check with your insurance company; many insurers offer limited coverage for therapy.

6 Discuss your child's issues with the therapist and find out what experience he or she has in dealing with similar problems. Discuss the treatment plan. Find out how the therapist establishes trust with a potentially defiant patient – will he or she take the child for a walk? Play football? Talk sports or Britney Spears for a while? Play therapy and art therapy are commonly used with children. A therapist's approach is key to the success of the relationship and will vary with the age of the child.

7 Learn what happens in a typical session. Some therapists offer a trial session for a reduced fee or allow parents to sit in on one session. Whether this is advisable depends on the child's age.

8 Use your intuition above all. You are your child's best advocate and should feel confident and supported throughout treatment.

What to Look For

- Your child's needs
- Referrals
- Professional qualifications
- Insurance coverage
- Appropriate experience and approach

Tip

If your child needs medication, ask your doctor to refer you to a child psychiatrist.

316 Gear Up for a New Baby

Most expectant parents want to buy their new baby the world – and there is a whole world of gear out there for little ones. But you don't need to spend a bundle on your little bundle. Before you blow the budget on all-new gear, consider borrowing as much as possible or buying much of it used. Check out online sources for reviews and recommendations and then selectively purchase new items with safety, durability and adaptability in mind.

Steps

1 Talk to people about what baby items they've used, and what they like or don't like about them. Other parents who have been in your boat are your best source of information. This is also a great way to find out if someone has something (like a travel cot) that they'll lend you or let you test drive.

2 Consult *Which?* Online (which.co.uk) for comparisons of major baby products by brand and price.

3 Visit car boot sales and National Childbirth Trust (NCT) fairs for access to used baby equipment. You'll be able to find almost everything you need in good condition from other parents whose child has outgrown it. Usability on most of these items is counted in months, not years.

4 Ask a friend who is a parent to make a list of those items you should borrow or buy used and those you definitely want to buy new. You'll want to borrow or find used such items as a travel cot, activity mat and baby bouncer.

5 Make sure any used gear is safe and in good working order, and give it a good scrub before using it. Check the Safety Warning List at tradingstandards.gov.uk for product recalls. Contact the Royal Society for the Prevention of Accidents (rospa.co.uk) for useful information and safety tips.

6 Always invest in a cot and check that the mattress conforms to European safety standards. A changing table that eventually converts to a useful piece of bedroom storage is also a good investment.

7 Follow safety instructions for all items. Similarly, adjust baby seats and baby bouncers as needed as your child grows. As a rule of thumb bear in mind that your baby's legs should never fully extend while jumping – he or she should always have slightly bent knees.

What to Look For

- Other parents' advice
- Bargains
- Used items
- Solid construction
- Up-to-date safety features
- Compliance with the latest safety standards

Tips

To get the most for your money, don't restrict your search to baby shops – check out department stores and furniture shops (especially during seasonal sales). You might find top-quality goods at reduced prices, and a few modifications (adding drawer stops or replacing protruding drawer knobs) will keep your baby safe.

Cot alternatives – cradles and Moses baskets – can keep a newborn snug and make it easier to move him or her from room to room. But because a baby outgrows them within six months – and you'll need that cot eventually – borrow or buy these items second-hand.

Always send off your product registration card in case of recalls.

See 318 "Choose a Pushchair".

ITEM	FEATURES	PRICE, POPULAR BRANDS
Changing Table	Look for a sturdy table with handy storage space. Some have extra drawers. Concave pads and straps keep babies from rolling off. Chests-of-drawers with removable pad revert to a dresser later.	Simple open-shelf tables, start at £50. Deluxe dresser models, £160 to £350.
Nappy Disposal	A plain bin with a tight-fitting lid works for nappy disposal if it is emptied frequently. Odour-free disposal systems hold 25–180 nappies before they need emptying.	Around £30 for disposal system; refill, £4 to £5. Safety 1st, Tommee Tippee
Baby Monitor	Sound indicator lights allow you to do noisy things (like vacuum). Most plug in as well as use batteries; make sure reception is clear in either mode. Some models monitor temperature and breathing.	£20 to £130. Tomy, Philips, Tommee Tippee
Front Packs and Slings	Indispensable from birth until too heavy. Allows you to "wear your baby" while doing other things. Some let baby face in or out. Look for adjustable straps. Slings are favoured by some parents even into the toddler years.	Slings, start at £30. Front packs, £30 to £70. Baby Björn, Tomy, Wilkinet
Backpack	For babies who can hold their head up. Test drive with baby inside to check fit. Make sure you can get the weight off your shoulders and onto your hips with the tummy band. Look for adjustability, secure baby harness and sturdy support stand.	£50 to £130 plus Trekabout, Bushbaby, some major outdoor gear suppliers
Movers and Shakers	Bouncing cradles (until baby can sit unaided), doorway jumpers (from 3 months) and activity gyms (from birth) run the gamut from stripped down to decked out. Choose sturdy, adjustable heights. Check for safety restraints that are easy to use and don't pinch.	Bouncing cradles, £12 to £55. Doorway jumpers, £20 to £40. Gyms, £35 to £45. Mamas and Papas, Galt, Chicco
Portable Cots and Playpens	Look for a safe, sturdy model that is easy to set up and take down.	£50 to £100. Graco, Baby Dan
Swings	Birth until can sit unaided. Look for variable speeds, and sturdy belt so baby doesn't slip out.	£60 to £100. Graco
Highchairs	For babies who can sit up comfortably. Get a tray that releases with one hand. Make sure crotch strap is securely tethered and that there are no parts that pinch. Up-market models have wheels and adjustable heights. Space saver option is a booster seat plus tray that belts securely to a chair.	£30 to £130. Mamas and Papas, Chicco, Stokke. Booster seat with tray, £30. Safety 1st, First Years
WARNING	Quilts, duvets, pillows and stuffed animals do not belong in your baby's bed. Any of these items are suffocation hazards since babies do not have the strength to move their head or body out of harm's way. The ties that attach some cot bumpers pose a strangulation risk: do not use until your baby is a year old.	

317 Buy a New Cot

Cots run the gamut from Fiestas to Ferraris in looks, materials and the price sticker. Shop for a cot that's built to last. It will be shaken, rattled and rolled (and sometimes slept in) for years.

Steps

1 Buy a reputable brand, such as Mamas and Papas or own brands of stores such as Mothercare or John Lewis, for safe, beautiful hardwood cots in sizes and styles that range from simple (£100) to completely over the top (£500 or more).

2 Check that the frame and headboard are strong. Jiggle the bars to make sure they don't twist or move. Make sure the mattress support frame is snug and doesn't easily pull apart from the corners.

3 If you're buying a used cot or inheriting a hand-me-down, be sure to get a model that is only a few years old so it meets safety standards and its components are not worn. Don't get a cot with split or loosened wood joints, missing or cracked bars or slats, or splinters. If the cot is painted, strip it down and repaint with lead-free paint so there is no danger of lead poisoning. Top rails should have plastic gum protectors.

4 On older cots, check that spaces between slats are no more than 4.5 to 6.5 cm (1¾ to 2½ in) apart.

5 Test the drop-side mechanism (on one or both sides) to make sure you can lower it easily with only one hand. When lowered, the top rail should be at least 23 cm (9 in) above the mattress.

6 Look for a cot with at least 66 cm (26 in) between the top of the side rail and the mattress support frame. Many cots let you lower the height of the mattress frame to keep a growing child safely inside. Your baby will no doubt attempt a daring cot escape at some point, and tall sides make it more difficult.

7 Explore cots with special features. Cot beds you can convert into toddler or child beds are costly up front, but may save money in the long run since you can do without an intermediate bed and go straight from a cot to a full-size single.

8 Buy the best cot mattress you can afford (£30 to £100). Look for firm support, fire retardancy, and a good-quality waterproof cover. Most mattresses come in a standard size, but check the fit: if you can put more than two fingers between the mattress and the cot frame, it is not safe.

What to Look For

- Cot that complies with BS EN 716
- Solid construction
- Style
- Snug-fitting mattress that complies with BS EN 1877 and BS EN 7177

Tips

Turn your mattress regularly top to bottom and side to side to maintain its shape.

It is recommended that you buy a new mattress for a new baby. A mattress that has been used by an older child may be compressed and so offers little support. Also, dust mites and bacteria may build up in an older mattress.

318 Choose a Pushchair

A pushchair will be one of your most-used items, so buy the best quality you can afford or request one as a gift. Most parents use it several times a day, loading it in and out of the car, wandering with baby from the zoo to the shops. Most manufacturers offer a variety of styles, from 2-in-1s to 3-wheelers to lightweight strollers; talk to other parents about their recommendations.

TYPE	DESCRIPTION	PRICES
Pushchairs	Look for seat with multiple positions so child can lie flat, sit up, and use positions in-between. Many can take a car seat to become a travel system. From birth on.	£50 to £500
2-in-1s	A chassis that can take a carry cot for small babies and converts into a pushchair. From birth on. Many can take a car seat to become a travel system (often called 3-in-1).	£150 to £600
Lightweight stroller	Usually the second pushchair. Lightweight and compact (usually under 7 kg/15 lb). Few recline for infants; most suitable from 3/6 months.	£50 to £200
3-wheeler	Designed to absorb the shock of running, jogging and going over rough terrain. Can include carrycot for infants. Most suitable from birth on.	£100 to £500 (quad)
Multiple	Carries two or more children.	£100 to £500
Accessories	Fleece	£40 to £50
	Raincover	£10 to £40
	Changing bag	£15 to £60
	Cosytoes/Footmuff	£15 to £75
	Parasol	£10 to £15
	Buggy board	£45
TIPS	Save your back by buying a pushchair with wheels that navigate easily and handlebars that fit properly. Buy a handlebar extension if necessary.	
	Ask if you can test drive the pushchair, with child inside, to see how the pushchair handles the reality factor. Check it fits in the boot of your car.	
	Choose a pushchair that complies with BS 7409.	

319 Buy Baby Clothes

Let's face it – babies are messy. They spring leaks in all sorts of places. You'll be changing your newborn's clothes several times a day, so put together a basic and inexpensive baby wardrobe, and be ready for anything. Also check out 519 "Buy Kids' Clothes".

ITEM	HOW MANY TO BUY	FEATURES
One-Piece Outfits	Five to seven	These make dressing and layering easy. Look for easy-entry head openings with shoulder press studs, and leg and sleeve cuffs that aren't too tight.
One-Piece Pyjamas	Five to seven	Soft, cotton-footed pyjamas keep your baby toasty. Gowns with drawstring hems keep infant feet covered and allow quick nappy changes, especially for newborns.
Vests	Five to seven	Shoulder press studs or boat neck openings make it easy to slip on and off. Crotch press studs keep vests from riding up.
Jumpers or Jackets	One or two	A button-up or zipped garment is best, as many babies hate anything pulled over their head, especially something tight. Fleece is a great choice for lightweight protection from the elements.
Cap, Sun Hat	Two or three caps, one sun hat	Soft caps hug baby's head to keep warmth in. Wide-brimmed sun hats protect tender skin. Look for hats with neck flaps for extra protection, and a chin tie to keep on when tiny hands discover what they can do.
Socks	Seven pairs	Pick socks with enough of a cuff to keep them on without gripping too tightly. Choose a few heavier pairs (or slipper socks) for colder days. For babies that are trying to stand, look for socks with rubberised grips on the soles.
Baby Shoes	One pair	Since very young babies' feet hardly touch the ground, they don't really need shoes (and shouldn't have "real" shoes until after they start to walk). Leather or cloth booties with elastic are great for crawlers (see 520 "Choose Children's Shoes").
Special Outfits	One or two	Indulge yourself with an adorable outfit. Don't buy more than a couple, since the next growth spurt is just around the corner. Avoid difficult-to-manage one-piece outfits that fasten at the back.
WARNING		Check that any sleepwear you buy is flame retardant. Do not put your baby to bed in any other type of clothing.

320 Choose Nappies

Before your child is potty trained, you'll have changed about 6,000 nappies. So think long and hard about whether you'd rather be dealing with cloth or disposables at 3 a.m. Cloth nappy advocates are concerned about the rate at which disposable nappies are filling our landfill sites. Disposable fans argue that the water, energy and chlorine it takes to clean cloth nappies have an equally harsh impact on our environment. Even the costs are comparable.

Steps

Disposable nappies

1 Get at least one small package of nappies in newborn size, and one larger package in the next size. Some newborns are already too big for newborn-size nappies when they come home.

2 Test drive supermarket own-brand or generic nappies on your baby for comfort and leak protection. Many have the same features (like expandable sides) as premium nappies such as Huggies and Pampers. Don't stock up on any one brand until you know what works for you and yours.

3 If you have the storage space, order in bulk online. Many sites offer free delivery for large purchases, so you won't have to cart huge packs around. Disposable nappies and wipes can run to £35 a month.

Cloth nappies

1 Get three-dozen pre-folded nappies plus four or five snap-on or Velcro waterproof covers, and pins or plastic clips, if you choose the type of nappy without sewn-on attachments. Look online for service-quality nappies. Many parents love the newer, all-in-one cloth nappies, which combine a nappy with a cover and don't require pins. These look and perform like disposables, although they can take a long time to dry completely.

2 Avoid the hassle of washing and drying nappies by getting a professional nappy service. These services pick up soiled nappies and drop off clean ones once a week. They provide the nappies so you don't have to buy them (you will still need covers). Call several services in your area to compare rates and start-up special offers. You'll pay more for a service, but your washing machine will thank you.

3 Budget about £30 a month for a nappy service (depending on where you live). Using cloth nappies requires an investment of about £50 for three-dozen nappies and covers (for each growth stage), plus energy costs.

What to Look For

- Correct size
- Leak-proof design
- Good price

Tips

Nurseries usually insist on disposables.

Eco-friendly disposables are available, though often expensive.

One type of nappy is no more likely than another to cause a rash, as long as you change your baby promptly. However, if your baby suffers from chronic rashes, you may want to rethink your nappy brand and talk to your doctor.

Warning

If you choose cloth nappies, while you are out and about, you will be carrying around dirty nappies until you get home. Many parents keep a stash of disposables for out-and-about convenience.

321 Buy or Rent a Breast Pump

If you're a nursing mother, you have milk on demand for your baby. But what happens when you are in demand somewhere else? For a back-up milk supply, you need a breast pump. All pumps, whether manual or mechanical, use suction to pull milk into a container for later feedings. The basic difference between models is how quickly, comfortably and conveniently they work – and at what price.

Steps

1 Consider how often you will be using the pump. Will you be expressing milk only occasionally, or do you want to give your baby a bottle regularly or continue to provide breast milk while you go back to work? If you will only be pumping occasionally, consider an inexpensive (£30) manual pump, such as the Avent Isis breast pump. Manual pumps are compact but can be slow – and sometimes painful – to use. Many models require both hands, tying you up completely. Still, for occasional at-home use, these do the trick.

2 Rent top-of-the-line motorised breast pumps used in hospitals at a low cost if you plan to express milk on a regular basis. Fees average £10 to £15 a week. Keep in mind that a security deposit is required. You'll also need to buy a personal accessory kit for about £35. If something goes wrong with a rental, you can get another. Rental machines can be bulky, making them a poor choice if you're short on space or on the move.

3 Consider buying your own pump if you'll be using it for a long time or plan to have more children. You get what you pay for in terms of motor quality. Some machines let you pump both breasts at once so you finish in half the time. Pumps run from £40 for a simple battery-powered model to around £250 for a powerful double-pumper like the Medela Pump In Style.

4 Look for a model that suits your needs, like a pump that packs neatly into its own carry case and comes with an ice pack to get your "white gold" home safely. Choose a double-pumper if you will be using it at work; you'll be finished in half the time. If you're in the car a lot, look for a pump with a car-lighter adapter.

5 Take the pump out of its packaging and get comfortable with its parts and operation a few weeks after the baby is born. Choose a time when you're not overwhelmed, or ask a friend to give you a hand.

What to Look For

- Manual pump
- Rental options
- Battery operated
- Portability

Tips

Although you don't need to buy a pump before your baby is born, you do need to get used to handling the pump well before you start using it.

Talk to your health visitor about the right time to start pumping and offering your baby a daily "acclimatising" bottle. Too early and he or she may develop "nipple confusion" and stop breast-feeding. Too late and the baby may refuse a bottle altogether.

A breastfeeding counsellor from the National Childbirth Trust (tel: 0870 4448708) can help you work out which pump is right for you and suggest where to buy or rent them.

322 Choose a Car Seat

Choosing the right car seat can be an agonising process for nervous new parents, and a significant expense as well. Research, talk to other parents and buy the best seat you can afford to keep your child as safe and comfortable as possible.

Steps

1 Do your research. Car seats come in five different weight categories: 0, 0+, 1, 2 and 3. Babies from newborn to nine months and weighing up to 10 kg (22 lb) fall into group 0 and need a rear-facing seat. Babies weighing up to 13 kg (29 lb) fall into group 0+ also need a rear-facing seat. If a baby is heavier than the maximum weight for a rear-facing seat but is not sufficiently developed to go in a forward-facing seat, he or she should still have a rear-facing seat.

2 After the first year, graduate to a group 1 seat designed for passengers weighing 9–18 kg (20–40 lb). A forward-facing seat with a 5-point harness will keep your child safe and comfortable for several years. It should be easy to install and have a locking mechanism your child can't unfasten. The straps should not get twisted or jammed.

3 Give a child over 15 kg (33 lb) a boost. A child weighing 15–25 kg (33–55 lb) will need a group 2 booster seat; a child weighing 22–36 kg (48–80 lb) will need a group 3 booster seat. Booster seats generally thread the standard seatbelt through a back or headrest at a height suitable for small bodies. Research and shop around for the best booster for your youngster.

4 Learn about safety. Visit childcarseats.org.uk, which gives advice on buying and fitting child restraints. The Royal Society for the Prevention of Accidents (rospa.co.uk) produces a video that shows parents how to choose and fit a seat correctly. Consult consumer reports and confirm that any seat you are considering meets the European safety standard ECE44-03.

5 Ask other parents about what works for them (easy to install, comfy armrests) and what doesn't (hard to adjust, poor padding). If a parent says his or her child can unbuckle a particular seat, and you have a little monkey, keep looking.

6 Baby car seats are installed rear-facing to cradle the baby's head and back as securely as possible. You can buy some group 1 baby seats as part of a complete travel system, such as the Mamas and Papas Freestyler Completo (£350). These car seats clip straight onto the chassis of the pushchair, allowing smooth transition from car to pushchair for sleeping babies.

What to Look For

- European safety standard ECE44-03
- Appropriate for your child's age and weight
- Safety harnesses

Tips

Try to borrow an infant car seat from a friend or family member who is no longer using it. Babies grow fast and most infant seats can withstand several years of use. Just make sure the seat is still compliant with safety regulations and has not been in an accident.

Your child is more likely to fall asleep in a car seat that's comfortable.

Ask if you can install a car seat before you buy it to make sure it fits your car and is easy to install correctly.

Warnings

Don't buy a second-hand car seat. It may have been in an accident and its ability to keep your child safe in another crash could be greatly compromised.

Never fit a rear-facing baby car seat in a seat with an airbag.

323 Buy Child-Proofing Supplies

Your baby's job is to explore every inch of his or her world. Your job: make sure that the terrain is safe for the intrepid explorer. It isn't too early to start baby-proofing your home before your baby arrives. You'll need to reassess the safety of your home and outdoor areas regularly, as your little Houdini grows and becomes more mobile.

Steps

1 Review the manufacturer's guidelines for your newborn's equipment (cots, pushchairs, car seats, travel cots, baths and monitors) to make sure you're using everything safely and correctly. If you purchased an item second-hand, contact its manufacturer to obtain a copy of the guidelines or check online.

2 Move items above the cot out of baby's reach as soon as he or she learns to roll over or push himself up on his hands (typically between three and six months).

3 Make sure that by the time your baby is crawling (around eight months), you've made your home as safe as possible. Strap tall, heavy furniture to the wall. Place fragile items out of reach. Crawl around yourself and see what looks dangerous (or enticing) from that vantage point.

4 Count electric sockets, cupboards, doors and openings that need to be made safe before going shopping for baby-proofing supplies.

5 Install wall-mounted safety gates at the top and bottom of staircases. You may want to create baby-safe zones with additional gates. Bathrooms and kitchens pose the most hazards. Avoid finger-pinching, accordion-fold gates.

6 Keep handbags out of reach – especially when Grandma comes to visit. They're full of fascinating dangers, from coins and medicines to nail files and make-up.

7 Stay current and reassess dangers at each developmental milestone. Every time your child is able to do something new and fabulous – roll over, sit up, grasp, crawl, cruise, climb, walk, run, bolt into the street – hazards that were previously out of reach suddenly come into play. Stay one leap ahead and don't be lulled into a false sense of complacency however sensible your child seems.

What to Look For

- Safety guidelines
- Age-specific hazards
- Appropriate equipment

Tips

Take a fresh look at your safety measures when your child starts to walk. He or she is picking up speed and can reach much higher than a baby on all fours.

Keep an eye out for older children who can disable safety gates and locks. Tell them you need their help to keep the baby safe.

Warning

Lock away medicines, toiletries, cleaning materials, matches and anything else that could pose a hazard to your baby.

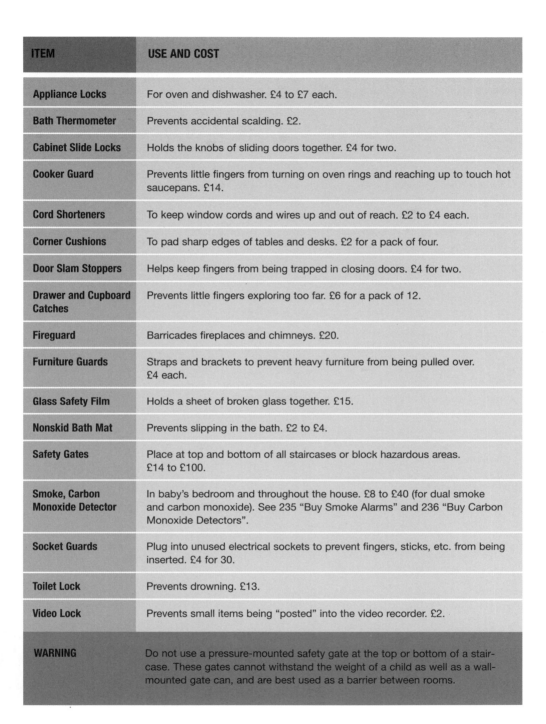

ITEM	USE AND COST
Appliance Locks	For oven and dishwasher. £4 to £7 each.
Bath Thermometer	Prevents accidental scalding. £2.
Cabinet Slide Locks	Holds the knobs of sliding doors together. £4 for two.
Cooker Guard	Prevents little fingers from turning on oven rings and reaching up to touch hot saucepans. £14.
Cord Shorteners	To keep window cords and wires up and out of reach. £2 to £4 each.
Corner Cushions	To pad sharp edges of tables and desks. £2 for a pack of four.
Door Slam Stoppers	Helps keep fingers from being trapped in closing doors. £4 for two.
Drawer and Cupboard Catches	Prevents little fingers exploring too far. £6 for a pack of 12.
Fireguard	Barricades fireplaces and chimneys. £20.
Furniture Guards	Straps and brackets to prevent heavy furniture from being pulled over. £4 each.
Glass Safety Film	Holds a sheet of broken glass together. £15.
Nonskid Bath Mat	Prevents slipping in the bath. £2 to £4.
Safety Gates	Place at top and bottom of all staircases or block hazardous areas. £14 to £100.
Smoke, Carbon Monoxide Detector	In baby's bedroom and throughout the house. £8 to £40 (for dual smoke and carbon monoxide). See 235 "Buy Smoke Alarms" and 236 "Buy Carbon Monoxide Detectors".
Socket Guards	Plug into unused electrical sockets to prevent fingers, sticks, etc. from being inserted. £4 for 30.
Toilet Lock	Prevents drowning. £13.
Video Lock	Prevents small items being "posted" into the video recorder. £2.
WARNING	Do not use a pressure-mounted safety gate at the top or bottom of a staircase. These gates cannot withstand the weight of a child as well as a wall-mounted gate can, and are best used as a barrier between rooms.

324 Find Reliable Childcare

There's no doubt about it – leaving your child in someone else's care can be agonising. But good quality childcare is available in most areas if you're willing to look for it, and there are many options for parents to choose from. Do your homework to find the right arrangement for your children and for yourself.

Steps

General tips

1 Decide when you want to make use of childcare. Some parents prefer to look after a child full time themselves until he or she is around three years old, while others hanker to return to work. Consider how much you can expect to earn and offset it against the cost of childcare to see your actual financial gain.

2 Ask friends with children, family and mothers' group members for recommendations. Find out what their experiences have been like. Listen to what they say and see if your instinct tells you those same things would work well for you and your child.

3 Consider the available options and decide which type of childcare best meets your needs. Be clear about how long each day and how many days a week you need the child looked after, as well as how much you can afford.

4 Decide whether to have your child looked after at home or to take the child to a childminder, nursery or playgroup. Your child's personality will play a role in this decision – social, active children may benefit from the stimulation and activity offered in a group environment.

Home-based care

1 If you want your child looked after in your home, employ a nanny (see 325 "Find a Great Nanny") or find an au pair (see 44 "Employ an Au Pair"). Note that you cannot use an au pair to look after a child under the age of three and that they will only provide care on a part-time basis.

2 Consider a nanny share. This is a particularly attractive option if you have only one child, as your child will get one or two playmates. If a solo nanny is out of your price range, splitting the cost with one or two other families can make it affordable. The parents decide whose home will host the children each day – it may always be the same home, or you can switch back and forth. This is also a good option if you only want childcare for two or three days a week. Split the week with the other family.

Childminders, nurseries and playgroups

1 Consider the options for childcare out of the home. Know that the choice is between a childminder, a nursery and, when the child is over two-and-a-half, a playgroup.

What to Look For

- Childcare to suit your child
- Nanny or au pair
- Registered childminder
- Nursery place
- Secure, nurturing environment

Tips

If you find a childminder through a card in a shop window, be sure to ask to see evidence that they are registered with the council.

Pay careful attention to the location of a nursery or childminder's home. You will have to travel there before and after work every day. An hour's journey each way stuck in traffic will be good neither for you nor the child.

2   Check out childminders in your area. A childminder cares for children in his or her home. They may range from babies up to secondary school age. All childminders must be registered with the local authority, which carries out checks and enforces safety standards in the home. Contact your local council for a list of registered childminders.

3   Meet a selection of childminders and interview them. Decide whether you feel happy with the idea of this person looking after your child. Ask about their experience. Be aware that they are not required to have received any training in childcare. Ask about the ages of the other children the childminder looks after. Are they a match with your child's age?

4   If you feel comfortable about the childminder, negotiate terms and hours. Expect to pay between £60 and £120 a week. Know that one of the advantages of childminders is that they can be flexible, fitting in with the hours you need.

5   Consider the advantages of nursery care. Nurseries have trained staff, will place your child with other children of the same age, and offer structured play and good facilities. Draw up a shortlist of nurseries and contact them. Ask for brochures or visit their website. Find out if there is space available when you need to enrol or if there is a waiting list. Make appointments to visit nurseries in person.

6   Compare the nurseries, taking account of their facilities, ethos and general atmosphere. The space should be well maintained and cheerful, with separate areas for quiet play and group activities, and plenty of toys. Check the outdoor space. Is there room to run around? Are there climbing frames, a sandpit and lots more toys? Is there a lively, engaged atmosphere that doesn't seem out of control? Do the children seem happy?

7   Use your instincts as a parent and look for a fit. Some nurseries have an extended family feeling, while others tend to be more businesslike. Make sure the structure of the scheme and its philosophy are suited to the temperament of your child. One situation may be great for one child but not for another.

8   Take your child for a short visit after you've narrowed down your choices. How does he or she respond to the environment?

9   When you have chosen a nursery, settle the detail of terms. Be sure you know of any extras – for example, what are the fees for late pick-ups.

10 Consider a playgroup once your child is potty-trained – they will not take children before that stage. Know that a playgroup will not take your child for a whole day. Typically, they offer sessions lasting about two-and-a-half hours either before or after lunch. Playgroups are thus not a solution for working parents.

Warning

Know that nurseries will not care for your child when the child is ill. Childhood illnesses are very common, so this can seriously eat into your working time.

325 Find a Great Nanny

Employing a nanny may remind some people of the days when children had a governesses, but it is in fact a highly practical modern-day solution to the problem of childcare. Choose wisely: not only will this person be responsible for your child's safety and happiness, but he or she is likely to become an integral part of your family.

Steps

1 Decide if you want your nanny to live with you or not – there are potential benefits and drawbacks to both choices.

2 Contact local nanny agencies. Discuss your requirements and find out what's involved in the placement process. Ask how background checks are done and how applicants are screened. Find out what the placement fee is and what the cancellation fees are.

3 Read up on prospective candidates. Ask for CVs, references and evidence of background checks.

4 Arrange interviews with possible candidates. Go over your job description, air any concerns you have and ask each applicant to do the same. Discuss potential behavioural and discipline issues to get a feel for how various situations would be handled and how each potential nanny would respond to your baby or child's disposition. Watch how each candidate interacts with your child, and how your child responds to him or her. Discuss a few hypothetical situations that require good judgement and see how each applicant responds.

5 Call the references provided and have an honest conversation about the prospective nanny. Most parents have similar concerns for their children and are happy to discuss their experiences.

6 If you've met your match, call the agency to arrange for a contract and pay your final fee. Most agencies have a short trial period before finalising the contract. Agencies have procedures in place in the event a nanny doesn't work out. Find out what they are.

7 Alternatively, avoid agency fees by advertising for a nanny yourself or asking for a copy of the nanny register drawn up by members of the National Childbirth Trust (NCT). You'll save money, but you'll have to deal with the phone calls, background checks, interviews and contract issues yourself, which requires considerable time and effort.

8 Draw up a contract specifying salary and conditions in detail, including holiday entitlement. Arrange to pay employer's national insurance, and income tax and national insurance for the nanny. If this is a daunting prospect, employ an accountant to handle the tax matters.

What to Look For

- Qualified agency
- References
- Great fit with your family
- Provisions if it doesn't work out

Tips

Check each reference thoroughly, even if the agency has already done so. You will be trusting this person with the physical and emotional care of your child.

Consider a nanny share if footing the bill alone is too difficult and you don't require a live-in nanny (see 324 "Find Reliable Childcare").

If you are not taking your nanny with you on family holidays, try to arrange for the nanny to take at least part of his or her annual holidays at the same time that your family goes away.

Warning

When budgeting for a nanny, remember the extra costs involved, such as employer's national insurance, the nanny's income tax, national insurance, sick pay, holiday pay, and possible higher premiums on your car insurance if you wish the nanny to drive your car.

326 Find the Right Private School

Families choose a private education for their children for many reasons, but finding the right school takes a lot of homework (and legwork). The process can be gruelling and requires considerable time and effort, but if you research carefully and involve your child, you're likely to find a school that suits your child and meets your expectations.

Steps

1 Decide between day and boarding school options. Decide if a particular focus suits you and your child best, such as university preparation, religious, military, athletic, artistic, linguistic or musical. Do you need a school that serves students with special needs or specific populations, such as gifted students?

2 Gather information. Ask for brochures, videos and application information. Visit school fairs. Get recommendations from teachers and other parents. Browse school websites to compare curricula and timetables.

3 Match your child's abilities and accomplishments to particular schools. For example, if you're looking at elite secondary schools, a very strong academic record and solid extra-curricular interests will form the foundation of the application. Prep school applications can be less stringent, but require a parent application and at least one interview.

4 Schedule visits and interviews during school hours so you can get a feel for the pupil population and the structure of a typical day. Are the pupils happy, engaged and lively? Do the teachers seem approachable and professional? Is there a wide range of facilities for the pupils to enjoy?

5 Take into consideration teacher-student ratio, staff qualifications, counselling services and standardised test scores. Examine the curriculum to determine if it meets your child's needs. Interview the head teacher to get a sense of the school's philosophy and vision for its pupils. Ask about the success ratio of school leavers entering universities or the job market.

6 Discuss school fees. These vary enormously: some schools can cost in the region of £6,000 a term, with add-ons for inclusions in sports, art courses and more. Boarding fees will, of course, increase the cost. Ask about additional financial obligations such as fundraising; before- and after-school care; and coverage during school holidays. Get a copy of the school calendar and note school closure dates. Ask how much parental involvement is required.

What to Look For

- Good fit for your child
- Curriculum meets interests
- Application requirements
- School's mission and philosophy
- Affordable tuition

Tips

Do your research well in advance. School entrance exams usually take place in the January before the September intake of pupils. As a rough rule of thumb, start looking in the April of the previous year and submit your application well in advance of the entrance exam date.

If footing the bill is a hardship, apply for financial help. Many schools offer their own assisted places as well as scholarships.

327 Find Good After-School Care

School's out, but you need to be at work for another three hours every day. The challenge is finding a convenient programme that offers your children a stimulating environment for playing, relaxing and doing homework.

Steps

1 Know that after-school clubs are organised at most large primary schools. If your child's school does not have an after-school facility, check whether there are arrangements for pupils to be bussed to a club at a neighbouring school.

2 Visit the after-school club while it is in operation so you can see at first hand what goes on. Do the children seem well supervised, happy and engaged? Is there positive interaction with the staff? Are there age-appropriate activities? Does it look safe and fun?

3 Find out exactly what the fees are. Expect to pay around £2 an hour per child. Ask if any meals and snacks are included. Find out what penalty fees are charged for late collection of a child – they may be quite stiff, as late collection is highly unpopular.

4 Check whether the scheme runs a holiday programme. Care for a day is likely to cost around £12.

5 Be aware that childminders will also pick up children from school and look after them for a few hours. Check out this option.

What to Look For

- After-school club
- Good supervision
- Appropriate activities
- Affordable fees

Tip

Look out for breakfast clubs run by some schools for children whose parents need to go to work early.

Warning

The children attending after-school clubs may include an above-average percentage of rough and disruptive children.

328 Sign Your Child Up for Lessons

Is your child a tiny dancer or a karate kid? A diva, a diver or a go-kart driver? Sign her or him up for classes. Your child will have fun, make friends outside school and maybe even discover a lifelong passion.

Steps

1 Follow your child's lead. More than anyone, he or she can tell you what interests him or her the most: you might be dying to see your daughter in a tutu, while she would rather put on jodhpurs.

2 Start the search as early as possible. Spaces fill up quickly, especially in the summer months.

3 Ask other parents and your child's teachers for recommendations. Check listings at the local library, in local newspapers, at the park and online.

4 Determine how much various lessons cost. Will you also have to fork out for uniforms or expensive equipment?

5 Make sure the classes are offered by a reputable organisation and that they're held in a safe, secure environment. Instructors should have experience with kids and medical emergencies.

What to Look For

- Fun and appropriate for your child
- Reasonable price
- Excellent safety standards
- Trained instructors

Tips

Encourage other families you know to enrol a child in the same class. A friendly face will reassure your child.

Ask if your child can attend a trial session for free or for a reduced rate before you commit.

329 Buy a Garden Play Structure

Shopping for a play structure? It's a jungle out there. A well-chosen set can provide years of stimulating fun for your monkeys, but the price range and variety of choices can make anyone's head spin. And with an alarming number of playground injuries treated in the hospital each year, safety is a top concern.

Steps

1 Evaluate how much space you have before you shop. You'll need a level area at least 1.8 m (6 ft) away from your house or garage and clear of hazards such as trees, electrical wires, fences and standing water.

2 Make safety your first priority. Inspect the structure: climb on it, shake it, stomp on it and look closely at the construction.

3 Reduce the risk of serious injury with an appropriate surface material. Dirt and grass don't offer enough padding for falls; instead look into pea gravel, wood chips or rubberised mats. Keep in mind that the "fall zone" extends 1.8 m (6 ft) beyond the structure itself.

4 Set your budget while keeping in mind that you get what you pay for. First consideration is materials, and while you can find a metal play set for a few hundred pounds, don't expect it to last – either your child will outgrow it or it will fall apart.

5 Step up to a wooden set if you're willing to invest in long-lasting durability. Make sure the wood used is not prone to splintering or treated with toxic chemicals.

6 Climb all over maintenance-free, sturdy plastic play structures. Relatively inexpensive (£40 to £350), they're great for toddler adventures. Visit Toys'R'Us.

7 Choose a set your children can grow into. Adjustable-height swings, for example, offer a few extra years' use. Pay attention to the different climbing options since kids spend a significant amount of playtime scrambling up the structure.

8 Keep an eye out for hidden costs, such as delivery and assembly charges. Ask about payment plans for more expensive sets.

9 Read the fine print. Ask how long and how difficult it is to assemble the set. What tools are required? Some sets are so hard to put together that it's no fun for anyone. Line up skilled and willing hands to help you set up your kid's new dream-come-true.

What to Look For

- Safety features
- Durability
- Play options
- Can grow with your child

Tip

Reeling from price label shock? Remember that the play structure can go with you when you move. Smaller structures, particularly plastic ones, are always in demand from other parents looking for used bargains.

Warning

Structures made from pressure-treated wood can leach toxic chemicals, including arsenic.

330 Find a Family-Friendly Hotel

Hotels can be more hard work than relaxation if they don't cater for children. Do some research to find one that suits your needs and those of your family to ensure that you all have a good break.

Steps

1 Decide what you all want from the holiday, bearing in mind the age of your child or children. Do you want organised entertainment and childcare for your child, or simply a child-friendly environment? Involve your child in the search if he/she is old enough.

2 Ask friends for recommendations. Browse the internet, looking at some of the parenting sites and travel sites, then narrowing the search to individual hotel websites. Send off for brochures.

3 Look at the facilities on offer. Is there plenty for kids to do? Are there facilities like a gym or spa for parents? Check what else is nearby so that you can plan daytrips.

4 Check out the eating arrangements. Do the timings of meals fit in with your family? Will the menu suit your child? Can provision be made for special diets?

5 Find out what is included in the cost. Many hotels only provide babysitting services in high season and for an extra fee. Check that the hotel is affordable and offers good value.

6 Take out insurance in case you need to cancel (see 434 "Get Travel Insurance").

What to Look For

- Good recommendations
- Well-trained staff and a good ratio of staff to guests
- Affordability
- An atmosphere that suits your child

Tips

Look for star ratings awarded by the AA and RAC and crowns awarded by the English Tourist Board.

Always ask about free child places, reductions for children, and how prices vary outside school holidays.

331 Organise a Fund-Raising Event

Whether you are planning a stall at the annual fête to raise funds for the school, or a sponsored event for charity, an individual effort or one that involves lots of others, you need to keep in mind the end result you want, and plan carefully

Steps

1 Come up with a suitable idea. This could be anything from a concert, in which the proceeds are donated to the school or charity, to a sponsored swim.

2 Work out the costs involved for an event that involves the public, and how you are going to cover them (can others donate their services free?), and how much you are likely to raise at the end. Check if you need insurance and if you need to inform the police or local authorities (raffles, performances and money collections may all need a licence). Can you manage the organisation or should you enlist others? Who will want to come?

What to Look For

- A good idea
- Meticulous organisation
- A clear idea of how much you want to raise

Tips

E-mail everyone you know and tell them about the event.

After the event, thank all your supporters.

3 Choose a number of impartial people who can confirm what has been achieved if you are organising an individual event where sponsorship is involved.

4 Set a date and publicise the event. This may involve producing posters, contacting the local press, or simply producing a sponsorship form to take to everyone you know.

5 Ensure there are people and arrangements at the event to look after any volunteers and keep things running smoothly. Take your own photos, and arrange for the local press to be there. Send a press release to the local paper or radio station after the event, with details including how much you raised.

Warnings

If the event is dangerous in any way, seek the advice of professionals.

Where children are involved adults should always be present, particularly in a public place.

332 Buy Braces for Your Child

Is orthodontics in your child's future? You'd better brace yourself for the bill if you decide to go private. While orthodontic work is a great investment in overall dental health, the final bill bites: a jaw-dropping £2,000 to £5,000.

Steps

1 Start early. Problems detected early are generally easier and cheaper to fix.

2 Ask other parents and your family dentist to recommend an orthodontist. Since you'll be making a lot of trips to his or her surgery, find a qualified orthodontist who is close to your home or your child's school.

3 If you have insurance, consult with your insurance company to find out what is and isn't covered.

4 Call the orthodontist's practice manager and ask about payment plans. You may be offered a reduced fee if you pay for treatment in advance. Others may be able to arrange relatively inexpensive financing through a third-party lender.

5 Talk with your child about which features are important to him or her when choosing braces. The clunky metal models are no more – modern braces almost disappear on the wearer's teeth, while designer braces can sparkle in school colours. While designer features can add to the total bill, they may be important to your child and result in him or her cooperating more fully with the treatment.

What to Look For

- Recommended, qualified orthodontist
- Location
- Health coverage
- Payment plans

Tip

Often orthodontists are happy to accept a large initial down payment, then arrange monthly payments until the balance is paid in full.

333 Buy Toys

Nothing is more exciting – and potentially overwhelming – than a trip to the toy shop with your child. The aisles of tempting toys seem to stretch for miles. So how do you choose developmentally appropriate toys that do not break the bank?

Steps

1 Review the list of recommended toys in the chart opposite. These guidelines will help you select toys that appeal to your child's current developmental stage. See also 334 "Buy Books, Videos and Music for Your Children".

2 Put safety first. Packaging is labelled with a suggested age range, to use as a guideline when buying a gift. If the toy is for your own child, use your judgement about what is appropriate, but remember that the age guidelines are generally well researched.

3 Go to a big retailer for good prices and selection but don't over-look independent toy shops. Although prices can be higher in these than at large retailers, the atmosphere is less frantic and it is easier to find a knowledgeable staff member who can make recommendations. You can find unique items in small shops.

4 Shop on the internet, especially during holiday times. Internet shopping works particularly well for gifts, since postage and packing are often included in the price. See 3 "Buy Products and Services Online".

5 Cruise car boot sales, second-hand shops and school fêtes for used toys. Make sure they don't have any broken or missing parts before you buy.

6 Choose toys that are well made and can handle lots of wear and tear. Also remember that the best toys can be used over and over for many different types of play. These toys allow the chid's imagination to take over, rather than the child feeling there is only one thing to do with it and becoming bored. Good examples are blocks, art supplies and train sets.

What to Look For

- Age-appropriateness
- Safety
- Quality

Tips

Try before you buy, at a friend's house or a shop that provides toys to play with. Some libraries lend out toys as well as books. Check with your children's librarian.

If your child doesn't seem interested in a toy, or if he or she is overwhelmed after receiving a lot toys at Christmas or a birthday, stash the toy away and re-introduce it after a few months. More than likely, your child will be excited about the "new" toy.

AGE	DEVELOPMENTAL STAGE	RECOMMENDED TOYS
Birth to 1 year	Babies are developing their motor skills and hand-eye coordination. Choose toys that appeal to sight, hearing and touch.	Big blocks of plastic or wood; teethers with different textures; mobiles; play pots and pans; soft, washable animals and dolls; books with fun textures; activity centres; easy-to-grab squeeze toys and rattles; shape sorters; baby-safe mirror.
1 to 2 years	Young toddlers like to imitate and explore. They are developing language, rhythm and motor skills. Pick toys that stimulate curiosity, satisfy building urges and can take a beating.	Sturdy board books; musical tops; push and pull toys (no long strings); stacking toys; musical instruments; train sets; nesting blocks; toy telephones; large cars; sandbox with lid; sturdy dolls; play keys; bath toys; balls; building bricks, such as Duplo; wooden puzzles.
3 to 5 years	Imagination starts to develop. Focus on toys that foster creativity and imaginative play.	Books; crayons, nontoxic clay, washable markers; blackboard and chalk; building kits such as Lego; housekeeping toys; puzzles; train sets; dressing-up clothes; slide, swing set, playhouse; musical instruments; tricycle, mini-car; play kitchens and dishes; pretend tools. Storybooks are also a big hit.
6 to 9 years	Bigger kids are on the move, perfecting fine motor skills by doing more involved crafts. Find toys that help your child develop skills and creativity.	Puppets; sports equipment; bicycles; craft kits; skateboards; skipping ropes; roller skates; board and card games; electronic games; information books; science experiment kits.
10 to 14 years	Teens and pre-teens have definite preferences. Pick toys that build on their interests.	Computer games; hobby kits; science sets; microscopes/telescopes; sports gear; more complex craft kits or science experiments.
WARNING	Choking, strangulation and suffocation are major causes of death among children under three. Do not buy toys with small parts or balls that are loose or can break off and end up in your child's mouth. Use a toilet paper tube to test the size: if any loose parts fit inside the tube, they are potentially lethal. Strings and balloons also pose a significant hazard. Make sure strings are not long enough to encircle your child's neck, and never let children play with uninflated balloons.	

Every parent knows that exposing your kids to books and music fosters a lifelong appreciation for both. Not only that, but it's so much fun to see your daughter enjoy reading her own stories, or watch your two-year-old son dancing to pop music. Films can also be great learning tools. But how to select from so many choices? Talk to your local librarian or bookseller, browse the age-appropriate recommendations at online stores and preview all films first before handing over the remote.

AGE	BOOKS	VIDEOS	MUSIC
Birth to 1 year	Any touch and feel book; nursery rhymes; lift-the-flap books; *Goodnight Moon, Peekaboo Baby.*	The *Baby Einstein* Series; *So Smart;* Gymboree series; *Babymugs!*	Classical music of all kinds; traditional lullaby compilations; *African Lullaby.*
1 to 3 years	Board books; lift-the-flap books; *Guess How Much I Love You; Elmer; Kipper; Wibbly Pig; Thomas the Tank Engine;* Dr. Seuss titles; *Mother Goose; The Very Hungry Caterpillar* and other Eric Carle titles; first word books; ABCs, numbers, shapes, colours primers; Richard Scarry books; television character stories.	Television character videos; *Bob the Builder; Pingu; Bing and Bong; Fun Song Factory* compilations; *Thomas the Tank Engine* series; *Winnie-the-Pooh; Peter Rabbit; Maisy; Kipper; Teletubbies; Tweenies.*	Traditional children's song collections; Fun Song Factory compilations; kids' compilation of adult music; singalong compilations for the car or for joining in the actions; television themes
4 to 5 years	*Bread and Jam for Frances; The Tiger who Came to Tea;* Maurice Sendak titles; television character stories; *Madeline;* Dr. Seuss titles; Tove Jansson's Moominland picture books; Disney stories; *Grimm's Fairy Tales;* Hans Christian Andersen folktales.	Television character videos; *Pinocchio; The Little Princess;* Disney films (with discretion); *Thumbelina; Toy Story, Toy Story II; Bugs; Antz; Monsters Inc; Thomas the Tank Engine; Winnie-the-Pooh; The Muppets.*	*The Sound of Music* soundtrack; Peter, Paul & Mary; Bob Marley; *Peter and the Wolf; The Nutcracker;* Disney soundtracks/compilations.

AGE	BOOKS	VIDEOS	MUSIC
6 to 9 years	*Harry Potter* series; Lemony Snicket titles; Dick King-Smith titles; Anne Fine titles; Roald Dahl titles; *Scooby Doo*; *Captain Underpants*; *Madeline*; *Horrid Henry* titles; *Charlotte's Web*; *Stuart Little*; *Little House on the Prairie* series; *Pippi Longstocking*; *Winnie-the-Pooh*; *The Velveteen Rabbit*; *Horrid Henry* titles; *The Worst Witch*; *The Owl Who Was Afraid of the Dark*; *Horrible Histories* series.	Disney films; *Finding Nemo*; *The Sound of Music*; *The Princess Diaries*; *Scooby Doo*; *Pokemon*; *Rug Rats*; *Gigi*; *Mulan*; *Charlie and the Chocolate Factory*; *Charlotte's Web*; *Harry Potter* series; *Spy Kids*; *Captain Scarlet*, *Stingray* and *Thunderbirds*; *Looney Tunes*; *The Simpsons*.	Pop music with age-appropriate lyrics, soundtracks from their favourite films. Kids at this age are curious but still open, so it's a good time to expose them to world music, jazz and other favourites if you haven't already.
10 years and up	Above titles plus Judy Blume titles; *Holes; Wizard of Oz* series; J.R.R. Tolkien books; Tove Jansson's Moominland books; Jacqueline Wilson; *The Chronicles of Narnia*; Sport biographies; *Little Women; Anne of Green Gables; The Silver Sword*.	Above titles plus *Holes; Shrek; James and the Giant Peach; Wizard of Oz; Cool Runnings; Mr. Bean; E.T. the Extra-Terrestrial; Star Wars* films; *Grease; Lord of the Rings*.	Find versions of popular music that have been edited for younger listeners. It is important to preview these, however, as it is not only the language that is inappropriate, but often the subject matter.
WARNING	Be very cautious about film content. Disney films, for example, are too intense for children under four or five years of age even though many grown-ups think they're harmless.		

335 Buy a Video Game System

Are you shopping for a console-based video-game system, but don't know an Xbox from a mailbox? To start off with, take a look at 415 "Buy Video and Computer Games". The popular systems all offer spectacular graphics and special effects, and run from £100 to £200. Before you go to the next level, check out the special features.

Steps

1 Start by doing your homework. Check online at Amazon.co.uk and in gaming magazines for product reviews, or ask video-game fanatics you know which system they prefer.

2 Stick with one of the big brand names: Sony, Microsoft and Nintendo. The system will require updates, upgrades and support in the future – and a company that is still around to provide them.

3 Shop at a retailer that stocks different systems and compare them. Ask a salesperson to define the differences between them and describe any additional features like internet connectivity, expandability and CD/DVD capability.

4 Give each system a test run. Is it easy to use?

5 Ask about the library of game titles available for each system. Make sure you can play the games you want. If you are upgrading from an older system, find out if you can play your old games on the new machine.

6 Find out what the basic price includes. Peripherals can bump up costs considerably, but many new systems have starter packs that include several options like a second controller.

7 Compare shop prices with game sites online.

What to Look For

- Positive reviews
- Reliable manufacturer
- Ease of use
- Large game library
- Compatibility with your existing system
- Pricing

Tip

Look for special offers that bundle a few games with a console purchase.

336 Hire a Tutor

Tutoring benefits all kinds of students, whether they are performing above, below or at expected levels for their age group. A trained tutor can provide one-on-one attention, an individualised approach and a big boost for your child's self-esteem.

Steps

1 Determine your goals. They may be very specific, such as raising a maths grade from a C to a B, or more general, such as getting your child more excited about learning.

2 Talk to your child about why you feel tutoring is so important. He or she may be resistant to the idea of needing extra help, or be embarrassed about it. Taking the time to be supportive and encouraging can make a big difference.

What to Look For

- Relevant education and experience
- Shared expectations
- Encouraging results

3 Ask for recommendations from your child's school, other parents, or local colleges and universities.

4 Interview prospective tutors about their qualifications, experience, areas of expertise and teaching style. After a first meeting with the tutor, ask your child what he or she thinks. Without a connection between the two of them, your efforts may be in vain. Be clear with the tutor about your expectations.

5 Discuss the hourly fee. Choose a location that works for both your child and the tutor. Get references from the tutor's other clients and contact them. Talk to the students themselves if it's appropriate.

6 Check in with your child, the child's teacher at school, and the tutor as lessons progress. Find out if they feel tutoring is making a difference and how you can help.

7 Ask for regular updates about your child's progress.

337 Adopt a Child

Adopting a child is a long and emotional process that can take several years. While you will encounter obstacles, disappointment and frustrating delays along the way, with persistence you will stand a good chance of finding your heart and your hands full.

Steps

1 Be clear about the age of the child you want to adopt. Know that very few babies or young children are available for adoption in Britain. Also be aware that almost all children up for adoption are to some degree disturbed. Contact Adoption UK (adoption.org.uk) for information and support. Their Helpline is 0870 7700 450.

2 Decide whether to apply to your local social services or to a voluntary agency. Social services have a broad range of children. Agencies tend to deal with special-needs and older children.

3 Contact BAAF (baaf.org.uk), which offers a free agency search to help you find a suitable agency. Or look in the *Yellow Pages*, where you will find both voluntary agencies and local social services advertised.

4 Expect to undergo a rigorous and intrusive vetting process. You and your partner will be interviewed and a judgement made on your emotional suitability and the commitment of your relationship. Your house will be examined and so will the area in which you live. Former partners may also be contacted and you will have to submit to a medical examination. Do not expect anything about the process to be quick or easy.

Tip

Match your child's personal style with his or her tutor's. Would your child benefit from lots of structure or a more flexible approach? Will cracking jokes help your child crack the books?

What to Look For

- Local spocial services
- Voluntary adoption agency
- Extensive vetting
- Advice helplines

Tip

For advice on adopting a child from another country, call the Overseas Adoption Helpline on 0870 516 8742. Be aware that, although there may be more suitable children for adoption in some foreign countries, vetting procedures are still lengthy and strictly enforced.

338 Get Your Child Hired as a Model

Can't you just see your gorgeous child in a magazine ad – once you get that icing sugar off his or her face? Modelling is not a piece of cake. It's tough, demanding work for you and your child, and involves dealing with tight schedules, rejection and impatient art directors. But if your child is patient, easy-going and comfortable in front of strangers, it may be worth a try.

Steps

1 Be realistic. Child models must live in or very near a city where work is routinely available.

2 Contact reputable modelling agencies (check the internet or *Yellow Pages* for "Model Agencies") with a brief letter stating your interest. Include two or three clear photos of your child (both head shots and full body). Write your contact details and your child's name, age, hair and eye colour, and clothing and shoe sizes on the back of each picture (not with a ball point).

3 Visit the agencies that offer you and your child appointments. Arrive on time, come armed with questions and trust your instincts. If you don't like what you see or hear, try another agency.

4 Review contract offers carefully, and understand the fees and how they're paid. Be aware that most contracts require you to release control of all photographs; read all provisions and make sure you consent to them.

5 Hit the pavement once you've signed the contract. The agency will send you and your child on "go-sees" (short meetings with prospective clients). You may face countless go-sees without ever seeing a job. Ask how you should dress your child and bring several changes of clothing, a hairbrush, wipes, snacks, drinks and toys to keep your child happy through all the hurry up and wait.

6 Prepare yourself and your child for rejection. Agencies usually have a very specific look in mind, and not even a child as adorable as yours may sway them.

7 Help your child be comfortable throughout the process. Try not to get stressed. Be as natural with him or her as you can, as you are the anchor in a chaotic situation. Listen to the director at the shoot and do what she says. Help your child succeed under the lights by translating the director's instructions into words he or she better understands. Photoshoots can be long, hot and tedious. If you see that your child needs a break, tell the crew.

What to Look For

- Reputable agency
- Reasonable contract

Tip

You don't need to spend money on professional photos. Your own regularly updated pictures are fine. Your child will build up a portfolio over time.

339 Sell Used Baby Gear, Toys, Clothes and Books

Is a tidal wave of gear, toys and books taking over your house? It's time to clear out. Most kids don't play with the majority of their toys and books, and they certainly can't wear clothes that no longer fit. If you can't bear to give away those expensive new sandals your kid refuses to wear, it's time for eBay, baby!

Steps

1 Sort baby gear, toys, clothes and books into categories – the discard pile, the pass-on-to-someone-else pile and the sell pile. Dole out the "pass on" items to family and friends. Sort toys by age and/or category: blocks, cars, dolls, electronic toys.

2 Sort books by age. Repair torn pages as much as possible. Wipe down board and plastic books.

3 Sort clothing by gender and size. Wash clothes, removing stains if possible. Fold neatly or hang on hangers.

4 Decide to take part in a car boot sale. Check when and where the next one is due to take place in your area, then register your car with the organisers. Take stock of your "sell" pile and decide which items will sell best at a car boot sale – these will be the fairly old and not in great shape items for which you don't expect to get that much cash. When the time comes, take them and sell them, for knock-down prices if necessary (see 42 "Take Part in a Car Boot Sale").

5 Take the "sell" pile of clothes to a second-hand clothes shop. Call the shops in your area to find out what they accept, what their buying hours are and how they pay (see 498 "Sell Used Clothing").

6 Sell expensive or nearly new items online. Browse eBay.co.uk to see what is selling and for how much. Sell by the lot if you have a group of smaller toys or bags of clothes. You can make a decent return on items like individual *Thomas the Tank Engine* pieces and sets, bicycles, and up-market clothing and shoes. See 6 "Sell Products and Services Online", spruce up your goods, post quality digital photos and get ready to haul in some cash.

7 Donate whatever doesn't sell or seem salesworthy to a local children's charity, charity shop or nursery.

What to Look For

- Sorted piles – discard, giveaway, sell
- Clean items
- Car boot sales
- Online auctions

Tip

Fresh, clean toys and clothes in particular are more appealing to buyers and will fetch a higher price. Wash or wipe down everything that's plastic or wood with disinfectant.

340 Find a Couples Counsellor

Let's face it, being in a relationship can be tricky. Almost every couple can benefit from a little objective help now and then, to put the relationship back on the rails. A skilled couples counsellor can offer new approaches to making things work. The key is to find someone you and your partner both feel comfortable with.

What to Look For

- Qualifications
- Specific experience
- Good fit

Steps

1 Sit down with your partner, if possible, and talk about what each of you expects to get out of counselling. Try to be specific about your goals and be considerate of each other's wishes. Write them down if you feel it's helpful.

2 Get a professional referral or follow up on personal leads (see 352 "Hire a Mental-Health Professional"). Relate is the UK's largest provider of relationship counselling (relate.org.uk). Use the *Yellow Pages* as a last resort.

3 Contact therapists and ask about their qualifications, licensing, experience and education. If you have special issues (such as substance abuse, depression or anger management), ask about their experience in those areas.

4 At your first meeting with the counsellor, discuss what you and your partner hope to accomplish. You'll also need to talk about appointment times and fees.

5 Consider working with someone still in training if finances are an issue – they often offer reduced rates and will be supervised by a trained professional. Relate expects to receive a fee for its counselling, although the organisation does not make a profit from the services it provides. Some Relate centres offer subsidised counselling.

6 Ask a potential counsellor how long it may take to work on your issues. If you cannot afford in-depth work, a shorter solution-based approach may be helpful.

7 Trust your instincts and respect your partner's point of view. A wall covered in diplomas and professional awards can't substitute for the right fit for you and your situation.

Tips

Think carefully before asking relatives or friends for referrals. It may prove helpful, or it may compromise your security and privacy, making an already tough task harder.

A sense of trust and security with your therapist is critical. Therapy often raises difficult issues, and working through them will be easier if you feel comfortable with your counsellor.

341 Hire a Family Solicitor

They say death and taxes are certain, but these days, so is the need for a good solicitor. Over the years, there will be times you might require legal assistance: resolving divorce and custody issues, preparing a will or settling an estate.

Steps

1 Ask family, friends and co-workers to recommend an honest and dependable solicitor. Have they crossed paths with a not-so-honest solicitor? Find out who to avoid.

2 Hit the shelves at your public library and look for Chambers and Partners Guide to the Legal Profession, which lists and rates lawyers. Alternatively, use the internet: chambersandpartners.com. The Law Society also offers details of solicitors and their area of expertise at solicitors-online.com.

3 Put together a short list of candidates. Call them and ask for references. Then call their references. Were they happy with their services?

4 If you don't have time to search for a solicitor yourself, call the Law Society's Helpline on 0870 606 6575.

5 Establish your price range. Hourly rates can vary.

6 Set up initial meetings with your candidates, but ask first if they will charge for these. Be prepared to ask about fees (hourly as well as for phone calls), the solicitor's track record, and his or her education and experience.

7 Make a smart choice. A trustworthy, quick-to-respond solicitor is like an honest mechanic; once you've found one, you'll rely on that person for years to come.

What to Look For

- Excellent track record
- References
- Reasonable fees
- Quick response

Tip

Many people don't look for a solicitor until a time of stress – when they're facing a lawsuit or getting divorced. Choose a solicitor for the long run, not for a quick fix.

342 Buy or Rent Sheltered Housing

Sheltered, or retirement, housing is ideal for active retired people who like living independently but want the reassurance of knowing that help is nearby if there is an emergency. Most schemes have a live-in warden as well as a community alarm, and there may be community facilities such as a communal lounge and guest flat.

Steps

1 Consider your present needs, and think about what lies ahead. Your goal may be to hold on to your independence for as long as possible.

2 Be aware of the costs beyond the price of the property (which may start at £100,000). Service charges vary enormously, depending on the location and the level of service offered, but for most ordinary sheltered schemes expect to pay in the region of £80–£160 per month.

3 Decide in which part of the country you want to live. Do you wish to stay locally or move away to be closer to family?

4 Ask for referrals from your doctor or social worker. You can also get lists of nearby retirement homes online or in your phone book. The charity EAC (Elderly Accommodation Counsel – HousingCare.org) offers advice and information on sheltered housing schemes around the country. Check with your local council for council-run rented sheltered housing.

5 Visit as many properties as possible and talk to the warden. Find out if any social events are organised.

6 Find out exactly what the service charge includes.

7 Chat with residents and ask for their honest opinions about the facility. If everyone is hiding in their flat, that's not a good sign. Also, what is the average age of the people you see? Do they look like people that you would get along with?

What to Look For

- Affordability
- Location
- Likeable warden
- Social activities

Tips

"A Buyer's Guide to Retirement Housing", published by Age Concern (ageconcern.org.uk) gives useful information about buying sheltered housing.

There is usually a minimum age for sheltered housing, often 60 or 55. Check with individual schemes.

343 Choose a Care Home

At some time in our lives, you may have a parent, spouse or relative who needs around-the-clock care. Choosing a care home is a truly difficult but often necessary choice. You'll want the best medical care possible, in a setting that retains the comforts of home, for a price that doesn't drain all reserves.

Steps

1 Long-term care homes are no longer referred to as residential or nursing homes, but simply as care homes, although they do still provide different levels of care. If your spouse or relative just needs help with day-to-day activities, look for a home that provides personal care. When the person can no longer look after himself or herself, research care homes that provide nursing care.

2 Gather recommendations from your family doctor, friends, co-workers and social workers. All care homes should be registered and regulated by the local care standards authority.

3 Contact the local authority for a list of accredited facilities. Care homes can be run by local authorities or health authorities, voluntary organisations or privately, by individuals or companies on a commercial basis.

4 Focus on these basics: dignified care, quality medical care, good food, meaningful interactions with staff, stimulation and a pleasant, secure environment. Be specific about the needs of the potential resident, and make sure the staff is qualified to meet them.

5 Make as many visits and see as many people as you can. You need to feel positive about this difficult and emotion-laced decision. Don't stop searching until you do. You'll want to make at least three visits – one unannounced, if possible – at different times during the week and day, and once during a meal.

6 Chat with residents to find out what the brochures may not cover. Are they getting the assistance they need? Do they appear to be well cared for?

7 Ask what is included in their social and recreational activities. Look for exercise, art and music classes, film or theatre nights, social hour and excursions. Find out if transportation to doctors' appointments, shopping and religious services is provided.

8 Look at different rooms to see how the floor plan would work for your relative or spouse. Ask if adjustable beds and other mobility-enhancing equipment are available. Find out if your relative may furnish the living quarters with his or her own furniture.

9 Ask for information about admissions procedures and contracts. Don't be shy about asking questions. Ask about fees and find out exactly what they cover. Find out from your local authority if you are liable for the full cost of residential or nursing accommodation or whether you qualify for financial help.

What to Look For

- A good (and realistic) fit
- Registered and regulated
- Excellent medical care
- Safe and well-maintained environment
- Caring staff

Tips

Start your search long before you need to, if possible.

Spot anything worrying on a visit? Mention your concerns to the care home's manager.

Get a sense of the level of basic kindness and compassion that the staff demonstrates to and for its residents.

Contact Help the Aged (helptheaged.org.uk) for help and advice.

344 Write a Living Will

You've chosen how to live; you can also make choices about dying. A living will, which will come into effect only if you are terminally ill, spells out your preferences regarding the use of medical treatment to delay an inevitable death. It also spares your family the anguish of making a heart-wrenching decision as well as guaranteeing that your wishes are followed should you be unable to communicate them. Living wills are legal documents, encouraged by the British Medical Association and the Law Commission.

Steps

1 Discuss your beliefs and wishes with your partner or spouse, family members, friends, clergy, solicitor and doctor.

2 Write down your wishes and get a solicitor to check that they comply with the law. Alternatively, research a living will form on the internet.

3 Review the form carefully. You may need the advice of your doctor when specifying which types of treatment you do not want. You can differentiate between life-prolonging procedures and those that alleviate pain. Detail specific wishes you have about your care that the form doesn't cover.

4 Sign the living will form and get it witnessed. An improperly signed or witnessed form may be ruled invalid.

5 Give copies to your family members and doctor. Put a copy in your home medical file.

What to Look For

- Compliance with the law
- Accurate reflection of your wishes
- Legally signed and witnessed

Tip

Look for a living will form on the internet.

Warning

Don't put off writing a living will until you're elderly or seriously ill, particularly if you have a family.

345 Buy a Cemetery Plot

Most cemeteries are run by local authorities, and a number of them will allow you to arrange the pre-purchase of a cemetery plot. Prices vary enormously: expect to spend between £200 and £2,000. You can include the purchase of a cemetery plot with a pre-paid funeral plan, which is organised through a funeral home. As with buying other property, it's all about location, which can significantly affect the cost.

Steps

1 Pick a cemetery. Consider family preferences, but look for a reasonable price. Some cemeteries that are connected with a specific place of worship may restrict entry to people who meet specific criteria.

2 Tour the grounds of the cemetery and ask for a map of available plots. Find out if there are any price differences at the cemetery;

What to Look For

- Family wishes
- Reasonable fees
- Clear rules and guidelines
- Ability to transfer ownership

Tips

Buying your own final resting place? Make sure you have left clear instructions in your will regarding your intentions for example, a plot with a view may be more expensive. If necessary, enquire about less expensive options at the same cemetery.

3 Check if there are any additional costs (the cost of the actual interment will not be included). How will payments be made?

4 Find out what happens if you change your mind. Can you sell the plot or transfer ownership to someone else?

5 Ask about the cost for adjacent plots if several family members want to be buried together. (If you don't want to lie next to Uncle Reg for eternity, speak up or forever rest in peace.)

(see 346 "Pay for Funeral Expenses").

Some cemeteries have restrictions about grave markers and decorations.

346 **Pay for Funeral Expenses**

It's difficult to arrange a dignified and appropriate service for someone you love when you're suffering their loss. Take a steady friend or relative with you to help sort it all out.

Steps

1 Find out from a close family member or a solicitor if the deceased left special requests regarding funeral arrangements. Check if the deceased took out a pre-paid funeral plan.

2 Set a budget. Prices for coffins and services vary hugely.

3 Contact undertakers. Family members may have their preferences.

4 Ask for an itemised price list, and make sure you understand exactly what it includes.

5 Find out what fees members of the clergy charge for their services, if applicable.

What to Look For

- Wishes of the deceased
- Price within budget
- No hidden charges

Tip

You may be eligible for assistance with funeral costs from the Department of Social Security (DSS). Apply at your local office.

...CTION SITES • BUY BARGAIN CLOTHING • BUY WHOLESALE • GET OUT OF DEBT • BUY NOTHING • BUY HAPPINESS • BUY A BETTER MOU...
...BUY YOUR WAY INTO SOMEONE'S FAVOUR • BUY LOVE • FIND THE RIGHT RELAXATION TECHNIQUE FOR YOU • BUY HEALTHY FAST FOOD •
...ATING SERVICE • SELL YOURSELF ON AN ONLINE DATING SERVICE • SELL YOURSELF TO YOUR GIRLFRIEND/BOYFRIEND'S FAMILY • BUY FL...
...CHOOSE FILM FOR YOUR CAMERA • BUY RECHARGEABLE BATTERIES • GIVE TO A GOOD CAUSE • TAKE PART IN A CAR BOOT SALE • EMPL...
...UDENT DISCOUNTS • BUY FLOWERS WHOLESALE • GET A PICTURE FRAMED • EMPLOY A REMOVAL COMPANY • EMPLOY A LIFESTYLE MA...
...Y FOR A HALLOWE'EN PARTY • BUY A GREAT BIRTHDAY PRESENT FOR UNDER £10 • SELECT GOOD CHAMPAGNE • BUY A DIAMOND • BUY...
...T A GIFT LIST • BUY WEDDING GIFTS • SELECT BRIDESMAIDS' DRESSES • HIRE AN EVENTS ORGANISER • HIRE A BARTENDER FOR A PART...
...NNOUNCEMENTS • SELL YOUR WEDDING DRESS • BUY AN ANNIVERSARY GIFT • ARRANGE ENTERTAINMENT FOR A PARTY • COMMISSION...
...RSON WHO HAS EVERYTHING • BUY A GIFT FOR PASSING EXAMS • SELECT A CHRISTMAS TURKEY • BUY A HOUSEWARMING GIFT • PURC...
...LAND • WRITE A MESSAGE IN THE SKY • HIRE A BIG-NAME BAND • GET INTO A PRIVATE GAMBLING ROOM IN LAS VEGAS • BUY SOMEONE...
...E TIMES • EMPLOY A BUTLER • BUY A FOOTBALL CLUB • BUY A PERSONAL JET • SELECT A CLASSIC CAR • ACQUIRE A BODY GUARD • B...
...REYHOUND TO RACE • BUY A RACEHORSE • BUY A VILLA IN TUSCANY • EMPLOY A PERSONAL CHEF • BUY A JOURNEY INTO SPACE • EMP...
...ORTUNE • HIRE AN EXPERT WITNESS • MAKE MONEY FROM ACCIDENT COMPENSATION • DONATE YOUR BODY TO SCIENCE • MAKE MONE...
...NANCIAL ADVISER • PLAN FOR RETIREMENT • COPE WITH HIGHER EDUCATION COSTS • BUY AND SELL SHARES • CHOOSE A STOCKBROK...
...SS INSURANCE • BUY LIFE INSURANCE • GET PRIVATE HEALTH INSURANCE • BUY PERSONAL FINANCE SOFTWARE • CHOOSE AN ACCOU...
...KE OUT A PATENT • MARKET YOUR INVENTION • FINANCE YOUR BUSINESS IDEA • BUY A SMALL BUSINESS • BUY A FRANCHISE • LEASE F...
...EBSITE • HIRE A GRAPHIC DESIGNER • ACQUIRE CONTENT FOR YOUR WEBSITE • BUY ADVERTISING ON THE WEB • SELL YOUR ART • HIR...
...UBLISH YOUR BOOK • START A BED-AND-BREAKFAST • SELL A FAILING BUSINESS • BUY A HOT DOG STAND • SHOP FOR A MORTGAGE • G...
...OUSE AT AUCTION • SHOP FOR A HOUSE ONLINE • BUY A PROPERTY FOR RENOVATION AND RESALE • EVALUATE BEFORE BUYING INTO A...
...UY A PLOT OF LAND • HAVE YOUR HOUSE DESIGNED • HIRE AN ARCHITECT • HIRE A BUILDER • GET PLANNING PERMISSION • BUY A HOL...
...BROAD • BUY TO LET • RENT YOUR HOME FOR A LOCATION SHOOT • FURNISH YOUR HOME • FURNISH YOUR STUDIO FLAT • BUY USED F...
...BUY HOUSEHOLD APPLIANCES • BUY FLOOR-CARE APPLIANCES • BUY EXTENDED WARRANTIES ON APPLIANCES • FIND PERIOD FIXTURE...
...OME • SELECT PAINT, STAIN AND VARNISH • CHOOSE DECORATIVE TILES • CHOOSE A DEHUMIDIFIER • BUY A WHIRLPOOL BATH • BUY A S...
...ALLPAPER • BUY A WOOD-BURNING STOVE • SELECT FLOORING • SELECT CARPETING • CHOOSE KITCHEN CABINETS • CHOOSE A KITCH...
...MOKE ALARMS • BUY CARBON MONOXIDE DETECTORS • BUY FIRE EXTINGUISHERS • CHOOSE AN ENTRY DOOR • BUY A GARAGE-DOOR C...
...UTDOOR FURNITURE • BUY THE PERFECT ROSE • BUY FLOWERING BULBS • BUY FLOWERS FOR YOUR GARDEN • SELECT PEST CONTRO...
...UTOMATIC WATERING SYSTEM • START A NEW LAWN • BUY A LAWN MOWER • BUY KOI FOR YOUR FISH POND • BUY A STORAGE SHED • ...
...RODUCE • CHOOSE A PERFECT PEACH • BUY AND SELL AT FARMERS' MARKETS • SELECT KITCHEN KNIVES • DECIPHER FOOD LABELS • ...
...ERFECT BURGER • PURCHASE A CHRISTMAS HAM • BUY ORGANIC BEEF • BUY HAGGIS • PURCHASE LOCAL HONEY • CHOOSE A CHICKE...
...UT TRUFFLES • BUY ARTISAN BREADS • BUY ARTISAN CHEESES • PURCHASE KOSHER FOOD • BUY SENSIBLY IN SUPERMARKETS • CHOO...
...RDER A GREAT CUP OF COFFEE • BUY A COFFEEMAKER OR ESPRESSO MACHINE • PURCHASE PARTY BEER • CHOOSE THE RIGHT WINE •...
...PERM • CHOOSE AN OVULATION PREDICTOR KIT • PICK A PREGNANCY TEST KIT • CHOOSE BIRTH CONTROL • CHOOSE WHERE TO GIVE E...
...UY BABY CLOTHES • CHOOSE NAPPIES • BUY OR RENT A BREAST PUMP • CHOOSE A CAR SEAT • BUY CHILD-PROOFING SUPPLIES • FIN...
...UY A GARDEN PLAY STRUCTURE • FIND A FAMILY-FRIENDLY HOTEL • ORGANISE A FUND-RAISING EVENT • BUY BRACES FOR YOUR KID •...
...S A MODEL • SELL USED BABY GEAR, TOYS, CLOTHES AND BOOKS • FIND A COUPLES COUNSELLOR • HIRE A FAMILY SOLICITOR • BUY C...
...URCHASE A TOOTHBRUSH • BUY MOISTURISERS AND ANTIWRINKLE CREAMS • SELECT PAIN RELIEF AND COLD MEDICINES • CHOOSE A...
...RODUCTS • BUY WAYS TO COUNTER HAIR LOSS • BUY A WIG OR HAIRPIECE • BUY A NEW BODY • GET A TATTOO OR BODY PIERCING • C...
...EETH • SELECT SPECTACLES AND SUNGLASSES • HIRE A PERSONAL TRAINER • SIGN UP FOR A YOGA CLASS • TREAT YOURSELF TO A DA...
...AN ANTIQUE MARKET • BUY AT AUCTION • KNOW WHAT YOUR COLLECTIBLES ARE WORTH • BARTER WITH DEALERS • GET AN ANTIQUE...
...OINS • BUY AN ANTIQUE QUILT • BUY FILM POSTERS • LIQUIDATE YOUR BEANIE BABY COLLECTION • SCORE AUTOGRAPHS • TRADE YU-...
...ND SELL SPORTS MEMORABILIA • SELL YOUR FOOTBALL-CARD COLLECTION • CHOOSE A DESKTOP COMPUTER • SHOP FOR A USED CO...
...OMPUTER PERIPHERALS • CHOOSE AN INTERNET SERVICE PROVIDER • GET AN INTERNET DOMAIN NAME • NETWORK YOUR COMPUTER...
...VD PLAYER • BUY A VIDEO RECORDER • CHOOSE A PERSONAL DIGITAL ASSISTANT • CHOOSE A MOBILE PHONE SERVICE • GET A BETTE...
...IGITAL CAMERA • BUY A HOME AUTOMATION SYSTEM • BUY A STATE-OF-THE-ART SOUND SYSTEM • BUY AN AUDIO/VIDEO DISTRIBUTION...
...A SYSTEM • BUY VIRTUAL-REALITY FURNITURE • BUY TWO-WAY RADIOS • BUY A MOBILE ENTERTAINMENT SYSTEM • GET A PASSPORT,...
...EAL LUGGAGE • FLY FOR NEXT TO NOTHING • TAKE A TRIP ON THE TRANS-SIBERIAN EXPRESS • BUY DUTY-FREE • SHIP FOREIGN PURC...
...ALIAN CYCLING HOLIDAY • CHOOSE A CHEAP CRUISE • BOOK A HOTEL PACKAGE FOR THE GREEK ISLANDS • RAFT THE GRAND CANYO...
...CKSHAW IN RANGOON • TAKE SALSA LESSONS IN CUBA • BUY A CAMERA IN HONG KONG • BUY YOUR WAY ONTO A MOUNT EVEREST E...
...ALL TEAM • BUY ANKLE AND KNEE BRACES • CHOOSE RUGBY PROTECTION KIT • BUY GOLF CLUBS • SELL FOUND GOLF BALLS • BUY F...
...MPLOY A SCUBA INSTRUCTOR • BUY A SKATEBOARD AND PROTECTIVE GEAR • BUY SKATES • GO BUNJEE JUMPING • GO SKYDIVING • ...
...OOTS AND BINDINGS • BUY SKI BOOTS • BUY A BICYCLE • BUY AN ELECTRIC BICYCLE • BUY CYCLE CLOTHING • BUY A PROPERLY FITT...
...UIT • BUY A SURFBOARD • BUY FLY-FISHING GEAR • BUY ROCK-CLIMBING EQUIPMENT • BUY A CASHMERE JUMPER • PURCHASE VINTA...
...OCKTAIL DRESS • BUY DESIGNER CLOTHES AT A DISCOUNT • CHOOSE A BASIC WARDROBE FOR A MAN • BUY A MAN'S DRESS SHIRT •...
...EATHER JACKET • BUY MATERNITY CLOTHES • GET A GREAT-FITTING BRA • CHOOSE A HIGH-PERFORMANCE SWIM SUIT • BUY PERFORM...
...CTORY SHOPS • BUY A NEW CAR • BUY THE BASICS FOR YOUR CAR • BUY A USED CAR • BUY OR SELL A CAR ONLINE • BUY A HYBRI...

BUY TIME • BUY A BOUQUET OF ROSES • BUY SOMEONE A DRINK • GET SOMEONE TO BUY YOU A DRINK • BUY YOUR WAY INTO THE BES
SCREEN • BUT FURTHER EDUCATION • ORDER EXOTIC FOOD • ORDER AT A SUSHI BAR • BUY DINNER AT A FRENCH RESTAURANT • EMPLC
SAY SORRY TO YOUR PARTNER • BUY MUSIC ONLINE • EMPLOY MUSICIANS • ORDER A GOOD BOTTLE OF WINE • BUY AN ERGONOMIC C
NER • EMPLOY AN AU PAIR • BUY A GUITAR • BUY DUCT TAPE • GET A GOOD DEAL ON A MAGAZINE SUBSCRIPTION • GET SENIOR CITIZE
IND A VET • BUY PET FOOD • BUY A PEDIGREE DOG OR CAT • BREED YOUR PET AND SELL THE LITTER • BUY OR RENT FOR A FANCY DRES
RY MADE OF PRECIOUS METALS • BUY COLOURED GEMSTONES • CHOOSE THE PERFECT WEDDING DRESS • BUY OR RENT MEN'S FORMA
PHOTOGRAPHER • HIRE A CATERER • FIND THE IDEAL CIVIL WEDDING VENUE • THE COST OF MARRYING • ORDER PERSONALISED INVITAT
KS SHOW • BUY A MOTHER'S DAY GIFT • BUY A FATHER'S DAY GIFT • SELECT AN APPROPRIATE COMING-OF-AGE GIFT • GET A GIFT FOR T
ISTMAS CARDS • BUY CHRISTMAS STOCKING FILLERS • BUY CHRISTENING GIFTS • PURCHASE A PERFECT CHRISTMAS TREE • BUY A PRI
AY A RANSOM • GET HOT TICKETS • HIRE A LIMOUSINE • BUY A CRYONIC CHAMBER • RENT YOUR OWN HOARDING • TAKE OUT A FULL-PA
URY CRUISE AROUND THE WORLD • BUY A TICKET TO TRAVEL FOR A YEAR • BOOK A TRIP ON THE ORIENT-EXPRESS • OWN A VINEYARD •
OSTWRITER TO WRITE YOUR MEMOIRS • COMMISSION ORIGINAL ARTWORK • IMMORTALISE YOUR SPOUSE IN A SCULPTURE • GIVE AWAY
ICAL GUINEA PIG • SELL YOUR STORY TO THE TABLOIDS • SELL YOUR SOUL TO THE DEVIL • NEGOTIATE A BETTER CREDIT CARD DEAL •
RADE (OR NOT) • BUY ANNUITIES • BUY AND SELL MUTUAL FUNDS • BUY BONDS • SELL SHORT • INVEST IN PRECIOUS METALS • BUY SEF
D CASUAL WORK • SELL YOUR PRODUCT O   HEADHUNTER • SELL YOURSELF IN A JOB INTEF
E • LEASE INDUSTRIAL SPACE • LEASE OFFI   MENT • HIRE SOMEONE TO DESIGN AND BUILD YC
ACH • SELL ON THE CRAFT CIRCUIT • HIRE A   RY • SELL A SCREENPLAY • SELL YOUR NOVEL •
R MORTGAGE DEAL • SAVE ON YOUR MORT   • OBTAIN HOUSE INSURANCE • BUY A HOUSE •
EXCHANGE CONTRACTS ON A PROPERTY •   AN ESTATE AGENT • RELEASE CAPITAL FROM YOL
RENT A HOLIDAY HOME • BUY A FLAT • REI   COUNTRY • BUY A LOFT APARTMENT • BUY PRO
BUY DOOR AND WINDOW LOCKS • CHOOSE   IGHT FIXTURES • BUY A PROGRAMMABLE LIGHTIN
ED AND MATTRESS • HIRE AN INTERIOR DES   NCORPORATE A GREATER SENSE OF SPACE INTO
UY A TOILET • CHOOSE A TAP • BUY GLUES   MENTS • GET SELF-CLEANING WINDOWS • CHOOS
P • BUY GREEN HOUSEHOLD CLEANERS •   SECURITY SYSTEM • BUY A HOME ALARM SYSTI
Y TIMBER FOR A DIY PROJECT • HOW TO S   R, PAINTER OR ELECTRICIAN • HIRE A GARDENEF
L IMPROVERS • BUY MULCH • BUY A COMF   BLE GARDEN • HIRE A GARDEN DESIGNER • BUY
SURGEON • BUY BASIC GARDEN TOOLS • B   BUY AN OUTDOOR LIGHTING SYSTEM • BUY OF
S AND SPICES • STOCK YOUR KITCHEN WIT   RESH PRODUCE • SELECT MEAT • STOCK UP FOI
RESH FISH • SELECT RICE • PURCHASE PR   LTON • GET FRESH FISH DELIVERED TO YOUR DOC
OILS • SELECT OLIVE OIL • SELECT OLIVES   VINEGAR • CHOOSE PASTA • BUY TEA • BUY COFF
REAL ALE • ORDER A COCKTAIL • CHOOSE   STOCK A WINE CELLAR • STOCK YOUR BAR • DC
A MIDWIFE OR DOULA • PLAN A HOME BIRTI   R A NEW BABY • BUY A NEW COT • CHOOSE A PU
HILDCARE • FIND A GREAT NANNY • FIND T   TER-SCHOOL CARE • SIGN YOUR CHILD UP FOR I
BUY BOOKS, VIDEOS AND MUSIC FOR YOUF   HIRE A TUTOR • ADOPT A CHILD • GET YOUR CH
TERED HOUSING • CHOOSE A CARE HOME   LOT • PAY FOR FUNERAL EXPENSES • GET VIAGF
ARY MTHERAPY • SEE A MENTAL-HEALTH F   BUY HOME-USE MEDICAL SUPPLIES • SELECT HA
IMPLANTS • GET WRINKLE-FILLER INJECT   ACTITIONERS • CHOOSE A MANICURIST • GET WH

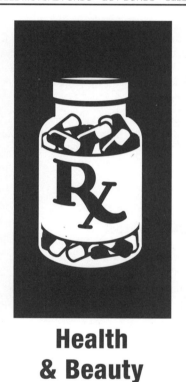

**Health
& Beauty**

• BOOK A MASSAGE • GET ON ANTIQUES R   SHOP AT AN ANTIQUE FAIR OR FLEA MARKET • RI
BUY SILVERWARE • EVALUATE CARNIVAL GLASS • BUY AND SELL STAMPS • BUY ANTIQUE FURNITURE • GET CLUED UP ON CLARICE CLI
• SEIZE STAR WARS ACTION FIGURES • SELL YOUR VINYL RECORD COLLECTION • SELL TO A PAWNSHOP • BUY AND SELL COMIC BOOK
ERIPHERALS • CHOOSE A LAPTOP OR NOTEBOOK COMPUTER • SELL OR DONATE A COMPUTER • BUY PRINTER PAPER • BUY A PRINTEF
THE MEMORY IN YOUR COMPUTER • BUY COMPUTER SOFTWARE • CHOOSE A CD PLAYER • BUY BLANK CDS • BUY AN MP PLAYER • CH
YOUR PHONE COMPANY • BUY VIDEO AND COMPUTER GAMES • CHOOSE A FILM CAMERA • CHOOSE A DIGITAL CAMCORDER • DECIDE C
Y A SERIOUS TV • CHOOSE BETWEEN DIGITAL TV PROVIDERS • GET A DIGITAL VIDEO RECORDER • GET A UNIVERSAL REMOTE • BUY A H
HASE CHEAP AIRLINE TICKETS • FIND GREAT HOTEL DEALS • HIRE THE BEST CAR FOR THE LEAST MONEY • GET TRAVEL INSURANCE • F
UNITED KONGDOM • TIP IN A FOREIGN COUNTRY • TIP PROPERLY IN THE UK • BRIBE A FOREIGN OFFICIAL • GET AN INTERRAIL PASS • T
EAP BUT FANTASTIC SAFARI • RENT A CAMEL IN CAIRO • GET SINGLE-MALT WHISKY IN SCOTLAND • BUY A SAPPHIRE IN BANGKOK • HIR
IRE A TREKKING COMPANY IN NEPAL • RENT OR BUY A SATELLITE PHONE • BUY YOUR CHILD'S FIRST CRICKET BAT • ORDER A STRIP FC
BUY A RACKET • BUY A HEALTH CLUB MEMBERSHIP • BUY AN AEROBIC FITNESS MACHINE • BUY SWIMMING EQUIPMENT • BUY A JETS
TING EQUIPMENT • CHOOSE A CAR RACK • BUY SKIS • BUY CLOTHES FOR COLD-WEATHER ACTIVITIES • SELL USED SKIS • BUY A SNOV
BUY THE OPTIMAL SLEEPING BAG • BUY A TENT • BUY A BACKPACK • BUY A CAMPING STOVE • BUY A KAYAK • BUY A LIFEJACKET • BU
• SELL USED CLOTHING • ORDER CUSTOM-MADE COWBOY BOOTS • BUY CLOTHES ONLINE • FIND NON-STANDARD SIZES • BUY THE PI
• BUY A WOMAN'S SUIT • BUY A MAN'S SUIT • HIRE A TAILOR • BUY CUSTOM-TAILORED CLOTHES IN ASIA • BUY A BRIEFCASE • SHOP F
JT CLOTHES • BUY A HEART-RATE MONITOR • SELECT A WATCH • BUY KIDS' CLOTHES • CHOOSE CHILDREN'S SHOES • PURCHASE CLO
CAR • BUY A MOTORCYCLE • BUYING AND CHANGING MOTOR OIL • WASH A CAR • WAX A CAR • BUY CAR INSURANCE • SPRING FOR

347 Get Viagra

All that stands between a man's impotence problems and revived virility is a credit card, an internet pharmacy and a subtly packaged delivery of those famous blue, diamond-shaped pills – right? Not so fast. If you buy Viagra online or by mail order, you could end up with fake pills that aren't effective or safe.

Steps

1 See your GP first to evaluate possible causes of impotency, check your overall health, assess Viagra's suitability in your case, rule out medication conflicts and make sure you're fit for sex. The two of you will discuss possible side effects of the drug. If you have a specific medical condition, such as diabetes or MS, your doctor may give you an NHS prescription for Viagra. If you do not have any of the specified medical conditions, he or she may offer you a private prescription.

2 If you must buy online, go to a UK-based online pharmacy. Online pharmacies in the UK have to be registered with the Royal Pharmaceutical Society (RPS) in order to trade legally.

3 Get assurance of the drug's authenticity, precise dosage instructions and a list of possible side effects.

What to Look For

- Your doctor's prescription
- Online pharmacies registered with the RPS
- Assurance of drug authenticity
- Precise dosage instructions

Warning

Avoid herbal products that claim to function like Viagra. They aren't subjected to quality control or scientific rigour like prescription drugs, so there's no way to know what (or how much of it) you're getting, or if it works.

348 Purchase a Toothbrush

A power toothbrush can make you feel as if it's whirring you straight towards smile nirvana. If you want to splurge on one of these plug-in or switch-on toothbrushes, check out the benefits you'll enjoy.

Steps

1 Ask your dentist to recommend a toothbrush. Depending on the state of your teeth and gums, he or she may give you a soft-bristled regular toothbrush or steer you towards an electric one. Always get soft-bristled brushes or heads to avoid pushing gums up.

2 Get a buzz with vibrating toothbrushes. They work better because people brush longer and more debris is loosened by the vibrations.

3 Buy an electric toothbrush with a rotational oscillation design; although it costs more, it gives you tangibly better results.

4 Experiment with tufted, angled or rounded-end bristles and easy-grip, curved or flexible-grip handles to see which type of toothbrush is the best for helping you reach the nooks and crannies.

What to Look For

- Rotating or vibrating bristles
- Head size
- Bristle softness

Tips

If you have proper brushing technique and do it for two to five minutes at least twice daily, you'll do just as well with a manual toothbrush as you would with a power toothbrush.

If your teeth have gaps or you wear braces or any kind of bridge, use floss threaders.

349 Buy Moisturisers and Antiwrinkle Creams

Most basic moisturisers – both chemists' own brands and more expensive products – contain the same key ingredients (water, propylene glycol, lanolin) to soften your skin and help with surface dryness. Wrinkles? That's another story. Here's the rub.

Steps

1 Choose moisturisers, foundation and other daily-use beauty products with built-in sun protection factor (SPF) 30. Sunscreen really can prevent new wrinkles from forming. Look for at least one of these active ingredients: titanium dioxide, zinc oxide or avobenzone (aka Parsol 1789). These protect you from harmful UVA and UVB rays.

2 Mind your skin's moisture needs. Dry skin drinks up rich moisturisers, while oily or acne-prone skin does better with *non-comedogenic* or *nonacnegenic* products. (These are better than "oil-free" products, which often include pore-clogging oil imitators.)

3 Study the active ingredients, which are listed on labels in order of the amount contained. If soothing aloe vera or vitamin C is 15th on the list, you're not getting much of it.

4 Be sceptical of products that claim to augment your own natural collagen or elastin, whose job it is to keep skin plumped up and youthful. The molecules in these products are too big to actually penetrate the skin.

5 Ask your doctor about *tretinoins,* one of the few active ingredients shown to truly reverse sun damage, reduce fine lines and soften wrinkles. These medications, which include Retin-A, are available by prescription only. Because of their ability to actually change your skin's structure, they are designated as drugs rather than cosmetics.

6 Sample other weaker, non-prescription vitamin A relatives like alpha hydroxy acids (AHAs) and beta hydroxy acids (BHAs). You need at least 8 per cent AHA for any visible results, though, which is just as likely to be present in a chemist's own brand product as in an expensive brand.

7 Experiment with antioxidant ingredients like coenzyme Q10, vitamin C and alpha lipoic acid. Some dermatologists make great claims for them (with promising research), while others are sceptical about visible results given the low concentrations used.

What to Look For

- SPF 30 sunscreen
- Active ingredients
- Right ingredients for your skin type
- Prescription treatments
- AHAs and BHAs
- Antioxidant ingredients

Tip

Reduce long-term risks of skin ageing, skin cancer and other harmful effects of the sun by limiting sun exposure, wearing protective clothing and using sunscreen. While it's true that genes play a large part in how you age, with care, your skin will appear younger – for free.

Warnings

Never use tretinoin or AHA products on the sensitive skin around your eyes. Because these are mildly exfoliating, they can cause redness or flaking en route to revealing fresh new skin. They also make your skin more photosensitive.

Hypoallergenic products should be free of fragrance and other common irritants like preservatives, but can still aggravate your skin.

350 Select Pain Relief and Cold Medicines

If your congested head is occupied by a sadist pounding a pneumatic drill, you need the right relief, right away. The main thing you need to look at in over-the-counter (OTC) products are the active ingredients and what they do. Then home in on the one that's tailor-made for your symptoms without extra ingredients you don't need. The following information is for adults only.

ACTIVE INGREDIENTS	BRAND NAME	WHAT IT'S USED FOR	POSSIBLE SIDE EFFECTS
Acetylsalicylic Acid or Aspirin	Alka-Seltzer, Anadin	Nonsteroidal anti-inflammatory drug (NSAID). Reduces inflammation, fever, minor aches and pains, and headaches.	Don't take with ibuprofen, especially regularly. Never give to children or teenagers due to a link to Reye's syndrome. Can be harsh on the stomach.
Ibuprofen	Nurofen, Motrin, Advil	An NSAID. Reduces inflammation (swelling), fever, headaches, minor aches and pains, including sprains, arthritis and muscle pains.	Gentler on stomach than aspirin. Maximum adult dosage is 1,600 mg in 24 hours to avoid hurting stomach.
Naproxen Sodium (available on prescription only)	Naprosyn	An NSAID. Alleviates minor pain from headache, colds, toothache, muscle ache, backache, arthritis and period pains. Reduces fever. Works for 12 hours.	Works slowly. Can cause indigestion, nausea, heartburn and diarrhoea; irritate stomach; and cause gastro-intestinal bleeding. Available in a range of strengths on prescription only.
Ketoprofen	Orudis	An NSAID. Relieves the pain, tenderness, inflammation (swelling) and stiffness caused by arthritis, muscle cramps, period pains, and pain after surgery, dental work or childbirth.	Can cause drowsiness, indigestion, nausea, heartburn and diarrhoea; can irritate the stomach; and cause gastrointestinal bleeding. Avoid if you have a history of gastrointestinal problems or ulcers.
Paracetamol	Panadol	Works well for many headaches, period pains or muscle aches. Good choice for fevers and sore throats.	Ideal for those who can't tolerate NSAIDs' side effects, although less effective at reducing inflammation. Used in allergy, cough and sinus medication. May be mixed with caffeine to increase effectiveness. No adverse effects on stomach.
Guaifenesin	Robitussin	Cough expectorant designed to liquefy phlegm. Relieves coughs caused by colds, bronchitis and other lung infections.	Doesn't help congested nose.

ACTIVE INGREDIENTS	BRAND NAME	WHAT IT'S USED FOR	POSSIBLE SIDE EFFECTS
Dextromethorphan	Robitussin	Cough suppressant	May not be beneficial if chest is congested; may prolong cough. Can be useful at night, as sleep aid.
Chlorpheniramine, Diphenhydramine, Pheniramine, Clemastine, Tripolidine	Benadryl, Piriton	Antihistamines relieve hay fever and allergy symptoms, including sneezing; runny nose; and red, itchy, runny eyes. Common in cold and flu medication.	Can cause drowsiness, sluggishness and dry mouth. Don't take with antidepressants or other medication without doctor's supervision.
Loratadine	Clarityn	Nonsedating antihistamine (doesn't cause as much drowsiness).	May be less effective than sedating antihistamines.
Phenylephrine, Pseudoephedrine	Sudafed, Actifed	Relieves nasal or sinus congestion due to colds, sinusitis, hay fever and other respiratory allergies. Relieves ear congestion caused by inflammation or infection.	Doesn't help runny nose. Do not use if have high blood pressure, diabetes, heart problems, asthma and for other conditions.
Nasal Saline	Sold as a generic medicine	Nonmedicated. Thins nasal secretions and relieves congestion. May be advised following sinus or nasal surgery.	Multiuse containers are subject to bacterial growth over time unless antimicrobial preservatives are in the solutions. Using sprays for more than a few days can cause rebound congestion and may lead to severe dependency.

OTC terms you need to know:

- Enteric: Coated to be kinder on the stomach because the medication doesn't dissolve until it reaches the intestines.

- Buffered: Added antacid to help avoid upset stomach, but it's likely to be too little to be effective.

- Migraine-relieving: Ingredients same as in nonmigraine counterparts, just with tailor-made package instructions.

- PM: Indicates a pain-relief and sleep-aid combination. Often paracetamol for pain and diphenhydramine for sleeplessness.

351 Choose a Complementary Therapy

Many people today are discovering that complementary therapies, such as aromatherapy, shiatsu and kinesiology can be beneficial not only when you are ill, but also if you wish to improve your general fitness and increase your energy levels. Based on a holisitic approach to health, these therapies are viewed as being complementary to conventional medicine, and not in opposition to it.

Steps

1 Consult your doctor first if you are suffering from any illness as you may need conventional medical treatment.

2 Discuss alternative treatments with your GP. Be prepared for him to be dismissive of the more esoteric therapies, such as crystal healing, but more amenable to, say, acupuncture and osteopathy.

3 Research the various therapies and how much they all cost. Look in *Yellow Pages* under Alternative Medicine/Therapies for the therapies available in your area or visit a local alternative medicine centre to discuss the treatments it offers. Alternatively, visit therapypages.com and consult the Directory of Complementary Therapies.

4 Decide which therapy would most suit you and your personality. Some alternative therapies may sound too New Agey, while others will strike a chord. A range of therapies can treat the same problem, so consider how the treatment is done. For example, you will need to remove your clothes for an aromatherapy massage to ease tension in your back, but to treat the same symptoms with a shiatsu massage you will remain fully clothed.

5 Meet the therapist in advance to discuss the treatment.

What to Look For

- GP consultation
- Research
- Cost
- Meeting with therapist before treatment

Tips

Some homeopaths are also trained GPs. Check the British Homeopathic Association (trusthomeopathy.org).

See 362 "Find Alternative and Holistic Practitioners".

352 See a Mental-Health Professional

If you've just experienced a traumatic event – the death of a loved one, loss of a job – or you are at a transition point, you may want to talk through your feelings with a trusted professional. Here are some ways to help you find the right therapist, psychologist or psychiatrist.

Steps

1 If you want non-NHS treatment and you have medical insurance, find out if your insurance policy covers mental-health providers. If it does, find out what kind of provider and how many sessions are covered. Ask if you must see a doctor to be reimbursed.

What to Look For

- Insurance coverage
- Professional credentials, Licence
- Appropriate therapy method
- Comfort, trust

2 Verify that the provider is properly qualified, which indicates
   they've undergone rigorous, standardised training. For more
   information, contact the General Medical Council
   (gmc-uk.org).

3 Book a consultation. Ask the provider to explain his or her predominant theoretical orientation and discuss favoured methods.
   Expect to talk frankly about any issues and how they affect your
   ability to work, sleep, eat, concentrate, relate to family and so
   on. Establishing a good rapport is essential to effective therapy.

4 Ask the provider to explain any proposed treatment.

Tips

The Samaritans (thesamari-
tans.com) offer counselling
on 08457 909090.

See 315 "Hire a Child
Therapist".

DEMYSTIFYING THE CREDENTIALS

Psychotherapist	Anyone can claim to be a psychotherapist. Choose those registered with the UK Council for Psychotherapy (UKCP), the largest umbrella body for all psychotherapies in the UK (psychotherapy.org.uk).
Social Worker	Social workers should have a Diploma in Social Work (DipSW) or, for those now in training, a newly introduced university-level degree in social work. The degree will involve at least 200 days of practical work.
Family Therapists	Specialise in helping clients deal with major life changes or transitions, such as marriage, divorce, job change and death in the family. Can also help when communication is an issue for families, couples or individuals. Should have a qualification approved by the Association for Family Therapy, which guarantees at least 320 hours clinical practice.
Counsellor	Counsellors vary in their experience and qualifications, although they should be accredited or approved by the British Association of Counselling. Usually involves listening sympathetically and not giving direct advice. They are generally not trained doctors or nurses, and tend not to advise on medication.
Clinical Psychologist	Specialists in testing and assessing mental-health problems. A clinical psychologist generally has a degree in psychology (or other good university degree) and then studies for a further three years to become a Doctor of Clinical Psychology (ClinPsyD).
Psychiatrist	Qualified medical doctors who then undertake basic psychiatric training, which usually takes three years. Can write prescriptions for antidepressants, antianxiety drugs and other psychiatric medication.

353 Choose a Wheelchair

The fanciest wheelchairs cost more than some cars, but competition has brought down the cost of basic manual models. It's an intensely personal choice, with many features to think about.

Steps

1 Seek a physiotherapist's advice on special features that would enhance your quality of life.

2 Check if the NHS can supply you with the right kind of wheelchair. Some insurers will cover electric wheelchairs, but don't assume that they all do. Factor in what you can spend out of your own pocket and decide what your budget is. Keep in mind that popular powered models go from £3,500 to nearly £20,000.

3 Determine how you will control a motorised chair. For example, if you have C7 tetraplegia, you may use a joystick as the input device, but the top of the joystick may need to be modified to accommodate for your lack of grip.

4 Decide what kind of back height and support you require. Criteria include head control, trunk control, upper extremity function and propulsion, as well as personal preference. Physiotherapists generally recommend that people with little or no upper body strength need a chair that tilts back 45 degrees to avoid bedsores. A range of cushion options are available such as visco-elastic memory foam, which provides unparalleled relief from seat pressure as well as great back support. Air cushions are equally effective for other people. Take a test drive before you decide.

5 Research different foot and leg supports, as well as armrests and attachments, such as trays. The style you want or need might determine the specific wheelchair frame that you will order. For instance, a fixed tapered front-end cannot be ordered on a lightweight wheelchair frame.

6 Obtain measurements of potential environment obstacles, such as doorframes, hallways and desk clearance, and compare these to the chair's overall width, overall length, turning radius and seat height from the floor. There's nothing worse than buying a new chair and finding out the hard way that it can't make the tight turn into your bedroom.

7 Find a local supplier that lets you put a range of models through their paces and sit in them long enough to make sure you'll really be comfortable.

8 Compare weights. Manual chairs range from 1.8 to 13.6 kg (4 to 30 lb), so the strength of the wheelchair mover – be it you or an aide – is a big consideration. Motorised chairs can weigh as much as 115 kg (250 lb).

What to Look For

- Professional advice
- Insurance coverage
- Suitability to lifestyle and ability
- Manoeuvrability
- Lightweight
- Easy transfer to vehicle

Tip

Wheelchair manufacturers unveil new models annually and, more important, consult wheelchair users during the design process. As with cars or computers, you pay more for the very latest model.

9 Test how easy it is to move smoothly from the chair to your car and back again, and to fold and pack (manual) chairs into your vehicle. (Motorised wheelchairs do not fold.) If you have a van, make sure the chair fits both the ramp and the vehicle's interior.

10 If you'll only need help getting around or are fatigued easily, give a scooter, or personal mobility vehicle, a test-drive. Three- and four-wheel models are available, depending on mobility requirements and terrain.

11 Look into a custom-made chair. Some models have a dozen different seat widths and even more colours.

12 Research performance wheelchairs if you are active in competitive sports or marathons at such sites as bromakin.co.uk and gblwheelchairs.com.

354 Buy Home-Use Medical Supplies

Whether your need is permanent or temporary, here's how to get hold of home-use medical supplies like trapezes, walkers, bathroom aids and adjustable beds. With hospitals pressing for more home care and recuperation, manufacturers are pursuing this expanding market very aggressively, so smart shopping really pays.

Steps

1 Ask your doctor, rehabilitation therapist, occupational therapist or carer what specific pieces of equipment are necessary and whether they are available on the NHS.

2 If you have medical insurance, discuss your options with your insurance provider, so you know what's covered.

3 Have a professional rehabilitation expert visit your home. They can advise on constructing a wheelchair ramp, for example, or the positioning of a bath grab bar or trapeze over the bed.

4 Home in on details. Something as simple as crutches can be made much more comfortable (and safe) when correctly adjusted for height. Or, if you lack upper body strength, you may opt for crutches with an adjustable flexible cuff that goes around the forearm just below the elbow and minimises arm strain.

5 Recognise your needs. Equipment that the NHS can provide you with may be sufficient for your needs, particularly if your disability is short-term.

What to Look For

- Informed expert advice
- Insurance coverage specifics
- Suitable, reasonably priced equipment
- Good selection

Tip

The website Patient UK (patient.co.uk/equipment) has helpful leads on all kinds of medical equipment.

355 Select Hair-Care Products

Are you finding your bad-hair days outnumber the good ones? It could be due to your hair-care products. You may be using one made for hair that's a different texture from yours. Consult this chart, then head to the hairdresser's or chemist's. Soon your tresses will go from terrible to terrific.

PRODUCT	FEATURES
Moisturising Shampoos and Conditioners	Good for very dry hair. Restore moisture lost in blow-drying. Products containing aloe, seed oils or shea butter are especially rich. Generally too heavy for oily or fine hair, although can be used just on the ends.
Clarifying Shampoos or Conditioners; Build-up Removers	Clean hair that's dulled by too much build-up of hair-care products or from hard-water residues. Help greasy hair if used periodically. Can be drying; limited use recommended. Special antidandruff shampoos are far more effective for flaking or itchy scalp.
Colour-fading Shampoos and Conditioners	Gentle, moisturising; won't strip colour or natural oils from hair. Easy to confuse colour-protecting products with colour-boosting or colour-enhancing products. The latter two deposit colour (and can stain highlights) and thus might be more than you bargained for, especially on dry or processed hair.
Regular Conditioners	Panthenol is a cosmetic cover-up found in most shop products. Look for dimethicone, a mineral emollient, which helps smooth and straighten a mop of thick hair before blow-drying. A light conditioner tames static and untangles normal to oily hair. Deep, rich conditioners resuscitate dry or damaged hair. Using too much can flatten thin, fine or oily hair, so use on midshaft and ends. If hair is very fine, use very little to create shine and smoothness.
Leave-in Conditioners and Reconstructive Detanglers	A light leave-in conditioner is great for giving shine and body to straight hair and for taming. Also tames frizz and defines curls in wavy hair.
Hair Masks, Hot Oil Treatments, Deep-conditioning Protein Packs	Restore softness and shine by penetrating into the hair shaft and filling in "pockets" of missing protein. Indulge yourself and your hair with a 20-minute treatment that rejuvenates and replenishes lost moisture, protein and shine.

PRODUCT	FEATURES
Volume-enhancing Sprays and Root-lifting Products	Apply to damp roots, then again when dry to add volume to flat, limp, thin or very straight hair. Not for bushy or thick curly hair.
Hair Gels and Cremes	Add texture and shape. Good for defining curls; holding styles. Cremes can be softer and lighter; gels are harder and stiffer. Use sparingly and experiment with different effects.
Styling Cremes or Pomades	Stop flyaway hair and static. Tames frizz when worked into dry curls with fingers. Can be too greasy and weigh down hair. Best to start with coffee bean-size amount and add more later if needed.
Shine-enhancing Gels or Sprays; Glossing Cremes	Calm curls and fix frizzies on dry, processed (coloured or permed) or curly hair. Add shine. Look for silicone in ingredient list to help hair reflect light and look shinier. Too much product weighs down oily hair. Use very lightly or just on ends. Sprays are the least oily; spray on hands and smooth over hair.
Hair Balms	Handy to carry around for touch-ups on frizzies or flyaways. Is a cosmetic cover-up and doesn't restore moisture, but gives a healthier look to hair.
Straighteners, Spray Relaxers, Relaxing Cremes	Straighten all hair types for people of all skin colours. Can transform curls into waves. Temporary products often contain moisturising ingredients like glycerin, coconut oil and plant extracts. Permanent straighteners and relaxers are serious business and should always be applied by professionals. Use at-home products sparingly and monitor how they affect your hair.
Hair Sprays	Tame flyaways, add volume, seal coiffure. Try spraying on brush, then brush through hair. Use light varieties for natural-looking hold. Firm-hold sprays can give a bulletproof, rigid look.

356 Buy Ways to Counter Hair Loss

The loss of one's hair can be a grievous blow to self-image and confidence. Medication, illness, heredity, pregnancy, menopause, changing hormone levels and stress can all contribute to hair loss. Other culprits are chemotherapy, hereditary baldness or alopecia.

Steps

1 Consult your doctor, dermatologist or an endocrinologist to eliminate medical causes such as thyroid issues or alopecia. Rule out any dietary contributors by making sure you're getting all the vitamins, protein and calories you need.

2 Apply over-the-counter minoxidil (Regaine) to thinning or balding patches twice a day. The exact way this medicine works is not known, but it is thought to cause dilation of the blood vessels in the scalp. If you stop treatment once you've started, hair loss will resume within a few months.

3 Try prescription-only Propecia or Proscar, which have been found to work rather well for women. The active ingredient finasteride blocks the formation of active testosterone and allows those hairs predisposed to inactivity to become active again and make new hairs. The two brands have different dosages of finasteride.

4 Explore hair-replacement surgery options. Mini- or micrografting may offer the most natural results. A strip of scalp with hair is divided into a few hundred tiny grafts with just a few strands apiece, then inserted into minuscule slits in the scalp. Skilled surgeons ensure all hair is growing in the same direction. Make sure you see live examples of the surgeon's work before proceeding.

5 Discuss treatment options with your doctor for alopecia. While very little is known about the disorder, there is evidence of a genetic component as well as a link to autoimmune problems. Depending on the variety (*areata:* spots on the head; *totalis:* the entire head; or *universalis:* all body hair), there's a good chance that cortisone injections on the head and eyebrows will spur hair growth. Injections can be painful but may offer a huge morale boost for people who would do just about anything to look the way they used to.

What to Look For

- Underlying cause
- Your doctor's opinion
- Topical treatments
- Hair-replacement surgery

Tip

Talking to other people who've lost their hair can be enormously helpful, as are supportive friends and family. Contact the Alopecia Patients Association at hairlineinternational.com or, for cancer patients, cancerindex.org.

Warning

Be aware that 5 per cent minoxidil is not recommended for use by women, due to the potential for greater drug penetration. Women using this percentage in clinical trials were inclined to grow hair in areas where minoxidil was not applied.

357 Buy a Wig or Hairpiece

Bald might be beautiful in the eyes of some people, but not for those with gradual or drastic hair loss who just want to look like their old selves again. With a wide range of colours and styles, wigs have never looked more fabulous, darling.

Steps

1 Talk to your doctor and insurance provider and find out what's covered.

2 Find a hairstylist experienced in working with wigs and ask about style and shape. They can take your measurements and order your wig, as well as cut and style it after it's delivered. Ask about each wig's scalp and hairline. A bad hairline is the biggest give-away, so ask to see and try on samples.

3 Work out the prices of various kinds of wigs. Prices reflect whether the wig was made by hand or by a machine.

- Synthetic wigs are affordable and easy to style, and cost from £65 to £350. They're not quite as durable, and frizz more, but are ideal if you're experiencing temporary hair loss due to chemotherapy. Wigs available on the NHS are synthetic.

- Human hair, of course, has the most lifelike look and bounce. You'll pay around £660 for a net-based wig, and up to £4,000 or more for a custom-moulded polyurethane vacuum base. These top-quality cranial hair prostheses adhere securely to the head and, since hairs are injected through the base one at a time, look the most natural.

4 Consider a partial wig if you have a few bald or very thin spots (common with alopecia). They can be custom-made to blend in with and bulk up your own remaining hair.

5 Feel confident your wig won't take flight with different anchoring options. Many wigs have adjustable fasteners or straps in the back; tape tabs at the hairline and ears also provide security. A nonirritating head band is helpful if you've lost all your hair. Custom-fit caps help smooth any remaining hair underneath (stretch lace costs around £15).

6 Ask if extra hair can be added to the wig later if it thins in places. While a quality wig starts showing wear at two or three years, spot repairs can extend its life to four or five years.

7 Ask for tips on care and styling. Depending on how dirty the wig gets, you might need to wash it every 10 to 14 days, following the manufacturer's instructions. Store the wig on a wig block when it's not in use.

8 Find out if the hairstylist can revitalise colour later if the wig fades.

What to Look For

- Insurance coverage
- Hairstylist with wig experience
- Synthetic or human-hair
- Custom-moulded base
- Secure fasteners
- Wig care and maintenance

Tips

A wig is much easier to match for style and colour when you still have your natural hair.

Helpful information on wigs and headwear is available from cancerbacup.org.uk.

358 Buy a New Body

Fed up with those bags and sags? Buy yourself a head-to-toe body transformation. Courtesy of recent advances in cosmetic surgery, almost anything is possible to enhance your physical appearance and buy back your long-departed youthful looks. A new you won't be cheap, though, and there are other important health considerations to take into account before taking the plunge.

Steps

1 Interview several surgeons and ask how many procedures similar to yours each has performed, which is particularly important with new treatments. Identify a top-notch plastic surgeon via referrals from your doctor and satisfied friends.

2 Choose a surgeon who is a member of the British Association of Aesthetic Plastic Surgeons. Members should have completed six years of specialist training.

3 Ask to see living examples of the surgeon's work, not just photographs in a book. Ask to be introduced to satisfied patients, but frank talk with all former patients is valuable.

4 Consider a rushed consultation a red flag. If a surgeon doesn't thoroughly advise you on possible side effects, potential problems and how much discomfort or disability you can expect, you aren't getting what you need to give informed consent to surgery, which is your right.

5 Confirm exactly what the quoted prices cover, since some plastic surgeons' offices quote the surgeon's fee separately. You might need to factor in other costly items like the consultation, anaesthesia, supplies, medication, facility fees, hospitalisation, compression garments and blood testing.

What to Look For

- Personal referrals
- Surgeon's expertise and credentials
- Testimonials from patients
- Living examples of surgeon's work
- Clear explanation of prices

Tip

See 352 "See a Mental-Health Professional".

PROCEDURE	DESCRIPTION	PROS AND CONS	COST
Face-lift (Rhytidectomy)	Heredity, personal habits, the pull of gravity, and sun exposure contribute to the ageing of the face. The skin is raised outwards before the surgeon repositions and tightens the underlying muscle and connective tissue. Some fat, as well as excess skin, may be removed.	A face-lift cannot stop ageing, nor can it turn back the clock. What it can do is help your face look its best and give you a healthier and more youthful appearance. Recovery usually takes two to three weeks. Insurance does not generally cover surgery that is done purely for cosmetic reasons.	£3,500 to £10,000

PROCEDURE	DESCRIPTION	PROS AND CONS	COST
Nose Job (Rhinoplasty)	Reshapes nose by reducing or increasing size, removing hump, changing shape of tip or bridge, narrowing span of nostrils, or changing angle between nose and upper lip. May also relieve some breathing problems.	One- to two-hour outpatient procedure. Patients are back to work in one to two weeks. Must avoid strenuous activities for two to three weeks. Side effects: temporary swelling, bruising around eyes and nose, headaches, some bleeding and stiffness. Risks include infection.	£2,500 to £3,500
Eye Lift (Blepharoplasty)	Correct drooping upper eyelids and puffy bags below the eyes by removing excess fat, skin and muscle.	One- to three-hour outpatient procedure. Patients are back to work in 7 to 10 days. Can cause temporary discomfort, tightness of lids, swelling, bruising; dryness, burning or itching of eyes; watering, sensitivity to light. Risks include temporary blurred or double vision; infection, bleeding; swelling at the corners of the eyelids.	£2,000 for upper and lower lids, plus £450 for anaesthesiologist, £550 for operating theatre
Neck Lift	Endoscopic surgery, performed under local anaesthetic, gets rid of neck sag. Good for those prone to fat deposits and drooping under chin.	Minimal scarring. Back to normal life in two or three days. Endoscopic neck surgery is relatively new, so look for an expert.	£5,500 to £6,000
Breast Reduction or Breast Lift (Mastopexy)	Nipple and areola can be repositioned and reduced for balance and aesthetic purposes. Can also rebalance breasts after one has been reconstructed after a mastectomy. (For breast enlargement, see 360 "Obtain Breast Implants".)	Can be huge relief for women with large, heavy breasts, which can be truly uncomfortable and cause years of backache and neck pain. Surgery may be covered by insurance. Hospitalisation after breast-reduction surgery, four to six weeks to return to normal activity. Risk of infection, bleeding, loss of feeling in the breast and permanent visible scars.	£2,000 to £3,500 for breast lifts; £3,500 to £4,000 for reductions.
Upper-arm Lift (Brachioplasty)	Lifts skin that is drooping below tricep from ageing or weight loss.	Reduces circumference of upper arm; contours and tightens. Visible scars. Ask about how much scarring to expect. Nerve injury, change in sensation and swelling are possible complications. Requires a couple of weeks to recover.	£2,000 for surgeon's fees alone

PROCEDURE	DESCRIPTION	PROS AND CONS	COST
Liposuction (Suction-assisted Lipectomy)	Contours the fat layer beneath the skin. Removes excessive fat when exercise doesn't help. New ultrasound-assisted liposuction can liquefy fat deposits first, making them easier to remove. The power-assisted lipoplasty method is less traumatic for the body and lets the few surgeons experienced in using it sculpt the body more easily.	New fat can build up afterwards in untreated areas. Expect bruising and swelling after surgery. May need to wear supportive garments. Removing too much fat can cause dangerous blood loss. Serious nerve damage, although rare, can occur. Can result in lumps and bumps or even sagging.	£650 to £1,500 surgeon's fee, plus at least £550 per site
Tummy Tuck (Abdominoplasty)	Spot-shaping treatment that slims and trims, removing excess fat and skin that hasn't responded to dieting and exercising. Doctors can be adamant about requiring patients to make a serious effort to lose weight before surgery. Incisions don't show much as they're just above or within pubic area. New shape lasts for years barring substantial weight gain.	Removing excess sagging skin is a major undertaking. Support garment must be worn for a few weeks. Benefits take several months to become fully apparent. Not for the overweight. Won't remove cellulite.	£2,500 for surgeon's fees alone
Buttock Implants	Add curve to a flat bottom by inserting silicone implants.	A little more shape, a little more lift. Risk of thrombosis (a blood clot).	£2,000 to £6,500 a pair

359 Get a Tattoo or Body Piercing

Body piercings and tattoos, ancient forms of adornment and beautification, are now found on all sorts of bodies. Before you let a stranger puncture your skin, shop around and find out how to mutilate your body safely.

Steps

1 Think hard about what designs you want. Collect art, leaf through books and make sketches. A good tattoo artist will take what you bring in and transform it into beautiful art.

2 Place temporary tattoos on different parts of your body until you're clear where you want yours: tattoos on your back or shoulder may look incredible, but you'll never see them without a mirror. Designs on your arms may be appealing, but you may tire of always having something there.

3 Consider long-term social or professional implications for visible piercings and tattoos. While a particular style of body art may be appealing right now, ask yourself whether you will love it for the rest of your life. Will the indulgence of a moment eliminate certain career options down the road?

4 Evaluate your ability to handle pain. Does a tattoo hurt? Not as much as childbirth, but pain is considered part of the experience. Piercings are briefer. Location also determines pain levels – anything near major nerves (down the side of the leg, for example, or on or near bones) can be excruciating; the bigger the tattoo, the longer your agony lasts.

5 Ask about hygiene practices. In the age of AIDS, cleanliness is taken very seriously. Artists should wear gloves, sterilise their tools and work space, and use packaged, single-use needles.

6 Take your time and review lots of portfolios when choosing a tattoo artist. When you see a great tattoo, ask who did it. Look for clean, smooth outlines and excellent use of colour.

7 Be prepared to pay for an experienced, reputable piercer or tattoo artist. Tattoo artists usually charge by the hour and have a minimum fee (about £35), but designs can run into the thousands for large, intricate work. Common piercings (including jewellery) range from £35 to £50.

8 Insist on surgical-grade stainless, niobium, platinum or titanium steel jewellery, or solid 18-carat gold for all piercings until they're healed.

9 Review all procedures and risks in advance. Be clear on the after-care regime.

What to Look For

- True artistry
- Surgery-standard hygiene
- Experienced practitioner

Tips

Check that the salon is registered with the local health authority.

Professional tattoo artists will not work on a client who is under the influence of judgement- or pain-altering substances, legal or otherwise.

Warnings

Piercing in particular, but also tattooing, damages the body's natural infection barrier. Serious problems can include viral hepatitis, nerve and vein damage, and sexually transmitted diseases (most commonly with genital piercing). Tongue piercings are particularly prone to complications. If a piercing site looks infected, don't touch the jewellery, just get to a doctor.

A new tattoo is dressed with a bandage and takes up to two weeks to scab and heal. One medical journal reported that people with tattoos are nine times more likely to be infected with hepatitis C. However, you can avoid many problems by choosing a sterile establishment.

360 Obtain Breast Implants

Breast augmentation can be a powerful morale booster, but it's not something to take lightly. Whether you've opted for implants for cosmetic reasons alone or as a part of breast reconstruction surgery after a mastectomy, here's how to go about it safely.

Steps

1 Read up on implants at the Department of Health's website (doh.gov.uk/bimplants) or request a copy of their leaflet from the Department of Health, PO Box 777, London SE1 6XH. Do your visual homework at ImplantInfo.com, where you can see scores of before and after photographs.

2 Be referred to a surgeon by your GP.

3 Find out if the surgeon is on the GMC Specialist Register for Plastic Surgery, or a member of a relevant association, such as the British Association of Plastic Surgeons, British Association of Aesthetic Plastic Surgeons or British Associatiaon of Surgical Oncology.

4 Consult with several surgeons, taking along photographs of breast sizes and shapes you like. Ask if your body type is suited to implants; very thin women aren't always good candidates, as wrinkling in the implant can show through the skin.

5 Ask surgeons for patient referrals before you go under the knife. Also check out the doctor with medical organisations to find out if there have been any complaints or malpractice lawsuits filed against him or her.

6 Enquire about the incision. Will the surgeon go in under the breast or armpit, through the belly button or the nipple? Most implants go in beneath the chest muscle for more natural-looking results and easier mammograms, but this method takes longer to heal.

7 Ask what kind of implants are used.

8 Wear a bra in your desired cup size to the consultation and ask to try it with an implant. Most women go up two cup sizes, but many later wish they'd gone bigger. Discuss this with the surgeon.

9 Make sure you receive comprehensive advice about potential complications and all aspects of the surgery and recovery.

10 Prepare to pay about £850 for saline implants or about £1,200 for silicone, with an additional £2,000 for surgeon's fees.

11 Expect scarring. Ask about possible future problems such as difficulty with breast-feeding. Complications can range from ruptures and leakage to infections and tightening of the scar tissue around the implant. The implants themselves can wrinkle, deflate, harden and develop an unnatural feel.

What to Look For

- Qualified and accredited surgeon
- Thorough consultation
- Clear explanations
- Implant costs and surgeon's fees

Tip

Although breast reconstruction can do so much for cancer patients after a mastectomy, some doctors neglect to refer their patients for this surgery. However, women can explore this option and safely benefit from the surgery right after their mastectomy.

Warnings

Implants make diagnostic mammograms less effective because they literally cloud the picture.

Implants aren't forever; they often need to be replaced within 15 years. Patients sometimes return years earlier than this to have them removed, change their shape and size, or have repair or maintenance work done. One study found more than a quarter of the women receiving saline implants underwent more surgery within five years – about two thirds for corrective work, the remainder to get a different shape or size.

361 Get Wrinkle-Filler Injections

If you're not squeamish about needles and don't mind the cost, a few tiny injections of Botox, collagen or even your own fat can temporarily turn back the clock. Watch frown lines, crow's-feet and lip creases all but disappear. But first, weigh these safety concerns and be sure to put your face in the right hands.

Steps

1 Find a skilled cosmetic surgeon or dermatologist who injects Botox, collagen or fat as a part of his or her daily practice. A medical qualification alone isn't enough; it's a specialised, aesthetic field. Ask to see living examples of the doctor's work. (See 358 "Buy a New Body".)

2 Ask your doctor which substance will work best for you given the location and severity of your facial lines.

   • Botox is a diluted form of a powerful nerve toxin. Minuscule amounts are injected to temporarily paralyse or relax facial muscles so they don't – and can't – contract into wrinkles.

   • Collagen injections fill out lines from underneath – smile lines, lipstick bleed lines, crow's-feet, acne scars, even wrinkling on lips and hands. This synthetic filling agent derived from cows requires an allergy patch test before treatment.

   • Your own body's fat is good for filling in deep lines and poses no allergy problems. It can be removed from hips or buttocks then stored. The results can last longer than with Botox or collagen.

3 Factor in the cost of upkeep. With Botox and collagen, you'll need to repeat the injections every three to six months. Depending on the number of injections, Botox can cost £200 to £700 each time, and collagen £200 to £450.

4 Expect some irritation or redness afterwards, and perhaps a little bruising with collagen, but nothing that make-up can't cover. You'll notice collagen's benefits right away. Botox's effects can take a few days or even up to three weeks to peak, then the effects gradually disappear as nerves regenerate. Getting injections may be a little uncomfortable, but it isn't painful because the needle is so fine.

What to Look For

• Doctor's expertise
• Right type for you
• Funds for upkeep

Tips

Look out for a new treatment called Artefill – bovine collagen coupled with microscopic plastic spheres. Although it has some risks (it can turn lumpy or cause rashes), expect to hear more about it, as its results can be permanent. All the more reason to have a great surgeon do the treatment.

Botox and collagen injections work best on people under 65 because the skin has more natural elasticity. Sun-damage wrinkles in older people don't always respond as well. Ask for a realistic assessment of expected improvement, given your age and skin.

Warning

There are no known allergy problems with Botox, but short-term problems can occur, such as drooping eyelids or eyebrows, a frozen expression and even dribbling if it's used near the mouth. The usual cause for such problems is off-target placement.

362 Find Alternative and Holistic Practitioners

Government and medical research institutions have poured millions of pounds into studies on promising complementary and alternative medicine (CAM). You'll still need to check with your doctor, but here's how to find legitimate CAM professionals.

Steps

1 Ask your doctor for a referral. You may face possibly well-warranted scepticism in regard to some alternative practices but encouragment in others.

2 Ask friends, family, nutritionists or physiotherapists for their recommendations. If you know someone who has suffered from the same health problem as you, ask if they found any particular complementary medicine helpful in the relief of their symptoms. Some alternative-medicine professional organisations have CAM referral services.

3 Find out what your health insurance covers; many costly CAM treatments are not covered. While some insurers include chiropractic treatments in their policies, far fewer cover acupuncture, let alone Ayurvedic medicine or homeopathy.

4 Ask about practitioners' educational background and training, and if any formal complaints have ever been filed against them. Enquire if any scientific research supports specific treatments you may be considering.

5 Check qualifications, if possible, despite the patchy regulations that exist for CAM. For example, to be a member of the British Acupuncture Council (BAcC), practitioners must have completed a two-year full-time or equivalent part-time accredited course. However, some medical doctors, nurses or physiotherapists who practise acupuncture may have taken just a weekend course.

What to Look For

- Doctor's referral
- Additional recommendations
- Health insurance coverage
- Legal requirements

Tips

Research studies underway – like the massive clinical trials testing the supplements glucosamine and chondroitin sulphate, separately and together, against Celebrex and a placebo on osteoarthritis sufferers – for clues to remedies with the best potential. Check with your doctor first; these supplements might cause elevated blood sugar, for instance.

Keep your GP informed about your treatment plans.

363 Choose a Manicurist

Have you been going sans-trowel in the garden? Using your nails to tighten screws and scratch off labels? Regain your glamour and pamper yourself with a soothing manicure or pedicure. Choose the beauty salon wisely, though, or you may end up with sore cuticles – or worse.

Steps

1 Study how the manicurists work at a prospective salon. Metal tools should go straight into disinfectant after use, and nail files and buffing blocks should be brand-new for each client. Ask how their tools are cleaned. Since dirty nail-care equipment can harbour and pass on tenacious fungal infections, consider taking your own tools and polish for your manicurist to use. They can be kept at the salon for you.

2 Observe how the foot baths are cleaned and if fresh hand towels are used for each customer. Is the salon clean in general?

3 Stop any snip-happy manicurist who tries to clip your cuticles. They tear more easily as they grow back, can look ugly and are more vulnerable to infections and fungus. A manicurist should use cuticle softening oil after a warm soak, then gently ease them back with an orangewood stick. Too many manicurists try to remove the cuticle, which only brings on infection.

4 Discuss the length and shape you like – oval, squared-off, rounded. A good manicurist has the eye and artistry to shape nails uniformly. Don't file them down at the sides because that weakens nails and can cause splitting.

5 Go glam and get acrylic nail tips for £13 to £30, but bear in mind that you'll need to return regularly for fills as the nail grows out. Or get a silk wrap to strengthen existing nails. Tips soften and weaken nails, but can cure chronic nail-biting.

What to Look For

* Disinfected tools
* Excellent hygiene
* Pristine premises

Tip

Nail-polish remover can be drying. Moisturising and protecting cuticles makes them less likely to split or crack; use cuticle cream, facial moisturiser, hand and body lotion – whatever's handy. Cuticles are near the nail growth centre and also protect the proximal nail groove, which, if exposed, is vulnerable to bacteria, fungus and paronychia, a common nail infection.

Warning

If your nails ever look discoloured, see your doctor. Onychomycosis (nail fungus) is serious and can lead to deformed nails or even loss of nails.

364 Get Whiter Teeth

If your pearly whites, well, aren't – blame it on caffeine, sweets, prescription drugs or ageing, all of which dull the gleam. Whiten and brighten dingy teeth with high-tech treatments at your dentist's surgery or over-the-counter bleaches you use at home. Here's how to bring that sparkle back.

Steps

1 Ask your dentist if you're a good candidate for whitening, since results can vary. Yellowed teeth generally lighten well; darkened greyish or brownish teeth may not.

2 Try over-the-counter products, which have low concentrations of hydrogen peroxide. A dental tray and gel kit can be used for a short time each day to lighten teeth one to two shades in two weeks, at best. Whitening strips cover the six front teeth – which must be even – for similar results, and keep peroxide on teeth and off gums. Paint-on gels get similar results and cover more teeth, but can be messy to use. Hydrogen peroxide works faster than carbamide (see Step 3), but takes longer to get results and deactivates faster. These are the least expensive treatments to use when staining recurs due to beverages and smoking.

3 Use a dentist-made tray at home twice daily for an hour for a couple of weeks, or wear it overnight. The gel's active ingredient is 10, 15 or 20 per cent carbamide peroxide, which is gentler than hydrogen peroxide. Teeth could lighten several shades depending on the strength of the gel used. Higher percentages work faster but also increase the chance of teeth sensitivity. Ask your dentist for whitening products that include fluoride to reduce sensitivity. Cost: £200 to £300.

4 Whiten your teeth by up to ten shades in one 60- to 90-minute session with a potent, light-activated bleaching formula of 35 per cent hydrogen peroxide. Cost: £300 to £750.

5 Consider porcelain veneers or bonding if you have conditions where bleaching isn't effective, such as tetracycline or intrinsic staining. Bonding is a resin that's contoured over teeth. Veneers are thin porcelain manufactured in a laboratory. Cost: £300 to £1,000 per tooth for porcelain veneers, £100 to £200 for bonding.

6 Bear in mind that two to three weeks of whitening by over-the-counter products equals one week of overnight tray treatment from the dentist – and may well equal one hour of the light-activated treatments.

What to Look For

- Dentist's options
- Over-the-counter kits
- Percentage of active ingredient

Tips

See 348 "Purchase a Toothbrush".

The results of whitening treatments, even the costly ones, aren't permanent. Touch-ups may be required every six to 24 months.

Warnings

If you experience severe sensitivity after using a product, let your dentist know.

Since whitening treatments have no effect on artificial materials such as crowns, fillings or veneers, monitor your progress closely to keep colour uniform with your natural enamel.

Avoid restaining brightened teeth with red wine, fizzy drinks, tea, coffee or tobacco. Bonded teeth can be affected but to a lesser degree. Veneers will not be affected at all.

"Whitening" toothpastes contain polishing agents that improve tooth appearance by removing surface stains. It can take months to see results, if any.

365 Select Spectacles and Sunglasses

Prescription glasses and sunglasses have to be functional but also look good. Fortunately, there are so many styles that it's easy to find the right pair. Learn the technical details first, then shop around.

Steps

Prescription eyewear

1 Consider frame materials. Aluminium and titanium frames are very durable and offer custom fitting options. Plastic frames are light and durable but usually can't be bent to offer a custom fit.

2 Assess overall weight. Glasses need to be comfortable. Large lenses and thick frames add up to heavy glasses, something most people find uncomfortable. If you need thick lenses, get the smallest diameter lens that looks good on you.

3 Understand lens materials. Glass lenses resist scratching but are heavy and have lower shatter resistance. Polycarbonate (plastic) lenses are light and shatter resistant but demand care to prevent scratches. Custom options for lenses include an antireflective coating to cut glare, enhanced thinness for light weight and good looks, and photoreactive tinting that gets darker in bright light. Beware: these options can easily double your total cost.

4 Shop for metal frames that can withstand vigorous bending without damage. Opt for a separate set of specialised sports glasses with an impact-resistant frame and lenses secured by a strap.

Sunglasses

1 Read the label carefully. You want 100 per cent UV (ultraviolet light) protection from both UVA and UVB rays. Some lenses are labelled as UV400, which means the same thing.

2 Own several pairs of sunglasses since one pair can't do everything. Leave a pair in the car for driving – cheap ones if you tend to sit on them. A slim stylish pair will not protect your eyes from debris while riding your bike. Expensive, sporty wrap-arounds will make you look ridiculous at work.

3 Look for shatter-resistant polycarbonate lenses for water and snow sports, which require protection against strong reflected rays. Glass lenses, with their increased scratch resistance and fine optical quality, are a good choice for pricey, dress-up glasses. Polarised lenses, which reduce glare, are always a good idea.

4 Choose lens colour carefully. Sensitive eyes need dark lenses. Grey or grey-green are good for general use. Brown works well for daytime driving or golf. Yellow and amber provide depth perception in low-light conditions. Avoid light blue and pink for driving or sports as they distort colour. Some models have interchangeable lenses.

What to Look For

- Durability
- Comfort
- UV protection
- Lens colour
- Style

Tips

Talk to your optician and get prescription sunglasses if you need them. Or get clip-ons that attach to your everyday glasses.

You don't have to spend a lot to get good protection. Moderately priced sunglasses, around £15, frequently offer good eye protection. Designer sunglasses can cost £60 to £200. Ask about a warranty.

Take a Polaroid camera along when you shop for glasses. If you're undecided, get a picture of you wearing them to bring home.

If you're under 20, your eyes let in more UV rays. Since children spend a lot of time outside, protect their eyes from UV exposure and glare.

Warning

Too much UV radiation can lead to blindness. Not all tinted glasses – even very dark ones – protect against UV radiation, so be sure to check the label.

366 Hire a Personal Trainer

Whether you want to become the next Demi or Arnold, or just get back in shape, working with a personal trainer will do the job. Trainers' expertise and work-out styles vary enormously. Here's how to find the best person for you – and that six-pack just waiting to be discovered.

Steps

1 Determine which fitness activities are most likely to keep you feeling happy, enthused and committed: kickboxing, spinning, free weights, Pilates, walking, step aerobics, dance, rock climbing, circuit training, cardio-focused training... Doing what you love will keep you doing it.

2 Get a referral from a satisfied (and toned) friend or call nearby fitness centres, gyms or studios and find out what programmes are offered by their personal trainers.

3 Find out if the trainer is certified by a nationally recognised body such as the YMCA. The term "personal trainer" is not yet fully defined by the health and fitness industry in the UK, although the Register of Exercise Professionals (reps-uk.org) has been established to regulate the industry. Check if dance or martial arts teachers have had proper training as well.

4 Schedule a trial work-out to see if a trainer is suited to your personality and shows a genuine interest in you and your goals.

5 Choose a trainer or teacher with a good grasp of your work-out level – and limitations. You want someone who motivates and challenges you without setting impossible goals or pushing you too fast or too hard. Creative work-out planning will help avoid burn-out.

6 Some gyms employ only trainers with fitness qualifications. However, there are many trainers out there who have no qualifications at all. Check credentials carefully.

What to Look For

- Favourite work-out activities
- Referrals
- Qualifications
- Motivating personality
- Good pacing

Tip

Check on your trainer's cancellation policy to avoid wasting money on classes you can't make.

367 Sign Up for a Yoga Class

Interest in yoga, with its allure of peace, enlightenment, physical flexibility and fitness, has exploded in recent years. Choose between the many different schools, and find a yogi with the wisdom and advanced training to help you best. Check with the British Wheel of Yoga (bwy.org.uk).

TYPE	DESCRIPTION
Iyengar	Developed by Yogacharya B.K.S. Iyengar, this type of yoga focuses on an in-depth study of asanas (posture) and pranayama (breath control). Helps increase flexibility, strength and connection of mind, body and spirit.
Kundalini	Brought to the West in 1969 by Yogi Bhajan, kundalini focuses on unleashing spiritual (and sexual) energy, and is used to increase strength, movement and balance. It can promote greater physical wellbeing and awareness, while also helping the participant feel more relaxed.
Hatha	Hatha is the most widely practised form of yoga in the world, and is used to promote flexibility and relaxation. Combining postures and stretches with proper breathing techniques, it encourages strength and proper body alignment while decreasing stress. There are many styles of hatha yoga, some of which use props such as blocks or belts to assist the postures.
Mantra	A mantra is a sound or word, and mantra yoga is a meditation practice that helps quieten the mind. The goal is to focus on a single thought (your mantra) until the mind and emotions are transcended and the superconscious is revealed.
Bikram	Taught in a gruelling 90-minute session and a 38°C (100°F) room, this form of yoga developed by Yogiraj Bikram Choudhury is for those wanting to combine yoga with an intense work-out. The sweltering heat so loosens the muscles and ligaments that they stretch much further than they normally would. Beginners should work slowly to avoid strains and other injuries.
Ashtanga	An ancient form of hatha yoga composed of a series of postures, connecting movements and rhythmic deep breathing. One of the purposes of ashtanga is to rid the body of toxins through vigorous movements that create sweat. It is a challenging practice, but enhances mental focus and relaxation, while developing strength and flexibility.
TIPS	• Most yoga classes provide the props that are used in class, such as blocks and belts, but it is a good idea to bring your own mat and towel. Bring a water bottle as well, especially if participating in "hot" yoga such as Bikram or Ashtanga.
	• Videos are widely available, but it is best to learn the techniques in a class first, to avoid injury.
	• Specialised classes are available at many yoga studios including pre- and post-natal and restorative yoga, and yoga for elderly people and children.

368 Treat Yourself to a Day at the Spa

Need to rejuvenate but don't have the time or money for a weekend getaway? A day spa could be the perfect solution. Popping up in towns across the country, day spas offer a variety of treatments and pampering techniques that are sure to leave you feeling refreshed.

Steps

1 Get personal referrals, worth their weight in gold, since there are so many levels on which to assess the day spa experience.

2 Take a tour of the spa before you commit to spending a day there. Look for beautiful, clean surroundings and ample plush towels. Do you like the atmosphere? It can vary from alluring and relaxing with candlelight, flowers and water fountains, to more spartan and natural with soft music.

3 Scan the treatment menu. Full packages can be more economical than several à la carte treatments.

4 Ask about the qualifications of beauty therapists, massage therapists and spa personnel. Where were they trained? What methods or styles do they use? How long have they worked there?

5 Decide how lush you want to go and what your body is really crying out for. Is it a deep-tissue massage and a facial? Or a stimulating salt rub and then a pedicure? Choose your treatments accordingly. Throw in at least one exotic-sounding full-body treat, the kind that sounds like a dessert-trolley delicacy with tasty ingredients like pineapple, chocolate or papaya.

What to Look For

- Personal referrals
- Clean, attractive environment
- Staff expertise
- Relaxing, get-away-from-it-all ambience
- Menu of treatments

Tip

Enquire if robes, slippers and towels are provided. And although many spas have lockers that lock, it is best to leave valuables at home.

Warning

Don't drive yourself home. If you're truly as relaxed as a limp noodle, as prescribed, you'll be a road hazard – and rallying to negotiate traffic will kill the mood.

TREATMENT	DESCRIPTION AND PRICE
Facial	Types include anti-ageing, stress-reducing and therapeutic. Includes thorough cleansing as well as product application and generally a mini massage of the head and neck. Cost: £50 to £85 for 60 minutes.
Reflexology	Using the foot as a map of the entire body, apply pressure to different areas of the foot to reduce stress, improve circulation and cleanse the body of toxins. Cost: £45 for 60 minutes.
Aromatherapy	Uses therapeutic, essential oils to soothe or regenerate the body. May be used in conjunction with other treatments like massages and facials. Cost: £55 to £100.
Body Wrap	Using mud, paraffin, seaweed or aromatherapy-infused cloth to cover the body, these treatments stimulate the circulation, release muscle tension and promote general relaxation. Cost: £60 to £100 for 60 minutes.

369 Book a Massage

Massage has enormous potential to do a body good if you're in the right hands. But the way people like to get rid of knots and tension is highly personal. Get the lowdown on the rubdown.

TYPE	TRADEMARK TOUCH	BENEFITS
Swedish	Technique includes kneading, shaking, tapping, long sweeping strokes and circular pressure. Oil is generally used.	Energises, eases sore muscles and joints, improves blood flow.
Deep-tissue	Strokes are intentionally firm and can be painful as therapist gradually breaks through muscle spasms and layers of tension and goes deeper to slowly release it. Oil is generally used.	Can give remarkable relief. Should never be horribly painful; if it is, the therapist isn't tuning into your body, so ask for a lighter touch.
Acupressure	For the faint of heart who can't face acupuncture needles. Finger pressure is applied to the same spots and pathways. Acupressure points that are initially painful to the touch hold more pain, stress and tension.	Puts the body into balance, rejuvenates and relaxes. Gives sense of wellbeing. During the massage, pain gradually ebbs away.
Shiatsu	A Japanese art; widely available variation on acupressure.	Puts the body into balance, rejuvenates and relaxes. Gives sense of wellbeing. During the massage, pain gradually ebbs away.
Thai	Therapist uses his or her hands, arms, feet, legs and whole body to ease you into yoga poses. Fully clothed. Involves rhythmic stretching and pulling, plus pressing key energy points for total relaxation.	Makes you feel loose and supple. Gives feeling of peace and wellbeing followed by rush of energy. Can help chronic pain.
Reflexology	Stimulation of specific points on feet and hands believed to connect to specific internal organs.	Can remove energy blockages and improve overall health. Finds tender spots you didn't know you had.
TIPS	• Let your massage therapist know about any injuries or tender spots you'd prefer to avoid. • Check that your massage therapist is certified. Ask to see evidence of special training in methods like Thai or Swedish massage. • Contact local massage schools for less expensive services.	

CTION SITES • BUY BARGAIN CLOTHING • BUY WHOLESALE • GET OUT OF DEBT • BUY NOTHING • BUY HAPPINESS • BUY A BETTER MOUS
JY YOUR WAY INTO SOMEONE'S FAVOUR • BUY LOVE • FIND THE RIGHT RELAXATION TECHNIQUE FOR YOU • BUY HEALTHY FAST FOOD •
TING SERVICE • SELL YOURSELF ON AN ONLINE DATING SERVICE • SELL YOURSELF TO YOUR GIRLFRIEND/BOYFRIEND'S FAMILY • BUY FLC
HOOSE FILM FOR YOUR CAMERA • BUY RECHARGEABLE BATTERIES • GIVE TO A GOOD CAUSE • TAKE PART IN A CAR BOOT SALE • EMPLC
JDENT DISCOUNT$ • BUY FLOWERS WHOLESALE • GET A PICTURE FRAMED • EMPLOY A REMOVAL COMPANY • EMPLOY A LIFESTYLE MAN
Y FOR A HALLOWE'EN PARTY • BUY A GREAT BIRTHDAY PRESENT FOR UNDER £10 • SELECT GOOD CHAMPAGNE • BUY A DIAMOND • BUY
T A GIFT LIST • BUY WEDDING GIFTS • SELECT BRIDESMAIDS' DRESSES • HIRE AN EVENTS ORGANISER • HIRE A BARTENDER FOR A PARTY
NOUNCEMENTS • SELL YOUR WEDDING DRESS • BUY AN ANNIVERSARY GIFT • ARRANGE ENTERTAINMENT FOR A PARTY • COMMISSION A
RSON WHO HAS EVERYTHING • BUY A GIFT FOR PASSING EXAMS • SELECT A CHRISTMAS TURKEY • BUY A HOUSEWARMING GIFT • PURCH
AND • WRITE A MESSAGE IN THE SKY • HIRE A BIG-NAME BAND • GET INTO A PRIVATE GAMBLING ROOM IN LAS VEGAS • BUY SOMEONE A
E *TIMES* • EMPLOY A BUTLER • BUY A FOOTBALL CLUB • BUY A PERSONAL JET • SELECT A CLASSIC CAR • ACQUIRE A BODY GUARD • BC
EYHOUND TO RACE • BUY A RACEHORSE • BUY A VILLA IN TUSCANY • EMPLOY A PERSONAL CHEF • BUY A JOURNEY INTO SPACE • EMPI
RTUNE • HIRE AN EXPERT WITNESS • MAKE MONEY FROM ACCIDENT COMPENSATION • DONATE YOUR BODY TO SCIENCE • MAKE MONEY
ANCIAL ADVISER • PLAN FOR RETIREMENT • COPE WITH HIGHER EDUCATION COSTS • BUY AND SELL SHARES • CHOOSE A STOCKBROKE
SS INSURANCE • BUY LIFE INSURANCE • GET PRIVATE HEALTH INSURANCE • BUY PERSONAL FINANCE SOFTWARE • CHOOSE AN ACCOUN
LE OUT A PATENT • MARKET YOUR INVENTION • FINANCE YOUR BUSINESS IDEA • BUY A SMALL BUSINESS • BUY A FRANCHISE • LEASE RE
BSITE • HIRE A GRAPHIC DESIGNER • ACQUIRE CONTENT FOR YOUR WEBSITE • BUY ADVERTISING ON THE WEB • SELL YOUR ART • HIRE
BLISH YOUR BOOK • START A BED-AND-BREAKFAST • SELL A FAILING BUSINESS • BUY A HOT DOG STAND • SHOP FOR A MORTGAGE • GE
USE AT AUCTION • SHOP FOR A HOUSE ONLINE • BUY A PROPERTY FOR RENOVATION AND RESALE • EVALUATE BEFORE BUYING INTO A N
Y A PLOT OF LAND • HAVE YOUR HOUSE DESIGNED • HIRE AN ARCHITECT • HIRE A BUILDER • GET PLANNING PERMISSION • BUY A HOLIC
ROAD • BUY TO LET • RENT YOUR HOME FOR A LOCATION SHOOT • FURNISH YOUR HOME • FURNISH YOUR STUDIO FLAT • BUY USED FU
JY HOUSEHOLD APPLIANCES • BUY FLOOR-CARE APPLIANCES • BUY EXTENDED WARRANTIES ON APPLIANCES • FIND PERIOD FIXTURES
ME • SELECT PAINT, STAIN AND VARNISH • CHOOSE DECORATIVE TILES • CHOOSE A DEHUMIDIFIER • BUY A WHIRLPOOL BATH • BUY A SH
LLPAPER • BUY A WOOD-BURNING STOVE • SELECT FLOORING • SELECT CARPETING • CHOOSE KITCHEN CABINETS • CHOOSE A KITCHE
OKE ALARMS • BUY CARBON MONOXIDE DETECTORS • BUY FIRE EXTINGUISHERS • CHOOSE AN ENTRY DOOR • BUY A GARAGE-DOOR O
TDOOR FURNITURE • BUY THE PERFECT ROSE • BUY FLOWERING BULBS • BUY FLOWERS FOR YOUR GARDEN • SELECT PEST CONTROLS
TOMATIC WATERING SYSTEM • START A NEW LAWN • BUY A LAWN MOWER • BUY KOI FOR YOUR FISH POND • BUY A STORAGE SHED • H
ODUCE • CHOOSE A PERFECT PEACH • BUY AND SELL AT FARMERS' MARKETS • SELECT KITCHEN KNIVES • DECIPHER FOOD LABELS • SE
RFECT BURGER • PURCHASE A CHRISTMAS HAM • BUY ORGANIC BEEF • BUY HAGGIS • PURCHASE LOCAL HONEY • CHOOSE A CHICKEN
T TRUFFLES • BUY ARTISAN BREADS • BUY ARTISAN CHEESES • PURCHASE KOSHER FOOD • BUY SENSIBLY IN SUPERMARKETS • CHOOS
DER A GREAT CUP OF COFFEE • BUY A COFFEEMAKER OR ESPRESSO MACHINE • PURCHASE PARTY BEER • CHOOSE THE RIGHT WINE • •
ERM • CHOOSE AN OVULATION PREDICTOR KIT • PICK A PREGNANCY TEST KIT • CHOOSE BIRTH CONTROL • CHOOSE WHERE TO GIVE BI
Y BABY CLOTHES • CHOOSE NAPPIES • BUY OR RENT A BREAST PUMP • CHOOSE A CAR SEAT • BUY CHILD-PROOFING SUPPLIES • FIND
Y A GARDEN PLAY STRUCTURE • FIND A FAMILY-FRIENDLY HOTEL • ORGANISE A FUND-RAISING EVENT • BUY BRACES FOR YOUR KID • E
A MODEL • SELL USED BABY GEAR, TOYS, CLOTHES AND BOOKS • FIND A COUPLES COUNSELLOR • HIRE A FAMILY SOLICITOR • BUY OF
RCHASE A TOOTHBRUSH • BUY MOISTURISERS AND ANTIWRINKLE CREAMS • SELECT PAIN RELIEF AND COLD MEDICINES • CHOOSE A C
ODUCTS • BUY WAYS TO COUNTER HAIR LOSS • BUY A WIG OR HAIRPIECE • BUY A NEW BODY • GET A TATTOO OR BODY PIERCING • OB
TH • SELECT SPECTACLES AND SUNGLASSES • HIRE A PERSONAL TRAINER • SIGN UP FOR A YOGA CLASS • TREAT YOURSELF TO A DAY
AN ANTIQUE MARKET • BUY AT AUCTION • KNOW WHAT YOUR COLLECTIBLES ARE WORTH • BARTER WITH DEALERS • GET AN ANTIQUE A
NS • BUY AN ANTIQUE QUILT • BUY FILM POSTERS • LIQUIDATE YOUR BEANIE BABY COLLECTION • SCORE AUTOGRAPHS • TRADE YU-G
D SELL SPORTS MEMORABILIA • SELL YOUR FOOTBALL-CARD COLLECTION • CHOOSE A DESKTOP COMPUTER • SHOP FOR A USED COM
MPUTER PERIPHERALS • CHOOSE AN INTERNET SERVICE PROVIDER • GET AN INTERNET DOMAIN NAME • NETWORK YOUR COMPUTERS
D PLAYER • BUY A VIDEO RECORDER • CHOOSE A PERSONAL DIGITAL ASSISTANT • CHOOSE A MOBILE PHONE SERVICE • GET A BETTER
ITAL CAMERA • BUY A HOME AUTOMATION SYSTEM • BUY A STATE-OF-THE-ART SOUND SYSTEM • BUY AN AUDIO/VIDEO DISTRIBUTION S
SYSTEM • BUY VIRTUAL-REALITY FURNITURE • BUY TWO-WAY RADIOS • BUY A MOBILE ENTERTAINMENT SYSTEM • GET A PASSPORT, QL
AL LUGGAGE • FLY FOR NEXT TO NOTHING • TAKE A TRIP ON THE TRANS-SIBERIAN EXPRESS • BUY DUTY-FREE • SHIP FOREIGN PURCHA
LIAN CYCLING HOLIDAY • CHOOSE A CHEAP CRUISE • BOOK A HOTEL PACKAGE FOR THE GREEK ISLANDS • RAFT THE GRAND CANYON •
KSHAW IN RANGOON • TAKE SALSA LESSONS IN CUBA • BUY A CAMERA IN HONG KONG • BUY YOUR WAY ONTO A MOUNT EVEREST EX
L TEAM • BUY ANKLE AND KNEE BRACES • CHOOSE RUGBY PROTECTION KIT • BUY GOLF CLUBS • SELL FOUND GOLF BALLS • BUY PO
PLOY A SCUBA INSTRUCTOR • BUY A SKATEBOARD AND PROTECTIVE GEAR • BUY SKATES • GO BUNJEE JUMPING • GO SKYDIVING • BL
OTS AND BINDINGS • BUY SKI BOOTS • BUY A BICYCLE • BUY AN ELECTRIC BICYCLE • BUY CYCLE CLOTHING • BUY A PROPERLY FITTIN
T • BUY A SURFBOARD • BUY FLY-FISHING GEAR • BUY ROCK-CLIMBING EQUIPMENT • BUY A CASHMERE JUMPER • PURCHASE VINTAC
CKTAIL DRESS • BUY DESIGNER CLOTHES AT A DISCOUNT • CHOOSE A BASIC WARDROBE FOR A MAN • BUY A MAN'S DRESS SHIRT • PI
THER JACKET • BUY MATERNITY CLOTHES • GET A GREAT-FITTING BRA • CHOOSE A HIGH-PERFORMANCE SWIM SUIT • BUY PERFORMA
CTORY SHOPS • BUY A NEW CAR • BUY THE BASICS FOR YOUR CAR • BUY A USED CAR • BUY OR SELL A CAR ONLINE • BUY A HYBRID

BUY TIME • BUY A BOUQUET OF ROSES • BUY SOMEONE A DRINK • GET SOMEONE TO BUY YOU A DRINK • BUY YOUR WAY INTO THE BES
SCREEN • BUT FURTHER EDUCATION • ORDER EXOTIC FOOD • ORDER AT A SUSHI BAR • BUY DINNER AT A FRENCH RESTAURANT • EMPLO
O SAY SORRY TO YOUR PARTNER • BUY MUSIC ONLINE • EMPLOY MUSICIANS • ORDER A GOOD BOTTLE OF WINE • BUY AN ERGONOMIC [
ANER • EMPLOY AN AU PAIR • BUY A GUITAR • BUY DUCT TAPE • GET A GOOD DEAL ON A MAGAZINE SUBSCRIPTION • GET SENIOR CITIZE
FIND A VET • BUY PET FOOD • BUY A PEDIGREE DOG OR CAT • BREED YOUR PET AND SELL THE LITTER • BUY OR RENT FOR A FANCY DRE
RY MADE OF PRECIOUS METALS • BUY COLOURED GEMSTONES • CHOOSE THE PERFECT WEDDING DRESS • BUY OR RENT MEN'S FORMA
PHOTOGRAPHER • HIRE A CATERER • FIND THE IDEAL CIVIL WEDDING VENUE • THE COST OF MARRYING • ORDER PERSONALISED INVITA
RKS SHOW • BUY A MOTHER'S DAY GIFT • BUY A FATHER'S DAY GIFT • SELECT AN APPROPRIATE COMING-OF-AGE GIFT • GET A GIFT FOR
RISTMAS CARDS • BUY CHRISTMAS STOCKING FILLERS • BUY CHRISTENING GIFTS • PURCHASE A PERFECT CHRISTMAS TREE • BUY A PR
PAY A RANSOM • GET HOT TICKETS • HIRE A LIMOUSINE • BUY A CRYONIC CHAMBER • RENT YOUR OWN HOARDING • TAKE OUT A FULL-P
URY CRUISE AROUND THE WORLD • BUY A TICKET TO TRAVEL FOR A YEAR • BOOK A TRIP ON THE ORIENT-EXPRESS • OWN A VINEYARD
OSTWRITER TO WRITE YOUR MEMOIRS • COMMISSION ORIGINAL ARTWORK • IMMORTALISE YOUR SPOUSE IN A SCULPTURE • GIVE AWAY
DICAL GUINEA PIG • SELL YOUR STORY TO THE TABLOIDS • SELL YOUR SOUL TO THE DEVIL • NEGOTIATE A BETTER CREDIT CARD DEAL •
RADE (OR NOT) • BUY ANNUITIES • BUY AND SELL MUTUAL FUNDS • BUY BONDS • SELL SHORT • INVEST IN PRECIOUS METALS • BUY SE
ND CASUAL WORK • SELL YOUR PRODUCT O   A HEADHUNTER • SELL YOURSELF IN A JOB INTER
CE • LEASE INDUSTRIAL SPACE • LEASE OFFI   MENT • HIRE SOMEONE TO DESIGN AND BUILD Y
ACH • SELL ON THE CRAFT CIRCUIT • HIRE A   RY • SELL A SCREENPLAY • SELL YOUR NOVEL •
ER MORTGAGE DEAL • SAVE ON YOUR MORTG   D • OBTAIN HOUSE INSURANCE • BUY A HOUSE •
• EXCHANGE CONTRACTS ON A PROPERTY •   AN ESTATE AGENT • RELEASE CAPITAL FROM YOU
• RENT A HOLIDAY HOME • BUY A FLAT • RE   COUNTRY • BUY A LOFT APARTMENT • BUY PRO
BUY DOOR AND WINDOW LOCKS • CHOOSE   GHT FIXTURES • BUY A PROGRAMMABLE LIGHTI
ED AND MATTRESS • HIRE AN INTERIOR DES   NCORPORATE A GREATER SENSE OF SPACE INTO
UY A TOILET • CHOOSE A TAP • BUY GLUES   MENTS • GET SELF-CLEANING WINDOWS • CHOO
OP • BUY GREEN HOUSEHOLD CLEANERS •   SECURITY SYSTEM • BUY A HOME ALARM SYST
UY TIMBER FOR A DIY PROJECT • HOW TO S   R, PAINTER OR ELECTRICIAN • HIRE A GARDENER
IL IMPROVERS • BUY MULCH • BUY A COMP   BLE GARDEN • HIRE A GARDEN DESIGNER • BUY
SURGEON • BUY BASIC GARDEN TOOLS • B   BUY AN OUTDOOR LIGHTING SYSTEM • BUY OF
BS AND SPICES • STOCK YOUR KITCHEN WI   RESH PRODUCE • SELECT MEAT • STOCK UP FO
FRESH FISH • SELECT RICE • PURCHASE PR   LTON • GET FRESH FISH DELIVERED TO YOUR DO
G OILS • SELECT OLIVE OIL • SELECT OLIVES   VINEGAR • CHOOSE PASTA • BUY TEA • BUY COF
REAL ALE • ORDER A COCKTAIL • CHOOSE A   STOCK A WINE CELLAR • STOCK YOUR BAR • D
A MIDWIFE OR DOULA • PLAN A HOME BIRT   R A NEW BABY • BUY A NEW COT • CHOOSE A PU
CHILDCARE • FIND A GREAT NANNY • FIND T   TER-SCHOOL CARE • SIGN YOUR CHILD UP FOR
BUY BOOKS, VIDEOS AND MUSIC FOR YOU   HIRE A TUTOR • ADOPT A CHILD • GET YOUR CH
LTERED HOUSING • CHOOSE A CARE HOME   PLOT • PAY FOR FUNERAL EXPENSES • GET VIAG
TARY MTHERAPY • SEE A MENTAL-HEALTH P   BUY HOME-USE MEDICAL SUPPLIES • SELECT HA
T IMPLANTS • GET WRINKLE-FILLER INJECT   ACTITIONERS • CHOOSE A MANICURIST • GET WI
A • BOOK A MASSAGE • GET ON ANTIQUES   SHOP AT AN ANTIQUE FAIR OR FLEA MARKET •
• BUY SILVERWARE • EVALUATE CARNIVAL GLASS • BUY AND SELL STAMPS • BUY ANTIQUE FURNITURE • GET CLUED UP ON CLARICE CL
• SEIZE STAR WARS ACTION FIGURES • SELL YOUR VINYL RECORD COLLECTION • SELL TO A PAWNSHOP • BUY AND SELL COMIC BOOK
PERIPHERALS • CHOOSE A LAPTOP OR NOTEBOOK COMPUTER • SELL OR DONATE A COMPUTER • BUY PRINTER PAPER • BUY A PRINTEI
THE MEMORY IN YOUR COMPUTER • BUY COMPUTER SOFTWARE • CHOOSE A CD PLAYER • BUY BLANK CDS • BUY AN MP PLAYER • CF
YOUR PHONE COMPANY • BUY VIDEO AND COMPUTER GAMES • CHOOSE A FILM CAMERA • CHOOSE A DIGITAL CAMCORDER • DECIDE
UY A SERIOUS TV • CHOOSE BETWEEN DIGITAL TV PROVIDERS • GET A DIGITAL VIDEO RECORDER • GET A UNIVERSAL REMOTE • BUY A F
CHASE CHEAP AIRLINE TICKETS • FIND GREAT HOTEL DEALS • HIRE THE BEST CAR FOR THE LEAST MONEY • GET TRAVEL INSURANCE •
E UNITED KONGDOM • TIP IN A FOREIGN COUNTRY • TIP PROPERLY IN THE UK • BRIBE A FOREIGN OFFICIAL • GET AN INTERRAIL PASS •
EAP BUT FANTASTIC SAFARI • RENT A CAMEL IN CAIRO • GET SINGLE-MALT WHISKY IN SCOTLAND • BUY A SAPPHIRE IN BANGKOK • HIF
HIRE A TREKKING COMPANY IN NEPAL • RENT OR BUY A SATELLITE PHONE • BUY YOUR CHILD'S FIRST CRICKET BAT • ORDER A STRIP FC
• BUY A RACKET • BUY A HEALTH CLUB MEMBERSHIP • BUY AN AEROBIC FITNESS MACHINE • BUY SWIMMING EQUIPMENT • BUY A JET
ETING EQUIPMENT • CHOOSE A CAR RACK • BUY SKIS • BUY CLOTHES FOR COLD-WEATHER ACTIVITIES • SELL USED SKIS • BUY A SNO
BUY THE OPTIMAL SLEEPING BAG • BUY A TENT • BUY A BACKPACK • BUY A CAMPING STOVE • BUY A KAYAK • BUY A LIFEJACKET • BU
• SELL USED CLOTHING • ORDER CUSTOM-MADE COWBOY BOOTS • BUY CLOTHES ONLINE • FIND NON-STANDARD SIZES • BUY THE P
• BUY A WOMAN'S SUIT • BUY A MAN'S SUIT • HIRE A TAILOR • BUY CUSTOM-TAILORED CLOTHES IN ASIA • BUY A BRIEFCASE • SHOP
UT CLOTHES • BUY A HEART-RATE MONITOR • SELECT A WATCH • BUY KIDS' CLOTHES • CHOOSE CHILDREN'S SHOES • PURCHASE CLC
CAR • BUY A MOTORCYCLE • BUYING AND CHANGING MOTOR OIL • WASH A CAR • WAX A CAR • BUY CAR INSURANCE • SPRING F

Collectibles

370 Get on Antiques Roadshow

This wildly popular BBC programme has been largely responsible for the growing awareness of antiques among the general public. If the Antiques Roadshow comes to your town, don't miss a chance for a free appraisal – and an opportunity to be on national television.

Steps

1 Check the BBC's website (bbc.co.uk/antiques/antiquesroadshow) for tour stops. The Antiques Roadshow visits a number of locations around the country for each series that it films.

2 Apply to appear on the show via the website.

3 Choose the antique that you take along with you wisely. There's no item that will guarantee you an on-air appraisal, although unusual and older items tend to receive more attention.

4 Weigh your options. If you decide to bring along a large piece of furniture like a sideboard, you'll have to work out how to get it safely from home to the show and home again. You and your back might be happier carting around a lightweight piece of jewellery instead.

5 Wear an outfit that's suitable for TV, but also dress comfortably, especially when it comes to shoes. You'll spend a lot of time on your feet.

6 Be a star. If appraisers see something rare or unusual in what you've brought, they might film your appraisal. You won't receive any information about it until the cameras roll – the show is looking for a genuine reaction from you. If you and your antique are chosen to be filmed, don't assume you'll receive good news. Some treasure hunters learn the hard way that, if they bought the antique, they paid too much for it, or that a cherished family heirloom has only sentimental value.

What to Look For

- Tour stops
- Tickets
- Chance at stardom, riches

Tip

Share everything you know about your antique, such as how long it's been in your family, who the previous owners were or what it was used for. It not only helps the appraiser put the right price on something, but it's also good television.

Warning

If you're worried about damaging an item while transporting your antique to the show or while you're waiting in the queue to get in, don't bring it.

371 Buy and Sell Used Books

In the estate agent game, the mantra is location, location, location. In the book trade, it's condition, condition, condition. Even the dust jacket figures into a book's value.

Steps

Buying

1 Determine what kind of collector you are. Will you collect by author? Subject? First editions only? Answering these questions will set your course.

2 Do your homework. Yes, there are books about books. They tell you who published the book first and when, as well as how to approximate a book's value.

3 Surf for pricing information on the internet. Be aware that some of the listings are asking prices, not actual selling prices.

4 Visit a few used bookstores and introduce yourself to the owners. Let them know what kinds of materials interest you. Bookstore owners frequent many more auctions and shows than you will.

5 Buy only the best. Once you've established what you're looking for, get the best example you can find.

6 Keep your books in good condition by storing them upright on bookshelves. If you must pack them away in boxes, lay them one on top of another, keep weight evenly distributed and pack them tightly so they don't rub against one another. Don't put any weight on top of the books that might cause the binding to bend or the top to wear.

Selling

1 Lower your expectations – most sellers tend to place a value on books far above what they are really worth. Finding a rare gem among a pile of books you inherited is highly unlikely. Invite a local book dealer to see what you've got and ask for an off-the-cuff appraisal.

2 Sort paperbacks in one pile, hardcovers in another. Only in rare cases do paperbacks possess more than just word value. Sell them at a car boot sale or trade them in at a second-hand book shop.

3 Find out what you can about any hardcover books you have in good condition. Check the library for reference books and search the internet for used-book sales venues.

4 Sell your rare examples on an internet auction site or at an auction house. If you're selling online, set a reserve (a price that must be met for a sale to take place) to ensure that you will get what you expect. See 374 "Buy at Auction" and 10 "Use Online Auction Sites".

What to Look For

- Pricing info
- Second-hand book shops
- Best quality
- Library
- Internet auction sites

Tips

Look for the words *first edition* and *first printing* in the front of the book (usually just after the title page) on a page that also lists copyright date, publisher, printing location and reference numbers.

Not all first editions are marked as such. You may have to determine age by points of issue, such as spelling corrections or changes in illustrations made between printings.

Warning

Books made especially for a book-club distributor have little worth, except for people who choose to collect them. If a book is a book-club edition, it will say so on the copyright page.

372 Shop at an Antique Fair or Flea Market

These fairs and exhibitions offer the opportunity to view the wares of hundreds of dealers from all across the country in one location. Go with a partner and a plan.

Steps

1 Make a list. It's easy to get distracted by all the wonderful antiques and collectibles on display. Set some priorities so you won't waste precious time.

2 Decide how much you're willing to pay for items on your wish list. A quick internet search will reveal what similar items are selling for. Work at least one splurge item into your budget, to reward yourself for being in the right place at the right time.

3 Get there early, because the best items are snatched up quickly. The serious shoppers will be waiting at the gate when it opens. Find out if the event offers a preview party. You will pay to get in, but you'll see the best material.

4 Be prepared. Take a bag or a trolley to put purchases in so you can keep shopping. If you're buying furniture, bring blankets, ropes and a vehicle that will enable you to transport the item safely home. Take a partner. Two people can cover more ground than one. Some high-tech shoppers use two-way radios or mobile phones to stay in touch.

5 Bring your own bottled water and snacks. Even though there may be food and drink stands, you don't want to have to fight the crowd or spend precious shopping minutes standing in a queue.

6 Wear comfortable walking shoes so you can be on your feet all day and navigate uneven ground. If the market is held outdoors, bring a hat to protect yourself from the sun.

7 Bring cash, credit cards and your chequebook. Different dealers accept different forms of payment. Dealing in cash can sometimes land a better price for an item.

8 Ask for what you want. If a dealer has items similar to but not exactly like the ones you're looking for, there's a chance he or she may have just what you want back at the shop.

9 Make quick decisions. Few dealers will hold an item while you take time to think about it. They're at the fair to sell, sell, sell.

10 Ask dealers if they are open to trading or purchasing the items you bring to the show. Grab a business card for later contact.

11 Ask if a dealer will take less for a blemished or flawed item. The worst that can happen is that he or she will say no.

What to Look For

- Shopping list
- Budget
- Partner
- Cash
- Dealers who trade

Tips

Search antiquing newspapers and magazines for listings of antique fairs in your area and beyond.

One of the best-known antique centres is in Battlesbridge, Essex (battlesbridge.com), with around 80 dealers selling most types of antiques.

Most large shows offer a map of exhibitors and the types of merchandise they sell. Get one to help focus your shopping efforts.

These are some hot items to look for: vintage cookbooks and '50s kitchenware, and anything for the garden.

Warning

Big shows bring out large numbers of shoppers. Find a landmark that will help you remember where you parked, or tie a ribbon to your car aerial so you can find it in the car park.

373 Rent Space at an Antique Market

If you've been toying with the idea of opening your own antique shop, take that notion for a test drive by setting up shop at a local antique market. Here, many different dealers rent space to display their wares, creating a one-stop shopping bonanza for collectors.

Steps

1 Do an inventory to see if you have enough merchandise to fill up the space you rent. Remember, the more diverse your inventory, the more shoppers you'll entice.

2 Choose a market that appears popular and has a friendly staff. Ask yourself, "Would I shop here?"

3 Weigh your commitment. You will pay the market owner rent for the space you choose, plus a portion of your sales income.

4 Choose a space. A display case may be all you need if you're selling small items like jewellery. Some antique markets even rent single open shelves. If you have furniture, you'll want a booth.

5 Know the local market and what appeals to the market's clientele. If you have a lot of diverse items but not what shoppers want, the merchandise won't move.

6 Display your wares in a way that makes it easy for passers-by to see what you have for sale. Don't stack items on top or in front of each other.

7 Give customers room to shop. Don't pack your booth so full of merchandise that people can't get close to items they want to look at. Collectors are hands-on shoppers.

8 Price your goods appropriately and fairly. Consult price guides and compare your merchandise to that of other sellers in the market when pricing items. If something doesn't sell, mark it down. Discounted tickets will attract attention.

9 Keep your booth or display case looking fresh by bringing out new merchandise. If it appears the same from week to week, repeat shoppers will walk by without a second glance.

10 Review your progress, keeping a close eye on profits. Contracts for market space tend to be short-term, and either party can terminate them, which is to your advantage if you find the antique market route isn't for you.

What to Look For

- Diverse inventory
- Good location
- Friendly staff
- Rent rates
- Market-owner's commission
- Contract terms

Tips

Think like a business owner. Keep items dusted and looking their best. Faded price tags indicate to shoppers that no one is minding the booth.

Label items with as many facts as you have, including the date an item was made, its rarity and any information on its provenance. All those factors will help make a sale.

Warning

Make sure your insurance is sufficient and up to date. If merchandise is stolen, broken or lost in a fire, the owner of the items, not the owner of the market, is responsible for their loss.

374 Buy at Auction

Auctions put your antiques and collectibles in front of the greatest number of serious buyers at one time. If you're in the mood to buy rather than sell, auctions offer an exhilaration you can't get from just walking into an antique shop. See also 10 "Use Online Auction Sites".

Steps

1 Find the type of auction that works for you. Online auctions are the most time-consuming option and the riskiest for buyers, as you never get to see the merchandise in person. Auction houses like Sotheby's and Christie's feature up-market items you won't find anywhere else. Country auctions offer the best chance for finding a diamond in the rough.

2 Know the purchasing rules of the auction house. Sellers pay a commission to the house for their services, from 5 to 15 per cent, depending on the value of the piece. Similarly, buyers may be required to pay a premium to auction owners for up-market sales.

3 Get the timing down. Country auctions and auction house events will last from just a few hours to a day. Online auctions are timed; items are usually posted for a week or so. Bidding really heats up as the deadline approaches.

4 Ask questions about the provenance (ownership history) of a piece. It's especially important to find out from online sellers if anything was left out of their description of the piece. As a seller, you need to be able to provide this type of feedback.

5 Decide on a bid limit for yourself, after inspecting merchandise. It's easy to get swept up in the excitement of a live auction and overbid.

6 Register so you can be identified as a bidder. No matter what type of auction you participate in, you'll need to do this – by name on the internet, by number in person. You may also be asked for proof of payment to show your seriousness as a bidder.

7 Get the auctioneer's attention if you enter late in the bidding on a particular item at an auction house. His or her assistants will be concentrating on bidders already in the fray.

8 Have fun. A live auction is pure entertainment, from fast-talking auctioneers to fast-spending collectors. Auctions are free and open to the public, and you don't have to bid if you don't want to. In fact, attend a few auctions without bidding to learn the rules of the game.

What to Look For

- The right auction
- Rules of engagement
- Auction fees
- Information
- Reasonable budget
- Registration
- Preview

Tips

When selling expensive pieces, set a reserve (a minimum price you will accept for sale) to guarantee that you either get the amount you're after or get to keep the item.

Many auctions benefit charities so bids often exceed the item's worth.

Warning

The hammer price (the final bid amount when the gavel closes bidding) is not all you'll pay as a buyer. The auction house receives a percentage of the hammer price, and you'll have to pay for shipment (unless you transport it yourself).

TYPE	LOCATION	MERCHANDISE VALUE	HOW TO PLACE A BID	SCOPE	MARKETING MATERIALS
Auction House	Sale rooms sometimes at an estate	Upmarket, usually from £350 up to millions	Bidding paddle, rub of nose	International	Catalogue with photos, descriptions, sometimes minimum bids
Country Auction	Garden, farmyard	Mid-range, from hundreds into the thousands	Wave of hand, tip of hat	Regional	Flyers listing highlights, newspaper advertisements
Online Auction	Internet	Wide range, from a few pounds to thousands	Click of mouse	Global	Online listing with photos, descriptions

375 Know What Your Collectibles Are Worth

When you start collecting, always buy things you love and you'll never regret your investment. It's important to do some research before buying and selling. Finding information you can trust is key.

Steps

1 Consult price guides, which list collectibles and their price ranges. General guides list a number of collecting categories in one book. You'll also find more specific single-topic guides.

2 Visit shops or antique markets to see how items similar to yours are priced. Establishing a relationship with a dealer may get you a better price when you're ready to sell or buy.

3 Contact auction houses to obtain a report of the most recent sales. Look for items similar to yours and the price they fetched.

4 Scour the internet for antiques and collectibles that are for sale through online auctions or stores.

5 Search newspapers and other publications devoted to antiques to find collecting clubs.

6 Find an experienced mentor who can tell you if you're getting a fair offer. Some of these experts work as pickers (regional buyers) for antique dealers and see a lot of merchandise.

7 Get a verbal appraisal from a dealer for free. If you have an item you think is really valuable, you might want to contact a professional appraiser, who will charge for that service.

What to Look For

- Price guides
- Antique experts
- Auction houses
- Internet sources
- Other collectors
- Mentor
- Appraisals

Tips

If you're selling to a dealer, expect to get only 50 per cent or less of the price listed in the price guides. Selling to another collector may bring a better price.

If you want to buy or sell a valuable collectible, such as a piece of fine art, always seek a second opinion on its value before you go ahead.

376 Barter with Dealers

Part of the fun of going to antique and collectibles shows is feeling like you've made the deal of the century. Many dealers love to barter and leave room for negotiating in their pricing. Brush up on the rules of the game.

Steps

1 Be serious about your offer. Know what you can pay for the merchandise and then be ready to follow through. While bartering can be fun for novice buyers, it's serious business for dealers.

2 Gather all the merchandise you're interested in from a particular booth before tallying your take. The more items you buy, the more room you have to negotiate.

3 Prioritise the merchandise. Decide what you can do without just in case you and the owner can't make a deal and you don't want to raise your price.

4 Make only one deal a day at any given booth. Don't come back a second time and try to make another deal. Dealers might not remember you from show to show, but they will remember someone who tried to barter them down twice in one day.

5 Build a relationship with the dealer. If you bought from a dealer before, remind him or her of that fact. He or she may offer a better price even before you ask. Dealers like to know that they are getting repeat customers and sales they can count on.

6 Say, "What's your best price on these things?" or "Would you take X amount for this?" Don't say, "I saw something like this a couple of booths away for only X amount." The dealer's reaction will probably be, "Then go and buy that one."

7 Deal in cash or a cheque for more leverage. If you're paying by credit card, the dealer will have to figure credit card company charges into the final price.

8 Negotiate a compromise. If the merchandise adds up to £250 and you have £200 in your pocket, offer to buy it all for £200. Expect the dealer to ask for something between those two totals.

9 Show your hand. The last step is to pull the cash out of your pocket and say, "But £200 is all the cash I've got." The dealer doesn't want to repack merchandise after the show and might be willing to drop the price for cash. If not, you might have to let something go to get your total down to an affordable amount.

What to Look For

- Serious offer
- Strength in numbers
- The right questions
- Compromise
- Cash offer

Tip

Keep your poker face on. If you're salivating slightly, the dealer will know he or she doesn't have to bother with a discount because you'll buy it at any price.

Warning

Don't insult the dealer with a ridiculously low price for merchandise or by calling into question the authenticity of what he or she is selling. That's a sure way to kill a deal and a potentially profitable relationship.

377 Get an Antique Appraised

An appraisal is just one person's opinion, whether it's free or for a fee. Get a second opinion (and even a third or fourth) if you have a lot of money on the line.

Steps

1 Find out what you have, but don't buy £200 worth of books to research an item that may bring only £100. Price guides and printed estimates of value are just guidelines. What someone's willing to pay dictates the real worth of an item, and for that you need an expert in the field.

2 Look in the *Yellow Pages* under "Valuers". Often they will include their speciality in the listing.

3 Look for valuers that are members of organisations like LAPADA (Association of Art and Antique Dealers – lapada.co.uk) and NAVA (National Association of Valuers & Auctioneers – nava.org.uk).

4 Show the item in its original condition. If you refinish furniture or polish your coin collection, you might actually diminish the item's value. (See 381 "Buy Antique Furniture" and 383 "Buy Coins".)

5 Find out what a written appraisal is likely to cost before you give the OK. An appraiser's research time can add up quickly.

6 Try to get a free verbal appraisal as part of an antiques show or exhibition. You can also ask an antique dealer to give you an idea of what your piece may be worth.

7 Find an online appraiser. The drawback here, of course, is that the appraiser isn't in the same room with the item.

8 Beware of the appraiser who offers to buy your item after appraising it, especially if you've never conducted business together before. Unscrupulous people may give you a low estimate to get a better deal.

What to Look For

- Price guidelines
- Experts in the field
- Professional associations
- Estimates for written appraisals
- Verbal appraisals
- Online appraisals

Tips

When presenting your item, don't say that you don't know anything about it. Simply say, "Tell me what you think about this."

Check with your insurer to see what's required to insure an item. You might not need a professional appraisal; a detailed bill of sale might be enough.

378 Buy Silverware

Back when entertaining meant a formal meal rather than a garden barbecue, people set ornate tables full of unusual pieces, a treasure trove for today's collector.

Steps

1 Select a conversation piece to collect, like a crumb knife (looks like a sugar scoop with a flat bottom and one open side; used to sweep up crumbs between courses) or a butter pick (looks like a mini corkscrew; used to grab individual curls or balls of butter).

2 Choose large serving pieces you can use for special occasions, or pick a silver pattern you like and try to collect a complete set. One fun collectible category is ladles. Our ancestors relied on ladles for serving (from smallest to largest) mustard, mayonnaise, sauce, gravy, bouillon, oysters, soup and punch.

3 Look for the silver hallmark on the back of the handle. If it's not there, it's silver-plated. Look for the name of the manufacturer as well. An 18th-century find may have the craftsman's initials.

4 Avoid badly worn pieces if you plan to use them at your own table. Over the years, the silver plate on the back of a spoon or along a fork's tines can wear off.

5 Collect cutlery for an affordable hobby. You can find teaspoons for less than a pound. Large serving forks and spoons in fine condition can be had for £15 or less. Harder-to-find patterns will cost more, of course.

What to Look For

- Usable pieces
- Complete set
- Sterling
- Cutlery

Tip

Collecting silverware is not a labour-free hobby. Silverware needs to be polished to look its best. Buy products expressly meant for silver cleaning. Never substitute toothpaste, which may include abrasives like baking soda that will damage silver. Rub polish back and forth instead of in a circular motion for a uniform finish. Rinse immediately with warm water and pat dry with a cotton dish towel. Silverware used and washed frequently is less likely to tarnish.

379 Evaluate Carnival Glass

No one knows how carnival glass got its name in the 1960s, although it's been suggested that pieces may have been given away as prizes at fairs. Although cheap then, carnival glass today is collectible. Made from the 1900s until the 1930s, this vividly coloured iridescent glassware was created by spraying metallic powder onto pressed glass. This distinctive effect mimicked much more expensive Tiffany art glass, hence its other name of "poor man's Tiffany".

Steps

1 Research the pieces you own. Since carnival glass was mass-produced, rarity determines value. As plates were more difficult to make, fewer examples were produced; as a result, they are more valuable today. Black and red pieces also have rarity value.

2 Attend an antiques show and look for glass dealers. Remember that the prices you see at the show are retail; you'll get half that or less if you sell your wares to a dealer.

What to Look For

- Rare pieces
- Antique dealers

Tip

Collectors are on the lookout for undamaged pieces and rare shapes and colours.

380 Buy and Sell Stamps

Stamps won't make the casual collector rich, but as a hobby they're almost unbeatable. They don't take up much room, and your postman brings new opportunities every day – for free!

Steps

Buy

1 Decide what you want to collect. Topical collecting (looking for any stamp with a flag, train or other specific item on it) is the latest trend. For example, an extensive collection can be made from collecting the Christmas stamps of just one country, especially if you include all the varieties of each issue. Some people even collect postmarks.

2 Look in the *Yellow Pages* for a shop that specialises in stamps. The shop owner will know of forthcoming stamp shows in the area.

3 Ask the shop owner about auction houses that sell stamps. Order an auction catalogue. Expect big-ticket items; most auction houses want their lots to sell for more than £60 to make it worth their while. Look in collector magazines for advertisements by mail-order stamp sources.

4 Search online. Some stamp dealers have set up shop online, and a few auctions feature stamps. Royal Mail (royalmail.com) also has information on starting a collection.

5 Select stamps with a bright colour – fading can be caused by sunlight, artificial light, dirt, pollution and natural skin oils. The stamp should not be torn or damaged, and all perforations should be complete. It should be centred inside the white border.

Sell

1 Look through your collection for pre-1940 stamps for investment-quality material. Far fewer stamps were printed in the old days, making good specimens more difficult to find. For the most part, today's stamps are not going to appreciate greatly in value over the years because so many are in circulation.

2 Join a stamp club – it's a great way to find fellow collectors looking to buy. Clubs often hold their own stamp shows for members.

3 Ask a stamp dealer to assess your collection if you want your money right away. Face-to-face meetings are best.

4 Keep in mind that auction houses won't even look at your collection if they don't think it will sell for hundreds of pounds, and it may take a month or more to receive the proceeds.

5 Sell your stamps online. This method can be time-consuming: you must submit a photo and description for each stamp or lot.

What to Look For

- Stamp shops
- Auction houses
- Mail-order sources
- Websites
- Stamp clubs
- Stamp shows

Tips

Glue on the back of a stamp means it has never been circulated. Removing stamps from letters also removes the glue.

Don't bother trying to soak a stamp off a coloured envelope. The ink in the envelope will bleed and ruin the stamp.

Store your stamps using hinges or mounts on acid-free paper, all available at craft shops. You'll also need tongs, a magnifier, a watermark detector and a perforation gauge.

See 374 "Buy at Auction".

Warning

As it's so easy to sell items online, keep in mind that the seller might not be an expert and could overstate the quality of the item.

381 Buy Antique Furniture

You can find antique furniture to fit any decor, from country to contemporary. Let the buyer beware: reproductions abound in the furniture field. Do your homework to make sure you're purchasing the real thing.

Steps

1 Become familiar with terms like *cabriole legs* that you're going to come across in advertisements and auction catalogues. (By the way, cabriole legs curve out like a cowboy's after too long in the saddle.)

2 Study the names (there can be more than one) of the styles you like best. Sellers classify their furniture by style: Louis XV, Queen Anne, Chippendale and so on.

3 Check the antiques section of your local book shop or library for reference guides. The internet is another good source for information and photographs of different furniture styles.

4 Visit a local museum. Seeing antique furniture up close will help you identify it in the field. Ask the curator for the names of trustworthy local dealers.

5 Learn to spot features that could affect the value of a piece such as damaged finish or joints, or unauthentic metalwork (see chart, opposite).

6 Get to know the local antique dealers and show them your wish list. They'll have contacts around the country who can further your search. They will also be able to help you recognise a reproduction.

7 Go to an auction. For top-quality, top-price furniture, choose an auction house that guarantees what it sells. If you're not looking for a museum-quality piece, try a country auction, where you could find a bargain. (See 374 "Buy at Auction".)

8 Watch for estate sales. If you're lucky, a family member will be at the sale to tell you about the piece's provenance or history.

9 Look through collectors' newspapers and magazines for ads, or search the internet for antique fairs specialising in furniture. (See 372 "Shop at an Antique Fair or Flea Market".)

10 Curb your desire for perfection in a piece of furniture that might be more than 100 years old. It should show signs of wear in places where you'd expect it, like the bottoms of chair legs and underneath drawer runners.

What to Look For

- Style
- Reputable dealers
- Auctions
- Estate sales
- Furniture shows
- Wear and tear

Tips

Definitions vary, especially regarding more recent items, but generally speaking, an antique is at least 100 years old. Everything newer than that falls into the collectible category.

Buy pieces you can use. Few of us have extra rooms we can fill with an untouchable collection of antique furniture.

If you know how to date a piece of furniture, you won't fall for a reproduction. Read one of the many books on the subject.

WHAT TO LOOK FOR	WHERE TO LOOK	IS IT OLD?
Hand-planing	The bottom of a chair or drawer.	If a seat bottom shows signs of hand-planing, it was probably made before 1810.
Construction Joints	The joints between two pieces of wood.	18th-century furniture was often pegged and glued, not nailed. Look for irregularly shaped and spaced dovetails (notches cut in wood so pieces fit together like puzzle pieces). Until the last half of the 19th century, these were cut by hand and shouldn't be perfectly spaced or formed.
Size of Boards	Tabletops and backs of dressing tables, sideboards.	These should be built with one solid piece or different pieces of various widths if the piece is truly old. Perfectly sized and spaced boards indicate new construction.
Saw Marks	On the backs of chests and under tables.	Straight saw marks indicate the piece was made before the mid-18th century. Wavy lines (cut with a band saw) show it was made in the mid-18th to 19th century. Look for circular saw patterns in furniture made after that.
Secondary Wood	Inside drawers and on dressing table backs.	The builders of old furniture used less expensive wood in places where it wouldn't show. No secondary wood is a sure sign of new construction, and any plywood is a dead giveaway.
Original Paint Finish	Cracks or dents in painted furniture.	If the paint finish is original, exposed wood should appear in any cracks and gouges. If you spy paint down in the cracks and crevices, then it's been painted since the dent occurred.
Antique Glass	Mirrors.	Antique glass is very thin. Test by placing a coin on edge against the mirror. If the reflection is very close to the coin itself, almost touching it, the glass is old.
Worm holes	On the surface of any wood piece.	Stick a pin in the hole. If the pin goes straight through, the hole is manufactured. True worm holes are winding paths.

382 Get Clued Up on Clarice Cliff

Clarice Cliff pottery, with its brightly coloured, geometric patterns inspired by contemporary art, flowers and botany, had its heyday in the 1930s. Cliff's famous "Bizarre Ware", launched as cheerful, inexpensive domestic pottery, was an immediate success and it's especially popular with collectors today, fetching high prices. Here's how to spot a valuable Clarice Cliff piece.

Steps

1 Check the manufacturer's mark on the underside. A piece is unlikely to be of any great value without one of the following words: "Bizarre", "Fantasque", "Inspiration", "Latona" or "Appliqué".

2 Be on the lookout for Clarice Cliff candlesticks. These are quite rare and attract high prices. Chargers (large dishes), "Lotus" jugs, vases and plates are very popular and also fetch high prices.

3 Be on your guard for fakes. Thickly applied, uneven glazes and smudged designs usually mean that the piece is a fake, as does poor-quality painting.

4 Visit the Clarice Cliff Collectors Club (claricecliff.com), which offers valuations via the internet.

What to Look For

- Manufacturer's mark
- Bright, colourful and geometric shapes are very popular with collectors
- Condition

Tip

The value of a piece is likely to be reduced if it is damaged or worn.

Warning

Visible brushstrokes are a hallmark of some of Clarice Cliff's best work – don't mistake these for poor-quality painting as found on fakes.

383 Buy Coins

When it comes to buying coins, buy the best example you can find. And if you get serious about coin collecting, you can call yourself a numismatist – it'll look great on your CV!

Steps

1 Look for lustre – the shine on a new coin. If you're collecting old coins, however, lustre is less of a concern.

2 Get a lucky strike. The strike is the impression on the coin. Look for a design that's perfectly centred on the coin.

3 Examine a coin for sharp details. One that has been in circulation for years will show a wearing down of high points on the design.

4 Avoid coins with small scratches on their surface: hairlines decrease its value. Cleaning the coin can also create hairlines, so learn the correct cleaning method from an expert.

What to Look For

- Lustre
- High-quality strike
- Sharp details
- Absence of hairlines

Tips

The use of silver for coins in general circulation practically ceased after World War II. However, it is still used for Maundy Money and for special collector coins.

Contact the Royal Mint (royalmint.com) for more information on collecting coins.

384 Buy an Antique Quilt

When it comes to craftsmanship, hand-made quilts, especially traditional American quilts, can rival the best examples of antique furniture that you'll find. Expect to pay hundreds, even thousands, of pounds for quilts in very good condition. A quilt writes a history with every stitch. Here's how to read it.

Steps

1 Look at authentic antique quilts, which usually date from the 19th and early 20th centuries, at living history museums, local quilt guilds or antique shops to train your eye. For example, old fabrics tend to have a tighter weave (more threads per inch) than new ones.

2 Ask to touch the quilts so you can learn how vintage material feels. Watch out for old quilt tops that have been given new cotton-polyester backs. To spot new batting (material sandwiched between the quilt top and back), gently rub the batting between your fingers. Polyester batting feels slippery.

3 Turn the quilt over and look for a label attached by the quilter. These list occasions, such as birthdays, weddings or national events, or names and dates.

4 Inspect the entire quilt. If the composition looks wrong, it may have been altered. Look for signs of wear in the binding (the edging on the quilt). Sometimes consistency of stitching is easier to see on the back than on the front.

5 Revel in the beautiful colours and craftsmanship of Amish quilts, one of the most prized categories of American quilts. Look for plain, solid-colour fabrics in bold, geometric designs. Amish beliefs reject adornments, including floral and stripe patterns. Quilts made from the late 19th century to the first half of the 20th century, with brilliant contrasting colours on black backgrounds, can command £1,500 to £6,500.

What to Look For

- Authenticity
- Label
- Flaws

Tips

In the 1950s to 1970s, borders were sometimes added to older quilts so they would fit on modern beds.

The fabric patches of antique quilts were often stuffed with newspaper or scrap paper templates to stiffen them. These may indicate the date and maker of the quilt.

Warning

Learn to recognise fakes and Asian imports. As with any deal, if it sounds too good to be true, it probably is.

385 Buy Film Posters

If film is your passion, then you'll love collecting original film posters. Posters from the country of a film's original release are usually the most popular with collectors, and the most sought-after sizes are the one sheet posters (68 x 105 cm/27 x 41 in) and British quads (76 x 102 cm/30 x 40 in). Original posters advertising 1930s films, such as *King Kong* and *Robin Hood*, command the highest prices because of their rarity value.

Steps

1 Get a theme going. As so many different films have been adver-rtised on posters, focusing on one theme, such as films directed by Alfred Hitchcock or starring James Stewart, will give coherence to a collection.

2 Look out for posters by the designer Saul Bass and by the artist Robert Peak. Striking images and posters for cult films or films that caught the public's imagination are also very desirable.

3 Check for tears and serious folds and creases. Most posters from before 1970 were folded for storage, so you are unlikely to find a poster from before that time in mint condition.

4 Beware of reproduction posters. These can usually be identified quite easily because poster paper is used and the image is reproduced photographically. Fake posters are relatively scarce.

What to Look For

- Size
- Era
- Theme
- Designer/artist
- Condition

Tips

Visit an auction or a dealer to see original posters so you can learn to tell the difference between the real thing, a reproduction and a fake.

Re-issue posters are produced when a film is re-released; they are not reproductions.

Visit brucehershenson.com for buying online.

386 Liquidate Your Beanie Baby Collection

If you were swept up in the collecting craze of the 1990s, chances are you've got a few drawers heaped with bean-filled plush toys. Here's how you can reclaim that storage space.

Steps

1 Check the label. If it doesn't say Ty, forget it. Ty made the original Beanie Babies. Look for the words *first generation;* these toys have the most value. Also, the value goes up for those sporting a clear plastic label protector.

2 Don't let toy price guides fool you. They will list some Beanie Babies for hundreds of pounds, but finding someone willing to pay that much is almost impossible now that the craze is over.

3 Browse the internet for your best chance of finding a Beanie Baby lover who's trying to complete a collection. Otherwise, find a flea market seller who will give you a few pounds apiece for the items in your collection.

4 Give the toys to a local hospital or children's home. The pleasure you'll get from watching kids enjoy the toys is reward enough.

What to Look For

- Ty label
- First generation
- Rare examples

Tip

See 6 "Sell Products and Services Online".

387 Score Autographs

You never know where your next brush with fame may be. Here are a few tips for adding to your collection of David Beckhams without relying on serendipity to put you in the right place at the right time.

Steps

1 Start a collection fast by purchasing autographs at memorabilia shows and auctions. Get proof of authenticity.

2 Join the queue. A sports show might book a Premiership footballer to sign autographs. A car dealership might feature a rally driver. Sometimes players or speakers sign autographs before or after an event. Bring the kids along for a chance to meet a hero. Stars are usually good about signing items for their younger fans.

3 Write letters to famous people asking for signatures. Be sincere and include a self-addressed stamped envelope and blank cards.

4 Protect your investment by keeping autographs in their original state. Don't glue or tape an autographed paper onto cardboard or any other surface. Don't laminate. Craft shops sell boxes or albums appropriate for storing autographs.

5 Don't give up your day job. While some autographs are very valuable (Ernest Hemingway, £700; JFK, £1,000), for the most part, this isn't a money-making hobby. Still, time will tell. Today's Brad Pitt (£15) could be tomorrow's Bruce Lee (£400).

What to Look For

- Memorabilia shows
- Promotional events
- Stars' addresses

Tips

You can find addresses for agents or representatives of famous people in Who's Who (whoswhoonline.co.uk) or through fan clubs.

Keep a supply of blank index cards and a permanent black marker with you at all times.

388 Trade Yu-Gi-Oh Cards

Two years ago, this item would have been titled "Trade Pokémon Cards". By the time you read this, there's sure to be a hot new card game for the preteen scene. Trading a craze card by any other name is done in the same way.

Steps

1 Keep cards in top shape. Only those in mint condition (as they came out of the pack) will retain top value.

2 Know what your cards are worth so you can be sure to get a fair trade. You don't want to trade a £40 first-edition Gate Guardian for a £15 Dark Magician.

3 Keep a poker face, no matter how badly you need the card. Some cards are necessary to play combinations. Everyone knows you can't play Great Moth without a Cocoon of Evolution.

What to Look For

- Card condition
- Fair value
- Combinations

Tips

First-edition cards have more value – sometimes twice as much – than later versions of the same card. Check for the words *first edition* under the photo.

Once a deal is made, there's no going back.

389 Seize Star Wars Action Figures

Star Wars may seem like a galaxy far, far away, but to many collectors, the adventure is here and now. Stalking these hot sellers can turn into an epic quest. Your search will take you beyond your local toy shop.

Steps

1 Focus your intergalactic collection. For example, narrow your search to just vintage (1977 to 1985) items, such as loose figures, vehicles or light sabres. Or choose a favourite character, scene or ship. Internet auctions are your best bet for these items.

2 Watch for new-releases dates in collector magazines and online forums. Visit sci-fi gatherings to get an idea of what's hot and what's not.

3 Keep in mind future resale value. It's not always the hero who wins the day. Bad-guy Boba Fett may earn you more than Luke Skywalker. As with any collectible, it all depends on rarity. More Lukes were made, another reason why this character goes for less.

4 Do not open, bend or damage the packaging. The best prices go to items in mint condition.

What to Look For

- New releases
- Resale value
- Packaging

Tips

Buy three of your favourite new figures – one for your kid, one for your own collection and one to sell someday.

Store items out of direct sunlight, away from excessive heat or cold and in a dry place. Moisture, including high humidity, can damage the packaging and reduce resale value.

390 Sell Your Vinyl Record Collection

With CDs on the scene, vinyl records seem to be going the way of cassettes and eight-track tapes. But there are still plenty of collectors out there interested in your Louis Armstrong albums.

Steps

1 Understand the supply and demand of selling records. Owning a chart-topping Elvis record is like owning a first-edition Harry Potter book. Because there were so many printed, they're easy to find and the value goes down. That's why *Baby It's You* by the Beatles is listed in price guides at £3 while *Ragtime Cowboy Joe* by David Seville and the Chipmunks is £10.

2 Check for damage. To fetch the top price, the record itself can't be scratched or warped. The album jacket should have sharp corners and few signs of wear.

3 Go to a local second-hand record shop to find a buyer, or look in the back of price guides and collector magazines for advertisements.

4 Scrutinise the cover, which can often be even more valuable than the record inside. Collectors frame them as works of art. Especially popular are album covers with portraits of a singer like Frank Sinatra or Doris Day.

What to Look For

- Unusual artists
- Scratches
- Warping
- Buyer's advertisements

Tip

An out-of-town buyer may want to judge the condition of your collection. Send only a few albums or you might pay more in shipping than he whole collection is worth.

Warning

Don't stack your records – the weight leaves a ring on the album cover.

391 Sell to a Pawnshop

The debt collector will be by tonight to take your new sports car unless you have cash in hand. When it comes to fast money, there's no place like the pawnshop. Sometimes, though, cashing in on an antique can be difficult.

Steps

1 Think small. Items like antique jewellery, a piece of silver, old guns or artwork are most likely to get a shop owner's attention. Fewer pawnshops are equipped to deal with big furniture pieces or rare pottery.

2 Put yourself in the shop owner's shoes to judge the sales appeal of your item. He or she is only going to buy what will easily resell. If you have an antique to pawn, finding a pawnshop in an area known for its antique shops may bring a better deal. That shop will have more customers looking to get a deal on an antique.

3 Lower your expectations. The shop owner may offer only about 30 per cent of value for your item. The offer will be lower still if the shop owner is not familiar with the piece.

4 Ask the owner how long he or she is legally required to hold onto an item before offering it for resale, on the off chance you come down with a case of seller's remorse or your mum finds out.

What to Look For

- Small items
- Sales appeal
- Low return
- Seller's rights

Tips

If your need for cash is short-term, ask the pawn-shop owner for a loan on the item. Keep in mind that the interest rate you pay is per month, not per year. Fees could get out of control fast if you took a year or more to pay back the loan.

Check if the broker is a member of The National Pawnbrokers Association (thenpa.com).

392 Buy and Sell Comic Books

Collecting comic books isn't just for kids anymore. A copy of *Action Comics #1,* the first appearance of Superman, sold for 6p in 1938. Today it could bring £¾ million. Windfalls like that are extremely rare, but who knows what you might find in your parents' attic.

Steps

1 If you're looking to sell your old collection for a packet, it'll help to have some #1s (the first comic in a series) or issues that introduce popular characters.

2 Condition is key whether you're buying or selling; the cover is especially critical. Keep comics in top condition by sliding them into plastic sleeves with a piece of acid-free cardboard. Store protected comics upright on bookshelves in a cool, dry place.

3 Internet auctions offer the best access to other buyers and sell-ers of older comic books. Another good place to make a deal on older material is at one of the many comic book conventions.

4 If you're looking to unload more recent comics (five or six years old), try a local comic book shop. That's also the place to look if you need just a couple of comics to fill out a series.

What to Look For

- Superheroes
- Condition
- Internet auctions
- Conventions
- Local sources

Tip

As a rule, the older the comic book, the more value it has. Before the 1970s, people treated comic books like magazines; many ended up in the bin. Today, collec-tors treat them more like books, coveting creative storylines and colourful artwork.

393 Buy and Sell Sports Memorabilia

In the past 25 years, the value of sports memorabilia has only gone up. Because of that, this collecting category offers some good investments. It can also quickly become a very costly hobby.

Steps

Buy

1 Pick a category to collect. Sports cards? Which sport? One team only? One player only? The options are endless.

2 Look in periodicals and internet sources to find out what items sell for.

3 Go to a sports memorabilia show to get a feel for the variety and quality of items for sale.

4 Go to an auction. Some auction houses specialise in sports memorabilia; order one of their catalogues for a forthcoming sale. Send in a bid or hire a proxy if you can't be there in person. Of course, check out internet auction sites like eBay.co.uk.

5 Ask about the item's authenticity – proof of its provenance is essential to making a good investment. Buying from a reputable dealer will give you some level of assurance.

6 As with every collecting category, a lot of fakes circulate in the marketplace. There are businesses that specialise in authenticating sports memorabilia. You might want to get some off-the-cuff, free opinions from dealers first. You don't want to pay £200 to authenticate an object that's only worth £50.

Sell

1 Find someone qualified to give you an appraisal if you're not sure about the value of what you own. You'll want more than one opinion, and you might have to pay for it. Collectors' magazines are filled with ads for authentication services.

2 Sell it yourself. If your collection doesn't contain any high-price items, you can try to sell them one at a time or in small lots on the internet. A local dealer might be interested in your collection.

3 Take any really high-quality items among your sports collectibles to an auction house for the best return on your investment.

4 Bring any documentation you have to help you get the best price. If you have a famous footballer's shirt, that's good; if you have a photo of him handing it to you after a match, that's better.

What to Look For

- Price guides
- Local outlets
- National outlets
- Authenticity

Tips

Prices vary from year to year and month to month on articles related to current players. The smart money is in retired players, who won't have any more scoring slumps or legal woes to affect their status.

"Older is better" doesn't hold true in all collecting categories, but it's a good rule of thumb in sports memorabilia. Materials from the 1940s and 1950s are relatively rare and therefore more valuable.

Warning

When selling sports memorabilia to a dealer, expect to get about half the wholesale price listed in popular price guides.

ITEM	COLLECTOR TIPS
Football Cards	Condition is key. Look for sharp corners and no creases. Cards depicting star players at the start of their football careers tend to fetch the highest prices.
Signed Footballs	Look for footballs that are clean and white, and that have a very clear autograph. Value depends on availability. The best find is a ball from the footballer's playing days. Many players hit the memorabilia circuit after retirement.
Team Shirts	This is one of the few collecting categories in which sweat stains are a plus. Shirts worn in matches are the only way to go. Ask for authentication; don't be fooled by a new shirt that's been passed off as the real thing.
Equipment	Shoes, golf balls, gloves, bats, hockey pucks and sticks, and tennis rackets; again, it's key that the items were used in a game. Even a cracked cricket bat will sell for a lot of money if a famous player used it.
Stadium Items	Seats, signs and even turnstiles are available to collectors. Especially valuable are those from old stadiums that have been renovated or that hosted a historic sports moment.
Ticket Stubs and Programmes	World Cup items are especially coveted – a ticket stub from the 1966 World Cup lists at £150.
Bobble Heads	These ceramic dolls have a bobbing, oversize head on a spring. Early examples represented an entire team; newer examples depict a particular player.

394 Sell Your Football-Card Collection

Are those old boxes stashed full of football cards taking up precious space? Don't throw them out; you might have a Michael Owen there before he became famous!

What to Look For

- Full sets
- Cards of players before they became famous
- Mint condition

Steps

1 Sort your cards according to manufacturer (Topps, Futera, Panini, and so on). Try to get a complete set, which is all the cards in one manufacturer's series for a particular year.

2 Look for names you recognise and put those cards aside. Cards of popular players sell well individually.

3 Search for stars before they became famous. The card's condition will play a big part in its price.

4 Try to find a buyer among fellow supporters at your football club or try selling over the internet. Sell rare and valuable cards at auction.

5 Look out for retired players' cards, which hold their value. Prices vary for cards of current players.

Tip

Wear is expected in old cards. If it's a rare card, it will have great value despite some flaws.

CTION SITES • BUY BARGAIN CLOTHING • BUY WHOLESALE • GET OUT OF DEBT • BUY NOTHING • BUY HAPPINESS • BUY A BETTER MOUS
Y YOUR WAY INTO SOMEONE'S FAVOUR • BUY LOVE • FIND THE RIGHT RELAXATION TECHNIQUE FOR YOU • BUY HEALTHY FAST FOOD • BU
RVICE • SELL YOURSELF ON AN ONLINE DATING SERVICE • SELL YOURSELF TO YOUR GIRLFRIEND/BOYFRIEND'S FAMILY • BUY FLOWERS T
OOSE FILM FOR YOUR CAMERA • BUY RECHARGEABLE BATTERIES • GIVE TO A GOOD CAUSE • TAKE PART IN A CAR BOOT SALE • EMPLOY
JDENT DISCOUNTS • BUY FLOWERS WHOLESALE • GET A PICTURE FRAMED • EMPLOY A REMOVAL COMPANY • EMPLOY A LIFESTYLE MAN
Y FOR A HALLOWE'EN PARTY • BUY A GREAT BIRTHDAY PRESENT FOR UNDER £10 • SELECT GOOD CHAMPAGNE • BUY A DIAMOND • BUY
T A GIFT LIST • BUY WEDDING GIFTS • SELECT BRIDESMAIDS' DRESSES • HIRE AN EVENTS ORGANISER • HIRE A BARTENDER FOR A PARTY
NOUNCEMENTS • SELL YOUR WEDDING DRESS • BUY AN ANNIVERSARY GIFT • ARRANGE ENTERTAINMENT FOR A PARTY • COMMISSION A
O HAS EVERYTHING • BUY A GIFT FOR PASSING EXAMS • SELECT A CHRISTMAS TURKEY • BUY A HOUSEWARMING GIFT • PURCHASE CHR
ESSAGE IN THE SKY • HIRE A BIG-NAME BAND • GET INTO A PRIVATE GAMBLING ROOM IN LAS VEGAS • BUY SOMEONE A STAR • PAY A RA
PLOY A BUTLER • BUY A FOOTBALL CLUB • BUY A PERSONAL JET • SELECT A CLASSIC CAR • ACQUIRE A BODY GUARD • BOOK A LUXURY
CE • BUY A RACEHORSE • BUY A VILLA IN TUSCANY • EMPLOY A PERSONAL CHEF • BUY A JOURNEY INTO SPACE • EMPLOY A GHOSTWRI
PERT WITNESS • MAKE MONEY FROM ACCIDENT COMPENSATION • DONATE YOUR BODY TO SCIENCE • MAKE MONEY AS A MEDICAL GUIN
N FOR RETIREMENT • COPE WITH HIGHER EDUCATION COSTS • BUY AND SELL SHARES • CHOOSE A STOCKBROKER • DAY-TRADE (OR NO
E INSURANCE • GET PRIVATE HEALTH INSURANCE • BUY PERSONAL FINANCE SOFTWARE • CHOOSE AN ACCOUNTANT • FIND CASUAL WO
RKET YOUR INVENTION • FINANCE YOUR BUSINESS IDEA • BUY A SMALL BUSINESS • BUY A FRANCHISE • LEASE RETAIL SPACE • LEASE IN
SIGNER • ACQUIRE CONTENT FOR YOUR WEBSITE • BUY ADVERTISING ON THE WEB • SELL YOUR ART • HIRE A LIFE COACH • SELL ON TH
D-AND-BREAKFAST • SELL A FAILING BUSINESS • BUY A HOT DOG STAND • SHOP FOR A MORTGAGE • GET A BETTER MORTGAGE DEAL • S
JSE ONLINE • BUY A PROPERTY FOR RENOVATION AND RESALE • EVALUATE BEFORE BUYING INTO A NEW AREA • EXCHANGE CONTRACTS
JSE DESIGNED • HIRE AN ARCHITECT • HIRE A BUILDER • GET PLANNING PERMISSION • BUY A HOLIDAY HOME • RENT A HOLIDAY HOME •
ME FOR A LOCATION SHOOT • FURNISH YOUR HOME • FURNISH YOUR STUDIO FLAT • BUY USED FURNITURE • BUY DOOR AND WINDOW L
Y FLOOR-CARE APPLIANCES • BUY EXTENDED WARRANTIES ON APPLIANCES • FIND PERIOD FIXTURES • BUY A BED AND MATTRESS • HIR
NISH • CHOOSE DECORATIVE TILES • CHOOSE A DEHUMIDIFIER • BUY A WHIRLPOOL BATH • BUY A SHOWER • BUY A TOILET • CHOOSE A
OVE • SELECT FLOORING • SELECT CARPETING • CHOOSE KITCHEN CABINETS • CHOOSE A KITCHEN WORKTOP • BUY GREEN HOUSEHOL
NOXIDE DETECTORS • BUY FIRE EXTINGUISHERS • CHOOSE AN ENTRY DOOR • BUY A GARAGE-DOOR OPENER • BUY TIMBER FOR A DIY F
FECT ROSE • BUY FLOWERING BULBS • BUY FLOWERS FOR YOUR GARDEN • SELECT PEST CONTROLS • BUY SOIL IMPROVERS • BUY M
V LAWN • BUY A LAWN MOWER • BUY KOI FOR YOUR FISH POND • BUY A STORAGE SHED • HIRE A TREE SURGEON • BUY BASIC GARDEN
D SELL AT FARMERS' MARKETS • SELECT KITCHEN KNIVES • DECIPHER FOOD LABELS • SELECT HERBS AND SPICES • STOCK YOUR KITCH
Y ORGANIC BEEF • BUY HAGGIS • PURCHASE LOCAL HONEY • CHOOSE A CHICKEN • SELECT FRESH FISH • SELECT RICE • PURCHASE PR
ISAN CHEESES • PURCHASE KOSHER FOOD • BUY SENSIBLY IN SUPERMARKETS • CHOOSE COOKING OILS • SELECT OLIVE OIL • SELECT
FFEEMAKER OR ESPRESSO MACHINE • PURCHASE PARTY BEER • CHOOSE THE RIGHT WINE • CHOOSE A REAL ALE • ORDER A COCKTAIL
• PICK A PREGNANCY TEST KIT • CHOOSE BIRTH CONTROL • CHOOSE WHERE TO GIVE BIRTH • HIRE A MIDWIFE OR DOULA • PLAN A HO
RENT A BREAST PUMP • CHOOSE A CAR SEAT • BUY CHILD-PROOFING SUPPLIES • FIND RELIABLE CHILDCARE • FIND A GREAT NANNY •
RIENDLY HOTEL • ORGANISE A FUND-RAISING EVENT • BUY BRACES FOR YOUR KID • BUY TOYS • BUY BOOKS, VIDEOS AND MUSIC FO
THES AND BOOKS • FIND A COUPLES COUNSELLOR • HIRE A FAMILY SOLICITOR • BUY OR RENT SHELTERED HOUSING • CHOOSE A CAR
D ANTIWRINKLE CREAMS • SELECT PAIN RELIEF AND COLD MEDICINES • CHOOSE A COMPLEMENTARY MTHERAPY • SEE A MENTAL-HEALT
Y A WIG OR HAIRPIECE • BUY A NEW BODY • GET A TATTOO OR BODY PIERCING • OBTAIN BREAST IMPLANTS • GET WRINKLE-FILLER INJE
SONAL TRAINER • SIGN UP FOR A YOGA CLASS • TREAT YOURSELF TO A DAY AT THE SPA • BOOK A MASSAGE • GET ON ANTIQUES ROAL
JR COLLECTIBLES ARE WORTH • BARTER WITH DEALERS • GET AN ANTIQUE APPRAISED • BUY SILVERWARE • EVALUATE CARNIVAL GLAS
JIDATE YOUR BEANIE BABY COLLECTION • SCORE AUTOGRAPHS • TRADE YU-GI-OH CARDS • SEIZE STAR WARS ACTION FIGURES • SELL
RD COLLECTION • CHOOSE A DESKTOP COMPUTER • SHOP FOR A USED COMPUTER OR PERIPHERALS • CHOOSE A LAPTOP OR NOTEBO
OVIDER • GET AN INTERNET DOMAIN NAME • NETWORK YOUR COMPUTERS • UPGRADE THE MEMORY IN YOUR COMPUTER • BUY COMPL
TAL ASSISTANT • CHOOSE A MOBILE PHONE SERVICE • GET A BETTER DEAL FROM YOUR PHONE COMPANY • BUY VIDEO AND COMPUTE
THE-ART SOUND SYSTEM • BUY AN AUDIO/VIDEO DISTRIBUTION SYSTEM • BUY A SERIOUS TV • CHOOSE BETWEEN DIGITAL TV PROVIDE
IOS • BUY A MOBILE ENTERTAINMENT SYSTEM • GET A PASSPORT, QUICK! • PURCHASE CHEAP AIRLINE TICKETS • FIND GREAT HOTEL D
NS-SIBERIAN EXPRESS • BUY DUTY-FREE • SHIP FOREIGN PURCHASES TO THE UNITED KONGDOM • TIP IN A FOREIGN COUNTRY • TIP P
KAGE FOR THE GREEK ISLANDS • RAFT THE GRAND CANYON • BOOK A CHEAP BUT FANTASTIC SAFARI • RENT A CAMEL IN CAIRO • GET
JG KONG • BUY YOUR WAY ONTO A MOUNT EVEREST EXPEDITION • HIRE A TREKKING COMPANY IN NEPAL • RENT OR BUY A SATELLITE F
JY GOLF CLUBS • SELL FOUND GOLF BALLS • BUY PORTS SHOES • BUY A RACKET • BUY A HEALTH CLUB MEMBERSHIP • BUY AN AERO
TES • GO BUNJEE JUMPING • GO SKYDIVING • BUY WEIGHTLIFTING EQUIPMENT • CHOOSE A CAR RACK • BUY SKIS • BUY CLOTHES FO
JY CYCLE CLOTHING • BUY A PROPERLY FITTING HELMET • BUY THE OPTIMAL SLEEPING BAG • BUY A TENT • BUY A BACKPACK • BUY A
Y A CASHMERE JUMPER • PURCHASE VINTAGE CLOTHING • SELL USED CLOTHING • ORDER CUSTOM-MADE COWBOY BOOTS • BUY CLO
A MAN • BUY A MAN'S DRESS SHIRT • PICK OUT A TIE • BUY A WOMAN'S SUIT • BUY A MAN'S SUIT • HIRE A TAILOR • BUY CUSTOM-TA
FORMANCE SWIM SUIT • BUY PERFORMANCE WORKOUT CLOTHES • BUY A HEART-RATE MONITOR • SELECT A WATCH • BUY KIDS' CLO
SELL A CAR ONLINE • BUY A HYBRID CAR • SELL A CAR • BUY A MOTORCYCLE • BUYING AND CHANGING MOTOR OIL• WASH A CAR • W

JY TIME • BUY A BOUQUET OF ROSES • BUY SOMEONE A DRINK • GET SOMEONE TO BUY YOU A DRINK • BUY YOUR WAY INTO THE BEST
EEN • BUT FURTHER EDUCATION • ORDER EXOTIC FOOD • ORDER AT A SUSHI BAR • BUY DINNER AT A FRENCH RESTAURANT • EMPLOY A
RY TO YOUR PARTNER • BUY MUSIC ONLINE • EMPLOY MUSICIANS • ORDER A GOOD BOTTLE OF WINE • BUY AN ERGONOMIC DESK CHAIR
R • EMPLOY AN AU PAIR • BUY A GUITAR • BUY DUCT TAPE • GET A GOOD DEAL ON A MAGAZINE SUBSCRIPTION • GET SENIOR CITIZEN OF
D A VET • BUY PET FOOD • BUY A PEDIGREE DOG OR CAT • BREED YOUR PET AND SELL THE LITTER • BUY OR RENT FOR A FANCY DRESS
MADE OF PRECIOUS METALS • BUY COLOURED GEMSTONES • CHOOSE THE PERFECT WEDDING DRESS • BUY OR RENT MEN'S FORMAL W
HOTOGRAPHER • HIRE A CATERER • FIND THE IDEAL CIVIL WEDDING VENUE • THE COST OF MARRYING • ORDER PERSONALISED INVITATIO
S SHOW • BUY A MOTHER'S DAY GIFT • BUY A FATHER'S DAY GIFT • SELECT AN APPROPRIATE COMING-OF-AGE GIFT • GET A GIFT FOR TH
RDS • BUY CHRISTMAS STOCKING FILLERS • BUY CHRISTENING GIFTS • PURCHASE A PERFECT CHRISTMAS TREE • BUY A PRIVATE ISLAN
T HOT TICKETS • HIRE A LIMOUSINE • BUY A CRYONIC CHAMBER • RENT YOUR OWN HOARDING • TAKE OUT A FULL-PAGE AD IN *THE TIME*
OUND THE WORLD • BUY A TICKET TO TRAVEL FOR A YEAR • BOOK A TRIP ON THE ORIENT-EXPRESS • OWN A VINEYARD • BUY A GREYHO
E YOUR MEMOIRS • COMMISSION ORIGINAL ARTWORK • IMMORTALISE YOUR SPOUSE IN A SCULPTURE • GIVE AWAY YOUR FORTUNE • H
L YOUR STORY TO THE TABLOIDS • SELL YOUR SOUL TO THE DEVIL • NEGOTIATE A BETTER CREDIT CARD DEAL • CHOOSE A FINANCIAL A
NUITIES • BUY AND SELL MUTUAL FUNDS • BUY BONDS • SELL SHORT • INVEST IN PRECIOUS METALS • BUY SERIOUS ILLNESS INSURAN
OUR PRODUCT ON TV • HIRE A CAREER COU͏ — YOURSELF IN A JOB INTERVIEW • TAKE OUT A PATENT
PACE • LEASE OFFICE SPACE • BUY LIQUID — TO DESIGN AND BUILD YOUR WEBSITE • HIRE A G
CUIT • HIRE A LITERARY AGENT • PITCH A N — ELL YOUR NOVEL • SELF-PUBLISH YOUR BOOK • S
R MORTGAGE • GET A MORTGAGE YOU CA — UY A HOUSE • BUY A HOUSE AT AUCTION • SHOP
ERTY • SELL A HOUSE • SELL A HOUSE WIT — L FROM YOUR HOME • BUY A PLOT OF LAND • HAV
• RENT A FLAT OR HOUSE • BUY A PLACE — • BUY PROPERTY ABROAD • BUY TO LET • RENT Y
OSE AN ORIENTAL CARPET • BUY LAMPS A — LE LIGHTING SYSTEM • BUY HOUSEHOLD APPLIAN
R DESIGNER • HIRE A FENG SHUI CONSULT — SPACE INTO YOUR HOME • SELECT PAINT, STAIN A
GLUES AND ADHESIVES • CHOOSE WINDOW — OWS • CHOOSE WALLPAPER • BUY A WOOD-BURN
• STOCK YOUR HOME TOOL KIT • BUY A VI — RM SYSTEM • BUY SMOKE ALARMS • BUY CARBO
OW TO SELECT ROOFING • HIRE A BUILDER — E A GARDENER • BUY OUTDOOR FURNITURE • BUY
A COMPOSTER • BUY FERTILISER • START A — IGNER • BUY AN AUTOMATIC WATERING SYSTEM
Y SHRUBS AND TREES • BUY A SPA POOL • — Y ORGANIC PRODUCE • CHOOSE A PERFECT PEA
PLES • EQUIP A KITCHEN • CHOOSE FRESH — R THE PERFECT BURGER • PURCHASE A CHRISTM
AND PEPPER • BUY A REAL STILTON • GET — NIFF CUT TRUFFLES • BUY ARTISAN BREADS • BU
Y ETHNIC INGREDIENTS • PURCHASE VINE — FEE • ORDER A GREAT CUP OF COFFEE • BUY A
RESTAURANT FOR A BUSINESS FUNCTION • — R • DONATE SPERM • CHOOSE AN OVULATION PRE
RE A CHILD THERAPIST • GEAR UP FOR A N — USHCHAIR • BUY BABY CLOTHES • CHOOSE NAPP
HT PRIVATE SCHOOL • FIND GOOD AFTER-S — ESSONS • BUY A GARDEN PLAY STRUCTURE • FIN
DREN • BUY A VIDEO GAME SYSTEM • HIRE — LD HIRED AS A MODEL • SELL USED BABY GEAR,
TE A LIVING WILL • BUY A CEMETERY PLOT — RA • PURCHASE A TOOTHBRUSH • BUY MOISTUR
NAL • CHOOSE A WHEELCHAIR • BUY HON — CARE PRODUCTS • BUY WAYS TO COUNTER HAIR
D ALTERNATIVE AND HOLISTIC PRACTITIONE — TEETH • SELECT SPECTACLES AND SUNGLASSES

Computers & Home Electronics

AND SELL USED BOOKS • SHOP AT AN AN — AT AN ANTIQUE MARKET • BUY AT AUCTION • KN
SELL STAMPS • BUY ANTIQUE FURNITURE • GET CLUED UP ON CLARICE CLIFF • BUY COINS • BUY AN ANTIQUE QUILT • BUY FILM POSTE
RECORD COLLECTION • SELL TO A PAWNSHOP • BUY AND SELL COMIC BOOKS • BUY AND SELL SPORTS MEMORABILIA • SELL YOUR FO
R • SELL OR DONATE A COMPUTER • BUY PRINTER PAPER • BUY A PRINTER • BUY COMPUTER PERIPHERALS • CHOOSE AN INTERNET SE
RE • CHOOSE A CD PLAYER • BUY BLANK CDS • BUY AN MP PLAYER • CHOOSE A DVD PLAYER • BUY A VIDEO RECORDER • CHOOSE A P
HOOSE A FILM CAMERA • CHOOSE A DIGITAL CAMCORDER • DECIDE ON A DIGITAL CAMERA • BUY A HOME AUTOMATION SYSTEM • BUY
GITAL VIDEO RECORDER • GET A UNIVERSAL REMOTE • BUY A HOME CINEMA SYSTEM • BUY VIRTUAL-REALITY FURNITURE • BUY TWO-W
HE BEST CAR FOR THE LEAST MONEY • GET TRAVEL INSURANCE • PICK THE IDEAL LUGGAGE • FLY FOR NEXT TO NOTHING • TAKE A TRII
HE UK • BRIBE A FOREIGN OFFICIAL • GET AN INTERRAIL PASS • TAKE AN ITALIAN CYCLING HOLIDAY • CHOOSE A CHEAP CRUISE • BOOK
WHISKY IN SCOTLAND • BUY A SAPPHIRE IN BANGKOK • HIRE A RICKSHAW IN RANGOON • TAKE SALSA LESSONS IN CUBA • BUY A CAM
YOUR CHILD'S FIRST CRICKET BAT • ORDER A STRIP FOR A FOOTBALL TEAM • BUY ANKLE AND KNEE BRACES • CHOOSE RUGBY PROTE
MACHINE • BUY SWIMMING EQUIPMENT • BUY A JETSKI • EMPLOY A SCUBA INSTRUCTOR • BUY A SKATEBOARD AND PROTECTIVE GEAR
HER ACTIVITIES • SELL USED SKIS • BUY A SNOWBOARD, BOOTS AND BINDINGS • BUY SKI BOOTS • BUY A BICYCLE • BUY AN ELECTRIC
OVE • BUY A KAYAK • BUY A LIFEJACKET • BUY A WET SUIT • BUY A SURFBOARD • BUY FLY-FISHING GEAR • BUY ROCK-CLIMBING EQUIP
• FIND NON-STANDARD SIZES • BUY THE PERFECT COCKTAIL DRESS • BUY DESIGNER CLOTHES AT A DISCOUNT • CHOOSE A BASIC WAF
ES IN ASIA • BUY A BRIEFCASE • SHOP FOR A LEATHER JACKET • BUY MATERNITY CLOTHES • GET A GREAT-FITTING BRA • CHOOSE A H
E CHILDREN'S SHOES • PURCHASE CLOTHES AT FACTORY SHOPS • BUY A NEW CAR • BUY THE BASICS FOR YOUR CAR • BUY A USED
Y CAR INSURANCE • SPRING FOR A NEW PAINT JOB • BUYING AND CHANGING A BATTERY • BUY THE RIGHT FUEL • BUY FUEL TREATME

395 Choose a Desktop Computer

Shopping for a computer doesn't need to be that hard. First think about what you need. Are you looking for a computer to perform basic tasks or to meet special requirements? Then do a little homework, and finally go shopping armed with that knowledge. You'll get a computer you can be happy with, and you'll get the best value for your money.

Steps

Before you shop

1 Decide whether a PC/Windows or Apple Macintosh computer would be best suited to your needs. You can generally get a faster computer for the same amount of money by choosing a PC machine, but Macs are easier to use and have a reputation for greater reliability.

2 Think about whether this machine will need to work with your office or school server. Exchanging files between platforms is less of an issue than it used to be, but it's still worth noting.

3 Ask your friends and colleagues in similar lines of work what machines they have, where they bought them, if there were any problems, and whether they're happy with their choices.

4 Although it is possible to pay anything from £250 to £5,000 for a desktop computer, expect to spend £800 to £1,000 for a decent general-purpose machine.

The basics

1 If you buy a cheap computer from a discount centre, you may find yourself alone when it comes to troubleshooting. Technical support from the major manufacturers tends to be better.

2 Buy as much random-access memory (RAM) as you can afford. As a bare minimum, go for 256 megabytes (MB). Memory is as critical as having a fast processor.

3 Your machine should have at least two universal serial bus (USB) connections – preferably the more recent USB 2 protocol – and a FireWire (also called IEEE 1394) connection. These will allow you to connect peripheral devices, such as a printers and scanners.

4 Make sure your machine has a DVD drive if you want to watch movies on your computer. Get a CD burner so you can make your own music CDs and back up valuable data on CD-R. Better still, a DVD burner will enable you to back up about eight times as much data onto a DVD-R. Also look for an internal modem.

5 Computer technology dates at an alarming rate, so ask about upgradability if you intend to get more than three years from it.

6 If you simply want to do word-processing, send e-mails or surf the web you can choose any current computer produced by one of the major manufacturers with a high degree of confidence.

What to Look For

- 256 MB RAM (minimum)
- USB (preferably USB 2) and FireWire connections
- CD or DVD burner
- DVD drive
- Internal modem
- 3D graphics card
- Soundcard
- 120 GB hard disk
- Video input/output

Tips

The term *desktop computer* can be misleading. *Desktop* refers to computers that aren't laptop or notebook computers. *Personal computer* (or *PC*) also used.

Computers continue to get faster and cheaper. Don't torture yourself by second-guessing your purchase, or by waiting for the next jump in power or drop in price.

Warnings

Don't throw old computers away with your household rubbish (see 398 "Sell or Donate a Computer"). Like many other electronic devices, they contain toxic chemicals and need to be recycled.

Special considerations

1 You'll need high-quality graphics and sound if you plan to play games or watch DVDs on your computer. Look for a system that includes a graphics card with a co-processor, and – to get the best out of your DVDs – a soundcard that can play Dolby 5.1 surround sound. You'll want a broadband internet connection to play online games and to improve your internet experience overall (see 402 "Choose an Internet Service Provider").

2 Buy the largest hard drive you can afford – 120 to 180 gigabytes (GB) is now commonplace. You will need more than 200 GB if you're planning to store music and/or edit video. (Note: For video editing, you'll also need a video input/output card and a FireWire connection.)

3 Add a TV capture card, and you can even have your computer function as a DVR (see 424 "Get a Digital Video Recorder").

You might be able to use your existing monitor, printer, and other peripherals with a new computer if you're happy with them. Write down their specifications and take your notes to the store. But remember that many computers come packaged with hardware pre-configured to work together and with the latest operating systems.

396 Shop for a Used Computer or Peripherals

If you've got your computer and are looking for a usable one for your kids – or if the kids want a computer for you so they can keep the good one to themselves – you can save substantial amounts if you buy a used machine. Hundreds of computers go on sale daily on internet auction sites.

Steps

1 Ask your most technically clued-up friend to shop with you.

2 Follow half a dozen online auctions of used systems and make a note of what people were willing to pay. Unfortunately, there's no unbiased, reputable source for used computer prices.

3 If viewing before purchase – always a good idea if possible – give the computer a thorough physical inspection to ensure it's not damaged. Then turn it on and run it; be alert for obvious glitches. Insist on doing this yourself, rather than watching the seller do it.

4 Make sure that the sale includes the original operating system software discs and manuals. Get the manuals, discs and licences for any software applications and fonts on the computer.

5 Old computers depreciate at a rapid rate, so take care not to overpay. It doesn't matter how much the seller paid for it; the important thing is how much it's worth now. Be brutal.

6 Don't buy used printers, scanners or disk drives unless you know exactly what you're doing. These peripherals have moving parts that inevitably wear out or break down.

What to Look For

- Intact hardware
- Bug-free operating
- System and program software

Tip

Refurbished computers from major manufacturers can be a good alternative. They're cheaper than new but may also carry a full warranty.

Warning

Hundreds of thousands of laptops are stolen every year. Use common sense to avoid buying a hot machine.

397 Choose a Laptop or Notebook Computer

Today's laptops are more powerful than top-of-the-range desktop computers produced only a few years ago. They're also lighter and much more stylish. An increasing number of people are choosing a laptop to take care of all their computer needs. If you're thinking of going this route, check out these shopping tips.

Steps

1 Read through 395 "Choose a Desktop Computer". The "Before you shop" points and most of "The basics" apply similarly when shopping for a laptop.

2 Before you buy, pick up the laptop that interests you. Choose one that feels sturdy and solid but not too heavy.

3 Test the keyboard. Since you can't replace it (except with the exact same item), make sure you're comfortable with its touch and responsiveness. Test it on a desk and on your lap.

4 Test the pointing device, track pad or track ball, the laptop alternatives to a mouse. Some of these can be hard to master. You'll be able to connect an external mouse, but the built-in device is more handy when you're mobile.

5 Check if the base of the computer gets uncomfortably hot when it's running – a problem if you actually use the laptop on your lap.

6 Pay attention to screen size and resolution. Current liquid-crystal display (LCD) screens on laptops measure from 30 to 43 cm (12 to 17 inches) diagonally. Screen resolution may be as low as 800 x 600 pixels or as high as 1,600 x 1,200. The more pixels, the crisper the screen image. View the screen in a variety of settings: a screen that looks great in normal room lighting can look terrible in bright or dim light.

7 Choose a laptop with at least two USB connections (preferably USB 2). A FireWire (IEEE 1394) connection is also useful for such high-speed peripherals as external hard disks or CD burners.

8 Consider buying an internal wireless card if you really plan to be mobile. A wireless network card (also called Wi-Fi or 802.11) will free you from having to be wired to your internet connection (see 404 "Network Your Computers"). Bluetooth capability will let you share information wirelessly with other Bluetooth-equipped devices, such as your mobile phone or personal digital assistant.

9 Get an internal DVD player so you can watch movies on the road. (Go for a higher resolution screen if you plan to do this.)

10 Hundreds of thousands of laptops are stolen every year, so get an anti-theft device. Look for cables that will secure your laptop to a desk. Install software that can disable a stolen laptop or – better still – will report the laptop's location when it connects to the internet.

What to Look For

- Overall sturdiness and solidness
- Weight
- Keyboard
- Pointing device
- Temperature while in use
- Screen size and resolution
- USB (or USB 2), FireWire connections
- Wireless networking
- DVD player
- Anti-theft device

Tips

Don't always believe claims about battery life. In practical everyday use, battery life is almost always less than what the manufacturer advertises.

What's the difference between a laptop and a notebook? Nothing. Use the two terms interchangeably.

If you're style-conscious check out the Apple iBook; PC/Windows users should investigate the Sony Vaio range of laptops.

398 Sell or Donate a Computer

We've all been there. The gear that cost you thousands of pounds a few years ago is now worth a fraction of your investment. But don't throw it out with your household rubbish – it contains toxic materials that really shouldn't go in landfill sites. Here's how to recycle, donate or sell it to recoup some of your cash.

Steps

1 Uninstall any applications you plan to use on your next computer. (Make sure you have the installation disks and serial numbers.)

2 Purge the computer of all personal information. It's not enough simply to drag documents to the Trash. Use a utility program that will permanently delete or overwrite sensitive documents, then reformat the hard drive and reinstall the operating system.

3 Collect the original software disks and manuals for the operating system that came with the computer.

4 Value your computer by following online auctions, then put it up for auction too, or sell through classified advertisements. Don't expect to make a fortune; old computers aren't worth much.

5 Donate the computer to a school, charity or recycling centre. Recyclers may charge a fee.

What to Look For

- Original software disks and manuals
- Delete-overwrite utility software

Tip

Experts have recently found credit card numbers, medical records and financial data on hard drives bought randomly at online auctions. ALWAYS make sure that you reformat hard drives before you sell or donate your computer. (Replacement drives are so cheap nowadays – for the ultimate in peace of mind, remove the hard drive and destroy it with a hammer!)

399 Buy Printer Paper

How do you choose the right paper? Answer just two questions: What type of printer do you have, and what do you want to print?

Steps

1 Determine what type of printer you have. Most domestic users own ink-jet printers, but some have laser printers.

2 Decide what weight of paper you want. Everyday paper is around 50 to 80 gsm (grams per square metre) and works with any type of printer. The higher the number, the heavier the paper. Card weights begin at around 200 gsm.

3 Pick ink-jet stock for important projects. The printing is crisper because the paper is smoother and less absorbent.

4 Select photo paper to print pictures on an ink-jet printer. This coated stock is very smooth and somewhat stiff, so that the finished prints feel like a real photograph. Matt photo paper is less shiny than glossy.

5 Choose colour laser printer paper only if you have a colour laser printer. It won't work well for ink-jet printing. Laser prints are more permanent than ink-jet prints, and less likely to run and bleed because they use toner rather than water-based ink.

What to Look For

- General-purpose paper
- Ink-jet paper
- Photo paper (matt or glossy finish)
- Colour laser printer paper

Tips

Ink-jet prints will always run or bleed when wet, no matter what sort of paper you use.

Make sure that transparencies, labels, stickers and other speciality media work with your type of printer.

400 Buy a Printer

With printers costing anything from £50 to £5,000, how do you choose a machine that's right for you? Comparing your needs with the features of different printers will make your decision an easier one.

Steps

1 Consider the various sizes, shapes, and capabilities. They range from portable printers to printer/copier/scanner/fax combinations the size of a small filing cabinet. Combination units are great if you're short on space, but be sure to test the features that are most important to you.

2 Decide between ink-jet and laser printers. How you'll use the printer will guide your decision.

   • Choose ink-jet if you print infrequently, or if you're going to print colour pictures. Ink-jet printers are less costly, but can work out more per printed page because of expensive inks.

   • Go for a laser printer if you mainly print text (and lots of it), and you want fast, permanent printing. They cost more up front, but less in the long run due to cheaper supplies. Longer lasting laser printers can be repaired more easily and less expensively.

3 Buying a brand name will ensure that you get service, software, support and supplies in the future. Brother, Canon, Epson, Hewlett-Packard and Lexmark are among the leading brands.

4 Confirm that your computer's operating system supports the printer you intend to buy. Printer drivers are provided with the printer, but can also be downloaded from the manufacturer's website. (Search for the driver to confirm that the printer will work with your computer.)

What to Look For

- Size and shape
- Capabilities
- Ink-jet versus laser
- Brand names
- Operating system support

Tips

By law, the printer's warranty remains in effect even if you use toner or ink produced by a company other than the original manufacturer.

It's almost certainly not going to be worth having an inexpensive ink-jet printer repaired if it breaks.

ANY PRINTER FEATURES	
Quality of Text Printing	• Test print to see quality of text.
Cost of Supplies	• How much are ink or toner cartridges, and how long do they last? Divide cost of cartridge by number of pages it can print. Add the cost of premium or photo paper to determine the real lifetime cost.
Connectivity	• Most new printers have USB or FireWire connections. If you have an older computer, look for a printer with a parallel port or SCSI socket, or look into fitting a USB or FireWire card. Some high-end printers have network connections. This is useful if you have a home network and will share the printer among several machines (see 404 "Network Your Computers").
Warranty	• If you rely on your printer for business, look for a warranty that supplies you with an immediate loan machine if yours goes in for repairs.
Paper Handling	• Look for a large paper tray to handle multiple-page jobs. Look for manual feed trays, multiple trays and envelope handling if you print a variety of materials or large formats. Some models can also print onto blank CD-Rs.

ANY PRINTER FEATURES (continued)

Straight Paper Path	• If you print on card stock, labels or envelopes, look for printer with a straight paper-path option (sometimes called a bypass). Paper path should not have any 90-degree or tighter bends.
Image Resolution	• Measured in dots per inch (dpi). How dots are formed – a function of printer and computer software – can be as important as number of dots, so use resolution as only one indicator.
Speed	• Measured in pages per minute (ppm). Take manufacturer's speed claim with a pinch of salt. It indicates how quickly the printer can send paper through its mechanism, not how quickly the machine will actually print. If speed is important, bring a variety of documents when you shop, and test them on several printers using the same computer.

LASER PRINTER FEATURES

Expandable Memory	• Get at least 8 megabytes (MB); 64 MB or more is better, especially if you're printing graphics or pages with lots of fonts.
PostScript Capability	• A printer description language used to produce high-quality images and fonts. Vital for Macintoshes or working with complex graphics.
Resolution	• Resolution of 600 dpi is usually sufficient for most uses.
Economy Mode	• Extends life of toner cartridges without sacrificing print quality.
Energy-saving Features	• Energy Star designation means the unit uses less electricity when idle.
Colour	• Colour laser printers are much more expensive than non-colour models.
Price	• Black-and-white laser printers start at around £200 with many good deals around £500. Colour laser prices are dropping, but they're still expensive (starting at around £1,000) compared with ink-jets.

INK-JET PRINTER FEATURES

Photo Quality	• How do prints of pictures look? Bring your own images to print, rather than relying on test prints.
Ink Cartridges	• Look for separate ink cartridges for each colour (blue, yellow and red), so you'll only need to replace the one that's empty. The best quality photo printers may use seven or more different coloured ink cartridges.
Colour Print Speed	• Some printers slow dramatically if there's even just a little colour on the page.
Water-resistant Inks	• This is valuable if you know your prints will be exposed to the weather.
Removable Memory Media	• On some new models, memory cards from a digital camera can be plugged directly into the printer, bypassing the computer altogether. Make sure the printer works with your camera's media type.
Price	• Prices for ink-jet printers can range from free (included with purchase of new computer) to over £1,000.
WARNING	Some manufacturers void a printer's warranty if you use refilled ink cartridges.

401 Buy Computer Peripherals

As complex as computer technology can sometimes be, buying peripherals – such as printers, scanners and CD writers – is becoming easier. This is principally because most modern devices connect with either universal serial bus (USB/USB 2) or FireWire (also called IEEE 1394). Both high-speed connections work easily and almost automatically. If your computer is relatively new (Windows XP or 2000 or Mac OSX), you should have very few problems at all. NOTE: users of older versions of Windows, or Mac OS 9.2 or earlier, should check that drivers are available before making a purchase.

DEVICE	FEATURES TO CONSIDER
Monitor	• Video connector. • Flat-panel liquid-crystal display (LCD) monitors cost more, but are easier on the eyes and use less energy than cathode-ray tube (CRT) monitors. • Flat shadow mask and flat aperture grille CRT monitors have sharper pictures than regular CRTs. • CRT monitors can operate at multiple resolutions, but LCDs operate optimally only at maximum resolution. Before you buy an LCD monitor, make sure your computer can handle it. Resolution information should be in the computer manual. • The higher the refresh rate of a CRT monitor, the less the screen will flicker. Look for a refresh rate of 85 hertz (Hz) or higher. • USB or FireWire.
Scanner	• Scanner resolution is measured in dots per inch (dpi) and typically appears as two numbers, such as 2,400 x 1,200. Higher resolution results in better-quality scans. • Bit depth tells you how many colours a scanner can recognise. Choose at least 24-bit; 48-bit is preferable. • Make sure that you get a scanner with a transparency adaptor or lid if you plan to scan slides or film negatives. • A good-quality scanner includes photo-editing software. • Use optical character recognition (OCR) software to convert scanned printed pages to editable word-processing documents.
Speakers	• Audio out connections (soundcard) or headphone jack. • For surround sound, you need a soundcard that supports multiple audio outputs or speakers. Check your manual. • Most computer speakers need to be shielded or they will hum when positioned alongside a CRT monitor. Regular stereo speakers are fine as long as they aren't right next to the monitor or drive.
CD Burner	• USB, USB 2 or FireWire. • CD burners are described by three numbers: the first is the maximum speed it can write a CD-R; the second, the speed for a re-writable CD; the third is the speed a CD-R can be read. These are "real-time" multiples, so a 24 x 12 x 24 burner will take around three minutes to write a full disk (plus a couple of minutes extra for verification). Get the unit with the highest write speed you can afford. • CD-RW burners can use both CD-R and CD-RW disks (see 408 "Buy Blank CDs"). • Don't use your CD burner to read CDs if your computer also has a CD drive.

If you have more USB peripherals than your machine has USB sockets, buy a USB hub, which plugs into a single USB connection and provides two, four or even eight more connections. Choose a powered hub for better performance. If you have a choice between FireWire and USB 1, go for the faster FireWire. For the faster USB 2 to operate at full speed, all three elements – computer, cable and peripheral – must support it. Check packages carefully. USB 1 peripherals can plug into USB 2 sockets.

DEVICE	FEATURES TO CONSIDER
Keyboard	• USB or PS/2. • For flexibility, choose a USB keyboard rather than a PS/2 model. • Never buy a keyboard without typing on it. If the shop doesn't have display models available, ask for models to test. • Special controls on the keyboard (for Internet access or speaker volume) may require special software to be installed on your computer. • Wireless keyboards are available. Infrared (IR) models require a small receiver on your desk and a line-of-sight connection between keyboard and receiver. Radio frequency (RF) or Bluetooth models allow receiver to be out of sight.
Mouse	• USB or PS/2. Choose a USB mouse rather than a PS/2 model. • Feel how the mouse fits in your hand; see how it responds on screen. • Opt for an optical mouse, which works on many surfaces and won't be affected by dirt and fluff. • If you go wireless, get a rechargeable mouse. Mice eat batteries like cheese. • Some mice with extra buttons and scroll wheels may require installation of software to use all features.
Media Reader	• USB or FireWire. • Popular with people who own digital cameras, MP3 players, and PDAs. Remove the memory product (Compact Flash, Smart Media, SecureDigital/MMC, Memory Stick) from the device and plug it into the media reader for fast access to data. • Some media readers can read multiple formats. Check your electronic devices to see what types of memory they use.
Game Controller	• USB or game port. • Computer games may use joysticks, game pads and steering wheels instead of (or in addition to) keyboard and mouse. • Look for a model that feels right in your hands and makes sense for your needs. • Most game controllers require special software – this should be included. • Most computers lack game ports, so look for controller with a USB connector. • Wireless game controllers are also available.
WARNING	If you want to install an internal CD burner or media reader, be sure you know how to safely open your computer and connect devices to its internal circuitry.

402 Choose an Internet Service Provider

The internet is one of the great wonders of the modern world. To get online, you first need to find an internet service provider (ISP). You have two general choices: dial-up service, which is cheap but slow; and broadband service, which is more expensive and much faster.

Steps

1 Determine your needs. Do you want to send and receive e-mail and occasionally surf the web? An inexpensive dial-up account, which uses a regular telephone line, is probably enough. If you want to connect to your office network, play online games, or download and exchange music and video files, you'll want a speedy broadband connection, such as ADSL or cable.

2 Find out what hardware is needed. For a dial-up account, a modem is required – this is included with most new computers. Broadband services will also require a modem or a network interface card (NIC); a visit from a telephone engineer might also be needed.

3 Ask your friends and neighbours what internet service they use and whether they're satisfied with it. Customer service varies from region to region, especially with broadband providers, so seek out a local recommendation.

4 Dial-up users should make sure an ISP has local access numbers (telephone numbers) in your area to avoid long-distance charges. Alternatively, look for "unmetered" internet access, where you pay a one-off monthly subscription that covers the cost of your telephone calls.

5 Check for ADSL and cable broadband providers in your area. (ADSL ISPs use telephone wiring, while cable ISPs use cable TV wiring.) ADSL or cable may not always be available in rural areas, so check that your local BT exchange is equipped to provide broadband services.

6 Ask potential broadband providers about package deals. Cable companies may discount internet access if you subscribe to a cable TV service.

7 Consider other broadband options. Although very expensive, investigate the possibility of satellite or radio broadband if you live in a rural area. Some new housing developments have built-in fibre-optic internet access.

8 Consider your internet usage before selecting an ISP. Some offer broadband for not much more than the cost of a dial-up line. Be aware, however, that this may not be full-speed broadband, or may limit the size or frequency of files you wish to download.

9 Some ISPs offer their customers unique content, such as online access to magazines or websites not available to non-subscribers.

What to Look For

- Broadband versus dial-up service
- Appropriate hardware connections
- Recommendations
- Local access numbers
- Package deals included with telephone or cable TV service
- Satellite, fixed wireless, or fibre-optic connections

Tips

A broadband connection can be shared by several computers (see 404 "Network Your Computers").

Some experts recommend choosing an ISP that does not require you to install its own specialised software on your computer.

Warnings

With a broadband connection, your computer can always be connected to the internet. Get firewall software to protect against potential snoopers (see 406 "Buy Computer Software").

In the fast and furious internet world, even big name ISPs go out of business. This means you'll have to find a new service, and possibly a new e-mail address. See 403 "Get an Internet Domain Name" for an easier solution.

403 Get an Internet Domain Name

Tired of changing e-mail addresses each time you change internet service providers? Want to put up a website but don't want an address that's two lines long and full of slashes and squiggles? Then register your own domain name.

Steps

1 Consider a suitable name. If you are a business, remember that a short and sweet domain name will be easier to remember. Make a short list of possibilities.

2 Visit the WHOIS website (www.whois.org). using Whois, you can type in your chosen names to see if they have already been taken, and by whom. Enter the name you want to register (don't forget the part after the dot) and click on Submit.

3 Read the search results on the screen. If the name you want is available, it'll read "No match for domain".

4 If the popular ".com" name is taken, try other suffixes, such as ".co.uk", ".net", ".org" or ".tv". Since users randomly searching for your site may be directed to the ".com" site first, ".net", ".org" and ".tv" suffixes may be better for personal rather than business uses.

5 If the name you want is taken, try variations, such as adding a middle initial, a city name or meaningful number to your search.

6 When you find a name you like, return to InterNIC.net and click on the link to the Accredited Registrar Directory. You'll see a list of more than 150 registrars, or companies that can register your domain name for you. Alternatively, you will find the names of companies offering domain registration and server facilities advertised in any of the popular monthly computer magazines.

7 Survey these companies for services. Most people want e-mail forwarding (automatically sending e-mail from john@*yourown-name*.com to jsmith2424@*yourISP*.com) and website forwarding (sending people who go to www.*yourownname*.com directly to www.members.*yourISP.com*/~jsmith2424/index.html).

8 Registering the domain name and details of your e-mail and web forwarding requirements can usually be achieved immediately by filling in an online form and paying by credit card.

9 The company that registers your name doesn't have to host your website. If your monthly ISP fee includes web hosting, you can save money by using website forwarding. Your ISP may also be able to register a domain name for you, but they don't always offer prices or service to match specialist companies.

10 Now you need a website: See 157 "Hire Someone to Design and Build Your Website".

What to Look For

- Available domain name
- E-mail forwarding
- Web site forwarding
- Web site hosting

Tip

There's no single, objective, authoritative place to check the reputation of a domain registrar. However, typing the registrar's name into a search engine, alongside words such as "complaints" or "reliability" might give you some clues about how happy its customers are.

The more unusual the name, the more likely it is to be available. Most common or well-known corporate names are taken.

If the domain name you want to register is already taken and you desperately want it, you may contact the owner with an offer to buy it.

Warning

Registering a domain name trademarked by another company is commonly known as "Cybersquatting". Even if you have bought the domain name legitimately, you may still find yourself on the wrong end of legal action.

404 Network Your Computers

With an increasing number of British households owning more than one computer, home networking is an increasingly important topic. If you want all your computers to share a single internet connection, this information will help you make the right choices.

Steps

Learn the jargon

1 A *router* relays data between your broadband internet connection and your individual computers.

2 A *network adaptor* connects to each computer. It sends data from the computer to the router.

3 An *Internet protocol (IP) address* is your computer's unique identification on the internet. When you have a home network, all your computers share one IP address.

4 A *print server* is a special network adaptor that's used to connect a printer to a network. With a print server, several computers can share one printer.

Choose a network type

1 Network your computers wirelessly over radio waves using a special type of router called an *access point*. One access point can serve most average-sized homes. The trade name for this technology is Wi-Fi or 802.11 (802.11b or its faster cousin, 802.11g). Wi-Fi products are largely compatible with each other regardless of brand. Wireless networks work for people who move from room to room with their laptops, or want to use them in cafés, airports and other places with a wireless service.

2 Hook up with the most secure home network, a *wired network,* sometimes called Ethernet, 10-Base-T or 100-Base-T. If your broadband connection, router and all computers are in the same room, it's probably the best choice for you. However, because of its special wiring, it's also the least flexible if your needs change.

Buy the equipment

1 Get one router. If you're going wireless, this router is called an access point or base station.

2 Get a network adaptor for each computer. The simplest ones plug into the computer's universal serial bus (USB) port. If you're using a wired network, your computer probably already has an Ethernet network interface card (NIC) in it. For wireless networks, each computer will require a card allowing it to transmit and receive signals from the base station. On laptops, these are either fitted internally or via a PC card.

3 Purchase extra-long Ethernet cables (also called Category 5 or Cat5 cables) if you're using a wired network.

What to Look For

- Router or access point
- Network adaptor
- Print server
- Ethernet cable
- Technical support

Tips

Hybrid networks are very popular. For example, you can have wired Ethernet going to a desktop computer and printer in your home office, and a wireless access point for a roaming laptop and a desktop in a bedroom.

Microwave ovens and some types of cordless phones can interfere with wireless networks. If you have such a problem, move the access point and experiment with different channels.

Different competing network technologies may brag about their speed differences, but if you're sharing a broadband internet connection, the claims will be irrelevant. Even the fastest domestic broadband connections will run considerably slower than the rated speed of any home network.

4 Buy a print server if you want to put a printer on your network. Make sure the connectors on your print server and printer match. Some wireless routers – such as Apple's Airport Extreme base station – have built-in USB connections for connecting printers.

Set it up

1 Start reading and experimenting. Many networking products have surprisingly good manuals and online support, and many web-sites are packed with good advice, such as HomeNetHelp.com, PracticallyNetworked.com and compnetworking.about.com. Some manufacturers offer online advice. Good technical support can make a huge difference in your installation, especially if you're not particularly patient or computer literate.

2 If you're putting in a wired network, consider running cables to your stereo or home cinema. Many new home entertainment components including digital video recorders and game systems, are internet-enabled.

Warning

When you first fire up a router, change its default password. Every hacker and mischief-maker on the internet knows how default passwords are created. Wireless network owners should also enable wireless encryption protocol (WEP) to keep information private.

405 Upgrade the Memory in Your Computer

One of the best ways to improve your computer's performance is to add random-access memory (RAM). Unless you're confident of your abilities, have a professional do the work.

Steps

1 Find out how much memory your computer has. Here's how:

- In Windows XP, click on Start, then Control Panel, then Performance and Maintenance, then System. In other versions of Windows, double-click on My Computer, then double-click on Control Panel, then double-click on System.

- In Mac OS X, find the Applications folder, double-click on the Utilities folder, and double-click on Apple System Profiler. In Mac OS 9 or earlier, select the Apple System Profiler or, in the Finder, click on About This Computer in the Apple menu.

2 Check your manual or manufacturer's website to determine whether there are open memory slots on the motherboard. Also see what the maximum amount of memory your computer can take, as well as the type, category and speed of memory it uses. For example, PC2100 DDR 133 MHz RAM means that PC2100 is the type, DDR is the category, and 133 MHz is the speed in megahertz.

3 Compare your current memory with the maximum. You have two choices: add new memory in open slots; or, if all slots are full, replace the existing memory with new, greater-capacity modules.

What to Look For

- Current memory
- Maximum allowable memory
- Type, category and speed of memory
- Open slots

Tip

Good tools for choosing memory are available online, including Crucial.com (you don't need to purchase from them to use the selector tool). You can also check the shopper sections of most computer magazines.

406 Buy Computer Software

These days, most big-name personal computers come with a software bundle that can handle most people's basic needs. However, if you buy a bare-bones machine, you may find yourself spending a lot of time and money to properly equip it. Here's how you can get started.

Steps

1 Collect your computer's vital statistics. You should know the operating system, the amount of random-access memory (RAM), and the available hard-disk space before you shop. Knowing whether it's Windows or Mac OS isn't enough; you need the operating system version number (Windows 98, 2000, Me or XP; Mac OS 8.*x*, 9.*x* or OS X). To locate this information:

   • In Windows XP, click on Start, then Control Panel, then Performance and Maintenance, then System.

   • In other versions of Windows, double-click on My Computer, then double-click on Control Panel, then double-click on System. You may need to click on the Performance tab.

   • In Mac OS X, open the Applications folder, double-click on the Utilities folder, then double-click on Apple System Profiler.

   • In Mac OS 9 or earlier, select the Apple System Profiler or, in the Finder, click on About This Computer in the Apple menu.

2 Think about the kind of work you want to do on your computer. Software applications are organised into broad categories:

   • Office applications are for word processing, spreadsheets, databases and presentations. Most new computers come with some sort of office software. Whatever you choose, make sure it works with industry standards Microsoft Word and Excel.

   • Internet applications include web browsers and e-mail, and come with most computers. E-mail software is sometimes categorised as "communications" software.

   • Personal finance software includes money-management and tax-preparation tools. Ensure you buy UK tax software – a program that helps you complete a US tax return won't be much use.

   • Utilities include virus protection, internet firewall, back-up and recovery, and disk-management software. Every computer should have current virus protection, and, for security, machines that are permanently connected to the internet via broadband should have a firewall.

   • Graphics and multimedia applications include digital image manipulation, drawing, video editing and sound. These often demand huge amounts of available disk space and memory.

   • Entertainment software refers to games. Most run best with graphics or soundcards; some require external controllers such as joysticks. See 415 " Buy Video and Computer Games".

What to Look For

• System requirements
• Software categories
• Reviews
• Version number
• Support options
• Trial versions
• Packaged versus down-loaded
• Freeware
• Shareware

Tips

Students can sometimes get educational discounts on computer products.

What is the difference between software programs and applications? Some IT people say that the *software* includes operating systems, but *applications* do not.

Note that some software can cause conflicts with others; ask manufacturers or read online reviews to learn if you have these.

Some companies create "home" and "professional" versions of the same pieces of software. Find out what the difference is, and whether you need the more expensive pro version.

- Educational software includes language instruction, typing tutors, and maths and reading learning programs for children.

- Reference software includes dictionaries, atlases, road maps and encyclopedias.

- Development applications are for advanced computer users and programmers who want to create their own software.

3 Learn about which specific software will best serve your needs by talking with friends and colleagues and reading reviews. You can read software reviews on ZDNet.com and Cnet.com and in magazines such as *MacUser* and *PC World*.

4 As you narrow your choices, compare the system requirements of the software with the information you collected in Step 1. In shops, look for the system requirements on the package. Catalogues and online stores list requirements with the product description. NOTE: before purchasing, make sure your system can handle the application.

5 Find out the current version of the software. If a newer version exists (or is expected soon), make sure that the version you buy can be upgraded to the most current version for free. Updates and patches can sometimes be costly.

6 Find out what technical support comes with the software. The options vary greatly, from free lifetime support to by-the-minute telephone help. Most software companies are moving towards self-service web-based support, so visit the manufacturer's web-site to see if it seems helpful and complete.

7 If you can't decide between two products, take a look on the manufacturers' websites for a free trial version. Some versions will become inactive after a set time period; others lack some basic functionality (such as the ability to save or print work). Most can be upgraded to full versions online for a fee. Many computers come loaded with trial versions of popular software.

8 Purchase packaged software if you like having a printed manual and an installer disk you can file away. (Check that the package actually contains a printed manual – they're increasingly being presented as Acrobat PDF files, intended to be read on screen. You do, of course, have the option of printing it out yourself.)

9 Buy software online and download it if you have a broadband internet connection and need to use the software right away. This can often be done from manufacturers' websites.

10 You can spend little or nothing by using either freeware (no-cost software) or Shareware (low-cost software that you can choose to buy if you like it). Many of these products, as well as trial versions of commercial software, are available from such sites as Tucows.com, VersionTracker.com and Download.com.

Warning

Software is licensed, not purchased. This means that it's actually illegal to borrow a CD-ROM from a friend and install his or her software on your computer.

407 Choose a CD Player

CD players are the hardest-working piece of equipment in most home music systems. When you're out shopping, look for the features you use most. Decent machines can be found for well under £200.

Steps

1 Think about how you listen to music. Do you routinely drop in several CDs and hit Shuffle, or listen to one at a time? Do you burn your own CDs? Your habits should drive your choice.

2 Check the CD connection on your current stereo. If it accepts digital optical inputs (which provide better sound quality than normal wire jacks), find a CD player with digital optical output.

3 Bring some home-burned CDs when you go shopping to play on any unit you're considering. Some CD players can't play CD-RWs, and many can't play MP3s.

4 If you have lots of CDs and rarely take them out of the house, consider a CD jukebox or a carousel that can holds dozens – or even hundreds – of discs.

5 DVD players can also play audio CDs. Consider a machine that does both jobs.

6 Serious listeners should look at high-definition compatible digital (HDCD), DVD-Audio or super-audio CD (SACD) players. These new formats provide better sound quality. All will play traditional CDs, but the formats are often not compatible with one another.

What to Look For

- Shuffle/random/program-mable playback
- Digital optical output
- CD-RW capability
- MP3 capability
- Carousel or jukebox
- Cataloguing feature
- HDCD capability
- DVD-Audio
- SACD capability

Tips

Manufacturers use such terms as *shuffle* and *random* differently. If a CD player has both features, find out what they mean.

Broken CD players can be repaired, but are not usually worth the expense.

408 Buy Blank CDs

Blank CDs can cost anything from 10 pence to over a pound each. The kind you buy depends on your equipment and what you want to do.

Steps

1 Check your computer manual to see if your CD burner is a CD-R (recordable) or a CD-RW (re-writable). Recordable discs can be used only once, but re-writable discs can be used over and over.

2 Keep in mind that blank CD-Rs will work in a CD-RW burner, but CD-RWs won't work in a CD-R burner.

3 Buy blank CDs with gold-tone on the bottom to record archival material, such as family photographs or financial records.

4 Get less-expensive green-toned CDs if you're making everyday copies of documents, photos and music.

5 Buy CD-Rs (not CD-RWs) if you're recording music to be played on a portable or car stereo. Choose blank CDs labelled "Music", "Digital Audio" or "DA" if your CD burner is part of your system.

What to Look For

- CD burner (CD-R or CD-RW)
- Gold-tone CDs
- Green-tone CDs
- Music CDs

Tip

Blank CDs labelled "Music" cost more, as a portion of the price goes to recording artists as royalties. However, they are the only CDs that work in stereo-component CD burners.

409 Buy an MP3 Player

An MP3 player is the perfect tool for people on the go who have moved their music collections onto their computers. And because they're digital – some with absolutely no moving parts – MP3 players don't skip or warble if you're running, skiing or biking.

Steps

1 Shop for price. MP3 players range from £30 for a bare-bones model to £400 for the top-of-the-line Apple iPod. Other popular brands are Creative Labs, SonicBlue, Archos, Samsung, Sony and Panasonic.

2 Get a player with as much storage as you can afford. The more storage, the more music it can hold. One minute of MP3 music takes up about 1 megabyte (MB) of memory, so a 128 MB MP3 player can hold about two hours of tunes. Unlike computers, memory and storage are sometimes used synonymously in MP3 players, since the storage in smaller devices (under 128 MB) is usually made of Flash memory chips. At the top end, an Apple iPod can hold 40 gigabytes of data – that's good for at least 5,000 albums! Don't forget, some of the larger FireWire or USB models can double up as mobile hard drives.

3 Make sure any potential purchase works with your computer. Many MP3 players don't work with Macintosh computers, although that's improving.

4 Try the controls. Less-expensive players often have transport control panels that can at best be described as "minimalist". Make sure they make sense to you.

5 Pick up the unit to gauge its size and weight. Would you find it comfortable in your pocket or on your belt? How about when you're moving around?

6 Check out the player's advertised battery life. Manufacturers' claims aren't exact, but they can be used for comparison.

7 Choose a unit with USB or FireWire, rather than a parallel connection to your computer. USB and FireWire are fast and flexible.

8 If you are interested, look for a player with an FM radio receiver. Some models can record music from the radio, and will identify the artist and title the next time you connect the player to your computer. Some also double as digital voice recorders.

9 Look for expandable storage, especially on units without much built-in memory. CompactFlash, MemoryStick and SecureDigital media are common choices. Newer models with more storage have internal hard disks that can store computer data.

10 Have a listen. MP3 players use standard stereo headphones. If you don't like the headphones that come with a player, there are a variety of alternatives you can purchase.

What to Look For

- Maximum storage
- Computer connectivity
- Easy-to-use controls
- Size and weight
- Battery life
- USB or FireWire
- FM receiver
- Expandable storage
- Headphones

Tips

A few high-end MP3 players have built-in FM transmitters to send music wirelessly to a car stereo. You can do the same with a pocket-sized FM transmitter; if you don't mind wires, use a cassette-on-a-cable device from a portable CD player car kit.

Some MP3 players double as portable CD players, so you can burn your MP3 files to a CD and pop it in the player.

Some MP3 players can also play ".wav" and ".aif" files, making it possible to listen to CD-quality recordings.

Warning

Although the legalities of MP3 music-swapping are constantly changing, the vast majority of MP3 activity remains illegal. There are, however, many internet sites where music can be downloaded legally (see 35 "Buy Music Online").

410 Choose a DVD Player

The thing that convinces some people to move up to a DVD player is the great picture quality. Or, maybe it's just being able to click to hear Tony Soprano speak French. There's a DVD player to match almost any pocket, and even the cheapest ones have features galore.

Steps

1 Inspect your TV and home cinema connections. You'll want your DVD player to take advantage of the best-quality inputs: for audio, look for coaxial or optical inputs. For video, look for component-video, S-Video, composite-video or SCART inputs. At the shop, look for DVD players with corresponding outputs.

2 Bring a home-made DVD with you when you shop. There are three competing – but incompatible – formats: DVD-R, DVD-RW and DVD-RAM. Even if a player says it takes your format, test it.

3 Get a progressive-scan player if you have an HDTV. These deliver higher resolution for more natural-looking output. Better still, purchase a DVD player with 3:2 pulldown, if you can afford it, for even better picture quality. See 422 "Buy a Serious TV".

4 Remember that the audio encoding – Dolby Digital or Digital Theater System (DTS) – on the DVD itself is critical. Proprietary audio features on a DVD player are less important than having a good home cinema receiver and speakers. See 426 "Buy a Home Cinema System".

What to Look For

- Digital audio output: coaxial or optical
- Component-video output
- S-Video output
- Composite-video output
- Progressive scan
- 3:2 pulldown
- Good receiver and speakers

Tips

If your home cinema system includes DTS and/or Dolby Digital decoding, you don't need these features in your DVD player.

DVD players can also play audio CDs. If you burn CDs on your computer, bring along a homemade disc to test it.

411 Buy a Video Recorder

Have you shopped for a video recorder lately? Models comparable to units that once cost a fortune are now available for under £50. Maybe you don't have to replace all of those VHS movies with DVDs right away after all.

Steps

1 Check the connections on your television set or home cinema receiver. Look for a machine with the best possible connectors – in descending order of quality, they're S-Video, composite-video and SCART inputs.

2 Choose a video with S-VHS (super VHS), high-fidelity stereo audio, and four or six heads for best recording and playback.

3 Pick a model with audio-video connectors on the front panel if you plan to transfer movies from a video camcorder to tape.

4 Expect a raft of standard features. Even on the lowest-priced models you should find stereo sound and high-speed rewind.

What to Look For

- S-VHS
- Four or six heads
- Audio-video connectors in front
- Auto clock set
- Commercial skip
- Fast rewind

Tip

Avoid combination VCR/DVDs unless you don't have room for both. You get more for your money with stand-alone components, and one is sure to break before the other.

412 Choose a Personal Digital Assistant

Tired of lugging around an address book, a calendar, a pad of paper, a photo album, your journal, a game machine, the newspaper and a calculator? With today's handhelds – sometimes called personal digital assistants (PDAs) or pocket computers – you can consolidate them all into one handy device. All your information is readily available and searchable. And PDA prices are now cheaper than ever.

Steps

1 Think about how you might use a handheld. What would you like to do on it? (If you're not sure what PDAs can do, read up on them in speciality magazines or on the web.)

2 Look at your computer. What operating system (Windows or Macintosh) does it have, and what sort of connectors (USB 1, USB 2, FireWire) does it have? Make sure that any handheld you consider is compatible with your computer. You don't need a computer to use a handheld, but it helps. Your computer can back up the information on your handheld, give you another way to enter information, and act as a bridge between your handheld and the internet.

3 Compare the two leading handheld operating systems: Palm OS and Pocket PC. They serve the same basic functions (calendar, address book, notebook, calculator), but they differ in features and approach. Try out a few models in the shop.

4 Focus on screen display; quality is vital. Is text on the screen easy to read in a variety of settings? If you're intending to view photographs, look at colour screens. Utilitarian black-and-white screens might be acceptable for text-only tasks.

5 Pick up the handheld and get a feel for its weight, sturdiness and comfort.

6 Learn how you'll enter text on your handheld. If the handwriting-recognition method isn't comfortable for you (it takes some practice), look for a model with a built-in thumb-operated keyboard. Add-on keyboards are available but have drawbacks.

7 Look at the battery type. Rechargeable handhelds usually need recharging every week or two, while those with disposable batteries need replacements monthly. (Your mileage may vary.)

8 Get as much memory as you can afford, especially if you plan to load lots of pictures, games or documents from your computer.

9 Look for handhelds with slots for expanding memory and adding functions. Popular add-ons include MP3 players, Global Positioning System (GPS) receivers, modems and wireless network adaptors (Wi-Fi).

What to Look For

- Compatibility with your computer
- USB or FireWire connectors
- Palm OS or Pocket PC
- Screen display
- Weight, sturdiness, overall feel
- Text-entry method
- Battery type
- Memory
- Expansion slots

Tips

You don't need a Microsoft-based Pocket PC just because you run Windows on your computer. Palm OS devices are reportedly better at handling Word and Excel documents.

Avoid cheap address book–only devices. Palm OS and Pocket PC handhelds are generally much more useful, and don't usually cost much more money.

Warning

If you are upgrading from an older Palm OS device to one of the new handheld models with Palm OS 5, make sure the programs you use are enhanced for, or at least compatible with, the new operating system.

413 Choose a Mobile Phone Service

Who said competition makes everything better? If you've shopped for mobile phone service lately, you know that the variety of service plans and phones is overwhelming. Companies often entice customers with great new phones, but that's the last item you should think about. First choose a provider, then a service plan, then think about your hardware.

Steps

Compare competing providers' coverage

1 Make sure a prospective provider's service works where you do. Providers have maps of their service areas. If you travel a lot, look for national – or international – coverage.

2 Ask your friends and colleagues which providers they use and how satisfied they are with the services provided. Ask them to check reception by making calls in your home and office – there's nothing worse than discovering that there's a dead spot where you spend all your time.

3 If required, check where data services – such as e-mail, internet access, games and photographs – are available.

Compare service plans

1 Look carefully at your needs. If the main reason you want your phone is to receive calls, then a pay-as-you-go package may be more economical than one which allows you a set amount of call time for a fixed monthly fee.

2 Think about how much time you intend to spend making calls. If it's more than 120 minutes a month it will be more economical to choose a monthly package rather than paying for calls as you make them.

3 Think about when during the day you intend making calls. If you use a pay-as-you-go tariff, calls made during the day will cost you much more than those made at evenings and weekends.

4 Ask if standard features such as call waiting, voicemail and caller ID are included in your plan at no extra charge.

5 Look for a plan with roll-over minutes; make sure that if you don't use your full monthly quota the remainder will be carried forward to the next period.

6 Some providers round call time up to the nearest minute. Be aware.

7 Check into package plans for data services if you plan to use their services heavily. They can add a hefty additional charge per month – often at a cost per kilobyte of data.

8 Look for a plan with a low (or no) cancellation fee if you think your needs might change. Before you pay such a fee, ask your provider to switch you at no cost to a plan that makes better sense for you in the future.

What to Look For

- Coverage
- Service plan
- Phone

Tips

If you know you'll use data services heavily, getting hold of the right phone may be more important for you than the right service plan.

Mobile phone companies must give you the ability to take your mobile phone number with you if you move to a new provider.

Select a telephone

1 Ask about free phones. You can get some great full-featured phones when you agree to sign a one-year contract.

2 Make sure the phone's basic features work simply and well: an easy-to-use keypad, clear sound, long battery life, clock and voicemail are important for most people.

3 Get a hands-free headset with your phone if you need to talk on the move.

4 Consider advanced features, like colour screens, speaker-phone operation, built-in cameras, address books that synchronise with your computer, or custom ring tones.

5 Look for Global Positioning System (GPS) location capability if you need to be found in an emergency.

6 Consider a combination mobile phone and PDA if you rely on these services heavily. They are costly, but can reduce the load in your briefcase or purse.

Some of the bigger mobile phone companies will let you terminate a contract without paying a cancellation fee if you do so within a set time, usually 14 to 30 days.

414 Get a Better Deal from Your Phone Company

Not so long ago, if you wanted a telephone there was only one real option – you subscribed with British Telecom. With the introduction of Carrier Pre-Selection (CPS) there are ever more players in the telephone provider market. Competition can be great for the consumer, but how do you work your way through the maze of ever-changing tariffs?

Steps

1 Review several months of existing phone bills to understand your calling patterns. Think about how might they change in future. If you're on an economy drive, try to discipline yourself to making calls when they are at their cheapest – peak day use may be two or three times more expensive than making your calls during evenings and weekends.

2 Go to the internet and log onto www.uswitch.com. This is a free service that compares the cost of tariffs being offered by all of the telephone service providers in your area. Enter your postcode and study the results. Another useful website is lower-my-bills.co.uk. (Both can also advise you of better deals in other areas, such as gas and electricity.)

3 If you are a heavy phone user, look at deals that offer "free" unlimited off-peak calls for fixed monthly fee.

4 Check for special deals with your mobile phone provider – strange though it may seem, it's sometimes cheaper to make an international call from your mobile than from a land line.

What to Look For

- Calling patterns
- Internet comparison services
- Unmetered call packages
- Comparison with mobile phone companies
- Switching costs

Tips

Check your plan every few months to make sure you're still getting the best deal.

When you subscribe to a new phone provider make a note of penalty costs that may result from switching to a competitor.

415 Buy Video and Computer Games

Fun and games aren't just for kids anymore. Video games – both computer and console games – are now mainstream entertainment for adults. Indeed, technology magazines talk of the "battle for the living room", with some game consoles up there with DVD players in terms of power and features.

Steps

1 Since not all games are available on all platforms, it's a good idea to start your shopping by deciding what type of games you want to play. Genres include action/adventure, role-playing/strategy, simulation and sports.

2 See what platform the games you want are on. Games fall into two general categories: computer games (for PC or Apple Macintosh) and console games (usually played on a Sony PlayStation2, Microsoft XBox or Nintendo GameCube).

3 Look for these features in a computer game.

- System requirements: make sure your computer's processor, memory and video card meet the minimum requirements. Also be alert for special hardware, such as game pads or joysticks (see 401 "Buy Computer Peripherals").

- Multi-player internet capability: this allows you to play computer games online against other people. Some games don't even have a single-player mode. A broadband internet connection will improve game performance.

- Free demonstration versions: demos are available for many computer games from manufacturer websites. You can upgrade them to full versions later.

4 Look for these features in a console game.

- Compatibility: XBox, GameCube and PlayStation 2 games are not interchangeable. Older PlayStation games can be played on a PlayStation2, but not vice versa.

- Special controller needs: most games use the standard console controls, but some work better with other types.

- Advanced audio needs: newer game consoles and games can handle Dolby 5.1 surround sound.

5 Understand the rating system established by the British Board of Film Classification (BBFC) or the European Leisure Software Publishers Associaton (ELSPA). Ratings are based on violence; sexual content; language; depiction of drug use; gambling; and other factors. Ratings are especially important for people who are buying games for children. (See 335 "Buy a Video Game System".)

What to Look For

- Computer versus console
- System requirements
- Multi-player capability
- Demo versions
- Special controllers
- Internet connectivity requirements
- Audio-video needs
- Suitability ratings

Tips

Most game consoles can double as DVD and music CD players. However, the sound and picture quality is often not up to regular DVD standards.

The best games – especially the "first-person shooters" – are released as computer games before they come out on consoles.

416 Choose a Film Camera

The massive boom in digital photography hasn't killed the market for film cameras. Many people with digital cameras still use film cameras occasionally, and great choices are available in all price ranges. There are a couple of important issues to consider when shopping for a film camera, and lots of features to choose from.

Steps

1 Decide what you intend to shoot. If you want great holiday and family snapshots, a point-and-shoot camera will do fine. Don't underestimate the quality you can find in these easy-to-operate cameras – many are full-featured and fitted with a high-quality lens. For more serious photography you should look for a single lens–reflex (SLR) camera, which gives you manual control over a number of features.

2 Consider your film choices. For most uses, you'll choose between 35 mm and Advanced Photo System (APS) film. The former is easier to find, cheaper to buy and process, and easier to develop, while the latter (in the proper camera) lets you shoot panoramic and wide-angle shots on the same roll as normal pictures. See 39 "Choose Film for Your Camera".

What to Look For

- Point-and-shoot versus SLR
- 35 mm versus APS
- Special features

Tips

The majority of SLR cameras use 35 mm film, not APS.

You will be able to find good deals on SLRs and lenses at reputable used-camera shops or online auctions.

Some film cameras have LCDs like digital cameras so you can see the photo you just took (although you won't be able to erase it).

POINT-AND-SHOOT CAMERA FEATURES	SLR CAMERA FEATURES
Flash: look for red-eye reduction and fill-in modes. The further the flash is from the lens, the less likely you are to get red-eye in your pictures.	Interchangeable lenses.
Timer and/or remote control: these let you appear in your own photos.	Manual exposure control: you'll want to be able to adjust both the shutter speed and the aperture.
Date stamp: this marks the photo with the date you took it.	Automatic exposure control: look for both shutter speed and aperture priority.
Automatic film loading, winding and rewinding.	Automatic and manual focus: some cameras will even track your eye movements in the viewfinder and focus on the element you're looking at.
Zoom lens.	Film handling features: look for automated loading, winding, re-winding and DX sensing. With DX sensing, the camera reads a bar code on the film can and adjusts itself accordingly.
Panorama mode (in APS cameras).	Flash capability: some SLRs have a built-in flash. Make sure the camera also has a "hot shoe", which will enable you to connect an external flash.
Price: £20 and up, with many very good cameras under £100.	Price: £100 and up, with very good cameras from around £300.

417 Choose a Digital Camcorder

Now that you've written your screenplay (see 166 "Sell a Screenplay"), it's time to start shooting. Digital camcorders, many selling for under £500, can capture remarkably high-quality images and are great fun to use. Combine one with editing software on your computer, and capture your family's favourite moments in style.

Steps

1 Forget about analogue camcorders. When it comes to image quality, even the cheapest digital camcorder will outperform the very best analogue models. And analogue models won't connect to your computer – at least not without additional hardware – so you can forget about editing your home movies.

2 Choose a digital recording format: MiniDV (the most popular format, with easy-to-find blank tapes), Digital 8 or MicroMV.

3 Pick a model with a liquid-crystal display (LCD) screen that measures at least 6 cm (2.5 inches) diagonally. The bigger and brighter the screen, the easier the camera will be to focus and use. Ask to view it outside, in bright daylight. (Many cameras have a black-and-white viewfinder in addition to the LCD.)

4 Look for a front-mounted microphone rather than a top-mounted one. For the best sound, make sure there's a jack socket for an external microphone.

5 Pay attention to the optical zoom. The higher the numbers, the closer your camera will bring you to the action. However, digital zoom simply reduces the resolution of the recorded image.

6 Try the controls and the on-screen menus. Make sure that you're comfortable using them and they make sense to you.

7 Picture-stabilising circuitry and low-light operation can be useful. Ask to see what they do and how well they work.

8 Weigh the features of the camera against its bulkiness, weight and price tag. A large, heavy camera won't be comfortable for you to use. Tiny, palm-sized camcorders can be bought, but at a hefty price.

9 Make sure to get a camcorder with a FireWire (IEEE 1394) or USB 2.0 connection socket if you're planning to edit your movies on your computer.

10 Have fun with video-editing software and turn your raw footage into entertaining movies complete with professional-looking cuts, transitions and soundtracks. Basic editing programs come with some computers and digital camcorders. For example, new Apple Macs come standard with easy-to-learn iMovie. More expensive models are kitted out with hardware and software that allow you to burn your finished movie onto a DVD.

What to Look For

- Digital format
- LCD screen at least 6 cm (2.5 in) in size
- Front-mounted micro-phone
- Optical zoom
- Easy-to-use controls
- Picture-stabilising circuitry
- Low-light operation
- FireWire or USB 2.0 connection

Tip

As you shop you may see the term *i.LINK*. It's another name for FireWire and is used mostly with digital camcorders.

418 Decide on a Digital Camera

The price of digital cameras is falling as swiftly as their quality is soaring. That means great opportunities for shoppers. Remember that, while they seem expensive when compared to film cameras, digital cameras never need film. And you can create photo-quality prints using your home computer and a good-quality ink-jet printer. The only downside is the dizzying array of choices. Here's some help.

Steps

1 Decide what you want to get out of your camera. Are you shooting family snapshots, professional portraits or something in between? A good basic digital camera costs under £300, while professional models are upwards of £2,000. Spend what you need to get a camera that covers the high end of projected uses.

2 Understand image resolution, measured in megapixels (mg). The more megapixels, the higher the resolution of the final image. The way you want to show your images should be your guide: A 1 mg camera can create a 7.5 x 13 cm (3 x 5 in) photo-quality print; a 2 mg camera will make a 13 x 18 cm (5 x 7 in) print; a 3 mg camera will make a 20 x 25 cm (8 x 10 in) print, and a 6 mg camera will make a 23 x 33 cm (9 x13 in) print.

3 Find out if the camera includes a cable for your computer (USB or FireWire). If it doesn't, it's not the end of the world (see 401 "Buy Computer Peripherals: Media Reader").

4 See if a camera comes with image-editing software that works with your computer (Windows or Mac OS). Adobe Photoshop Elements and ULead PhotoImpact are two popular programs.

5 Choose a camera with removable memory in addition to built-in memory. The most popular formats are CompactFlash, MemoryStick, SmartMedia and MultiMedia/Secure Digital (MMC/SD). (The differences between formats are irrelevant for most uses.) They cost roughly the same, with 128-MB cards usually giving the best value.

6 Expect an LCD screen for viewing pictures, a built-in flash, a timer and a time/date stamp on even the most basic camera. Some models let you record short snippets of video.

7 Insist on optical zoom, not digital, if you need zoom capability. Mid-range cameras should have high-quality optical zoom lenses.

8 Get manual exposure control – a feature on mid-range cameras – if you plan to shoot in low-light conditions or otherwise need to override automatic settings.

9 Expect features equivalent to those of the best single lens–reflex (SLR) cameras on the best digital models. Features include removable lenses, full exposure control, a "hot-shoe" mount for an external flash and a through-the-lens focus system.

What to Look For

- Image resolution
- Battery life
- Cable and software
- Removable memory
- LCD screen
- Built-in flash
- Timer
- Time/date stamp
- Video recording
- Optical zoom lens
- Manual exposure control

Tips

Ignore claims of digital zoom. When you use digital zoom, the image resolution drops accordingly. For example, 2X digital zoom will reduce the resolution of your finished pictures by half.

Digital cameras eat batteries, especially to power an LCD screen. For longer life, avoid using the LCD and use lithium batteries – but always carry extras. Ignore the claims of manufacturers when it comes to projected battery life (see 40 "Buy Rechargeable Batteries").

Look for software that helps you organise and manage your digital photos, such as Jasc Paint Shop Photo Album, Apple iPhoto and Adobe PhotoAlbum.

Take lots of pictures and trash the unwanted shots later, on your computer.

Most digital cameras have a slight delay between tripping the trigger and actually exposing the picture. This can cause you to miss shots, especially when you're first learning to use the camera.

419 Buy a Home Automation System

If you've seen so-called smart houses with remote controls for lights, heating and cooling, security, home cinema and even window blinds, you've probably been amazed – and they're not exclusively available for upmarket homes. Here's how to put automation into your home.

Steps

1 Start feeding your fantasies. Pore through any of the popular DIY, design or electronics magazines for ideas, or go online to see what's available. Since such systems are increasingly being built into new houses, an architect may be a good source of advice.

2 Think about what you'd like to automate. If you plan to start small – with just lights, perhaps – get a system that can be expanded when you want to add other functions.

3 Calculate your budget. Prices can range from a few hundred pounds for basic systems to hundreds of thousands of pounds for whole-house automation systems

4 Make sure that any system you're considering installing will work with your current heating and air conditioning, security and home entertainment systems. You may need to replace light switches, alarm controllers and thermostats.

5 Place the master control panel, also known as the "headend", in a convenient, central spot. This is where your home automation systems come together.

6 Consider a powerline or radio frequency controls if you're installing home automation in an existing house. These don't require extra wiring for controls, but tend to be less useful or flexible than systems that operate with low-voltage wiring.

7 Get a system with external remote control capabilities so you can turn on your home's system as you approach, check its status when you're away and shut down the house as you leave. Remote controls include telephone and internet-based controls.

8 Look for a system with a "Holiday mode". This tracks your lighting patterns while you're home, and re-creates them when you're away so your house appears to be occupied. Separate programs for weekdays and weekends should be standard.

9 Check out the wireless touch-screen controllers to be sure they are programmable, make sense, and will work anywhere in the house.

10 Install an uninterruptible power supply with your system to maintain service even if the power goes off.

What to Look For

- Fantasy ideas
- Plan that fits your budget
- Compatibility with your existing systems
- Remote access
- "Holiday mode"
- Programmable touch-screen controllers
- Uninterruptible power supply
- Compatibility among products
- Maximum flexibility

Tip

The best time to install a home automation system is when you're in the building or renovation process.

11 If you're looking to combine top-of-the-range products from a variety of vendors, make sure they're compatible with each other before you go ahead.

12 Shop for a system that gives you maximum flexibility. The more preset options there are, the better.

SYSTEM	FACTS AND FEATURES
Lighting Control	• Look for timer that adjusts to seasons. Lights can turn on automatically later in summer than in winter. • An All Off command is useful if you tend to leave lights on. • An All On setting can quickly illuminate the whole house in emergencies. • Scene or Event controls let you create multi-room lighting schemes (for small dinner parties or large-group entertaining) with a single command. • "Light paths" lead from one room to another and can be turned on with one command. • See 206 "Buy a Programmable Lighting System".
Heating	• Automating your central heating can save money on energy costs. • Combined with remote controls, central heating makes sense for holiday homes that get very cold when unoccupied. • It should be easy to switch between home and away settings.
Security	• System should let you monitor and control security cameras and motion detectors remotely, within the house, by telephone or via the internet. • Look for ability to arm or disarm alarm by zones, rather than the whole house. • Remote control–powered curtains or blinds are good for home security, privacy and home cinema rooms.
Audio/video	• See 421 "Buy an Audio/Video Distribution System".
Other Controls	• Systems can control appliances. For example, you can pre-heat the oven as you leave work. • Pools, spas and saunas can be tied into the system. • Temperature sensors can control curtains and ceiling fans to save energy and maintain comfortable rooms.

420 Buy a State-of-the-Art Sound System

If music is important to you – indeed, if you find that your daily life *requires* a soundtrack – then having the best-quality sound may be your top priority. Forget those department-store all-in-one-systems. There's a whole world of upmarket, high-priced audio equipment just waiting for your discriminating ears (and discretionary income).

Steps

1 Let your listening habits and desires be your guide. You should assemble a system that sounds great to you, not a salesperson.

2 Assess your living and work spaces. A system that sounds incredible in a small demonstration room might sound dreadful in a huge loft apartment.

3 Bring your own music when you shop. You'll know the nuances of that music better than demonstration CDs, which are designed to highlight an audio system's strengths.

4 Listen to systems without regard to price range, at least at first. You want to *hear* – if it's perceptible – why prices vary so much. Try to listen to various components in isolation. If you're trying to compare two amplifiers, use the same combination of CD player, CD and speakers during your test.

5 Select a system with separate components (including amplifiers and pre-amps). Each component should have its own power supply to reduce electrical interference between components. Get a power conditioner to further reduce interference.

6 Splurge on speakers, if you're making budget trade-offs. Crank up the music as loud as you're likely to play at home.

7 Shop for a digital audio receiver if you want your stereo to play internet-based music or MP3s from your computer. Digital audio receivers are a new and varied breed of component. Some connect directly to the internet via your broadband connection; others connect via your computer and can access MP3s (or the CD-quality ".wav" or ".aif" files) on your hard drive. They require a network connection in addition to stereo cables (see 404 "Network Your Computers").

8 Buy high-quality cables. It makes little sense to connect top-end audio components with cheap cables. (This is especially important when connecting loudspeakers to a power amplifier.)

9 Link your upmarket audio system into whole-house media and control systems. (See 426 "Buy a Home Cinema System", 419 "Buy a Home Automation System", and 421 "Buy an Audio/Video Distribution System".)

What to Look For

- Separate components
- Power conditioner
- Good-sounding speakers
- Digital audio receiver
- High-quality cables

Tips

Don't be intimidated by any salesman. He or she may be on a commission and so not totally unbiased.

The most expensive system won't necessarily be the best. Remember, what sounds great to one person may sound very average to another.

421 Buy an Audio/Video Distribution System

You've sprung for the home cinema system and kitted out the hi-fi with a 300-CD changer. Now what happens when you're downstairs and want to listen to a CD that's trapped in the player upstairs, or when you're watching a pay-per-view movie in the home cinema but need to cook your dinner? What you need is a whole-house audio/video distribution system.

Steps

1 Count the number of audio and video sources (DVD player, CD player, cable or satellite box, FM receiver) in your current set-up.

2 Determine the number of outputs (rooms or zones in your house) where you want to listen or view.

3 Shop for a controller – the central brain of the system – that can serve your entire house. The cost of the controller will vary depending on the number of inputs and outputs. Most controllers can be linked: if one controller handles six outputs but you have nine zones, you can chain together two six-output controllers.

4 Look for control panels that are sensible and easy to operate. Most systems employ touch-screen pads in each room to control the audio and video, and come with handheld remotes.

5 Look for an internet-enabled system if you listen to internet radio and streaming media. Some systems can work with dial-up connections, but they work much better with broadband. Some will have a built-in hard disk for storing MP3s.

6 Get a system with a built-in intercom if you have a large house. Some systems can alert you when the doorbell rings.

7 Remember that these systems require wiring to each room, so it's easiest to install one while you're building or renovating. If you're installing one in an existing house, hire an experienced contractor (see 242 "Hire a Builder, Plumber, Painter or Electrician"). Audio/video systems can also be tied in to home automation systems (see 419 "Buy a Home Automation System").

What to Look For

- Input/output controller
- Sensible control panels
- Internet radio connectivity
- Hard disk for MP3s
- Intercom
- Extras

Tips

Because of their complexity, audio/video distribution systems are usually installed by the manufacturers. If you want to buy and install your own, you'll probably have to shop online.

Some systems have flashy extras. For example, you can have cover art for the CD or DVD that's playing displayed on an LCD keypad in individual rooms. You can decide if that's worth the money.

422 Buy a Serious TV

Over the past few years, television has made a giant leap into the realm of high fidelity. If you visit even the most modest TV showroom you'll find yourself faced with an almost mind-numbing array of serious, big-screen models, packed to the brim with seemingly exotic features. To the uninitiated this choice can be quite intimidating. So what's the difference between a rear-projection TV and a plasma screen? You'll need to know before you go shopping.

Steps

1 Look at the size of your TV room. The bigger the screen, the further away you'll need to sit for the picture to look good. Here's a simple formula to help you out: multiply the diagonal size of the screen by 3 and 5 to get the optimum viewing distance. Let's take an example using a 30-in (75 cm) screen. (Note: TV screens are always described in imperial measurements.) The ideal viewing distance for a 30-in television screen will be between 225 cm (90 in) and 375 cm (150 in). If you watch from closer than the minimum recommended distance, the picture quality may not appear to be as well defined.

2 Go for a widescreen TV (16:9 aspect ratio), especially if you watch a lot of feature films on DVD.

3 Learn the difference between flat screens and flat panels. Flat-screen TVs have a heavy glass picture tube just like regular TVs, but are flat rather than curved on the front. Flat panels – which include plasma and liquid-crystal displays (LCD) – can be as thin as 9 cm (3.5 in) and can hang on the wall like a picture.

4 Avoid unnecessary duplication. If your viewing set-up includes a cable or satellite box, or a high-fidelity surround receiver and speakers, then look at flat-panel plasma models that have no TV tuner, amplifier or speakers built in. The sound quality possible from "separates" will inevitably be higher than those built in.

5 If you're looking for anything above a 48-in (120 cm) screen, the best results will come from a projector system. This will require a special screen on which the picture is projected. On a pound-per-screen-inch basis, rear-projection TVs – where the image is projected from within the unit onto the rear side of the screen – are the best value. However, they generally provide the lowest resolution, and so can look poor if viewed too closely. Plasma flat-screen models look the most stylish and provide the best pictures on 28- to 50-in (70- to 130-cm) screens.

6 Make sure that your TV has enough audio and video connections for your DVD, digital video recorder, cable, satellite, VCR and other devices.

What to Look For

- HDTV or HD-ready
- Screen size
- Widescreen (16:9 aspect ratio)
- Flat-screen versus flat-panel
- Rear-projection
- Component-video, S-video, or composite-video inputs
- Sufficient audio and video connections

Tips

Nothing ruins the effect of a cool-looking, flat-panel TV like a tangle of wires and cables. If you're going to spend a wad on a top of the range plasma model, run cables and wires inside your walls.

Some projectors designed for computer presentations also have component-video or S-video inputs. With a home cinema system and a blank wall, you've got a ready-made big-screen TV.

Go for a plasma TV if your home cinema is the centre of your entertainment universe. These are the most stylish, the best-viewing and – not coincidentally – the most expensive.

423 Choose Between Digital TV Providers

The revolution in digital television has meant that where only a few years ago most of us had to select our programmes from – at best – five terrestrial channels, we have potential access to any of several hundred channels at the press of button. Digital television reaches our homes via cable or a satellite dish. Which system is best depends on your specific needs.

Steps

1 Contact local cable companies for their price lists – in most areas there will only be one or two providers. For satellite systems, contact Sky TV. Prices range from £10 a month for basic services to £50 a month and more for premium packages. Be aware that companies may have separate costs for hardware – control boxes and/or satellite dishes – and programming. Ask about all the costs, including contract commitments.

2 Satellite systems require a receiver dish to be fixed to the outside of the house. Some find these ugly or offensive – and in some areas or on listed buildings they may not even be allowed.

3 Cable systems are only available if the wiring is already in place in the road outside your home. Your local cable company will tell you if you are already wired up.

4 Check out the channel packages each provider offers. Decide what combination of TV channels, movies and sports is best for your household. There are separate charges for some specialist channels, such as FilmFour or ArtsWorld.

5 Satellite TV generally has better broadcast quality than cable, but is more prone to interference from heavy snow or rain. Also, satellite service requires a south-facing surface on which to mount the dish.

6 If you do your viewing through a high-quality home cinema system ask if modern feature films are broadcast in Dolby 5.1 surround. Note: you may need to buy a different cable or satellite box to pick up such broadcasts.

7 If you have multiple televisions, you may need a cable or satellite box for each one. You may also be required to pay separate subscriptions for each additional unit.

8 Enquire about package deals. The main cable companies also offer telephone and broadband internet services, so if you are an existing subscriber you may be able to get your cable TV packages at reduced prices (see 402 "Choose an Internet Service Provider").

9 For satellite subscribers, for an additional premium, Sky offer packages that include their own digital video recording system, Sky+. (See 424 "Get a Digital Video Recorder").

What to Look For

- Hardware versus programming
- Channel packages
- Regulations about dish installation
- Broadcast quality
- Per-room charges
- Broadband internet packages
- Digital video recorder packages

Tips

If you live in a block of flats, or rented housing you should check with your landlord or freeholder about mounting a satellite dish on the building roof. You shouldn't need such approval to mount a dish on a balcony or patio.

If you want to enjoy digital TV – and by the end of the decade you'll have no choice, since the "terrestrial" analogue systems are going to be switched off – but don't care for the monthly subscriptions, then FreeView is another possibility. You pay a one-off charge for a set-top box, and plug it into your existing TV system. However, the choice is VERY limited when compared to even the most basic cable or satellite package. (Note: FreeView is still not available in all areas – check it out on www.freeview.co.uk.)

424 Get a Digital Video Recorder

With so many channels from which to choose your viewing, it's easy to miss programmes of interest. The good old video cassette recorder is all well and good, but how about an alternative that won't run out of tape five minutes before the end of nail-biting movie? You'll need a digital video recorders (DVR) to do that. Instead of recording onto tape, it records on its own hard drive and can store at least 20 hours' worth of programmes. It's almost like creating your own personal TV channel.

Steps

1 Decide if you want a generic or subscription-based DVR. Generic models are programmed like a VCR: you choose the channel and the viewing time and set the DVR to record. Subscription-based DVRs have many other features, among them the ability to record entire series of programmes, meaning that you'll never again have to miss a single episode of your favourite show.

2 If you decide on a subscription-based DVR, choose between a monthly fee and a one-off charge. The one-off charge is usually cheaper in the long run.

3 Compare the features of a subscription-based DVR with that of a generic DVR. Subscription systems may provide an interactive list of upcoming programmes or intelligently select the shows it thinks you might want to see. A generic DVR is simply a digital version of a video cassette recorder – and hence of considerably higher quality.

4 Compare prices. Subscription-based DVRs run from £150 up to £500, depending on the size of the machine's hard disk (and hence how many hours of viewing it can store). The subscription service can cost a one-off fee of several hundred pounds, or a few pounds per month. The lowest prices are available through package deals with satellite or cable companies.

5 Take a look at the remote. Pausing live TV, doing instant replays, fast-forwarding or creating the David Hasselhoff Channel is fun only if you know how to work the remote.

6 Make sure you have a phone line available near to your DVR. Subscription-based DVRs regularly connect to their service provider to update their software and programming information. Some newer DVRs may also connect via the internet if you have a broadband connection.

7 Get as much recording time as you can afford. A gigabyte of disk space will store about an hour of programming at the lowest-quality resolution; that same hour recorded at the highest quality will use about 4 gigabytes of storage. Most DVRs have a number of quality settings.

8 Look into package deals. Some satellite and cable TV companies sell a bundled TV service with DVRs at reduced subscription fees (see 423 "Choose Between Digital TV Providers").

What to Look For

- Generic or subscription-based
- Monthly fee versus one-time charge
- Onscreen programme guide
- Remote control
- Phone or broadband internet connection
- Disk size
- Package deals with cable or satellite TV

Tips

DVRs are fast becoming internet-enabled. On some models you can adjust your programming choices online; others let you share recorded videos over the internet.

You can copy programmes from DVR to videotape or a DVD recorder. This is handy when your disk fills up (and it will).

If your entertainment centre is tight for space, you can find combination DVR-DVD players on the market.

425 Get a Universal Remote

If your collection of remote controls is getting so big and confusing that only an eight-year-old can sort it out, it's time to shop for a universal remote control unit. There is a good chances that a single device may be able to handle all of your video and audio equipment and reduce the clutter on your coffee table.

Steps

1 List all the remote-control devices in your home. Note the type of device (CD player, TV, VCR) and the manufacturer.

2 You may be able to pick up a fairly basic unit for under £20 in some department stores. Special universal remotes with large, colourful buttons are good choices for the elderly, people with limited vision or other disabilities.

3 Go to a specialist electronics store or shop online if you want something more powerful. Some remotes have LCD screens that change depending on the device you're controlling. Some of the more sophisticated units may even be voice-activated. Prices can go as high as £300.

4 Consult your list to make sure the remote you choose will control all your components. The remote's package should have a chart specifying what brands and types of devices it will control. Alternatively, look on the manufacturer's website.

5 Some universal remote controls are terribly complex to use, and may even require interface with a computer to get the most out of them. Some manufacturers will provide a downloadable copy of the operating manual on their websites – check it out first if you are lacking in technological confidence.

6 Look for a device that lets you program "macros" if you want to simplify lots of complicated gear. Macros can perform a number of functions in sequence with the press of a single button. For example, a home-cinema user might create a macro that turns on the TV, sets it to DVD, turns on the DVD player, turns on the amplifier, sets the volume to level 5, and opens the DVD tray (see 426 "Buy a Home Cinema System").

7 Some units may also be able to handle other automated tasks, such as lights or electronically controlled blinds.

8 Similarly, some remote-control systems can also handle some functions of a universal remote (see 419 "Buy a Home Automation System").

What to Look For

- Department store
- Electronics store
- Online store
- Compatibility with your home-entertainment components
- Macro capability

Tips

If your needs are simple, see if the remote that came with your most recent audio or video purchase can be programmed to support multiple devices. You might save yourself a shopping trip and some money.

Very complex remotes can be attached to a computer for programming.

426 Buy a Home Cinema System

So now you've got a CD player, a DVD and digital video recorder (DVR), a plasma-screen TV and a satellite dish. The perfect way to tie all these media components together is with a state-of-the-art home cinema. Everything from a cheap and cheerful cinema-in-a-box to custom systems costing thousands of pounds is available. Here's how to create the ultimate private screening room.

Steps

1 Take stock of your current components. A home cinema system connects video sources (DVD, VCR, DVR, and cable or satellite boxes), a TV or monitor, and a set of five or six speakers through a home cinema receiver. Many people may also attach audio components (CD and MP3 players) into their receiver. It may be that all you need is a receiver and speakers.

2 Look at your space. If you have a dedicated room for the home cinema, get a more powerful system (measured in watts per channel). For a bedroom, 40 watts is plenty; 40 to 80 watts is good for an average-sized living room. Get at least an 80-watt receiver if you have a large room with high ceilings.

3 Buy a receiver with a minimum of Digital Theater System (DTS) or Dolby Digital. (These are competing, incompatible formats for home cinema sound, although most high-quality receivers can play both.) Avoid receivers that can only handle Dolby Surround or Dolby ProLogic – these are older, inferior systems. Dolby Digital EX and DTS-ES are the next step up. THX is the top of the line, although relatively few films have yet been made that can take advantage of its capabilities.

4 Check out the universal remote that comes with the receiver. You'll want to operate several components with this remote, so make sure it's easy to use and makes sense.

5 Listen carefully to the speakers when you shop. Six speakers make up the ideal home cinema: left and right front-channel speakers, left and right surround speakers, a sub-woofer, and a centre-channel speaker. The centre-channel speaker is probably the most important, since most movie dialogue comes from it. If you're worried about your budget, forgo the sub-woofer.

6 Consider cinema-in-a-box systems if your space is average to small or you're technically challenged. Combining receiver, speakers and cables (and often a DVD player), these systems offer easy installation and operation as well as a smaller price tag. Read up on these systems online or in speciality magazines, since their quality ranges from surprisingly good to very bad.

What to Look For

- Home cinema receiver
- DTS or Dolby Digital
- Universal remote
- Speakers, especially centre channel
- Cinema-in-a-box system

Tips

Got kids? Dolby Digital includes a feature for late-night viewing that plays dialogue and quiet scenes a little louder, and noisy scenes a little quieter.

Always hook up components using connectors that provide the highest-quality signal. For video components, they are (in descending order) component-video, S-Video, composite-video, and antenna/cable inputs. For audio components, they are digital optical, co-axial, and RCA connectors.

427 Buy Virtual-Reality Furniture

You've got the biggest home cinema system, the best video screen, and the fastest game system out there. Take the leap and immerse yourself in the action with a virtual-reality chair or motion simulator. These systems employ a motion track electronically keyed to the movie's soundtrack and literally move you, giving new meaning to the phrase "poetry in motion".

Steps

1 Get a handle on your budget. Choices range from £30 for seat cushions, to digitally controlled platforms (like that of Odyssee Motion Simulator) that cost in excess of £20,000 and will rock the entire sofa.

2 Find out how the furniture connects to the entertainment system. Most virtual-reality chairs are made for video games but will also connect to the speaker jacks of home theatre systems. Just make sure that the person in the chair isn't the only one who can hear the sound.

3 Choose a chair system if you play a lot of video games. Most of these look like high-tech office chairs. They contain an array of speakers to surround you with sound and shake your innards in sync with the game. (If that doesn't sound like fun, you may want to skip virtual-reality furniture altogether.)

4 Rock your world with a sofa-shifting system. Consult with a home cinema specialist, as these require lots of space, extra components for the home cinema and actuators that generate the motion under your furniture.

5 Use the system for a good hour before you buy – watch an entire movie or play your favourite game. This way, the initial surprise of the effect will wear off, and you can decide if it truly enhances your experience.

What to Look For

- Connects to entertainment system
- Virtual-reality chair systems
- Motion-generator sofa systems

Tips

Most virtual-reality furniture isn't available to try out at your local electronics store. That's unfortunate, since this is a product you want to try before you buy. If you buy online, make sure the seller has a good returns policy.

Check out sites such as HighTechHomeTV.com for information on other impossibly cool equipment.

428 Buy Two-Way Radios

Taking the family to a playground, amusement park or camp site and want to stay in contact? Or are you in a remote part of the countryside where no mobile phone signal can reach you? The answer to your prayers could well be a two-way radio system. Cynical? Forget about the old CB radios of the past, there's now a new generation of models that boast a clearer sound, better range and more channels – a far cry from the "walkie-talkies" of old.

Steps

1 Think about usage. Once you've set up a two-way radio system the cost of calls is free. If, however, you're an infrequent user, you might find it more economical to use a mobile phone, or hire a system for the duration.

2 Consider the transmission range. Most systems are limited to a range of about two miles.

3 You no longer need a licence. In 1998 the European Union agreed a number of frequencies – PMR446 – that the general public could use for personal communication. In theory, any radios you buy for use in the UK can be legally used elsewhere in Europe.

4 If you are new to the world of two-way radio, start by looking on the internet for basic information. Type something like "Two-Way Radio FAQ" into Google, or an alternative search engine. (Note: most of the websites you turn up will be based in the US; use this information as a general introduction to the subject since specific systems will not be relevant outside of the US.)

5 Take the range claims of manufacturers with a pinch of salt – walls, hills, trees, people and almost anything else may easily reduce that range.

6 Pick units with a vibrating call feature if you need to remain quiet while you use them.

7 Buy from a specialist radio shop. Trained staff should be able to show you how to set up and use your system, and should provide you with a reliable after-sales service.

8 More experienced users can expect a better deal buying on the internet or from an auction site. HOWEVER: be aware that whilst US FRS and GMRS sets may work in the UK, they are, in fact, illegal. This is because they transmit outside of the EU's agreed PMR446 frequencies. While risk of prosecution may be low, you should be aware that using illegal systems could interfere with frequencies used by the emergency services.

What to Look For

- Hire companies
- PMR446 compliance

Tip

You can add an external antenna to extend the range of some two-way systems.

Warnings

American FRS and GMRS radios are illegal in Europe.

Never say anything on a two-way radio that you wouldn't say in public. They're not secure lines.

429 Buy a Mobile Entertainment System

For better or worse, it seems that nowadays kids want to do more than count cows or play licence-plate bingo on road trips. Fantastic mobile entertainment systems have high-quality video and surround sound.

Steps

1 Look at what you can afford. Mobile entertainment gear ranges from simple, portable units that sit between the seats and plug into the cigarette lighter, to full-blown in-car cinema systems (from £100 to £2,500 and more).

2 Decide between video or DVD units. Most people will want to future-proof their purchase by choosing DVD players.

3 Buy an all-in-one unit or individual components if your budget is small (under £250) and your needs are simple. An all-in-one unit includes a video player (VCP) or a DVD player, speaker and screen. Many electronics retailers carry them.

4 Choose a component system (£400 and up) where a single video source can run several screens, usually liquid-crystal displays (LCDs). The screens can drop down from the car's ceiling or mount in the back of the headrests. Component systems can tap into your vehicle's stereo and pipe sound directly to headphones for quiet viewing. Most quality car stereo retailers will carry these systems.

5 Make sure any component system is expandable, so you can add more or different screens and input devices in the future.

6 Get a double-antenna system – known as a *diversity antenna* – for better TV reception when the car is moving.

7 Make sure your vehicle's electrical system can handle the demands of a mobile entertainment system. You may need a professional installer to determine this.

8 Large four-wheel drives, vans and recreational vehicles can incorporate a back-up camera into the mobile video set-up.

What to Look For

- Video versus DVD
- All-in-one versus components
- LCD screens
- Audio connections
- Expandability
- Diversity antenna
- Back-up camera

Tips

A laptop computer with a DVD drive can serve as an entertainment system for smaller cars with one viewer.

Mobile entertainment systems are theft targets. Invest in a good car alarm (see 546 "Buy a Theft-Prevention Device").

Warning

Front-seat viewing is illegal – not to mention pretty stupid – while a car is in motion.

JCTION SITES • BUY BARGAIN CLOTHING • BUY WHOLESALE • GET OUT OF DEBT • BUY NOTHING • BUY HAPPINESS • BUY A BETTER MOI
JY YOUR WAY INTO SOMEONE'S FAVOUR • BUY LOVE • FIND THE RIGHT RELAXATION TECHNIQUE FOR YOU • BUY HEALTHY FAST FOOD • E
ERVICE • SELL YOURSELF ON AN ONLINE DATING SERVICE • SELL YOURSELF TO YOUR GIRLFRIEND/BOYFRIEND'S FAMILY • BUY FLOWERS
HOOSE FILM FOR YOUR CAMERA • BUY RECHARGEABLE BATTERIES • GIVE TO A GOOD CAUSE • TAKE PART IN A CAR BOOT SALE • EMPLO
TUDENT DISCOUNTS • BUY FLOWERS WHOLESALE • GET A PICTURE FRAMED • EMPLOY A REMOVAL COMPANY • EMPLOY A LIFESTYLE MA
JY FOR A HALLOWE'EN PARTY • BUY A GREAT BIRTHDAY PRESENT FOR UNDER £10 • SELECT GOOD CHAMPAGNE • BUY A DIAMOND • BUY
ET A GIFT LIST • BUY WEDDING GIFTS • SELECT BRIDESMAIDS' DRESSES • HIRE AN EVENTS ORGANISER • HIRE A BARTENDER FOR A PART
JNNOUNCEMENTS • SELL YOUR WEDDING DRESS • BUY AN ANNIVERSARY GIFT • ARRANGE ENTERTAINMENT FOR A PARTY • COMMISSION A
HO HAS EVERYTHING • BUY A GIFT FOR PASSING EXAMS • SELECT A CHRISTMAS TURKEY • BUY A HOUSEWARMING GIFT • PURCHASE CH
MESSAGE IN THE SKY • HIRE A BIG-NAME BAND • GET INTO A PRIVATE GAMBLING ROOM IN LAS VEGAS • BUY SOMEONE A STAR • PAY A F
MPLOY A BUTLER • BUY A FOOTBALL CLUB • BUY A PERSONAL JET • SELECT A CLASSIC CAR • ACQUIRE A BODY GUARD • BOOK A LUXUR
ACE • BUY A RACEHORSE • BUY A VILLA IN TUSCANY • EMPLOY A PERSONAL CHEF • BUY A JOURNEY INTO SPACE • EMPLOY A GHOSTWF
XPERT WITNESS • MAKE MONEY FROM ACCIDENT COMPENSATION • DONATE YOUR BODY TO SCIENCE • MAKE MONEY AS A MEDICAL GUII
LAN FOR RETIREMENT • COPE WITH HIGHER EDUCATION COSTS • BUY AND SELL SHARES • CHOOSE A STOCKBROKER • DAY-TRADE (OR N
FE INSURANCE • GET PRIVATE HEALTH INSURANCE • BUY PERSONAL FINANCE SOFTWARE • CHOOSE AN ACCOUNTANT • FIND CASUAL WO
ARKET YOUR INVENTION • FINANCE YOUR BUSINESS IDEA • BUY A SMALL BUSINESS • BUY A FRANCHISE • LEASE RETAIL SPACE • LEASE
ESIGNER • ACQUIRE CONTENT FOR YOUR WEBSITE • BUY ADVERTISING ON THE WEB • SELL YOUR ART • HIRE A LIFE COACH • SELL ON T
ED-AND-BREAKFAST • SELL A FAILING BUSINESS • BUY A HOT DOG STAND • SHOP FOR A MORTGAGE • GET A BETTER MORTGAGE DEAL
DUSE ONLINE • BUY A PROPERTY FOR RENOVATION AND RESALE • EVALUATE BEFORE BUYING INTO A NEW AREA • EXCHANGE CONTRAC
DUSE DESIGNED • HIRE AN ARCHITECT • HIRE A BUILDER • GET PLANNING PERMISSION • BUY A HOLIDAY HOME • RENT A HOLIDAY HOME
DME FOR A LOCATION SHOOT • FURNISH YOUR HOME • FURNISH YOUR STUDIO FLAT • BUY USED FURNITURE • BUY DOOR AND WINDOW
JY FLOOR-CARE APPLIANCES • BUY EXTENDED WARRANTIES ON APPLIANCES • FIND PERIOD FIXTURES • BUY A BED AND MATTRESS • HI,
RNISH • CHOOSE DECORATIVE TILES • CHOOSE A DEHUMIDIFIER • BUY A WHIRLPOOL BATH • BUY A SHOWER • BUY A TOILET • CHOOSE
OVE • SELECT FLOORING • SELECT CARPETING • CHOOSE KITCHEN CABINETS • CHOOSE A KITCHEN WORKTOP • BUY GREEN HOUSEHO
ONOXIDE DETECTORS • BUY FIRE EXTINGUISHERS • CHOOSE AN ENTRY DOOR • BUY A GARAGE-DOOR OPENER • BUY TIMBER FOR A DIY
RFECT ROSE • BUY FLOWERING BULBS • BUY FLOWERS FOR YOUR GARDEN • SELECT PEST CONTROLS • BUY SOIL IMPROVERS • BUY N
EW LAWN • BUY A LAWN MOWER • BUY KOI FOR YOUR FISH POND • BUY A STORAGE SHED • HIRE A TREE SURGEON • BUY BASIC GARDE
ND SELL AT FARMERS' MARKETS • SELECT KITCHEN KNIVES • DECIPHER FOOD LABELS • SELECT HERBS AND SPICES • STOCK YOUR KITC
JY ORGANIC BEEF • BUY HAGGIS • PURCHASE LOCAL HONEY • CHOOSE A CHICKEN • SELECT FRESH FISH • SELECT RICE • PURCHASE F
RTISAN CHEESES • PURCHASE KOSHER FOOD • BUY SENSIBLY IN SUPERMARKETS • CHOOSE COOKING OILS • SELECT OLIVE OIL • SELEC
DFFEEMAKER OR ESPRESSO MACHINE • PURCHASE PARTY BEER • CHOOSE THE RIGHT WINE • CHOOSE A REAL ALE • ORDER A COCKTAI
T • PICK A PREGNANCY TEST KIT • CHOOSE BIRTH CONTROL • CHOOSE WHERE TO GIVE BIRTH • HIRE A MIDWIFE OR DOULA • PLAN A HC
R RENT A BREAST PUMP • CHOOSE A CAR SEAT • BUY CHILD-PROOFING SUPPLIES • FIND RELIABLE CHILDCARE • FIND A GREAT NANNY
-FRIENDLY HOTEL • ORGANISE A FUND-RAISING EVENT • BUY BRACES FOR YOUR KID • BUY TOYS • BUY BOOKS, VIDEOS AND MUSIC FC
LOTHES AND BOOKS • FIND A COUPLES COUNSELLOR • HIRE A FAMILY SOLICITOR • BUY OR RENT SHELTERED HOUSING • CHOOSE A CA
ND ANTIWRINKLE CREAMS • SELECT PAIN RELIEF AND COLD MEDICINES • CHOOSE A COMPLEMENTARY MTHERAPY • SEE A MENTAL-HEA
JY A WIG OR HAIRPIECE • BUY A NEW BODY • GET A TATTOO OR BODY PIERCING • OBTAIN BREAST IMPLANTS • GET WRINKLE-FILLER INJ
ERSONAL TRAINER • SIGN UP FOR A YOGA CLASS • TREAT YOURSELF TO A DAY AT THE SPA • BOOK A MASSAGE • GET ON ANTIQUES ROA
DUR COLLECTIBLES ARE WORTH • BARTER WITH DEALERS • GET AN ANTIQUE APPRAISED • BUY SILVERWARE • EVALUATE CARNIVAL GLA
QUIDATE YOUR BEANIE BABY COLLECTION • SCORE AUTOGRAPHS • TRADE YU-GI-OH CARDS • SEIZE STAR WARS ACTION FIGURES • SEL
ARD COLLECTION • CHOOSE A DESKTOP COMPUTER • SHOP FOR A USED COMPUTER OR PERIPHERALS • CHOOSE A LAPTOP OR NOTEB
ROVIDER • GET AN INTERNET DOMAIN NAME • NETWORK YOUR COMPUTERS • UPGRADE THE MEMORY IN YOUR COMPUTER • BUY COMF
GITAL ASSISTANT • CHOOSE A MOBILE PHONE SERVICE • GET A BETTER DEAL FROM YOUR PHONE COMPANY • BUY VIDEO AND COMPUT
-THE-ART SOUND SYSTEM • BUY AN AUDIO/VIDEO DISTRIBUTION SYSTEM • BUY A SERIOUS TV • CHOOSE BETWEEN DIGITAL TV PROVID
ADIOS • BUY A MOBILE ENTERTAINMENT SYSTEM • GET A PASSPORT, QUICK! • PURCHASE CHEAP AIRLINE TICKETS • FIND GREAT HOTEL
RANS-SIBERIAN EXPRESS • BUY DUTY-FREE • SHIP FOREIGN PURCHASES TO THE UNITED KONGDOM • TIP IN A FOREIGN COUNTRY • TIP
CKAGE FOR THE GREEK ISLANDS • RAFT THE GRAND CANYON • BOOK A CHEAP BUT FANTASTIC SAFARI • RENT A CAMEL IN CAIRO • GE
DNG KONG • BUY YOUR WAY ONTO A MOUNT EVEREST EXPEDITION • HIRE A TREKKING COMPANY IN NEPAL • RENT OR BUY A SATELLITE
BUY GOLF CLUBS • SELL FOUND GOLF BALLS • BUY PORTS SHOES • BUY A RACKET • BUY A HEALTH CLUB MEMBERSHIP • BUY AN AER
CATES • GO BUNJEE JUMPING • GO SKYDIVING • BUY WEIGHTLIFTING EQUIPMENT • CHOOSE A CAR RACK • BUY SKIS • BUY CLOTHES FC
BUY CYCLE CLOTHING • BUY A PROPERLY FITTING HELMET • BUY THE OPTIMAL SLEEPING BAG • BUY A TENT • BUY A BACKPACK • BUY
JY A CASHMERE JUMPER • PURCHASE VINTAGE CLOTHING • SELL USED CLOTHING • ORDER CUSTOM-MADE COWBOY BOOTS • BUY CL
)R A MAN • BUY A MAN'S DRESS SHIRT • PICK OUT A TIE • BUY A WOMAN'S SUIT • BUY A MAN'S SUIT • HIRE A TAILOR • BUY CUSTOM-T.
ERFORMANCE SWIM SUIT • BUY PERFORMANCE WORKOUT CLOTHES • BUY A HEART-RATE MONITOR • SELECT A WATCH • BUY KIDS' CLC
R SELL A CAR ONLINE • BUY A HYBRID CAR • SELL A CAR • BUY A MOTORCYCLE • BUYING AND CHANGING MOTOR OIL• WASH A CAR •

Travel

430 Get a Passport, Quick!

You've just been invited on an all-expenses-paid foreign trip, but the departure date is next week and your passport expired last year. What to do?

Steps

1 Get an passport application form at a post office. Although application forms can be downloaded from the UK Passport Service website (passport.gov.uk), online applications may take up to four weeks.

2 Fill in the application form in black ink. Obtain two identical passport photos at a photo booth or photographer's. The photos need to be 45 x 35 mm (1¾–1⅓ in). They can be colour or black-and-white and should be on a light background with your face fully visible. Spectacles are allowed.

3 Make an appointment at the nearest passport office to you by phoning the Passport advice line on 0870 521 0410. There are offices in Belfast, Durham, Glasgow, Liverpool, London, Newport and Peterborough.

4 Decide which service you need to use to obtain your passport. The Premium service is a one-day service and costs £89; it is not available for first passports or those that are being replaced if lost, stolen or damaged. The Fast Track service guarantees that your passport will be returned to you by first-class post within one week of submission and costs £70.

5 Check that you have filled in your form correctly and supplied all the documents requested – any incomplete information or missing documents are likely to cause a delay.

What to Look For

- Passport photos
- Nearest passport office
- Airline tickets or itinerary
- Expired passport
- Additional fees

Tips

Always include your departure date and travel plans on your passport application.

Some countries require that your passport be valid at least six months beyond the end date of your trip.

Check whether or not you will need to apply for a visa before you travel.

Someone else can collect a passport for you if you use the Premium service, but they must take evidence of their identity and a letter of authorisation signed by you.

Warning

If using the Premium service, check the latest time for an appointment to guarantee you receive your passport the same day – usually this is before lunchtime.

431 Purchase Cheap Airline Tickets

Passengers on the same flight rarely pay the same price for their tickets. Numerous factors determine ticket prices, but the surest way to get the best deal is to be thorough, flexible and know where to shop.

Steps

1 Be thorough. Don't rely just on travel websites for the best deal; call airlines and travel agents, and ask about promotional fares from major airlines or those just starting up. Look for internet specials on websites of budget airlines such as EasyJet (easyjet.com), Ryanair (ryanair.co.uk) and bmibaby (bmibaby.com). Airlines start up and get taken over at quite a rate so browse your Sunday newspaper's travel section and major travel magazines for the latest information.

2 Be flexible. Avoid peak holiday months and school holidays, buy as far in advance as possible, or last-minute, fly midweek and at anti-social hours, and stay over on Saturday night. Better yet, put your holiday on standby until a fare war erupts.

3 Research all the major online travel agencies such as ebookers.com, Expedia.co.uk, Travelocity.co.uk, opodo.co.uk and lastminute.com. Each has a unique arrangement with the airlines and may offer different fares on the same flights. Each site also offers numerous package deals and last-minute bargains that change daily.

4 Book your flight as part of a travel package that includes car hire and hotel accommodation. Such deals are sold in bulk to tour operators who resell them to the public at prices that are usually far less than standard à la carte rates. Most major airlines offer their own holiday packages.

5 Consider the name-your-own-price ticket providers, such as Priceline.com. You can save up to 40 per cent over the lowest published airfares, but it's not without risk: the exact airline, flight times and routes may not be disclosed to you until after you've purchased your tickets: think red-eye and stopovers.

6 Purchase from a consolidator or "bucket shop" – a wholesaler that buys discount tickets in bulk. It's an excellent resource for cheap international tickets. Your Sunday newspaper's travel section is the best source for consolidator fares, but they're often nonrefundable or have brutal cancellation penalties.

7 Look into courier flights, where companies hire a courier (you) and use your excess baggage allowance for their time-sensitive business cargo (see 436 "Fly for Next to Nothing").

What to Look For

- Promotional discount fares
- Small and regional airlines
- Fare wars
- Package deals
- Last-minute bargains
- Holiday packages
- Internet rates
- Consolidators
- Courier flights

Tips

Many charter operators sell their discount holiday packages only through travel agents, so don't rely solely on web-based fares.

Try to book a ticket in its country of origin. For instance, if you're planning a one-way flight from Paris to Rome, a France-based travel agency will probably offer the lowest fares.

Warning

Lowest-price fares often require one to three weeks' advance purchase, are non-refundable, require a certain length of stay, and carry stiff penalties for changing dates and destinations.

432 Find Great Hotel Deals

To find a deal on a hotel room, be thorough, be flexible, and know where to look and what to ask. The steepest price a hotel charges for a room is likely to be in high-season, when the hotel demands a standard price for a room *sans* discounts. Your goal is to get well below that inflated figure with package deals, low-season rates and savvy bargaining.

Steps

1 Plan your holiday well in advance and during the low-season when hotel rates are far cheaper – up to 50 per cent – due to less demand. Call the hotel and ask for the exact day its low-season rates start. Timing is everything.

2 Call the hotel and ask about package deals, promotions and special discounts for pensioners, students or family rooms. When you're quoted a rate, ask if less expensive rooms are available.

3 Book your room via the web: many hotels offer discounts for commission-free online transactions. Major online agencies, such as CheapHotelBookings.com, uk.hotels.com, Expedia.co.uk and Travelocity.co.uk, have special arrangements with thousands of hotels, offering room rates you can't get on your own.

4 Ask if kids stay free if you're travelling with your family. Find out if the rooms have kitchens – you'll save a fortune by preparing your own meals.

5 If you're very flexible about the type and location of a hotel, let name-your-own-price online travel agencies such as Priceline.com do the haggling for you. You save up to 40 per cent on published room rates, but there's a catch: the hotel, room, exact location and rate are not disclosed to you until after your room is already charged to your credit card (however, they usually come pretty close to meeting your requests).

What to Look For

- Low-season rates
- Package deals
- Special discounts
- Internet rates
- Family rates
- Online travel agencies

Tip

If you're staying at a hotel for longer than seven days, haggle for one free night per week or ask about weekly rates.

Warning

Beware of hidden costs. Taxes, surcharges, resort fees and "incidental" fees tacked on to your bill are common and rarely mentioned until you check out, so be sure to ask if there are *any* extras charges on the agreed room rate. If they are tacked on without your prior approval, refuse to pay them.

433 Hire the Best Car for the Least Money

Thousands of hire cars go unused every day – a good reason to drive a hard bargain. Car reservation agents rarely volunteer money-saving suggestions, but if you follow this advice, you could save hundreds on your next car hire.

Steps

1 Make a reservation online through one of the major car hire companies. It's by far the easiest and cheapest way to rent a car either locally or internationally. Just about every car hire website offers internet-only discounts (about 10 per cent) and upgrades as well as various special offers. Compare deals before you hire.

What to Look For

- Internet discounts
- Upgrades
- Online travel agencies
- Package deals
- Special discounts

2 Hire through a name-your-own-price online travel agency such as Priceline.com, particularly if you're not choosy about the car. These agencies will get the best deals with the car hire companies for you, including upgrades and unlimited mileage. Note: once your request is accepted, you can't cancel or change your reservation or get a refund.

3 Search for package deals. Fly-drive holiday packages offer huge discounts on car hire. Many online travel agencies also offer fly-drive discounts as well. Avoid reserving a hire car through an airline. It's convenient, but you rarely get the best deal.

4 Ask for more discounts that may apply to you, even when you think you've scored the best deal: being a member of a motoring organisation, or a frequent-flier programme, or being a pensioner may qualify you for a special discount.

434 Get Travel Insurance

Travel insurance includes trip-cancellation insurance and 24-hour emergency assistance. It helps you get your money back if, for example, you have to cancel your holiday or go home early. It's a smart purchase if you've planned a major holiday well in advance, but the trick is knowing which policy to buy, if any.

Steps

1 Check your existing insurance policies and credit card coverage before you buy travel insurance. You may already be covered for medical expenses, cancelled tickets or lost luggage.

2 Decide which type of travel insurance is best suited for your destination (for example, emergency medical rescue insurance during an ocean cruise). Keep in mind that the cost varies widely, depending on your age, your health, and the cost and length of your trip. Holidays including particular sports may require additional specialised insurance.

3 Determine whether the following is included in your policy: international medical insurance, emergency medical rescue (including helicopter transport), accidental death or bodily injury, repatriation of remains, and family travel benefits.

4 Have your travel agent purchase an insurance plan for you or shop commission-free online. You'll find a wide selection of reputable insurance companies on the web that can get you a policy within 24 hours.

5 Make sure your travel insurance provider offers a 24-hour hotline service. Don't buy trip-cancellation insurance from the tour operator that may be responsible for the cancellation, and don't overbuy – you won't be reimbursed for more than the cost of your trip.

Tip

If you've been asked to return the car full of fuel, always fill it up yourself or you'll get landed with a service charge to have the hire company fill it for you – at an inflated price per litre.

Warning

If you don't have car insurance, you'll need to buy it from the hire company.

What to Look For

- Baggage loss/delay insurance
- Personal accident
- Personal liablility
- Cancellation/curtailment
- International medical insurance
- Emergency medical evacuation
- Accidental death
- Repatriation of remains
- Family travel benefits
- 24-hour hotline service

Tip

Many travel-related injuries and thefts are not fully covered by your credit card company, home or medical insurance.

Warning

Read the small print to make sure your cruise line or airline is on the list of carriers covered in case of bankruptcy.

435 Pick the Ideal Luggage

Few things are more worthless and frustrating than a cheap piece of luggage that falls apart during your holiday. It's crucial to invest in quality luggage that can withstand a baggage handler's bad day. Somewhere out there is your dream luggage set.

Steps

1 Consider where you're going and what you're packing before you shop for new luggage. This will determine the quantity and size of luggage you'll need.

2 Determine your budget before you shop. This will help steer you in the direction of quality luggage brands you can afford. A reputable luggage shop or department store that specialises in all types of luggage will give you advice based on your budget and travel needs.

3 Decide whether you want soft or hard-case luggage. Heavier, hard-sided suitcases offer far better protection for fragile items (if packed properly). Soft luggage is lighter.

4 If you choose a roll-along model, look for heavy-duty wheels (some have durable in-line skate wheels) and a sturdy base.

5 When buying soft luggage, check the denier of a fabric, a measurement that refers to the fineness of the yarn. Generally speaking, the higher the denier the more durable the fabric.

6 Look for a quality zip that's heavy-duty enough to support the weight the bag was designed to hold. Critical seams and attachment points for webbing should be securely oversewn.

7 Make sure the bag fits airlines' approved carry-on size. Most bags within the 61 x 35.5 x 23 cm (24 x 14 x 9 in) size restriction are considered legal on all planes.

8 Choose a size that's appropriate for the length of your trip. Keep in mind the possibility of needing to accommodate unexpected items or expand for a longer trip.

What to Look For

- Prices in your budget
- Reputable luggage shop
- Soft case or hard case
- Heavy-duty wheels
- Expandability
- Denier of fabric
- Appropriate sizes

Tips

Look for luggage that isn't too heavy to carry long distances. For larger suitcases, a difference of 2.3 kg (5 lb) or less doesn't matter much in the overall weight of a fully packed bag.

Consider a colour other than black. Brightly coloured luggage stands out better on the airport carousel.

The majority of airlines allow bags up to 18 kg (40 lb).

Warnings

Is the pull-out handle protected? It won't work if the shaft gets bent.

If you unintentionally buy a cheap imitation, the warranty is also likely to be fake.

LENGTH OF TRIP	SUGGESTED LUGGAGE SIZE
1 to 3 days	56 cm (22 in) upright-wheeled carry-on
3 to 7 days	61 cm (24 in) suitcase
7 to 14 days	66 to 69 cm (26 to 27 in) suitcase
14 to 21 days or longer	74 to 76 cm (29 to 30 in) suitcase

436 Fly for Next to Nothing

Aching for an exotic holiday but short on funds? Drastically discounted fares can be yours if you're willing to travel solo and work for a courier. Complete a few simple tasks, save yourself hundreds of pounds.

Steps

1 Decide where and when you'd like to go. The main destinations from London are Bangkok, Miami, New York, Sydney and Tokyo.

2 Find a courier company. Contact the major flight courier companies or find recommendations through an organisation such as the International Association of Air Travel Couriers (aircourier.co.uk).

3 Be prepared to offer a deposit for your flight and pay the remainder when you collect the ticket. You can save 50–75 per cent of the cost of the ticket, sometimes more at short notice.

4 Book at least two weeks ahead, more at busy holiday times, to get the flight you want. Call the airline a few days ahead of your flight to verify your reservation and request a seat assignment. Your stay is often for 14 days, or longer by arrangement. You will usually be required to act as a courier on the return trip.

5 Pack sparingly. You may have the normal baggage allowance or may be restricted to one item or hand luggage only.

6 Deliver your package at your destination as agreed, then you are free to do as you wish until the return flight.

What to Look For

- Reputable courier companies
- Carry-on bag

Tips

Couriers must join a courier organisation such as the International Association of Air Travel Couriers.

Ask about earning frequent-flier miles.

There is only one courier seat per courier company on each flight.

437 Take a Trip on the Trans-Siberian Express

One of the world's greatest train journeys, this trip takes you from Moscow, through Russia and Mongolia to Beijing (or vice versa).

Steps

1 Start your research on the internet, visiting sites such as transsiberian.co.uk and some of the sites that give a forum for travellers' experiences – these can be a source of good, up-to-date information. Get hold of a copy of *The Trans-Siberian Handbook* by Bryn Thomas (Trailblazer Publications, 2003).

2 Decide in which direction you want to travel and how long you want your trip to be. The basic train journey takes six days, but with stops along the way your trip can be extended considerably. Apply for your visas – you'll need Russian, Chinese and Mongolian visas to do the whole trip, and if you are visiting other countries on the way there or back check their visa requirements.

3 Price varies hugely according to whether you are travelling independently on a budget or as part of a luxury package or something in between. It also rises in high season (June to September).

What to Look For

- Websites and books
- Visa requirements
- Length of trip and route to and from the Trans-Siberian

Tips

If comfort is a priority, travel first class.

For budget travellers, it is often much cheaper (and many say tastier) to eat from the station food vendors rather than in the restaurant carriage.

438 Buy Duty-free

Duty-free allowances vary widely on items such as perfume, currency, cameras, and agricultural material. For travel to and from non-EU countries, it's easy to save on the world's two favourite vices: alcohol and tobacco.

DESTINATION	ALCOHOL LIMIT	TOBACCO LIMIT
Argentina	2 litres	400 cigarettes and 50 cigars
Australia	1 litre	250 cigarettes or 250 g tobacco/cigars
Brazil	2 litres	400 cigarettes and 250 g tobacco and 25 cigars
Canada	1 bottle wine/spirits and 24 bottles beer	200 cigarettes and 50 cigars and 200 g tobacco
Chile	2.5 litres	400 cigarettes and 500 g tobacco and 50 cigars
China	2 litres	400 cigarettes
Egypt	1 litre	200 cigarettes or 25 cigars or 200 g tobacco
Hong Kong	1 bottle wine/spirits	200 cigarettes or 50 cigars or 250 g tobacco
India	1 litre	200 cigarettes or 50 cigars or 250 g tobacco
Japan	3 bottles	200 cigarettes or 50 cigars or 250 g tobacco
Kenya	1 bottle	200 cigarettes or 50 cigars or 225 g tobacco
Morocco	1 bottle	200 cigarettes or 50 cigars or 250 g tobacco
New Zealand	4.5 litres	200 cigarettes or 50 cigars or 250 g tobacco
Peru	3 litres	400 cigarettes or 50 cigars or 50 g tobacco
Philippines	2 litres	400 cigarettes or 50 cigars or 250 g tobacco
Russia	1.5 litres spirits and 2 litres wine	1000 cigarettes or 1 kg tobacco
Singapore	1 litre spirits, and 1 litre wine and 1 litre beer	No tobacco to be brought into Singapore
South Africa	1 litre spirits and 2 litres wine	400 cigarettes and 50 cigars and 250 g tobacco
South Korea	1 litre	200 cigarettes or 50 cigars or 250 g tobacco
Taiwan	1 litre	200 cigarettes or 25 cigars or 450 g tobacco
Thailand	1 litre	200 cigarettes
Turkey	700 ml wine/spirits	200 cigarettes or 50 cigars or 200 g tobacco
United States	1 litre	200 cigarettes and 100 cigars
Venezuela	2 litres	200 cigarettes and 25 cigars
WARNING	Be sure to stay within the allowance limits set by the country you're heading to next and keep a lid on your purchases – or you might have some explaining to do at customs.	

Duty-free allowances have been abolished on journeys within the EU; you simply pay the duty rates of the country from which you are travelling as long as the goods bought are for personal use or as a gift. The limits set as reasonable for personal use are:

Alcohol: 90 litres wine; 10 litres spirits; 20 litres intermediate products (e.g. fortified wine); 110 litres beer. Tobacco: 800 cigarettes or 400 cigarillos or 200 cigars or 1000 g tobacco.

439 Ship Foreign Purchases to the United Kingdom

Byzantine might be the best word to describe the process of shipping purchases to the United Kingdom. Every country has its own confusing set of shipping regulations, and then you have to factor in duty, taxes and customs fees. Cramming the item in your luggage is your best bet; otherwise, follow these steps and hope for the best.

Steps

1 Many shops abroad are happy to arrange wrapping and shipping for you for a fee. This may seem expensive at the time, but can often take a lot of the hassle and legwork out of the process.

2 Wrap your purchase as carefully as possible to avoid breakage. Write on the postal address clearly (don't forget to write *UK* below the postcode). You may need to fill in a Customs declaration; if not, mark the outer wrapping with (1) the contents' identity, (2) the retail value and (3) whether the package is for personal use or a gift (this determines the exemption limit).

3 Send the purchase via the nearest large post office. International shipping companies such as Federal Express (fedex.com) and UPS (ups.com) are available in most countries (check before you leave the UK), but you pay a steep premium for their services. Be sure to ask about insurance for valuable items.

4 Be prepared to pay a duty fee for your package when you return home. HM Customs raise a charge on all packets arriving from abroad for which duty must be paid. These customs charges and a clearance fee are collected from the addressee by Royal Mail upon delivery.

5 Keep all receipts for items you buy overseas: You might need them to solve potential problems with customs. If you feel you've been charged too much duty on a package sent from abroad, you may file a complaint with the HM Customs.

What to Look For

- Post office or shipping company
- Insurance
- Duty fees upon return

Tips

Some countries waive the sales tax on items that you ship home.

Warnings

Be especially careful when shipping wildlife souvenirs (possibly illegal), and antiques that could be construed as national treasures. At best you could be detained and fined; at worst, arrested.

Beware: no matter what a foreign postal employee or store owner may tell you, you cannot prepay duty fees.

440 Tip in a Foreign Country

When you're abroad, tipping can be a perplexing experience: in some countries it's expected, in others it's an insult – and the rules are constantly changing. As corporate mentality replaces traditional ideology (that the honour of providing hospitality is reward itself), tipping etiquette has become more mainstream.

COUNTRY	GRATUITY PROTOCOL
Australia and New Zealand	Round up taxi fares and restaurant bills to nearest dollar.
Austria	Service charges generally included in bill.
China and North Korea	Tipping is illegal.
Czech Republic	Round up the bill to nearest koruna.
France and Germany	Service charges generally applied to bills; customary to add 5 per cent extra.
Hong Kong	Tipping is common – about 10 per cent in most situations – even when a service charge has already been applied.
Hungary	10 per cent tip is customary.
Indonesia	Service charges are usually included in bill.
Israel	Restaurants and hotels typically add 10 per cent service charge to bills; otherwise, tipping not expected.
Italy	Tipping is customary, about 10 per cent, even when a service charge is already included.
Japan	Tips are usually included in hotel and restaurant bills; otherwise, tipping is not expected.
Malaysia	Tipping is expected for porters and room service.
Mexico	Tipping is customary, about 10 to 15 per cent. Service charges rarely applied.
Philippines	10 per cent tip is common for most services.
South Korea	Tipping is not expected.
Spain	Offer a 10 to 15 per cent tip even when service charges have been added.
United States	Tip at least $1–$2 for most personal services.
WARNING	Double-check the tipping protocol at South Pacific and Asian hotels. Many prohibit tipping to prevent staff from hustling guests for money.

441 Tip Properly in the UK

Holidaymakers and business travellers using larger hotels often ask "How much should I tip?" when they are on their home territory. The answer is complex when you consider various protocols around the world, but general rules do apply. Commit these tipping tips to memory to avoid getting either fleeced or forgotten.

Steps

1 Don't tip if it's not deserved. You're essentially buying good service, and if it's not earned it shouldn't be rewarded. You're only promoting poor service habits and wasting money.

2 Tip above the norm for two reasons: if service is exceptional, and if you plan on returning to the hotel or restaurant in the future. Big tippers are rarely forgotten by the staff.

3 Tip discreetly. There's an art to passing money: fold the note three times, cup it in your palm with your thumb, and hand it to the staff member with a casual handshake while saying, "Thank you".

4 Tip big when first checking into a hotel to assure better service throughout your stay.

Tips

When in doubt, tip. Failure to tip – or not tipping enough – can have dire consequences to your holiday, from lost luggage to slow restaurant and room service.

See 440 "Tip in a Foreign Country".

SERVICE	TIPPING CONVENTION
Airport Porters	£1 per bag for normal sizes, £2 per bag for large or heavy items.
Chauffeurs	10 to 15 per cent of fare.
Cloakroom	£2 to £4 upon retrieval.
Hotel Concierges	£10 to £20 depending on the complexity of the service – theatre tickets, restaurant reservations, tour bookings, last-minute arrangements.
Hotel Door Persons	£2 for summoning a taxi by phone, £1 for hailing from street, £2 to £4 if they opened the door for you each time you entered and left the hotel.
Hotel Porters	£1 to £2 per bag, £5 minimum.
Housekeeping Staff	£2 to £5 per night, paid daily or as a sum at checkout.
Parking Valets	£2 to £5 for parking and delivery.
Restaurant and Bar Service	15 to 20 per cent of the total bill.
Room Service	£5 minimum.
Taxicabs and Hotel Courtesy Cars	10 per cent of fare. Add £1 per bag placed in boot.

442 Bribe a Foreign Official

Take a shortcut through a minefield, and you'll either get where you're headed sooner or end up wishing you'd never left home. Bribing an official is a lot like that. In many developing countries an unofficial travel "tax" is *de rigueur*. Although every bribery situation is unique, there are a few universal rules you'll want to follow to successfully negotiate a mutual agreement.

Steps

1 Verify that bribery is customary in the country you'll be travelling through. The X-rated magazine you proffered up to get you past a Mexican army checkpoint would get you imprisoned in some Muslim countries. Travel guidebooks are typically good sources of information about dealing with foreign officials.

2 Determine who is in charge before offering a bribe. If you deal with anyone other than the superior, you may offend him and create a face-losing confrontation. Be extremely careful not to insult or upset anyone.

3 Identify exactly what the problem is. If you're in violation of some law, ask to pay the fine on the spot. If you're carrying something they want, offer some of it. Your ultimate goal is to agree with the official on both the problem and a mutually beneficial solution.

4 Offer a legitimate explanation for the bribery to put a veneer of legality to the situation. For example, say that you're afraid the fine will get lost in the mail and that you'd rather pay the proper authorities right now. The way in which you offer a bribe is sometimes more important than the bribe itself.

What to Look For

- Local bribery traditions
- The official in charge
- Exact problem
- Speedy solution
- Legitimate explanation

Tip

Carry small amounts of US currency to offer as bribes. Offer cash first, then other items.

Warning

Only reveal the amount of money you're willing to part with. If you show the official £500, the fine will most likely be £500. Hide the bulk of your money along with all valuable personal items.

443 Get an Interrail Pass

An Interrail Pass lets you travel like a local to almost every corner of Europe – up to 28 countries, to be exact. The problem is figuring out which of the many Interrail Pass options best suits your travel plans.

Steps

1 Decide which countries you want to visit and how long you plan to travel, then choose which type of Interrail Pass best complements your itinerary. Countries are grouped into eight zones (the UK is not included in any of the zones), and you can purchase one-, two-, three-, or all-zones for your Interrail Pass.

2 Determine if you will be on the train overnight or be needing to get somewhere quickly. An Interrail Pass is for 2nd-class travel and does not include sleeper cars or high-speed rail (TGV). An additional payment and reservation is required in most cases.

What to Look For

- Multiple-country deals
- Sleeping arrangements
- Interrail.com
- Special fares

Tip

The Interrail Pass is available only to European citizens or those who have lived in Europe for at least six months. If you do not qualify for an Interrail Pass you can apply for a Eurail pass

3 Log onto the Interrail website (Interrail.com), or if you wish to compare other passes try europeanrailguide.com. You can obtain all the information you need about the various types of passes and can order online.

4 Find out about special fares for those under the age of 26 as discounts are considerable. Children aged from 4 to 11 pay about half the price of an adult (over 26) ticket.

5 Purchase your pass online using a credit card. Allow two or three business days for standard delivery. Passes can also be sent overnight for an additional fee. Have a nice trip!

Warning

There are myriad quirky rules and limitations that apply to each type of Interrail Pass. Be sure to carry a list of all the rules that apply to your pass at all times.

444 Take an Italian Cycling Holiday

If sweating your way through *la bella Italia* is your idea of a good time, you're in luck: dozens of companies offer packaged bicycle tours throughout Italy. But to pick the one that best fits your interests, you'll need to do your homework.

Steps

1 Start by asking yourself these questions: Where in Italy do I want to ride? During what season? In what type of terrain? What distance, pace and level of difficulty am I comfortable with? How much am I willing to spend?

2 Make an honest assessment of your riding skills and endurance. Most trips cater for the out-of-shape tourist (hence the full-time van support); this means a lot of waiting around. If you're a strong rider, a more challenging tour operator such as Cycle Italia would be a better match.

3 Cruise the web. Type "Italian cycling holiday" in a search engine and spend a few hours shopping for the tour outfits that best suit your requirements.

4 Call and ask these questions: What's the typical riding day like in terms of duration and difficulty? What is the accommodation like? How much experience does the tour leader have? Is transport from the airport provided? What's the leader-to-client ratio? What's not included (for example, meals, bikes and helmets)? Is there a maximum number of people? Will the trip be cancelled if not enough riders sign up? Will there be van support? Are marked maps and written route instructions included? How many days do riders actually ride?

5 Budget in tips for your guides along with other trip expenses. Ten per cent is standard; 15 per cent will reward superior service.

6 *Pedala forte, mangia bene.* (Ride hard, eat well.)

What to Look For

- Suitable level of challenge
- Experienced leader
- Bike hire/transport costs
- Extra costs
- Full-time van support
- Desired accommodation

Tips

The more challenging itineraries – 70 to 140 km (45 to 85 miles) per day on varied terrain – tend to be the most scenic and least crowded.

Call or visit a local bike club for tour company recommendations.

Warning

Check the daily itinerary for the word *transfer*, a euphemism for a requisite van, bus or train ride to your next destination. Make sure these transfers are few and brief.

445 Choose a Cheap Cruise

Cruising is one of the fastest-growing segments of today's suffering travel industry. Hard times for the travel trade spell lower prices for the budget-minded passenger seeking a great deal. Packages offering a wide range of activities and destinations are now easy to find.

Steps

1 Ask about theme packages that are tailored for your lifestyle (single, pensioner, gay and lesbian). If it's going to be a family affair, ask about money-saving family discount packages.

2 Look for departures close to home. Many cruise line companies are adding departures from new ports to drum up more business, which cuts airfare expenses for you.

3 Book early – or late. Cruise lines are eager to make bookings far in advance and to fill up last-minute cancellations. If your schedule is flexible, you may find even hotter deals at the last minute.

4 Use a cruise-only travel agent. These agents have access to the best deals on the lines they do the most business with. A good agent will also recheck prices close to the departure date and refund part of your money if the rate has gone down. Some fares are so low that the agents aren't allowed to publicise them; you have to ask if they're available.

5 Budget for tips to shipboard waiters and service personnel. Ships often have suggested amounts, depending on cruise length.

6 If you've got some time on your hands, book a slow boat to China – on one of 150 freighters worldwide that accept passengers. Voyages last for 21, 45, even 90 days, cost the actual fares charged by the shipping lines with no margin added, and offer many amenities. Visit FreighterWorld.com.

What to Look For

- Theme trips
- Family discount packages
- Departures nearest you
- Last-minute bargains
- Reputable cruise-only agent
- Freighters

Tips

It's wise to purchase cruise insurance to protect you and travelling companions (see 434 "Get Travel Insurance").

Stick with your favourite lines; many offer special discounts for repeat customers.

Warning

Port fees are often not included in advertised prices and can add significantly to your cruise cost.

446 Book a Hotel Package for the Greek Islands

There are a multitude of gorgeous Greek isles to choose from when planning an Aegean island-hopping excursion, not to mention the many hotels and resorts on each. With the right amount of research, you'll be swilling ouzo and yelling "Opa!" in no time.

Steps

1 Work out when you want to go and how long you'd like to stay. Factors such as climate, public holidays and political crises (skip a Greek refuse strike) are important considerations.

2 Choose which islands you'd like to explore on your trip by researching what each island has to offer. If you've never been to

What to Look For

- Optimum travel periods
- Reputable travel agent
- Web-based discount packages

Greece before, spend at least a few days touring the glories of Athens before you hit the islands.

3 Surf the internet for package options or hire a reputable travel agent who specialises in trips to Greece to book your package.

4 Contact the hotel(s) directly before you arrive to be sure that all your arrangements are in correct order, especially if you've booked your trip through a travel agent, no matter how reputable.

Tip

It's wise to purchase travel insurance for international holidays (see 434 "Get Travel Insurance").

447 Raft the Grand Canyon

Rafting the Colorado River through the Grand Canyon is one of North America's greatest adventures. The wet 'n' wild ride is an expensive thrill, however, so be sure to choose wisely when hiring a rafting outfitter. Here's what you need to know.

Steps

1 Plan the trip at least a year in advance. Most of the rafting trips through the Grand Canyon book quickly – National Park regulations allow a limited number of boats through the canyon each season – and require a deposit. If you can't plan that far in advance, go standby and ask the rafting outfitters to call you if there's an opening. The Colorado's water releases are controlled, so the best rafting conditions are typically in the spring (April) and autumn (September and October).

2 Review your budget – you may be draining more than your raft every day. Costs run at a minimum of £140 per person per river day. (All food and nonalcoholic beverages are included.) Add more for travel to and from, tips, hotels and alcohol.

3 Choose from four types of watercraft: oar rafts (the guide does all the work), paddle rafts (you paddle and the guide steers), motorised rafts (long raftlike boats with a specialised outboard motor), and traditional dories (charming 5.2-m/17-ft wooden boats that carry three passengers and a guide). Hybrid trips, where you paddle one day and rest the next, are also available.

4 Scrutinise potential outfitters. Visit the websites of commercial rafting companies licensed to run the Grand Canyon, then call them, ask for brochures and grill the staff. Where possible, try contacting previous clients via e-mail or phone numbers provided by rafting companies.

5 Expect to spend 6 to 16 days: six to seven days for Upper Canyon trips, nine days for Lower Canyon trips, and 13 to 16 days for full-canyon trips. Rapids range from class I to V; however, Grand Canyon water levels are based on the water being released from Lake Powell through the Glen Canyon Dam.

What to Look For

- Advance planning
- Advance deposit policy
- Last-minute cancellations
- Unexpected costs
- Boat types
- Websites and brochures

Tips

You don't need to know how to swim to take a rafting trip, but you do need to let your guide know if you can't swim.

Include in your budget tips for your guides. They're doing the work because they love it, certainly not for the pay. Ten per cent is standard; 15 per cent will reward superior service.

Warning

If you get tossed from the raft, *never* attempt to stand up: if your foot gets wedged between rocks, you could drown.

448 Book a Cheap but Fantastic Safari

There are hundreds of safari companies competing for your business, which means incredible deals await the savvy safari hunter armed with a computer. Be aware of the political climate in any destination country before booking your trip.

Steps

1 Get a clear idea of the type of safari you'd like to experience, from viewing Egypt from camelback to touring a Kenyan wild game preserve to camping in Australia's famed Outback. Begin by researching safari companies on the internet.

2 Settle on where and when you'd like to go based on the type of safari you've chosen. Be sure to take the regional climate into account. High-season prices vary dramatically from low-season rates, which correspond with seasonal weather conditions.

3 Work out whether you'd like to be part of an organised tour or if you'd prefer a tailor-made tour. Money-saving packages are often available depending on how you book your safari.

4 Decide on the type of accommodation, service, transport and food you'd like to experience on your safari. Consider how much roughing it you're willing to do before you plan your adventure. If the lodge sounds like your cup of tea, check the amenities.

5 Determine what you can realistically afford, and bear in mind that you will get what you pay for. Generally speaking, a budget safari runs from as little as £45 to as much as £100 per person per day.

6 Consult with travel agents who specialise in adventure travel. They can find the deals you're looking for and offer more specific safari information than a general travel agent would.

What to Look For

- Locations and climate
- Package deals
- Organised versus tailor-made safaris
- Adventure-travel agents

Tips

Staying at a hotel or a beach resort is often less expensive than a safari camp.

If you really want to splurge on location, transport, accommodation and food, safaris can add up to thousands of pounds.

Travel insurance is often mandatory for safaris (see 434 "Get Travel Insurance").

Warning

Before traveling to Africa and Asia, contact your local GP or travel immunisation centre for recommended vaccines and immunisations.

449 Rent a Camel in Cairo

Planning to visit Egypt's capital and Great Pyramid of Giza? The absolute best way to soak in this wonder of the ancient world is on the back of a camel – a truly Egyptian experience. But there are a few rules you should follow when hiring a camel and guide.

Steps

1 Rent your camel just outside the entrance to the Giza Plateau. Alternatively, you can pick up a camel behind the Sphinx once you're inside the Plateau.

2 Expect to pay about 25 Egyptian pounds (£2.50) per person plus tip for a camel. It's customary to pay after you return with the camel.

What to Look For

- Healthy-looking camels
- Clean stables
- Recommended guide

Tip

Choose a calm, clear day for a camel ride. Desert sunsets behind the pyramids are breathtaking.

3 Check out the condition of the camels before you rent one. Sadly, it's normal for the camels to appear undernourished, but they should not have sores or look beaten. Also, the stables in which they are kept should appear clean. If you're not satisfied, move on to the next spot.

4 Tip your guide between 5 and 10 pounds (50 pence to £1). The only people who get out of tipping are those who ride on their own camels.

Warning

Hire a recommended guide in advance. Dubious guides have a tendency to hassle unaccompanied travellers.

450 Get Single-Malt Whisky in Scotland

What could be more pleasant than delving into the fine art of single-malt whisky tasting while you're on a trip to Scotland. What wine tasting is to Bordeaux, whisky sipping is to Scotland – so much so that an entire tourism industry is built around Scottish whisky tours.

Steps

1 Plan a tour of Scotland's distilleries. If you just want to buy single-malt, you'll get a great choice in Scotland, although you're unlikely to save any money on prices elsewhere in the UK. Visit the scotchwhisky.net website for lots of good background information and a list of distilleries.

2 Get hold of some books, such as *Michael Jackson's Malt Whisky Companion* (Dorling Kindersley) and the *Collins Gem Whisky* (Collins), and try the *Collins Whisky Map of Scotland* (Collins).

3 Using the books, website and map, plot a course among the dozens of distilleries open to the public throughout Scotland, particularly on Islay and in the regions of Speyside, Scotland's famed malt whisky country.

4 Look into one of the many organised tours of Scotland's distilleries that include lodging, meals and transport. Taking such a tour is often the only way to get a real behind-the-scenes look into traditional distillery techniques and sample rare Scotches.

5 Join the Scotch Malt Whisky Society (smws.com). If you're a die-hard Scotch lover, fork out the membership fee and join the worldwide fraternity of single-malt Scotch whisky connoisseurs. Privileges include access to The Vaults, a 19th-century members-only whisky lounge in Leith, the historical port of Edinburgh.

What to Look For

- Scotland distillery guidebooks
- Organised distillery tours
- Private whisky clubs

Tips

Plan your trip to coincide with one of Scotland's many whisky festivals, such as the Spirit of Speyside Walking Festival held each May.

451 Buy a Sapphire in Bangkok

Gem scams have ruined the holidays of many a visitor to Thailand. Before you set out shopping, read 63 "Buy Coloured Gemstones". Then consult the Thai Gem and Jewelry Traders Association's information booklet (thaigemjewelry.or.th), which lists reputable stores and members of the association.

Steps

1 Determine your budget before you shop – it will give you a good foundation for your shopping negotiations.

2 Explore the wholesale jewellery market on Mahesak Road just off Silom. Here you'll find Thai, Chinese, Iranian, Israeli and Indian dealers who import and export cut stones.

3 Compare gem quality and prices at several stores before you buy, and never feel rushed in your decision. The educated buyer gets the best deals, especially in a place where negotiation is critical.

4 Pay a fair price by negotiating with the knowledge you've gained from comparison shopping. Nearly all jewellery shops negotiate, so always ask for a "special discount" on the quoted price.

5 Know what you're buying and purchase your sapphire with a credit card so that you can cancel payment if you've been defrauded. Gem receipts should always be marked "Subject to identification and appraisal by a registered gemologist".

6 Carry your sapphire home with you rather than having it shipped.

What to Look For

- Wholesale market
- Competitive prices
- Quality stones
- Credit card protection

Tip

If you intend to make a sizable purchase, ask the jeweller to accompany you to a facility for an independent appraisal.

Warning

For every reputable gem dealer, there are hundreds of crooks waiting to snare you. The Tourism Authority of Thailand receives more than 1,000 complaints a year about fake jewellery.

452 Hire a Rickshaw in Rangoon

Whether you call it a rickshaw, trishaw or pedicab, a ride on one of these historic cycles offers much more than just a way of getting from A to B. Travel in a virtual time machine that adds an exotic element to your trip to Rangoon (Yangon), the rickshaw capital of the world.

Steps

1 Decide where you're going and for how long. Rickshaw drivers can go the distance, but a bus may be more comfortable for long trips.

2 Find your rickshaw along the outer edge of the city. You can hail one just as you would a taxi. Otherwise, step up to a rickshaw stand and put your order in.

3 Bargain for your fare in advance. You can charter a rickshaw for a full day for about 400 to 500 kyat (£36 to £45) and less for shorter trips around town, but you must bargain.

What To Look For

- City perimeter
- Rickshaw stands
- Good deal

Tip

Rickshaws are not allowed in the central area of Rangoon during the daytime.

453 Take Salsa Lessons in Cuba

Anyone can take salsa lessons at the local gym or village hall, but only the truly inspired make the pilgrimage to the Mecca of salsa – Cuba. The ardent salsa afficionado can easily book dance lessons from home and land in Havana a few days later.

Steps

1 Evaluate your salsa skills before arranging your trip. This will help you enrol in the most appropriate class for your level. If you don't know salsa from the macarena, take a few lessons before you go to be one step ahead when you arrive.

2 Book an "educational" excursion to Cuba through a travel agent who features salsa dancing. Several travel companies offer packages designed exclusively for those in search of salsa lessons during their visit.

3 Get to Cuba. Avoid travelling via the US as direct travel from the States to Cuba is currently prohibited.

4 Ask your hotel concierge for the best discotheque that offers salsa lessons. Arrive early to catch a few expert tips before the crowds arrive to show off their moves.

What to Look For

- Educational excursions
- Salsa lessons at discotheques

Tip

Although travel restrictions in Cuba are relaxing, virtually all visitors require a Cuban visa or tourist card, which is available through the Cuban government.

454 Buy a Camera in Hong Kong

Cameras may be a bit cheaper in Hong Kong, but if you don't shop wisely, you may end up paying the difference in headaches. Visit the Hong Kong Tourist Association office in Tsim Sha Tsui at the Star Ferry Pier and ask for its brochure. The Hong Kong Tourism Board website (hkta.org) lists recommended shopping areas and stores.

Steps

1 Make specific decisions about what brand and model of camera you want to buy. Researching on the internet is a fast and effective way to make informed decisions.

2 Check the prices among different shops at home as well as in Hong Kong to know whether you're getting a good deal.

3 Shop at Hong Kong's reputable establishments. To help discern which retailers are reputable, look for the Quality Tourism Services Scheme symbol of quality on shop display windows.

4 Visit Stanley Street in the Central District. This is where local professional photographers shop.

5 Get a proper receipt. If you're not satisfied with your camera, you'll have an easier time returning it with a receipt than without.

What to Look For

- Specific brands and models
- Reputable stores
- Stanley Street
- Receipt

Tip

Shop early for the best prices. Chinese merchants consider the first sale of the day to be very important and will offer special prices just to make that first sale.

455 Buy Your Way onto a Mount Everest Expedition

So you want to climb the world's highest mountain? It's just spooky how easy it is to sign on with an Everest expedition. In fact, you can join an expedition in minutes via the web. Essentially all you need is a lot of cash and rudimentary mountaineering experience. It's prudent to get your affairs in order first: many climbers – even experienced ones – die on Everest each year.

Steps

1 Stump up at least £35,000 in cash, most of which has to be wired to the expedition company's bank account before you start the 62-day journey. Might as well write your will while you're at it.

2 Get in the best shape of your life and join as many serious mountaineering climbs as possible. There are numerous companies offering mountaineering clinics. Whether a climbing team will take you on depends on your skills and value as a team member.

3 Choose an ascent route. Everest's southeast ridge on the Nepal side is the classic first ascent route. Less technical and dangerous than the northern Tibetan route, it's usually more expensive.

4 Make sure the expedition's guides are highly trained and have serious Everest experience. Numerous companies will take your money and your word that you have the skills and stamina to summit. Just fill out an online trip application form (scary, eh?).

5 Watch out for hidden costs such as rubbish disposal (£2,200 per team), entry visa, oxygen and regulator, Sherpa and porter tips, extra yaks and customs duty for all your gear.

6 Buy at least £30,000 in emergency medical insurance in case you need to be helicoptered out.

What to Look For

- Large cash reserves
- Mountaineering experience
- Physical stamina
- Highly experienced guides
- Hidden costs

Tips

Purchase accident insurance before you depart, particularly for helicopter evacuation and rescue. Travel and trip cancellation insurance is highly recommended as well (see 434 "Get Travel Insurance").

Check with your doctor what vaccinations are needed well before you go.

Everest summit expeditions typically depart in late March and late August.

See 344 "Write a Living Will".

456 Hire a Trekking Company in Nepal

OK, so summitting Everest is out of the question, but trekking to Base Camp (5,300 m or 17,388 ft)? Now you're talking. If you don't book a trip with an adventure travel company and instead choose to do it all yourself, here's what's involved.

Steps

1 Figure out exactly where in Nepal you'd like to explore and with whom you will be trekking. The person in your group with the least mountaineering skills and weakest physical condition determines which regions everyone can safely explore together.

2 Determine how many days you want – and can afford – to trek. You can find trekking packages that offer short or longer treks based on your interests and financial commitment.

What to Look For

- Physical limitations
- Online trekking companies
- Prebooked space
- Insurance and liability

Tips

In high-season base camp can be packed; consider less-frequented regions.

3 Get recommendations from personal contacts. Talk to people who have been there, ask if they enjoyed the trip, what route they took and how the food was. Find out which companies ran the trip. Browse through some of the many books on the topic.

4 Plan your trek with the size, fitness level, and interests of trip members in mind as well as the size of the crew, number of porters and desired comfort level. Trail accommodation ranges from tents to comfy tea house lodgings.

5 If just one or two of you need reservations in a prebooked group trek, inquire about cancellations. In the high season – October to December – this may be the only way openings are available in Nepal.

6 Be sure to buy travel insurance that includes at least £30,000 in emergency medical evacuation insurance. Then if you need to be helicoptered out of the mountains (the only other way out is to get carried on someone's back), you can repay the trekking company (up to £6,000) by credit card, then place a claim with your insurance (see 434 "Get Travel Insurance").

A trekking permit is required for all Himalayan destinations and may be obtained only in Nepal. Pick one up at the Immigration Offices in Kathmandu or Pokhara.

Budget in tips for your crew. Ten per cent is standard.

Warning

Get into shape well before your trek starts. Flat trails are rare in Nepal: the mountains are steep and require strong legs and good lungs.

457 Rent or Buy a Satellite Phone

Purchasing a satellite phone is very much like shopping for the best mobile phone plan, just much more expensive – sky high, you might say. First choose a satellite phone, then a provider, then a plan. Or the smarter move may be just to rent one for your off-the-grid odyssey.

Steps

1 Choose between buying a new or used satellite phone or just renting one. For example, a top-of-the-range Motorola 9505 handheld unit is about £1,100 new, £800 used, and £10 a day to rent. If you're heading to an ultra-remote location, be sure to bring along a solar-powered battery charger (about £30).

2 Choose a provider. Satellite telecommunications companies such as Iridium, Globalstar, Thuraya and Inmarsat offer competitive plans and varied coverage zones.

3 Make sure the provider you choose offers service to wherever you're headed. Thuraya, for example, offers coverage of Africa and Asia, which some other networks do not.

4 Choose a plan that best suits your needs. Like mobile phone plans, satellite phone companies offer package deals, prepaid SIM cards and airtime, and free e-mail and text messaging.

5 Shop online for the best price. There are dozens of satellite phone retailers offering very competitive package deals.

What to Look For

- Buying versus renting
- Noncoverage zones
- SIM card plan
- Package deals

Tips

Don't confuse Global System for Mobile Communications (GSM) mobile phones with satellite phones that offer cellular service. GSM phones don't use a satellite network.

Most satellite phone rental companies require a one-week minimum rental period and a large deposit. Call charges and insurance can be steep.

CTION SITES • BUY BARGAIN CLOTHING • BUY WHOLESALE • GET OUT OF DEBT • BUY NOTHING • BUY HAPPINESS • BUY A BETTER MOUS
JY YOUR WAY INTO SOMEONE'S FAVOUR • BUY LOVE • FIND THE RIGHT RELAXATION TECHNIQUE FOR YOU • BUY HEALTHY FAST FOOD • B
RVICE • SELL YOURSELF ON AN ONLINE DATING SERVICE • SELL YOURSELF TO YOUR GIRLFRIEND/BOYFRIEND'S FAMILY • BUY FLOWERS T
OOSE FILM FOR YOUR CAMERA • BUY RECHARGEABLE BATTERIES • GIVE TO A GOOD CAUSE • TAKE PART IN A CAR BOOT SALE • EMPLOY
DENT DISCOUNTS • BUY FLOWERS WHOLESALE • GET A PICTURE FRAMED • EMPLOY A REMOVAL COMPANY • EMPLOY A LIFESTYLE MAN
Y FOR A HALLOWE'EN PARTY • BUY A GREAT BIRTHDAY PRESENT FOR UNDER £10 • SELECT GOOD CHAMPAGNE • BUY A DIAMOND • BUY
A GIFT LIST • BUY WEDDING GIFTS • SELECT BRIDESMAIDS' DRESSES • HIRE AN EVENTS ORGANISER • HIRE A BARTENDER FOR A PARTY
NOUNCEMENTS • SELL YOUR WEDDING DRESS • BUY AN ANNIVERSARY GIFT • ARRANGE ENTERTAINMENT FOR A PARTY • COMMISSION A
RSON WHO HAS EVERYTHING • BUY A GIFT FOR PASSING EXAMS • SELECT A CHRISTMAS TURKEY • BUY A HOUSEWARMING GIFT • PURCH
AND • WRITE A MESSAGE IN THE SKY • HIRE A BIG-NAME BAND • GET INTO A PRIVATE GAMBLING ROOM IN LAS VEGAS • BUY SOMEONE A
TIMES • EMPLOY A BUTLER • BUY A FOOTBALL CLUB • BUY A PERSONAL JET • SELECT A CLASSIC CAR • ACQUIRE A BODY GUARD • BO
EYHOUND TO RACE • BUY A RACEHORSE • BUY A VILLA IN TUSCANY • EMPLOY A PERSONAL CHEF • BUY A JOURNEY INTO SPACE • EMPL
RTUNE • HIRE AN EXPERT WITNESS • MAKE MONEY FROM ACCIDENT COMPENSATION • DONATE YOUR BODY TO SCIENCE • MAKE MONEY
ANCIAL ADVISER • PLAN FOR RETIREMENT • COPE WITH HIGHER EDUCATION COSTS • BUY AND SELL SHARES • CHOOSE A STOCKBROKE
SS INSURANCE • BUY LIFE INSURANCE • GET PRIVATE HEALTH INSURANCE • BUY PERSONAL FINANCE SOFTWARE • CHOOSE AN ACCOUNT
E OUT A PATENT • MARKET YOUR INVENTION • FINANCE YOUR BUSINESS IDEA • BUY A SMALL BUSINESS • BUY A FRANCHISE • LEASE RE
BSITE • HIRE A GRAPHIC DESIGNER • ACQUIRE CONTENT FOR YOUR WEBSITE • BUY ADVERTISING ON THE WEB • SELL YOUR ART • HIRE A
BLISH YOUR BOOK • START A BED-AND-BREAKFAST • SELL A FAILING BUSINESS • BUY A HOT DOG STAND • SHOP FOR A MORTGAGE • GE
USE AT AUCTION • SHOP FOR A HOUSE ONLINE • BUY A PROPERTY FOR RENOVATION AND RESALE • EVALUATE BEFORE BUYING INTO A N
A PLOT OF LAND • HAVE YOUR HOUSE DESIGNED • HIRE AN ARCHITECT • HIRE A BUILDER • GET PLANNING PERMISSION • BUY A HOLID
ROAD • BUY TO LET • RENT YOUR HOME FOR A LOCATION SHOOT • FURNISH YOUR HOME • FURNISH YOUR STUDIO FLAT • BUY USED FUR
JY HOUSEHOLD APPLIANCES • BUY FLOOR-CARE APPLIANCES • BUY EXTENDED WARRANTIES ON APPLIANCES • FIND PERIOD FIXTURES
ME • SELECT PAINT, STAIN AND VARNISH • CHOOSE DECORATIVE TILES • CHOOSE A DEHUMIDIFIER • BUY A WHIRLPOOL BATH • BUY A SHO
LLPAPER • BUY A WOOD-BURNING STOVE • SELECT FLOORING • SELECT CARPETING • CHOOSE KITCHEN CABINETS • CHOOSE A KITCHEN
OKE ALARMS • BUY CARBON MONOXIDE DETECTORS • BUY FIRE EXTINGUISHERS • CHOOSE AN ENTRY DOOR • BUY A GARAGE-DOOR OP
DOOR FURNITURE • BUY THE PERFECT ROSE • BUY FLOWERING BULBS • BUY FLOWERS FOR YOUR GARDEN • SELECT PEST CONTROLS
OMATIC WATERING SYSTEM • START A NEW LAWN • BUY A LAWN MOWER • BUY KOI FOR YOUR FISH POND • BUY A STORAGE SHED • HIP
DDUCE • CHOOSE A PERFECT PEACH • BUY AND SELL AT FARMERS' MARKETS • SELECT KITCHEN KNIVES • DECIPHER FOOD LABELS • SE
FECT BURGER • PURCHASE A CHRISTMAS HAM • BUY ORGANIC BEEF • BUY HAGGIS • PURCHASE LOCAL HONEY • CHOOSE A CHICKEN
TRUFFLES • BUY ARTISAN BREADS • BUY ARTISAN CHEESES • PURCHASE KOSHER FOOD • BUY SENSIBLY IN SUPERMARKETS • CHOOS
ER A GREAT CUP OF COFFEE • BUY A COFFEEMAKER OR ESPRESSO MACHINE • PURCHASE PARTY BEER • CHOOSE THE RIGHT WINE • C
RM • CHOOSE AN OVULATION PREDICTOR KIT • PICK A PREGNANCY TEST KIT • CHOOSE BIRTH CONTROL • CHOOSE WHERE TO GIVE BIR
BABY CLOTHES • CHOOSE NAPPIES • BUY OR RENT A BREAST PUMP • CHOOSE A CAR SEAT • BUY CHILD-PROOFING SUPPLIES • FIND F
A GARDEN PLAY STRUCTURE • FIND A FAMILY-FRIENDLY HOTEL • ORGANISE A FUND-RAISING EVENT • BUY BRACES FOR YOUR KID • B
A MODEL • SELL USED BABY GEAR, TOYS, CLOTHES AND BOOKS • FIND A COUPLES COUNSELLOR • HIRE A FAMILY SOLICITOR • BUY OR
CHASE A TOOTHBRUSH • BUY MOISTURISERS AND ANTIWRINKLE CREAMS • SELECT PAIN RELIEF AND COLD MEDICINES • CHOOSE A CO
DUCTS • BUY WAYS TO COUNTER HAIR LOSS • BUY A WIG OR HAIRPIECE • BUY A NEW BODY • GET A TATTOO OR BODY PIERCING • OBT
LECT SPECTACLES AND SUNGLASSES • HIRE A PERSONAL TRAINER • SIGN UP FOR A YOGA CLASS • TREAT YOURSELF TO A DAY AT THE
IQUE MARKET • BUY AT AUCTION • KNOW WHAT YOUR COLLECTIBLES ARE WORTH • BARTER WITH DEALERS • GET AN ANTIQUE APPRAIS
AN ANTIQUE QUILT • BUY FILM POSTERS • LIQUIDATE YOUR BEANIE BABY COLLECTION • SCORE AUTOGRAPHS • TRADE YU-GI-OH CARD
RTS MEMORABILIA • SELL YOUR FOOTBALL-CARD COLLECTION • CHOOSE A DESKTOP COMPUTER • SHOP FOR A USED COMPUTER OR F
PHERALS • CHOOSE AN INTERNET SERVICE PROVIDER • GET AN INTERNET DOMAIN NAME • NETWORK YOUR COMPUTERS • UPGRADE T
A VIDEO RECORDER • CHOOSE A PERSONAL DIGITAL ASSISTANT • CHOOSE A MOBILE PHONE SERVICE • GET A BETTER DEAL FROM YOU
A HOME AUTOMATION SYSTEM • BUY A STATE-OF-THE-ART SOUND SYSTEM • BUY AN AUDIO/VIDEO DISTRIBUTION SYSTEM • BUY A SER
UAL-REALITY FURNITURE • BUY TWO-WAY RADIOS • BUY A MOBILE ENTERTAINMENT SYSTEM • GET A PASSPORT, QUICK! • PURCHASE C
NEXT TO NOTHING • TAKE A TRIP ON THE TRANS-SIBERIAN EXPRESS • BUY DUTY-FREE • SHIP FOREIGN PURCHASES TO THE UNITED KO
OOSE A CHEAP CRUISE • BOOK A HOTEL PACKAGE FOR THE GREEK ISLANDS • RAFT THE GRAND CANYON • BOOK A CHEAP BUT FANTAS
SA LESSONS IN CUBA • BUY A CAMERA IN HONG KONG • BUY YOUR WAY ONTO A MOUNT EVEREST EXPEDITION • HIRE A TREKKING COM
E BRACES • CHOOSE RUGBY PROTECTION KIT • BUY GOLF CLUBS • SELL FOUND GOLF BALLS • BUY PORTS SHOES • BUY A RACKET • E
A SKATEBOARD AND PROTECTIVE GEAR • BUY SKATES • GO BUNJEE JUMPING • GO SKYDIVING • BUY WEIGHTLIFTING EQUIPMENT • CH
TS • BUY A BICYCLE • BUY AN ELECTRIC BICYCLE • BUY CYCLE CLOTHING • BUY A PROPERLY FITTING HELMET • BUY THE OPTIMAL SLE
FISHING GEAR • BUY ROCK-CLIMBING EQUIPMENT • BUY A CASHMERE JUMPER • PURCHASE VINTAGE CLOTHING • SELL USED CLOTHIN
THES AT A DISCOUNT • CHOOSE A BASIC WARDROBE FOR A MAN • BUY A MAN'S DRESS SHIRT • PICK OUT A TIE • BUY A WOMAN'S SUIT
THES • GET A GREAT-FITTING BRA • CHOOSE A HIGH-PERFORMANCE SWIM SUIT • BUY PERFORMANCE WORKOUT CLOTHES • BUY A HEA
THE BASICS FOR YOUR CAR • BUY A USED CAR • BUY OR SELL A CAR ONLINE • BUY A HYBRID CAR • SELL A CAR • BUY A MOTORCYCL

Sports & Outdoor Recreation

458 Buy Your Child's First Cricket Bat

Buying the right bat is essential for any youngster who intends to develop skills at the crease. Give plenty of time and thought to the purchase – and learn to treat the bat right after you have bought it.

Steps

1 Decide what you can afford to pay. Junior bats range from about £25 to over £100.

2 Go to a reputable sports shop or the sports section of a big department store. Don't buy a bat without the person who is going to use it having held it in their hands.

3 Choose a bat of the right size. If the top of the handle is level with the top of your child's thigh, it is the right size.

4 Choose a bat of the right weight. Have your child try holding the bat with the top hand only – the left hand for a right-hander. If he or she can comfortably execute strokes such as a drive or a hook one-handed, the bat is the right weight.

5 Have the child practise a few strokes holding the bat with both hands. Does the grip feel comfortable? Does the balance of the bat – the weight distribution – suit?

6 Ask the salesperson about the size of the "sweet spot" – the area of the bat's face where the ball is struck with maximum effect. A larger sweet spot gives a higher chance of successful strokeplay.

7 Buy linseed oil at the same time that you purchase the bat. Oil the bat as soon as you get it home. When the oil has soaked in, oil it a second time.

What to Look For

- Right weight
- Right size
- Comfortable grip
- Good weight balance
- Large "sweet spot"

Tips

Buy a bat with a "toe guard". This protects the bottom edge of the bat from damage through frequent contact with the ground.

"Knock in" a new bat by striking it repeatedly with a soft mallet or old cricket ball for a half an hour a day during the first ten days after purchase.

459 Order a Strip for a Football Team

You may not play like Real Madrid or Arsenal, but you can look like true professionals if your team turns out in a well chosen strip. Choose carefully, because your efforts will be on display all season.

Steps

1 Select a supplier. Sports shops may provide team strips. If not, visit websites such as footballkit.co.uk to search for what you want. Make sure the supplier can arrange an appropriate delivery deadline before the start of your season. Ask for a price guarantee and any bulk-order discounts that apply.

2 Agree on a strip with the rest of the team members, choosing from those on offer. Know the strips of all other teams in your league to avoid conflicts.

3 Create a form that lists each player's name and number, shirt, shorts and sock sizes. Distribute to all team members to fill out.

What to Look For

- Delivery-date guarantee
- Price guarantee
- Large-order discounts
- Team colours

4 Set a deadline for returning both form and money. You'll need to make final decisions on styles and fabrics, subject to availability.

5 Decide if you want any special features, such as badges or logos, on the strip. Some suppliers will offer a range of logo designs to choose from, but you can create your own artwork and present that to the supplier to use.

6 Get out on the field and practise so that your football looks as good as your kit!

Tips

Expect suppliers to be very busy at the start of the season, so order early.

Ask if you can get a bulk rate if you buy a change strip at the same time.

460 Buy Ankle and Knee Supports

Preventing knee and ankle injuries is simple – never leave your armchair. For most of us, that's not an option, nor is it good for our health. But you can stay active and protect yourself with a few precautions. Modern supports provide an impressive amount of lightweight protection.

Steps

1 Determine what type of support you need. The following can be purchased at sports equipment shops, orthopaedic suppliers and chemists'.

- Knee braces provide lateral support while allowing full flexion and extension. They also protect against hyperextension, which is a common cause of major knee ligament injuries. Those with a hole for the kneecap can supply some pain relief. Hinged neoprene supports (from about £60) with extension stops offer compression and are best for protecting previously injured knees. Knee straps (£15 and upwards) relieve pain and pressure caused by an irritated kneecap by helping the kneecap track correctly.

- The best types of braces for stabilising the ankle provide good lateral support. Most sports ankle injuries occur when the ankle is rolled inward. Lace-up ankle supports slip on like a sock with laces to provide rigid side-to-side support while allowing freedom of motion. There are also rigid, plastic ankle braces with air-filled bladders that can be adjusted to provide varying degrees of support. Fitted with figure-8–shape elastic that wraps around the ankle and is designed to fit into sports shoes they provide excellent support and free range of motion.

2 Get a custom-built brace. Usually requiring a referral from an orthopaedist, these braces are given to post-operative or injured patients. Using a plaster mould of your knee or ankle, a rigid brace is constructed allowing the maximum safe range of motion while preventing unwanted lateral movement. It needs to be fitted by a doctor or nurse.

What to Look For

- Fit
- Lightweight or rigid
- ·Custom-built

Tips

By itself, an athletic support is a second-best solution. The best idea is to strengthen the problem area through appropriate exercises, which in the long run may eliminate the need for a support entirely.

Be sure to see your doctor about any injuries.

Verify that your sport allows participants to wear supports. Some sports do not allow certain kinds.

461 Choose Rugby Protection Kit

The time was when rugby players prided themselves on taking to the field with no more defence against bone-jarring impacts than a shirt, a pair of shorts and, if you were lucky, a thick head of hair. Now more sensible attitudes prevail. Buy yourself some protection.

Steps

1 Use a mouthguard if you want to keep your teeth. It will also give some protection to your head and jaw. Mouthguards are sold in packs of ten, retailing at around £15 a pack.

2 Buy a lightweight headguard, tagged as "IRB Approved". The IRB is the International Rugby Board. Its website, irb.com, provides a list of approved headguards. Expect to pay at least £25–£30 for a basic model.

3 Protect your shoulders and torso with padding. This usually comes in the form of a lightweight undervest. Again, this must conform to IRB regulations. Visit irb.com for a comprehensive list of approved products. Prices are in the £25-£40 range.

4 Wear shinpads (£10–£15) and forearm guards (about £15) if you want extra protection.

5 Protect vulnerable points on the body with special supports (see 460 "Buy Ankle and Knee Supports").

What to Look For

- Mouthguard
- Shoulder pads
- Headguard

Tip

The best defences against injury at rugby are a high state of fitness and good technique. Exercise regularly and train thoroughly.

462 Buy Golf Clubs

There are two schools of thought about golf clubs. You can buy a cheap set and then blame the clubs when you miss, or buy an expensive set and look good while you miss. Joking aside, even a beginner will benefit from the right clubs. Golf is a demanding game, and if you're going to make the effort, give yourself every advantage.

Steps

1 Experiment with different clubs before you buy by hiring or borrowing a set from a reputable golf store.

2 Find the right shaft length. Shaft length affects the feel of the club, but most players will fit an off-the-shelf club. If you have questions or are exceptionally short or tall, find a knowledgeable shop willing to match you to a shaft length. If necessary, ask if they have clubs made specifically for children.

3 Know the various clubs and how they are sold. Because it is important that they match, irons are sold as sets, usually consisting of the 3, 4, 5, 6, 7, 8 and 9 irons and a pitching wedge. For a basic set expect to pay about £150. Woods may be sold individually or in sets. A set, consisting of a driver, a 3 wood and a

What to Look For

- Knowledgeable shop
- Comfortable putter
- Perimeter-weighted or bladed clubs

Tips

Do not buy expensive balls at first. You'll lose many of them.

Unless you're planning to always ride in a buggy, look for a lightweight golf bag with a stand.

A wire brush and towel for cleaning clubs are handy items to keep in your golf bag.

5 wood, starts at £50–£100. Woods do not need to match. Some novices buy only a 3 wood instead of a full set of woods.

4 Select a putter based on what feels good to you. You can get one for about £15, but spend what it takes for a putter that makes you feel confident.

5 Understand the differences in club design. Most new clubs are perimeter weighted, with a larger hitting area to reduce the chances of an errant shot. Experts prefer bladed clubs, which demand great precision but deliver more power in skilled hands.

6 Wait to buy expensive clubs until your game has developed. There are many design options available; eventually, your style of play and preferences will determine the clubs you'll want to own.

463 Sell Found Golf Balls

Living next to a golf course brings many benefits. For one, you get regularly to replace your old, worn-out windows with fresh new ones. Also, you get a large supply of golf balls delivered to your garden. Serious scroungers stroll the course and comb through the rough for lost balls. The question is, how do you turn found balls into cash?

Steps

1 Clean the balls thoroughly. No one will buy grubby golf balls.

2 Sort the balls. Place the shiniest ones into one bucket, the moderately shiny ones into another, and old-looking balls into a third. Driving-range balls (identified by a solid colour stripe around the middle) go into their own bucket. Balls with cuts go into another or possibly into the dustbin. If they sell at all, damaged balls will go for a very low price.

3 If you have a large supply of balls, consider sorting them by brand. Many golfers prefer a specific brand.

4 Take your balls to the clubhouse for sale to the club, or approach individual golfers. Discreetly enquire whether they would be interested in buying balls.

5 Experiment with prices until you have a feel for what the market will bear. Encourage haggling. This can be fun and also allows you to shift more balls. If the golfer says "Three pounds? No way, I'll give you two," you say, "Great, two pounds each, but you have to buy five of them."

What to Look For

- Golf balls
- Good price to sell at

Tips

Dress respectably and act in a friendly manner to reduce the likelihood that club officials will chase you away.

Try to avoid offering a golfer the very same ball he or she hit into the stream 10 minutes ago.

464 Buy Sports Shoes

The choices in sporting footwear are overwhelming. Dozens of new designs are spawned every year, some changes purely cosmetic and others representing real technical advances. Avoid buying shoes that pinch your toes, which should have room to move and never touch the tip of the shoe. To make your sports shoes last, use them only when needed. Get another pair of trainers for everyday use.

ACTIVITY	SHOE DESCRIPTION
Running	• Get fitted correctly with shoes designed for your foot. The salesperson at a quality store will be able to offer you specific models that correct pronation or supination (where your foot turns inwards or outwards), or aid flat feet or high arches. Decide if you prefer more stability or more cushioning. Replace your shoes at least once a year: Even with infrequent use, running shoes wear out as the sole pad hardens. If you run every day, check the cushioning often and replace the shoe as soon as it feels stiff. • You can buy adequate running shoes for £30. But if you're running more than a few kilometres per week, spend what it takes to get the right fit. Once you've been fitted properly and know what type of shoe you need, shop by mail or online – great deals can be found at websites or in catalogues. • Track runners use different shoes for competition. Racing is done in flats, which have almost all padding removed to reduce weight. While some people use flats for road running, the lack of cushioning can cause injury. • Sprinters wear spikes – flats with small spikes attached. Different track surfaces require specific spike types; check with your coach or other runners to make sure you have the proper spike for the track. Racing shoes are intended to fit snugly and not provide long-wearing comfort or durability.
Walking	• Walking shoes often have a sole with an upward-curving toe to allow the walker to roll through the gait. With less cushioning than running shoes, long-distance walkers training on road might want to stay with a good running shoe. • Florsheim, Mephisto and Ecco make high-quality walking shoes. They are expensive but can be worn with a wide range of clothing styles for people who don't want to look like a Nike ad. Costs range from £30 to over £150.
Golf	• Most courses no longer allow metal golf spikes. Modern golf shoes have short plastic prongs on the sole for traction. Some models have replaceable prongs. • Look for soft leather uppers that require little or no break-in time. Your toes should have room to move, and the arch should be adequately supported. • If you play in a wet climate or in the early morning when the grass is damp, consider paying more for a waterproof model. Many golf shoes are now designed in a casual trainer look, as well as traditional styles. Costs range from £25 to over £100.
Cricket	• Cricket boots may come with sharp metal spikes, half spikes or studs. "Triple option" boots have all three of these available to suit weather conditions. In general, cricket boots emphasise lightness and cushioned soles to avoid jarring. Specialised boots for bowlers – especially pacemen – have extra padding for heels and reinforced toes, as well as features to increase lateral stability and reduce the risk of ankle injury. Expect to pay from £30 to £50.

ACTIVITY	SHOE DESCRIPTION
Basketball	• Whether you usually play indoors or outdoors will dictate the type of shoe you buy. Indoor shoes have a softer outsole (the very bottom of the shoe). For outdoor play on asphalt, get a shoe with a harder, more durable outsole. • Powerful or aggressive players usually choose a slightly heavier shoe for more support and durability. Faster players prefer lighter weight at the expense of durability. Expect to pay from £50 to £150 if you want to look fashionable.
Hiking	• Shop for a boot that matches your intended use. Unless you're on a serious trek, the days of the heavy, all-leather hiking boot are over. Modern lightweight designs offer comfort, good protection and durability. • Many models are not water-resistant. If this is an issue, look for a model with a higher top, a water-resistant upper, and a waterproof welt (the connection between the sole and the upper). A bellows tongue, attached to the upper at its edges, keeps out water and dirt. • Avoid wide, soft, running-shoe type soles which are very unstable on rough terrain. Boots should not fit tightly anywhere, but when fully laced with a medium-weight pair of socks, should hold your heel firmly in place. (Consider sock liners for blister prevention.) You can also find boots made specifically for women's feet. High-quality, long-lasting models cost about £50 to over £100.
Cross-training	• Advances in shoe construction have ushered in lightweight but sturdy shoes suitable for a variety of sports, such as a tennis shoe you can use for short running sessions. Look for a light-coloured sole for use on various courts without marking the surface. If you are primarily a runner, get a model with maximum cushioning. If you're mostly playing tennis, opt for more lateral support. Prices range from about £30 to £70 or more.
Aerobics	• Resembling a lightweight basketball shoe, aerobics shoes feature ankle support and durable soles. Look for complete freedom of movement with a secure fit. If you already own a cross-trainer shoe, you probably don't need to buy a separate pair for aerobics. Prices range from £30 to over £100.
Football	• Basic football boots use moulded plastic soles, a good choice for growing children. Better models have removable studs, which you can change to suit different playing surfaces and weather conditions. Some boots are specifically designed for playing on astroturf. Experienced players prefer a thin, supple leather shoe with a very tight fit and narrow toe box for maximum feel and ball control. If you want the name of your team or favourite player on your boots, there are companies that provide this service. Prices run from £20 to £140.
Tennis	• A secure feel and lateral stability should be your primary concern. Shoes not specifically designed for tennis's side-to-side action can be unstable and may lead to ankle injuries. • The shoe should be reinforced on high-wear areas, such as the top of the toe, for quick stopping. Competitive players may prefer lightweight shoes, while those purchased for recreation or practice may be heavier and more durable. You can also find tennis shoes tailored specifically for grass, clay or hard courts. A good-quality pair costs between £30 and £90.

465 Buy a Racket

Eliminate your romantic notions about that old wooden racket in your attic. It won't help your game, whether you play tennis, squash or racquetball. Today's rackets are lighter, larger and stiffer. Popular brands including Wilson, Head, Prince, Slazenger and Dunlop offer a range of design options; test as many as possible. With a price to fit any game (£20 to £200), you're sure to keep your eye on the ball.

TYPE	FEATURES	WHAT TO LOOK FOR
Tennis	Grip Size	• Too small a grip is hard to hold securely. Too large a grip tires your hand and arm. To test, grasp the racket and place your thumb along the shaft, pointing away from you. You should see a space about the width of your index finger between your fingertips and palm.
	Frame Material	• Heavier frames generate more power and less vibration. Aluminium rackets are inexpensive but may cause excessive vibration. Carbon, graphite and titanium composite rackets are more expensive and offer increased durability and stiffness. As you move up in price, rackets generally become stiffer, an advantage for advanced players who want more power.
	Head Size	• Rackets are frequently identified by the size of the head. A smaller head appeals to many experienced players seeking more control, while larger racquets appeal to beginners and to intermediate players who are seeking more power and a larger "sweet spot". Larger rackets naturally tend to weigh more. A common head size is from 610 to 710 sq cm (95 to 110 sq in).
Squash	Grip Size	• Grip size is the same for all squash rackets, but different manufacturers have slightly varied shapes. Sample brands to find what feels best. You can increase the size with a grip wrap, if necessary.
	Frame Material	• The majority of rackets are composites of carbon, graphite or fibreglass. Inexpensive rackets are heavier. Experienced players prefer stiffer, lighter-weight rackets for increased control of the ball and better vibration dampening. Squash rackets break frequently from court contact. Check for a replacement guarantee.
	Head Size	• Head sizes are usually measured in square centimeters. Most rackets are around 500 sq cm (77 sq in) although some beginners' rackets are larger and advanced rackets are smaller. Larger rackets offer a larger hitting area, but are harder to swing quickly. Advanced players are more likely to choose a small racket to minimise weight.
Racquetball	Grip Size	• Grip sizes are coded like clothing, using letters – for example, S for small and XS for extra small. A racquetball grip is much smaller than a tennis racket grip. Select a grip that gives you maximum flexibility of movement.
	Frame Material	• Advanced players prefer lighter rackets, which offer superb control but are more likely to break from contact with the court. A novice can ignore weight in favour of durability. Most rackets are made from composites of carbon fibre, fibreglass or graphite.
	Head Size	• These rackets vary less in head size than tennis rackets. Most are 645 to 710 sq cm (100 to 110 sq in). The racket's weight and feel are likely to be more important than its head size and shape.

466 Buy a Health Club Membership

This may seem simple, but many factors can affect ultimate satisfaction with a health club or fitness club membership. Make a fully informed choice to have the best chance of achieving fitness goals.

Steps

1 Proceed slowly. Many people join a fitness club on impulse, then never follow through. True fitness is based on your total lifestyle, not on a short-lived training programme.

2 Research the gyms of prospective clubs. Buy a guest pass that allows several visits. Go during peak periods or when you're most likely to use the gym, and check the availability of equipment. Observe the clientele in the gym. Are they people you feel comfortable with?

3 Weigh up any opposing factors. Are you more likely to use a large, well-appointed club located on the other side of town, or a small club in your neighbourhood? For many people, convenience is the most important factor – and that is determined by when you're most likely to go.

4 Review the facilities. Are they clean and in good working order? Does the club offer activities geared towards your entire family? Are there swimming pools, squash and tennis courts? Can you do aerobics and Pilates? Many clubs may also offer childcare, physical therapy, saunas, sunbeds and massage services.

5 Sample classes you're interested in. Are they easy to get into, or do you have come early and reserve a slot? Are they geared just for experts or are they suitable for newcomers?

6 Talk to current members. What do they like and dislike? Talk to the staff. Are the trainers full-time employees or freelancers? Is there a rapid turnover or will you be able to stick with a trainer?

7 Examine the contract. If the club has a high initial fee, you will be reluctant to change clubs once you are signed up. Is it easy to get out of the contract if you are not satisfied?

8 If you travel frequently, a club with nationwide affiliates (such as Holmes Place, David Lloyd or Cannons) may be a good deal. Check to see that you have full access to all locations.

What to Look For

- Convenient location
- Comfortable with clientele
- Activities, services and classes
- Cleanliness
- Helpful staff
- Flexible contract

Tips

Some health insurers offer discounts to health-club members. Employees of large companies may also get discounts at some gyms.

See 367 "Sign Up for a Yoga Class".

467 Buy an Aerobic Fitness Machine

Aerobic conditioning is the foundation of fitness. The ability to take in and use oxygen allows your body to perform; the more oxygen you can process, the more you can do. That's why aerobic workout machines are so popular. One major benefit of buying one is that it's in your house, not at the gym. However, it provides a less varied workout.

GENERAL ISSUES	SPECIFICATIONS
Price	• All types of machines have several quality and accessory levels. The least expensive aerobic machines sell for under £100, while the most expensive cost £2,000 or more. Expensive models are usually identical to those found in fitness clubs. Used machines, especially factory refurbished ones, may be a great deal. Be sure to ask about the warranty and maintenance records.
Quality	• Inexpensive machines don't provide the smooth operation of elaborate machines, and they may not maintain consistent resistance during a workout. Seats may not be as comfortable, and the machine itself may not be as stable. On the other hand, inexpensive machines tend to be small and easy to store, an important consideration for those with limited space.
Construction	• Many aerobic machines provide resistance by applying pressure to a flywheel, set spinning by the user's musclepower. The heavier the flywheel, the smoother the operation. Look for a large metal flywheel and a smooth, precise, sturdy resistance mechanism with a wide range of adjustment. Make sure your body weight does not exceed the machine's weight rating.
	• Inexpensive machines frequently use a system of hydraulic pistons (oil-filled cylinders) to control resistance. These can be subject to fading (lessening resistance) or leaking, which may render the machine useless.
	• High-quality machines have well-padded handrails. Any place where your body comes into contact with the machine (seat, pedals, rail and footrest) should be wide, secure and sturdy. Beware of wobbly connections and flimsy materials. Look for adjustable positioning for a wide range of body sizes.
Features	• Many machines have jazzy features like computerised workout displays. Basic machines may have no such functions, while most mid-level machines have a timer and an electronic display of your energy output, distance travelled or strides per minute. Look for pre-programmed workouts and the ability to store data on past workouts.
Maintenance	• Most machines require little or no maintenance. However, don't expect inexpensive machines to last more than a few years before numerous parts wear out. Many expensive machines are designed specifically for frequent use in fitness clubs, with the expectation of periodic professional servicing. Ask the seller about maintenance requirements before making a purchase.
Size	• All professional-quality machines are large. Check that you have sufficient space before buying one. Many exercise bicycles and rowing machines are designed for small spaces. If you have space restrictions, these may be your best choice.
Noise	• How noisy is the machine? It may need separate quarters.

MACHINE TYPE	FUNCTION	FEATURES
Steppers	Provides vigorous and intense workouts with minimal impact.	Look for a stable machine – if it feels wobbly, it may be unsafe and you won't feel comfortable or secure using it. Secure handrails are mandatory. StairMaster and Lifestep are recognised leaders in professional stepping machines, but many other companies offer acceptable models.
Rowing	The ultimate total-body workout that can accurately simulate rowing on water (without freezing weather).	For occasional use, a small, collapsible machine is fine. Larger units offer variable resistance, longer life and smoother operation. Test any machine for several minutes to assess seat comfort and pulling motion. The Concept II (concept2.com) is favoured by collegiate, club and Olympic rowers worldwide. The WaterRower (waterrower.com) employs a water-resistance system mounted on an attractive wooden frame. Both models feature impact-free resistance and a motion that accurately simulates rowing on water; the handle pulls straight out, allowing for better technique and stronger body positioning.
Treadmill	Good for runners and walkers wanting a killer aerobic workout and weather-proof convenience. Set it up with a VCR and you're ready to roll.	While inexpensive machines do the job, they tend to be noisy and have a rough action. If you have the space and the budget, a high-quality machine will probably maintain your interest longer and provide more enjoyable workouts. Look for variable speed control, adjustable incline, sturdy pad and roller construction, and quiet operation. Life Fitness, Matrix, Tunturi, Johnson and Trimline are all manufacturers of good quality treadmills.
Exercise Bike	Convenient, often compact units offer great aerobic workout – while you read or watch TV.	Get the model that feels best. It should have a comfortable, adjustable seat, secure feet attachment and smooth action. York, Beny and Reebok are makers of affordable exercise bikes, Tunturi offers mid-range machines, and Life Fitness is a recognised manufacturer of top-of-the-range machines.
Elliptical Machine	Provides a non-jarring workout with a smooth, elliptical motion that mimics the natural running stride.	A good choice when low impact is your main concern. York, ProForm and Tunturi produce more moderately priced machines, while Life Fitness, Johnson and many others manufacture higher priced examples.
WARNING	Make sure you are using any aerobic machine correctly. Incorrect body mechanics and bad posture may cause serious injury, particularly on rowing machines. Ask a salesperson or trainer for tips on safe technique before you buy.	

468 Buy Swimming Equipment

OK, so you've got your speedy swimsuit (see 515 "Choose a High-Performance Swimsuit") and are now ready to start training. If you're really serious about improving your stroke and times, you'll need to invest in some equipment.

Steps

1 First of all you'll need a cap to keep your hair out of your eyes and your contour streamlined. Speedo (Speedo.com) and Tyr (tyr.com) both offer lightweight latex caps for around £2 each, and longer-lasting, thicker silicone caps for about £6 each.

2 Next, you'll need a pair of goggles so that you can see where you're going while keeping your eyes protected from the heavily chlorinated water. For £10 to £15, choose from sleek, low-profile goggles that do not interfere with your speed through the water to curved lens and mask-style goggles for wide peripheral vision.

3 To improve the power of your kick, you'll need to work those thigh muscles. Invest in a kickboard (about £8) and a pair of fins (from £15 to £20) to get your legs working and your body propelled through the water at speed. Kickboards come in a variety of shapes and sizes, some with elbow rests to reduce back strain. Buy short-bladed fins for optimum propulsion and less water resistance, longer blades for maximum thrust and stability.

4 To improve your stroke and build upper body strength, invest in a pair of hand or finger paddles by Zogg or Speedo for about £7. They vary in size but all have adjustable finger and wrist straps. A pull buoy (also around £7) is also helpful for improving stroke technique. Place the contoured polythene foam board between your legs and grip with your thigh muscles, then propel yourself forwards with your arms on your front or your back.

What to Look For

- Swim cap
- Pair of goggles
- Pair of fins
- Kickboard
- Hand paddles
- Pull buoy

Tips

Try out a variety of styles of goggles in the shop to see which feel most comfortable. Some are designed especially for female facial dimensions. Junior goggles are also available to fit smaller faces up to the age of six.

Start with short-bladed fins (or flippers), as these require less strength in the legs. As your stroke and fitness levels improve move on to longer-bladed fins.

469 Buy a Jetski

Most people refer to personal watercraft (PWC) as Jetskis, although this was originally a trade name applied only to a model by Kawasaki. No matter what you call them, PWCs range from small single-seaters to huge four-seater models. Costs are in the £5,000 to £10,000 range.

Steps

1 Determine if you want a sit-down or stand-up PWC. Also decide if you want a craft powerful enough to pull a water-skier.

2 Examine the various size classes. This includes both engine sizes and hull sizes. Most manufacturers make a variety of both. Engine sizes are rated in cubic centimetres. Larger engines produce more horsepower and more speed, although the hull design has a big influence on performance.

What to Look For

- Sit-down or stand-up PWC
- Engine size
- Hull size
- Performance

Tips

Lifejackets are required by law (see 491 "Buy a Lifejacket").

3 Look at how performance and hull design are related. Short, narrow machines are manoeuvrable and very rewarding for skilled riders but may be difficult for beginners. Wider, longer designs are more stable, carry more people, and deflect spray better, but have reduced manoeuvrability.

4 See 551 "Buy a Trailer" to transport your new PWC from home to the beach.

Old-style two-stroke engines generated excessive noise and pollution. New models with four-stroke or direct-injection two-stroke engines are a little quieter and satisfy most emissions standards.

470 Employ a Scuba Instructor

To employ a scuba instructor, you need to establish his or her technical credentials. You need to be comfortable with their style of instruction and be able to trust his or her communication skills when underwater. If not, that person's not right for you, regardless of expertise.

What to Look For

- Qualifications
- Up-to-date certificate
- Appropriate class size
- Safety equipment

Steps

1 Locate potential instructors. Get a referral from a diving shop or centre; most work with or recommend particular instructors. Ask the centre why it chooses an instructor. Your best bet could be an instructor who is affiliated with a reputable diving centre.

2 Ask about the instructor's credentials. The largest training organisation certifying instructors is the Professional Association of Diving Instructors (PADI). A knowledgeable instructor should have an up-to-date PADI certificate.

3 Inquire about the classes. What is the student-to-instructor ratio? Ask where the pool is located. If it's not easy to get to, you may find it difficult to complete the programme.

4 Find out how long the programme to gain a scuba-diving certificate runs and how the sessions are scheduled. A responsible instructor gives classroom lectures before taking to the water. The schedule should allow sufficient time for personal attention from the instructor and questions from the students. Find out how to make up missed classes if necessary.

5 Review the equipment provided to students. While it is not always possible to tell if equipment is worn out just by looking at it, it shouldn't be obviously old or faulty. Check for dry, cracked rubber on suits, fins (or flippers) and hoses. Check for condensation inside gauges.

6 Inquire about open-water dive locations. Instruction should take place in an area where rescue personnel and medical facilities are available. If you will be transported to a dive site by boat, verify that the boat is seaworthy and equipped with a radio, fire extinguisher and lifejackets for all passengers.

Tips

If you feel an additional check is required, contact the instructor's certifying organisation to verify his or her standing.

Hire scuba gear until you become committed enough to buy your own equipment.

471 Buy a Skateboard and Protective Gear

The skateboard industry is extremely dynamic. Fashions change rapidly and new products are constantly hitting the shelves. If you're buying gear for children, understand what they want and are willing to use. The best helmet in the world will not provide much safety if it's thrown into the bushes.

Steps

1 Shop for safety gear. Gloves, wrist guards, elbow pads and knee pads are usually labelled simply "youth" or S, M, L and XL. These should fit comfortably but must be snug enough to stay in place when you hit the ground.

2 Check the helmet fit. It should fit snugly and have a secure chin strap. Make sure the helmet can't rotate backwards, exposing your forehead. The further the helmet extends over the ears, forehead and back of the skull, the more protection it offers (see 485 "Buy a Properly Fitting Helmet").

3 Determine whether you need a skateboard package or separate components. Inexpensive skateboards are usually sold as a complete package. These can be great for small children but probably won't bear the weight of an adult or teenager. Good-quality gear is usually sold as separate components, consisting of the deck, the wheels and bearings, and the trucks (the metal devices that hold the wheels to the deck).

4 Decide on a skateboard deck. The most common deck type is around 80–82 cm (31–32 in) long, with a slight upturn at each end. They are designed for manoeuvrability and cost around £40. Longer decks, called *longboards*, are anywhere from 89 to 127 cm (35 to 50 in) long and are for speed riding. Decks vary slightly in width. Smaller riders should look at narrower decks.

5 Examine your wheel choices. Small wheels, up to about 55 mm (2 in) in diameter, are for tricks and general street use. Larger wheels are for carving long, fast turns on a longboard. A set of wheels costs about £25–£40.

6 Choose a wheel hardness, which is rated using the durometer scale. The hardest wheels have a rating of 100. A wheel with a durometer rating of less than 90 is considered soft and is generally used on a longboard. A rating of 95 is about average for street and park use. A harder wheel can be better for tricks, while a softer wheel grips better.

7 Choose a truck width. Most trucks designed for a common 81 cm (32 in) board are about 13 cm (5 in) wide. A wider truck offers more stability, while a narrower one makes tricks easier. Many longboard riders prefer wider trucks. Trucks cost in the region of £40–£50.

What to Look For

- Snug safety gear
- Skateboard package versus components
- Appropriate deck size
- Wheel diameter and hardness
- Proper truck width

Tips

Take your time. Find a deck and wheel combination that fits your needs and also appeals to your sense of style, rather than buying the first board you see.

Ask plenty of questions in a shop. Any responsible shop will welcome you as a new customer.

See 140 "Get Private Health Insurance".

Warning

If your new board doesn't have non-slip tape on the deck, buy a roll. Cut it into any pattern you wish and apply for traction and grip.

472 Buy Skates

Skating was once restricted to just a few people in the frozen North. Now every little girl is training to be the next Olympic skating champion, in-line skates are everywhere, and ice hockey is played in Streatham. Before you commit to a purchase, know what you need in a pair of skates.

SPORT	HOW TO BUY
General	• For maximum performance, skates should fit snugly. Many experienced skaters opt for skates that are a size or more smaller than their normal shoes. Try on several different skates. Make sure your heel, ankle and instep are securely held in place but you don't feel any pressure points; toes should be able to move for balance. • Buy blade guards for figure skates for under £10. • If you want to play ice hockey, accessories including sticks, shin guards and helmets can be found online at sites such as icehockeykit.co.uk and skateoftheart.com.
Ice Hockey	• For children, it probably doesn't make sense to buy snugly fitting skates, but they shouldn't be too large either. Too large a skate provides insufficient ankle support and leads to lack of control and security. • Higher-priced models offer improved ankle support, fit and protection from stiffer and more-sophisticated materials. Stainless-steel blades offer increased durability. Expect to pay about £100 for basic skates and up to £400 for top-quality skates.
In-line Skating	• More expensive skates feature higher-quality wheel bearings, which roll faster and last longer than those of less expensive skates. • The unique feature of in-line skates is their wheels. Choose wheels that suit your skating style and the type of surface you're most likely to skate on. Hard wheels last longer, but lose traction on slick indoor surfaces. Soft wheels wear down quickly on abrasive surfaces like asphalt. Smaller-diameter wheels allow you to change direction quicker, and larger-diameter wheels roll faster. In-line skates run from £80 to around £200.
Figure Skating	• Figure skates should have stiff leather boots to provide adequate ankle support. The more advanced your skating, the stiffer boot you need. • Inexpensive figure skates lack ankle support and have poor-quality blades. If you're serious about pursuing figure skating, get good equipment. • Talk to other skaters or a coach about where to get skates. Expect to pay £75 for basic skates and hundreds for custom-fit skates.

473 Go Bunjee Jumping

The first bunjee jumps in Britain were made as recently as 1979. Since then thousands of people have paid good money to scare themselves witless by jumping off a crane with a rubber rope tied to their ankles. They can't all be wrong – so why not try it yourself?

Steps

1 Be sure that you are fit for a bungee jump. Know that the sport is not suitable for people with heart conditions, high blood pressure, asthma, or a damaged neck or spine. You mustn't be pregnant, or massively overweight.

2 Look for local or nationwide organisations that carry out bungee jumps. BERSA, the British Elastic Rope Sports Association (tel: 01865 311179), will give a list of its approved organisations. Or search the internet. The UK Bungee Club (ukbungee.com) and Bungee Extra (bungee.co.uk) are among the more popular bungee-jump organisers.

3 Check out the organisation. Does it have adequate public liability insurance? Are its staff fully trained? Does it have a safety certificate from an independent body and a clear safety code? How many jumps has it organised and has it had any accidents? If the organisation shows any hesitation or evasiveness in answering your queries on such issues, steer clear.

4 When you turn up for your jump, watch that safety procedures are being properly observed. First, someone should talk you through what is going to happen. Then you should be weighed, with the weight independently checked by two trained staff.

5 Next you should be harnessed and attached to bungee cables at the ankle and, for back-up, at the waist. Make sure the attachments are scrupulously checked – one staff member checking them is not enough. If you are not happy with any part of the procedure, back out. It's your life on the line!

6 Enjoy your death-defying jump. Savour the adrenaline rush. Tell your friends afterwards how your whole life flashed before your eyes.

7 Expect to pay £40–£50 for a first jump, with a reduced rate of around £10–£25 if you choose to repeat the experience.

What to Look For

- Local or nationwide bungee-jumping organisations
- Safety record and safety code
- Independent certification
- Safety procedures

Tips

Children under 14 cannot perform a bungee jump. Youngsters under 17 will need parental approval.

If you are over 50, you may be able to jump, but the organisers are likely to ask to see a medical certificate from your doctor.

Warnings

Bungee-jumping is an extreme sport. If safety procedures are not adequate, there is a serious risk of sudden death.

474 Go Skydiving

Skydiving can be the one-off experience of a lifetime, or an addictive adrenaline-rush activity to develop to a high level of skill. Make the right choice to suit your interests and the state of your nerves.

Steps

1 Assemble a group to go with you. You need witnesses to your bravery.

2 Contact an organisation that runs skydiving courses. Look in *Yellow Pages* or search the internet. Visit the British Parachute Association website (bpa.org.uk) for a list of the association's skydiving centres and useful information on the sport. Also go to the websites of companies providing courses, for example skydiveaurora.co.uk or ukskydiving.co.uk.

3 Phone the organisation and establish that they will take the time to answer your questions; and that they present a professional demeanour. Ask if they have had any accidents.

4 Decide on a type of jump. Doing a jump by yourself (a *solo jump*) requires that you complete an instruction course, then jump using a static line. This line automatically opens your parachute as you exit the plane, eliminating free fall. A *tandem jump* allows you to experience a free fall immediately. After brief instruction, you jump out of an aircraft strapped to an instructor. He or she does all the work, pulling the chute and controlling the jump. A one-off tandem jump may cost around £200.

5 Make certain that you understand every element of the instruction before the jump. Do not allow yourself to be rushed through it. If the instructor is not answering your questions to a degree that makes you feel secure and confident, do not proceed.

6 Enrol in an Accelerated Free Fall (AFF) course if you wish to pursue skydiving further. An eight- to ten-jump course, followed by ten individual jumps, will make you a certified skydiver. In your first jumps, you will be accompanied by two instructors. An AFF course costs upwards of £1,500. As a certified skydiver, you'll be allowed to perform jumps at will.

What to Look For

- British Parachute Association list
- Professional demeanour
- Good safety record
- Type of jump

Tip

Enquire about options for photographing or video-taping your jump. Most sky-diving companies provide this service – at a price.

Some skydiving companies sell gift vouchers, so you can buy a free-fall dive as a present for a friend.

475 Buy Weightlifting Equipment

Weight training benefits people of all ages by increasing bone density (preventing osteoporosis) and muscle endurance. It even lifts your spirits. But make sure you have the right equipment.

TYPE	FEATURE	WHAT TO LOOK FOR
Weight Machines	Basic Set	• A weight machine has stacks of iron plates fixed in a frame. A range of exercises are performed at different stations on the machine with adjustable weight loads. Costs run from £500 into the thousands.
	Size	• Allow enough room to set up the machine properly. If you have limited space, consider smaller individual machines. With one machine to work the arms and back and one for the lower body, you can get a complete workout. Powertec and Body-Solid are longtime manufacturers of professional-grade machines. You'll pay over £1,000, but get a set-up that would satisfy a professional.
	Construction	• Check that the machine is sturdy and that the framework remains immobile even during heavy lifting. Any point where your body contacts the machine will get lots of wear and tear; they should be padded with dense foam and covered by thick plastic or vinyl.
	Weight	• Check that the machine has sufficient weight for the type of lifting you plan to do, and that you can add more weight in the future.
	Exercises	• Test all the workout stations on the machine to make sure it performs the exercises you want. Read instructions for proper use. Investigate your options for adding stations.
	Alternative Designs	• Some machines replicate the weight resistance through springs or elastic bands. These systems are lighter and more compact but still provide a good workout and range of motions. Bowflex makes a popular machine. However, some people miss the satisfying feel and sound that comes from moving a serious stack of iron.
Free Weights	Basic Set	• Free weights provide a variety of strength-training exercises. Dumbbells are handheld weights. Barbells consist of a long steel bar with cast-iron plates that slide on and are secured. Weights are added or removed for various exercises. Choose a simple system with compatible parts for expandability and buy additional components as your training progresses. Verify that newly purchased plates fit your bar, but don't worry about mixing brands or types.
	Bench	• The first accessory most people add is a bench, which allows you to lie on your back and work your chest, shoulders and triceps. The bench should have a rack at one end for holding the weight bar, and you should be able to set it flat or at an incline.
	Squat Rack	• An upright rack that holds a bar and heavy plates at about shoulder height. Lifters add weight while the bar is secured in the rack, then move it onto their shoulders and squat, increasing explosive strength in the back, legs and glutes. A squat rack needs to be extremely strong and should be bolted securely to the floor, wall or ceiling.
WARNING		Free weights are more likely to cause injury than weight machines. To prevent injuries, emphasise proper technique and develop a warm-up and stretching routine before lifting.

476 Choose a Car Rack

Between the dogs, the children and the car seats, there isn't much room left in the car for equipment. That's where the rack comes in. Your needs and preferences, along with the type of vehicle you drive, will dictate your choice, but start by identifying models built to fit your specific car. Thule (roofracks.co.uk) is one of the best upmarket suppliers of rack systems. Expect to pay slightly more for a brand like this, but know that you are getting good quality. Many other brands exist, particularly for roof racks. A word to the wise: make sure you only need one key to operate all locks.

RACK TYPE	SET UP	FEATURES	PRICE
General Purpose Roof Rack	Basic roof rack consists of mounted stanchions and horizontal poles. Serves as the base unit for additional carriers, such as those for bikes, kayaks, skis or boards.	Check the rack's weight rating to make sure it can carry all your gear. Some people buy a basic rack and fashion their own systems to carry specific items. Quality racks can be locked.	£40 to £120
Tow-Bar Mounted Rack	For vehicles already equipped with a tow ball, get an equipment rack that uses the tow-bar mount.	This system is easier to load than a roof rack due to its lower height. But, this also means other cars can more easily damage your gear, and the gear collects more road grime. Check rack is compatible with your tow ball.	£100 to £200
Rear-Mounted Rack	Fits to the back of suitable vehicles, such as estates and hatchbacks. Typically carries up to three bicycles.	The main problem with these racks is that they need to fit your car. Make sure to keep bike tyres well clear of car exhaust to prevent warping.	£50 to £120
Roof Box	Considered by some an essential car complement, roof boxes are very slick, weather-proof luggage compartments.	Advantages over roof racks include security, watertightness, ease of loading, and improved aerodynamics. If you plan to carry bicycles, you still need a separate bike rack.	£250 to £600
Ski and Snowboard Rack	Simple to store when you don't need it; usually easy to install and remove.	A major disadvantage is that if later on you want to carry a bicycle, you'll have to buy a whole new rack. If you're buying a rack with individual slots, make sure the slots are compatible with newer, wider skis. Check out magnetic systems.	£50 and up
Roof-Mounted Cycle Rack	The cyclist's equivalent of the ski and snowboard rack.	The disadvantage of cycle roof racks is generally considered to lie in the difficult of loading and unloading. Look out for recent products that have ingenious ways of improving the ease of these operations. Roof racks get your bikes well out of harm's way.	£25 to £75

477 Buy Skis

Ski technology advanced dramatically during the 1990s when new materials and designs came together in easy-to-use, high-performance skis. Ski design used to be race-driven, so everyone skied on slalom or giant slalom skis. Today, it's largely driven by free-skiers who favour all kinds of terrain, and skis now commonly defy categorisation. If you only spend the occasional week on a winter sports holiday, you may prefer to hire equipment. But buying can be economical, especially if you sell your old skis

ALPINE	FEATURES
General	• Specialised for travelling downhill, with your boot rigidly fixed to the ski. For getting back uphill, most skiers rely on chairlifts.
Shopping for Deals	• Beginner and intermediate skis sell for £300–£400. You can pay a lot more for advanced equipment. • Shop around on the internet for great deals. Buying any of the recognised brands – for example, Salomon, Rossignol, Volki and Atomic – generally guarantees you a ski of acceptable quality. • Look for websites selling ex-hire skis in the spring. Shop early, they go fast.
All-mountain Skis	• Where skis used to be 200 cm (6 ft 6 in) or longer, that much length isn't needed anymore. A versatile, do-everything ski for an average-height adult runs between 160 and 180 cm (5 ft 2 in and 5 ft 10 in) in length. For cruising prepared runs and making occasional forays into other terrain, look for a ski up to about 75 mm (3 in) in width under the foot for versatile performance across most terrain. If you like skiing on powder, consider a wider ski. If you frequently ski icy snow, stick to a narrower design.
Mid-fat and Fat Skis	• Shorter skis, from 75 to 100 mm (3 to 4 in) in width under the foot, excel in deep powder and soft snow. If you have always struggled in powder, this is your ticket to the next level. Many of these skis are stiff and demanding, and are designed for accomplished skiers. If you're a beginner, make sure you aren't buying too stiff a ski, as you will not be able to turn it properly.
Slalom Racing Skis	• Racing skis have become incredibly short. The fastest racers in the world commonly use skis of about 160 cm (5 ft 2 in), while a few years ago they would consider nothing less than 205 cm (6ft 7 in). Flexible and responsive, they offer incredibly quick turning on firm snow, but are not a great choice for deep snow and ungroomed terrain.
Parabolic Skis	• This is an outdated term referring to the first generation of shorter, wider skis. All current skis reflect some elements of this design, but none use the original parabolic shape. For convenience (if not total accuracy), old-style skis are referred to as *straight*, and new, wider skis are referred to as *shaped*.
Twin-tip Skis	• Favoured by skiers who enjoy the challenges presented by special course features, twin-tips are very soft and forgiving with a turned-up tail to land jumps backwards. Bindings are mounted further forward than normal. Make sure to try out a pair to see if that's what you're after. Twin-tips can be skied in the same length as all-mountain skis, or slightly shorter, depending on preference.

periodically and replace them with more up-to-date kit (see 479 "Sell Used Skis"). Start looking for skis in the early spring and plan to buy that year's models by late spring. If you wait to buy until the snow starts to fall, you'll pay a premium for the new models. Give the latest gear a try – you might be surprised by how much your skiing improves. Talk to the experts at ski shops and general sports shops to help you choose the right skis for you.

CROSS-COUNTRY	FEATURES
General	• Cross-country skis differ from alpine skis in that they're lightweight and designed for self-propelled travel over a wide variety of terrain, not just down hills. The bindings let your heels lift off the ski, allowing a normal striding motion, which is why cross-country skis are also referred to as free-heel skis. Waxless skis are far easier to use and preferred by many. They achieve grip for forward movement by means of a texture set into the skis' base. Waxable skis require different wax for different snow conditions.
Shopping for Deals	• An inexpensive set of cross-country touring skis sells for around £100. Racing and telemark skis cost about £200–£400. Ski shops are your best source for equipment. Shop early in spring for the best deals.
Racing Skis	• Fast, narrow skis intended strictly for use on prepared cross-country trails, racing skis are not for exploring untracked areas. Each of the two racing styles – skating and the traditional diagonal stride – have specialised skis. Your skiing style, weight and the snow conditions in the locality will determine what ski is best for you.
Touring Skis	• Offered in a variety of widths and styles. Wider models, especially ones with metal edges, are designed for touring rugged terrain or ski camping. Narrower, lighter-weight models are for gentler terrain and for use on prepared trails.
Telemark Skis	• A telemark skier turns by sliding one ski forwards, bending deeply at the knees, and arcing both skis into a turn as though using one long ski. • Unless you are a skilled, high-speed skier, a forgiving, easy-turning model will work best. Stiff or long skis are very challenging for a beginning telemark skier. For deep snow where weight matters, look for lighter-weight skis at least 70 mm (3 in) wide under the foot. If you are an aggressive skier, avoid very lightweight skis; durability is a far more important factor than a little extra weight.
Accessories	• Off-piste skiers will need a pair of skins to make ascents. These attach to ski bottoms for uphill traction. • Different types of skiing require different types of poles. Ask a ski shop for suggestions, but know that some poles cost £100 and more. Unless you're racing, a £25 pair is fine. • Bindings also differ for different ski types. Talk to a ski shop for advice. • See 481 "Buy Ski Boots".

478 Buy Clothes for Cold-Weather Activities

Many people invite disaster when they are selecting winter clothes. Not wearing a hat is the number one mistake. If you use fashion as your guide instead of function, rest assured you'll be miserable when that first icy blast strikes.

Steps

1 Conduct research if possible. If you've just arrived in a winter sports resort, check out what the locals wear. In bad weather, they'll dress more like mountaineers than fashion models.

2 Layer clothing for maximum warmth and convenience. Layers allow you to add and remove items as your body temperature rises and falls. Begin with a base layer of synthetic polyester underwear, top and bottom. You can purchase these inexpensively at many outdoor wear shops. Brand-name items don't always deliver better quality, despite their higher costs.

3 Add one or more fleece layers as dictated by your comfort range. Again, these needn't be expensive to provide effective warmth. A vest is a good option, paired with a long-sleeved layer.

4 Add an outer waterproof, breathable shell. This layer does not need heavy insulation unless you expect to encounter below-zero temperatures. For jackets, get something that extends below your waist and has a hood. Trousers should be loose fitting and should rise above your waist to keep out snow. Look for sealed seams and elastic or drawstrings at cuffs and hems.

5 If you need an insulated top layer, decide on either synthetic or down filling. Synthetic filling will perform better if it gets wet, while down loses its warmth when wet. If weight is your primary consideration, however, buy goose down. It is warmer for its weight than any synthetic insulator.

6 Inspect the seams of insulated clothing. High-quality items have baffled seams. This means the stitching on the outside and inside layers doesn't meet, creating cold spots. Clothes without baffled seams are sewn straight through the two layers, and allow cold air to enter (see 486 "Buy the Optimal Sleeping Bag").

7 Wear a hat that completely covers your head, or even one that has earflaps, to prevent a potentially life-endangering loss of body heat. Look for itch-free fleece headbands on warm wool hats.

8 Waterproof, gauntlet-type gloves that extend over your jacket's sleeves provide the most protection from snow and water. Some people's fingers stay warmer in mittens.

9 Boots present the biggest challenge for the novice at winter holidays. The most successful boot design incorporates a rubber lower boot with a leather top and removable felt liner. Boot temperature ratings are particularly important if you will be outside for long periods of time and need your feet to stay warm.

What to Look For

- Layers
- Materials
- Baffled seams
- Waterproof gloves
- Winter boots

Tips

Many outdoor clothing retailers sell both online and through catalogues. Reputable names include Field & Trek (field-trek.co.uk) and, for skiwear, Sur la Piste (surlapiste.com).

Be sure to select a pair of boots designed for your anticipated needs, paying attention to temperature ratings. For bargains try the-outdoor.co.uk, which sells army surplus clothing, including all-weather boots.

Remember that with outer layers, more money usually does buy better quality.

See 516 "Buy Performance Workout Clothing" for more information on fabrics.

Warning

Be careful of drying your clothes too close to the fire or other heat source. Synthetic fabrics and insulators may not be able to withstand high temperatures.

MATERIAL	CHARACTERISTICS
Cotton	Avoid cotton, because once it gets wet, it stays wet and heavy. Snow country survival experts have a saying: Cotton kills.
Down	Lightweight down is a great insulator for extreme cold, but can be too warm for active sports, and loses its ability to insulate when wet. Not all down provides the same warmth: the higher the fill power, the warmer it is. (Fill power is the volume filled by 31.1 g (1 oz) of down, and is the standard measure of down quality and performance.) Look for a rating on the label – 650 fill power is good quality, 850 fill power is top quality. Items that don't specify the fill power are generally lower quality (see 486 "Buy the Optimal Sleeping Bag").
Synthetic Insulation	Clothing with high-quality synthetic insulation usually lists the brand name. Hollowfill and Thinsulate are popular types. They are slightly heavier than down, but stand up to wetness better and dry quickly.
Waterproof Fabric	The first truly breathable waterproof fabric, Gore-Tex (gore-tex.com), remains one of the best and is unbeatable for strenuous activity in wet weather. This is an outer shell layer, not an insulator. Expect to pay more for outer clothing that features sealed seams, watertight pockets and covered zippers.
DuPont Cordura	This is a brand name for a tough nylon fabric used to reinforce clothing. Durable gear frequently includes Cordura (cordura.com) patches on heavy-wear areas like knees and seat.

479 Sell Used Skis

Skis are expensive, so you'll want to sell your old pair before you get new ones. Unfortunately, they depreciate quickly. Leave the bindings in place because most buyers will want them.

Steps

1 Estimate their worth. Skis one season old in good shape might sell for about half what you paid. After two seasons, with light use, expect to get 30 to 40 per cent of their original price. Between three and five seasons old, expect about £50 to £100. If they're more than five years old, consider them a permanent part of the house or sell for the price of a casual dinner for two.

2 Look for used skis for sale in newspapers and magazines or on the internet. Where other people are selling second-hand skis, so can you.

3 Run a classified ad or advertise on the internet at a skiing website. Alternatively, put the skis up for auction at eBay.

4 Bring your equipment to a ski shop and ask for ideas. Suggest part-exchange for new skis in the shop.

What to Look For

- Skis less than five seasons old
- Ski shop
- Internet selling sites

Tips

Consider keeping your old skis. They are great for perfecting your waxing and repair skills.

480 Buy a Snowboard, Boots and Bindings

Snowboarding used to be simple – young people mysteriously had the necessary skills and old people stayed away. But now that everyone's doing it, things have become more complicated. Unless you plan to specialise in one type of riding (slalom racing, for example), get a versatile snowboard and binding combination.

Steps

1 Rent equipment or borrow a friend's before you buy. You need to know what's right for you, not what's right for someone else.

2 Consider the type of snow you encounter most often. For hard snow and ice, you want a stiffer board. For powder, a softer board rides better.

3 Choose board length. For example, a 1.7 m (5 ft 8 in) novice will ride a board in the range of 150 to 160 cm (5 ft to 5 ft 4 in). More length provides stability and flotation in powder, while shorter boards are more manoeuvrable.

4 Look for a board that matches your needs rather than a particular brand. For research purposes, interesting brands include Burton, K2, Rome, Sims and Völkl.

5 Expect to pay £200 to £450 for a board. There is a range of materials for different riding preferences and abilities.

6 Take your snowboarding style into account when choosing a board. Young or adventurous riders develop an array of techniques for destroying their board. This is normal and expected. Stick to boards in the lower price ranges if you plan to trash yours. More conservative riders can buy higher-priced models that will last them many years.

7 Select a binding system. The Snowboard Asylum website (snowboard-asylum.com) offers useful advice on binding options. Strap bindings, which hold your feet in place, can be slow to put on and remove, but step-in bindings give limited foot support and can clog up with snow, making them a chore to use in deep powder. Bindings range from £100 to £200.

8 Make sure the boots fit the bindings and that you can attach the bindings to the board. Not all gear is compatible.

9 Buy the boot that provides the best fit, even if it means moving to a different binding system. Look for boots that fit snugly in the calf and heel but do not crush your toes; get the smallest boot that is comfortable when you're wearing one medium-weight sock. If you require very large boots, consider purchasing a wider-than-average board to prevent your toes from dragging in the snow. Boots range from around £100 to over £200.

What to Look For

- Board, binding and boot compatibility
- Appropriate board length and stiffness
- Proper boot fit

Tips

A secondhand board can be a good deal. Check to see that it isn't bent or warped and that the edges are intact.

Long jackets and waterproof bottoms with a reinforced seat will keep you dry and protected. Even experienced snowboarders spend considerable time on the ground.

See 478 "Buy Clothes for Cold-Weather Activities".

Warning

Even the most accomplished snowboarders can encounter the random tree or, worse, another body moving at high speed. Always wear a helmet (see 485 "Buy a Properly Fitting Helmet").

481 Buy Ski Boots

Even if you ski only a few days per year, there's no substitute for good boots. Proper fit, appropriate level of stiffness, and comfort are essential for a great day of skiing. If you've been renting ski equipment, at least consider buying boots. Although the initial purchase price can be high, they last for years and provide a consistent foundation for improving your skills. Spending the time to find a skilled boot fitter will pay off every day you enjoy fun, pain-free skiing.

BOOT TYPE	FUNCTION, FIT AND PRICE
Downhill Ski (Alpine)	• Have a stiff plastic shell designed to hold your foot and ankle firmly in place. For the best performance, buy the smallest boot you can comfortably wear and use only one thin synthetic sock. All boots expand in size slightly after you have worn them several times. • Plan on spending at least an hour with a skilled boot fitter, and try on many different boots. A bargain boot that doesn't fit is no bargain. As you move up in ability, you generally want a stiffer (and more expensive) boot designed for faster, more aggressive skiing. If you're a beginner or an intermediate, you don't need this stiffness unless you're of above-average size. • Boot prices start from around £150 for good beginner and intermediate boots, rising to £300 and upwards for advanced boots. If your foot is very difficult to fit or you simply want the best fit possible, inquire about custom fitting. Some manufacturers recommend special moulding systems that make the boot conform exactly to your foot. All downhill boots are compatible with all downhill bindings. Expect to pay £100 or more on top of the standard price.
Cross-country	• Cross-country boots need to provide ankle and heel support but still allow your toes some freedom of movement. Because you will be lifting your heel as you ski, the boot needs to be comfortable as you bend your foot. Check to see that the sole is laterally stiff, meaning that you can't wring the boot like a dishrag. Plan on wearing one pair of medium-weight socks. For racing, weight matters, and lightweight boots cost more. • If you already own skis, check that new boots are compatible with your current bindings (not all are). • Prices range from around £70 to over £200.
Telemark	• A telemark boot used to be just a heavy-duty cross-country boot. Now it looks more like a downhill boot, with some important differences. First, decide where you will spend most of your telemarking time. If you only go to downhill areas, get a tall, stiff boot. If you prefer touring, get a shorter, lighter boot for easier and faster ascents. • As with alpine boots, spend time with a qualified boot fitter and experiment with different boots. A properly fitting boot holds your heel firmly yet allows your toes to move around even with the sole flexed. It should fit snugly around your calf without crushing your foot. All telemark boots expand in size slightly after you wear them several times. Your toes should never hit the end of the boot. A standard telemark boot measures 75 mm (3 in) across the front of the sole, and all 75-mm boots fit all 75-mm bindings. • Prices range from around £150 to £300 and upwards.

482 Buy a Bicycle

There are so many different types of bicycles that making a decision can be difficult. The primary consideration is to get a bike that matches your needs and fits you properly. After that, it's a matter of test-driving to see what you like at a price you can afford.

Steps

Any bike

1 Go to a reputable bicycle shop. A bike is a serious piece of equipment. Buy from someone who is serious about bikes.

2 Be clear what you want a bike for. Are you going to use it to cycle to work or to make a trip across Africa? Do you want speed or comfort? Express your needs and preferences clearly and an experienced salesperson will be able to direct you to suitable bikes at a range of prices.

3 Test-ride before buying. Look for a smooth gearshift and good handling. Ensure the bike is the right size for you – sizing systems are confusing, so personal testing is the only way to tell. Is the riding position what you want? On some bikes you crouch forwards over the handlebars; others make you sit upright.

4 Be aware that bikes differ in the comfort of ride they give over rough surfaces. For example, aluminium alloy frames are stiff and good for short rides, but titanium frames absorb more road vibration, making longer rides more comfortable.

5 Choose pedals depending on your need. Your options are a basic flat pedal; a basic pedal with a cage around it (called a *toe clip*); and clipless pedals for which you have to buy special shoes that attach directly to the pedal.

Mountain bike

Mountain bikes are designed to tolerate rough treatment. They also give comfort and stability over rough terrain, on a bona fide mountain or over curbs and potholes. They have knobbly tyres, a tough frame and lots of gears.

1 Decide what you can afford. You will have to spend upwards of £300 for a decent mountain bike. For aggressive riding with hard climbs and descents, plan on spending much more.

2 Stand over the top tube of a prospective bike and make sure your feet touch the ground comfortably.

3 Look for a frame that allows you a comfortable, upright riding position. A cramped frame with too short a distance between handlebar and saddle will not allow you to stand up and pedal, and will tend to tip backwards on steep climbs.

What to Look For

- Good handling
- Smooth gearshift
- Smooth suspension
- Strong wheels
- Tyre width

Tips

The more you know about bicycle components, the more likely you will be to spot good deals. Expensive bikes have top-of-the-range component packages that you would be hard-pressed to equal in price if you tried to purchase individually. Cheap bikes have cheap components, and mid-range bikes have a mixture. As a buyer, it's your job to spot the differences.

Unless you are, in fact, a racer, extremely lightweight frames and wheels are not the best choice. They're designed to win races, not to provide stability and durability, and won't always tolerate riders who weigh over 67 kg (180 lb).

4 Decide if you want front suspension, full suspension or neither. Most mountain bikes include front suspension, as the majority of riders consider it essential. Full suspension is fun for fast down-hills but adds weight, cost and a decrease in pedalling efficiency.

5 Do a subjective assessment of how the bike feels. You'll usually achieve a proper fit by feel more than by numbers. How does the bike climb? Can you stand up and steer easily?

Racing and touring bikes

Most road bike designs are race-driven, designed for light weight and aerodynamic efficiency at the expense of comfort. Touring bikes may have upright handlebars, mudguards, carrying racks and other amenities. A £200 bicycle is fine for moderate riding. A £400 bicycle will last longer, have better brakes and smoother gearshift. For serious racing or high-mileage touring, plan to spend £700 or more.

1 Decide on your comfort needs. Don't let the salesperson talk you into a racing-style bike if you don't want one. Instead look for one with higher handlebars to take the strain off your back.

2 Examine wheel and tyre widths. Wider tyres are comfortable and more secure but slower. Racing bikes are equipped with narrow, high-pressure tyres, which are fast but require more skill and concentration.

3 Consider the bike's weight. A 15 kg (40 lb) bike is generally not as pleasant to ride as a 8 kg (22 lb) bike.

4 Pay attention to the length of the tube that forms the top of the bike frame and determines the distance between the saddle and the handlebar. Too long a distance and you'll be uncomfortably stretched out. Too short and you'll be cramped. Look for a frame length that allows you to move your hands to different positions on the handlebars without placing too much weight on them.

City and folding bikes

City bikes are specifically designed for short trips around town. They are similar to racing bikes, but with a wider range of gears and a more comfortable riding position. Folding bikes are for carrying on the train or in your car.

1 Choose a city bike using the same criteria that apply to racing or touring bikes.

2 For a folding bike, decide whether your priority is lightness, for maximum portability, or performance. Very light folding bikes, easy to unfold and suitable for carrying on trains or the tube, are only good for short and easy cycle journeys. Heavier models, less handy to fold and unfold, are suitable to carry in your car and give better performance. Prices start at around £200.

There's no need to spend a lot on children's bicycles because they're quickly outgrown. Spend enough to get important safety features like good brakes.

You can replace handlebars with a shape that suits your grip comfort needs and riding style.

483 Buy an Electric Bicycle

If you really like the idea of cycling but find it a too much of an effort, think about an electric bicycle. This is a bike that you pedal, but with a battery-driven electric motor to give you assistance. It will save you arriving at work in a sweat, and help you up those unforgiving hills.

Steps

1 Know that most electric bikes have a sensor on the pedal linked to a small computer, which automatically determines how much help you need from the motor. You cannot ride them without pedalling – the motor won't work if you don't pedal at all.

2 Seek out shops selling electric bikes in *Yellow Pages* or visit websites like electricbikedirect.co.uk or electric-bike-uk.co.uk.

3 Check the weight of the bike and the distance it will travel without recharging. These are the variables that determine price. The lighter the bike, and the further it will travel at one go, the more it will cost: 16 kg (35 lb) and around 30 km (19 miles) are top range. More power is not an option – this is limited by law, unless you want to get into paying road tax and insurance.

4 Check what batteries the bike uses. NiCads are the longest lasting, NiMHs the lightest (see 40 "Buy Rechargeable Batteries"). You will need to buy a battery charger as part of the package.

What to Look For

- Lightweight model
- Durable batteries
- Websites and electric bicycle shops

Tip

Consider the option of adding an electric motor to your existing bike. This will cost around £250. Good purpose-made electric bikes cost in excess of £1,000.

Warning

Check the law on electric bikes, which is fast-evolving. Ensure the bike you buy is legal for road use. Children can't ride electric bikes.

484 Buy Cycle Clothing

Cycle clothing is more than a fashion statement. It is designed to maximise comfort and protection. There is plenty of cycling gear on offer in shops and on the internet, but you need to reflect a little to know what to choose that suits your needs.

Steps

1 Consider the comfort needs of your sensitive lower parts glued to a saddle bouncing over potholes and other boneshaking obstacles. Padded cycling underwear and shorts are designed to offer the necessary protection.

2 Think of the perspiration problem in warm-weather cycling. Look for a cycling top advertised as "high wicking". This means that it will soak up the sweat and release it into the atmosphere.

3 Recognise the need for protection for your hands from the wear of gripping the handlebars. Buy fingerless gloves for use in summer and warm skiing-style gloves for the winter.

4 Buy waterproofs and a fleece top for those days of typical British weather. Make sure that the clothing still allows your body to breathe – perspiration does not stop when it rains.

What to Look For

- Padded underwear and shorts
- High wicking fabrics
- Mitts and gloves
- Bad weather gear

Tip

If you are worried about breathing in fumes while cycling in the city, acquire a filtration protection mask. They cost from £10–£30, although you will also have regularly to buy replacement filters, priced at around £7.

485 Buy a Properly Fitting Helmet

Ah, the good old days, before seat belts, bike helmets and car seats. But were they really that good? Probably the staff at accident and emergency have an opinion about that. We seem to be moving faster, jumping higher and falling harder than ever before, so helmets just make sense.

TYPE	FEATURES	PRICE
Motorcycle	Look only at helmets that confrom to British and European safety standards. A helmet with a chin bar and visor offers the most protection and blocks the most noise, but some riders prefer open-face helmets. Bright colours increase visibility to car drivers. Buy a snug-fitting helmet with no pressure points that will cause pain and headaches. They loosen up slightly with use, so don't buy one that is too big.	You can get complete pro-tection from a £70 helmet, but can pay £500.
Ski or Snowboard	A winter sports helmet must meet many conflicting demands. It needs to keep out snow but allow ventilation. It should keep you warm on cold days but not stifle you on warm ones. Look for ventilation points that you can seal up on cold days and removable insulation around the ears. Make sure the helmet fits snugly but allows you to hear. Buckle the chin strap and test the fit by trying to rotate the helmet forward off your head – you shouldn't be able to. Then rotate the helmet back until your forehead is exposed. If you can do this, you need a smaller helmet.	Children's helmets cost around £40. Adult models range from £60 to around £180.
Bicycle	Look for a helmet that provides plenty of ventilation. Some brands have pads you can add to or remove from the helmet for a better fit. Fasten the chin strap: if you can rotate the helmet back until your forehead shows, it doesn't fit properly. Find an experienced salesperson when shopping for your child's helmet. Be aware that bicycle helmets only provide protection against a headfirst fall on to the pavement – they are not designed to resist a head-on impact with a car.	£20 buys a good helmet.
WARNING	A helmet that has been in a crash or one that's been dropped on a hard surface may no longer protect your head. If you suspect it's damaged, replace it.	

486 Buy the Optimal Sleeping Bag

For many people, crawling into a snug sleeping bag is the best (and perhaps the only) reason to go camping. Getting a bag that best fits your body means you don't carry excess weight or spend a lot of time trying to heat up one that's too big for you. Know your options before heading for the hills.

FEATURE	DESCRIPTION
Down	Down is the most efficient insulator available, with the highest warmth-to-weight ratio. Cared for properly, it will last a lifetime. Down does not perform well when wet but is perfect for very cold climates where moisture is less of a concern, and any time that weight concerns are paramount. Not all down is the same – the higher the fill power, the warmer it is. Two bags rated for –7°C (20°F), one with 650 fill and the other with 850, will keep you equally warm. The key is that it takes less 850 fill down to reach that degree rating, making it a lighter, more compressible bag than the 650.
Synthetic Insulation	Synthetics are cheaper than down but slightly heavier for the same warmth rating. They retain their warmth when wet because they dry better, retaining their loft. Polarguard, Hollowfill and Thinsulate are popular brands.
Outer Material	Most bags use polyester or nylon fabric for both the shell and lining. The shell is coated with a lightweight durable water repellent to allow small amounts of water to bead up but not penetrate to the insulation. Higher-priced bags are made with waterproof, breathable laminates that allow body vapour to escape to the surface of the bag while prohibiting moisture from coming in. These bags are used exclusively in high-altitude mountaineering.
Construction	Check the stitching. If it runs directly through the inner and outer layers of the bag, it's a low-quality bag good only for temperatures above 7°C (45°F). This quilted construction creates cold spots along the seams. High-quality baffled construction has inner and outer stitches that do not meet.
Shape	Bags come in either rectangular or mummy shapes. The reduced volume of a mummy means it insulates better and compresses to a smaller size. Rectangular bags are bulkier and heavier but can open flat. Some models are made in large or tall sizes for people over 1.8 m (6 ft) tall, or in short sizes for children. Better-quality bags are offered in men's and women's versions, wider at the shoulders or hips, respectively, and insulated in different patterns, which take into account anatomical and sleep differences.
Temperature Rating	Most bags list the lowest temperature at which the bag will be comfortable. An average backpacking bag, for example, might be rated for –7°C (20°F). These ratings are a handy way to compare bags, but they don't mean you'll always be comfortable at that temperature – you still need a secure tent, an insulated sleeping mat and proper clothing.
Hood	Cold-weather performance requires a hooded bag. Climb into the bag to test the hood; you should be able to seal it snugly around your face. Make sure your feet don't push against the bottom of the bag when the hood is fastened.
Price	The better a bag's warmth rating, the more it costs. A good down bag, rated to –7°C (20°F), costs from around £150 to over £300. A synthetic bag with the same rating costs about £50 to £150.

487 Buy a Tent

Some claim to have fond memories of sleeping out in old canvas tents. When pressed for details, they're likely to confess the tents were draughty, musty, leaky and heavy. Modern tents, lightweight and simple to set up, come in a variety of designs to fit your precise needs.

Steps

1 Decide what type of tent you need. For warm-weather use – that weekend at a music festival – a £20–£30 tent from a sports shop or department store will work fine. For general backpacking and hill walking, a three-season tent is best. For mountaineering and winter use, you need a four-season or high-altitude tent.

2 Step up to a speciality brand if weight, durability, speedy set-up, and resistance to wind noise (tautness) are issues. For a variety of tent options, check out sites such as venturesport.co.uk. Added money buys a lighter tent that lasts a lifetime (if well cared for), pitches easily, resists crumpling in wind (so that you don't wake up and find your tent collapsed across your face) and keeps out the rain.

3 Investigate prices. Three-season tents cost more than two-season tents. The larger and/or better built the tent, the more it will cost. An average four-person, two-season tent costs around £100. An eight-person, four-season tent can cost £1,500 and up.

4 Assess usable space. Some small two-person tents are fine in good weather, but can feel cramped if two people plus equipment and a dog are waiting out a storm. On the other hand, two hikers don't want to carry a heavier tent designed for four.

5 Shop for tents in person, then buy online if you find a better deal. Crawl in and stretch out. Make sure your feet and head are well clear of the ends. Imagine spending 24 hours in there during a storm. Cosy or torture? Keep looking until you find a cosy one.

6 Consider design trade-offs. Taller tents are comfortable but more subject to wind buffeting. A shorter tent is more secure in high winds and is likely to be warmer, but may feel claustrophobic. Many tents offer a "porch" to stash your gear or to cook in during rough weather. Some tents need staking to stay upright, while others don't. All backpacking tents, even free-standing ones, perform better when staked out. Unless you have a single wall tent, you'll need a rain flysheet for protection from bad weather.

7 Practise pitching different tents. Most are erected using a system of collapsible poles. Some are easier to set up than others. The simplest tents have two interchangeable poles; more complex designs have non-interchangeable poles. If tent assembly seems like a mysterious art to you, go for the simplest design.

8 Buy a single-wall tent, with one waterproof layer, for high-altitude mountaineering when weight and wind-resistance are crucial.

What to Look For

- Appropriate size
- Sufficient weather protection
- Add-on features
- Ease of assembly

Tips

Practise setting up your tent at home. You don't want to be learning how it works in the field.

Tents are generally sold by how many seasons they can be used for. *Three-season* tents are designed for all seasons except heavy snow. Choose a *four-season* tent if snow camping is your thing.

Interior space is designated by how many people the tent can comfortably accommodate, ranging from two to five. This, of course, depends on the size of the people and their comfort level. Also take into account the need to tuck in small children and dogs when looking at sizes.

Better-quality tents come with a lifetime warranty. Keep your receipt in a safe place.

488 Buy a Backpack

Almost any backpack will carry your stuff. The trick is to find one that's comfortable, durable, versatile and convenient.

Steps

1 Define the primary use of your pack. Any one pack is unlikely to be ideal for both short day trips to the beach and carrying all your gear on an overnight camping trip.

2 Look at various sizes. Packs are rated by capacity with internal volume in litres. Small packs, called *daypacks*, are 20 to 30 litres. Serious rucksacks generally range from 60 to 70 litres.

3 Examine pack construction. The simplest packs consist of a polyester bag with straps – fine for short hikes and light loads. Select better-built packs for backpacking and serious use. The pack should have dense padding anywhere the pack touches your body, including the straps, the waist belt and along your back. Make sure the straps are securely sewn to the bag. Better packs have an "airflow system" which increases air circulation around the back.

4 Try on the pack. The thick part of the shoulder straps should rest on top of your shoulders. The waist belt, if any, should rest on top of your hip bones. If possible, place a load in the pack while testing. Larger rucksacks are often adjustable for different torso length; make sure this works for you.

5 Examine the pack's other features. Is the material sturdy and rip-resistant? Are the zippers durable and lockable? Is it water-repellent? Are the outside pockets easy to access and large enough for your needs? Is there a pocket for a water container? If the pack is for winter use, can it carry skis, ice axes or snowshoes? Packs that consist of one compartment without many pockets carry large gear well, but fishing around for small items can be annoying.

6 Understand the frame structure, if any. Large packs used to incorporate an external metal frame to support the load. Most now have a smaller, internal frame, allowing greater freedom of movement and easier manoeuvring in tight places. Some people prefer the additional support of an external frame.

7 If you are a woman, look for a pack specifically created for female backpackers. Frames are designed to fit shorter torsos; hip belts are anatomically constructed to effectively transfer weight without crushing the hip bones; shoulder harnesses and sternum straps fit women's bodies more comfortably.

8 Consider costs. Reasonable quality daypacks can be had for between £15 and £50. A larger rucksack, suitable for serious backpacking, usually costs from £50 to £150, although you can pay more for a top-of-the-range product.

What to Look For

- Total volume
- Comfortable straps and waist belt
- Heavyweight material
- Durable zippers
- Water resistance
- Pockets
- Frame structure

Tips

Carrying books is very hard on a pack. Buy a basic daypack for books and save your outdoor gear for adventures. Single-strap bags or packs, while not recommended for serious hiking or load carrying, might be a good way to carry everyday items.

If your pack hits part of your body wrong or feels uncomfortable, it might just need readjusting.

Make sure a rucksack loaded for an extended trip has the heavy items at the bottom to keep the centre of gravity low.

489 Buy a Camping Stove

Stoves come in a variety of styles and sizes, but most follow the same basic design of a burner attached to a separate fuel source. Your intended uses and destinations will determine which stove and fuel type is the best choice for you.

Steps

1 Think of the most likely type of use for your stove. If you do lots of family camping with children, a sturdy camp stove is your best bet. A popular model made by Coleman has two burners and uses either proprietary liquid fuel or unleaded petrol. For back-packing, explore the many lightweight stoves that are available (see venturesport.co.uk for ideas and prices).

2 Understand the pros and cons of fuel types, primarily refillable liquid fuel bottles or pressurised gas canisters. Liquid fuel performs well in cold weather. It can be purchased in large cans and poured into the stove's fuel bottle. Liquid fuel stoves come in many models, at a typical price of around £60.

3 Choose pressurised gas canisters if simplicity of use is your main concern. These canisters are usually a blend of butane and other gases. Some but not all gas mixtures perform well in cold weath-er. There are many inexpensive stoves that use pressurized gas, costing as little as £20. They are small and easy to pack but not always highly durable. Gas canisters cost a few pounds each.

4 Consider other trade-offs. Gas canisters are not refillable and must be thrown away when empty. It is impossible to determine exactly how much fuel remains in a canister. With a stove using liquid fuel, it is easy to check remaining fuel. Liquid fuel can spill but a canister can't.

5 Buy a stove that can use a variety of fuels for global travel. These are usually referred to as multi-fuel stoves and can be operated on paraffin (kerosene), petrol or even jet fuel.

6 Set up a prospective stove and examine it. Is it easy to assemble and use? Pressurised gas stoves can be lit as soon as the fuel canister is in place. Liquid fuel stoves must be manually pumped then primed by preheating the burner. Make sure you understand the instructions before buying the stove, and learn how to use it at home instead of out in the field.

7 Check stability. Will the stove hold a large pot of water securely? This is a major consideration in the field, where a tip-over might be truly disastrous.

8 Be sure your stove or cooking set includes a windbreak that shields the burner. This is helpful at any time but an absolute necessity in cold or windy weather.

What to Look For

- Appropriate fuel source
- Easy to assemble
- Ease of use
- Stability

Tips

Look for manufacturers that sell pots, plates and cooking utensils in combined sets with a stove. A cooking set and stove that are designed to complement each other will pack neatly together. Expect to pay £40–£50.

Some liquid fuel stoves come with cleaning and repair kits. Don't be scared off by this. Cleaning is only likely to be an issue if you're travelling in parts of the world where paraffin (kerosene) of variable purity is the primary fuel source.

Some stoves have a built-in starter mechanism. These can be handy but unreliable. Always carry a lighter.

Warnings

Never use a stove in an enclosed area, such as a tent. In addition to the fire hazard, you can die from carbon monoxide poisoning.

For long trips, or those where your life depends on your stove's performance, be sure to pack more than one.

490 Buy a Kayak

Many modern kayaks barely resemble the long, narrow traditional crafts of a few years ago. These days you can choose between sea, family, tandem, touring, sit-on-top and white-water kayaks.

Steps

General

1 Look at boats designed for the type of water you are most likely to encounter. Do not expect a single model of kayak to excel in all bodies of water. A touring kayak, for example, would be downright dangerous on river rapids.

2 Understand kayak design. White-water kayaks tend to be less than 2.7 m (9 ft) long and are intended for tight manoeuvring. Sea kayaks range from 3 to 6.7 m (10 to 22 ft) long, with shorter boats more appropriate for beginners. Longer boats are less manoeuvrable but are favoured by more experienced paddlers for speed, paddling ease and improved tracking.

3 Spend time inspecting and paddling kayaks before you buy. Make sure you're comfortable sitting in the boat. Check the footrest, seat and backrest adjustments. Bring a paddle you're comfortable with to isolate differences between boats. Take several boats out for a paddle.

4 Bring any kayak equipment you already own. Check that your spray deck is compatible with any new boat you're trying out.

Sea kayaks

1 Analyse hull advantages: shorter moulded plastic hulls are a good choice for beginning sea kayakers. This material, while not indestructible, is extremely durable and will tolerate scrapes and bumps. Inexpensive moulded plastic may not be rigid enough to satisfy some users. Fibreglass hulls are more rigid but won't tolerate a lot of bumping and scraping. Wooden hulls, while very beautiful, require extra care and frequent maintenance.

2 Move up to faster, lighter and longer hulls of Kevlar or Kevlar-fibreglass combinations as you gain expertise and can handle a less stable sea kayak. Experts savour the even longer ultralight, super-fast hulls made of Kevlar and carbon fibre.

3 Consider the kayak's aesthetic qualities. Many people find a high-quality fibrerglass boat better looking than a moulded plastic one. If this is important to you, get a fibreglass boat, but understand that it may require more care and attention.

4 Buy a boat with a rudder if you're a long-distance paddler. Rudders help the boat track, which means less work for you.

5 Perception, Old Town and Dagger are among the popular brands of touring boats with a wide range of models. Prices vary widely, ranging from around £350 to £800 and upwards.

What to Look For

- Boat to match water
- Hull options
- Boat material
- Watertight

Tip

Some kayaks have a rigid frame covered with water-proof material. Designed to come apart for storage and travel, they are lightweight and convenient, but they don't paddle as well as a rigid boat and won't carry gear either.

Warning

Inspect the watertight compartments. If you can test the boat in the water, check for leaks. If not, check to see that it has been tested and guaranteed. Examine the compartment seals; they need to fit very securely.

OTHER KAYAKS	FUNCTION, FEATURES AND PRICE
Whitewater	Shorter boats are more manoeuvrable. Some are designed for spins and rolls, others for slalom. White-water boats can be good for riding ocean waves. You should be concerned primarily with durability and performance, not aesthetics. Get advice from a shop to match a boat to your preferred use. There are numerous brands of white-water kayaks, although the most popular are Dagger and Perception. Expect to pay £600 to £900.
Inflatable	Inflatables can be convenient and easy to store, but they don't paddle as well as a rigid boat. Some can be used successfully in white water. Cheap boats for use on flat water can cost under £200. More sophisticated models are £400 and up.
Sit-on-top	Paddlers sit directly on the exposed hull, in moulded seats. Sit-on-tops are reassuring to beginners who are not confined in the boat. Basic models start at under £300. Higher-performance models, designed for white water or wave-riding, are £450 and up. Ocean Kayak is one of the most popular brands of this type.

491 Buy a Lifejacket

Many people used to risk death rather than wear a cumbersome, bulky lifejacket. But now a wide range of slick and comfortable buoyancy aids are available, with types designed specifically to meet the needs of different watersport activities.

What to Look For

- Correct type
- Correct size
- Secure fit

Steps

1 Know that all lifejackets and other buoyancy aids sold in the UK must by law conform to European safety standards. Never let yourself be sold an item that is not "CE approved".

2 Understand that lifejackets and vests are classified into four categories, depending on the buoyancy they provide. Buoyancy is measured in Newtons, which gives an N number for different products. The minimum buoyancies for the categories are 50 N, 100 N, 150 N and 275 N. A product in the lowest category is suitable for anglers, waterskiers and lake canoeists. The highest category is needed for boating in the open sea.

3 Be clear what activities you intend to undertake and take care to select a product suitable to that activity. If in doubt, seek advice. Find excellent detailed information on the Marine Warehouse website at lifejackets.co.uk.

4 Make sure the lifejacket or vest fits correctly. With the jacket or vest on and all fasteners closed, you should be able to move your arms freely, and should not be able to pull it off over your head. Ask someone to give it a good tug while you raise your arms. If it moves more than 2.5 cm (1 in) or so, your jacket could be swimming up around your ears just when you need it most.

Tip

Children use identical lifejackets or vests to adults, but in smaller sizes.

Warning

Automatic lifejackets contain a CO2 cylinder, which inflates the jacket when needed. It is vital to ensure that the cylinder is correctly installed and full. Also be aware that gas cylinders differ. Check that the cylinder you are buying is compatible with your lifejacket.

492 Buy a Wetsuit

There are many types of wetsuits, but surf-style suits are perfect for swimming and many watersports. They offer freedom of movement and span a range of water temperatures. Suits designed for scuba diving are vastly different – talk to an instructor before buying one.

Steps

1 Understand the relationship between suit thickness, designated in millimetres, and body warmth. A 4-3 full suit is 4 mm thick in the body and 3 mm thick in the arms and legs, and is the best choice for water that's 10 to 16°C (50 to 60°F). For even colder water, get a 5-mm hooded suit. If you rarely see temperatures this low, consider one that's 1 or 2 mm thick.

2 Decide what kind you need. A suit with cut-off arms and legs is called a *shorty* and is good whenever maximum freedom of movement is needed. A *full suit* extends to your wrists and ankles, and is necessary for colder water. A *long john* has full legs and no arms. It's favoured by paddlers and is the bottom layer for scuba divers.

3 Inspect the seams. The better the construction, the warmer the suit. In a high-quality seam, the edges of the material meet flush, are glued and sewn into place, and are then covered by a strip of cloth. Cheaper seams can leave a small hump and exposed stitching.

4 Try on different brands. You want a snug fit that doesn't constrict your movement or breathing. All suits enlarge slightly with use. Avoid suits that bag around your waist or ankles.

5 Set your budget according to how often you'll use your wetsuit. An inexpensive shorty costs about £50, while a better-quality one may be £80. A top-quality full suit may cost £200 or more.

6 Choose a wetsuit for children based on the same criteria. Small-sized wetsuits range from £30 upwards. Keep in mind that children often grow out of a wetsuit before they wear it out, which makes finding a good used one a smart move. As they grow, children want to spend more time in the water, which requires buying a better suit.

What to Look For

- Appropriate thickness
- Suitable type
- Glued and taped seams
- Snug fit

Tips

The zipper on a surf suit runs up your back. Avoid embarrassment in the shop by remembering this. All zippered wetsuits are hard to get on and off; you just have to practise.

Rinse out suits used in salt-water after every use.

Warning

Adults should not buy used wetsuits unless they like being cold. Even the best suits wear out rapidly, begin to leak and lose their suppleness.

493 Buy a Surfboard

Most accomplished surfers are unemployed for a reason. Surfing requires total commitment. Even buying a board is tough. However, surfboard selection is surprisingly non-technical. Experienced surfers choose boards based on feel, intuition and experience as much as on any hard data. So leave your job, select a board and get in the water.

Steps

1 Find a comfortable spot and watch some surfers. Study the boards. Big boards glide easily but turn slowly. Small boards turn quickly but glide poorly.

2 Decide on a type of board. Small boards – less than about 7 ft (210 cm) in length, with pointed noses – are called *shortboards*. These are ideal for aggressive, rapid manoeuvres. Larger boards – usually 9 to 10 ft (240 to 270 cm), with rounded noses – are called *longboards*, and excel at graceful, smooth turns.

3 If you're a beginner, get a cheap board that you can knock around while learning, not an expensive and stylish board. If you buy a used board, check that the fins are securely in place and that there are no holes in the fibreglass. Small repairs are fine, but avoid boards that have been broken in half and repaired.

4 Inspect the dimensions, usually written on the bottom. For beginners, concern yourself with the length, width and thickness. Ignore the nose and tail dimensions. Width ranges from about 18 to 21 in (20 to 53 cm). Most thicknesses fall between 2 and 3 in (5 and 7.5 cm).

5 Larger surfers need larger boards. A 220-lb (82-kg) person might choose a 7-ft (210 cm) shortboard, 21 in (53 cm) wide and 3 in (7.5 cm) thick. An 80-lb (30-kg) child will surf better on a 5-ft (150-cm) board, 18 in (45 cm) wide and 2 in (5 cm) thick. For longboards, most people choose 9-ft (240-cm) boards. People of above average size should consider slightly longer boards, such as 9 ft 6 in (285 cm).

6 Avoid very old boards; they just won't surf very well. Old long-boards are easy to identify because they weigh over 20 lb (7.5 kg). If it's hard to lift, it will be hard to surf with. Also avoid shortboards with only one fin. A modern shortboard has three or more fins.

7 Expect to pay at least £150 for a reasonable shortboard. Better shortboards cost £300 and upwards. A good longboard will set you back around £500 or more.

What to Look For

- Appropriate type
- Correct dimensions
- Affordable price

Tips

Most shops make their own boards. Ask about having a board custom-made. The shop will have ideas about what will work for you, based on your experience and size, and the local waves.

Wax is applied to the top of a surfboard for grip. If you buy your board from a surf shop, it will usually throw in a few bars of wax for free.

Surfboards around the world are sold in feet and inches, not in metric measurement.

494 Buy Fly-Fishing Gear

For many seasoned enthusiasts, shopping for the right fly-fishing gear resembles the quest for the Holy Grail. The best advice for the new-comer is to spend as little as possible until you're committed to the sport, then reward yourself with the best gear you can afford.

Steps

1 Establish a relationship with a knowledgeable shop. In addition to getting help with gear, you will also gain access to important fishing information and news.

2 Buy only equipment you want. A shop that is willing to work with you should understand this immediately and shouldn't push you into making unnecessary purchases. Some people enjoy owning every bit of gear they can carry. This is fine if you enjoy it, but not essential.

3 Start by purchasing a rod-reel-line combination. Decent basic combos – often described as "classic" – can be had for £120. You needn't concern yourself with rod materials and characteristics at first – you want an inexpensive set with which to learn the basics. Later, get a high-quality rod with a lifetime guarantee. Materials range from wood-laminates to fibreglass.

4 Buy a good pair of waders, which allow you to stay dry while entering the water and are mandatory for comfort in cold water. Thigh waders are essentially a high-leg version of wellies. Chest waders are dungarees with attached boots. All waders need to fit securely to provide stability on wet rocks. Inexpensive waders for about £35 are fine for occasional use. For frequent use, spend over £100 to get a longer-lasting pair.

5 Save money on expendable items. Some of your stock of flies, line and leaders will end up decorating the bushes at your favourite fishing spot. There's no need to waste money on top-quality items at first.

6 Befriend an old pro, or buy an instruction book and video, and start tying those flies. Fly-fishing requires knowledge of specific knots – practise at home before you go fishing.

7 Embrace two competing concepts when buying flies. First, seek and listen to advice. Don't expect the experts to share all their secrets, but most will be happy to set you on the right path. Second, experiment with your own ideas.

8 Experiment with different rods as you develop your casting style. Your technique will determine the rod length and stiffness that works best for you.

What to Look For

- Knowledgeable shop
- Basic rod-reel-and-line set for beginners
- Accessories
- Pair of waders
- Fly-tying book and video

Tip

Try out new flies and fishing spots. In addition to an adventure, you may also get some stories to tell your fellow enthusiasts.

495 Buy Rock-Climbing Equipment

Aspiring rock climbers may find the equipment intimidating at first – but if you ask lots of questions and buy over time, it can be fun. Only buy new equipment, and only from a reputable shop. Treat your gear as if your life depends on it, because it does. Here are a few tips on some of the kit to look for.

ITEM	WHAT TO LOOK FOR
Rope	Various rope systems are in use today, but for the majority of climbing needs, a single rope, 10.5 mm (4 in) diameter and 50 m (160 ft) long, will do. Make sure you buy a dynamic climbing rope, not a static rope: £100–£130.
Harness	An inexpensive harness is fine for most climbing. More money will add clever features but will not necessarily be safer. Spend more for a harness that is easy to get in to. It should be comfortable but able to be tightened until it is very snug. From £30.
Climbing Shoes	Fit is the most important consideration for shoes, and the only way to find that perfect fit is to try on different models. Buy the smallest shoe you can comfortably wear for long periods: £50–£70.
Karabiners	These metal links attach ropes to harnesses and slings. They come in two major styles – locking and non-locking. Locking karabiners are more secure but can sometimes be cumbersome. All types are strong enough for general use, so don't worry about strength ratings unless you really enjoy engineering trivia or are doing some specialised climbing. An introductory climbing set should include four locking and four non-locking karabiners: £5–£15 each.
Slings	Slings are strong, flat, ribbonlike materials with numerous climbing applications used to secure a climber or karabiner to the rock. While slings are now made from a variety of materials, the most common and affordable type is nylon. You can buy a sling 4 m (13 ft) long and 10 mm (0.4 in) wide for around £20. Consider buying different colours for ease of identification.
Pitons	Steel pegs hammered into the rock to secure a climber. State-of-the-art equipment for decades, they have been supplanted by newer, easier-to-use tools that do not scar the rock. An introductory climbing set does not require pitons, but it may be fun to own one for practice or as a paperweight. Understand that it is considered bad form to hammer pitons indiscriminately into the rock at popular climbing spots.
Nuts (Chocks)	A small metal block with cable or wire attached, which can be inserted into a crack in the rock, creating a secure anchor. Well-equipped climbers on extended climbs carry a large selection of nuts in different sizes. Again, an introductory climbing set does not require these, but eventually you will want to become skilled in their use. Consider buying a few small nuts for practice: £7.50 to £10 each.
Cams	A cam is essentially a nut that can expand or contract to fit a variety of crack widths. They perform the same function as nuts, although they are much more sophisticated and offer great flexibility of use. Not required in a basic set-up, but aspiring climbers should practise with them as soon as possible: £40–£80 each.
Instruction Book	There's no substitute for climbing instruction from a qualified guide, but you can learn a lot while sitting in your armchair. Purchase a book that covers the basics, including a section on climbing terminology and etiquette. Most important, make sure the book has a section on rock-climbing knots, and practise whenever you can.

CTION SITES • BUY BARGAIN CLOTHING • BUY WHOLESALE • GET OUT OF DEBT • BUY NOTHING • BUY HAPPINESS • BUY A BETTER MOUS
Y YOUR WAY INTO SOMEONE'S FAVOUR • BUY LOVE • FIND THE RIGHT RELAXATION TECHNIQUE FOR YOU • BUY HEALTHY FAST FOOD • BU
RVICE • SELL YOURSELF ON AN ONLINE DATING SERVICE • SELL YOURSELF TO YOUR GIRLFRIEND/BOYFRIEND'S FAMILY • BUY FLOWERS TO
OOSE FILM FOR YOUR CAMERA • BUY RECHARGEABLE BATTERIES • GIVE TO A GOOD CAUSE • TAKE PART IN A CAR BOOT SALE • EMPLOY
DENT DISCOUNTS • BUY FLOWERS WHOLESALE • GET A PICTURE FRAMED • EMPLOY A REMOVAL COMPANY • EMPLOY A LIFESTYLE MAN
Y FOR A HALLOWE'EN PARTY • BUY A GREAT BIRTHDAY PRESENT FOR UNDER £10 • SELECT GOOD CHAMPAGNE • BUY A DIAMOND • BUY
A GIFT LIST • BUY WEDDING GIFTS • SELECT BRIDESMAIDS' DRESSES • HIRE AN EVENTS ORGANISER • HIRE A BARTENDER FOR A PARTY
NOUNCEMENTS • SELL YOUR WEDDING DRESS • BUY AN ANNIVERSARY GIFT • ARRANGE ENTERTAINMENT FOR A PARTY • COMMISSION A
O HAS EVERYTHING • BUY A GIFT FOR PASSING EXAMS • SELECT A CHRISTMAS TURKEY • BUY A HOUSEWARMING GIFT • PURCHASE CHR
ESSAGE IN THE SKY • HIRE A BIG-NAME BAND • GET INTO A PRIVATE GAMBLING ROOM IN LAS VEGAS • BUY SOMEONE A STAR • PAY A RA
PLOY A BUTLER • BUY A FOOTBALL CLUB • BUY A PERSONAL JET • SELECT A CLASSIC CAR • ACQUIRE A BODY GUARD • BOOK A LUXURY
CE • BUY A RACEHORSE • BUY A VILLA IN TUSCANY • EMPLOY A PERSONAL CHEF • BUY A JOURNEY INTO SPACE • EMPLOY A GHOSTWRIT
ERT WITNESS • MAKE MONEY FROM ACCIDENT COMPENSATION • DONATE YOUR BODY TO SCIENCE • MAKE MONEY AS A MEDICAL GUINE
N FOR RETIREMENT • COPE WITH HIGHER EDUCATION COSTS • BUY AND SELL SHARES • CHOOSE A STOCKBROKER • DAY-TRADE (OR NO
E INSURANCE • GET PRIVATE HEALTH INSURANCE • BUY PERSONAL FINANCE SOFTWARE • CHOOSE AN ACCOUNTANT • FIND CASUAL WOR
RKET YOUR INVENTION • FINANCE YOUR BUSINESS IDEA • BUY A SMALL BUSINESS • BUY A FRANCHISE • LEASE RETAIL SPACE • LEASE IN
IGNER • ACQUIRE CONTENT FOR YOUR WEBSITE • BUY ADVERTISING ON THE WEB • SELL YOUR ART • HIRE A LIFE COACH • SELL ON THE
-AND-BREAKFAST • SELL A FAILING BUSINESS • BUY A HOT DOG STAND • SHOP FOR A MORTGAGE • GET A BETTER MORTGAGE DEAL • S
USE ONLINE • BUY A PROPERTY FOR RENOVATION AND RESALE • EVALUATE BEFORE BUYING INTO A NEW AREA • EXCHANGE CONTRACTS
USE DESIGNED • HIRE AN ARCHITECT • HIRE A BUILDER • GET PLANNING PERMISSION • BUY A HOLIDAY HOME • RENT A HOLIDAY HOME •
ME FOR A LOCATION SHOOT • FURNISH YOUR HOME • FURNISH YOUR STUDIO FLAT • BUY USED FURNITURE • BUY DOOR AND WINDOW L
' FLOOR-CARE APPLIANCES • BUY EXTENDED WARRANTIES ON APPLIANCES • FIND PERIOD FIXTURES • BUY A BED AND MATTRESS • HIRE
NISH • CHOOSE DECORATIVE TILES • CHOOSE A DEHUMIDIFIER • BUY A WHIRLPOOL BATH • BUY A SHOWER • BUY A TOILET • CHOOSE A
VE • SELECT FLOORING • SELECT CARPETING • CHOOSE KITCHEN CABINETS • CHOOSE A KITCHEN WORKTOP • BUY GREEN HOUSEHOLD
NOXIDE DETECTORS • BUY FIRE EXTINGUISHERS • CHOOSE AN ENTRY DOOR • BUY A GARAGE-DOOR OPENER • BUY TIMBER FOR A DIY P
FECT ROSE • BUY FLOWERING BULBS • BUY FLOWERS FOR YOUR GARDEN • SELECT PEST CONTROLS • BUY SOIL IMPROVERS • BUY MU
LAWN • BUY A LAWN MOWER • BUY KOI FOR YOUR FISH POND • BUY A STORAGE SHED • HIRE A TREE SURGEON • BUY BASIC GARDEN
SELL AT FARMERS' MARKETS • SELECT KITCHEN KNIVES • DECIPHER FOOD LABELS • SELECT HERBS AND SPICES • STOCK YOUR KITCH
ORGANIC BEEF • BUY HAGGIS • PURCHASE LOCAL HONEY • CHOOSE A CHICKEN • SELECT FRESH FISH • SELECT RICE • PURCHASE PR
SAN CHEESES • PURCHASE KOSHER FOOD • BUY SENSIBLY IN SUPERMARKETS • CHOOSE COOKING OILS • SELECT OLIVE OIL • SELECT
FEEMAKER OR ESPRESSO MACHINE • PURCHASE PARTY BEER • CHOOSE THE RIGHT WINE • CHOOSE A REAL ALE • ORDER A COCKTAIL •
PICK A PREGNANCY TEST KIT • CHOOSE BIRTH CONTROL • CHOOSE WHERE TO GIVE BIRTH • HIRE A MIDWIFE OR DOULA • PLAN A HOM
RENT A BREAST PUMP • CHOOSE A CAR SEAT • BUY CHILD-PROOFING SUPPLIES • FIND RELIABLE CHILDCARE • FIND A GREAT NANNY • F
FRIENDLY HOTEL • ORGANISE A FUND-RAISING EVENT • BUY BRACES FOR YOUR KID • BUY TOYS • BUY BOOKS, VIDEOS AND MUSIC FOR
THES AND BOOKS • FIND A COUPLES COUNSELLOR • HIRE A FAMILY SOLICITOR • BUY OR RENT SHELTERED HOUSING • CHOOSE A CARE
ANTIWRINKLE CREAMS • SELECT PAIN RELIEF AND COLD MEDICINES • CHOOSE A COMPLEMENTARY MTHERAPY • SEE A MENTAL-HEALTH
A WIG OR HAIRPIECE • BUY A NEW BODY • GET A TATTOO OR BODY PIERCING • OBTAIN BREAST IMPLANTS • GET WRINKLE-FILLER INJEC
SONAL TRAINER • SIGN UP FOR A YOGA CLASS • TREAT YOURSELF TO A DAY AT THE SPA • BOOK A MASSAGE • GET ON ANTIQUES ROAD
R COLLECTIBLES ARE WORTH • BARTER WITH DEALERS • GET AN ANTIQUE APPRAISED • BUY SILVERWARE • EVALUATE CARNIVAL GLASS
IDATE YOUR BEANIE BABY COLLECTION • SCORE AUTOGRAPHS • TRADE YU-GI-OH CARDS • SEIZE STAR WARS ACTION FIGURES • SELL
D COLLECTION • CHOOSE A DESKTOP COMPUTER • SHOP FOR A USED COMPUTER OR PERIPHERALS • CHOOSE A LAPTOP OR NOTEBOO
VIDER • GET AN INTERNET DOMAIN NAME • NETWORK YOUR COMPUTERS • UPGRADE THE MEMORY IN YOUR COMPUTER • BUY COMPU
TAL ASSISTANT • CHOOSE A MOBILE PHONE SERVICE • GET A BETTER DEAL FROM YOUR PHONE COMPANY • BUY VIDEO AND COMPUTER
HE-ART SOUND SYSTEM • BUY AN AUDIO/VIDEO DISTRIBUTION SYSTEM • BUY A SERIOUS TV • CHOOSE BETWEEN DIGITAL TV PROVIDER
IOS • BUY A MOBILE ENTERTAINMENT SYSTEM • GET A PASSPORT, QUICK! • PURCHASE CHEAP AIRLINE TICKETS • FIND GREAT HOTEL DE
NS-SIBERIAN EXPRESS • BUY DUTY-FREE • SHIP FOREIGN PURCHASES TO THE UNITED KONGDOM • TIP IN A FOREIGN COUNTRY • TIP PRO
KAGE FOR THE GREEK ISLANDS • RAFT THE GRAND CANYON • BOOK A CHEAP BUT FANTASTIC SAFARI • RENT A CAMEL IN CAIRO • GET S
G KONG • BUY YOUR WAY ONTO A MOUNT EVEREST EXPEDITION • HIRE A TREKKING COMPANY IN NEPAL • RENT OR BUY A SATELLITE PH
Y GOLF CLUBS • SELL FOUND GOLF BALLS • BUY PORTS SHOES • BUY A RACKET • BUY A HEALTH CLUB MEMBERSHIP • BUY AN AEROB
TES • GO BUNJEE JUMPING • GO SKYDIVING • BUY WEIGHTLIFTING EQUIPMENT • CHOOSE A CAR RACK • BUY SKIS • BUY CLOTHES FOR
Y CYCLE CLOTHING • BUY A PROPERLY FITTING HELMET • BUY THE OPTIMAL SLEEPING BAG • BUY A TENT • BUY A BACKPACK • BUY A C
A CASHMERE JUMPER • PURCHASE VINTAGE CLOTHING • SELL USED CLOTHING • ORDER CUSTOM-MADE COWBOY BOOTS • BUY CLOT
A MAN • BUY A MAN'S DRESS SHIRT • PICK OUT A TIE • BUY A WOMAN'S SUIT • BUY A MAN'S SUIT • HIRE A TAILOR • BUY CUSTOM-TAIL
FORMANCE SWIM SUIT • BUY PERFORMANCE WORKOUT CLOTHES • BUY A HEART-RATE MONITOR • SELECT A WATCH • BUY KIDS' CLOTH
SELL A CAR ONLINE • BUY A HYBRID CAR • SELL A CAR • BUY A MOTORCYCLE • BUYING AND CHANGING MOTOR OIL • WASH A CAR • WA

Clothing & Accessories

496 Buy a Cashmere Jumper

Cashmere is synonymous with softness and luxury, and the finest garments are still manufactured in Scotland. Quality counts, though, so be a savvy shopper. After all, it took four years for a goat to grow enough wool for your jumper, and if taken care of well, it will last a lifetime.

Steps

1 Prepare to part with some cash: this high-quality, soft wool is an investment, averaging £130 for a 100 per cent cashmere jumper.

2 Pull gently and release the sides of the jumper. A high-quality garment returns to its proper shape; a loosely knit one doesn't.

3 Feel the fabric. If it feels coarse or fuzzy, it's a sign of poor quality. In the world of cashmere, softer is better. Lighter-coloured garments are softer since darker dyes are harsher on the yarn.

4 Check if the jumper is two-ply knit, which is sturdier than one-ply but still lightweight. Ply refers to weight, not quality.

5 Beware of bargains and mislabelling. In recent years, cashmere and sheep wool blends have been sold as 100 per cent cashmere. If the price seems too good to be true, it probably is.

What to Look For

- Quality weave
- Soft texture
- At least two-ply knit
- Pure cashmere

Tips

Many cashmere items can be hand-washed safely. Use baby shampoo or gentle-wash detergent and rinse well. Washing actually makes cashmere softer, allowing the yarns to bloom.

Use a lint brush to remove pills, which should be minimal on a good-quality garment.

497 Purchase Vintage Clothing

Whether your style is a 1970s Adidas jogging suit or a 1950s Chanel suit, an authentic disco shirt or a period zoot suit, going retro is a way to stand apart from the crowd.

Steps

1 Search out local and online sources that specialise in high-quality vintage clothes from a particular era or style.

2 Scour charity shops, car boot sales and flea markets for bargain-priced treasures, from wedding gowns and embroidered aprons to leather jackets and 1960s flares.

3 Plan to shop frequently because the availability of vintage clothing is, by its nature, hit or miss.

4 Consider having a quality item altered if it's too big. Some damage can be repaired – it's easy to sew up a split seam but not a moth hole. Odours and stains are often permanent. Factor in the complexity and cost of alterations. For example, it's easier and cheaper to take up a trouser hem than to take in a lined jacket.

5 Examine the garment's quality and condition. Check stress points such as under the arms for wear, and make sure zips work.

What to Look For

- Correct size and flattering fit
- Garment condition

Tips

Vintage fabrics can be fragile. A cleaner can advise you on whether to dry-clean or hand-wash the garment.

Don't go by the size on the label; always try the garment on.

498 Sell Used Clothing

If your wardrobe is bursting at the seams with clothing you've barely worn, turn your clutter into cash – and make room for that next purchase you can't live without – by selling your clothes online or at second-hand clothes shops.

Steps

1 Clean out your wardrobe. Toss worn-out or stained clothes in the ragbag. Pull out clothes, shoes and accessories that are in good shape, still in fashion and will be in season for the next few months. Sort kids' clothes by size and gender.

2 Clean and iron the clothes. You are more likely to sell them if they look good.

3 Act as your own retailer by selling your clothes, especially designer or vintage items, on your own website or auction sites like eBay.co.uk. To get the best possible price, write clear, accurate descriptions, give specific dimensions and include quality colour photos.

4 Walk away with cash – or more clothes – by selling casual styles to second-hand shops. They normally pay about 30 to 40 per cent of the price that they intend to charge for your items – more if you take store credit instead.

5 Look around for up-market second-hand shops that specialise in designer clothes. If necessary, make an appointment to take in your clothes. Check to see if there is a maximum number of garments that you can bring in. The more up-market the area, the more money you are likely to get for your couture cast-offs.

What to Look For

- Clothes clean and in season
- Appropriate shop for your clothing

Tips

Donate your unsold clothing to a local charity shop.

Think a season ahead or target the very beginning of seasons with weather-sensitive items such as winter coats and boots, and shorts and sandals.

499 Order Custom-made Cowboy Boots

Not just for cowboys – or cowgirls – these boots are classy and time-less and, in some places, the ultimate fashion statement. Exquisitely comfortable and intricately tooled, custom boots are an investment that can run from £150 to £16,000 or more.

Steps

1 Find a good custom bootmaker – *Yellow Pages* is a good place to start – and find out whether they will make cowboy boots. Alternatively, shop online.

2 Choose the leather or skin. Cowhide is common, tough and cheap, but if you're willing to pay a little more for dress boots and aren't squeamish, choose something exotic, such as eel, ostrich, lizard, shark, kangaroo, goat, deer, python or alligator. Get a feel for the texture and ask about a particular material's durability. A range of colour options are available.

3 Select a boot style and height. Western boots go all the way up the calf. Stockman, packers and work-style boots are a few inches shorter. Others come up a few inches above or fit right at the ankle.

4 Look at heels and soles. There are riding heels, walking heels and combinations; the standard height is 4½ cm (1¾ in). Soles are made from leather, thick crepe or rubber. What you plan to be kicking while wearing the boots will determine the type of heel height you need.

5 Specify a toe shape. Western boots have a very pointy toe. Ropers and work boots are more rounded. There are many other options including French toes and square-cut hog noses.

6 Indulge your wildest fantasies with decorative options. Bootmakers pride themselves on exquisite stitching, wingtips, inlay patterns, silver or gold toe and heel plates, and intricate custom designs. For the ultimate gift, have your sweetheart's name inlaid in green lizard.

7 Measure your feet according to the instructions provided by the bootmaker. Unlike shoes or boots that lace, a cowboy boot is held snug to the foot by the instep alone. Proper fit is critical: make sure you take accurate measurements.

8 Get all design options, costs and the delivery date, if applicable, in writing. Ask what recourse you have if you're unhappy with the finished results. Most artisans proudly guarantee both the work and your satisfaction; many have repeat customers who come back again and again over the years.

9 Pull on your boots, kick up your heels and enjoy.

What to Look For

- Local artisan or online store
- Type of leather
- Style and height
- Heel, sole and toe
- Decorative details
- Foot measurements
- Guarantee
- Delivery date

Tips

If you're unsure about measuring your feet yourself, visit a local shoe shop and ask a sales assistant to do it for you.

A bootmaker can take a few months to over a year to finish a pair of boots.

Scallops – the shape of the top of the boot – vary from a straight cut to a deep scallop cut, plus more decorative shapes.

500 Buy Clothes Online

Although you can't finger the fabric or try on the item, the payoff in convenience and an almost unlimited selection may make you a convert once you master the basics of buying clothes online.

Steps

1 Ask a friend, a tailor or a clothes shop assistant to help you measure your chest, waist, hips, arm length and inside leg (the distance from your crotch to where you want the hem of your trousers to fall). Another way to get your inside leg is to measure a pair of trousers that fit perfectly.

2 Look for sites that provide you with lots of information about their clothes via high-quality photos and detailed descriptions, dimensions and sizing information.

3 Contact customer service by phone or e-mail with any questions not addressed by the site's frequently asked questions (FAQ) area. Representatives often have additional notes about the fit or care of items. Some sites let you converse with customer service reps by typing in questions and receiving instant answers.

4 Buy several items at the same time to avoid paying individual postage and packing. Look for retailers that offer free shipping when you spend a certain amount.

5 Understand the returns policy. Some online retailers let you return clothes to their local store, which saves you shipping charges. Be sure to bring your shipping invoice. Some stores provide a prepaid postage label for returns, which reduces the hassle of returns. Many stores don't charge additional postage and packing when exchanging an item for a different size (see 4 "Take Goods Back").

6 Read the fine print before you click the button to finalise your order. Reputable retailers have secure sites to keep your credit card and personal information safe and private, but you may have to click on a specific box to prevent your name from being sold to other mailing lists or to avoid receiving additional catalogues.

What to Look For

- Accurate body measurements
- Detailed product information
- Customer service
- Postage and packing charges
- Returns policies
- Fine print

Tips

If you have a favourite web retailer, sign up to be notified about upcoming sales via e-mail.

Online clothing sites are often packed with images, which can make web pages load slowly. Save time and frustration by browsing through a retailer's catalogue before you go online.

See 65 "Buy or Rent Men's Formal Wear".

501 Find Non-standard Sizes

Do you have trouble buying clothes or shoes off the peg? You're not alone if you fall outside the limits of what the fashion industry considers standard sizes. Here are some resources for finding clothes and shoes that actually fit.

Steps

1 Start with local retailers, especially department stores and speciality shops, such as High & Mighty for men's clothes.

2 Ask shops if they will custom order items for you from the manufacturer. Sales assistants may also recommend other sources.

3 Take advantage of online and catalogue shopping. A number of companies offer clothes in tall sizes, but sometimes in their catalogue or on their website only. Take advantage of search engines, chat rooms and newsgroups to find retailers that carry your size. Sites that let you search multiple merchants at one time, such as uk.shopping.yahoo.com, are also good resources.

4 Find brands that cater to your size. For example, New Balance trainers come in varying widths, and Liz Claiborne makes lines of petite and outsize women's clothing. Larger department stores tend to carry clothing in a wide range of sizes.

5 Consider having shoes or clothes made to measure if you have difficulty finding your size. Some up-market shops will tailor custom clothing, especially suits. Working one-to-one with a tailor gives you more options and control over the design (see 509 "Hire a Tailor").

What to Look For

- Helpful sales assistants
- Department stores
- Informative websites
- Brands that cater to special sizes
- Made-to-measure shoes or clothing

Tip

Understand the returns policies, especially on custom orders. Just because an item is the right size doesn't mean it's going to be comfortable or fit well.

502 Buy the Perfect Cocktail Dress

Picture Audrey Hepburn in *Breakfast at Tiffany's.* Elegant, timeless and tasteful, a stylish cocktail dress has long been a must-have item for any woman's wardrobe.

Steps

1 Shop at good department stores, such as John Lewis and House of Fraser, to find options in the £70 to £100 range. If you intend to spend more or want something unusual, head to a boutique.

2 Buy an all-season fabric, such as lightweight wool or silk. Linen and cotton are also options, but their colour may fade faster. Test how easily the fabric wrinkles: grab and release a handful.

3 Ignore hemline fads and select a flattering length just above or around the middle of the knee. Shorten a dress that's too long.

4 Look for a versatile style that you can dress up or down with different shoes, jewellery and other accessories. A sleeveless or short-sleeved dress works year-round, either alone or with a jacket, jumper or shawl.

What to Look For

- All-season fabric
- Flattering fit and cut
- Timeless lines
- Versatile style

Tips

When you try the dress on, walk, sit and dance around to make sure it's comfortable.

Go from day to night in a flash: replace a canvas bag, denim jacket and sandals with a beaded bag, pashmina shawl and stilettos.

503 Buy Designer Clothes at a Discount

So you're a believer that it's better to have fewer high-quality items than a wardrobe packed with cheap clothes? The sales racks at department stores and boutiques aren't the only way to hunt out a bargain.

Steps

1 Remember the cardinal rule: everything eventually goes on sale. When new clothes arrive, shops have to clear out anything that's been on the racks too long. Keep checking back to find out if the price of your designer treasure has been reduced.

2 Shop at up-market factory shops and villages to find seasonal overstock from designers and lots of specially made merchandise at deep price cuts.

3 Visit second-hand, vintage clothing and charity shops. You never know when you might spot a designer bargain.

4 Check the internet. You may also be able to find designer clothes at heavily discounted prices on eBay.co.uk.

What to Look For

- Sales
- Second-hand, vintage clothing and charity shops
- Discount designer websites

Tip

There are usually heavy mark-downs at January and summer sales.

504 Choose a Basic Wardrobe for a Man

A man's wardrobe – and his ability to coordinate that wardrobe – expresses his personal style and taste. But comfort and care also play a big part. This chart demonstrates the basics for a stylish wardrobe, plus some suggestions for injecting more personality.

ITEM	QUANTITY	COLOUR	STYLE	FABRIC	FOR FLAIR
Blazer/ Sports Jacket	1	Navy blue or tan camel hair	Proper fit	100 per cent wool	Nubuck suede in chocolate brown
Formal shirts	2 or 3, more if worn daily	Basic white, then light or French blue, or ecru	Button-down or straight collars	100 per cent cotton or cotton-polyester blend (depending on ironing skills)	French cuffs with cuff links
Casual Shirts	1	White, black or other solid neutral	Polo shirts, T-shirts, turtlenecks	Cotton knit or cotton-lycra blend	Retro '50s style
Jumper	1	Neutral	V-neck or crew-neck	Cotton, wool or cashmere	Silk; deeper colours
Smart Trousers	1	Navy, mid-grey, tan or charcoal	Pleats	100 per cent wool	Lightweight wool; pinstripe; flat front
Chinos	1	Tan, stone or olive	Pleats	100 per cent cotton	Corduroys; flat front
Jeans	1	Medium wash	Not too baggy, not too tight	Denim, of course!	Black
Ties	2 or 3, more if worn daily	Red, burgundy or patterns	Width and length according to current fashion	Silk	Graphic prints, vibrant colours
Belt	2	Black and/or brown; should match shoes	One for casual trousers, one for smart trousers	Leather	Suede with contrast stitch-ing
Smart Shoes	1	Black or cordovan (reddish-black)	Cap-toe or wing tip	Leather	Square toe; tassel
Casual Shoes	1	Brown or black	Loafers or oxfords	Leather	Low-rise boots
TIPS	To save time, take advantage of free personal shoppers at department stores. Read care labels. Don't buy a garment that requires hand-washing or dry-cleaning if you throw everything in the washing machine.				

505 Buy a Man's Shirt

Men are no longer limited to the standard white shirt. While it remains a classic choice, options have expanded to include many more colours and styles. Prices start at about £25 and go up to hundreds of pounds for a hand-stitched shirt.

Steps

1 Buy all-cotton, which breathes and offers the greatest comfort. Look for cottons that have been treated to resist wrinkles.

2 Examine the collar. Though styles differ, every collar should be aligned, lay flat and fit snugly but comfortably around the neck. The best shirts have removable stiffeners, which hold the collar's points and keep them in place. Never wear a button-down collar with a suit; instead opt for a spread collar.

3 Inspect the shirt's stitching. A higher-quality shirt has single-needle stitching and 22 stitches per inch, and cross-stitched buttons for durability. The design on any patterned shirt should meet perfectly at the seams.

4 Select a cut to accommodate your build. Shirts come in either a fitted cut or a standard cut, which is looser.

What to Look For

- All cotton
- Collar details
- Stitching and seams
- Standard versus fitted cut

Tips

Have the sales assistant measure your neck size and sleeve length, if you are not sure of your correct size or if your weight has fluctuated since your last shopping trip.

French cuffs with cuff links add a dash of style.

Ceramic buttons are nearly indestructible.

506 Pick Out a Tie

Ties allow for a bit of creativity in what might otherwise be a straight-forward ensemble. While colour and pattern depend on personal preference, the right tie should have excellent construction.

Steps

1 Inspect the tie's lining. It should extend from the bottom of the tie to its narrowest point. A fully lined tie costs more; most ties these days are not fully lined.

2 Check the stitching along the back of the tie, which helps maintain the shape. Slip stitching runs vertically, while bar tacking runs horizontally across the bottom and top ends. An up-market tie has bar tacking on the top and bottom.

3 Get a feel for the fabric. Silk is the most popular because it holds its shape, and it's lightweight and durable. Polyester blends also hold their shape, but don't take dye as well as natural fabrics do. Excessive wrinkling can be a problem with cotton ties.

4 Expect to pay at least £30 to £65 for a nice tie. Prices can exceed £200 for a designer or a handmade tie.

5 Find extra-long ties – for taller or not-so-thin men – at some department stores.

What to Look For

- Lining
- Inner facing
- Stitching
- Fabric
- Handmade ties

Tips

Wear a white dress shirt to serve as a backdrop for viewing ties.

"Hand-finished" does not mean that a tie is handmade, only that the last few steps were performed by hand.

The background colour of the tie should match or complement your shirt or suit.

507 Buy a Woman's Suit

Whether you want a formal suit for an interview, a trouser suit for a wedding party or a classic Armani, look for a suit that's stylish, well made and fits like a dream.

Steps

1 Consider where you will wear the suit and how dressy your attire needs to be. Options include a formal skirt suit, a casual trouser suit or an interchangeable set with a jacket, skirt and trousers. If you wear different sizes on top and on bottom, your best bet is to buy matching separates.

2 Head to a clothes shop that matches your style and budget. Because fit is so important with a suit, buying online is riskier, but possible if you're familiar with a retailer or designer's fit and have a good tailor.

3 Anticipate spending at least £200 to £300. (Prices range from £130 to £1,500 or more.) Keep in mind that a higher price doesn't necessarily mean a better suit. Some manufacturers are coming out with stylish yet less expensive suits.

4 Get a high-quality, all-season fabric such as 100 per cent worsted wool, which looks and wears better better than polyester blends. If you're expanding your suit collection, you might consider more seasonal fabrics such as cotton twill, linen or silk.

5 Find a colour that fits your needs. Start with a neutral like navy, black or grey before adding other colours.

6 Find a jacket style that suits you. Choose from single- or less popular double-breasted jackets; with a lapel and collar (or neither); and a cut and length that flatters your figure. Once you've found a style you like, inspect the construction and fit in more detail.

7 Try the jacket on. You should be able to move your arms freely. The shoulders should be about 2½ cm (1in) wider than your shoulder bone, and the sleeves should extend to about the wrist bone. Button the jacket to test for comfort and to make sure the buttons don't gape across the chest or pull over the hips.

8 Choose a flattering style for the skirt or trousers. Flat-front trousers tend to be more slimming. Straight skirts aren't very forgiving but can be slimming when they fit just right. An A-line, pleated or slit skirt makes walking easier. You should be able to insert two fingers into the waistband. Choose a length that's appropriate for its intended use.

9 Examine the construction of each piece. They should be fully lined with straight hems, flat-lying collars and buttons that are even. Zips, buttons and other fasteners should lie flat. Pockets shouldn't gape, and the hem should hang straight.

What to Look For

- Appropriate style
- Wool fabric
- Colour, style
- Quality construction
- Comfortable fit

Tips

Investing in alterations can make an enormous difference in how the suit feels and looks.

Wear a blouse, smart shoes and hosiery, or try on matching garments with the suit.

Plastic buttons can be replaced with higher-quality ones of pearl or bone.

Make sure your freedom of movement is unrestricted – sit, walk and pick something up off the floor to test.

10 Have a knowledgeable sales assistant or, better yet, a tailor check the suit's fit before you buy it. Spend the money to have your suit altered to fit.

508 Buy a Man's Suit

Whether you need another suit for the office or want to dress to impress at an upcoming special occasion, a sharp suit is a wardrobe essential. The trick is to buy the best quality you can afford in an all-season fabric, and a style that won't look dated too soon.

Steps

1 Expect to pay at least £200 to £250. Suits can cost from £130 to £1,500 or more. The best value comes from finding originally expensive ones on sale. Watch for sales and get on the mailing lists of your favourite shops. But remember, even an expensive suit will lose its charm if it doesn't fit you well.

2 Get measured for your correct size of trousers and jacket. Sizes include a number (for example, even numbers between 36 and 48) plus a *short, regular, long* or *extra-long* designation.

3 Look for an all-season fabric. All-wool fabric wears longer and looks better than wool-polyester blends, but blends typically wrinkle less. Other options are twill, linen and wool crepe. If you choose a pattern, such as pinstripe, opt for a flattering, versatile colour, such as navy or charcoal.

4 Select a jacket style. The three-button jacket is a classic look, but some men prefer a two-button or double-breasted jacket, which is better for thin men. Make sure the jacket buttons up easily and doesn't pull on either side, whether you're standing or sitting. Make sure you can move your arms freely. The lapels should lie flat and show a 1 cm (½ in) rim of shirt collar. Shoulders cannot be altered, so make sure they aren't bulging or too boxy. The sleeves should extend to about the wrist bone. The jacket should be fully lined with no puckering seams.

5 Select a trouser style. Flat-front trousers tend to be more slimming, while pleats and turn-ups can make the trousers dressier. (Shorter men, however, should avoid turn-ups.) Go for lined trousers that rest comfortably on your waist. When they're hemmed, they should break at the laces of your shoes and hit just above your heel.

What to Look For

- Wool fabric
- Flattering style
- Comfortable fit
- Quality construction

Tips

Wear a button-down shirt and smart shoes when you shop for a suit, or plan to try them all on at the store.

Once you know your size, consider ordering online, then have a tailor do any alterations.

If you put your hands in the pockets of your trousers while wearing a jacket with a central vent, you expose your rear. You can decide if that's a good thing – or ask a friend.

Warning

Don't buy a suit without having a knowledgeable sales assistant or tailor check the fit. Some fitting problems, such as shoulder pads, cannot be fixed.

509 Hire a Tailor

If you can't find the clothes you're looking for at a shop, consider having them made. Good tailors can create garments that reflect your personal style and fit your figure impeccably. They can also perform minor miracles when you need an item updated or altered.

Steps

1 Ask friends or your favourite sales assistant for recommendations. A local fabric store is another possible source for referrals. Otherwise, look up "Tailors" in *Yellow Pages*.

2 Talk to tailors about their skills and experience. Do they specialise in a certain sort of work, such as bridal gowns or suits? Women's or men's clothing?

3 Check availability and turnround time. If possible, give the tailor a deadline that's a few weeks before you need an item, in case of an unexpected delay.

4 Enquire about their rates. Although tailors should be able to give you a rough estimate, they'll need specifics before they will give you a firm price.

5 For custom designs, ask to see examples of their work and get the names of some of their former clients. Call the clients to see if they were happy with the work and if it was delivered on time.

6 Bring any garments or pictures that would help illustrate what you'd like done. If a tailor is reluctant to try something, ask why; his or her expert opinion might change your mind.

7 Take advantage of what tailors can do to update or alter existing garments. Generally, it's far easier to take in or shorten clothes than to let them out or lengthen them. Adding turn-ups, narrowing trousers legs and changing necklines are all possible. Complexity adds to the price, and some alterations aren't worth it unless the piece is very high-quality or a beloved, irreplaceable garment.

8 Once the tailor has a firm idea of what you expect, get a description of the work, the price and the delivery date in writing.

What to Look For

- Personal recommendation
- Skills, experience, and specialisation
- Availability and price

Tips

Make sure the tailor measures both legs and arms for symmetry.

The more complex the job, the more often you may have to visit the tailor for fittings.

See 510 "Buy Custom-Tailored Clothes in Asia".

Warning

Try on the tailored clothes when you pick them up to make sure they fit.

510 Buy Custom-Tailored Clothes in Asia

Thailand, Vietnam, South Korea and other Asian countries are known for having tailors and seamstresses who make exquisitely crafted made-to-measure clothes in a few days (or even a few hours) for unbelievable prices. An evening dress can be as cheap as £10, while suits start as low as £15.

Steps

1 Pack any item of clothing that you want copied and bring magazines and clothing catalogues that show designs you want made. A talented tailor can copy many garments swiftly and skilfully.

2 Ask other travellers, locals, longtime foreign residents or the hotel concierge to recommend a tailor. A good recommendation will save you time and money.

3 Browse fabrics, either at the tailor's shop or in fabric stores. In addition to the variety of silks in Asia – such as raw silk, print silk, patterned silk and brocade – you can buy cotton and other fabrics. Flip through swatches in the store and show them the fabrics and patterns. A tailor will charge for any fabric or trims you do not supply.

4 Give the tailor adequate guidance. If you're using a picture for reference or duplicating an article of clothing, explain any modifications you want to the piece. For example, perhaps you like a shirt in a photo, but you don't want the chest pocket, or you may want a slit up both sides of a skirt, not just the left side.

5 Discuss price in advance. Expect to pay a flat rate that includes measurement and fittings. Prices drop when you select a tailor who designs the garment but contracts out for cutting and sewing. Be aware that Hong Kong is not a bargain for made-to-measure clothing: an up-market tailor may charge £300 to £550 to design and sew a man's suit.

6 Get the agreed-upon price in writing with a description of all design options and any additional charges, to eliminate any unpleasant surprises when you pick up your clothes later. Typically, you don't have to pay anything upfront, although some shops require a 50 per cent deposit.

7 Find out when the clothes will be ready. Remarkably, clothes are sometimes ready the same day or the following day. However, make sure you allow enough time. It may take three or more visits to order, be fitted and pick up your garment.

8 Try on the finished garment and check both construction and fit. Allow sufficient time to correct any problems.

What to Look For

- Clothing you want copied
- Magazines and catalogues
- Trusted referrals
- Quality fabrics
- Adequate guidance
- Upfront price agreement

Tips

The Vietnamese cities of Hanoi, Ho Chi Minh City and especially Hoi An are known for beautiful tailor-made clothing at bargain prices.

You can have clothes made-to-measure for friends and family if you have their measurements. Ask if the tailor will continue the relationship by post, if you want future garments created. Enquire about having shoes copied, too.

Warning

Often what is called "silk" in Asian countries is actually a synthetic. That said, this replacement looks just as good, doesn't wrinkle and wears better than the real thing.

511 Buy a Briefcase

In many circles, over-the-shoulder leather cases and padded computer bags have replaced the hard-sided briefcase that once was considered the standard of the business world. First determine your budget.

Steps

1 Think big. You may intend to travel light when heading to and from the office, but look for expandable compartments and outside pockets for stashing extra items.

2 Lift the case or bag. Leather is strong and classic, but can be heavy. Consider lighter-weight alternatives like canvas. If you routinely carry heavy books and files, a case with wheels and a retractable handle might work well for you.

3 Look for features that fit your needs: a padded laptop compartment, pockets for a phone and personal organiser; a back sleeve that allows the briefcase to slip over the handle of wheeled luggage; backpack straps or shoulder strap, and lockable zips.

What to Look For

- Large size
- Lightweight but durable material
- Useful features

Tip

Bicycle courier-style bags sell for £60 or less, while you can pay £350 and more for up-market leather cases.

512 Shop for a Leather Jacket

A leather jacket is a wardrobe staple and great way to express your personal style. Warm and durable, but also timeless and classic, leather is an investment that pays off over and over through the years.

Steps

1 Be prepared to spend at least £160. A good leather jacket costs £350 or more – not unreasonable when you consider how often and how long you'll wear this garment.

2 Slip into one of the classic styles, which include bomber, blazer and zip-up jackets. A medium-length jacket hits the top of your thigh. Waist or hip-length jackets are versatile. A trench coat can be sleek and slimming on the right figure.

3 Choose colour and texture. Although black is the most popular choice, with brown not too far behind, there is a wide range of colours to choose from. Textures vary from buttery soft, thin leather to thicker, more durable jackets. Suede (which requires a little more care) is another option.

4 Inspect the jacket's construction. Seams should be strong and perfect and the bottom hem straight. The collar and pockets should lie flat. Check the lining for strong seams, especially in the pockets where they get a lot of wear and tear. Motorbike jackets should have vents, a padded kidney panel and tough leather – all crucial for safe and comfortable riding.

What to Look For

- Style and length
- Softness
- Colour
- Detailing
- Quality construction

Tips

Store your leather jacket either flat or on a wide, sturdy, padded hanger to prevent stretch marks. Never use plastic covers.

Take care of stains immediately. When in doubt, take it to a dry-cleaner.

513 Buy Maternity Clothes

When your tummy expands beyond your baggiest waistbands, it's time to shop for maternity clothes. You don't need to spend a lot of money to get through your pregnancy in style. A few well-chosen pieces let you look professional and keep you comfortable.

Steps

1 Shop for maternity clothes labelled in your pre-pregnancy size. Maternity clothes are designed to give you extra room only where you need it – primarily in the tummy and the bust. If you're having twins or have a history of having big babies, you may need a larger size and might outgrow even maternity clothes. If necessary, outsize shirts and dresses can get you through the last few weeks (don't even bother with trousers).

2 Buy basic items in stretch fabrics. Cotton jersey is good, and a little lycra is even better. Buy inexpensive coordinating separates, such as a black skirt, dress, tunic and trousers. Try online sites such as maternityexchange.co.uk, a dress agency and clearance outlet, and maternityindex.org, which helps locate maternity shops in your area.

3 Buy only one or two bras at a time because you may grow several sizes over the course of your pregnancy, and wait to buy nursing bras until the last two months. Some women swear by the Bravado bra (bravadodesigns.co.uk), available at many maternity shops. These can be expensive, but the correct fit is crucial. Maternity shops are a good place to get expert advice on fitting, even if you end up buying elsewhere.

4 Splurge on at least one outfit that makes you feel great. Whether it's a slinky dress that shows off your shapely tummy or a funky pair of trousers, find something to wear when you want to look fabulous. Visit babyworld.co.uk for suggestions on where to shop online.

5 Remember, no woman leaves the hospital in her pre-pregnancy size. You may need to wear your maternity clothes for a while after the baby is born. Remember to pack a nursing nightgown for the hospital.

What to Look For

- Pre-pregnancy size
- Stretchy fabrics
- Comfortable basic items
- Undergarments that fit well
- Splurge outfit

Tips

Save money by borrowing from other recent mums or shopping in second-hand shops.

As your feet swell in the third trimester, you might need new shoes as well as clothes. Comfortable slip-on flip-flops, clogs or low-heeled shoes are a good choice, especially since you don't have to bend over to put them on. Make sure they fit well so you don't twist an ankle and fall over.

Two-piece maternity swim-suits provide the most flexible fit. Maternity shops and department stores are your best options for swimwear, but if you can, borrow one unless you'll be in it often.

514 Get a Great-Fitting Bra

A badly fitting bra is not only a fashion *faux pas*, it can be extremely uncomfortable. Yet, many women unwittingly wear the wrong size. Getting properly fitted is the first step to finding a bra that makes you look and feel your best.

Steps

Everyday bras

1 Go to a lingerie shop or department store and suss out an experienced sales assistant to measure you.

2 Try on a variety of styles. Underwires increase support, push-up bras enhance cleavage, and thicker padding adds inches.

3 Lean forwards at the waist and pull the bra away from your breasts by the straps so that your breasts fall naturally into the cups. The band should fit snugly but not dig into your flesh. If it's too tight, go to the looser hook or try a larger size. If the bra doesn't feel comfortably snug or it feels like your breasts might fall out below, tighten the hooks or go to a smaller band size.

4 Adjust the shoulder straps so that they feel snug but don't dig into your shoulders.

5 Walk around, jump up and down, and swing your arms around to test comfort and support.

Sports bras

1 Shop at a store where you feel comfortable. The staff should be helpful and able to answer your questions knowledgeably. Or shop online at a merchant such as figleaves.com/uk and lessbounce.com, which have a good selection of sports bras including very large sizes.

2 Put the bra on. You'll have three choices: pulling it on over your head, fastening it in front or closing it in the back. It should feel comfortable when you put it on. Large-breasted women should check that there's no pressure on the shoulders.

3 Inspect how the bra is built. There should be no exposed metal or hardware, which will irritate by the end of your work-out. Quality bras have plush lining surrounding all metal pieces.

4 Jump up and down to gauge movement. Women up to an average D cup are best off with a compression bra, while full Ds need an encapsulation bra to minimise movement. Ask if you can test-drive the bra and take a run around the block.

5 Read the label to find out what the fabric content is. Virtually every sports bra has a coolmax/lycra lining for wicking. The outer fabric, aside from looking great, lends support and maintains shape. Pure cotton won't wick, but a cotton/polyester/lycra blend is very supportive. Skin that chafes easily will be happiest in a

What to Look For

- Correct band and cup size
- Right bra for the purpose
- Comfortable fit

Tips

If you've never had one, get a professional fitting, even if you've been wearing the same size for years. Recheck your size if your weight changes appreciably.

One manufacturer's 32B may fit like another's 34C, so beware of buying a bra based only on the size.

When you find a bra you like, buy several. Styles are discontinued often.

poly/lycra blend. Many bras use a supplex/lycra/cotton mix for superior wicking. See 516 "Buy Performance Work-out Clothing" for more information on high-tech fabrics and blends.

6 Pick a fabric blend that maximises performance. Women with A and B cups can choose almost any fabric and still maintain their shape. Cs and Ds need to look for more supportive blends.

7 Live well and sweat hard even if you wear a prosthesis. Several bras accommodate prostheses, such as The Grace Bra. Try lessbounce.com and nicolajane.com.

First bras

1 Be supportive and buy your daughter a bra, even if you think she doesn't need one. If all her friends have bras, she'll want to fit in.

2 Take her to a lingerie shop or department store where an experienced, professional sales woman can properly fit her.

3 Skip the fitting if it's just too excruciating and select a sports-style bra that fits snugly but not tightly around her rib cage.

Wash your bras by hand or in a lingerie bag or pillowcase in the washing machine and allow them to air-dry.

When you purchase a bra online, make sure you can return it without penalty before you click that last send button.

515 Choose a High-Performance Swimsuit

Since the 1996 Atlanta Olympic Games, a new breed of performance swimwear has helped swimmers shave off more time than a Gillette Mach 3. Introduced to the mass market in 2000, these suits cover more of the body, and are revolutionising competitive racing.

Steps

1 Understand how the suits work. By enclosing the body with a fabric that is smoother than skin, they make the swimmer more streamlined in the water. These suits actually change the way water flows around the body to create less drag. They also compress the body, which reduces vibration.

2 Check out the Aquablade and Fastskin suits on Speedo.com. TYR Sport (tyr.com) offers Aquapel, a coated fabric with a water-repellent, hydrophobic finish in the Powerflow performance suit. Nike (nike.com) has a comparable suit called the Liftsuit.

3 Make sure you get fitted correctly, which means skin-tight and wrinkle-free. It should not be so tight as to limit your range of motion, which will reduce your effectiveness. Wrinkles cause added drag, which defeats the whole purpose of the suit.

4 Spend the money only if you're seriously committed. These swimsuits cost considerably more than traditional racing suits.

What to Look For

- Speedo, TYR Sport and Nike brands
- Correct fit

Tip

Performance may decline as the suit gets older.

516 Buy Performance Work-out Clothing

The old T-shirt and tracksuit trousers combo is only comfy until you get sweaty. Newer synthetic products offer the same freedom of movement while looking better and keeping you drier. Most modern athletic wear starts with some form of nylon or polyester, combined with other materials, to achieve the desired qualities. See 478 "Buy Clothes for Cold-Weather Activities" for more discussion of synthetic clothing.

MATERIAL	WHAT IT IS	WHAT IT'S GOOD FOR
CoolMax	A DuPont product, designed to enhance evaporation and cooling.	Gym work-outs, running wear, base layer under warm clothes.
Lycra	Another DuPont product, Lycra is designed to be close-fitting and stretchy, yet retains its shape well.	Swimwear and stylish work-out wear. Lycra is frequently added to other fabrics to add stretchiness and durability.
Fleece	A soft, lightweight material designed to provide maximum insulation with a minimum of weight and bulk. Quick drying and water resistant.	Fleece is everywhere, from jacket linings to gloves and underwear. Fleece has replaced wool as the all-purpose performance material.
Phase Change Materials	Fabrics that absorb and release body heat. Changes as skin temperature fluctuates to keep body temperature constant and increase comfort.	Outerwear constructed with these materials already exists. Look for increased use of phase change fabrics in work-out wear.
Supplex	Supplex, yet another DuPont product, is soft and comfortable. It recreates the comfort of cotton in a durable, quick-drying fabric.	Supplex is frequently combined with other synthetics to make stretchy, durable fabrics, suitable for everything from lightweight work-out wear to jackets.

517 Buy a Heart Rate Monitor

Monitoring your heart rate is easy: if you're living, you've got one. A heart rate monitor allows you to effectively train at your target heart rate for optimal results during competition.

Steps

1 Understand how monitors work. Most look like wristwatches and combine timekeeping functions with heart monitoring. For constant heart rate readout, purchase one with a chest strap transmitter that sends heart data to the wrist unit. Devices without a chest strap provide heart rate data but only when you are touching the unit with your hand.

2 Basic units cost about £50, more sophisticated units about £80. Popular makes include Polar and Reebok. You can buy online, but a knowledgeable shop can better educate you about the devices. Read the instructions.

What to Look For

- Easy to use
- Comfortable chest strap
- Knowledgeable shop

Tips

Get a unit with an audible signal if your heart rate falls above or below your specified range.

Some monitors can store data and download it to a computer to chart your progress.

518 Select a Watch

Watches serve a variety of functions, from work-out aid to fashion accessory. Some people even use them for telling the time. Before making a purchase, it's worth understanding the basics of watch construction. World-renowned designer models can cost many thousands, while fun disposable watches can be had for a few pounds.

Steps

1 Find out about the true origin. Switzerland has long been associated with fine watchmaking, and many manufacturers try to take advantage of that cachet. Watches identified as a "Swiss Watch" must meet certain requirements as to where production and assembly took place. Before making a major purchase, be sure to get a full explanation from the seller about the watch's origin.

2 Understand what keeps 'em ticking. Most modern watches use a battery-powered quartz crystal to keep time. Mechanical watches use gears and springs, which are charming and beautiful but require periodic servicing. A few companies, including Valjoux, make good mechanisms that are found in many popular brands. The very best watchmakers build their own mechanisms.

3 Examine the watch case. Any top-quality watch has a screw-on back and screw-down crown (the winding knob) for the most protection from water and dirt. Some watches feature a display back that allows you to see the mechanism. Common case materials include stainless steel, gold, silver, platinum and titanium. All of these are highly durable (except gold, which is fairly soft) and provide a distinctive, classy look.

4 Check the crystal, which is the transparent face that covers the watch (not to be confused with quartz crystal mechanisms). Acrylic crystals are the least expensive and offer good shatter resistance. Sapphire crystals are the choice for top watches, due to their clarity and scratch resistance.

5 Consider other features. Some models combine both digital and analogue faces on one watch. A water-resistant watch is fine for swimming and general use. For diving, be sure to check the depth rating. A chronograph (stopwatch) function is essential for a sports watch. For travel, an alarm is handy, as is the ability to track time in other cities. Gemstones are an elegant if expensive addition to up-market fashion watches.

6 Be sure the band is comfortable and secure. Segmented steel bands with their clean look and smooth feel are popular. Leather bands provide a timeless, understated look. Strong, secure, and quick-drying nylon bands are the best choice for sports watches.

7 Expect top-quality movements, materials (including gemstones) and construction from premium watches that cost several thousand pounds. Prestigious watchmakers include Rolex, Tag Heuer, Omega, Bulova and Cartier, with many others worldwide.

What to Look For

- Mechanism type
- Extra features
- Casual, sporty or dressy

Tips

While you will spend more on a designer watch, you won't necessarily get increased accuracy. Even moderately priced watches can keep accurate time.

Self-winding watches use the movement of your body to wind themselves; if you don't wear the watch for a few days, it has to be reset.

Warning

Do not be misled by a watch listing a large number of jewels. Tiny, low-value jewels are frequently employed within watch mechanisms, as a way to reduce friction and provide long wear. But overall workmanship is more important than the number of jewels. In other words, jewels by themselves do not guarantee quality and accuracy, and more jewels are not necessarily better.

519 Buy Kids' Clothes

Buying children's clothes can go from being a delight with your first baby to a challenge with your preteen. Whether you're shopping for a child who's growing like a weed or locked into a battle of wills with your toddler or preteen, planning before you shop is the key to saving time, money and sanity – all valued commodities for busy parents. Borrow as many baby clothes as possible, especially vests and sleep-suits. It's hard to have too many.

Steps

Shopping for babies and toddlers

1 Keep in mind that babies grow fast and have the next size ready to go. Many new parents and gift givers don't realise that some babies never fit, or fit only for a few days, in clothes sized zero to three months. If you receive a lot of gifts in this size, exchange most for sizes six to nine, or nine to twelve months.

2 Shop at a local second-hand clothing shop that specialises in children's clothes, and check out auction websites such as eBay.co.uk. Used clothes for babies and toddlers are a great deal because they outgrow clothes before they wear them out.

3 Shop when and where you can. Cruise the clothes department at supermarkets for deals when you're there buying nappies, or shop online at any time.

4 Remember that toddlers need clothes that pull on and off easily when they're in the "I can do it myself" and potty-training stages.

Shopping for older children

1 Take stock. At the start of each season, pull out and sort all the children's clothes. Box any outgrown items for selling, passing on, donating to charity or storing (see 339 "Sell Used Baby Gear, Toys, Clothes and Books").

2 Make a season-specific shopping list that includes categories such as basics, school clothes, outerwear, and athletic and extracurricular attire. When considering quantities, consider how frequently the washing gets done in your house.

3 Keep kids' preferences and ages in mind, and ask for their input. Many children will reach for tracksuits before chinos. By the time they're eight or nine, expect them to have firm opinions about what's cool and what's not. Look at websites and catalogues together at home to see what they like before venturing out shopping. Explain any limits you have regarding styles you're willing to purchase, but use your veto power sparingly.

What to Look For

- Second-hand clothes shops
- Online shopping
- Easy-to-use fasteners
- Season-specific list
- Budget
- Bulk socks in one colour
- Frequent-shopper schemes
- Durable basics

Tip

Make sure you understand returns policies, which have become stricter in many shops, and file your receipts, which are also important for any items with a wear-out warranty (see 4 "Take Goods Back").

4 Set a budget and use it as a teaching tool. As soon as your children are old enough to understand, tell them how much you plan to spend and let them help decide where to spend it. If the name-brand wardrobe your daughter must have costs too much, a compromise might be a few T-shirts from her favourite shop and less expensive jeans from a discount store.

5 Buy socks and underwear to fit, in bulk and in the same colour, style and/or brand for each child. These items wear out fast and are uncomfortable if they're too big. You don't want to have to throw out a good sock just because its mate got lost. If you have more than one child, assigning a colour or brand to each also decreases laundry mix-ups. Limiting styles to one choice also eliminates fussiness on busy mornings.

6 Take a child shopping if you have a question about size or an exceptionally picky child. Make sure everyone is well rested and fed to cut down on short tempers. Consider shopping without the kids for expediency. Just make sure you can return anything that doesn't work out.

Shopping for all kids

1 Purchase seasonal outerwear large to leave room for growth spurts.

2 Find the retailers that work best for you. Factory shops or outlets can have great prices but can be hit-or-miss for busy parents. Catalogues and websites, such as Next and Boden, let you shop from home and often have online specials.

3 Join frequent-buyer schemes and sign up for mailing lists for your favourite retailers.

4 Focus on buying durable basics such as jeans that will hold up after many washings. Inspect items for quality construction. Feel the fabric to see if it seems sufficiently heavy to withstand wear and tear. Check that buttons and zips fasten securely.

Warning

Don't waste your money buying clothes your children won't wear. You might think it's the bee's knees, but your rascal might not agree.

520 Choose Children's Shoes

Kids go through enough shoes that you may want to consider an insurance plan just for their feet. Toddlers' feet can grow an entire size or more every three months, and rough-and-tumble play takes its toll. Shopping for children's shoes, though, doesn't need to be daunting. The key is to keep up with growth spurts by having your child's feet properly measured on a regular basis.

Steps

Shopping for the first pair

1 Wait to buy shoes until your child starts to walk. Research suggests that children develop healthy, well-developed feet when they learn to walk barefoot. Keep their feet toasty and unrestricted with soft booties or warm skid-free socks. Robeez (robeez.co.uk) makes thin but warm leather moccasins in a range of colours and sizes that actually stay on little crawlers' feet.

2 When it's time for your baby's first pair of shoes, take your well-rested, recently fed child to a quality shoe shop that stocks brands such as Start-rite and Clarks. The best shops have patient and knowledgeable sales assistants who are expert at fitting children's feet.

3 Have the sales assistant measure the length and width of both of the child's feet. Many babies have an extra-wide foot and may need a special size.

4 Make sure the shoes aren't too big, which can cause a baby to trip. First shoes should be soft and pliable to let new walkers feel the ground.

As they grow

1 Have your child's feet measured on a regular basis at a shoe shop that specialises in children's shoes. Kids grow fast, and shoe sizes can change from month to month. Really good sales assistants can spot evasive manoeuvres like scrunched-up toes, and know how to woo a reluctant tot out of a parent's lap. Toys and play areas are added bonuses.

2 Have your child try both shoes on. Shoes vary in fit, even within the same brand. Toes should have a 1 cm (½ in) clearance, but not much more. Getting one size larger than their foot is typical. Watch your child walk and make sure that the heels don't slip out. If a heel is too wide but the rest of the shoe fits, try heel pads (available at some shoe shops and chemists).

What to Look For

- Precise measurements
- Proper fit
- Shoe quality

Tips

Some shoe shops offer warranties. If the shoes wear out before your kids outgrow them, they will replace them. Be sure to keep receipts.

Shoes with flashing lights are a huge hit with little kids and are found on both quality and discount brands.

Factory shops often sell brand-name shoes. The selection of sizes and styles may be limited, though.

If your child wears orthotics, bring them with you when trying on shoes.

3 Invest in a good pair of trainers that your child can wear every day. This pair will take a pounding, so look for quality. Leather holds up better than vinyl, and stitching lasts longer than glue.

4 Take advantage of Velcro fasteners. At some point, though, all children need to learn to tie shoelaces, so get your preschool-age child at least one pair that ties.

5 For summer months or warm climates, purchase cheap canvas trainers for playing in the sand pit or jumping in puddles. Velcro-strapped sandals are great for tender feet that want to have wet summertime fun.

6 Buy wellies and winter boots a size or two bigger. Kids can wear heavier or even doubled socks. Most retailers won't restock winter boots, even if they sell out of a size, until the following year's season. Be aware that most wellies don't come in wide sizes; you may have to go up in size to get them wide enough.

Warnings

Examine young children's feet regularly for red spots or blisters, evidence that their shoes don't fit properly.

Don't buy shoes more than one size too big for your toddler. You don't want your child to trip, and often he or she will wear them out before they actually grow into them.

521 Purchase Clothes at Factory Shops

When a clothing manufacturer can't sell items for full price, its loss is your gain. Factory shops stock slow-sellers and slightly flawed products, typically at 25 to 75 per cent off the retail price.

Steps

1 Call the factory shops or outlets you want to visit and ask about upcoming sales where already-reduced prices are sometimes slashed even more. Shoppingvillages.com lists factory shops all over the country.

2 Use the internet to familiarise yourself with the retail prices of the items you'd like to buy, so you'll know what kind of bargain you're getting at the factory shop. Set priorities.

3 Examine garments carefully for flaws. If you find a flaw in an item that isn't marked as a second, ask for an additional discount.

4 Ask about the store's returns policy. You may be looking at a long drive back to the shop, and many factory shop purchases are nonreturnable. Find out if you can return clothes to a shop's retail location near you, and get the answer in writing.

What to Look For

- Upcoming sales
- Retail price comparison
- Prioritised shopping list
- Flaws
- Returns policy

Tip

While most retail shops sell clothes for the following season, factory shops usually offer the current season.

UCTION SITES • BUY BARGAIN CLOTHING • BUY WHOLESALE • GET OUT OF DEBT • BUY NOTHING • BUY HAPPINESS • BUY A BETTER MOU

BUY YOUR WAY INTO SOMEONE'S FAVOUR • BUY LOVE • FIND THE RIGHT RELAXATION TECHNIQUE FOR YOU • BUY HEALTHY FAST FOOD •

ATING SERVICE • SELL YOURSELF ON AN ONLINE DATING SERVICE • SELL YOURSELF TO YOUR GIRLFRIEND/BOYFRIEND'S FAMILY • BUY FL

CHOOSE FILM FOR YOUR CAMERA • BUY RECHARGEABLE BATTERIES • GIVE TO A GOOD CAUSE • TAKE PART IN A CAR BOOT SALE • EMPL

TUDENT DISCOUNTS • BUY FLOWERS WHOLESALE • GET A PICTURE FRAMED • EMPLOY A REMOVAL COMPANY • EMPLOY A LIFESTYLE MA

JY FOR A HALLOWE'EN PARTY • BUY A GREAT BIRTHDAY PRESENT FOR UNDER £10 • SELECT GOOD CHAMPAGNE • BUY A DIAMOND • BUY

ET A GIFT LIST • BUY WEDDING GIFTS • SELECT BRIDESMAIDS' DRESSES • HIRE AN EVENTS ORGANISER • HIRE A BARTENDER FOR A PART

NNOUNCEMENTS • SELL YOUR WEDDING DRESS • BUY AN ANNIVERSARY GIFT • ARRANGE ENTERTAINMENT FOR A PARTY • COMMISSION A

ERSON WHO HAS EVERYTHING • BUY A GIFT FOR PASSING EXAMS • SELECT A CHRISTMAS TURKEY • BUY A HOUSEWARMING GIFT • PURC

LAND • WRITE A MESSAGE IN THE SKY • HIRE A BIG-NAME BAND • GET INTO A PRIVATE GAMBLING ROOM IN LAS VEGAS • BUY SOMEONE A

HE TIMES • EMPLOY A BUTLER • BUY A FOOTBALL CLUB • BUY A PERSONAL JET • SELECT A CLASSIC CAR • ACQUIRE A BODY GUARD • BC

REYHOUND TO RACE • BUY A RACEHORSE • BUY A VILLA IN TUSCANY • EMPLOY A PERSONAL CHEF • BUY A JOURNEY INTO SPACE • EMP

ORTUNE • HIRE AN EXPERT WITNESS • MAKE MONEY FROM ACCIDENT COMPENSATION • DONATE YOUR BODY TO SCIENCE • MAKE MONEY

NANCIAL ADVISER • PLAN FOR RETIREMENT • COPE WITH HIGHER EDUCATION COSTS • BUY AND SELL SHARES • CHOOSE A STOCKBROKE

ESS INSURANCE • BUY LIFE INSURANCE • GET PRIVATE HEALTH INSURANCE • BUY PERSONAL FINANCE SOFTWARE • CHOOSE AN ACCOUN

KE OUT A PATENT • MARKET YOUR INVENTION • FINANCE YOUR BUSINESS IDEA • BUY A SMALL BUSINESS • BUY A FRANCHISE • LEASE R

EBSITE • HIRE A GRAPHIC DESIGNER • ACQUIRE CONTENT FOR YOUR WEBSITE • BUY ADVERTISING ON THE WEB • SELL YOUR ART • HIRE

JBLISH YOUR BOOK • START A BED-AND-BREAKFAST • SELL A FAILING BUSINESS • BUY A HOT DOG STAND • SHOP FOR A MORTGAGE • G

OUSE AT AUCTION • SHOP FOR A HOUSE ONLINE • BUY A PROPERTY FOR RENOVATION AND RESALE • EVALUATE BEFORE BUYING INTO A N

JY A PLOT OF LAND • HAVE YOUR HOUSE DESIGNED • HIRE AN ARCHITECT • HIRE A BUILDER • GET PLANNING PERMISSION • BUY A HOLIC

BROAD • BUY TO LET • RENT YOUR HOME FOR A LOCATION SHOOT • FURNISH YOUR HOME • FURNISH YOUR STUDIO FLAT • BUY USED FU

BUY HOUSEHOLD APPLIANCES • BUY FLOOR-CARE APPLIANCES • BUY EXTENDED WARRANTIES ON APPLIANCES • FIND PERIOD FIXTURES

OME • SELECT PAINT, STAIN AND VARNISH • CHOOSE DECORATIVE TILES • CHOOSE A DEHUMIDIFIER • BUY A WHIRLPOOL BATH • BUY A SH

ALLPAPER • BUY A WOOD-BURNING STOVE • SELECT FLOORING • SELECT CARPETING • CHOOSE KITCHEN CABINETS • CHOOSE A KITCHE

MOKE ALARMS • BUY CARBON MONOXIDE DETECTORS • BUY FIRE EXTINGUISHERS • CHOOSE AN ENTRY DOOR • BUY A GARAGE-DOOR O

UTDOOR FURNITURE • BUY THE PERFECT ROSE • BUY FLOWERING BULBS • BUY FLOWERS FOR YOUR GARDEN • SELECT PEST CONTROLS

TOMATIC WATERING SYSTEM • START A NEW LAWN • BUY A LAWN MOWER • BUY KOI FOR YOUR FISH POND • BUY A STORAGE SHED • HI

RODUCE • CHOOSE A PERFECT PEACH • BUY AND SELL AT FARMERS' MARKETS • SELECT KITCHEN KNIVES • DECIPHER FOOD LABELS • SE

RFECT BURGER • PURCHASE A CHRISTMAS HAM • BUY ORGANIC BEEF • BUY HAGGIS • PURCHASE LOCAL HONEY • CHOOSE A CHICKEN

UT TRUFFLES • BUY ARTISAN BREADS • BUY ARTISAN CHEESES • PURCHASE KOSHER FOOD • BUY SENSIBLY IN SUPERMARKETS • CHOOS

RDER A GREAT CUP OF COFFEE • BUY A COFFEEMAKER OR ESPRESSO MACHINE • PURCHASE PARTY BEER • CHOOSE THE RIGHT WINE • C

ERM • CHOOSE AN OVULATION PREDICTOR KIT • PICK A PREGNANCY TEST KIT • CHOOSE BIRTH CONTROL • CHOOSE WHERE TO GIVE BIF

Y BABY CLOTHES • CHOOSE NAPPIES • BUY OR RENT A BREAST PUMP • CHOOSE A CAR SEAT • BUY CHILD-PROOFING SUPPLIES • FIND

Y A GARDEN PLAY STRUCTURE • FIND A FAMILY-FRIENDLY HOTEL • ORGANISE A FUND-RAISING EVENT • BUY BRACES FOR YOUR KID • E

A MODEL • SELL USED BABY GEAR, TOYS, CLOTHES AND BOOKS • FIND A COUPLES COUNSELLOR • HIRE A FAMILY SOLICITOR • BUY OR

RCHASE A TOOTHBRUSH • BUY MOISTURISERS AND ANTIWRINKLE CREAMS • SELECT PAIN RELIEF AND COLD MEDICINES • CHOOSE A CC

ODUCTS • BUY WAYS TO COUNTER HAIR LOSS • BUY A WIG OR HAIRPIECE • BUY A NEW BODY • GET A TATTOO OR BODY PIERCING • OB

ETH • SELECT SPECTACLES AND SUNGLASSES • HIRE A PERSONAL TRAINER • SIGN UP FOR A YOGA CLASS • TREAT YOURSELF TO A DAY

AN ANTIQUE MARKET • BUY AT AUCTION • KNOW WHAT YOUR COLLECTIBLES ARE WORTH • BARTER WITH DEALERS • GET AN ANTIQUE A

INS • BUY AN ANTIQUE QUILT • BUY FILM POSTERS • LIQUIDATE YOUR BEANIE BABY COLLECTION • SCORE AUTOGRAPHS • TRADE YU-GI

D SELL SPORTS MEMORABILIA • SELL YOUR FOOTBALL-CARD COLLECTION • CHOOSE A DESKTOP COMPUTER • SHOP FOR A USED COMI

MPUTER PERIPHERALS • CHOOSE AN INTERNET SERVICE PROVIDER • GET AN INTERNET DOMAIN NAME • NETWORK YOUR COMPUTERS •

D PLAYER • BUY A VIDEO RECORDER • CHOOSE A PERSONAL DIGITAL ASSISTANT • CHOOSE A MOBILE PHONE SERVICE • GET A BETTER D

GITAL CAMERA • BUY A HOME AUTOMATION SYSTEM • BUY A STATE-OF-THE-ART SOUND SYSTEM • BUY AN AUDIO/VIDEO DISTRIBUTION S

SYSTEM • BUY VIRTUAL-REALITY FURNITURE • BUY TWO-WAY RADIOS • BUY A MOBILE ENTERTAINMENT SYSTEM • GET A PASSPORT, QU

AL LUGGAGE • FLY FOR NEXT TO NOTHING • TAKE A TRIP ON THE TRANS-SIBERIAN EXPRESS • BUY DUTY-FREE • SHIP FOREIGN PURCHA

LIAN CYCLING HOLIDAY • CHOOSE A CHEAP CRUISE • BOOK A HOTEL PACKAGE FOR THE GREEK ISLANDS • RAFT THE GRAND CANYON •

KSHAW IN RANGOON • TAKE SALSA LESSONS IN CUBA • BUY A CAMERA IN HONG KONG • BUY YOUR WAY ONTO A MOUNT EVEREST EXP

LL TEAM • BUY ANKLE AND KNEE BRACES • CHOOSE RUGBY PROTECTION KIT • BUY GOLF CLUBS • SELL FOUND GOLF BALLS • BUY POP

PLOY A SCUBA INSTRUCTOR • BUY A SKATEBOARD AND PROTECTIVE GEAR • BUY SKATES • GO BUNJEE JUMPING • GO SKYDIVING • BUY

OTS AND BINDINGS • BUY SKI BOOTS • BUY A BICYCLE • BUY AN ELECTRIC BICYCLE • BUY CYCLE CLOTHING • BUY A PROPERLY FITTIN(

T • BUY A SURFBOARD • BUY FLY-FISHING GEAR • BUY ROCK-CLIMBING EQUIPMENT • BUY A CASHMERE JUMPER • PURCHASE VINTAGE

CKTAIL DRESS • BUY DESIGNER CLOTHES AT A DISCOUNT • CHOOSE A BASIC WARDROBE FOR A MAN • BUY A MAN'S DRESS SHIRT • PIC

THER JACKET • BUY MATERNITY CLOTHES • GET A GREAT-FITTING BRA • CHOOSE A HIGH-PERFORMANCE SWIM SUIT • BUY PERFORMAN

CTORY SHOPS • BUY A NEW CAR • BUY THE BASICS FOR YOUR CAR • BUY A USED CAR • BUY OR SELL A CAR ONLINE • BUY A HYBRID C

Cars & Other Vehicles

522 Buy a New Car

As exciting as it is to own a new car, many people dread shopping for one. Do your research before you head out, and the experience can be fairly painless. You can avoid haggling altogether by shopping online via a car broker (see 525 "Buy or Sell a Car Online").

Steps

1 Decide what you intend to use the car for – work; fun; weekends and evenings out; carrying things; towing a trailer; carrying more than one passenger; driving in the city, suburbs or country. Consider other factors that may be important to you, such as fuel efficiency, reliability and safety features.

2 Consider the type of fuel your chosen model uses. A diesel car will be more costly to buy than its petrol equivalent, but your fuel costs may be halved, so great savings are possible for high-mileage drivers. (Diesel cars have improved enormously over the past few years to the point where performance is usually comparable with equivalent petrol models.)

3 Set a realistic budget. If you're considering a trade-in, check the value of your current vehicle in publications such as *What Car?*, *Parker's Guide* or *Used Car Price Guide* – they will give you an indication of how much your car will be worth in the future. Factor your car's trade-in value into your total budget.

4 Find a model that interests you. Look out for in-depth magazine reviews that give a detailed specification as well as an impartial point of view. Look on the manufacturer's web pages or obtain a sales brochure for the model that interests you. (But be aware that these documents will be anything but impartial!)

5 Find the nearest car dealerships that sell your chosen model. Choose a number of dealerships to visit, preferably on a weekday. Remember to bring your driver's licence so you can test-drive.

6 Locate the car that interests you. Check its price – it will usually have a sticker on the windscreen. Seek out a sales representative. (That shouldn't be too demanding – in practice, he'll be more than likely to pounce on you the moment you step through the front doors of the dealership.)

7 Ask to look inside the car. Adjust the seat and mirrors, and check the leg room in each part of the car.

8 Check what the quoted price includes. Most new models are available with a bewildering variety of extras. Some of these – air conditioning, for example – can make a considerable difference to the overall price.

9 Ask for a test drive. Try as many different types of road as possible. Pay special attention to ease of steering, turning radius, braking response and acceleration. Adjust controls while you're driving to test convenience.

What to Look For

- Pricing comparisons
- Safety, cost of maintenance
- Financing options

Tips

If negotiations stall, don't be afraid to go to another dealer. Smart shoppers play dealers against each other to get the best price.

Shop at certain times of the year for a better deal. Late December is busy for nearly everyone except for car dealers, so they'll welcome your business.

You should be able to negotiate a better price on the biggest-selling models – especially from less prestigious marques such as Ford, Vauxhall or the cheaper Japanese brands.

Warnings

With very few exceptions, new cars depreciate at an alarming rate – your car could be worth half what you paid for it within a year. Buying "nearly-new" is better in terms of value for money.

Try to avoid setting your heart on one particular model or make. There are hundreds of excellent cars on the market, and getting attached to one of them will make you less hard-headed in your bargaining.

10 Return to the dealership. Inquire about availability, especially if you're interested in a popular model or want special features. If you like the car, ask for a business card and say you will return later. DON'T MAKE AN IMMEDIATE DECISION. Head to the next dealership and investigate other car models in the same way. Also consider calling a non-franchised car "superstore" to compare prices, or importing from mainland Europe.

11 Once you've decided to buy, treat marked prices as a starting point for negotiation. Make your first offer at least 10 per cent lower than what you're willing to pay. If the price is still too high, say you're not able (or willing) to afford that. If you really have reached your ceiling, ask him to talk to his manager. Continue negotiating until you can agree on a price within your budget. If you can't agree on a price, seek out another dealer.

Pay attention to customer surveys. These can give you important clues as to a car's potential reliability, or the level of service you are likely to receive from a manufacturer or dealership.

523 Buy the Basics for Your Car

Whether you like to work on your car at the weekends or need to top off fluids before a trip, it's good to have supplies on hand. Your owner's manual has the specifics of what your car needs.

LOCATION	PARTS, FLUIDS AND SUPPLIES	
Under the Bonnet	• Air filter • Automatic transmission fluid • Brake fluid • Clutch fluid • Engine coolant • Engine oil	• Fuses (for cooling fan, fuel injector and other circuits) • Oil filter • Power-steering fluid • Spark plugs • Windscreen-washer fluid
Interior	• Waterproof floor mats • Fuses • Gauges	• Oil for hinges • Light bulbs (overhead, dashboard, visor)
Exterior	• Battery for car alarm fob • Car polish • Car wash soap • Car wax • Headlamps • Leather/vinyl cleaner and conditioner	• Light bulbs (boot, side, licence plate and indicator lights) • Matching paint for touch-ups • Rear axle oil • Tyres • Windscreen wipers and blades
WARNINGS	Many car fluids are flammable, so make sure that they are stored with care. Keep them away from temperature extremes, and throw out greasy rags that were used on your car. Keep all fluids out of reach of pets and children.	

524 Buy a Used Car

If a brand new car is out of your price range – or you simply don't like the degree of depreciation that comes with buying new, there are plenty of bargains to be had in the used car market – so long as you know the pitfalls to avoid.

Steps

1 Decide on a number of models that interest you. Go along to second-hand car dealers or check adverts in magazines such as *Loot* or *Exchange and Mart*. Some new-car dealerships offer manufacturer-certified second-hand cars; they generally charge more, but may offer a limited warranty.

2 Make a list of the features you want, along with acceptable mileage limits and condition of the car you're willing to buy.

3 If you see a model that you like, compare the asking price with those printed in publications such as *What Car?*, *Parker's Guide* or *Used Car Price Guide* – these will supply you with a valuation based on the year in which the car was built.

4 Give the car a thorough inspection. Start with the exterior: if the paint finish is slightly different in some areas it is almost certainly a post-accident repair. Check the bumpers and wheel arches for signs of rust, dents or body filler. Check the tyres – uneven wear may be due to poor alignment or bent suspension components.

5 Open the bonnet. Look at the engine's overall level of cleanliness. Look for rust and oil leaks around the valve cover and head gasket. Unscrew the oil cap. If there is a deposit of white "cream", the car has been mostly used for short runs from cold starts. Such engines will have a reduced life expectancy.

6 Start up the engine. It should start immediately. Take the car for a test drive. Check the brakes. Test the transmission for slippage. Set the hand brake, depress the clutch pedal and shift through the gears. Check to make sure all the lights work, as well as the wind-screen wipers, indicators and in-car music system

7 Prepare to negotiate. Set yourself an upper limit beyond which you won't go. Make a fair offer that fits your budget. It's usually a waste of time coming up with a figure that greatly undervalues the car. Don't forget, the seller will probably have reached his or her own price by following the same valuation publications as you.

8 If the offer is not accepted, try to convince him rationally why your offer is fair – point out any problems you noticed about the car. Make a second offer reflecting your argument.

9 If you pay for the car with a building society cheque, take your pass book along – the buyer might want proof that the cheque is not a fake. If you pay by a bank draft, take it along during banking hours so that the seller can phone the issuing bank.

10 Take sensible security measures if you pay by cash.

What to Look For

- Pricing
- Acceptable mileage
- Maintenance and repair records
- No recalls
- Clean title
- Good running condition
- Good appearance

Tips

If the vehicle's mileage appears unusually low, have a mechanic determine whether someone has been tampering with the odometer. If so, steer well clear.

For peace of mind, have the car professionally inspected. The three main organisations are the AA (telephone: 0345 500610), ABS (telephone: 0345 419926), and Green Flag/National Breakdown (telephone: 01254 355606). Inspections usually cost from £50 to £150, depending on the car. You will receive a written report afterwards.

For a cheaper alternative, call the Institute of Automotive Assessors (01543 251346). They will put you in contact with your nearest affiliated independent assessor. They usually cost around half that charged by the motoring organisations.

Always ensure you see the log book of the car. The seller will have to return the registration documents to the DVLA, who will then send you new documentation.

525 Buy or Sell a Car Online

If you're selling a car, the internet offers a hassle-free way to reach an enormous number of potential buyers. And if you know exactly what type of car you're looking for, buying it online is as easy as pie.

Steps

Buy a new car online

1 Follow Steps 1 to 4 in 522 "Buy a New Car".

2 Look at the manufacturer's website and research the various options on offer. Write down exactly what you're looking for and the price you're willing to pay.

3 Go to a secure, reliable website that sells cars online or contains ads for new or used cars. Look in the business or automobile sections of a popular search engine, or try search strings like "internet car dealers uk" or "buy a car online uk". (Insert the "uk" suffix to avoid listing US dealers, who will be of no use to anyone trying to buy a car in Europe.)

4 You may be able to conduct the entire transaction online: Order the car via the site, arrange payment via e-mail without having to negotiate (new car prices are extremely competitive on the internet), and even have it delivered to your door.

5 Alternatively, you can use the internet to get the buying process started. After finding a local dealership online, work with the dealer in person to negotiate the deal and sign the paperwork.

6 Pick up your new car at a nearby dealership. Some dealerships will even deliver it to you.

Sell a used car online

1 Find a website that accepts online advertising. Newspaper, auto sales sites and local community sites all run ads for used cars.

2 Take some good-quality digital pictures of your car.

3 Take advantage of the ability of online ads to convey more facts about your car than print ads can, to reach more people and to feature multiple pictures of the car. To post your ad, sign up by entering your contact information and a description of your car, and pay a small fee (if required) with a credit card.

4 Create a web page with a simple design and good-quality images of your car. Include any other details you weren't able to fit in your online ad (such as a scanned copy of the vehicle's history report). You might be able to link it to your ad.

5 Wait for the offers to roll in. (See 527 "Sell a Car".)

What to Look For

- Secure websites
- Reliable service
- Clear communication
- Concise online advertising

Tips

Research auto sales websites just as you would any other company from whom you were contemplating making a major purchase.

Talk to anyone you know who's bought a car online about their experience.

Warning

Don't buy a used car online – not directly, anyway. You need to inspect it first. (See 524 "Buy a Used Car".)

526 Buy a Hybrid Car

A hybrid electric vehicle (HEV) has two engines: one electric and one combustion. The car generally runs on one or the other until the driver needs more power or faster acceleration than either of the two small engines can deliver alone. At that point they operate together. HEVs are low emission, fuel efficient and downright slick. This is sure to be a major growth area in auto technology.

Steps

1 Learn the jargon. Research has shown that a Super Ultra Low-Emission Vehicle is 90 per cent cleaner than an average new car. An Ultra Low-Emission Vehicle is about 50 per cent cleaner than the average new car. There are zero-emission cars on the road now, but they are electric vehicles, not HEVs.

2 Evaluate how and where you drive your current vehicle to decide whether an HEV is right for you. Hybrid vehicles are terrific for urban and suburban driving: if your car runs on an electric engine at low RPMs, the short trips and stop-and-go traffic make for impressive fuel savings. Long-distance commuters who drive such cars won't see the same savings as their urban cousins. Cars that run on combustion engines with electrical assistance – such as the Honda Civic Hybrid – will see less difference in fuel consumption between city and motorway driving.

3 Decide whether you can live with the limited choice of HEVs on the market. There are currently very few models to choose from, although many manufacturers claim to have hybrid concept cars in development or demonstration stages. If you're not satisfied with the current choices, be patient – plenty more will be coming on the market soon.

4 Be prepared to spend several thousand pounds more on an HEV than a comparable petrol- or diesel-powered vehicle, due to low production numbers and mechanical complexity. HEVs also have low resale value.

5 Research the availability of the car where you live and check the manufacturer's website to judge how easy it is to have repairs made. Some auto websites list the typical cost of ownership on available models.

6 Follow the steps in 522 "Buy a New Car".

What to Look For

- Super Ultra Low- and Ultra Low-Emission vehicles
- Availability of HEVs
- Local repair shops
- Cost of ownership

Tip

Hybrids – unlike electric cars – recharge their batteries as you drive and brake, so you never have to plug your car into the wall socket.

527 Sell a Car

When selling a car, private transactions almost always generate more money than selling to a dealer. Make the process smoother by putting yourself in the buyer's shoes (see 524 Buy a Used Car) and sell your car quickly, and possibly for more money.

Steps

1 Clear out your car, then wash, vacuum and wax it. Fix minor problems, or prepare to come down substantially in your asking price. Have a mechanic look at your car before you sell to help appraise its value. This will keep some buyers from telling you to lower the price by claiming the car needs significant work.

2 Check publications such as *What Car?*, *Parker's Guide* or *Used Car Price Guide* for the model and year of your car. Also, check the classified ads section of your local newspapers to get an idea of the going rate.

3 If you're selling a speciality car whose appeal is seasonal, sell when it's most in demand. Convertibles fetch the best prices in spring and summer, while autumn and winter weather is best for selling four-wheel-drive vehicles.

4 Advertise. The cheapest approach is to place a "FOR SALE" sign (including the price and a contact telephone number) in the window of your car while it's parked. This approach is only likely to work for the cheapest cars (below £2,000).

5 Adverts that feature a photograph of your car will be more costly, but will also sell the car more quickly. If you take this approach, use a good-looking picture with a simple uncluttered background that will reproduce well on low-quality newsprint.

6 Describe your car accurately and simply. The critical information is the marque, model, type of vehicle (hatchback, saloon, etc.), year, mileage, colour and price. Mention other features that may grab the attention of a potential buyer, such as full service history, power steering or multi-play CD system.

7 Confirm that anyone wanting to test-drive your car has a current driver's licence. Be prepared for potential buyers to ask if their mechanic can check out the car. If you've had a mechanic look at your car recently, you can show the receipt.

8 The buyer will almost certainly try to knock down your asking price. Never bother making a counter-offer to an insultingly low opening bid: politely decline and say you cannot accept anything so low. Lower your price only when the buyer gets closer to a price you might accept.

9 Unless you know the buyer personally, only accept cash, a building society cheque or bank draft as payment for the car.

10 Inform the DVLC that you have sold your car, otherwise you may find yourself with a future demand (and even fine) for road tax.

What to Look For

- Realistic price
- Advertisements
- Registration
- Cash or cheque

Tips

Always allow the buyer to inspect your car using an independent assessor. Be honest about both major and minor defects – rust, a bad engine, failing brakes – and subtract the cost of repairs from your asking price. Agree to meet the prospective buyer at a garage or accept a deposit of a few hundred pounds while the car is being inspected.

Write the buyer a receipt for the transaction, indicating that you are selling the vehicle "as seen" – this will help you to avoid future problems.

Warnings

Avoid using the expression "or best offer". You'll get the *worst* offers.

Don't forget to cancel or amend your insurance policy. Its clauses will specifically relate to your old car, and will not be transferred to its replacement automatically.

528 Buy a Motorcycle

Everyone loves motorcycles. Some people will tell you they're scary and dangerous, and they may be right, but they're lying when they say they don't like them. While many bikes look similar, they may behave in very different ways, depending on their engine size, configuration and intended use. Before deciding on a bike, be sure you understand these basic differences.

ENGINE CHARACTERISTICS	DESCRIPTION
Size	• Motorcycles are nearly always identified by their engine size. For example, a Honda CBR600 has an engine with a cylinder volume of 600 cubic cm (cc). • If you're not sure of the engine size, look for an identifying sticker on the frame, below the handlebars.
Power	• So, the larger the cylinder volume (cc) the more power, right? Not always. Engine configuration and design matter too. A highly tuned, four-cylinder 600 cc machine may have much more power than a single-cylinder 600 cc machine. The four-cylinder bike is also wider and heavier – important considerations for a novice looking for a stable ride.
Straight-four	• Most bikes that use a straight-four engine (four cylinders arranged in a straight line) are sport bikes. Japanese manufacturers have been associated with these engines since the 1970s and have been spectacularly successful in producing reliable, affordable machines with true racetrack performance.
V-twin	• This configuration is favoured by Harley-Davidson, a motorcycle brand that is as much a lifestyle as it is transportation. Harley V-twins are big, macho and heavy. Other manufacturers have produced their own successful V-twin lines to compete with Harley. Bikes using these engines are usually not designed for sportiness and quick handling, but for cruising and looking relaxed. • As an alternative to the straight-four, some sport bikes use a V-twin configuration although in a much more highly tuned format than in a Harley. V-twin sport riders claim their bikes are smoother, easier to ride and sound better than four-cylinder machines.
Single-cylinder	• Many bikes designed for both on and off the road use a single-cylinder engine. This keeps the overall weight of the bike relatively low but also reduces horsepower. • If simplicity, lightweight and ruggedness are important to you, these bikes are a great choice.
Two-stroke	• Two-strokes are simple and lightweight. They are also maintenance intensive, loud and smoky. And they are not ecologically sound machines. Research suggests that they produce more than 25 times the amount of carbon monoxide than a diesel car. There have even been calls to make them illegal in certain quarters. (Such bikes have not been street-legal in the USA for many years.)

MOTORCYCLE TYPES

Sport Bike

If you want more performance than a Ferrari will give you for one-tenth the price, this is for you. Sport bikes have a fairing to cut the wind, a very racy look and limited passenger room. They provide unmatched handling and acceleration but make few concessions to comfort. The most popular classes of these bikes are the 600 cc and 1,000 cc machines. Very few riders have the skill to truly utilise a 1,000 cc machine, even on a racetrack. (A & E doctors sometimes refer to them as "donor cycles".) If you're buying a used sport bike beware of race bikes, as they will have had heavy use. Small sport bikes cost under £4,000, large ones over £8,000.

Standard Street Bike

If you don't want the manic speed of a sport bike but are looking for more performance than a cruiser, there are many fine standard motorcycles available. Standard street bikes may have a small fairing (or sometimes none at all). They frequently use engines derived from those of sport bikes, but are built in a more user-friendly format. Performance is usually good enough to satisfy all but the neediest for speed. Comfort, particularly for passengers, is much higher than on a sport bike, while insurance costs are likely to be lower. BMW and Triumph are major makers of standard-style bikes, as are all the Japanese manufacturers. Prices span a wide range, from under £4,000 to over £10,000.

Motocross Bike

Motocross bikes are intended exclusively for off-road use and are usually powered by a two-stroke engine, although four-strokes are becoming popular. There are many different sizes available, but the majority of full-size motocross bikes are 125 cc, 250 cc or 500 cc. Unless you live near a riding area, you will need a trailer to transport your bike.

Touring

Built for long-distance travel, touring bikes have a windscreen, comfortable seating for two, and lots of storage. The Honda Goldwing is the recognised leader in this category, although BMW and Harley also make popular models. Average cost is about £15,000. A wide range of accessories are available to increase comfort on long rides.

Cruiser

Long, low and built for style, many cruisers utilise V-twin engines designed to have a retro look. Owners frequently add accessories to suit their own needs or tastes. Harley-Davidson is the recognised trendsetter in cruiser bikes, although many manufacturers produce high-quality machines. The average price for a Harley is about £18,000; Japanese cruisers average about half that.

Vintage

Bikes from the 1960s and earlier can be very beautiful and rewarding, but they can also be fragile and temperamental. Don't buy a vintage bike on a whim. Bargains are rare, and a cheap vintage bike is probably missing a lot of key parts. Do plenty of research and be honest about your abilities and enthusiasm for upkeep. Don't get a vintage bike with the expectation of using it for daily commuting, unless you're a skilled mechanic.

Dual-purpose

Street legal but designed to handle off-road use, dual-purpose motorcycles are usually powered by a single-cylinder, four-stroke engine of 600 cc or less.

Scooter

Low cost and ease of use are the primary attractions of a scooter, but they don't have the power to let you drive safely in anything but low-traffic town driving.

529 Buying and Changing Motor Oil

Plan to change your motor oil every 3,000 miles (4,800 km) or every three months. However, you may want to do it more often if you've been driving in very hot and/or dusty conditions.

Steps

Getting Ready

1 Gather the necessary tools and materials. Consult your owner's manual or an automotive-parts specialist to find out the weight of oil and type of oil filter your car needs.

2 Run the car's engine for ten minutes before you drain the oil. Warm oil drains faster than cold oil.

3 Park the car on a level surface, engage the handbrake and turn off the engine. If your car has a low ground clearance, raise it by driving it onto a ramp or by jacking it up and supporting it securely. You will need two jack stands to support the front of your car after jacking it up. Never get under a car supported only by a jack.

4 Open the bonnet and place the new oil and funnel on top of the engine to ensure that you won't forget to add oil afterwards (an expensive mistake that many do-it-yourselfers make).

Draining the Oil and Changing the Oil Filter

5 Locate the oil drain plug on the underside of the engine, usually near the front centre of the car.

6 Place an oil drain pan under the plug and loosen the plug with a socket wrench. Remember: turn the wrench anti-clockwise to remove the plug. Use the right size of wrench or socket – and avoid using an adjustable wrench – or you risk stripping the plug's threads and rounding the plug's hex head.

7 Carefully remove the plug by hand. Be prepared for the rush of warm oil. Wear rubber gloves to remove the plug if it's hot. Let the oil drain into the pan. Wipe off the drain plug and the plug opening with a rag when the oil finishes draining.

8 Reinstall the plug. Turn it by hand at first to prevent cross-threading. Tighten the plug with your socket wrench, but be careful not to over-tighten. Locate the oil filter on the side of the engine. Position the oil pan underneath the filter to catch any remaining oil. Use an adjustable oil filter wrench to unscrew the oil filter.

9 Use a rag to wipe the area where the filter mounts to the engine. Make sure the rubber seal of the old filter is not stuck to the engine. Open a new can of oil and use some to lightly coat the rubber seal of the new filter.

10 Screw the new filter into place by hand. It's usually not necessary to tighten the oil filter with the oil filter wrench, but have the wrench ready in case your grip's not strong (or large) enough.

What to Look For

- Correct tools
- Ramping facilities
- Safety

Tip

Record the date and mileage after you change the oil so you will know when your car is due for another oil change. It may help to put a small sticker on your windscreen to remind you.

Warnings

Handle hot automotive oil with extreme care.

Use extreme caution when jacking up the car. Make sure the jack stands are completely secure.

On some new vehicles, oil must be changed every three months or the warranty will be invalidated. Check your warranty carefully.

Adding New Oil and Cleaning Up

11 Locate the oil filler cap on top of the engine. Remove it.

12 Place the funnel in the opening and pour in the new oil. Typically, you will use 4.5 to 5.5 litres (8 to 10 pints) of oil. Check your owner's manual for the correct amount of oil.

13 Check the area around the oil drain plug and the filter for leaks. Tighten the plug or oil filter if you find leakage.

14 Use rags and newspapers to wipe away excess oil.

15 Pour the used oil into a plastic container after it cools.

16 Dispose of the used oil and filters at authorised locations: Take them to either a recycling centre or a garage that can recycle for you. Don't pour oil down a drain.

530 Wash a Car

To get your car gleaming for would-be buyers, work from top to bottom and do one side at a time.

Steps

1 Choose a shady spot, preferably away from trees that are dripping sap or dropping leaves.

2 Close all car doors and windows.

3 Put one cap of car soap into a bucket and fill it three-quarters of the way with warm water. Set the bucket aside.

4 Hose any excess dirt off the car, beginning at the roof and working down to the tyres.

5 Lather a sponge or old towel in the bucket of soapy water and sponge the roof of the car. Spray off excess soap when the entire roof has been cleaned.

6 Repeat for all four sides of the car, washing one full side, including the windows, bumpers and tyres, and rinsing completely before going to the next side.

7 Give the car one final rinse with the hose to get rid of any water spots when all four sides have been washed and rinsed.

8 Take a chamois leather ("shammy") or towel and dry the car thoroughly by setting the towel flat against the car's surface and dragging it along to pick up any water spots. Start at the roof and work your way down to the tyres.

9 Wash the windows with a rag soaked in plain water and dry them with a dry rag, or use window cleaner and pieces of wadded-up newspaper on both the inside and the outside of the windows.

10 Give metal or chrome an extra rubdown to get rid of water spots.

What to Look For

- Suitable location
- Necessary equipment

Tips

Wear old clothes for cleaning the car.

Soap dries fast. Wash one side at a time to keep the soap from drying on your car's paint. Otherwise, you'll have to re-wash to get the dried soap off.

Wet and wring out your chamois leather before you dry; it will be more absorbent.

531 Wax a Car

Nothing will pull in a prospective buyer like a beautifully clean car. You may not be able to beat a professional valet service using an electric buffer, but these steps will have your car's paint finish looking like new.

Steps

1 Remember that some waxes contain abrasives that can damage clear-coat and lacquer finishes, and may harm dark-coloured paint jobs. When in doubt, use a non-abrasive wax.

2 Park the car in a cool, shady spot. If you don't have access to a shady spot, wax one section at a time so the sun doesn't bake the wax onto your car. Avoid waxing if it's very hot or very cold.

3 Dip a damp wax sponge into the car wax, getting a clump on your sponge the size of a 10 pence piece. Rub the wax onto the car using small circles. Avoid getting wax into seams – if this happens, use a soft toothbrush to remove it.

4 Working on one section at a time, cover the car's entire surface, remembering the path you took. By the time you have finished, the wax will be ready to remove.Using soft terry cloth towels, wipe off the wax in the same order in which it was applied.

5 Shake out the towel or cloth as you work, in order to avoid wax build-up and streaking. Leaning as close to the surface of your car as you can, look down the sides and across the front, back and roof to spot any residual wax. Use a cheesecloth to polish the car's entire surface.

6 Wash your used towels, cloths and pads with liquid fabric softener to keep them from scratching your car the next time you use them.

What to Look For

- Suitable location
- Suitable weather conditions
- Correct equipment

Tips

Professionals differ on which car wax is best, but most agree that carnauba is better than other inexpensive varieties – it seals better, and is easier to apply and buff.

As a rule, the easier the wax is to work with, the more often you'll have to apply it.

Don't leave wax on your car for more than two hours or it will be very difficult to remove. Excess wax left on the car can damage the paint, especially if the car is exposed to direct sunlight.

532 Buy Car Insurance

Car insurance can be very expensive, but by choosing your coverage carefully you should be able to get affordable insurance. Don't forget, though, that the bottom line is that you are legally required to have some form of motor insurance to drive in the UK.

Steps

1 Determine the level of coverage you want. This means balancing how much you can afford to pay with how much you can afford to lose.

2 Although the specifics of each policy will differ from one insurer to another, there are essentially three types of insurance on offer:

Fully Comprehensive

This covers you fully for any accident that might take place. If your car is valued at over £5,000 you should go for this option.

What to Look For

- Cost
- Types of coverage
- No-claims bonus
- Competitive quote

Warning

If you've had an accident resulting in a previous claim, this information will follow you around, much like a bad credit rating.

Third Party, Fire and Theft

This covers any damages that you might cause, along with the theft and damage by fire of your own car. It's only really suitable for cars worth less than £5,000.

Third Party

This is the most basic insurance you can get, and covers any damage that you might cause to another person, but not the loss of your car if it is stolen or damaged. Only suitable for very low value vehicles – some insurers no longer offer it as an option.

3 Shop around for quotes based on the cover you've determined you need, instead of asking agencies what they think you need. You can get immediate quotes from most of the major motor insurers by filling in forms on their websites.

4 If you are an older driver, younger driver, female or owner of a high-performance car, you may be able to get a better deal by applying to companies that specialise in these markets.

5 Read your policy before signing. Make sure there are no surprise clauses.

6 Keep the policy in a safe place, and keep proof of insurance in the car.

533 Spring for a New Paint Job

No matter where you live, acid rain, UV rays, tree sap, falling leaves and bird droppings can all conspire to make your car look old and dull. A paint job can cost anything from £200 to beyond £4,000. In some cases it may even enhance the value of a car as it protects against rust and corrosion.

Steps

1 Look in the *Yellow Pages* for specialist auto body shops or contact local garages. Compare written estimates from several before you agree to go ahead.

2 Choose a colour, then decide from single-stage finish to multiple layers (primer, base, clear/tint and final coat). More layers result in a deeper shine, a more durable paint job – and a larger bill.

3 Save money by repainting your car the same colour, so sills and internal frame parts (such as the boot) don't have to be repainted to match. Special paint and designs add to the price.

4 Ask your body shop exactly how to care for and clean your new finish, as some paint jobs take weeks to cure. During that time, stay away from commercial car washes and don't use an ice scraper or spill fuel on the finish.

What to Look For

- Written estimates
- Warranties
- Matching colour
- Care instructions

Tips

Some car experts swear by a good wax job; some say new paints don't need wax. Ask your technician what's best for your paint job.

Unless your car's paint is damaged or is an old acrylic lacquer finish, you generally don't need to strip old paint before repainting.

534 Buying and Changing a Battery

A little maintenance will keep your battery charged throughout the cold months as well as the warmer ones.

Steps

1 If your battery is more than four years old, replace it.

2 Ask your mechanic to perform a "load test" on your battery. This tests whether the battery is capable of generating sufficient charge on below-freezing days. If it fails the test, replace the battery.

3 Clean the battery terminals if they are encrusted with deposits. Use a wire brush dipped in baking soda and water to clean them of corrosion and ensure that the deposits do not block the flow of electrical current.

4 Check to make sure the water level in the battery hasn't dropped. You can do this on conventional batteries by popping off the plastic cover and checking to see that the water inside reaches the plastic filler necks. Add distilled water if necessary. Maintenance-free batteries, however, generally have an indicator light that goes black when the battery needs service; take these types to a mechanic for service.

5 Check the tightness of the battery cable ends. A loose connection can prevent your car from starting and acts just like a dead battery. If you can move the battery cable ends that are attached to the battery terminals at all, they are too loose.

6 Check that the battery is securely fastened in the battery tray. A loose battery that is allowed to shift around can cause damage if it is able to tip over under the bonnet. Excessive vibration will also shorten the life of your battery.

What to Look For

- Current state
- Water level
- Cables

Tips

In severe cases, the battery may need to be recharged with a battery charger to bring it back to life.

Your car may not be starting because other components in the charging system are failing, or because of a bad starter motor.

Warnings

Keep open flames away from your battery – the chemicals inside it are combustible.

Battery acid is corrosive. When adding distilled water to the battery, take care that acid doesn't splatter on your skin or clothes.

535 Buy the Right Fuel

Different brands of fuel – even those with the same octane rating – can cause a vehicle to behave very differently. Your car may act sluggish or misfire (knock) on one oil company's product but not another's. As different refineries offer different formulations of oxygenates, detergents and even octanes, changing brands will often perk up sluggish performance.

Steps

1 Check your car owner's manual for any recommended fuel.

2 Try another company's brand if your car isn't running smoothly on the manufacturer's required minimum octane. Each refinery

What to Look For

- Manufacturer's fuel recommendation
- Octane rating
- No knocking sound
- Improved engine power

mixes its own blends with additives to encourage cleaner burning. Your car may simply need a higher-quality fuel to clean out its fuel system and run better. If switching fuels doesn't solve the problem, it may be time to ask your mechanic to search for a different cause.

3 Understand the difference between the different fuels on sale at your garage forecourt. Get to know the types that are applicable to your car. And, whatever you do, don't get them muddled up: if you put diesel in petrol engine – and vice versa – the results will be catastrophic. Not to mention very costly.

4 If your vehicle makes a knocking sound on acceleration, try a higher-octane petrol.

5 Try changing brands again if your engine runs rougher in winter, since fuel blends may change seasonally.

536 Buy Fuel Treatments

Fuel treatments or additives are fluids you put directly into your petrol tank. They're designed to reduce wear on your engine and deposits on intake valves and manifolds, carburettors and fuel injectors. Additives lubricate engine parts and generally enhance performance.

Steps

1 Check your car owner's manual to see what fuel treatments are recommended, or if the manufacturer recommends against using any at all. Don't gum up your engine with the wrong additive.

2 Figure out which problem with your engine's performance you need to correct. As with cold medicines, you want the specific treatment that addresses your engine's issues.

3 Find treatments for sale at garages or auto spares shops.

4 Add the treatment next time you fill your tank (usually a full bottle per tank) to the empty tank. You need to use such treatments regularly for maximum effectiveness.

Tip

If your car is running smoothly and getting top mileage, there's no need to use a higher-octane fuel.

What to Look For

- Manufacturer's recommendation
- Treatment for specific problem
- Regular use

Tip

Fuel treatment may be a simple solution for knocking or hesitating on acceleration. Higher-octane fuel, however, is often a cheaper solution (see 535 "Buy the Right Fuel").

537 Hire a Reliable Mechanic

It's not that hard to find a trustworthy mechanic – until you happen to be desperate. Have a good mechanic regularly maintain your car to help keep surprise breakdowns to a minimum.

Steps

1 As always, the most reliable way of choosing is to ask trusted friends for their recommendations. Talk to people who have cars similar to yours.

2 Check if the garage is a member of a recognised body (such as the Retail Motor Industry Federation or Institute of the Motor Industry) or listed by the local Trading Standards Office.

3 Ensure that the garage mechanics are qualified, and familiar with your car's make and model. Look for evidence of qualifications, such as certificates, on display.

4 Find out what the garage hours are. Will it be open when you finish work? Will you get a courtesy car while your car is being fixed?

5 Check that the price of the work being done includes the costs of service, parts, labour and VAT – you should know *exactly* what you are paying for. Insist that no additional work be undertaken without your prior permission.

What to Look For

- Recommendations
- Qualified mechanic

Tips

Don't wait until your car needs major repairs to find a good mechanic. Bring your car into the garage for small things like oil changes to get a feel for the place and develop a relationship.

Don't choose a garage based on price. The least expensive repair shop might not be the best place to take your car. Similarly, the most expensive garage (usually the dealership) may not give you the best service or quality.

538 Avoid Buying a Lemon

A "lemon" is any new or warrantied vehicle with a major problem that can't be fixed in a reasonable amount of time or number of attempts.

Steps

New vehicles

1 Find out from the manufacturer if there's ever been a recall on your model.

2 Research the model's safety recall and maintenance history through consumer safety agencies such as *Which*, or motoring magazines, newspaper articles and website reviews of the vehicle.

3 Ask your mechanic how often this model shows up at his garage for repairs.

4 Talk to other owners of this model: Are they satisfied? (Customer surveys carried out in motoring magazines give a good indication of such matters.)

Used vehicles

1 Follow the steps under "New vehicles".

2 Get a vehicle history report to make sure that the car you're considering is clean -- no salvage title issued and no major

What to Look For

New cars
- No recalls
- Safety, maintenance and repair history
- Positive recommendations

Used cars
- All of the above
- Vehicle history report
- Best possible condition
- No bodywork damage
- Seller not too hasty

crashes or any illegal activity in its history. Several commercial agencies sell this service.

3 If you're buying from an owner, have a trusted mechanic inspect the car. Alternatively, have the car professionally inspected by the AA (tel: 0345 500610), ABS (tel: 0345 419926) or National Breakdown (tel: 01254 355606). Inspections usually cost from £50 to £200, depending on the car. You will receive a written report afterwards.

4 Be wary of models offered for sale below prices quoted in such magazines such as *Parker's Guide* or *Used Car Price Guide*.

Tip

For a cheaper professional inspection, call the Institute of Automotive Assessors (tel: 01543 251346). They will put you in contact with your nearest independent assessor.

539 Sell Your Old Banger

Should you pay someone to haul away that beast in your driveway? Perhaps not: You might find someone willing to buy it. Before you advertise, though, take time to discover the inner beauty of the vehicle. The more selling points you can come up with, the better the pitch. Then clean it up to reveal any outer beauty it may still have.

Steps

1 See 527 "Sell a Car".

2 Clear out the interior, then wash, vacuum and wax the vehicle. Cleanliness impresses buyers and will make any old car look like less of a project.

3 Fix whatever's broken if it's inexpensive to repair: the more working parts it has, the more selling points you've got.

4 Research the vehicle's used-car value as well as other sellers' asking prices for the same "vintage" model in your area. It'll help you determine a realistic asking price (leave yourself room to comfortably drop the price when bargaining).

5 Bedazzle prospective buyers with whatever advantages you can find in writing: great crash-test results, clean title history.

6 Include "free with car" aftermarket parts or accessories you bought (such as the hammer you use to start it with). Maintenance records, too, indicate you had at least a little love for this vehicle.

7 Avoid volunteering bad news during bargaining (needs new tyres and a tune-up). Pitch the high points (has new brakes, is the same car Steve McQueen drove in *The Heist*).

8 Don't tell outright lies; they'll catch up with you and – at the very worst – you could end up in court.

What to Look For

- Cleanliness
- Inexpensive repairs
- Used-car value
- Positive points
- Accessories
- Maintenance records

Tips

Find ads for comparable cars to learn which selling points are hyped, and how to downplay an old car's character flaws.

Your invoice should include a phrase like "purchased as seen", meaning you're not responsible for any further repairs.

In a worst-case scenario, call a scrap yard – you should be able to get £20 on even the worst wreck.

540 Buy, Restore and Sell a Vintage Car

It might look like an old heap of rusted metal to some, but you know with a little elbow grease you can bring that beauty back to life. Nearly everyone who restores cars will tell you that they're in the business for the love of it, not the money – it's hard to beat the feeling of pride when new life has been given to an old classic.

Steps

Buying

1 Look in the mirror and tell yourself that whatever you may think, you're really unlikely to see a profit on this process. So don't be bitter if it doesn't turn out to be a money maker.

2 Be realistic when calculating the expenses of restoring a vintage vehicle to sell for profit. Get to know the car's market well. How much time and expertise you have to devote to the project will determine which cars you can restore. Find and talk to other people who have worked on the same model; members of car clubs and books are good sources of information. If you're starting from scratch, be prepared to spend a lot of money on tools and equipment in addition to parts for the car.

3 Follow the steps in 524 "Buy a Used Car", except be prepared to buy your car one piece at a time. The perfect chassis could be in someone's garage in Dublin, while the seats may have to be manufactured from scratch in Belgium. Go to car shows, scan the ads in collector and car parts magazines, check scrap yards, scour the internet, and ask friends if they have any car parts lying around.

4 Beware of cars that are heavily rusted. Some rust may be unavoidable, but make sure it's not corroding structural parts.

5 To be on the safe side, see any advertised car or parts you're considering buying in person. If this is not an option, ask for detailed photos. A third alternative is to arrange to have the vehicle inspected for a fee by a national organisation, such as the AA (tel: 0345 500610), ABS (tel: 0345 419926) or National Breakdown (tel: 01254 355606).

Restoring

1 Make sure you have enough room to do the work. A dismantled car takes up a considerable amount of space. Ideally, you need the equivalent of two adjacent garages: one to dismantle the car and keep the parts, and the other to build the car up again. Alternatively, store parts like the engine, gear-box, doors and bonnet in a dry basement or shed while you are working on the chassis and body.

2 Expect the unexpected: you'll always find that aspects of the restoration are more involved than anticipated. If you're not sure

What to Look For

Buying
- Car shows
- Scrap yards

Restoring
- Ample space
- Original equipment
- Vintage magazines

Selling
- Mint condition
- Complete sales package
- Vintage collectibles
- Car shows
- Museums

Tips

Pay attention to details that sell cars, such as a special number plate.

It's not a good idea to try selling the car based on how much money was sunk into its restoration.

With modern versions of the VW Beetle and Mini now out on the streets, the original models – if in good shape – are in demand.

you can do some of the work correctly or if it's dangerous (as is working with heavy duty suspension springs), always call in a professional. In the end it will save you time and money, if not your pride.

3 Use as much original equipment as you can get your hands on (dashboard ornaments, old mirrors, original radios) to enhance the value and raise the asking price. A successfully restored car is a trip back in time for car buffs.

4 Take your restoration cues (paint colour and more) from studying publications of the same era that show your vehicle. Magazines like these are also great to back up the work you've done when selling the car.

Selling

1 Clean the car extremely well. Steam-clean under the bonnet (car valeters can do this). Try to make sure its details are as complete and mint-looking as possible. Change the oil and service the car – the fact that the car doesn't require servicing right away may encourage some buyers.

2 Put together a complete sales package to market your car. Does it have its full set of chrome, for example?

3 Collect any artefacts or knowledge related to the car's history that might increase its allure and value. Was it a race car at some point? Car buffs love log books and proof of races won. Collect manufacturer medallions, racing badges, maintenance records, and original options and sales brochures as well as the manual.

4 Determine your asking price. Compare your car's make, model, year and condition to others listed in advertisements. Ask a fellow enthusiast for a valuation.

5 Choose advertising venues carefully, to get reasonable offers. The catalogues where you found parts for your car, magazines and automobile clubs devoted to your model, and online mailing lists of car buffs might turn up eager buyers.

6 Try not to limit the car's advertising to one geographic region. Different regions have different demands for the same vehicles, and buyers in another part of Europe – or further in some special cases – may pay thousands more than local buyers would.

7 Take it to car shows and museums, and park it prominently near the venue's entrance or exit. Car enthusiasts will appreciate this vehicle, so wave it under their noses. If you're going to a car show far away, transport your car on a trailer to eliminate road wear or damage.

8 Remind yourself, as the buyer hands over the cash, that you weren't planning to make a profit. Focus instead on that next rescue project.

Warnings

Lift with your knees, not your back.

Be realistic about how much you can afford to spend on restoration. Costs can mount quickly.

541 Locate Hard-to-Find Parts

The only thing missing from your beloved 1966 Ford Zephyr is that original chrome logo. No need to worry: new, original and reproduction parts – even the most obscure – can be found with a little bit of detective work.

Steps

1 Know the exact specifications of the part you are searching for. Ask yourself what kind of shape it needs to be in for you to buy it, and how much you're willing to spend. If you can't find the original parts, you could save money by having them rebuilt from scratch. (In some cases, it may be the only way for you to get the replacement part.)

2 Assuming you've already checked with your local car spares shop, browse the classified sections in both paid and free local newspapers. Some sellers (who advertise in the papers but aren't listed in the phone directory) offer cars for parts – a good source if you have a popular, hard-to-shop-for car.

3 Root around local scrap yards for a forgotten gem (look under "Salvage" in the *Yellow Pages*).

4 Check with local garages – they might be able to recommend a source for the elusive part.

5 Speak to local dealers who sell your car's make and model, if it's a new car.

6 Swap stories with auto-club members who own your model. Read the classifieds in speciality magazines.

7 Scour internet auction sites, online search services and bulletin boards. Check back often, as new items are listed frequently. An internet car spares locator service will put you in contact with dealers and private sellers for a fee.

8 Find out if you can use parts from another model of car on yours. Companies like Hollander Interchange (hollander-auto-parts.com) have manuals that identify interchangeable mechanical and body parts on all types of vehicles dating back to the 1920s.

What to Look For

- Acceptable condition and price
- Classified ads
- Scrap yards
- Garages
- Dealers
- Motor clubs
- Internet auctions
- Interchangeable parts

Tip

Buying original parts from car aficionados or dealers will probably cost you more, but are in better condition.

Warning

Saving money shouldn't be your goal for buying every replacement part. Some, such as tyres and brake parts, are vital to the safe operation of a vehicle.

542 Buy Basic Car Tools

Every car owner should have basic tools at home for keeping a car running or for doing minor repairs. Tools should have insulated grips (rubber or plastic-coated) for extra protection. Keep your tools in a box where they can stay dry, and clean off grease, dirt and water after using them. You'll find many of these tools at hardware stores and car spares shops.

ITEM	USES	PRICE RANGE
Adjustable Wrenches	Loosening and tightening everything properly.	£5 to £40
Circuit Tester	Testing electrical circuits.	£5 to £25
Funnels	Adding oil or other fluids. Clean after each use; designate a funnel for each fluid type.	From £1
Hand Degreaser	Works better than regular hand soap.	£1 to £3
Jack	Lifting car to change tyres.	£15 to £30
Jump Leads	Jump-starting a car.	£5 to £20
Oil-filter Wrench	Removing and securing filters.	£5 to £20
Pliers	Loosening and tightening everything improperly.	£5 to £10
Rags and Paper Towels	Checking oil and other fluids. The more the better.	£5 to £20
Rubber Gloves	Keeping hands grease-free.	Free to £2
Rubber Mallet	Tapping open stuck parts into position.	£2 to £5
Screwdrivers	Unscrewing screws, prying lids off cans.	£5 to £10
Socket Set	Tightening nuts and bolts.	£1 to £30 (for a set)
Spark-plug Wrench	Removing and tightening spark plugs.	£5 to £20
Stiff, Non-wire Brush	Cleaning battery contacts.	£3
Tyre Pressure Gauge	Checking air pressure.	£5
Tyre Wrench	Removing tyres.	£5 to £30
Utility Knife	Slicing rubber belts, tubes, etc.	£3 and up
Work Gloves	Keeping hands intact and blister-free.	£4 and up
WARNING	Never work underneath a jacked-up car. Jacks are not very stable and are meant for changing tyres only. Use a proper car lift or wheel ramps (along with tyre chocks and a set handbrake) designed for working under a car.	

543 Buying Car Tyres

Keeping your tyres in a healthy state is not only vital for the smooth running of your car, but also a critical safety factor. Here's everything you need to know about maintaining and replacing your tyres.

Steps

Checking Current State

1 Check your tyres out of doors where the lighting is good. Visually inspect all four tyres.

2 Remember that under normal driving conditions, all four tyres should wear evenly.

3 Check for even tread wear by using a tread-depth gauge, which costs less than £15. The depth of the tread (the grooves in the tyre) should be even all over.

4 Let some air out of your tyres if there is wear down the middle and not on the sides. It means there's too much air in them.

5 Add air to tyres with wear on both the inside and outside edges, which means there's not enough air in them.

6 If your tyres are worn more on one side than the other, pay a visit to an alignment shop for a front-end or four-wheel alignment.

7 Run your hand lightly over the tread surface of each tyre. If the treads feel bumpy or scalloped – even if the tread is still deep – you may need new shock absorbers or struts. (Some cars have shocks, some have struts and some have a combination – struts in front, shocks in back.)

8 Check the tyre pressure in all four tyres – and the spare tyre – at least once every month. The recommended tyre pressure will be listed in your vehicle's instruction manual or stamped on the side of the tyre.

Buying New Tyres

9 Think about how and where you drive. Tyre engineers design product lines for specific purposes, such as comfort, durability, sporty handling, or traction in rain and snow. But choosing one virtue usually means giving up a little of the others.

10 Consider an all-season tyre. It's a reasonable compromise for most drivers – that's why car manufacturers usually provide them as original equipment on new cars.

11 Know your current tyre. In general, it's best to replace your tyres with those of the same brand, design and size, all of which you'll find printed on your tyres.

What to Look For

- Current tread depth
- Even wear
- Consider alignment
- Regular maintenance

Tip

Depending on the type of tyre, the car and the kind of driving you do, tyres usually need to be replaced every 40,000 miles (64,000 km).

Have a servicing professional examine your tyres if you're not sure that they need replacing. For an unbiased opinion, use someone who doesn't sell tyres.

Get a front-end or four-wheel alignment if you are involved in an accident – even just a minor scrape. If anything is out of alignment, it will affect tyre wear.

Warnings

Driving on tyres that are bald or worn greatly increases your chance of a puncture, and is especially dangerous when the roads are wet or oily. Don't put off buying new tyres when you need them – not when your safety is at stake.

It is illegal to drive with a tyre with a tread that is less than 1.6 mm deep.

12 Decide where to buy your new tyres. In addition to car dealerships, tyre stores and garages and petrol stations, they can now also be bought at discount shops or ordered over the phone or the internet. Prices and service vary, so shop around if you can.

13 Have a mechanic or tyre dealer perform the installation. Special machines are needed to slip your new tyres over the car's wheels. And, anyway, it's hard and dirty work!

14 Keep tyre wear even by rotating your tyres as the manufacturer suggests – new cars are sensitive to tyres with differing degrees of wear. Keeping tyre wear even means your tyres will all need replacing at the same time, so monitor tread depth to help you budget ahead for the expense.

544 Select Tyre Rims

For some drivers, the biggest concern with their car's tyre rims (or wheels) is appearance. But an owner's choice of rims also affects the car's performance. New wheels run upwards of £60 apiece. If you're replacing a damaged rim, consider buying a used one.

Steps

1 Think about buying alloy wheels if you do a lot of driving on hills or in stop-and-go traffic. Some alloy wheels are designed to encourage cool air flow over the brakes to prevent overheating. The alloy itself can help dissipate heat, too.

2 "Plus-size" your rims if you want to improve performance and add a sportier look. With a larger inner diameter, you'll find that steering is more responsive and your car holds the road better. Purchasing rims that are one or two sizes larger than the ones you have means you'll have to buy new tyres as well. While the outside diameter of the tyre your car uses should remain the same, the inner diameter – wrapped around the rim – needs to be bigger to fit a bigger rim.

3 Look for rims that aren't too heavy for your vehicle. Big, steel rims on a small car can decrease handling ability. Heavy wheels are *unsprung* weight – not supported by your car's suspension – and therefore useless for smoothing out the ride or improving balance in driving manoeuvres.

What to Look For

- Alloy wheels
- Appropriate size and weight

Tips

Rims come in a wide array of designs. For something spectacular, check out custom car shows and speciality catalogues.

Be sure any wheels you buy have a maximum-load rating compatible with your vehicle.

Make sure your car's bolt pattern matches the new rims you're purchasing.

545 Outfit Your Car for Emergencies

Emergencies strike when you least expect them, so be prepared and carry an emergency kit in your car. They're commercially available, or you can easily put together your own. And it may make the difference between waiting hours for a breakdown truck and being able to make your way to your destination.

ROADSIDE KIT	FIRST AID KIT	DISASTER KIT	SNOW COUNTRY KIT
• Mobile phone, CB radio	• Pain killers	• Thermal blanket or sleeping bag	• Thermal blanket or sleeping bag
• Global positioning system (GPS) navigating device	• Medium-size adhesive-strip bandages	• Non-perishable food	• Additional warm clothing
• Spare tyre (inflated!)	• Small roll of sterile gauze	• 3-day supply of water	• Woollen socks
• Jack and tyre wrench	• Bandage tape	• First aid kit (see left)	• Waterproof jacket and trousers
• Jump leads	• Alcohol (isopropyl) or antibacterial wipes	• Change of clothes for each family member	• Snow boots, hat, gloves
• 4 litres (1 gallon) of water for radiator, drinking or squirters	• Saline or eye wash solution (to wash out eyes or wounds)	• At least £50 cash	• Hand warmers
• First aid kit (see right)	• Antibiotic ointment	• Medications	• Water
• Rechargeable torch with car recharger	• Quick-reference first aid card or book	• Baby food, formula, bottles	• Emergency food, energy bars
• Mini fire extinguisher	• Scissors	• Nappies	• Tyre chains
• Screwdrivers (one Phillips, one flathead)	• Antihistamines (to relieve itch and possibly limit severe allergic reactions)	• Wipes	• Salt or sand
• Adjustable wrench	• Disposable rubber gloves	• Dog and cat food	• Snow shovel
• Utility knife	• Plastic bags	• Heavy-duty gloves	• Ice scraper
• Hazard signs	• Paper tissues	• Shovel	• Matches or lighter
• Transmission/clutch fluid		• Torch	
• Can of oil		• Photos, names of family members, descriptions (for rescue and recovery)	
• Brake fluid		• Goggles, dust masks	
• Empty fuel can		• Bottle and tin openers	
• Rain coat and/or umbrella		• Whistle	
• Spare fuses		• Rucksack	
• Rags and/or paper towels		• Knife	
• Waterproof tape		• Nylon rope	
		• Personal hygiene items	
		• Matches or lighter	

WARNINGS	Not all medications are appropriate for all people. Before breaking out the first aid kit, consider the patient's age, special conditions (such as pregnancy) and health issues.
	Read your first aid quick-reference card before you put it in your car. It takes only minutes and may keep you from doing something foolish or harmful.

546 Buy a Theft-Prevention Device

Anti-theft devices for cars run the gamut from low-tech and cheap to fancy and expensive. Electronic engine immobilisers, for example, are extremely effective at keeping a car safe. They allow your car's engine to start only in the presence of a special key or device carried by the owner. But even a hunk of steel locked onto the steering wheel can deter opportunistic thieves.

Steps

1 Always lock your car doors, and close the windows and sunroof. Take your keys with you. A ridiculous number of cars are stolen simply because owners forget these basics.

2 Contact your insurance company to ask if anti-theft device discounts are offered on premiums.

3 Consider where you typically park your car: Would you be able to hear the alarm? Would it be ignored if it went off?

4 Deter thieves with alarm indicator lights, window stickers, and/or large and heavy-gauge steel objects, such as steering wheel or tyre locks (available from £50 to £200).

5 Consider how effective any theft-prevention measures you're considering actually are. Remember, a determined thief can cut through most steering immobilisers or shut off a simple alarm.

6 Look at the range of anti-theft devices. They include audible alarms, a concierge system or cellular alarms that notify police, or locking steering-wheel cover, steering-column covers, locking steering-wheel bars, electronic immobilisers (kill switches, secret switches), engine or fuel-system locks, tracking devices and delay devices.

7 Evaluate what level of protection you'd like. (Car ugliness is not usually a deterrent to car thieves.) Some alarms will arm automatically, as do tracking devices for locating the car after it's stolen. Steering-wheel and column locking devices must be manually put into place each time.

8 Budget for ongoing expenses. Low-tech solutions such as mechanical immobilisers (generally under £100) don't have to be professionally installed, nor are there monitoring fees attached.

9 Purchase your anti-theft device. Low-tech devices are often available at car spares shops or the car section of general retailers. Your local car dealer might install car alarms and immobilisers. Otherwise, specialist companies that sell and install car electronics (radar detectors, sound systems) will often also install car alarms and immobilisers.

What to Look For

- Common-sense safety measures
- Insurance discount
- Convenience and cost
- Environment and visibility
- Effectiveness
- Installation

Tip

If you use a steering-wheel immobiliser, attach it so the lock faces the dashboard, making it even harder for thieves to remove.

Warnings

Have any ignition immobiliser installed by a professional with lots of experience and who guarantees the work. As these link to the car's electrical system, shoddy work can harm the system or the immobiliser.

Don't rely only on standard car alarms – most members of the public ignore them when they go off.

547 Buy a Car From a Dealer in Europe

Once upon a time, British car buyers were bound by complex rules and dealership cartels, all of which left us paying over the odds for our vehicles. Now things are very different. Substantial savings – as high as 20 per cent – are possible when buying a new car from mainland Europe. What's more, it isn't even that difficult... if you know how.

Steps

1 Do your basic research in the UK. Choose suitable models and test drive them at a dealership before you make a move (see 522 "Buy a New Car").

2 Go to a good international newsagent and buy car magazines from the country in which you plan to make your purchase: *AZ*, *Motor Markt*, *Auto Motorrad Freizeit* and *Auto Motor und Sport* for Germany; *Auto Week* for Holland, *Coche Actual*, *Autopista* or *Top Auto* for Spain, *Irish Auto Trader* for Eire. Look for suitable dealerships. (Some overseas dealerships now advertise in the UK motoring press.).

3 If your grasp of foreign languages is poor, try dealerships in Holland where nearly everyone seems able to speak English. (Unless they specialise in exporting to the UK, most French and German dealers will expect to carry out business in their mother tongue.)

4 Call the dealer to agree pricing and availability. Overseas dealerships are likely to want higher deposits than are usual in the UK – up to 30 percent is normal. Send your deposit (and balance) by telegraphic transfer. Contact your bank for advice on how to do this safely.

5 Make sure that the price you pay is exclusive of local taxes; if inclusive, ensure that the dealership can provide you with the paperwork to reclaim the money.

6 The changes that should be made in order to register the car in the UK are: it must be right-hand drive rather than left-hand drive; the front lights should dip to the left not right; the speedometer must be shown in miles per hour. This needs to be incorporated in the dealer's price.

7 You may be able to save up to 50 per cent if you buy a left-hand drive car and choose not to get it converted. The delivery time will also be that much shorter. However, the car's resale value will be greatly reduced, and you may find it hard (or impossible) even to find a buyer.

8 Ensure that the dealer also provides you with English manufacturer's documentation.

9 To bring the car back to the UK, see 548 "Bring a Foreign-Bought Car into Britain".

What to Look For

- Suitable models
- Test drive in the UK
- Research foreign car journals
- Money transfer
- VAT and local taxes

Warnings

Don't forget to make allowances for VAT and local taxation. Subtract them from the source, but understand that you'll have to pay UK VAT (17.5 per cent) when you import your car. (In some territories you may have to pay the tax first and then reclaim it later – which will affect your cashflow.)

If a dealership goes bankrupt between taking your deposit and delivering, you will join the queue of creditors and are likely to come away empty handed. Although this is no different to having bought in the UK, higher deposits mean that there is more at stake. (You may be able to protect yourself from such an occurrence by using a credit card.)

10 If all of this fills you with dread, you can still save money (although not as much) by buying your car from a specialist importer. Many of these advertise in the back pages of the UK motoring press. (As always, the most reliable way of choosing is to get a personal recommendation from a satisfied customer.)

548 Bringing a Foreign-Bought Car into Britain

When you pick up a car from an overseas dealer (or a private seller) it must be in a legal state to drive on a UK road. Here's what you need to do before you return to Britain.

Steps

1 In the case of buying a new car from a dealership, make sure that it has been converted for use on UK roads. It should be right-hand drive, the front lights should dip to the left, and the speedometer must be shown in miles per hour. This can be done legitimately in the UK, but it's much easier to get it sorted out first (see 547 "Buy a Car From a Dealer in Europe"). It IS legal to use a left-hand drive car in the UK, but it will result in a greatly reduced resale value. Your driving experience will also be less safe.

2 When you pick up your car it should have temporary export plates. If these are not part of the deal you'll have to pay around £150 extra to organise them. The dealer must supply you with an EU-approved "Certificate of Conformity" (or "C-O-C"). *This is absolutely critical* – without it you won't be able to register your car in the UK.

3 Arrange import insurance covering your journey to the UK. (As your car won't yet be registered, regular car insurance policies won't be of any use.)

4 Find the nearest ferry to your pick-up point.

5 When in the UK, you have up to 30 days to pay the VAT on your car. For more information, read VAT Notice 728, which is available from HM Customs and Excise, Vehicle Appraisal Unit, PO Box 242, Dover, Kent, CT17 9GP (telephone: 01304 224372).

6 Register your car at your nearest DVLA office. Take with you your Certificate of Conformity and a valid certificate of insurance.

What to Look For

- Legal for UK use
- Insurance
- Certificate of Conformity

Warnings

Your car will be subject to the warranties that apply in the country of origin. This may not be the three years offered as standard in the the UK.

If a car bought overseas proves to be seriously faulty, it is not covered by the UK's "Sale and Supply of Goods Act 1994" and will have to be returned to the supplying dealer in that country. However, if you buy your car from an independent importer in the UK, *and that car was first registered in the UK*, then it is covered by UK law.

549 Get a High-Performance Car Audio System

Buying a car audio system can be more complex than buying the car. Audio components come with their own set of technical specifications, which may be unintelligible unless you're an electrical engineer. Find a salesperson who will help you cut through the marketing talk and evaluate what's really important to you.

Steps

1 Conduct enough research so that you're conversant with the basic terminology of audio systems. Audio and car magazines, knowledgeable friends and the internet are your best sources.

2 Set a budget. Complete systems range from £200 to many thousands of pounds, but you can find choices within any budget.

3 Determine what *high performance* means to you. If you like rock and rap, maximum power output is important. If you like classical music, you want moderate power and exceptional sound quality.

4 Avoid buying a system one piece at a time. Every component, regardless of quality, has its own sound characteristics. If you buy everything separately, you won't have a chance to preview the whole system before you own it.

5 Understand speaker options. Most speakers are two-way, with a low-range driver *(woofer)* and a high-range driver *(tweeter)*. Three-way speakers include a mid-range driver, which provides precise sound quality. Small car owners may opt to mount individual drivers, with the tweeters up front, and woofers and mid-range drivers in the back. Such systems require an *external crossover* device to synchronise the individual drivers. An audio shop will know the speaker limitations for your vehicle.

6 Research *head units,* also called *receivers,* which typically include a radio, an amplifier, and a CD or tape player. Head units list a power output figure in watts. Find a salesperson willing to explain the true power output. Higher-quality units usually have more power. Expect to pay £200 and up.

7 Check the *pre-outs* – plugs that allow for additional components on the head unit. If you plan on installing an MP3 player or an additional amplifier (for more volume), be sure enough pre-outs exist. If you're connecting the head unit to existing components, be sure the pre-outs are compatible.

8 Make sure the head unit is compatible with satellite radio, MP3 and home-recorded CDs. Even if you don't use these now, you might in the future.

9 Select speakers and a head unit that are compatible in terms of power. Don't use speakers with a lower power rating than the head unit. In fact, it's a good idea to get speakers with a slightly greater rating, allowing for the addition of an amplifier later. Expect to pay £200 or more for top-quality speakers.

What to Look For

- Quality of sound
- Room for speakers
- Adequate power
- Pre-outs for more components
- Head unit compatibility

Tips

Budget for installation costs. High-power systems require professional installation.

Bring along some of your own CDs when shopping. You want to test a system using familiar music.

Every system will sound different in your car than it does in the showroom. The best you can do is preview the entire system as a unit, prior to installation.

If you're worried about your flashy new audio system prompting a break-in, a head unit with a detachable face is a good idea. (See 546 "Buy a Theft-Prevention Device".)

Warning

Wattage figures have become a marketing tool and are thus subject to misrepresentation.

550 Buy a Motorhome

Buying a motorhome can be as complicated as buying a regular home. Start with the basics – running water, cooking and bathroom facilities, and a power source – then explore amenities such as entertainment systems, king-size beds and even hot tubs. Now you're ready to hit the road.

Steps

1 Understand that motorhomes are usually designated by length. The longer it is, the more opulent and expensive. Height and width measurements do not vary significantly.

2 Remember that you need to drive the vehicle. What size can you handle confidently? Are you comfortable reversing? Will your partner be comfortable driving it?

3 Decide which class of vehicle is right for you. "A-Class" motorised models are the largest – these are purpose-built mobile homes, with the driver's cabin forming part of the accommodation. These are sometimes also known by their American abbreviated name "RV" (recreational vehicles).

4 If your means are more modest, "Coachbuilt" models (sometimes known as "C-Class") are smaller with an "overcab" area that extends above the driver's cabin, and can be used as a sleeping area. For greater flexibility, demountable motorhomes have an accommodation area that can be unhooked from the vehicle itself.

5 A-Class motorhomes start at about £100,000 – many of these will have been imported from the US. Coachbuilt models start from around £30,000. Folding camper trailers and truck campers start at about £5,000.

6 Negotiate the purchase price just as you would with a car. If you can't find the style and options you want at a price that you think is reasonable, keep looking.

7 For advice and reviews of current models, buy magazines such as *Motorhome Monthly*, *Motor Caravan* or *Caravan, Motorhome and Camping Mart*. Attend caravan and camping trade shows, and talk to owners, dealers and other shoppers.

8 Consider renting before you buy. Ask your local motorhome dealers if this would be a possibility for any of the models that interest you.

9 Push for deals. Many manufacturers offer significant incentives to dealers, who will pass along some or all if they think it will make a deal. Late summer is the best time to shop, as dealers are looking to get rid of the previous year's stock.

What to Look For

- Appropriate class
- Motorhome shows
- Size
- Options and amenities

Warning

Look into insurance that specifically covers your mobile home. Your regular motor insurance may not cover total loss replacement, emergency living expenses or campsite liability.

551 Buy a Trailer

You've fallen in love with a horse, but you're reluctant to ride him down the road to your house. Now what? Time to get a trailer. Get the lowdown on general trailer options, and then look at issues specific to horse trailers.

Steps

Standard trailers

1 Research the maximum towing capacity of your vehicle. You should be able to find this information in the owner's manual. If not, contact your car's manufacturer.

2 Calculate the maximum load that will be hauled (for horse trailers, that's based simply on the number of horses you'll carry) and check the unloaded weight of any trailer you are considering. This should be stamped on the trailer. The unloaded weight plus maximum load is the total weight that you will tow. If that load surpasses your vehicle's maximum towing capacity, you need to either alter your plans or get a larger vehicle.

3 Understand trailer design. The smallest trailers have a single axle. Many of these are capable of hauling only small loads, such as recreational boats, although large single-axle trailers do exist. Double-axle trailers usually have a higher load capacity and always ride more smoothly. The additional wheels will also add stability when the trailer is unhitched. These are typically used for large sailing boats and carrying cars. Triple-axle trailers haul very large loads, such as tractors, and are difficult to manoeuvre due to their long wheelbase.

4 Trailers that connect to the back of a vehicle are known as *tag-along* trailers. They are also sometimes referred to as *bumper hitch* trailers, although only a tiny trailer can connect solely to a bumper. Most tag-alongs require a hitch that mounts to the frame of the vehicle. Larger trailers use a *fifth-wheel* or *goose-neck* mount that can be used only with a pickup truck that has a permanent hitch mount installed. These trailers ride more smoothly than tag-alongs.

5 Expect to pay about £750 for the smallest single-axle trailer. A medium-capacity, double-axle trailer costs in the region of £2,000. Fully enclosed trailers are more expensive.

Horse trailers

1 Decide on the number of horses you will transport. Single-horse trailers are few and far between – a two-horse trailer is likely to be the smallest type generally available.

2 Look for a double-axle trailer, which is preferable for horse transport because of the smoother ride. Hitch mechanisms are the same as for general trailers.

What to Look For

- Towing capacity
- Weight of load
- Weight of trailer
- Number of axles
- Hitch type

Tips

Electric brakes are adequate for most light trailers. Heavy-duty trailers should have air brakes.

Take a driving course to learn how to safely drive, turn and back a loaded trailer.

See 112 "Buy a Racehorse".

3 Decide between a *stock* trailer and a *show* trailer. Stock trailers contain few amenities and are designed to move horses and a small amount of feed or equipment. Show trailers are smarter and incorporate storage room for clothes and tack, and some even have human living quarters.

4 Expect to pay £5,000 for a basic two-horse stock trailer. A large show trailer can cost £25,000 or more.

552 Buy a Boat for Water Skiing

The changing nature of boat design reflects how the sport has evolved over time. Skiers prefer small, soft wakes. Wakeboarders, on the other hand, want big wakes from which to launch aerial manoeuvres. But what if you need both?

Steps

1 Review your basic options. An inboard engine is much the most powerful and is located in the boat's hull. Cheaper outboard motors clamp onto the side of the boat. Inboard/outboard engines combine the power of an inboard motor with the ease of use of an outboard motor.

2 Understand the trade-offs between inboard engine types:

• A direct-drive engine is located mid-boat and sends power directly from the engine to the drive shaft to the propeller. Direct drives with their flat bottoms are preferred by skiers because they produce small wakes, and handle and track better. The flat hull, however, makes riding on choppy water a bouncy ride; and the engine, smack in the middle of the boat, uses up prime seating.

• V-drive boats have rear-mounted engines and a deep V hull that cuts through chop without a blink, but produce a large wake. Some feature ballast tanks that can be filled for even bigger wakes – making wakeboarders ecstatic – then drained again for skiers. The engine location allows for quieter, more sociable seating. Tow lines attach from a tower high above the cockpit.

3 Meet in the middle. Recognising the market's changing needs, boat builders have designed crossover boats. Mostly featuring direct-drive engines, these "all-event" boats have ballast tanks that hold up to 600 kg (1,600 lb) with adjustable trim-plates. So fill it up and create monster wakes, or dial it back down for the skiers; one boat happily serves both camps.

4 Investigate available amenities. Swim platforms make it easier to climb into the boat after a hard run, and overhead racks stow gear safely away.

What to Look For

• Engine type
• Direct-drive or V-drive
• Crossover boats
• Amenities

Tip

Improved technology has boosted engines to over 300 horsepower. In the future, look for boats with new composite hull materials and engines that further reduce noise and water pollution.

Warnings

Check out the economics of buying. For infrequent skiers it will be cheaper in the long-run to rent a boat as and when it's needed.

If you're buying a used boat, hire a marine surveyor to perform an inspection. This may be costly, but will reveal any potential problems.

For further information try these websites:
• wakeboard,co,uk
• britishwaterski.co.uk

553 Find a Classic Wooden Powerboat

You've seen the gleaming Chris-Crafts racing across Lake Tahoe in *The Godfather: Part II.* If you're a true fan, sooner or later you'll be forced to confront "wooden boat affliction". The classic good looks of a finely crafted wooden boat are seductive – but do you really want to own one? Before you decide, better do your homework. Hire the necessary help and proceed carefully.

Steps

1 Set a budget and stick to it. Sounds simple, but it isn't. The first person you talk to is likely to say, "For a few thousand pounds more, you can get a…." Don't forget to include repairs and expenses in your budget. If your total budget is £20,000, look for boats with a £15,000 purchase price. Reserve £5,000 for transportation, repairs, insurance and docking fees. You'll also need a trailer (see 551 "Buy a Trailer").

2 Research boats thoroughly using the internet, telephone and boating magazines, such as *Yachting and Boating World* (ybw.co.uk). make sure that you attend the London Boat Show, held each year in January – this is the biggest boat show in Europe (londonboatshow.net).

3 Contact wooden boat dealers, restorers and owners' clubs. You'll find boats for sale as well as information about your favourites. Be flexible about the exact appearance or type of boat that you want. Most manufacturers make numerous changes to a given model over the years.

4 Suppress the urge to make an impulse buy. Be patient and wait for what you want. Prices can range from a few thousand pounds to millions.

5 Tell boat brokers what you're looking for. They can arrange boats for you to view or suggest places to look. Fibreglass boat dealers will tell you about the complications of wooden boats. Listen well.

6 Understand the commitment required by wooden boats, which reward you with great beauty but require attention. Budget at least £1,000 per year to have your boat professionally maintained if you're not prepared to do the work yourself.

7 Respond to classified ads, outside your area if necessary. Chase leads and ask lots of questions about the boat's condition: has it been out of the water for many years? Are the engine, electrical systems and gauges all functioning? Is the hull intact? Have any modifications been done that are likely to make the boat less desirable to collectors.

8 Hire a marine surveyor. This inspection may cost over £100 but will uncover any serious problems and may also enable you to negotiate price reductions for small issues. Be prepared to back out of the deal if the survey findings are bad.

What to Look For

- Wooden boat shows
- Dealers
- Restorers
- Owners' clubs
- Brokers
- Original condition
- Functioning engine
- Intact hull
- Marine surveyor

Tips

No matter how tempting, never buy a boat on impulse, especially an old one.

Ask a marine broker to recommend a transport operation that is experienced with boats. Research any necessary delivery costs.

Warnings

Don't expect to restore a boat, then sell it at a profit. Sales prices of classic boats are almost always lower than the cost of restoration.

Petrol-powered inboard boats require proper bilge ventilation to avoid build-up of explosive fumes. Be sure your boat is well equipped.

554 Hire an Aircraft

With a pilot's licence, you're not at the mercy of the timetables of the major airlines; you can hire yourself a plane at many airports across the country. Even if you don't have a flying licence, fleet operators and charter groups can usually get you where you need to go – if you can afford the luxury.

Steps

Get checked out

1 Look on the internet for fixed base operators (FBO), which manage and hire aircraft at an airport for training, charters and pleasure flights.

2 You'll be asked to go through the checkout with a qualified flight instructor to judge whether you can safely operate the aircraft. Unlike renting a car, it won't be assumed that you know how to operate the plane in question just because you have a licence. For a single-engine, fixed-gear aircraft, the check-out may be straightforward. Requiring a longer check-out are complex planes, which have retractable landing gear and variable pitch propellers, and include high-performance planes of 200 horse-power and above. Multi-engine aircraft have a different rating and require even more time.

3 The aircraft's owner will also require you to take out insurance. Your experience and previous record may determine the type of plane you can fly.

Join the club

1 Join a local flying club, which you can find in the phone book under "Aircraft Charter, Leasing and Rental", or do a search on the internet. These clubs may charge a membership fee plus regular dues and per-flight costs.

2 Go through the club's check-out to join. Once again, your past experience will determine the type of plane you're allowed to fly.

Charter a flight

1 Look in the telephone directory or do an internet search under "Aircraft Charter, Leasing and Rental". The group will find you an appropriate-size plane, cater the in-flight meal when needed, and take care of any necessary fleet liaison.

2 Charter a plane with a fleet operator. Choice and availability of planes may be limited, but the concierge services are comparable.

3 Check your bank balance – if there are less than seven figures to the left of the decimal point then you probably shouldn't consider this as an option!

What to Look For

- Fixed base operators
- Local liability insurance
- Flying clubs
- Renters insurance
- Planning companies
- Charter firms
- Fleet operators

Tip

The fastest way to board a plane (outside commercial flying) is to hire a planning company to charter a plane for you.

555 Sell Your Sailing Boat

How do you make your beloved boat attractive to buyers and stand out from the crowd? Unfortunately, the answer is hard work. Many sailing boats are neglected for years prior to the decision to sell. Don't force buyers to look past the dirt and mildew to see your beautiful yacht.

Steps

1 Survey the market for used sailing boats. Sailing publications, boat dealers, marinas and sailing enthusiasts' websites all have lists of boats for sale. Compare prices for boats of a similar size, age and condition as yours.

2 Identify areas where your boat is commonly found, then advertise locally. Your boat will sell best where it is a known entity and already popular. Don't bother placing ads in regular newspapers unless your local paper routinely carries a lot of sailing boat ads.

3 Include photos of your boat with any ad. A full or three-quarter profile shot is best. Some online bulletin boards let you include a variety of shots; take additional pictures of the interior and stern.

4 Be able to rattle off the facts about your boat. Know the overall length, year of construction, draught, sail area and displacement. Customers lose faith in sellers who can't answer basic questions.

5 Look for a racing fleet (a group of boats, identical in design, that get together to race) for your boat. Yacht clubs or boat dealers in the area know if a fleet exists and how to contact it. Your goal is to place an ad in the fleet organisation's newsletter. Be sure to inquire about a national organisation with additional advertising opportunities.

6 Boat prices vary widely, usually based on how well the boat is equipped, but also on appearance, recent overall maintenance, and condition of the sails. Be honest about how your boat ranks against others like it.

7 Empty everything off the boat, including seat cushions, anchor and fire extinguisher. Search all the compartments. Don't make a buyer dig through your junk.

8 Clean the boat. While everything is off, take a bucket of soapy water and a big sponge and go over the whole interior. Get rid of mildew, mould and rust stains. Clean the items that you removed from the boat. If you intend to sell them with the boat, return them to their proper storage compartment. Let everything dry completely before closing the boat back up.

9 Scrub the deck and cockpit with a stiff brush and soapy water. Oil any teak trim. Coil any loose lines. Check that the winches spin freely and all fittings operate. Oil any items that need it.

10 Check the lights and electrical systems. Be sure the engine runs and the batteries are fully charged. Repair any minor problems.

What to Look For

- Fair price
- Appropriate location
- Racing fleet
- Cleanliness
- Good condition
- Sails in good shape
- Clean hull
- Prospective buyers

Tips

A marine surveyor is likely to find the flaws in your boat. If you are aware of problems, it's best to be up-front about them early in the process.

Go to a local boatyard and practice being a customer. Ask yourself these two questions: What's effective about the presentation? What sort of information would be useful?

11 Fold all the sails neatly and store them in sail bags, either on the boat or nearby where they can be examined.

12 If the boat is on land, be sure the bottom is clean. Scrub off any algae or barnacles. If the boat is in the water, use a long handled brush to remove any visible growth.

13 If the boat is in a marina, inform the harbour master that your boat is for sale. He or she may be able to direct potential buyers to your boat.

14 Be prepared to spend considerable time with prospective buyers. Some buyers will want to go for a test sail. You may also need to be present when a marine surveyor inspects the boat on behalf of a buyer.

556 Purchase a Satellite Navigation System

A navigation system in your car, boat or motorcycle can use global positioning satellites (GPS) sending out synchronised signals to pinpoint your location anywhere in the world with great accuracy. When your position is compared with the GPS system's embedded maps, frustrating voyages of all kinds turn into precision-guided tours.

Steps

1 Take your budget into account. If you're lusting after a high-end GPS system for your car, buy a built-in unit from your car dealer. If cash outlay is a concern, dashboard-mounted and handheld systems are up to a quarter of the price of built-in models.

2 Imagine where you want to use your navigation system – driving around city streets, hiking up mountains or touring the Virgin Islands in your yacht? Each use has its unique needs, whether it's street maps and directions, topographical and altitude information or extra battery power.

3 Decide the kind of maps you'll need: general regional maps or precise street-level city-driving directions? This will determine the capabilities you'll need from your system. After you make your purchase, make sure all the appropriate maps are loaded.

4 Look for features such as audible alerts that warn you of road or traffic features ahead, and scrolling maps to track your progress. Opt for units with a larger display to avoid zooming in and out repeatedly to read street names and find turnings.

What to Look For

- Built-in system
- Dashboard-mounted or handheld system
- Maps and directions capabilities
- Audible alert and scrolling map features

Warning

Don't try to read a tiny, moving map while driving. If no one's riding shotgun with you, pull over and work out where you're going.

INDEX

CONTRIBUTORS

Sharon Beaulaurier is a writer who lives in the San Francisco Bay Area. She is the former managing editor of eHow.com and a former news producer. Her head is full of useful and useless how-to information, and she is frequently called upon by friends in need of how-to help.

Lori Blachford honed her collecting skills while working as managing editor of *Country Home* magazine. She now does a variety of freelance writing and editing from her home in Des Moines. Her current conquest: Yoda figures from the Star Wars series.

Laura Buller never met a thrift shop she didn't like. She spends so much time in them that her friends joke the film *Good Will Hunting* is about her. To pay for those 1970s transistor radios, miniature buildings and lunchboxes, she writes and edits books for children. Her own family affair (Alice and Sean) takes place in Los Angeles.

Julie Jares spent several years in the dot-com fray as a writer and editor for various websites, including eHow.com, Sidewalk.com and Concierge.com. Currently a freelancer, her recent projects include *Out to Eat in San Francisco* and *Hawaii's Big Island* guide, both from Lonely Planet.

Kathie Kull specialises in writing about building and remodelling and is the former editor of *Better Homes and Gardens Home Products Guide* magazine. Her Maine house (circa 1860) generates endless "to fix" and "to buy" lists.

Matthew Richard Poole is a freelance travel writer who has authored more than two dozen guides to California, Hawaii and abroad. Before becoming a full-time writer and photographer, he worked as an English tutor in Prague, ski instructor in the Swiss Alps, and scuba instructor in Maui. Highly allergic to office buildings, he spends most of his time on the road doing research and avoiding commitments.

Elaine Rowland is a freelance editor and writer who has rediscovered the thrill of cars since leaving Manhattan. She contributes regularly to several car owner magazines, but spends the rest of her time driving her new black Miata, giggling.

Sue Russell is an internationally syndicated, veteran reporter with over 1,500 articles published in numerous magazines and newspapers, including *Redbook, Us* and *Good Housekeeping*. She has been a health and beauty editor at a major women's magazine and has written on countless diverse topics. She is also the author of several non-fiction books on subjects ranging from beauty to true crime.

Fred Sandsmark is a freelance writer in the San Francisco Bay Area who covers technology-related subjects. A self-described "gadget freak on a budget," his prized geek possession is a Wi-Fi wireless network interface, bought (cheap) on eBay.com, that works with his ageing, beloved Handspring Visor.

Marcia Whyte Smart is a San Francisco food writer and editor who has contributed to *Cooking Light*, *Sunset*, Citysearch and *Parenting*. She's the associate food editor of *7x7* magazine.

Derek Wilson has bought and sold more sporting goods than any normal person should and if you don't believe him you're welcome to visit his garage and count the bicycles. He lives in the Lake Tahoe area of California and divides his time between economic consulting and writing projects which include *Burritos: Hot on the Trial of the Little Burro,* and contributions to *How to Fix (Just About) Everything*.

Marty Wingate is an author and teacher. Her features appear every Thursday in the *Seattle Post-Intelligencer's* Northwest Gardens. She also writes for national gardening publications including *Horticulture* and *Fine Gardening*. Her first book is *Big Ideas for Northwest Small Gardens*.

Contributing Editors to the UK Edition

Alison Bolus: Personal Finance
Terry Burrows: Careers, Property, Computers & Home Electronics, Cars and Other Vehicles
Reg Grant: Smart Strategies, Daily Life, Splurges & Rare Events, Sports & Outdoor Recreation
James Harrison: Special Occasions
Jane Laing: Family Affairs
Helen Ridge: Food & Drink, Health & Beauty, Collectibles, Clothing & Accessories
Jane Simmonds: Home & Garden, Travel